ART SINCE 1940

Strategies of being

Third Edition

ART SINCE 1940

Strategies of being

Third Edition

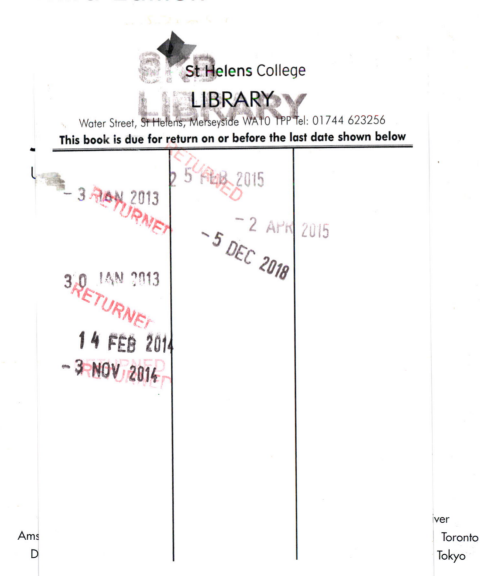

Ams

D

ver

Toronto

Tokyo

For Pearson Education, Inc.:
Editor-in-Chief: Sarah Touborg
Senior Editor: Helen Ronan
Editorial Assistant: Carla Worner
Assistant Managing Editor: Melissa Feimer
Project Liaison: Marlene Gassler
Senior Operations Supervisor: Brian K. Mackey
Director of Marketing: Brandy Dawson
Senior Marketing Manager: Kate Mitchell

Credits and acknowledgments borrowed from other sources and reproduced, with permission, in this textbook appear on the appropriate page within text or on the credit pages in the back of this book.

The third edition of *Art Since 1940: Strategies of being* has benefitted from the reflections and assessments of a distinguished team of scholars and educators. We are grateful to the following academic reviewers for their numerous insights and suggestions of improvement:

Jonathan P. Ribner, Boston University
Valerie Hellstein, Massachusetts College of Art
Greg Metcalf, University of Maryland
Robert Patrick Kinsman, Indiana University-Purdue University
    Indianapolis
James Romanie, New York Center for Art and Media Studies
Anne Swartz, Savannah College of Art and Design
Jennifer Quick, Harvard University
Shalon Parker, Gonzaga University
Marian Mazzone, College of Charleston
Mysoon Rizk, University of Toledo
Meredith Tromble, San Francisco Art Institute
John Ianelli, Eastern Maine Community College

This book was designed and produced by
Laurence King Publishing Ltd, London
www.laurenceking.com

For Laurence King Publishing:
Production: Simon Walsh
Development Editor: Robert Shore
Designer: Ian Hunt
Picture Researcher: Julia Ruxton

Printed in China

Frontispiece: Gabriel Orozco, *My Hands Are My Heart*, 1991. Two-part cibachrome, each 9⅛ x 12½in, edition of 5.
Courtesy Marian Goodman Gallery, New York.

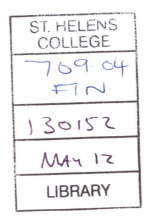
Library of Congress Cataloging-in-Publication Data

Fineberg, Jonathan David.
   Art since 1940 : strategies of being / Jonathan Fineberg. -- 3rd ed.
      p. cm.
   Includes bibliographical references and index.
   ISBN 978-0-13-193479-5 (alk. paper)
   1. Modernism (Art)--United States. 2. Postmodernism--United States. 3. Art, American. 4. Modernism (Art)--Europe. 5. Postmodernism--Europe. 6. Art, European. I. Title.
   N6512.5.M63F56 2011
   709.04'5--dc22
                                    2009051184
10 9 8 7 6 5 4 3 2 1

Prentice Hall
is an imprint of

www.pearsonhighered.com

ISBN 10:   0-13-193479-1
ISBN 13: 978-0-13-193479-5

To Marianne

"Painting is a state of being … self-discovery.
Every good artist paints what he is."

JACKSON POLLOCK

CONTENTS

FOREWORD TO THE THIRD EDITION

I have largely left the acknowledgments and preface to the previous editions stand as they still apply, though I want to add two names to my list of great mentors whose classes and writings shaped my approach: Erik Erikson and Rudolf Arnheim (who also became a dear friend). But I also want to add a few more remarks and acknowledgments for this edition.

This is a personal account. It is predominantly an American perspective (it is *my* perspective) on art since 1940 and there are many other possible and valid points of view from which this book could have been written. What matters here is not the specific list of works (my ideas on that continue to evolve as I learn more), but rather the style of my engagement with the works of my lifetime that have most enlarged or challenged the way I see the world. What I hope to have communicated through my encounter with these works is the seriousness of these artists and the way in which their art continues to give us all a fresh perspective on reality.

I was born in the months before Pollock's first drip picture, so this is very much an account of issues that have come to the fore in my own lifetime. Moreover, I have had the privilege of meeting (and often coming to know quite well) many of the artists in this book. That, along with the work they produced, helped me to experience both their work and our times on a deeper level. I want to acknowledge once again my gratitude to the artists discussed in this book.

I also want to thank several individuals by name, along with still more unnamed persons, for generously contributing time and insights to help me make this a better book: Laura Bandy, Jennifer Burns, Roy Campbell, Jessica Cash, Mary Coffey, Josef Helfenstein, Suzanne Hudson, Miriam Kienle, Dorothy Kosinski, Leng Lin, Jordana Mendelson, Hubert Neumann, Jordana Saggese, Meng Tang, Fred Tomaselli, Beth Turner, Wang Chang, Zhang Xiaogang, and Gary Xu.

In addition, I am very grateful to the staff at Laurence King Publishing, London, who worked on this book with great forbearance and skill to rescue this very tardy author—in particular my terrific editors Robert Shore and Kara Hattersley-Smith; I wouldn't have made it without them. I also want to thank Laurence King and Sarah Touborg (at Prentice Hall/Pearson) who miraculously made all the complicated issues work out so well. At the University of Illinois I feel so lucky to have an outstanding team from Nan Goggin, the Director of the School of Art and Design, to the Dean of the College Robert Graves, and the former Provost Linda Katehi who have made Illinois such an amazing place to work. But I want to single out the former Chancellor, Richard Herman, whose vision has done more for Illinois than any Chancellor or President in my thirty-five years there; his support played an indispensable role in my being able to write this edition, to make the *Imagining America* film for PBS, and to build the Illinois program at the Center for the Study of Modern Art at The Phillips Collection (and without Jay Gates, Bonnie Himmelman, Ruth Perlin, Vicki Sant, and George Vradenburg, that would never have succeeded and I am so grateful for their friendship and expertise too). I also want to warmly acknowledge five friends in particular from whom I have learned so much in conversation over the last decade about issues that touch directly on this book: Manuel Borja-Villel, John Carlin, Okwui Enwezor, Maya Fineberg, Larry Jeckel, and Buzz Spector. Without the continuing love and support of Marianne, as well as Maya, Noni, and Henry Fineberg none of this could have happened at all.

Jonathan Fineberg
Urbana, Illinois
October 2009

What's new in the third edition:

- Discussion of the forties and fifties expanded to include such important figures as Jacob Lawrence, Hedda Sterne, Bill Traylor, and Rufino Tamayo, and also now introduces the early work of Louise Bourgeois.
- Considerably expanded discussion of photography as an important medium for the artist: from Lisette Model and Weegee in the forties, to Aaron Siskind in the fifties and Diane Arbus in the sixties, Cindy Sherman and William Wegman in the seventies and eighties, and Andreas Gursky, Jeff Wall, Yto Barrada, and Nikki S. Lee in the last twenty years – just to mention a few of the photographers discussed.
- The contribution of film and video are re-evaluated from the heroes of sixties underground film Stan Brakhage and Bruce Connor to the revolutionary video work in the past two decades of Bill Viola, Gary Hill, William Kentridge, Shirin Neshat, and Andrea Fraser.
- Discussion of several of the major and enduring artists, such as Louise Bourgeois and Christo, has been updated to survey their work all the way up to the present.
- Discussion of work by non-Western artists has been considerably expanded and now includes Shazia Sikander (Pakistan), Ravinder G. Reddy (India), Mona Hatoum (Palestine), Ghada Amer (Egypt), Yinka Shonibare, MBE (Nigeria), Murakami (Japan), Sang-ah Choi (Korea) and Xu Bing, Zhang Xiaogang, Hai Bo, Fang Lijun, Cui Xiuwen, Zhang Huan, and Yue Minjun (China).
- New discussion on comics as art, introducing work in this genre by Jack Kirby, Chris Ware, Art Spiegelman, and Kerry James Marshall.

ACKNOWLEDGMENTS

Until I wrote this book I never understood those (as it once seemed to me) melodramatic expressions of gratitude to the author's husband or wife "without whom this couldn't have been written." I now realize that either those authors found their books easier to write than I have mine, or they discovered, as I have, that there is no way adequately to express the contribution my wife, Marianne, has made to this book, intellectually and spiritually. I am also deeply grateful for the patience of my children—Maya, Naomi, Henry—who gave up a lot of my time that was rightfully theirs over the decade when I sat buried in my library researching and writing this book. That Maya—the eldest—could tell me she wanted to be an art historian after watching this process touches me more deeply than I can say (though I secretly hoped for law school).

I also want to acknowledge the three greatest teachers of my life: Harold Rosenberg, Christo, and my father, Henry H. Fineberg, M.D. The influence of Harold's uncompromising commitment to intellectual values will never leave me: fifteen years after his death I can still hear his voice over my shoulder, needling me and scrutinizing my argument as I write. Christo's ideas about change and time, in particular, were too radical for me even to acknowledge at first, because they revolutionized my thinking so fundamentally: I still find the effects of his ideas continuing to unfold in my life in new ways. Finally, my father's psychoanalytic perspective on the influence of social interaction as the key to understanding the mechanisms of art shaped my perspective on the world and is at the very heart of this book's premise.

An ongoing conversation of now fifteen years' duration with my friend John Carlin has greatly enriched my life and I want to thank him warmly for that. Likewise, I am enormously grateful to many friends who have generously given their time and shared their ideas with me. Some of them even suffered through extensive parts of this text in draft (for which I am especially indebted): in particular, I want to acknowledge Katherine Manthorne, the late Robert Motherwell, Richard Shiff, and Larry Silver. I am also very grateful to Stephen Fineberg and Lois Fineberg for being there when I most needed them.

Important contributions to my understanding of various issues came from discussions with Manuel Borja-Villel, Mary Schmidt Campbell, Jeanne-Claude Christo, Renee Conforte, Caroline Cox, William J. R. Curtis, Gabriella de Ferrari, Jeffrey Deitch, Ebon Fisher, Henry Louis Gates, Jr., Alma Gottlieb, Anne Coffin Hanson, Michael Heizer, Gracie Mansion, Elizabeth Murray, John Neff, Jeannene M. Przyblyski, Margit Rowell, Martica Sawin, Charles Slichter, Tim Spelios, Robert Farris Thompson, Vicente Todolí, David Weinstein, and Angela Westwater. I thank them all. I have also been blessed with a succession of remarkably talented current and former graduate students at the University of Illinois who helped in numerous ways (and also graciously accommodated my preoccupation with this project during its various phases): I especially want to thank Mary Coffey, Sarah Eckardt, Charng-Jiunn Lee, Lorraine Menar, Mysoon Rizk, and Lisa Wainwright.

This entire enterprise rests in part on the outstanding work of other writers on postwar art whose books and essays I have read and admired.

I want to thank Jane Block, Christopher Quinn, and the staff of the Ricker Library at the University of Illinois, who have come to the rescue repeatedly. There are also a number of people on the staffs of museums and galleries who went out of their way to help: I am grateful to them all, especially Anita Duquette of the Whitney Museum, Bob Panzer at VAGA, and Katia Stieglitz and Janet Hicks of ARS whose help was particularly appreciated.

Everybody ought to have a friend like Carl Brandt: I want to thank him for many hours of listening patiently and then leading me out of my conundrums with unfailingly sound judgment. Bud Therien at Prentice Hall was wonderful to work with and I am enormously grateful that he had enough faith in me to keep an open mind about my radical transformation of this project as it went along. I could not have been more pleased with the work of everyone at Laurence King Publishing, where the production of this book was undertaken.

I owe a profound debt to the Research Board of the University of Illinois; I do not know another institution that does the job of supporting serious research so well. Finally, I want to say how much Ted Zernich's friendship and support have meant to me over the years since he assumed the directorship of the School of Art and Design at the University of Illinois. Ted always comes through for me somehow, and deserves a good deal of credit for helping me make my time at the University of Illinois the most productive years of my career.

Jonathan Fineberg
Urbana, Illinois
August 1994
(revised 2009)

PREFACE

Great works of art arise from the effort of exceptional individuals to come to terms with the facts of their existence—within themselves and in the world. Insofar as the artist's experience touches on the experience of others, his or her work offers a fresh perspective on events for someone else too, though that is not its purpose. In the sense that artists explore their ideals and speculate on the meaning of matters of defining importance to them in their art, it is a spiritual endeavor. That is the aspect of art most worth understanding, remembering, discussing.

Some may criticize this book for presenting "heroic narratives" when the collective aspect of history is being emphasized in contemporary criticism. So much the better. Artists stand against the corporate experience of culture; the models of "heroism" described here consist of great feats of imagination, insight, and thought. A culture without such "heroic narratives" to inspire us is a gloomy prospect indeed.

This book attempts to survey art from 1940 to the present as an accumulation of unique contributions by individual artists, interspersed with a few chapters that concern the broader context of the seven decades treated here. These broader sections include a number of other wonderful, if less historically defining, artists whom space does not permit me to discuss in greater depth. I have tried to take a long view about this subject and have made a judgment about which artists seem to me to have shaped their cultural moment in the most significant ways; in particular I have tried to be a careful field worker in listening to what artists have told me about the work that has influenced them. Nevertheless, this process of selection has also been painful for me since, by these criteria, I have said little about—or altogether left out—many artists whom I deeply admire.

I should add that the number of illustrations included by individual artists is not strictly proportional to my estimation of their influence; sometimes it merely happened that more pictures were needed to explain an idea. Also I have introduced the detailed coverage of important artists in the chronological context in which they had their most significant impact. Thus artists like Guston and Bearden, for example, come up in relation to their defining roles in the art of the seventies even though both were already well recognized artists for at least two decades by then. Finally, I want to point out what should be obvious—that this is intended as a survey of European and American art and that I chose the opening date of 1940 because it was then that a large part of the Paris art scene moved *en masse* to New York, transforming it into the art capital of the world. By the 1990s, the idea of a single art center was over; instead there are more and more magnificent microecologies of art dispersed across the globe, making a comprehensive survey impossible. So for the most recent work I have tried instead to survey some of the large issues in world culture which different artists can help us articulate.

It will become clear to the reader that on the whole I do not believe in movements. They simplify what needs to remain complicated. Whereas in science one aspires to the simplest explanation of the phenomenon under scrutiny, the whole point of art and the humanities is to open our minds to more alternatives and ambiguities in the way we see the world.

1.1 Vincent van Gogh, *Three Pairs of Shoes*, 1886–7. Oil on canvas, 19⅜ × 28½in (49.2 × 72.4cm).

Harvard University Art Museums, Cambridge, Mass. Bequest from the Collection of Maurice Wertheim, Class of 1906. 1951.66

1.2 Snapshot of a pair of work shoes, Les Baux, France, 1968.

1 INTRODUCTION

Approaching Art as a Mode of Thought

The simple premise of this book is that artists make things to see what they will look like. They have an intuitive grasp of something, an insight, an idea that they find deeply engaging and at the same time impossible to describe in words, so they seek to make it visible as a work of art. The great works of art are the ones that other people, besides just the artist, can also understand and use to gain a fresh perspective on their experience. Anyone who is deeply moved by Vincent van Gogh's *Three Pairs of Shoes* [fig. 1.1], for example, can never again look at a pair of old work boots [fig. 1.2] without a rich resonance from Van Gogh's worldview. In the painting, one sees the shoes through the artist's eyes and in so doing begins to know the artist. In this way the artist speaks to us through our empathic response to his account of experience. He is, as Wordsworth described the poet, "singing a song in which all human beings join with him."[1]

Making art is a form of thinking that we access through empathy more than through detached analysis. The thinking in a work of art is not necessarily verbal, though that may enter in too; it is visual thinking, which is different, but also quite rigorous in the way it articulates and connects visual ideas. Even in an abstract work, which may seem to concern only issues of color, form, and the like, the structure that the artist conceives for those pictorial elements provides a model for organizing experience. That model is an instance of the artist's "style" of thinking with traits of a clearly consistent character, like a personality, and like a personality the style continues to grow and change in response to new experience over time. "You've developed a little culture for yourself," the painter Willem de Kooning remarked. "Like yoghurt, as long as you keep something of the original microbes, the original thing in it will grow out. So I had—like most artists—this original little sensation."[2]

Any work of art worth thinking about is a tangible embodiment of the complex cluster of perceptions and emotions that the artist had with respect to her or his experience rather than simply a representation that attempts to "look like" what we see in the world. Gabriel Orozco's 1991 photograph *My Hands Are My Heart* [see page 2] testifies to this way in which an object (in this case a pair of photographs of an action) articulates the close, even bodily, connection for an artist between making something and the experience of being in the world. The implicit underlying subject matter of art is always the artist's encounter with reality—the alternately painful and exhilarating intersection of psychological forces, intellect, society, and events. Brushwork, line, composition, even representational subject matter constitute metaphors for the artist's experience of events (internal and external). In literally giving form to these subjective perceptions, the artist arrives at what the Oxford philosopher A. N. Whitehead called "symbolic truth."[3] What makes the great artists of any historical moment so fundamentally important is that (1) they have a heightened sensitivity to what is new or undisclosed in the world, (2) they perceive this in personal (human) terms, and (3) they find a way to express this insight as form so that we can all begin to look at these realities before we have the words to describe them or the distance to analyze them.

The definitively individual nature of this activity makes the classification of modern art into movements too simplistic to be interpretatively meaningful. At most one can say that artists necessarily share some common elements from the visual language and experience of their time and place. These shared traits or ideas connect them to other artists in ways that often lead to resemblances in style. Yet only rarely is there a conscious agreement among artists to do this on more than a very superficial level. In the end, making art is always an individual act, even in artistic collaborations (which consist more of symbiosis than sameness), and in today's corporate-controlled mass culture art is one of the only vehicles left for individual expression on a large public scale.

Modernism

Just as we have reason to be skeptical about lumping artists together into movements, sweeping characterizations of historical periods are also problematic. Yet we sometimes need these reductive categories (of both periods and movements) as a shorthand to help us sort our way through the inherent chaos of history and current events. Even with all the variations and exceptions, the terms "modernism" and "postmodernism" are particularly useful in this regard and they are so common in the art literature that it is worth trying to define them here, at least in simple outline.

Modernism is a worldview that parallels and embraces the industrial age. It is prefigured in the closely connected development of democracy, reason, and humanism that has its origins in the seventeenth- and eighteenth-century thought of Europe and America (the Age of Reason and the Enlightenment). But modernism itself emerged with the industrial revolution of the nineteenth century and flourished until after the mid-twentieth century, when it took on a greatly transformed and contested identity as we approached the new millennium. Postmodernism is often understood as paralleling the "post-industrial," or "late-capitalist," society of the last forty years. Some see it as a facet of a persevering modernism; others have argued that postmodernism has replaced modernism. But everyone seems to agree that we have come to see the world in an increasingly complex way since the end of the 1960s, embracing many constantly changing, overlapping, and even cross-tracking truths that run counter to the teleology of modernism (the idea of progress toward an ideal).

Modernism centers on a faith in the ability of human beings to examine and reshape the world around them using scientific knowledge, technology, and the power of reason. Modern science, from its beginnings in the "natural philosophy" of the eighteenth century, relied on observation and reasoned proof in search of a verifiable and stable truth. This reliance on reason also underlies democratic debate as a means of organizing social relations and leads naturally to secularism, since religious views cannot be verified rationally. Modernism orients itself in the present with a fundamental belief in progress and an assumption that change is inevitable and even desirable. Indeed, modernism has endowed progress with an aesthetic value and tends to reject traditional forms of art, literature, social structure, and economics as outdated almost immediately.

The Concept of the Avant-Garde

The concept of the avant-garde is a central driver in the modernist idea of progress. In Western art from ancient times well into the nineteenth century even the most innovative artists depended upon patrons and a public that measured quality in relation to well-known standards of subject matter, technique, and style. At the beginning of the twentieth century the art public began, increasingly, to value an artist's work most of all for its success in changing those standards by the force of its originality. But the more original an artist's vision, the more his or her frame of reference will vary from what the rest of us think and see. Thus the individuality that we prize so highly in an artist's work makes understanding the work a much more complex interpretive task; the meaning of art today is not readily accessible without the help of books like this one and a lot of time spent looking and questioning with an open mind.

The word "avant-garde" originated as a French military term, referring to the small group of soldiers that went out ahead of the main forces to scout for the enemy. In art "avant-garde" (or "vanguard" in English) describes the situation in which an artist thinks that (1) his or her art expresses ideas and that (2) those ideas not only differ from what the rest of society believes, but that they come closer to "the truth" about the world. In addition the concept implies that (3) art has a bearing on understanding the present and it aspires to have an influence on the future. Vanguardism places great emphasis on the newness and the profundity of insight in an artist's thinking.

For many, one important implication of this stress on innovation is the idea that if a work of art redefines standards, it must be measured against its success at fulfilling the standards it sets for itself. This dream of an autonomous work of art—an abstract idea that responds only to its own internal criteria rather than to external demands (as in copying "nature")—has often been understood as a signature of modernism. "I should like to write a book about nothing," the French writer Gustave Flaubert confided in 1852; "a book dependent on nothing external."[4]

Art critics of the 1920s and 1930s such as the British authors Clive Bell and Roger Fry celebrated as "dehumanized" art that deemphasized any reference to nature. This was not a criticism; they saw this as a positive virtue. For them, the form was the content; they rejected as inessential not only the representation of nature but the psychology of the artist.[5] Clement Greenberg, the American heir to Fry and Bell, took this to an extreme in portraying the avant-garde as being chiefly engaged with the purification of art as an autonomous abstraction. He defined "high art" as that which attempts to expunge all references to the world, and opposed it to "kitsch," or popular culture.[6]

So many critics from 1970 to the end of the century, especially in the United States, grew up on Greenberg's narrow definition that this drive toward purification is even now still assumed to be a defining trait of modernism in much contemporary writing on art. So, too, is the notion that the major twentieth-century artists subscribed to the separation of "high art" from life and from popular culture, as Greenberg did. But this is by no means the case; indeed, the eclecticism of modern artists, their radical openness to disparate sources of content, is one of the most constant—though not always the most explicit—features of modernism. In fact, much of the "historical avant-garde" of the earlier twentieth century (futurism, dada, and constructivism, for example) sought specifically to erase the boundaries between art and life and between "high" and "low" art as a means of undermining the "institution" of art (namely, the socially accepted values in and about art and their embodiment in museum installations, academic scholarship, and the like) and broadening the critique of values in society at large.[7] This wish to revolutionize mainstream values is the defining role of the avant-garde, and it is inseparable from modernism. While most modern artists have defined their practice as avant-garde, however, this is sometimes misleading because in giving us a fresh perspective on the world they do not necessarily intend to revolutionize mainstream values. What really motivates them is more personal; it is the wish to bring coherence to their experience when their insight has revealed something new and unsettling to their understanding.

Modernism's Radical Individuality and Self-Critique

The story of modernism is a double one of faith and doubt, hope and despair. In today's world the utopianism of early modernism seems quaint, like something from another era. But underlying this book is a faith in the creative ingenuity of the individual and of the artist, in particular, as an exemplary individual. Such individuals help us all recognize the present and envision a different future than the one toward which we may seem headed. They also act as a force against the spread of a statistical view of humankind as disposable units in the machinery of mass culture. Indeed, built into the origins of modernism is the idea, explained more than a hundred years ago by the French writer Charles Baudelaire, that imagination "decomposes all creation, and with the raw materials accumulated and disposed in accordance with rules whose origins one cannot find save in the furthest depths of the soul, it creates a new world."[8]

Baudelaire's faith in individual genius builds on "romanticism," another useful term that resists rigorous definition as much as modernism. Indeed, romanticism is built into the origins of modernism, which in some respects it simultaneously contradicts. Romanticism is above all a personality trait that transcends culture and time, although the paradigmatic examples are artists and writers of the late eighteenth and early nineteenth centuries, such as the English painter J. M. W. Turner, the French painter Eugène Delacroix, and the English poets Samuel Taylor Coleridge and William Wordsworth. The term, defined in this way, is nevertheless also usefully deployed in discussions of the twentieth and even the twenty-first centuries and need not be locked into an immutable historical construction. The romantic disposition favors the dynamic, the disordered, the soft-focused, the inner, the sensate world. The concept generally involves a faith in progress and change, the subversion of institutions, and an emphasis on the inspired individual in some special contact with nature or the cosmos.

The practical side of progress through open debate and reason also celebrates the individual thinker. In this sense the radical individuality of romanticism, despite its elevation of the irrational (as opposed to reason), belongs to modernism. But if we acknowledge that works of art give meaningful form to perceptions that we cannot verbalize, and that, in art, we can contemplate, rearrange, and structure the relations between such forms, then we might have to broaden our sense of what reason itself actually means, separating linear, verbal logic from more intuitive and complex forms of reasoning.

The intuitive and emotional in romanticism had their counterparts in the precise definitions, rules, and boundaries of contemporaneous classicism. Yet, a timeless duality in the human mind between our rational, analytical side and our emotions has preoccupied great thinkers from the earliest poets of antiquity to the present. In the later part of the nineteenth century Friedrich Nietzsche famously described it as a duality of the "Apollonian" and "Dionysian," in an epochal book of 1872 entitled *The Birth of Tragedy*. But the idea reemerges repeatedly in the history of human thought, as in the duality of romanticism and classicism in the early nineteenth century and in the famous debates between Claude Lévi-Strauss and Jean-Paul Sartre in the French press at the end of the 1950s pitting structuralism against existentialism. From the start, however, modernism has embraced this conflict within itself so that major exemplars of the one tendency frequently also embody aspects of the other.

Sigmund Freud, one of the most influential thinkers of the twentieth century, built on Nietzsche's dichotomy with his concept of the unconscious, first articulated in his book *The Interpretation of Dreams* of 1900. In this and in subsequent writings, Freud described the human mind as a complex and dynamic layering of conflicting primal impulses, self-imposed controls, and shifting symbolizations. If, as Freud argued, reality was subjective, filtered through the interplay of basic drives, instincts, and perceptions, the external and absolute truths of modern science were at least difficult to verify, if not inherently questionable. Freud's subject is something we can neither see nor measure directly. His psychoanalytic method relied on profound self-examination to distinguish reality from subjectivity and yet he acknowledges that he can never reach a complete interpretation nor a definitive separation of the two.

Self-examination and self-criticism are essential traits of modernism. The fact that vanguard artists have, to a great extent, come from the middle classes and that their radical art has been paid for largely by the bourgeoisie further affirms this model of self-revolutionizing on a larger scale; the avant-garde has consistently aimed its most vehement attacks at the bourgeoisie, making vanguardism a form of self-criticism. Self-criticism (especially in the form of self-examination) is, in turn, central to the aspirations for the objective analysis and innovation that modernism (and democracy) reveres. In the art of the late twentieth century, however, the vanguard attack on traditional values became such an expected aspect of new art that the avant-garde and even innovation ironically became traditions in themselves, as Harold Rosenberg pointed out in his famous essay "The Tradition of the New."[9] This observation is what underlies the most intriguing new element in the discussion of the avant-garde and modernism, namely the widespread sense of their demise.

Postmodernism

Whereas modernism emphasizes rationality, objectivity, and progress, the attitude that has come to be called "postmodernism" questions whether any of these can even exist. The sought-after universality and totality in modernist thought are rejected in postmodernism as untenable "metanarratives." The postmodernist denies the practical possibility of objectivity or even constancy in the meaning of symbols, believing that they can be redefined at will.

In 1979 the French philosopher Jean-François Lyotard wrote: "I define *postmodern* as incredulity toward metanarratives."[10] By this he meant to express his skepticism toward such fundamental, sweeping, and commonly held assumptions about the world as our belief in progress, our sense of individual uniqueness, and our faith in linear logic. In 1980 Gilles Deleuze and Félix Guattari, two of Lyotard's contemporaries in Paris, proposed a model for describing and interpreting the world that developed in many different directions simultaneously. They used the metaphor of "the rhizome," a root structure in plants that spreads out horizontally in multiple places at once and shoots off new growths in many sites at the same time and in a non-hierarchical, seemingly arbitrary manner.[11]

This was a radical departure from common ways of thinking, and yet at the same time there were a number of others, especially in this circle of thinkers in France, articulating a similarly decentered and unstable worldview. Among the most famous was Jacques Derrida, who founded "deconstruction"—an approach to reading that denied the possibility of a single, "correct" interpretation in favor of a permanent instability in meaning, engendered by inevitable contradictions within the text itself that collided and caused a "deconstruction" of the meaning into dynamic flux. Another was Michel Foucault, whose deeply nuanced writings on the relations of power and knowledge underscored the endlessly complex, contingent and dynamic nature of social relations. All of this so-called "post-structuralist" philosophy and sociology was indebted to the "structuralism" of the French anthropologist Claude Lévi-Strauss, who taught us to analyze culture like a language with a grammar and syntax. His successors used this method to demonstrate (among other things) how much the language we use to describe a thing frames the reality of what it is for us. At the same time, they also regarded this reality as an inherently unstable organizing fiction.

As early as 1960, a number of artists and writers were beginning to explore this instability. The 1959 novel *Naked Lunch*, by William Burroughs, consists of arbitrarily juxtaposed pages of text that were published in the random order in which they were received by the editor, rather than in any order proposed by the author. In the visual arts, Robert Rauschenberg's "combines" of the fifties (assemblages of found and painted elements) and his photosilkscreen paintings of the sixties center on his experience of constantly shifting, arbitrary juxtapositions of perceptions. "I was bombarded with television sets and magazines, by the excess of the world," Rauschenberg explained. "I thought an honest work should incorporate all of those elements, which were and are a reality."[12]

An American Perspective/the Perspective of this Book

Dan Flavin, one of the most important American artists of the 1960s, wrote at the end of that decade: "The quaint, exotic, pretentious, esoteric and hostile jargon of 'avant-garde' so frequently conveniently abused by a few American artists and several of their critics . . . ought to be relegated to a more plausible distinction than local contemporary arts, better to be descriptive of a tactic for a French army."[13] In the recent discussion about modernism, it has become increasingly clear how poorly modernism and the concept of an avant-garde fits an American context, as Flavin pointed out in this essay of 1969. Modernism is a European invention and a modernist avant-garde depends upon the normalizing force of a common history, inherited social class, and stable values against which to react. But the framers of the American Constitution constructed the nation without such a legacy; the United States came into being at the end of the Enlightenment as a society invented, more than inherited, and from the start it included a broad and constantly shifting diversity of cultures. The framers believed they could depend upon their own intellects to devise a code of laws that would guarantee for future generations the agreed-upon principles of equality, individual freedom, and religious tolerance. The themes of self-invention and self-reliance, cultural diversity, and the idea of starting afresh (as though there were no past) have recurred prominently in American cultural history from the beginning, though these core values have become increasingly corrupted over time by self-serving politicians and some of those with a disproportionate share of our society's wealth.

Thomas Jefferson and his contemporaries did want to create a common sense of an American identity and of a collective future. But unlike Europeans, who could look back to the ancient temples of Greece or the cathedrals of France, Americans had few visible symbols of human history on this continent. So the Founders turned to our geological and natural history. The discoveries of the Lewis and Clark Expedition (commissioned by President Jefferson) and the 435 "Birds of America" painted by John James Audubon in these same years took their place alongside Niagara Falls and Yosemite Valley as the emblems of our common culture. But these things existed outside of time. So we fashioned our national history in a collage of juxtaposed symbols rather than as a chronicle of a continuous past. In this way, America has embraced some of the underlying principles of what today we call "postmodernism" since its founding in the eighteenth century! This lack of history also unburdened Americans from a strong loyalty to tradition. American culture (both for better and worse) has tended to take up pragmatic innovation quickly and adapt to changing circumstances more freely than Europe.

The fundamental hybridity and mutability of American culture is implied in the multicultural identity of its founding self-conception; indeed, as a culture it is committed to a destabilizing fluidity in its forms—politically, economically, and socially. From Emerson, Thoreau, and Whitman, through O'Keeffe, Hemingway, and William Carlos Williams, right to the present, most of the greatest American artists and writers have always been engaged with a myth of self-reliance, grounded in practicality. Whereas European modernism and the European avant-garde have occupied themselves with breaking down inherited hierarchies in thinking, American culture has always seen itself as starting "from scratch"—which is how the American painter Barnett Newman put it in 1967.[14]

In everything from free-market capitalism to the myth of "pioneer" individualism, Americans have tended toward a broadly ahistorical approach to things, as though we could always begin with a *tabula rasa*. That attitude gave America in the twentieth century a Protean adaptability in economics and technology and art. It also means, as we have said above, that the European innovations of the avant-garde and modernism have never precisely fit the American situation. The American contribution to the twentieth century is postmodernism, with its journalistic vulgarity in accepting popular culture and respecting no canon of style or technique. American postmodernism is not so much an attack on history or aesthetic values as a brash disregard for their very premises in favor of a definitive uprootedness and creative instability.

At the same time it is worth pointing out that the real practice of all ideology is impure and, despite the underlying theory, the story of America is also complicated with tendencies in opposition to all these aspirations, notably the historical repression of minorities and continuing attempts by some to exploit fundamental human insecurities among the broad population in order to cement the privileges of the few. Unfortunately, as Jefferson wrote, "experience hath shown, that even under the best forms [of government], those entrusted with power have, in time, and by slow operations, perverted it into tyranny; and it is believed that the most effectual means of preventing this would be, to illuminate, as far as practicable, the minds of the people at large."[15]

In *The Ego and the Id* Freud described a persevering pressure from the unconscious mind to gratify its wishes directly in the world. The resistance to the attainment of such immediate gratification from others or from the material conditions of the world necessitates the creation of a mental mechanism—which Freud called the "ego"—that assesses what is possible and integrates the unconscious wishes with reality. A few years later, he expanded on the political implications of this idea in his book *Civilization and Its Discontents*. This tension between the inner self and the world is what,

in my view, provides the foundation for that "happening of truth" in art which Martin Heidegger described in 1935.[16] For him a work of art needed to be discussed in terms of the process of its creation precisely because creating is a form of seeing or knowing. The writings of both Derrida and Sartre grew out of this same basic principle from Heidegger and Edmund Husserl (another German philosopher and the one on whom Derrida wrote his first book).

The methods of this book are a formally based mode of analysis that look to the spiritual concerns of the individual (in a secular sense of the term) as the origin and defining rule for forms. Moreover, this approach assumes that through the form—together with other expressions of intention by the artist—one can make a meaningful and verifiable (though not a complete or final) interpretation. Many philosophically inclined academics have attempted to parse contemporary art into categories, or subject it to highly theorized arguments, which, however interesting, miss the essential impetus behind making a work of art and its most important task in illuminating the realities of the present. Art is a mode of discovery and experimentation. Theory has the effect of distancing and normalizing precisely what is so unsettling in new art. That unsettling content is what makes art so important. This is a danger with museums as well; even the simple picture frame distances us from a direct and often disturbing encounter with the chaotic revelations that are at the heart of aesthetic experience.

I began my introduction to this book with Van Gogh's painting of shoes in homage to Heidegger, who opened his seminal lectures of 1935–6 on the "Origin of the Work of Art" with the same example. These lectures affirm the foundations of modern art in the expression of being rather than in pure form. My persistent focus is on the work of extraordinary individuals. I have deliberately subordinated the concept of movements and of collective cultural constructs. This approach expresses my belief that the innovations of individuals, in response to what they themselves encounter in the world, play the most significant role in shaping the history of art (though I do not wish to discount the impact of vernaculars, tradition, or social, political, and economic factors in defining "what the artist encounters"). Moreover, this history is being continually revised to include previously neglected points of view that later acquire historical significance through the responses of subsequent audiences.

Artists' creative struggles to reconcile their individual imaginative life with their social existence can—through the empathic reading of viewers—affect the level on which others experience events. The structural strategies in a work of art (motivated by what I have called "strategies of being") can put the viewer in a certain frame of mind that he or she can then bring to bear, as a posture for questioning, on real events. One of the hazards of our educational system's concern with technical mastery has been to foreground "history" in the history of art at the cost of the more immediate but always baffling and inconclusive experience of the art itself. Art is a force against authoritarian modes of thinking. I hope this book will help us all recover a healthier state of ignorance.

2.1 André Masson, *Battle of Fishes*, 1926. Sand, gesso, oil,
pencil, and charcoal on canvas, 14¼ × 28¾in (36.2 × 73cm).
The Museum of Modern Art, New York. Purchase, 260.1937.

2 NEW YORK IN THE FORTIES

NEW YORK BECOMES THE CENTER

With the French and British entrance into World War II in September 1939, artists and intellectuals began fleeing Paris, which had been the world's art capital for more than a century. The surrealists had captured the spotlight in the thriving interwar art scene of Paris, but by 1942 the critical mass of the movement's key figures—André Breton, Salvador Dalí, Max Ernst, André Masson, Kurt Seligmann, Yves Tanguy, and the young Roberto Matta—had all gone to New York. In addition, great cubists, abstract artists, and others from the School of Paris had come over, too, among them Fernand Léger, Piet Mondrian, Marc Chagall, Jacques Lipchitz, and Amedée Ozenfant. Of the major artists only Pablo Picasso and the seventy-three-year-old Wassily Kandinsky remained in Paris for the duration of the war. This book begins at the turning point of 1940, when the center of the art world shifted to New York, setting the stage for the nascent New York School to form the new leading edge of the "avant-garde." This scattering of the Parisian art world also began a process of dispersing our focus in a way that would, by the end of the century, provide a new model of multiple centers, and with the rise of information technology at the beginning of the twenty-first century the whole notion of a single center to the global art world became moot.

Surrealism

Surrealism evolved from the shock tactics of dada around 1924, under the direction of the poet André Breton. Influenced by Freudian psychoanalysis, the surrealists looked to the unconscious mind as the source of artistic subject matter. In the first *Surrealist Manifesto* of 1924 Breton defined surrealism as "pure psychic automatism by which one intends to express verbally, in writing or by other method, the real functioning of the mind. Dictation by thought, in the absence of any control exercised by reason, and beyond any aesthetic or moral preoccupation."[1]

The French surrealist André Masson created his *Battle of Fishes* [fig. 2.1] by spilling glue on the canvas and then pouring on sand; the sand stuck where the glue fell and he used the forms produced in this random fashion as a springboard for free association. He then modified these chance shapes to accentuate the subject matter of his associations. The finished painting "reads" like a poem rather than a narrative; instead of interacting in logical ways, each image moves off into seemingly different trains of thought. The underlying coherence of meaning in the work relies on metonymy, as in the symbolism of a dream where ideas are represented, often cryptically, by ideas that are associated with the manifest content. This is a classically surrealist application of "psychic automatism." But it was as a device for generating form rather than a means of revealing content that automatism would become central to the artists of the New York School.

Wifredo Lam

Among the artists championed by Breton was a young Afro-Cuban painter named Wifredo Lam, who had come to Paris in 1938 at the age of twenty-six. In Paris he met Picasso, who in turn introduced him to Breton. After the German occupation in the fall of 1939, Lam fled home to Cuba, where he painted his best-known works. In 1945 the Museum of Modern Art in New York purchased *The Jungle* of 1942–3; he also had several exhibitions in New York during the 1940s, and his work appeared in New York surrealist publications such as *VVV* and *View* as well as publications associated with the New York School like *Tiger's Eye*. Yet he associated with the post-World War II surrealists in Paris

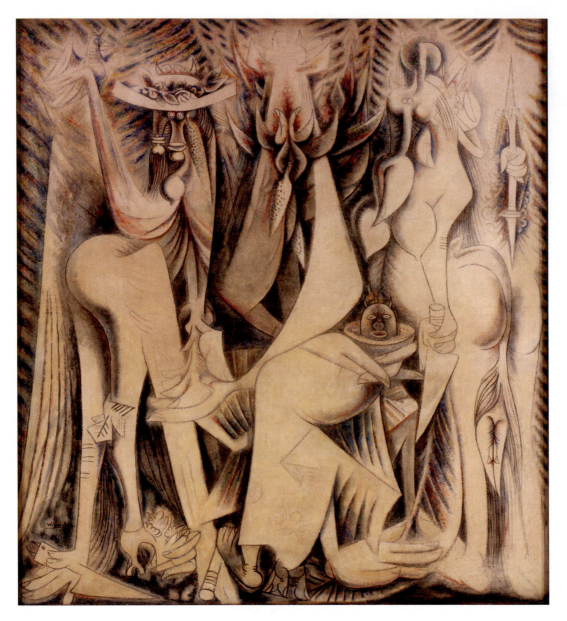

2.2 Wifredo Lam,
The Eternal Present, 1944.
Mixed media on jute, 85 ×
77½in (215.9 × 196.9cm).
Museum of Art, Rhode Island School
of Design, Providence. Nancy Sayles
Day Fund.

more than with the artists in New York; even after his return to Cuba, Lam remained close, above all, to Breton. In Cuba during the forties, Lam fashioned a highly original, hybrid surrealism that melded his Afro-Caribbean roots with both stylistic and theoretical aspects of French surrealism.

In *The Eternal Present* of 1944 [fig. 2.2], Lam created the three *femme cheval* (woman-horse) images through a partial process of metamorphosis of a woman into a horse; the transformation is especially evident in the heads. This transformation is surrealist in its genesis through unconscious association and dreamlike mutation. But it also has a dynamic black spirituality with clear connections to the Afro-Cuban voodoo practices in which a woman, in a state of spiritual possession by the *orisha* (or saint), is said to be ridden by the *orisha* like a horse. The New York filmmaker Maya Deren documented a Haitian voodoo rite of this kind in *The Divine Horsemen* of 1947–51 (see Chapter 7). Breton's continuing links to Lam not only demonstrate the internationalist

perspective that Breton and the other Europeans brought to the New York art scene in the early forties, but Lam's work and even the person of the artist himself (whose father was Chinese and mother Afro-Cuban) also exemplify the rich mix of cultures in the New World. In her book on Lam, Lowery Sims writes of the "permeability between the physical and metaphysical in the Afro-Cuban universe,"[2] while also pointing out the simultaneous connections to surrealism as well as to the nascent New York School's interest in mythic imagery. The hybridity of Lam's practice was emblematic of the whole of postwar art, particularly in the Americas.

Roberto Matta

In 1935, the young Chilean Roberto Matta (Echaurren) also headed for Paris. Trained in architecture, he discovered the work of Marcel Duchamp and the surrealists and became interested in the idea that he could explore time and change in drawing. In 1937, he worked on the famous Spanish Pavilion at the Paris World's Fair, for which Picasso painted his *Guernica*, and in 1938 Matta left architecture for painting. But he was scarcely into this new endeavor, when he had to flee from the Nazi invasion of Paris and in November of 1939, at the age of twenty-seven, he arrived in New York.

Breton embraced both Matta and his close friend Gordon Onslow Ford into the ranks of surrealism, and in New York he showed, along with other surrealists, at the Julian Levy Gallery (1940), in the 1942 "Artists in Exile" at the Pierre Matisse Gallery, and in the October "First Papers of Surrealism" at Peggy Guggenheim's Art of This Century gallery in which Marcel Duchamp famously hung miles of white string across the space in a web through which viewers had to walk (a kind of "dada" theatrics). Ford and Matta met William Baziotes through a mutual friend and, in 1942, Robert Motherwell and Baziotes brought a few more young American artists (including Jackson Pollock) to meet in Matta's studio. They met several times over the fall and winter of 1942–3 to experiment with collage and automatic drawing. Matta was a critical link between surrealism and the New York School, in part because he was of the same generation as Motherwell, Pollock, and their friends.[3] Matta moved back to Europe in 1948 [fig. 2.3], leaving his wife Anne, from whom he had separated in 1943, and his five-year-old twins, Gordon and Sebastien. Gordon was to become a major figure in the art of the 1970s.

2.3 Roberto Matta, *Je m'honte (I Shame Myself/I Ascend)*, 1948–9. Oil on canvas, 6ft 4¾in × 4ft 7⅞in (1.95 × 1.42m). Menil Collection, Houston.

Joseph Cornell

Joseph Cornell was a native New Yorker, but from his first collages of 1931, he demonstrates the formal influence of the surrealists with whom he soon began showing at Julien Levy's gallery—although, as he wrote in 1936, "I do not share in the subconscious and dream theories of the surrealists."[4] Cornell's work mostly consisted of little boxes filled with found objects and images assembled to suggest complex, mesmerizing stories. He wrote of an "intense longing to get into the boxes this overflowing, a richness & poetry."[5] He found inspiration for these self-contained fantastical worlds not only in the mysterious collages of Max Ernst, which he saw at the 1931 opening of Levy's gallery , but also in souvenirs and old cards he saw in the curio shops around Times Square, in the constellations painted on the ceiling of Grand Central Station, and in other things that a less imaginative mind might have overlooked as ordinary.

In Cornell's *Untitled (The Hotel Eden)* (1945) [fig. 2.4], the "Hotel Eden" seems to be a stopping place in a magical voyage, filled with exotic birds and strange scientific devices. Cornell seems deliberately to suggest a tattered Paradise after the Fall, linking the work to other boxes which refer to punished lovers—Adam and Eve, Paul and Virginia (from the eponymous nineteenth-century French novel), Paolo and Francesca (from Dante). The swirling spiral in the upper left may refer directly to the *Rotary Demisphere* of Marcel Duchamp, whom Cornell befriended after Duchamp's return to New York in 1942. Cornell read widely, especially in French literature, and had a fascination with Hollywood stars. But externally he led an utterly simple life. He lived on Utopia Parkway in the New York borough of Queens with an invalid brother, his mother, and his grandfather. He largely supported them by taking routine jobs in the garment industry until, in 1941, he was finally able to devote himself to art full time.

American Pragmatism and Social Relevance

The surrealists' preoccupation with the hidden content of the mind and the formal vocabulary of European modernism [figs. 2.10, 3.22, and 5.17] provided the intellectual and aesthetic ingredients for the New York School. "Today painters do not have to go to a subject matter outside of themselves," Jackson Pollock told an interviewer in 1950. "Most modern painters work from a different source, they work from within." And yet, even with the introverted Pollock, there was a sense that the artist should express his or her culture and moment in history. The modern painter, he said, had to "express his age, the airplane, the atom bomb, the radio."[6]

2.4 Joseph Cornell, *Untitled (The Hotel Eden)*, 1945. Assemblage with music box, 15 × 15⅝ × 4¾in (38.1 × 39.7 × 12.1cm). National Gallery of Canada, Ottawa.

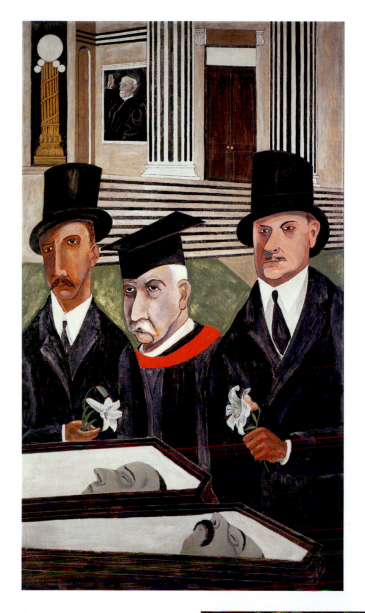

But for many of Pollock's contemporaries, the ingrained values of interwar American culture created a commitment to engage the outside world more directly. Reinforced by the experience of the Great Depression, government patronage (under the Federal Art Project of the thirties), and by the war itself, America's pervasive Protestant ethic had instilled in many a sense of obligation to make their art socially "relevant" or "useful." In American art of the thirties relevance meant either the easily recognizable treatment of political themes or the promotion of "American values." Ben Shahn's *The Passion of Sacco and Vanzetti* [fig. 2.5], an example of the former, concerned the famous 1927 trial and conviction of two Italian-American laborers in Boston for a hold-up and shooting. Many people at the time believed that the jury's attitude toward the defendants' radical leftist politics and their ethnicity resulted in an unjust verdict. Shahn portrayed the two as martyrs to the cause of social justice. Thomas Hart Benton's celebration of hairy-chested American masculinity in his painting *The Arts of the West* [fig. 2.6] and Grant Wood's well-known *American Gothic* exemplify the alternative to Shahn in their affirmation of the American national myths of the Wild West, country religion, and "the heartland." This kind of painting was referred to as "regionalism."

Meanwhile Mexico (like Germany and Russia) had undergone a leftist revolution in the teens, and the utopian aspirations associated with it engendered a brilliant efflorescence of fresco painting beginning in 1921. News of a "Mexican mural renaissance" spread through the New York art press in the late twenties, and the leading artists—Diego Rivera, David Siqueiros, and José Clemente Orozco—began receiving important public commissions around the United States.

Rufino Tamayo is another example of the vitality of the Mexican art scene. As Mary Coffey has pointed out,[7] Tamayo did not want to be seen as the fourth "great one" ("*Los Tres Grandes*" were Rivera, Siqueiros, and Orozco)

2.5 (above) **Ben Shahn**, *The Passion of Sacco and Vanzetti*, 1931–2. Tempera on canvas, 7ft ½in × 4ft (2.15 × 1.22m). Whitney Museum of American Art, New York. Gift of Edith and Milton Lowenthal in memory of Juliana Force, 49.22.

2.6 (right) **Thomas Hart Benton**, *The Arts of the West*, 1932. Egg tempera and oil on linen mounted on panel, 8 × 13ft (2.44 × 3.96m). New Britain Museum of American Art, Connecticut. Harriet Russell Stanley Fund.

because his ideas were so different artistically, even though he too contributed important murals to prominent sites like the Palacio de Bellas Artes in Mexico City. In a work like his *Girl Attacked by a Strange Bird* of 1947 [fig. 2.7] he took the inspiration of Picasso's cubist expressionism of the late thirties and forties and infused it with a brilliant Latin palette and rich narrative subject matter. This was the foundation of a powerful and unique postwar style; the expressive content of Tamayo's work had more in common with Pollock in the forties than the muralists did, although the latter's scale and technical experimentalism impacted Pollock greatly.

Julian Levy gave Tamayo a one-person show in 1937. In addition to a series of murals done in New York by the Mexicans, Siqueiros set up a workshop by Union Square,

in which he introduced his apprentices (among them the young Pollock) to experimental techniques, including paint splattering and the use of industrial "Duco" paints. Punning on Siqueiros's radical leftist politics, some of the younger painters at the time jokingly referred to him as "Il Duco:"[8]— a pun on Duco paint and "Il Duce" (the popular epithet of the Italian Fascist leader, Mussolini). Politics was very much in the air.

Of all the Mexican muralists, Rivera had the most powerful impact on the younger generation in the United States. In his *Detroit Industry* frescoes [fig. 2.8] he transformed the Ford Motor Company's Rouge River industrial complex into a symphony of modern industry and workers. Although he denied any connection to socialist realism, Rivera deliberately chose to work in a simplified, monumental style so as

2.7 Rufino Tamayo, *Girl Attacked by a Strange Bird*, 1947. Oil on canvas, 6ft 10in × 4ft 2⅛in (1.78 × 1.27m).
The Museum of Modern Art, New York. Gift of Mr. and Mrs. Charles Zadok, 200.1955.

2.8 Diego Rivera, *Detroit Industry*, 1932–3.
South wall, fresco, 43 × 67ft (13.11 × 20.42m).
The Detroit Institute of Arts. Gift of Edsel B. Ford.

to educate the masses in the ideals of the leftist utopia, and his mastery of figural composition on this public scale is unequaled in modern art.

Ben Shahn knew and admired Rivera's work and actually served as an assistant on Rivera's murals for Rockefeller Center. But Rivera's scale and his multilayered content also profoundly influenced Pollock and other young abstract artists. Rivera's style brings together a rich matrix of historical and conceptual references: the spirituality of Italian Renaissance frescoes, the idealism of classical proportions, a sense of the origins of his art in pre-Columbian civilization, shallow cubist space with its overtones of European modernism, constructivist compositional dynamism, and a utopian enthusiasm for the machine age.

Nevertheless, Rivera sought to create an indigenously "American" art (by which he meant Mexico even more than the United States) that was at the same time not provincial. In his autobiography he described himself as undergoing a kind of rebirth through native culture when he returned to Mexico from Paris in 1921.[9] In his *Detroit Industry* frescoes,

and even more obviously in the *City College of San Francisco* fresco of 1939, Rivera conceived the great machines as modern transformations of ancient Indian gods; indeed, one can find direct sources in Aztec statuary for some of Rivera's industrial images.[10] This transformation implies a sense of continuous and inevitable cultural evolution, which Rivera modeled on a Marxist view of history. It also suggests Rivera's sense of the rich and mysterious presence of ancient forces lingering behind the forms of the modern world.

Benton and his fellow regionalists, the Mexicans, and the social realists (like Ben Shahn) all sought idealistic transformations of society by programmatic appeals to the masses on an expansive public scale, using an easily legible style. They agreed on very little else than the imperative for social relevance and on their opposition to European modernism, whose rarefied language seemed to them elitist (though all of them had learned enduring formal lessons from it). The denial of sensibility and the retreat from cultivation (synonymous with Europe in the minds of most Americans) was also evident in such American writers of the period as Ernest Hemingway. Similarly the painter Georgia O'Keeffe and the contemporary imagist poets Wallace Stevens and William Carlos Williams sought a kind of matter-of-fact objectivity in their work. Yet they also seem to have experienced a sense of romantic transport in the closely observed detail of nature and, unlike Benton, felt torn between their "Americanness" and their reverence for the subtlety and depth of European modernism. Neither the paintings of O'Keeffe nor this kind of poetry were anti-intellectual, they merely sought an indigenous American character in their simple facticity.

The Depression and the Works Progress Administration (W.P.A.)

The stock-market crash of 1929 and the ensuing Great Depression intensified the pressure for social relevance in art. George Biddle, who came from a patrician Philadelphia family, studied painting in Paris, and went through Groton and Harvard with F.D.R., wrote to Roosevelt on May 9, 1933:

> The Mexican artists have produced the greatest national school of mural painting since the Italian Renaissance. Diego Rivera tells me that it was only possible because Obregon [president of Mexico, 1920–4] allowed Mexican artists to work at plumbers' wages in order to express on the walls of the government buildings the social ideals of the Mexican Revolution. The younger artists of America are conscious as they have never been of the social revolution that our country and civilization are going through, and they would be eager to express these ideas in a permanent art form.[11]

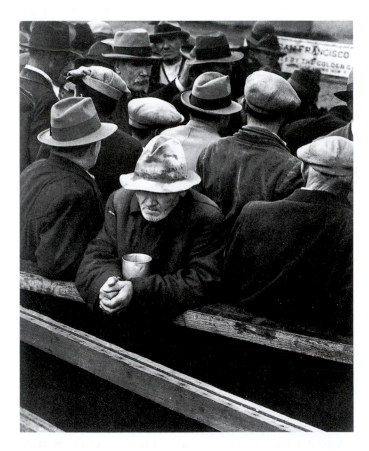

2.9 Dorothea Lange, *White Angel Breadline, San Francisco*, 1933. Photograph.

Courtesy of the Dorothea Lange Collection, Oakland Museum. Gift of Paul S. Taylor.

This appeal was not viewed unsympathetically; President Roosevelt had already had artists on the payroll while governor of New York. As the Depression deepened, the government stepped in with the Public Works of Art Project in 1934, commissioning murals (and distributing a booklet on Rivera's fresco technique to recipients of commissions). The Works Progress Administration (W.P.A.) began the Federal Art Project under Holger Cahill in 1935, expanding the types of commissions to easel painting, sculpture, and other media. In addition the Farm Security Administration commissioned an extensive photographic project, documenting the country's impoverished rural areas and workers as well as the plight of the urban poor [fig. 2.9].

The Project produced hundreds of thousands of works, and by 1936 employed around 6,000 artists, half to three-quarters of them living in New York. Although the stipend provided only enough to get by on (the equivalent of about $325 a week in today's dollars), government patronage offered artists dignity, a sense of value, and a place in American society. It also formed a real community of artists for the first time, especially in Greenwich Village in New York. Stuart Davis, Jackson Pollock, Willem de Kooning, Arshile Gorky, Lee Krasner, David Smith, and Mark Rothko—many of the most influential artists of the New York School—all worked on the Project. Those whose income or employment status disqualified them felt like outcasts. Barnett Newman, who had a teaching job in the Depression, said, "I paid a severe price for not being on the Project with the other guys; in their eyes I wasn't a painter; I didn't have the label."[12]

The Availability of European Modernism

Despite the wish among so many interwar artists in New York to throw off the weight of European modernism, they had also felt the opposite emotion too—true admiration; the influence of the Europeans continued to grow as their work became increasingly accessible in the thirties in New York. The founding of the Museum of Modern Art in 1929 made available magnificent works by Cézanne, Seurat, Van Gogh, Gauguin, Toulouse-Lautrec, Picasso, Matisse, and Léger as well as special exhibitions of cubists, surrealists, abstract artists, and Bauhaus art and design. The Valentine Gallery, which had held particularly notable shows of Matisse and Brancusi in the twenties, exhibited Picasso's enormously influential painting *Guernica* [fig. 2.10] in 1939, after which the Museum of Modern Art kept it on display continuously for nearly forty more years.

The New Art Circle gallery, founded by J. B. Neumann in 1923, was an early but by no means the only place where young artists might see German expressionism—including works by Beckmann, Klee, and Kirchner. In addition, the Gallatin Collection—with works by Cézanne, Seurat, the cubists, Mondrian, and such artists of the Russian avant-garde as Naum Gabo and El Lissitzky—went on loan to New York University in Washington Square; and although

2.10 Pablo Picasso, *Guernica*, May 1–June 4, 1937. Oil on canvas, 11ft 6in × 25ft 8in (3.5 × 7.82m).
Museo Nacional Centro de Arte Reina Sofia, Madrid. On permanent loan from the Museo del Prado, Madrid.

the Museum of Non-Objective Painting (later to become the Solomon R. Guggenheim Museum) did not open until 1939, Guggenheim regularly opened his definitive collection of Kandinsky's abstractions to young artists in his New York apartment from 1936.[13]

Picasso's *Guernica* had particular importance to younger painters because it combined a powerful political statement with the best of European formal sophistication. The title refers to the little Basque town of Guernica, which the German *Luftwaffe*, under directions from the Spanish Nationalist General Franco, leveled in 1937, wiping out most of the defenseless civilian population. When the Republican government of Spain (in the midst of civil war with Franco) commissioned Picasso to paint a work for its pavilion at the Paris Exposition Universelle of 1937, the artist responded with *Guernica*. The monumental scale and powerful expressionism of the work, and the use of a cubist vocabulary for a tragic theme, set an important precedent for American artists. Its influence can be seen in the use of a grand scale with a shallow cubist depth in the great drip paintings of Pollock [figs. 4.1 and 4.5–4.9]; it also underlies de Kooning's black paintings of the mid-forties [fig. 3.37] and Motherwell's "Elegies" [figs. 3.29 and 3.30].

Meanwhile, European surrealism had already affected younger artists even before the arrival of the surrealists themselves. The Julien Levy Gallery began exhibiting the European surrealists' work and publishing translations of their writings at the end of 1931, the Pierre Matisse Gallery showed Miró and Masson beginning in 1935, and the Museum of Modern Art's important "Dada, Surrealism, and Fantastic Art" exhibition of 1936 made available a stunning array of their paintings, objects, and writings. In 1942 the "Artists in Exile" show at Pierre Matisse and Marcel Duchamp's "First Papers of Surrealism" exhibition, staged in the former Whitelaw Reid mansion on Madison Avenue at 50th Street, celebrated the arrival of the artists themselves in New York.

The Europeans in New York

When the Europeans finally arrived in person, their self-confidence and bohemian lifestyles made it seem as if money never worried them—in fact, many were exceedingly poor. They communicated a sense of conviction about the importance of art and of New York as the center; indeed *they* made it seem that wherever *they* were was *ipso facto* the center. Moreover, Breton and the other surrealists had a strong sense of belonging to a unified avant-garde that comprised artists outside surrealism as well. When Breton edited the first catalog for Peggy Guggenheim's Art of This Century gallery in 1942, he included texts and manifestoes by futurists, by Gabo and Pevsner, by Ben Nicholson, and Mondrian, in addition to those by the surrealists.

So, having the Europeans personally on the scene in New York was very different from just looking at works by them. The European moderns not only connected New York in a vital way to a more international world, but they also provided a compelling new model of what an artist was. To the Europeans art and life were inseparable and they lived this heightened existence twenty-four hours a day. In conversation with the younger Americans they also

2.11 (opposite) **Jackson Pollock**, *Male and Female*, c. 1942.
Oil on canvas, 6ft 1¼in × 4ft 1¹⁵⁄₁₆in (1.86 × 1.24m).
Philadelphia Museum of Art. Gift of Mr. and Mrs. H. Gates Lloyd.

imparted their insights into the more subtle formal concerns of painting, thereby implicitly encouraging them to come up to the aesthetic level of European modernism. Associating with artists is a time-honored way for the young to learn not just the craft, but what it means to be an artist. The presence of the Parisian vanguard in New York finally gave young Americans an opportunity to see this firsthand, creating the fertile soil out of which the new American art grew.

The Europeans found life in New York quite different from that to which they were accustomed. Paris is a city of neighborhoods and the vitality of each neighborhood radiates from its cafés. The members of Parisian art movements had always frequented particular haunts in Paris; and for the surrealists it was above all the Café Cyrano near Pigalle at which they would run into one another almost daily and engage in protracted discussions. New York had no such tradition: The pace of life was too fast and the city too populous to make a café society possible. In addition,

the artists had to scatter to find housing quickly when they arrived, which effectively meant that no one neighborhood could be identified with a particular movement, although Greenwich Village had a tradition of attracting artists of all kinds and would become a focus for the New York School too because of the relatively low cost of living there.

The young Museum of Modern Art opened its doors to the surrealists, and to some extent the Julien Levy and Pierre Matisse galleries helped compensate for the loss of the established Paris meeting places. But the most important gathering spot was the private gallery of Peggy Guggenheim, called Art of This Century. In 1942 alone she showed work by Arp, Ernst, Miró, Masson, Tanguy, Magritte, Dalí, Brauner, and Giacometti. But Art of This Century also gave one-person exhibitions to the Americans Jackson Pollock [fig. 2.11], Hans Hofmann, Mark Rothko, Clyfford Still, William Baziotes [fig. 2.12],

2.12 William Baziotes, *Green Form*, 1945–6.
Oil on canvas, 3ft 4in × 4ft (1.02 × 1.22m).
Whitney Museum of American Art, New York. Gift of Mr. and Mrs. Samuel M. Kootz and exchange, 49.23.

2.13 Robert Motherwell, *Pancho Villa, Dead and Alive*, 1943. Gouache and oil with cut-and-pasted paper on cardboard, 28 × 35⅞in (71.1 × 91.1cm).

The Museum of Modern Art, New York. Purchase.

and Robert Motherwell [fig. 2.13]. In addition, there was by then a tradition of American "little magazines" that were actively publishing vanguard art, and the surrealists soon started up more of them. *View* and *VVV* were particularly significant. Its editorial staff included André Breton, Max Ernst, Marcel Duchamp, Claude Lévi-Strauss, and the Americans Robert Motherwell, Harold Rosenberg, Lionel Abel, and William Carlos Williams. Through such collaborations in the galleries and journals, the presence of the European moderns soon flowered into a close liaison with the young Americans of the emerging New York School.

THE SENSE OF A NEW MOVEMENT IN NEW YORK

By 1943 talk of the emergence of a new movement had already begun to spread in the New York art world. In the spring of 1945 Art of This Century gallery mounted a show called "A Problem for Critics," challenging the art press to identify this new "movement." The show included works by the abstract surrealists Hans Arp, André Masson, and Joan Miró, as well as by the Americans Hans Hofmann, Jackson Pollock, Arshile Gorky, Adolph Gottlieb [fig. 2.14], and Mark Rothko. Between 1942 and 1950, the Americans in that show (though it is worth pointing out that among them only Pollock was actually born in America)—together with others, of whom the most important were Willem de Kooning, Robert Motherwell, Barnett Newman, Clyfford Still, and David Smith—produced a body of work which placed American art at the forefront of the international

2.14 Adolph Gottlieb, *Romanesque Façade*, 1949. Oil on canvas, 48 × 36in (121.9 × 91.4cm).

Krannert Art Museum and Kinkead Pavilion, University of Illinois, Urbana-Champaign. Purchased out of the "Illinois Biennial" exhibition of 1951.

avant-garde for the first time. As a group (which they never were in any systematic sense) these American artists came to be known as "abstract expressionists" or, as the artists themselves preferred, "the New York School."

Commonalities and Differences Among the Artists of the New York School

Art historians had begun using the term "abstract expressionism" at the end of World War I to refer to Kandinsky and other Europeans who painted abstractly with expressionist brushwork. In a 1946 review for the *New Yorker*, Robert Coates applied the term for the first time to the work

of an American artist of the forties when he described the paintings of Hans Hofmann as "abstract Expressionist."[14] He capitalized the "E" to indicate that he regarded Hofmann's work as a type of "Expressionism" in the tradition of Kandinsky, which is precisely how Hofmann had been describing himself for some time. Ironically Hofmann, of all the major New York School artists, had the least in common with the rest. In addition to the difference in age and background, he continued to be preoccupied with the formal principles of European modernism over and above any conscious concern with an introspective subject matter.

Except for Hofmann, who was fifty when he left Germany and sixty-five by the mid-forties, the artists of the New York School faced many of the same formative cultural, philosophical, and aesthetic issues. These included: the imperative of social relevance; existentialism; the surrealists' interest in the unconscious mind leavened by an American matter-of-factness; the Mexican influence; and the formal vocabulary of European modernism—especially Kandinsky's abstract expressionism of 1910–14, Mondrian, Picasso's *Guernica*, interwar cubism, and abstract surrealism. From cubism they took the shallow picture space and the concern with the picture plane. The biomorphic forms and automatist elements came from surrealism and Picasso's work of the thirties. Early Kandinsky [fig. 3.17] inspired some of the freedom of brushwork and the painterliness, and his moral tone fueled the ethical seriousness of purpose. To these American artists of the forties Kandinsky represented romantic emotionalism and spontaneity, as opposed to Mondrian, who stood for strict planning, the denial of personality, and intellect.

Although each of the New York School artists responded differently to these sources, they were at roughly the same stage of personal development at the same time (the forties) and in the same place (New York). Except for Hofmann, they were all students in their twenties and early thirties when Benton and the Mexicans were prominent in New York. As young men and women, many of them worked on the W.P.A.—Gorky, Pollock, Lee Krasner [fig. 2.15], Willem de Kooning, Rothko, Gottlieb, Guston, and David Smith all did. Moreover, between 1942 and 1949 all the major artists of the New York School except Hofmann transcended their early influences to achieve a distinctive personal style, and all placed paramount emphasis on content or meaningful subject matter in their art, which was predominantly abstract (except for that of de Kooning and Gorky). They took this stance in opposition to the widespread practice of what they regarded as a banal formalist abstraction dominated by the American followers of Mondrian such as Ilya Bolotowsky and Burgoyne Diller [fig. 2.16]. In addition, they all believed in the absolute individuality of the artist, for which reason they unanimously denied the idea that they coalesced into a movement. Indeed, all but Hofmann objected to the term "abstract expressionism," which, they felt, linked them to the expressionist and abstract artists of preceding generations; by contrast, they saw their work as arising out of unique acts of individual introspection.

The artists in this circle also had a general interest in myth as a source for the universals of the human psyche. They looked to ancient Greek literature as well as to "primitive" cultures for a more authentic connection with the underlying forces of nature, especially human nature, than contemporary Western society seemed to provide. Around 1940 Pollock and Rothko in particular had begun reading the theories of the psychoanalyst Carl Jung, who postulated "archetypes" in the individual unconscious which belonged to a "collective unconscious," connecting all of humankind. These archetypes, he thought, manifested themselves in myth. Pollock had undergone some Jungian therapy, and in general the writings of both Jung and Freud were a major topic of discussion among educated people in the forties and fifties. Myths of rebirth and renewal had a particularly keen attraction for the artists of the New York School as a metaphor for their increasingly spontaneous methods of painting.

Yet for all that they had in common, the central figures of the New York School had important philosophical differences too. Hofmann, for example, disliked surrealism and shunned the psychological orientation of most of the others. Gorky centered his aesthetic on a hidden but predefined subject matter (in the manner of Kandinsky), which he transformed through psychic metamorphosis (using surrealist automatism). This procedure was directly at odds with the premises of his friends de Kooning and Pollock, who used painting as an act of discovery rather than representation (which such predetermination implies). Motherwell's persistent sense of formal continuity with French modernism, especially Matisse, set him apart from the others, and only de Kooning centered his attention for most of his career on the human figure. And Newman's automatist doodles in the early forties rapidly grew so involved with metaphysics that exploring the individual unconscious seemed at best tangential, especially after 1946.

The critic Harold Rosenberg (who was very much a part of the group) once remarked that the only thing on which these artists could all agree was that there was nothing on which they could agree.[15] In a broad sense their radical individuality stood in opposition to the emergence of mass culture, as Rosenberg pointed out in a 1948 essay entitled "The Herd of Independent Minds":

2.15 Lee Krasner, *White Squares*, c. 1948.
Oil on canvas, 24 × 30in (61 × 76.2cm).
Whitney Museum of American Art, New York. Gift of Mr. and Mrs.
B. H. Friedman, 75.1. Photograph by Geoffrey Clements, New York.

2.16 Burgoyne Diller, *Third Theme*, 1946–8. Oil on canvas, 3ft 6in × 3ft 6in (1.07 × 1.07m). Whitney Museum of American Art, New York. Gift of May Walter, 58.58.

exactly in so far as he touches the common situation of man in the twentieth century, Kafka goes against the common experience; he undermines the self-confidence of official high culture, which rests on a system of assumptions which are as "false to reality" as the formulas of behavior in a best seller; and for this reassuring common experience he substitutes only the tension of an individual struggling for self-knowledge, a cloudy and painful seeing and not-seeing. Along this rocky road to the actual it is only possible to go Indian file, one at a time, so that "art" means "breaking up the crowd"—not "reflecting" its experience.[16]

Automatism and Action in the Art of the New York School

Automatism seemed to be the ideal device for artists so concerned with radical individualism. The artists of the New York School viewed it as a technique for generating form that did not impose style. In the beginning Pollock, Motherwell, Rothko, and Gottlieb used automatism to create forms which they would develop through free association as the abstract surrealists Matta, Miró, and Masson had done. Then, in the mid-forties Pollock, and increasingly Motherwell too, departed from the surrealist concept by using automatism as a device for objectifying an intense *conscious* experience as it was unfolding, rather than as a means of bringing forth unconscious material.

Rothko abandoned automatism entirely as he entered his mature style in the late forties; and it remained only in a more limited role in Gottlieb's work. In Gorky's mature work (from 1944) he was selecting his subject matter in a deliberate classical fashion, using automatism only to camouflage and enrich the images. Hofmann, Kline, and de Kooning had never picked up on the surrealist technique, although the spontaneity of their improvisations resembled the gestural freedom which Pollock and Motherwell gleaned from automatism. In the mid-forties the artists of the New York School gradually stopped evoking classical myths (to which both surrealist artists and existentialist writers made frequent recourse) and they looked beyond surrealism toward a subject matter of even more immediate and personal introspection. The artists of the New York School reached universals of the human psyche as a by-product of the search for self.

Where the surrealists attempted to disorient the viewer and provoke unconscious revelations, for which they sought parallels in the myths of antiquity, the artists of the New York School turned away from the viewer altogether and wiped out the surrealists' theatrical distance. Increasingly Pollock, Motherwell, and by the end of the forties Smith, viewed automatism simply as a more direct means of conveying the subjective experience itself. For them content was intrinsic to the act of painting (or welding steel forms together, in the case of Smith), in that the process unearthed a vein of intensely felt experience on which the artist deliberated in his or her materials. The encounter was never oriented either to past sources (psychological or art historical) or to an anticipated future; the artist lived the work entirely in the present, and the object was left over as an artifact of that event.

In this sense a painting by Pollock, de Kooning, Kline, or the others in this circle embodied a spontaneous act of origination that aspired to an ideal state of defining the style of the painting, the identity of the artist, and even art itself, in the process of painting. These artists turned the conceptual enactment into an object. They sought an embodiment of the individual's act of making order out of chaos, but not an embodiment of the order itself, as Mondrian had. They conceived each work as an uncompleted thought, still in process, and their canvases engaged the immediacy of the present with such directness and spontaneity that today, more than half a century later, they look as if the paint is still wet.

In 1952 Harold Rosenberg coined the term "action painting," modeled on his intimate knowledge of de Kooning's working process. His essay "The American Action Painters"[17] brought into focus the paramount concern of de Kooning, Pollock, and Kline in particular (though Rosenberg did not single them out by name) with the act of painting. Lee Krasner, Elaine de Kooning, and other remarkable women at the time also shared these aspirations in their work but, as Ann Gibson has pointed out, "they were not *seen*."[18] The social hierarchy of the forties and fifties, even in the art world, simply wasn't open to the full participation of women or ethnic minorities. This began to change only at the end of the sixties. Nevertheless, for some of these women of the New York School, as for the male action painters, the canvas was not a representation but an extension of the mind itself, in which the artist thought by changing the surface with her brush. Rosenberg saw the artist's task as a heroic exploration of the most profound issues of personal identity and experience in relation to the large questions of the human condition.

The model of Greek tragedy was often raised as a metaphor for this heroic feat of introspection, although it was important as a conscious prototype only for Newman, Motherwell, and the early Rothko among the major artists of the New York School. Like the tragedy of Oedipus, which unfolds as the protagonist lives through each episode, what the painter's actions reveal about him- or herself takes the artist by surprise. Rather than dominating events with a pre-ordained scheme, the action painter throws him- or herself in with them and the art theory emerges only in hindsight. In 1939 Breton wrote a widely discussed article for the last issue of the French surrealist magazine *Minotaure* called "The Prestige of André Masson." In it he discussed "risk" and portrayed art as an "event," the significance of which derives not from its quality as a finished object but from its power of revelation. This essay no doubt influenced Rosenberg's idea of action painting.

Action and Existentialism

The Depression and the W.P.A., the Spanish Civil War, and World War II gave rise to political activism and a mentality of action. Pollock, de Kooning, and their friends sought to express this with a style in which the artist defined art in the act of making it. No part of the process in an action painting is purely technical; everything is a meaningful gesture inseparable from the artist's biography, according to Rosenberg. Likewise, in the writings of Jean-Paul Sartre, action was the means of knowing oneself in relation to the world.

In an essay of 1944 Sartre (the leading postwar existentialist) explained: "In a word, man must create his own essence; it is in throwing himself into the world, in suffering it, in struggling with it, that—little by little—he defines himself."[19] In his fiction Sartre wrote about situations rather than characters, as in "The Wall" (a classic short story of 1939) where a confrontation with death causes the characters to reexperience everything as if new. The dull terror of the absurd in the novels and short stories of Franz Kafka also created an existential dilemma for his characters that demanded a fundamental rethinking of experience. This sense of starting from scratch with only immediate experience is a precedent for the commitment of the New York School artists to the unpremeditated act of painting.

Like abstract expressionism, existentialism was also a non-movement. Its major exponents—Søren Kierkegaard, Fyodor Dostoyevsky, Friedrich Nietzsche, Rainer Maria Rilke, Franz Kafka, Martin Heidegger, Karl Jaspers, and Jean-Paul Sartre—were so concerned with individuality and the uniqueness of subjective experience that all (except Sartre) rejected the term as well as the idea that they belonged to any school of thought. As Nietzsche wrote: "No one can construct for you the bridge upon which precisely you must cross the stream of life, no one but you yourself alone."[20]

The existentialists rejected systems of belief and shared a dissatisfaction with traditional philosophy as shallow, academic, and, worst of all, remote from the immediacy of life. Jaspers, who disliked all doctrines, thought that genuine philosophy must well up from inside a man's individual existence. He regarded reason as subphilosophic and declared that philosophy begins only where reason fails. Heidegger insisted on going back to the pre-Socratics[21] because he believed that Latin mistranslations of Greek thinkers had vitiated all subsequent philosophy. This was an expression of Heidegger's sense of urgency about starting over from one's own immediate experience for an authenticity in philosophical thought that parallels the new world consciousness of the artists of the New York School.

From the point of view of American art, existentialism had its most significant influence from 1945, when the works of Kafka, Sartre, and then Heidegger began to appear in English. Sartre's preoccupation with dread, failure, and death, his focus on anxiety and ambiguity, and most of all his search for a direct and spontaneous encounter with oneself characterized all the existentialist writers. A person first exists, in Sartre's view, then one encounters oneself, and only then does one define oneself. As if embarking from precisely this position on behalf of the action painters, Harold Rosenberg asserted in 1947 that each artist "is fatally aware that only what he constructs himself will ever be real to him."[22] Similarly Motherwell described the abstract expressionist's "response to modern life" in 1951 as "rebellious, individualistic, unconventional, sensitive, irritable . . . this attitude arose from a feeling of being ill at ease in the universe . . . The need is for felt experience."[23]

Clyfford Still

No artist embodied Motherwell's characterization more dramatically than Clyfford Still, a testy, paranoid character who believed that he would change the world with his paintings. Blunt pronouncements like painting is "a matter of conscience," and "any fool can put color on canvas,"[24] conveyed the impression that he saw himself as the anointed prophet of painting and that his model was John Brown, not Christ. "He used terror tactics," Motherwell recalled. For example, "in his Jaguar (he had a passion for cars) Still had driven out from California; he wanted a painting back from Ossorio [a minor New York School painter and patron] and Ossorio had said no. Still drove out to East Hampton when Ossorio wasn't home; a servant let him in. He went into the house and cut a big piece out of the center of the picture with a razor, rolled it up and left."[25]

By 1945, when he came back to New York, Still was painting what seemed like cross-sections of geological strata with jagged peaks cracking through stratifications of color above them on a vertical plane [fig. 2.17]. These forms derived from Still's expressionistic figures of the thirties and retain an obscure sense of human presence without, however, being representational in even the most indirect sense. The compositions defy symmetry and even seem to deny the limits of the canvas, thus evoking a sense of boundlessness and primary force. In 1951 Rothko said, "Still expresses the tragic-religious drama which is generic to all myths at all times, no matter where they occur . . . For me, Still's pictorial dramas are all an extension of the Greek *Persephone* myth. As he himself has expressed it, his paintings are 'of the Earth, the Damned, and of the Recreated.'"[26]

2.17 Clyfford Still, *Untitled*, 1945. Oil on canvas, 42⅜ × 33⅝in (107.6 × 85.4cm).
Collection, Whitney Museum of American Art, New York. Gift of Mr. and Mrs. B. H. Friedman, 69.3.

In describing the experience of painting, Still portrayed himself as if possessed and spiritually transported: "A great free joy surges through me when I work," he wrote. "And as the blues or reds or blacks leap and quiver in their tenuous ambience or rise in austere thrusts to carry their power infinitely beyond the bounds of the limiting field, I move with them and find a resurrection from the moribund oppressions that held me only hours ago."[27] In Still's mature painting the complete absorption of the figurative elements provides a metaphor for the fusion of self and nature. This fusion amplifies the image of the artist as a microcosm of nature through which cosmic forces surge and it is doubtless influenced by the shamanism of the Indians from Still's native region, the Pacific Northwest.

Adolph Gottlieb

Adolph Gottlieb began painting his pictographs [fig. 2.14] around 1941. In stressing the importance of content, he set himself apart from the pervasive formalist abstraction of the time. In 1943 Gottlieb and Rothko collaborated on a letter to the *New York Times* in which they proclaimed: "There's no such thing as good painting about nothing."[28] The idea of creating free-associative episodes in boxes came from the sequential narrative frames in early Italian Renaissance paintings. From a compositional point of view, this allowed an isolation and simultaneity of symbols that paralleled the multiplicity of levels in the unconscious mind and, as a formal device, made it possible to use automatism freely while at the same time maintaining control over the pictorial structure.

Franz Kline

Franz Kline [figs. 2.18 and 2.19] came to action painting in 1948 from an expressionist style of figure painting, without working through the cubist and surrealist stages through which so many of the other New York School artists evolved. Kline grew up in northeastern Pennsylvania and his stepfather was a railroad foreman. Particular trains—like the "Chief"—as well as locations that Kline loved in the landscape of the Lehigh Valley recur persistently in the titles of many of his later paintings. As a boy he enjoyed watching the trains speeding by, and he later captured that sense of velocity and mass in motion in the brushwork of his paintings. Typically Kline started his paintings by first setting down the movement with fast gestural strokes in black and then cutting back the black with white, modifying and clarifying the idea. The paintings concern weight and movement rather than contours or forms.

2.18 Franz Kline, *Untitled*, 1948. Oil and collage on paperboard mounted on wood, 28⅛ × 22¼in (71.3 × 56.4cm).
Collection, Hirshhorn Museum and Sculpture Garden, Smithsonian Institution, Washington, D.C. Gift of Joseph H. Hirshhorn, 1966.

2.19 Franz Kline, *Chief*, 1950. Oil on canvas, 4ft 10¾in × 6ft 1½in (1.48 × 1.86m).
The Museum of Modern Art, New York. Gift of Mr. and Mrs. David M. Solinger.

Elaine de Kooning (a friend since 1943) recalled that around 1948 Kline enlarged some of his quick brush sketches in an opaque projector and "a four by five inch brush drawing of the rocking chair . . . loomed in gigantic black strokes which eradicated any image, the strokes expanding as entities in themselves, unrelated to any reality but that of their own existence . . . From that day, Franz Kline's style of painting changed completely."[29] Kline's powerful gestures, characteristically black on white and large in scale, are a kind of grand manifesto of the New York School's emphasis on the direct expression of personality.

Friends In and Around the New York School

The artists of the New York School met informally, but frequently, in certain bars (most famously the Cedar Tavern just above Washington Square), in automats and cafeterias, or in studios around Greenwich Village. The critics Clement Greenberg, Harold Rosenberg, and Thomas Hess, as well as the art historian Meyer Schapiro, were an integral part of this crowd. Greenberg—writing chiefly for the *Nation* and *Partisan Review*—liked Hofmann's "laws" and attacked surrealism for reversing the anti-pictorial trend of cubism and abstract art. He criticized Mondrian's *Broadway Boogie Woogie* as wavering and awkward and denounced Kandinsky for his non-cubist picture space. Writing in the *Nation* in 1944, he admonished: "The extreme eclecticism now prevailing in art is unhealthy and it should be counter-acted, even at the risk of dogmatism and intolerance."[30] Though he seemed to want everyone to march in step, he often demonstrated a keen eye for formal quality.

Rosenberg came from a literary background and loved to defend intellectual values deep into the night. Like the existentialists, he championed individuality and the unexpected and he felt genuine sympathy with the creative struggle of artists. Instead of laying down the law to artists, as Greenberg increasingly tried to do, Rosenberg entered into a dialog with them. He identified closely with their work, successfully extending the issues they raised pictorially into the realm of words. He would even caustically take artists to task when he found their ideas ethically questionable or intellectually shallow.

Hess provided a more objective account of the artists but probably influenced them and the scene less as a result. Schapiro's great contribution was as a teacher and friend whose eye the artists respected. Schapiro's lectures at Columbia, as Motherwell pointed out,[31] made art seem important and worthy of serious thought.

There was also much abstraction on the New York scene in the thirties and forties that had nothing to do with the motives behind the New York School, even though many artists had personal ties which crossed these boundaries. Burgoyne Diller [fig. 2.16], for example, took his inspiration from a formalistic reading of Mondrian and of the Parisian *Abstraction–Création* group; yet in the early forties he was an important supporter of Jackson Pollock. The classes of

Hans Hofmann also turned out many formalistic abstract painters—indeed, the hard core of geometric abstraction was a group founded in 1936 and called "The American Abstract Artists," more than half of whose organizers were former pupils of Hofmann's. Ad Reinhardt [fig. 6.12], who became a prophet of the sixties minimalists, was perhaps the most articulate and interesting member of this group.

Mark Tobey, who founded his abstract style on Zen Buddhism, lived primarily in Seattle, Washington and in Europe rather than in New York. He was nevertheless a contemporary of the artists of the New York School and showed at the Willard Gallery alongside David Smith. Like them he reacted against the materialism of the burgeoning mass culture of the late forties. "We have occupied ourselves too much with the outer, the objective," he said, "at the expense of the inner world."[32] During the forties he developed his so-called "white writing" [fig. 2.20] and acquired a major international reputation.

Similarly, the contemplative sculpture of Isamu Noguchi [fig. 2.21] owes more to Zen than to psychological introspection, but Noguchi's style also has an evident debt to the biomorphism of Arp. Noguchi went to Paris for two years on a Guggenheim Fellowship in 1927, worked briefly as a studio assistant to Brancusi, and befriended Alexander Calder. He was born in Los Angeles in 1904, but spent much of his childhood in Japan. His aesthetic reflects a Japanese feeling for natural materials and spaces, which Brancusi fostered in him as well. One of Noguchi's greatest gifts was in the design of spaces, particularly the dance stage and small sculpturally landscaped gardens [fig. 2.22] and playgrounds, where his sensitivity to subtle changes of form and material played an important role. He did his first

dance sets for the Martha Graham Dance Company in 1935; his ideas for outdoor parks began in the mid-thirties and reflected the influence of Japanese garden design. He also made beautiful design objects such as lamps and tables that are still manufactured today.

By the fifties the New York School was generally recognized as the leading edge of the international avant-garde and many younger artists adopted its stylistic grammar. But the starting-point of these second-generation artists tended to be an appreciation for the painterly quality of the abstract expressionist brushstroke rather than for existential concerns of the sort that prompted the work of the first-generation artists of the New York School. By 1960 other movements with their own radical ideas had emerged, and the New York School had turned into a disparate handful of old masters.

ALTERNATIVE NARRATIVES OF THE FORTIES

For most of the second half of the twentieth century, an influential group in the art world—art historians, critics, dealers, and curators (most prominently Alfred Barr, director of the Museum of Modern Art in New York, and his successors)—promoted a linear history of art as a sequence of dominant movements. But part of what made New York so important as an art center in the second half of the twentieth century was precisely its dynamic heterogeneity; the mix of artists around Breton in New York points, in microcosm, to this wider and more complicated story. Despite the important coalescence of ideas around the American artists who came to be seen as the leaders of the New York School

2.20 Mark Tobey, *Universal Field*, 1949. Tempera and pastel on cardboard, 27⅞ × 43⅝in (70.8 × 110.8cm). Whitney Museum of American Art, New York. Purchase, 50.24.

2.21 Isamu Noguchi, *Kouros*, 1944–5. Pink Georgia marble, on slate base, 117 × 34⅛ × 42in (297.2 × 86.6 × 106.7cm).
Metropolitan Museum of Art, New York. Fletcher Fund, 1953, 53.87a–i.

2.22 Isamu Noguchi, *Water Garden*, 1963. Black river stone, granite paving.
Chase Manhattan Bank Plaza, New York. Photograph courtesy Chase Manhattan Archives, New York.

in the forties—Jackson Pollock, Willem de Kooning, Robert Motherwell, Mark Rothko, David Smith, Philip Guston, Barnett Newman, Hans Hofmann, Arshile Gorky, Clyfford Still, Adolph Gottlieb, and Franz Kline being the most prominent—the New York art world had been and continued to be quite diverse. Nevertheless, it was nearly half a century before the important women working at the time came to be acknowledged—including such major figures as Louise Bourgeois, Hedda Sterne, Elaine de Kooning, Joan Mitchell, Grace Hartigan, and Lee Krasner. There were also artists of color like Jacob Lawrence whose great historical epics did not fit this "logical" narrative. Neither did an artist like Bill Traylor [fig. 2.23], who began his artistic career at the age of eighty-two when he moved to Montgomery, Alabama, from a rural town forty miles away and began living on the street and drawing on scraps of cardboard. The strikingly modernist simplicity of Traylor's drawings would only come to be appreciated fully in the late 1980s.

Jacob Lawrence

If Bill Traylor was invisible in the forties because of his location and his circumstances, Jacob Lawrence was a young star. He was twenty-three years old when he painted his great historical epic *The Migration of the Negro*, of 1941. This series of paintings was immediately published in *Fortune* magazine and shown at the well-known Downtown Gallery in New York; Lawrence was the first African American artist to have a one-person show in a major New York gallery. Alfred Barr and Duncan Phillips, two of the great connoisseurs of the

2.23 Bill Traylor, *Figures, Construction*, 1940–2. Watercolor and pencil on cardboard, 12¾ × 11⅝in (32.4 × 29.5cm).
Montgomery Museum of Fine Arts, Alabama. Gift of Charles & Eugenia Shannon, 1982.4.16.

teacher to the W.P.A. Harlem Art Workshop, sponsored in the local public library by the College Art Association. He dropped out of high school when his mother lost her job, but he continued to paint.

Lawrence completed his first historical series, *The Life of Toussaint L'Ouverture* (a founding figure of Haiti, the first black republic in the Americas), in 1938, at the age of twenty-one. He then went on to create multipanel narratives of the lives of the African American abolitionists Harriet Tubman and Frederick Douglass. He was hired in the easel-painting division of the Federal Art Project for a year and a half, and in 1940 he received a $1,500 fellowship (about $25,000 in 2010 dollars) from the Julius Rosenwald Foundation to embark on a historical narrative about the exodus of black labor from the South during World War I— *The Migration of the Negro*.

Lawrence grew up hearing about friends and family who had migrated north, and part of what makes these paintings so powerful is that they record history as lived experience.

2.24 Jacob Lawrence, *The Migration of the Negro Series*, *No. 16*, 1941.
The Museum of Modern Art, New York. Gift of Mrs. David M. Levy, 28.1942.8.

period, both wanted to buy the entire series and in the end agreed to split the work between their collections, with the even-numbered panels going to the Museum of Modern Art in New York and the odd numbers to the Phillips Memorial Gallery in Washington, D.C.

Despite this early success, it was more than half a century before Lawrence's work took its appropriate place in art history as one of the masterpieces of twentieth-century painting. One reason, perhaps, is that art historians wanted to segregate such work as "African American," categorizing it instead of acknowledging its powerful expression of radical individuality and humanness. But there was also a *de facto* segregation in the art world between the uptown (Harlem) and the downtown scene in New York at the time. Even an artist like Romare Bearden, an African American who showed abstract expressionist paintings in the Egan Gallery alongside major figures of the New York School during the forties, was nevertheless not visible in the art-historical narrative of the period.

Lawrence grew up in Atlantic City, New Jersey and Easton, Pennsylvania. When his parents separated in 1924, his mother moved with the children to Philadelphia for three years and then went to New York, leaving him in a sequence of foster homes until the age of thirteen (1930) when he reunited with her in Harlem. Lawrence began painting in an after-school program and at fifteen he followed his art

2.25 Jacob Lawrence, *The Builders—19 Men*, 1979. Gouache and tempera on paper, 30 × 22in (76.2 × 55.9cm). Private collection. Courtesy D.C. Moore Gallery, New York.

"I don't think about this series in terms of history," he said. "I think in terms of contemporary life. It was such a part of me I didn't think of something outside . . . It was a portrait of myself, a portrait of my family, a portrait of my peers."[33]

Each panel is accompanied by a line of narrative. With panel 16 [fig. 2.24], for example, he wrote: "Although the Negro was used to lynching, he found this an opportune time for him to leave where one had occurred." The upturned table, with a bowl teetering off the top edge, seems to echo the stark anxiety of the sad, attenuated figure of the woman with her head bowed down on her forearm. But the beautiful simplicity of the flat form of her red dress is at the same time a powerful modernist abstraction that seems to call on the tradition of the great frescoes of Diego Rivera and Parisian cubist abstraction of the 1920s. Half a century later in this artist's long career, one still sees in a painting like *The Builders—19 Men* (1979) [fig. 2.25] a masterful command of modernist vocabulary in a now more complex pictorial structure, balanced by a simple palette of flat, high-keyed colors, distributed in an active pattern across the surface. This later work has a late-style monumentality that can only come from the certainty of an eye and hand honed by a long career.

Hedda Sterne

On January 15, 1951, *Life* magazine published the now famous photograph of "The Irascibles"—fourteen members of the pathbreaking artists of the New York School. Thirteen were men. The one woman, Hedda Sterne, is unique among these artists in having waited half a century for a major museum retrospective and catalog devoted to her work.[34]

Sterne showed in the 1942 exhibition "First Papers of Surrealism" and, like Matta, her painting evolved away from the conventions of surrealism despite her ongoing use of automatism and other surrealist devices. Sterne's machine paintings garnered some recognition in the late 1940s and she showed them alongside the work of other New York School artists, though she took her subject matter from the city—the machines and the continual movement she saw there—rather than from an introspective journey. *Machine No. 5* of 1950 [fig. 2.26] is a delicate superstructure of interconnected moving parts, incised into a sensuous, painterly, red field. The drawing is about detailed articulation rather

2.26 Hedda Sterne, *Machine No. 5*, 1950. Oil on canvas, 51 × 38⅛in (130 × 97cm).

Krannert Art Museum and Kinkead Pavilion, University of Illinois, Urbana-Champaign, 1950-7-1. Festival of Arts Purchase Fund. Courtesy the artist.

than boundary contours, and the rich red surface seems to be scraped back under the drawing to allow articulation of the line with even more fineness.

Sterne never sought to paint as an assertion of identity. Her art was receptive and interactive with the context in which she found herself—she frequently uses the metaphor of a camera lens—prefiguring the postmodern instability of things and of style that emerges so clearly in the mid-fifties with Robert Rauschenberg, and in the sixties with Gerhard Richter and Sigmar Polke in Germany. Some of the fanciful machine parts in *Machine No. 5* are annotated with eyes or other linear commentary that resembles the brilliantly metamorphic line of Saul Steinberg, the *New Yorker* cartoonist whom she married at the end of 1944. Steinberg and Sterne were both among the initial stable of artists (with Cornell, Gottlieb, Ossorio, Baziotes, and Theodoros Stamos) to show with the Betty Parsons Gallery when it opened in 1946.

Steinberg still tends to be left out of the histories of the art of the period because he drew "cartoons." No one would leave Hogarth or Daumier out of the history of eighteenth and nineteenth century art because they drew cartoons, and today we look back at the work of Steinberg with great admiration for his draftsmanship, humor, and intellect. It is a lesson about categories which, although useful in sorting the complexities of history, can also sometimes prevent us from seeing what is right in front of us. As Harold Rosenberg pointed out, Steinberg often treated style itself—an abstract concept—as the main subject matter of his work. Within one work he might contrast several drawing styles, suggesting the artifice of each.[35] In contrast to the "heroic" assertion of identity in the brushwork of Pollock or de Kooning, Steinberg's pen line points away from that idea.

Louise Bourgeois

Louise Bourgeois was another great artist working among the New York School in the 1940s whose work only came to be well known much later. Although trained in Paris, Bourgeois had no direct contact with the surrealists until 1938, when she met and married the prominent art historian Robert Goldwater and moved to New York. Immediately upon her arrival, her circle of friends included most of the major figures in the New York art world. Yet she didn't have her public debut as a sculptor until 1949, at least in part because she kept her prolific practice of drawings, paintings, and sculptures deeply private in the 1940s. She lived with her sculptures; they belonged to her daily life; she moved them from room to room as though conversing with and among them [fig. 2.27]. "The process of making the sculptures, reworking them and exposing them to different, mostly

2.27 Louise Bourgeois, *Listening One*, 1947. Bronze, painted white, 80 × 20 × 12in (203.2 × 50.8 × 30.4cm).
Courtesy Cheim & Read, Galerie Karsten Greve, and Hauser & Wirth.

2.28 Louise Bourgeois, *Untitled*, 1947. Ink on paper,
11 × 8½in (27.9 × 21.5cm).
Private collection. Courtesy Cheim & Read, New York.

private milieus, was more important than showing them publicly," Josef Helfenstein wrote about her early work.[36]

Whereas Sterne showed often in the forties and fifties, Bourgeois scarcely exhibited at all. On the other hand, Sterne's presence diminished in the sixties and seventies as the mythology of the abstract expressionists solidified. In contrast, Bourgeois was suddenly rediscovered in the late 1960s and interest in her work grew exponentially in the 1970s and 1980s. The eccentricity of Bourgeois's drawing style [fig. 2.28]—especially the nonsymmetrical composition and the obsessive mark-making that drew attention to process over finish to a degree not even achieved in the radical drip pictures of Pollock—didn't fit into the aesthetic of the late forties and fifties. But in the emerging postmodernism of the late sixties this work seemed prescient.

Photography in the Era of the New York School

Most surveys of the art of the 1940s and 1950s limit themselves to painting and sculpture, leaving photography aside. Even a photographer like Aaron Siskind, who was very much a part of the social and intellectual circles of the New

York School, was left out. It wasn't until the 1970s, when Cindy Sherman and others began printing color photographs in high resolution on the scale of large paintings, selling them in limited editions on the market, that photography came to be seen as part of the "mainstream" of the art world. And yet, a number of well-established historical artists—Man Ray, Alexander Rodchenko, John Heartfield, to name a few—had already created major bodies of work in the medium during the first half of the century.

There was also a distinction made between news photography (photojournalism) and "fine art" photography. In 1940, the Museum of Modern Art in New York established a separate Department of Photography, with Beaumont Newhall as its first director. This greatly impacted the reception of photography, though it took another twenty-five years before the radical implications of the medium's distinct character were widely appreciated. In a famous essay of 1936, the German critic Walter Benjamin had explored the implications of photography's inherent reproducibility,[37] but Newhall displayed the work in his collection (even the photojournalism) like rare etchings, downplaying their reproducibility and instead focusing on a language of connoisseurship. This in effect subordinated photography in a hierarchy of mediums. The style of Newhall's successor, Edward Steichen, could hardly have been more different. He worked like a magazine photo editor, reproducing the collection of photographs in all different scales and formats from books to dynamic exhibition displays. His sensational "The Family of Man" exhibition of 1955 was mailed out in book form to members of the Museum of Modern Art all over the country. Steichen organized "The Family of Man" around universal themes and experiences, virtually erasing the artistic identity of the photographer.[38]

Like Newhall, Steichen neglected to provide a conceptual framework for grasping what was unique to the language of photography as an art medium, even though he successfully exploited aspects of it in his exhibition style. Nevertheless, photography—the work of self-described photojournalists as well as those with explicitly aesthetic projects—had been very much a part of the visual field with which all artists had been in dialog since the turn of the century. The importance of television images in relation to social and political issues in the 1960s may have had an effect on photography's status; certainly the economic expansion of the art market in that decade played a role, and the ethos around collecting photography had changed significantly by 1970.

As in painting, there were photographers in the 1930s concerned with social relevance. In the mid-thirties a group of politically conscious photographers, committed to documentary projects, founded the leftist New York Photo League. Aaron Siskind produced a famous series of Harlem documents under the banner of the League. Margaret Bourke-White and Berenice Abbott, who were among the most prominent magazine photographers of the interwar period, were founding members; Lisette Model and Weegee also exhibited there.

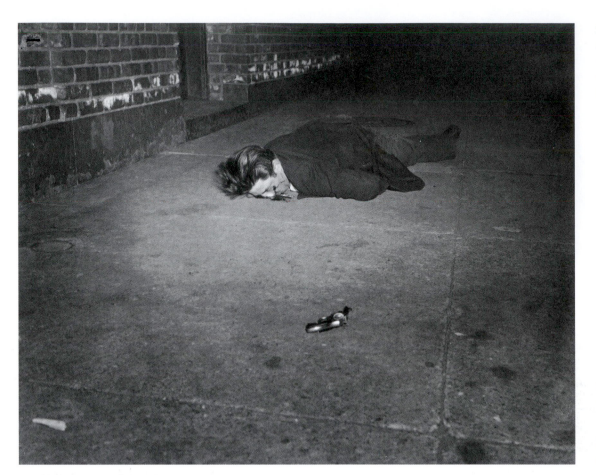

2.29 Weegee,
Murder in Hell's Kitchen,
1942. Gelatin silver
print, 13⅖ × 10½in
(34 × 26.9cm).

2.30 Lisette Model,
Coney Island Bather,
1942. Black-and-white
photograph.
Courtesy Hasted Hunt
Kraeutler, New York.

Weegee and Lisette Model

In the forties Weegee seemed like the quintessential city news photographer [fig. 2.29]—a straight documentarian. But in retrospect, nearly all of his work has the dated drama of a *film noir* detective story, revealing the depth of its expressive artifice. As one writer pointed out, Weegee "promoted himself in Hollywood as the quintessential hard-boiled, cigar-smoking, flashgun-popping"[39] photographer. "No bumping off was official until I arrived to take the last photo," Weegee stated matter-of-factly.[40]

Weegee (Arthur Fellig) first worked in the darkrooms at the *New York Times.* But he really began his career after leaving the paper in 1935 to work as a freelance photographer and developed his uncanny ability always to be the first photographer on the scene. In 1938 he obtained permission to install a police radio in his car, an innovation that catapulted him to celebrity status. His first one-person exhibition—"Weegee: Murder Is My Business"—took place at the Photo League in 1941, Beaumont Newhall included him in group shows at MoMA in 1943 and 1944, and Weegee published his first and most celebrated book, *Naked City*, in 1945.

Like Weegee, Lisette Model photographed the people and events of the city, making the ordinary, extraordinary. But unlike Weegee she was a European who came to America as an adult; she immediately saw a contrast with

Europe. The United States was a highly commercialized culture in which advertising played a much bigger role in shaping the reality of common things. In this sense she intuitively approached some of the issues raised by Walter Benjamin. "I found that America was the country, *par excellence*, of making images of everybody, everything," she explained. "Everything had to have an image, the car had to have an image, a shoe had to have an image, the politician had to have an image. One day I was sitting in a kind of bar, and I saw a politician projecting his image, and I said to myself: 'Glamour, the image of our image—that is my project.'"[41]

Trained as a musician, Model had studied with Arnold Schoenberg in Vienna in her teens, moved to Paris in her twenties, and, as a Jew, fled to New York in 1938. From 1941 to 1955 Model lived on her photographic work for *Harper's Bazaar*. Although the people at Coney Island [fig. 2.30] or on the streets of the Lower East Side were the flipside of the *Harper's Bazaar* fashion plates, Model found the same richness of visual experience in the ordinary sights of daily life. In 1951 she began teaching at the New School for Social Research, where she became the mentor of Diane Arbus, who created one of the great artistic *oeuvres* of the postwar period.

Aaron Siskind and the Chicago School

In the summer of 1943 Aaron Siskind had an epiphany about his work while photographing in Gloucester, Massachusetts. In contrast to the socially engaged documentary photography he had been doing, for which he conducted extended interviews and did a great deal of research, he suddenly found himself working spontaneously. "I made some pictures and these pictures revealed meaning to me, a way of making a picture . . . which I had never dreamed of before," he said. "In the pictures you have the object, but you have in the object or superimposed on it . . . my idea. And these things are present at one and the same time . . . the meaning is partly the object's meaning, but mostly my meaning."[42] Siskind had gone to City College with Barnett Newman and Adolph Gottlieb in the twenties and was friends with the painters of the New York School. But it wasn't until his discovery of this spontaneous process in 1943 that he engaged introspection as a source of content.

From 1947 to 1951 Siskind exhibited regularly at the Charles Egan Gallery as part of the New York School, with which he had developed close personal ties. In the summer of 1951 he taught at Black Mountain College with the photographer Harry Callahan, who invited him to the Institute of Design in Chicago where, over the next twenty years, they created a "Chicago School" of photography, fundamentally changing the artistic orientation that had been established there as a "New Bauhaus" by László Moholy-Nagy from one of experimentation and documentation to a philosophy motivated by an interior vision.[43]

In a work like *Acolman 1* of 1955 [fig. 2.31], Siskind used straight photography (no manipulation of the negative or any distortion) to create the apprehension of an abstract image. The strongly defined shadows accentuate the picture plane so dramatically that we don't at first see the subject matter. The subject is simultaneously "real" and intangible, infused with Siskind's own meaning.

2.31 Aaron Siskind, *Acolman I*, 1955. Gelatin silver print, 9½ × 13½in (26.9 × 34cm). Courtesy Center for Creative Photography, University of Arizona.

3.1 Alexander Calder, *Only, Only Bird*, 1951. Tin cans and wire,
11 × 17 × 39in (27.9 × 43.2 × 99cm).
The Phillips Collection, Washington, D.C.

3 A DIALOG WITH EUROPE

ALEXANDER CALDER

Alexander Calder showed none of the introspective focus of such artists as Pollock or Motherwell; but like them he successfully assimilated the momentum and subtlety of the interwar European vanguard into an American style. Calder had a playful openness, at once naive and self-confident, curious and filled with a lively sense of wonder about the world. His work is optimistic, gregarious, witty, irreverent, sometimes even bawdy. Indeed, a wry, Yankee sense of humor, in the tradition of Mark Twain, characterized both Calder's personality and his work.

Calder's Early Life and Themes

Alexander Calder was born outside Philadelphia in 1898. His grandfather (Alexander Milne Calder) and his father (Alexander Stirling Calder) were successful sculptors of public monuments and his mother was a painter. At the age of six the young Calder and his eight-year-old sister had to be left with friends for a year when his father was diagnosed with tuberculosis and went, along with Calder's mother, to a health ranch in Arizona. The family reunited on the ranch in the summer of 1906, and in the fall they all moved to Pasadena, California, where the climate seemed better for his father's health. In his *Autobiography* Calder dated his earliest interest in the planets and stars—which became especially important to the iconography of his mobiles—from evenings spent gazing up at the night sky with his parents on that ranch in Arizona at the time of the family's reunion.

Childhood memories set many themes for Calder's later art. Vivid recollections of trains, the San Francisco cable cars, and toys have echoes in his later sculpture [fig. 3.1]. Pasadena's Tournament of Roses, which he attended frequently between the ages of six and twelve, climaxed with a chariot race, just like the *Cirque Calder* (*Calder Circus*) he later created in Paris [fig. 3.2]. Even the wire jewelry which Calder made throughout his career began in his youth as a collaboration with his sister to adorn her dolls.

From the age of seven, Calder already displayed the unusual inventiveness with tools and found materials that characterized his artistic career and adult life. As an adult, he still tinkered incessantly with rudimentary inventions, made with the simple tools and materials he had at hand. At one point, for example, he rigged up an arrangement of pulleys by his bed to turn on the stove for coffee in the morning. If it didn't work he would get up, repair it, and then get back into bed rather than just turn on the burner in the normal way.

This mechanical aptitude attracted Calder to an engineering college (the Stevens Institute); but after a sequence of unsatisfying jobs he gave up on engineering in 1922. Feeling undecided about what to do, he took work as a common seaman on a ship sailing from New York to San Francisco via the Panama Canal, and in the course of the voyage Calder had an experience that significantly reinforced his childhood interest in the stars and planets. "It was early one morning," he recalled, "on a calm sea, off Guatemala, when over my couch—a coil of rope—I saw the beginning of a fiery red sunrise on one side and the moon looking like a silver coin on the other. Of the whole trip this impressed me most of all; it left me with a lasting sensation of the solar system."[1] This cosmic imagery figured importantly around 1930 in the artist's first stabiles and in the genesis of the mobile.

Calder studied at the Art Students League in New York from 1923 to 1926 and then worked his passage across the Atlantic to Paris (still the undisputed art center of the world). Calder had made a number of drawings of the circus in 1925, on commission from the *National Police Gazette*, and by the end of 1926 he had begun his great project of the 1920s, the wire circus. At the end of the twenties Calder had a few one-man shows in New York of his wire portraits and animals (including some carved in wood); in one exhibition his work appeared side by side with a display of eighteenth-century mechanical birds in cages that may have inspired the gear-driven sculptures like the *Fishbowl with Crank* [fig. 3.3], although they also grew naturally out of the aesthetic of the *Cirque Calder*.

Calder in Paris

Calder opened the performances of his *Cirque Calder* with a scratchy recording on the gramophone. As the voice of the ringmaster, "Monsieur Loyal," Calder would announce: "Mesdames et Messieurs je vous présente . . ." and then ceremoniously march in each of the animals and performers in his thick, pawlike hands. He performed the *Cirque Calder* on his hands and knees, making the sounds of the different animals as they entered the ring. The event included sword-swallowers, acrobats, clowns, lion-tamers, and a variety of other acts. Many of the performers actually moved, through some clever mechanical invention: Rigoulot, the weight lifter, bent over, hooked his wire hands on the barbell, and lifted it into the air; the seals tossed a ball back and forth; and the acrobats (using a simple catapult device) sprang, hilariously, from one place to another. People were fascinated by Calder's meticulous attention to detail: he put safety netting below the high-wire act, and using an air bulb and wooden blocks for legs, he figured out how to make the elephant move with the animal's typically awkward lumber.

The *Cirque Calder* grew from two suitcases full of performers and props in 1927 to five by 1930. Then Calder more or less stopped working on it, although he continued to put on performances to the end of his career and frequently returned to circus themes in his sculpture, as in the magnificent *Performing Seal* of 1950 [fig. 3.4]. In the early days Calder occasionally charged admission to these performances to make his rent, but he generally presented the *Cirque Calder* free to his friends and their friends, and in this way he met most of the advanced artists in Paris in the late twenties. It even made an appearance in Thomas Wolfe's 1934 novel *You Can't Go Home Again*[2] after a 1929 performance Wolfe witnessed in a New York apartment.

In Paris, Fernand Léger shared Calder's interest in machine culture and they established a fast friendship. But it was his encounter with Piet Mondrian that played the most important role in transforming Calder into an abstract artist. After Mondrian came to see the *Cirque*, Calder repaid the visit and later described the Dutchman's studio:

It was a very exciting room. Light came in from the left and from the right, and on the solid wall between the windows there were experimental stunts with colored rectangles of cardboard tacked on. Even the victrola [the record player], which had been some muddy color, was painted red. I suggested to Mondrian that perhaps it would be fun to make these rectangles oscillate. And he, with a very serious countenance, said: "No, it is not necessary, my painting is already very fast." . . . This one visit gave me a shock that started things. Though I had often heard the word "modern" before, I did not consciously know or feel the term "abstract." So now at thirty-two, I wanted to paint and work in the abstract.[3]

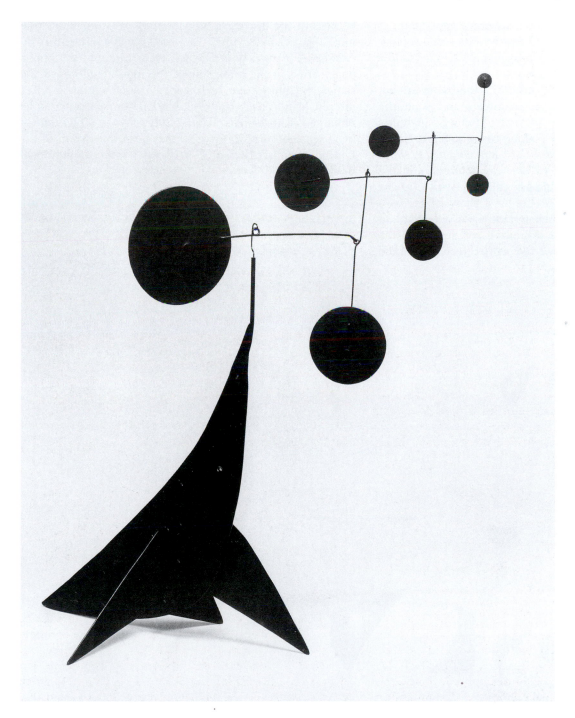

3.4 Alexander Calder,
Performing Seal, 1950.
Painted sheet metal and steel wire, 33 × 23 × 36in (83.8 × 58.4 × 91.4cm).
Museum of Contemporary Art, Chicago. The Ruth and Leonard Horwich Family, PG92.6.

Formally Mondrian inspired in Calder a new use of flat planes, primary colors—especially red—in opposition to black and white, a concern for the equilibrium of space and surface, and the idea of nonsymmetrical balance. He also made Calder more aware of the relation of style to the definition of a worldview. Calder understood that Mondrian saw the harmonies in his paintings as abstract blueprints for harmonizing the underlying structure of nature with a social utopia. In Mondrian's view, painting permitted the contemplation of the cosmic order and society in their purest forms. Although Calder's wire sculpture of the 1920s already embodied a fully elaborated character, the correlation of formal simplification and metaphysics that Mondrian's work brought home to him gave Calder's work a new depth. It began to take on a tone of formal concentration and sophistication that the more directly exuberant *Cirque Calder* lacked, for all its youthful brilliance.

In 1930, shortly after this visit to Mondrian's studio, Calder began his first abstract sculptures and soon the *Abstraction–Création* group in Paris (which included Mondrian and Arp) invited Calder to join. Such classic Calder sculptures as *Little Ball with Counterweight*, *The Pistil*, and *A Universe* evolved out of the wire sculptures in the service of this more philosophical content. In April 1931 the Galerie Percier in Paris gave Calder a show of his wire portraits and abstractions. Duchamp came to Calder's studio for the first time during this exhibition and suggested the term "mobiles" for his motorized works; Jean Arp asked Calder if the wire abstractions were "stabiles" (the term Calder adopted for his sculptures that do not move).[4]

Cosmic Imagery and the Mobiles

All of Calder's new abstractions of 1930 and 1931 made use of cosmic imagery. Indeed, it became a central theme in Calder's work, particularly in the movement of the mobiles. His friend Miró was using images of the sun, moon, and stars in the twenties and painted a series of "constellations" around 1940; Jean Arp constructed a series of wood reliefs entitled "constellations" in the early thirties. But cosmic imagery was also present in Calder's mind at the time because of the discovery on March 14, 1930 of Pluto (the ninth planet) by scientists at the Lowell Observatory in Arizona. This widely publicized event captured the public imagination in the same way as the moon landings of the sixties and must have reawakened Calder's long-standing interest, dating back to his childhood "star-gazing." As he remarked, with his characteristically dry wit: "The underlying sense of form in my work has been the system of the Universe, or part thereof. For that is a rather large model to work from."[5]

3.5 Alexander Calder, *Y Object*, 1951. Painted metal and wire, 5ft 4in × 9ft 6in (1.62 × 2.89m) (variable). Courtesy PaceWildenstein Gallery, New York.

The formal vocabulary of these abstractions appears to have been inspired by orreries (mechanized models of the universe) and tellurians (mechanical earth, moon, and sun systems) from the seventeenth and eighteenth centuries. In the first half of the thirties Calder motorized several of these pieces, but this regularized the relations of the parts into repetitive patterns that he found less interesting than the myriad arrangements created by chance in the unmotorized mobiles, as seen here in two configurations of the same piece [figs. 3.5 and 3.6]. Calder was especially interested in events he could not predict and sought to make work that would spontaneously respond to unpredictable interventions with an infinitely varied, adaptive equilibrium; the mobiles provided that. He described his mobiles as "abstractions which resemble nothing in life except their manner of reacting."[6] Their invention in 1930 was a radical innovation; they literally incorporated time (the fourth dimension), movement, and relative variations in speed and distance into sculpture. The time–space–matter continuum— a central concern of advanced science since 1905—tied in with Calder's cosmological interests. Movement undermined the seemingly fixed nature of the object. Calder also created a number of abstract drawings on cosmological themes around 1931–2, which, along with the circus drawings from the same time [fig. 3.7], are Calder's greatest works on paper.

Calder's mobiles asserted an utterly different definition of sculpture than that which had existed since antiquity. Where a work like Henry Moore's *Reclining Figure* [fig. 4.35] is a fixed form sitting on a pedestal that separates it from the real space of the viewer like the frame on a picture, Calder's mobiles [figs. 3.5, 3.6, 3.8] seem to float freely in the same space inhabited by the viewer. This idea of incorporating the real space around the sculpture into the work (called "open-form" sculpture) was pioneered by the prewar cubists and futurists and by the Russian avant-garde, especially Vladimir Tatlin, who insisted on "real materials in real space."[7]

In their precise outlines and sophisticated mechanics, the mobiles reflect Calder's engineering training at the Stevens Institute. In particular he recalled a wave machine from a kinetics course being a forebear of his fascination with mechanical action. As a genre Calder's mobiles have a celestial metaphor inherent in their structure, since they suggest the absence of a fixed frame of reference—an analog to objects in space. The parts of the mobiles move effortlessly, creating a seemingly infinite variety of form. Like the planets, they continually redefine their relations around the different centers of equilibrium and gravity that the artist has cunningly composed. The perpetually changing relations within the mobiles give them a metaphysical identity that relies on temporal memory to assemble the sequence of partial definitions comprising the more complex identity of the whole.

3.7 Alexander Calder, *The Circus*, 1932. Ink on paper,
20¼ × 29¼in (51.4 × 74.3cm).
Courtesy Perls Galleries, New York.

This gives each mobile a kind of physical transparency, revealing the internal processes in a manner that greatly extends the static transparency of prewar cubism and futurism.

The mastery of continuous, unpredictable change is a central theme in Calder's art. Its roots go back to the frequent dislocations of his unsettled childhood and the anxiety caused by his father's illness. This background seems to have produced in the adult artist a surface resilience and an ability to keep emotional ups and downs out of sight by way of sarcasm and a disinclination to look inward. A *Life* magazine reporter once asked if he ever felt sad and Calder replied: "No, I don't have the time. When I think I might start to, I fall asleep. I conserve energy that way."[8] The experience of the year-long separation from his parents in 1905 and 1906 must have caused considerable stress for the child, and yet in recounting the episode in his *Autobiography* Calder uses a strikingly cool tone and humor to negate the emotional charge. This mirrors the central metaphor for the mobiles: the regaining of equilibrium from the chaos of the unexpected and the out of control.

In January 1931 Calder married Louisa James (the grand-niece of both William and Henry James), whom he had met on a passenger ship for New York in June 1929. Two years later they moved back to New York and eventually bought a house in rural Roxbury, Connecticut, where he worked from 1938 to 1953. The Calders' first daughter, Sandra, was born in 1935 and Mary, their second, came four years later.

Both Calder's family life and his career settled into a good stride by the mid-thirties. The Pierre Matisse Gallery began showing his work on a regular basis, the Museum of Modern Art acquired one of his sculptures, he designed sets for Martha Graham's dance troupe, and was generally very much on the New York scene in the thirties and forties. In addition Calder had established close ties with the European moderns—indeed, the Spanish architect José Luis Sert asked him to create the *Mercury Fountain* for the Spanish Republican Pavilion at the 1937 Paris World's Fair (to accompany Picasso's *Guernica* and Miró's *The Reaper*). His dealer, Pierre Matisse, provided the primary showcase for the European surrealists in New York in the thirties and forties, and more and more of the artists Calder knew from Paris began emigrating to New York in person.

Calder's personal tie to surrealism and dada was important. His biomorphic abstraction was adapted from surrealism

3.8 Alexander Calder, *Gamma*, 1947. Painted metal and wire,
58 × 84 × 36in (147.3 × 213.4 × 91.4cm).
Courtesy PaceWildenstein Gallery, New York.

and Calder credited Miró with encouraging his brilliant
colors and preference for simple oval and circular forms.[9]
But Calder's work has none of the surrealists' concern with
the unconscious, psychological dynamics, nor any of the
soul-searching emotionalism that surrealism inspired in the
painters of the New York School.

In 1943, when aluminum grew scarce because of the war,
Calder made a series of wooden sculptures that he called
"constellations" [fig. 3.9].[10] They have a formal affinity with
the shapes in paintings by Tanguy and with Giacometti's *The
Palace at 4 a.m.* [fig. 5.11], which had been on display at the
Museum of Modern Art in New York since the mid-thirties.
Some of Calder's works come directly from natural subjects,
such as the plant forms in his *Bougainvillea* [fig. 3.10]; others

3.9 Alexander Calder, *Constellation*, 1943. Painted wood and
wire, 51 × 46½ × 10in (129.5 × 118.1 × 25.4cm).
Private collection. Photograph courtesy Whitney Museum of American Art, New York.

3.10 (left) **Alexander Calder**, *Bougainvillea*, 1947. Painted sheet metal, wire and weights, 6ft 4in × 6ft 11in (1.93 × 2.11m). Private collection.

are derived not from the appearance of nature but from an abstract idea, visualized in the mind with sufficient particularity to seem real, as in *Y Object* or the "constellations."

"Léger once called you a realist," Katherine Kuh reminded him. "How do you feel about this?"

"Yes, I think I am a realist . . . Because I make what I see. It's only the problem of seeing it. If you can imagine a thing, conjure it up in space—then you can make it, and *tout de suite* you're a realist. The universe is real but you can't see it. You have to imagine it. Once you imagine it, you can be realistic about reproducing it."[11]

By the forties Calder had become an established artist. The Museum of Modern Art gave him a one-person exhibition in 1943–4 and no less a figure than Jean-Paul Sartre wrote the catalog introduction for his 1946 gallery show in Paris. By the end of the forties he was receiving increasingly important commissions from around the world.

In 1953 the Calders bought a second house in Saché, France, and began spending more and more time in Europe again. Although Calder died in 1976 at nearly eighty years of age; his development never tapered off. In 1932 he took the mobiles off their supporting armatures and started hanging them from the ceiling. In the 1940s, he began to experiment with scale.

The stabiles, which also originated in that first body of abstract work of 1930 and 1931, started to take a different form around 1936. Calder defined the new stabiles with large flat planes of metal, fabricated in an industrial style. These grew in size during the forties too, and when the commissions for both mobiles and stabiles on an architectural scale started coming his way in the late fifties, Calder began collaborating with industrial fabricators in their construction. Calder's magnificent 1973 *Flamingo* [fig. 3.11] in the Federal Center Plaza in Chicago not only *appears* to

3.11 Alexander Calder, *Flamingo*, 1973. Painted steel plate, 40ft (13.5m) high.
Federal Center Plaza, Chicago.

be constructed like the hull of a great ship; it *is*. Yet this work also maintains a supple, avian grace on a scale and in a style that holds its own brilliantly against the steel and glass skyscrapers around it.

HANS HOFMANN

Stylistic Lessons from Europe

Like Calder, Hans Hofmann provided an important bridge between European modernism and the new American avant-garde, although Hofmann retained a European sensibility that neither Calder nor the American-born artists of the New York School ever had. This "European sensibility" is difficult to define precisely, but it has to do with a conception of the artist as a vehicle for the forces of nature and indeed as inseparable from nature in the artist's definition of him- or herself. The idea goes back to the romantics of the late eighteenth century and contrasts with the more pragmatic, matter-of-fact attitude that artists of the interwar period singled out as a characteristically American trait.

Hofmann was a German who emigrated to America, and from the mid-thirties through the late fifties taught young American painters the formal subtleties of European modernism: nuances of handling paint and color (based on his firsthand experience with fauvism and Kandinsky); an analytical approach to pictorial structure (from his study of Cézanne and cubism); and a spirituality (as in Kandinsky's

romantic abstraction). Hofmann's seriousness of purpose and his intensity with regard to the formal issues of painting set an example that the young Americans emulated. As a charismatic teacher on the scene, Hofmann helped bring the young Americans up to a level of formal sophistication hitherto the sole province of the European moderns.

In Stuart Davis's *House and Street* [fig. 3.12], one can see the limited extent to which interwar American painting had assimilated European styles. Davis was an important painter of the period. He had studied with Robert Henri and gone to Paris in the twenties. But like other advanced American artists between the wars he sought to remodel European modernism into a "description" of America with a sociopolitical and semiotic agenda. While he recognized that no American artist had "created a style which was . . . completely divorced from European models," he nevertheless wanted to distinguish himself from his influences: "I am an American, born in Philadelphia of American stock. I studied art in America. I painted what I see in America, in other words, I paint the American scene."[12]

Despite his radical simplification of the subject matter in *House and Street*, Davis still emphasizes the *description* (of an American city scene). The strength of the work lies in its presentation of "facts" in a disengaged style that is at the same time distinctly "modern" (in its shallow space and its flat planes of bright color, as in French cubism of the twenties) and also American in the formal execution. By contrast Picasso, even in those phases where his painting is very flat (as in *Guernica* or *The Studio* [figs. 2.10 and 3.22]), always has a formal elegance, a richly worked surface that is interesting to look at entirely on the level of paint surface.

Hofmann helped the younger Americans to understand this aspect of European modernism—what the French call *belle peinture* (the beautiful handling of paint). But on the whole, the best American painters never adopted this painterly refinement; indeed, dispensing with it implied a rejection of hierarchies that was at the heart of American art. Pollock, for example, always had a kind of awkwardness in paint handling that set off the freshness of the conception; de Kooning retained a mastery of brushwork from his European training, but he pushed bravura brushwork over the edge of refinement. What makes Davis so interesting and important is precisely that he pushed *belle peinture* aside for a distinctly American vulgarity that prefigures American pop art and was seminal for late-twentieth-century advertising.

Hofmann was born in Bavaria in 1880 and spent his youth in Munich during the symbolist period. He trained as an engineer and had some commercial inventions to his credit. From 1904 to 1914 he painted in Paris and frequented the Café du Dôme, where he met such artists as Picasso, Braque, Pascin, Rouault, Picabia, Matisse, and Léger. Although he had no personal contact with the German expressionists until after World War I, Hofmann stored some of Kandinsky's great prewar paintings in his Munich studio from 1914 to 1918 and later received two of them in thanks for his kindness.

3.12 Stuart Davis, *House and Street*, 1931. Oil on canvas,
26 × 42¼in (66 × 107.3cm).
Collection, Whitney Museum of American Art, New York. Purchase, 41.3.

A weak lung got Hofmann excused from military service
and enabled him in 1915 to open the Hans Hofmann School
for Modern Art in Schwabing (the artists' quarter of Munich).
The best known of the many American pupils he attracted
was the sculptress Louise Nevelson, who attended Hofmann's
last session there in the spring of 1931. In the summers of
1930 and 1931 he taught at the University of California in
Berkeley, and in the fall of 1931 he moved to New York City.
There Hofmann taught at the Art Students League for two
years before opening his own school. In 1935 he also started
up a summer school in Provincetown, on the tip of Cape Cod.

For Hofmann art had nothing to do with politics or
social consciousness. He stressed drawing and lectured on
pictorial structure, paint handling, and intuitive expression
through materials. Although Hofmann's interpretation of
fauvism, prewar cubism, Cézanne, and Kandinsky was formalistic and twenty years behind the developments on the
European scene, it nevertheless carried much authority for
his young American students. Hofmann had a heavy German
accent and a hearing problem, which made communication
difficult; but instead of interfering with his teaching, this
seems to have given an Olympian distance to his charismatic
personality.

Hofmann's Art Theory

In addition to teaching, Hofmann wrote essays on art theory,
pervaded by the spirituality of Kandinsky and Mondrian.
"The artist's technical problem," Hofmann wrote, "is how
to transform the material with which he works back into the

3.13 Paul Cézanne, *Mont Sainte-Victoire*, 1902–4. Oil on canvas,
27½ × 35¼in (69.9 × 89.5cm).
Philadelphia Museum of Art, George W. Elkins Collection, 1936.

3.14 (left) **Hans Hofmann,** *Landscape*, 1941. Oil on plywood, 30 × 35in (76.2 × 88.9cm). Private collection.

3.15 (below) **Henri Matisse,** *Promenade Among the Olive Trees*, 1905. Oil on canvas, 17½ × 21¾in (44.5 × 55.2cm). Metropolitan Museum of Art, New York. Robert Lehman Collection, 1975.

sphere of the spirit."[13] But Hofmann detached the spirituality of Kandinsky and Mondrian from their radical social aims and thus essentially missed the point of their work. What he understood well about their painting was its visual structure, and to this he intuitively attached an emotional dimension, which he identified as "spirituality." The main part of Hofmann's theories, however, concerns spatial dynamics and visual tensions. For example, he reasoned that "painting possesses fundamental laws. These laws are dictated by fundamental perceptions. One of these perceptions is: the essence of the picture is the picture plane. The essence of the picture is its two-dimensionality. The first law is then derived: the picture plane must be preserved in its two-dimensionality."[14]

This idea derives from Hofmann's study of the works of Paul Cézanne [fig. 3.13]. Cézanne's prominent brushwork, and such compositional devices as his tipped-up perspective and regularized system of simplifying forms, flattened out the pictorial space and emphasized the surface of the canvas. The work of the prewar cubists carried this accentuation of the picture plane, the shallow space, and the systematic application of paint still further. Hofmann extrapolated from these sources a theory of spatial dynamics in painting: "Depth, in a pictorial, plastic sense, is not created by the arrangement of objects one after another toward a vanishing point, in the sense of Renaissance perspective, but on the

contrary (and in absolute denial of this doctrine), by the creation of forces in the sense of *push and pull*."[15]

Hofmann's concept of "push and pull" asserts that all movement within a painting necessarily implies a reciprocal movement in the opposing direction; movement into pictorial space demanded a balancing advance toward the viewer. One can see the direct influence of this idea in

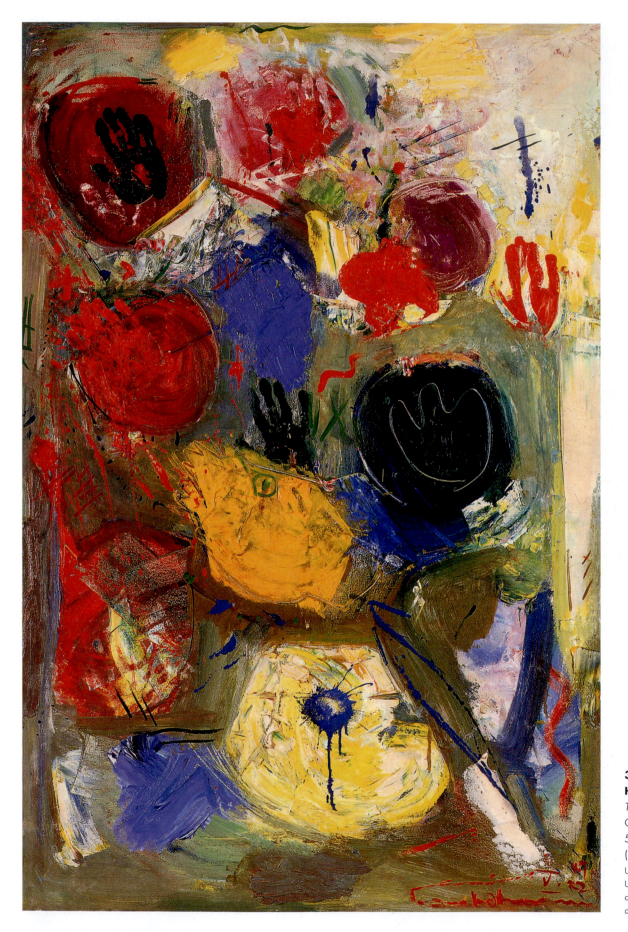

3.16 Hans Hofmann, *The Third Hand*, 1947. Oil on canvas, 5ft ⅛in × 3ft 4in (1.53 × 1.02m). University Art Museum, University of California at Berkeley. Gift of the artist.

Louise Nevelson's works [fig. 7.16], which simultaneously move forward and back from a hypothetical picture plane. Yet this and other aspects of Hofmann's teaching may have had their most profound influence through the interpretations of the formalist critic Clement Greenberg, who stated in 1945 that he owed "more to the illumination received from Hofmann's lectures than from any other source."[16]

Hofmann's Painting

Lee Krasner studied with Hofmann around 1940, and through her he met Jackson Pollock and other artists in their circle. Yet Pollock's existential introspection was too psychological for Hofmann. When Krasner brought Pollock to Hofmann's studio for the first time in 1942, Hofmann said to Pollock: "You don't work from nature. You work by heart. This is no good. You will repeat yourself." Knowing that Hofmann was at this stage more of a teacher than a practicing painter and had never even shown his work in New York, Pollock responded defiantly to this patronizing advice: "I *am* nature . . . Put up or shut up. Your theories don't interest me."[17]

As a painter, Hofmann did all of his important work in America, carrying fauvist color and handling into a free abstract expressionism. Though the painterly handling resembled Kandinsky's canvases of 1912–14, Hofmann's work lacked Kandinsky's depth of subject matter. The strength of Hofmann's work derives from a passionate engagement with the mastery of paint application and composition in themselves. In addition, Hofmann's work always maintained a shallow, orderly space, meticulously derived from Cézanne and cubism.

From the mid-thirties into the early forties Hofmann painted numerous summer landscapes of Cape Cod [fig. 3.14]. Although they are dated by their stylistic affinity with prewar Paris, the paintings' unique fusion of fauvist color and cubist space makes them powerful nonetheless. Throughout this period Hofmann remained committed to nature; whether in the studio or out of doors in the landscape, he constantly tested reality while simultaneously asserting the autonomy of these paintings as paintings. The translation of three-dimensional space onto the picture plane in this composition acknowledges the flatness of the canvas; the ecstatic palette of brilliant and energetically applied color agitates the entire surface with uniform intensity, further emphasizing the surface, as in the fauvist works of Matisse [fig. 3.15]. Hofmann's landscapes are raw; they brim over with excess energy, and so did he.

Under the pressure of the new formal devices of surrealism in the early forties, the visible link to nature in Hofmann's painting gave way to a more experimental mode. In a number of pictures of the forties, Hofmann stresses spontaneity by splattering the paint rather than applying it with a brush. This automatist technique frees the gesture of the hand. But Hofmann had no interest in using this technique as a means of probing or expressing his unconscious mind.

Indeed, Hofmann pointedly explained: "My work is not accidental and not planned. The first red spot on a white canvas may at once suggest to me the meaning of 'morning redness' and from there on I dream further with my color."[18] As distinct from surrealist free association, Hofmann insisted that his work proceeded from an "inner necessity" that was psychic rather than psychological; its claim to truth centers upon a revelation of the content to the artist (as it did for Kandinsky, from whom Hofmann borrowed the term "inner necessity"). "The spirit in a work," Hofmann asserted, "is synonymous with its quality. The *Real* in art never dies, because its nature is predominantly spiritual."[19]

The rich, heavily applied palette of Hofmann's painting *The Third Hand* [fig. 3.16] takes off from the romantic clouds of color in the early Kandinsky [fig. 3.17]. The individuality of Kandinsky's spatial vision and the secretive character of his iconography cast the artist as the medium for cosmic truths. Hofmann's vision remained more secular, focused as it was on a systematic exploration of technique and structure. Yet his declaration of presence in his own handprint provides the same kind of romantic counterpoint to his mysterious color actions as in Kandinsky. In addition, Hofmann (like Kandinsky and other symbolist-influenced painters) had a mystic fascination with synaesthetic correlations between color and sound, and invoked music in his titles and in the subjectivist "orchestration" of colors.

Hofmann had his first one-person show at the age of sixty-four; it took place in 1944 at Peggy Guggenheim's Art of This Century gallery. Writers frequently blame this late start on the energy that Hofmann's teaching siphoned off. But Hofmann was not a man in a hurry: he lived with his prospective wife, Miz, for twenty-eight years before making up his mind to marry her; he painted for forty-four years before his first one-person show; and he did not commit himself stylistically until he was seventy-eight years old (in 1958). He may not have felt confident enough about his work in the forties to commit himself to a single stylistic direction, and perhaps that held him back from showing his work initially. Not even his students saw his work in the thirties; he permitted only a small number of close friends into his studio. Samuel Kootz began showing Hofmann's paintings at the end of 1947; in 1948 this brought him an American museum show with an accompanying monograph and a major exhibition in Paris. But even as he gained visibility he continued to pursue a wide range of styles.

Art generated on a predominantly formal basis, rather than out of a commitment to the content, runs the risk of lacking stylistic continuity. Hofmann himself was evidently concerned about this when he took pains to construct a philosophy that deliberately rejected the adoption of a particular style; he insisted that he viewed painting as a dedication to individual, spontaneous expression, and took as his model the stylistic diversity of Paul Klee. "If I ever find a style," he told Kootz, "I'll stop painting."[20] Yet in 1958 Hofmann gave up teaching and for the last eight years of his life focused on

3.17 Wassily Kandinsky, *Sketch 1 for Composition VII*, 1913. Oil on canvas, 30¾ × 39⅜in (78.1 × 100cm). Private collection, Germany.

a unified stylistic development that resulted in some of the best paintings of his career.

Hofmann's late painting (from 1958 to 1966) centered on a defined opposition between hard geometry and painterliness, as in *The Golden Wall* [fig. 3.18]. Some late works include only loose gestures or precise, geometric forms. Most, however, involve a new synthesis of, on one hand, the fauvist palette and the Cézanne-inspired structural rationality of the late-thirties landscapes with, on the other hand, Kandinsky's free brushwork and his romantic spatial organization. These paintings reflect the precision of Hofmann's analysis of color relationships and their structural implications, as set out in his essay "The Color Problem in Pure Painting—Its Creative Origin":

> Since every color can be shaded with any other color, an unlimited variation of shading within every color scale is possible. Although a red can be, in itself, bluish, greenish, yellowish, brownish, etc., its actual color-emanation in the pictorial totality will be the conditioned result of its relationship to all the other colors. Any color shade within one color scale can become, at any moment, the bridge to any other color scale. This leads to an interwoven communion of color scales over the entire picture surface.[21]

With the rectangles, which dominate Hofmann's compositions by 1958, the artist leads the viewer around the space in a processional way, as in a plan for a classical building. The viewer discovers the spaces through these defining forms. Mondrian's writings on the contrast of rectangles to other forms helped Hofmann refine one aspect of this language, and the picturesque complexity of Kandinsky's spatial systems informed another. Hofmann's distinction between shifting and overlapping rectangles—both retreating and advancing in space—is a subtlety that grew out of his concept of "push and pull."

The large areas of intensely saturated color in Hofmann's paintings influenced the so-called "color field" painters of the late fifties and sixties [figs. 6.8–6.10]. In that period, in which much abstract painting was dominated by the formal questions discussed by Clement Greenberg, many artists and critics looked to Hofmann as a heroic pioneer. Meanwhile Hofmann himself sounded like something straight out of Clement Greenberg. Writing in 1962, Hofmann explained: "I am often asked how I approach my work. Let me confess: I hold my mind and my work free from any association foreign to the act of painting. I am thoroughly inspired and agitated by the actions themselves which the development of the painting continuously requires."[22] Hofmann was a master at assimilating stylistic ideas without regard to the content from which they originated; even his sensual landscapes of 1936–41 and the great last works of 1958–66 have an almost polite reserve in the way that the artist segregates the language of intuitive expression from an overtly personal content. In this respect Hofmann had a profound effect on such painters of the sixties as Frank Stella and Robert Ryman [figs. 10.1, 10.3, 10.4, and 10.21] but it set him apart from the likes of de Kooning and Pollock.

ARSHILE GORKY

Arshile Gorky was a self-educated intellectual, and thus all the more earnest in his reading of literature and in his dedication to art. He carried small books on artists around in his pockets and talked about art incessantly—on park benches in Washington Square, in bars, or at parties. He would stand in front of a great Vermeer or a Titian in the Metropolitan Museum and scrutinize it, sometimes expostulating aloud to himself as he examined each detail. Afterwards he and de Kooning or other friends would go out for coffee and discuss the painting for hours. For Gorky art was the vehicle through which he experienced everything and a matter of the utmost importance.

3.18 Hans Hofmann, *The Golden Wall*, 1961. Oil on canvas,
4ft 11½in × 5ft 11¾in (1.51 × 1.82m).
Art Institute of Chicago. Mr. and Mrs. Frank G. Logan Prize Fund, 1962.775.

Gorky's Life (Real and Imagined)

Gorky was born Vosdanik Adoian on April 15, 1904 in
Turkish Armenia. His mother descended from a noble line of
priests from the fifth-century Armenian Apostolic Church,
and she imbued him with a love of the ancient culture and
language. The rich manuscripts, architecture, sculpture, and
wall carvings in the 3,000-year-old city of Van inspired an
early interest in art and blended in his memory with his deep
emotional attachment to his mother and to the majestic

scenery of his native region. The central theme of his later
life and art was a vivid, animistic re-creation of his family
and childhood surroundings in the village of Khorkom and
on the shores of Lake Van in eastern Turkey.

Long victims of religious persecution by the Muslim
Turks, the Armenians suffered a systematic campaign of
genocide during World War I. When Gorky was four, his
father fled to the United States to avoid conscription into
the Turkish army. Two years later the young Gorky had to
evacuate to the stronghold of Van with his mother and sisters,
and in 1915 they set out on foot for Caucasian Armenia on
the infamous "death march." The Muslim Turks slaughtered stragglers and by the year's end had exterminated
a million-and-a-half Armenians. Gorky's family arrived in
July, and in the fall Gorky's elder sister and half-sister
emigrated to the United States, leaving him with his mother

and youngest sister, Vartoosh. Conditions for the refugees were appalling and in March 1919 Gorky's mother literally died of starvation in his arms.

On February 26, 1920—sixteen years old and destitute—Gorky arrived at Ellis Island in New York with Vartoosh. Three days later the husband of their half-sister, Akabi, picked them up and brought them home to Watertown, Massachusetts. After some odd jobs and a couple of years in a Boston art school, Gorky moved in late 1924 to Sullivan Street, near Washington Square in New York. He took more art courses and then joined the teaching staff at the Grand Central School of Art where, according to Harold Rosenberg, he stressed the idea of getting emotion into drawing, once even hiring a Hungarian violinist to play during the class![23]

Gorky systematically constructed an artistic image for himself, beginning by a change of name just prior to leaving Boston. "Arshile" is a cognate of Achilles, the heroic warrior of *The Iliad*, who flew into battle out of rage at the death of his beloved friend Patroclus; and "Gorky" means "bitter" in Russian. Thus Gorky, in effect, named himself "the bitter Achilles," no doubt in reference to his rage and sorrow at the death of his mother and his enforced exile. He also deliberately chose a Russian name, which seemed not only glamorous for a leftist artist in the twenties, but also registered his admiration for Chekhov and Dostoyevsky. He even claimed to be related to the Soviet writer Maxim Gorky in order to enhance his intellectual pedigree. Of course "Maxim Gorky" was also a pen name, prompting Rosenberg's crack that: "In making someone else's alias his own name, Arshile involved himself in the higher mathematics of pseudonymity."[24]

Almost everyone who knew him recollected Gorky's character as humorous in its melodramatic expressions and in his fabrication of biographical details. In the summer of 1936 he had a brief affair with the female painter Michael West and sent her love letters plagiarized from the French artist Gaudier-Brzeska with sections from Paul Eluard.[25] They were quite torrid too; he even signed one of them: "In flames, Arshile."[26] In addition, Gorky's friends joked about how he enjoyed playing the exotic Armenian peasant at parties, complete with shepherd dances and folk songs [fig. 3.19]. Even Stuart Davis, a close friend in the early thirties, described Gorky and his studio as if the artist had staged everything; it was an "artistic-type studio . . . equipped with the paraphernalia popularly believed to be the appropriate sign of the true artist [including] . . . a few plaster casts around, and a stringed musical instrument of some kind to complete the setting."[27]

At six foot three, the lean, dark-complexioned, handsome artist with large, "pleading war-orphan eyes," as Rosenberg described them, and a strong foreign accent made an unforgettable impression. Gorky accentuated the effect by pulling a black velour hat down low over his forehead and wearing a long, black overcoat that flowed like a monk's cassock down to the ankles and buttoned up tight under the chin. He staged everything in the sense that he carefully selected and systematically emulated certain famous artists and

3.19 Arshile Gorky dancing at a party, c. 1945.
Photograph by V. V. Rankine.

intellectuals as a means of incorporating what he admired. He did this at the easel and in shaping his artistic persona. In essence, he felt he had to invent the autobiography that would lead to the intellectual and artistic position he had taken. To the sophisticated New Yorker it seemed like a put-on, but even his friends may have underestimated the naive directness with which Gorky pieced together a self-image and a style. He came from a world that had literally disappeared and was in any case so foreign in every respect to New York that he had to redefine himself as though *ex nihilo*. In effect he was a natural embodiment of the existentialist hero, who creates his identity in the process of encountering himself, and experiences everything as if new. What Rosenberg learned from Kafka about starting from scratch, Gorky discovered in life.

Everyone who knew Gorky has remarked on the acuity and freshness of his visual insight. This rightly baffled them because it had the effect of substantiating the artist's otherwise unbelievable act. To Gorky, the false pretense of a blood relation to Maxim Gorky, the impossible claim of having studied with Kandinsky for three months in 1920,[28] and the sequence of stylistic charades of Cézanne, Picasso, and Miró in his painting—all had an intellectual vividness that made them "real" to him. Certainly nothing could be less credible than the actual facts of his early life. It is not that Gorky was out of touch with reality; rather, he believed that true intellectuals must construct their own reality and intellectual genealogy. The clarity and conviction with which he presented this notion was an important contribution. It was a new perspective on facts and it was an existential paradigm. Gorky's particular "history" was a completely authentic facet of his artistic statement. The intellectual position set out in his art was in turn his strategy for survival. Gorky lived his art with absolute dedication at all times and in doing so provided an example of the seriousness of the endeavor; his complete surrender of himself, both in his life and his art, to the demands of his aesthetic helped to pave the way for a deeper understanding of the modern movements of Europe for young American artists.

The Development of Gorky's Style

Between 1925 and the late thirties Gorky painstakingly aped the styles of one major modern master after another. He also learned about the European moderns through his contacts with other artists. In 1928 Gorky met John Graham, a Russian-born artist who began making annual trips to Paris in 1930, establishing friendships with Picasso and Breton and keeping abreast of the French art scene. Throughout the thirties Graham played a critical role for Stuart Davis, Willem de Kooning, and David Smith (all of whom Gorky befriended too in 1929 and 1930) as well as for Pollock and Gorky in keeping them up to date with current events in Paris. In 1929 Gorky also met David Burliuk, an old friend of Kandinsky's from the Blue Rider

3.20 Arshile Gorky, *The Artist and His Mother*, 1926–36. Oil on canvas, 5ft × 4ft 2in (1.52 × 1.27m).

Collection, Whitney Museum of American Art, New York. Gift of Julien Levy for Maro and Natasha Gorky in memory of their father.

period, and Gorky must have heard firsthand about Kandinsky's abstraction.

Gorky's career began to have some modest success in the thirties, highlighted by the inclusion of three works in a 1930 exhibition at the Museum of Modern Art and a one-person show in 1934 in a Philadelphia gallery. In 1935 the W.P.A. commissioned him, at roughly $100 a month, to work on a mural for Newark Airport. The mural showed the systematic transformation of airplane parts using a combination of biomorphic abstraction and cubist flatness, heavily influenced by the color and compositional rhythms of Fernand Léger. But this elegant mural did not have the studied derivativeness of Gorky's work of the twenties, and it received considerable attention.

During the Depression, radical politics took over from vanguard art in many quarters. Painting was widely viewed as a tool of agitation, best exemplified by the Mexican muralists. Gorky took quite the opposite view—that the genesis of a true work of art is in the history of art, not as a product of the wider socioeconomic milieu. Although he attended some of the recurring meetings that sought a Marxist approach to painting, it seems that he went to speak only on behalf of artistic values.

Around 1930 Gorky moved into a grimy commercial loft building in Union Square. Friends reported that he scrubbed the floor so thoroughly and so frequently that it came to have the washed-out look of driftwood. He wanted to create a beautiful refuge not only from the pressures for "social relevance" in art but from the desperation of his own poverty. He lived off occasional teaching and help from friends, but in his world of painting he made no concessions; despite the Depression he stockpiled supplies (only the best ones) with an air of aristocratic *noblesse oblige*. Stuart Davis remarked: "outside of an art store, I had never seen anything like this."[29]

Gorky had the same uncompromising idealism in his image of family life. Marny George, whom Gorky married in 1935, later remarked that Gorky had tried to mold her into what he imagined to be the ideal wife for him, but took little notice of who she actually was. This led to the break-up of their marriage in under a year.[30] A series of portraits

3.21 Arshile Gorky, *Organization*, 1934–6.
Oil on canvas, 4ft 1¾in × 5ft (1.26 × 1.52m).
National Gallery of Art, Washington, D.C. Alisa Mellon Bruce Fund, 1979.

of himself, his mother, and his sister Vartoosh (to whom he remained close throughout his life) provided the first deeply felt subject matter of Gorky's career. Although Gorky himself signed and dated many of these paintings as if they had been completed in the twenties, they probably date from the later thirties.

Gorky's painting of *The Artist and His Mother* [fig. 3.20] is the most moving of the portrait series. He worked from a 1912 photograph of himself with his mother, taken in the city of Van, three years before her tragic death. Making careful drawings from the photograph, he painted two full-sized versions, eliminating detail and refining his mother's face into a beautiful system of perfect ovals and arcs. Furthermore he composed the picture like an icon, with a tripartite division that suggests the throne of the Virgin. In one version the enlarged black pupils of the eyes and the transparent immateriality of the shoulder seem to transform his mother into a noncorporeal vision of pure spirit.

Gorky attained the shiny, glasslike surface by repeatedly scraping it down with a razor blade and repainting. This technique became a stock procedure for de Kooning too, who no doubt learned it from Gorky. Gorky may in turn have devised it from looking at the magnificent Ingres portrait of Madame de Haussonville which had recently been acquired by the Frick Collection. The anatomical segmentation in Gorky's portrait, which resembles his planar biomorphic

abstractions of the late thirties, also influenced the early figurative paintings of his good friend de Kooning. In 1949 the latter wrote that "when, about fifteen years ago, I walked into Arshile's studio for the first time, the atmosphere was so beautiful that I got a little dizzy and when I came to, I was bright enough to take the hint immediately . . . it is about impossible to get away from his powerful influence."[31]

In the mid-thirties Gorky began obsessively painting abstractions, like *Organization* [fig. 3.21], that derived from Picasso's work of the late twenties [fig. 3.22]. According to Rosenberg, Gorky came to be known as "the Picasso of Washington Square."[32] When Julien Levy went to Gorky's studio for the first time in 1932, he sensed Gorky's talent but couldn't reconcile himself to the artist's peculiar, almost superstitiously faithful, apprenticeship to Cézanne, Picasso, and then Miró. "I was *with* Cézanne for a long time, and now naturally I am *with* Picasso," he told Levy; Levy promised him a show, "when you are *with* Gorky."[33]

The series of paintings in homage to Khorkom (the village of Gorky's childhood) dominate the strikingly original abstractions of the late thirties. In these compositions

3.22 Pablo Picasso, *The Studio*, Paris, winter 1927–8; dated 1928. Oil on canvas, 4ft 11in × 7ft 7in (1.49 × 2.31m). The Museum of Modern Art, New York. Gift of Walter P. Chrysler, Jr., 213.1935.

3.23 Arshile Gorky,
Garden in Sochi, No. 3,
c. 1943. Oil on canvas,
31 × 39in (78.7 × 99cm).
The Museum of Modern Art, New York.
Acquired through the Lillie P. Bliss Bequest.

Gorky expanded upon the vocabulary of free abstract forms announced in *Organization* and anticipated in his drawings of 1931 and 1932. The rich, sensuous surfaces were so heavily painted that the pictures weighed as much as sculptures. It became a regular joke in his studio to ask some unsuspecting visitor to go over and pick one up.

Between roughly 1940 and 1943 Gorky also painted a series of paintings called "Garden in Sochi." Stylistically the sequence shows a transition from the strong influence of Miró's flat, brilliant colors, relatively thinly but opaquely painted, to an even denser impasto than the Khorkom paintings, and ending with a feathery and transparently brushed canvas set off by drawing with a fine black line [fig. 3.23]. The word "Sochi" probably comes from the Armenian *sos* or *sosi*, meaning a "poplar tree." Gorky's sister recalled, "it was the custom in our family at the birth of a son to plant a poplar tree which would later have the birth date and name carved on it. Gorky as a child loved his tree and took great pride in caring for it."[34]

In 1942 the Museum of Modern Art bought the 1941 version of *Garden in Sochi* and asked Gorky to write a statement about the series. His text indicated that his father's garden was the underlying theme of these works. He called it "the Garden of Wish Fulfillment" and recounted:

> often I had seen my mother and other village women opening their bosoms and taking their soft and dependent breasts in their hands to rub them on the rock. Above all this stood an enormous tree all bleached under the sun, the rain,

the cold, and deprived of leaves. This was the Holy Tree . . . people . . . would tear voluntarily a strip of their clothes and attach this to the tree. Thus through many years of the same act, like a veritable parade of banners under the pressure of wind all these personal inscriptions of signatures, very softly to my innocent ear used to give echo to the sh-h-h-h-sh-h of the silver leaves of the poplars.[35]

In the first version, the bare-breasted figure is still legible along the left edge, with a butterfly overhead, the trunk of a tree in the upper center, and perhaps the pennants of cloth in the upper right. The out-of-scale shoe in the center may refer to a pair of slippers given to Gorky by his father before leaving for America, and consequently it had great symbolic significance. But the shoe probably also relates to Miró's *Still Life with an Old Shoe* of 1937, which was at the Pierre Matisse Gallery in New York and featured a shoe filling a large area of the foreground. Gorky's use of automatist form control to transform natural subjects, especially figures, is heavily indebted to the metamorphic figures of Miró and Picasso [fig. 5.17]. The precise edges, thin planes, silhouettes, and flat grounds in the first *Garden in Sochi* painting also reveal the influence of Miró.

Gorky's Late Works

In 1942 everything came together in Gorky's painting; he clarified for himself what he wanted to paint and more or less how he had to do it. With this aesthetic self-assurance, the last six years of his life not only proved the most productive of his career but yielded work of uniformly brilliant quality, focused on a subject matter with highly specific referents. André Breton was right when he said that Gorky "maintains a direct contact with nature—sits down to paint before her."[36]

Scholars have pointed out that the seemingly abstract works which Gorky made in the forties contained figures, often family members before a fireplace, or details of plants or landscape.[37] Where the "Garden in Sochi" pictures still have a predominantly emblematic character, the new compositions begun after 1942 successfully embody the deep resonances of Gorky's Armenian past in the describable present of his family in Connecticut. In an April 1944 letter to Vartoosh about *The Liver Is the Cock's Comb* [fig. 3.24] Gorky wrote: "it is as if some ancient Armenian spirit within me moves my hand to create so far from our homeland the shapes of nature we loved in the gardens, wheatfields and orchards of our Adoian family in Khorkom. Our beautiful Armenia which we lost and which I will repossess in my art."[38]

The Liver seems to be populated with figures, one standing at the right edge, others on either side of the center, and there is perhaps a dog lying at the bottom, right of center. Gorky's metamorphic figures seem to condense multiple images into one form, as in a dream. Drawings make such guesswork easier, though one is always uncertain about the precise identity of the images. Those who knew Gorky well have confirmed that the images derive from natural forms—so, too, does Gorky himself, as in the letter to Vartoosh. Even the deliberate working-out of the forms in preliminary studies on paper makes it clear that Gorky had something specific in mind.

Gorky also conceived the picture titles of the forties to link up closely with their subject, providing multiple meanings and references. Many ancient and medieval texts refer to the liver (not the heart) as the center of passion. The "cock's comb," at once the headdress and the elaborately feathered genitalia of the figure along the right side of the canvas, as well as the brown phallus in the center of the left half of the painting, have to do with vanity and virility.

3.24 Arshile Gorky, *The Liver Is the Cock's Comb*, 1944.
Oil on canvas, 6ft 1¼in × 8ft 2in (1.86 × 2.49m).
Albright-Knox Art Gallery, Buffalo, New York. Gift of Seymour H. Knox, Jr., 1956.

On one level this invites the interpretation that the source of passion is physical lust, on another level that living itself is vanity (the "liver" meaning "one who lives").[39]

At the beginning of 1942 the young surrealist Matta encouraged Gorky to add more turpentine to his pigment;[40] this immediately gave Gorky's painting a looser, more spontaneous effect. But Matta conceived of the technique as a way of fostering free association, which he used for generating new forms, whereas Gorky already knew precisely what he wanted to paint. In a letter of 1939 Gorky rejected such surrealist devices for their lack of control: "I do not believe in anarchy in art. There must be some structure . . . For me, art must be a facet of the thinking mind . . . unrelenting spontaneity is chaos."[41] By 1947, when he described the surrealists as "drunk with psychiatric spontaneity and inexplicable dreams,"[42] his own concept of painting was firmly established as anything but automatist. For Gorky this looser technique of Matta's helped him to systematically disguise a consciously generated subject.

Gorky's debt to Kandinsky of 1913–14 [fig. 3.17] in his painting of the forties can be seen in the voluptuous pleasure of the surface application of paint, but also in the independence of color, form, and line from one another; in the flowing, often semitransparent, brilliant color; in the romanticism of brushwork and palette; and above all in the handling of the subject matter. Kandinsky's early abstract paintings contain many "disguised" objects which any careful

viewer can see. But in Gorky's work, as in Kandinsky's, one cannot necessarily identify the objects with any certainty. In 1943 Gorky wrote to Vartoosh that his father's garden in Khorkom was "a secret treasure to which I have been entrusted the key,"[43] and Gorky maintained the secrecy of this treasure by disguising the subjects of his paintings. Thus Gorky's claim to have studied with Kandinsky in 1920, although untrue, nevertheless reflects a real intellectual and aesthetic connection.

When Gorky married Agnes Magruder ("Mougouch") in 1941 and started his own family, she and the children joined the gallery of "loved ones" or "loveds" that included himself, Vartoosh, his mother, his paintings, and the landscape of his childhood, which he personified in his imagination. These "loved ones" are the "secret" subject matter of Gorky's paintings. For Gorky the security of a family, which he lost in childhood, took on the most profound importance. After his marriage and the births of his daughters, Maro (1943) and Natasha (1945), portrayals of the family became his obsessive subject.

The Calendars [fig. 3.25] shows just such a family scene, with Gorky standing at the right reading a magazine behind his seated wife Agnes (with black hair) rocking a cradle. The older child sits (at left) in a large gray chair looking out of the window at an orange sunset. A log is engulfed in flames in the fireplace (center) and in front of the fireplace is what may be a pram. A large dog sits in the center foreground

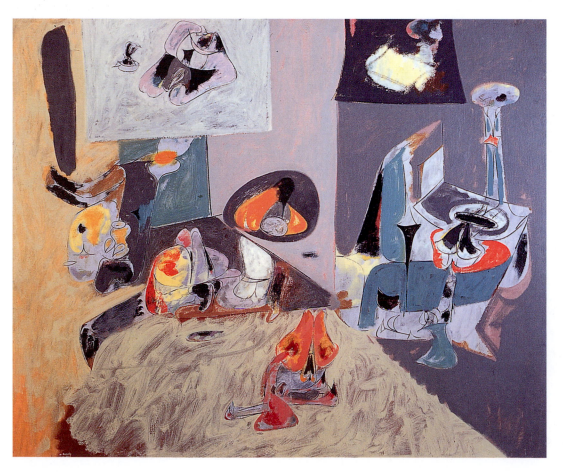

3.25 Arshile Gorky,
The Calendars, 1946–7.
Oil on canvas, 4ft 2in × 5ft
(1.27 × 1.52m).
Destroyed, former collection N. Rockefeller.

looking out. Two types of calendar are on the wall above this scene: a pink bathing beauty on a white beach with explicitly exposed genitals and a nature calendar with a fluffy bird. Perhaps the "cheesecake" calendar and the nature scene reflect two sides of his sexuality, a theme that resembles that of *The Liver Is the Cock's Comb*.

Tragedy pursued Gorky relentlessly. On January 26, 1946 he had a studio fire and lost about thirty canvases. After watching them burn, he produced two pictures called *Charred Beloved*, whose titles refer directly to the lost paintings. Late in February 1946 he underwent a cancer operation. He bounced back with an extraordinarily productive year in 1947, making nearly 300 drawings and twenty paintings. Then in December 1947 his father died.

Gorky's last works are filled with the sense of imminent death. Gorky's last painting was titled *Last Painting*, and the subtitle, *The Black Monk*, is a revealing allusion to a Chekhov play of the same name. In the play an apparition of a black monk tells Kavrin (the hero) that his frail frame cannot bear the weight of his genius, and then he dies. Gorky had suffered severe depression, which led in turn to marital problems, and during the winter of 1947–8 he tried killing himself several times. On one occasion his wife recalled seeing him take a rope and march up the hill; she sent the children out after him, telling them: "Look, Daddy is going to build a swing," so that they would unwittingly divert him long enough for the mood to pass.[44] But on June 26, 1948 Julien Levy and his wife were driving with Gorky in Connecticut and had an accident in which Gorky broke his neck. He temporarily lost the use of his right arm and became despondent and difficult; he thought he would never paint again. Agnes began to fear the effect of this depression on the children, so she took them to her parents' house. Three weeks later Gorky hanged himself in the woodshed, leaving a note on the wall that said, "Goodbye, my loveds."[45]

Gorky, more than anyone, gave New York painting in the forties a tragic image. Yet he also symbolized the triumph of aesthetic experience over the vagaries of (even a tragic) life. His work brought the individual's experience of the past (real and imagined) into the immediate present as an ineluctable element of one's ongoing definition of self (in the existentialist sense) and demonstrated that art, if not life, is an act of intellectual will.

ROBERT MOTHERWELL

Jackson Pollock came from a poor family and never finished high school, Gorky barely escaped with his life from the Armenian refugee camps, de Kooning stowed away on a ship from Holland and arrived in New York with nothing but the clothes he was wearing. By contrast Robert Motherwell attended prep school, toured Europe in the Depression, received a bachelor's degree in philosophy from Stanford, and was well on his way to a Ph.D. at Harvard, funded by his father, when in 1939 he decided to become a painter. He kept company with the other members of the New York School and lived frugally in the forties. Yet he never suffered the same poverty or went through the lengthy trial-and-error process of bad student works. Before Motherwell ever picked up the brush he knew precisely where he stood in terms of modernist styles and ideas; as a painter he sprang, so to speak, fully grown from the head of Zeus.

Motherwell's splendid education made him the most literate and articulate of the major New York School artists. But nowhere in his upper-class background or education did he have any exposure to the bohemian existence or commitment of genuine painters. Motherwell grew up in San Francisco amid affluent surroundings. The family summered by the sea in Aberdeen, Washington, and his father, a conservative bank chairman, fully expected his only son to head straight from college into business or law. De Kooning once quipped that all the best painters were lawyers and doctors;[46] the pressure on Motherwell not to be an artist was formidable.

Intellectual Affinities with the European Moderns

Instead of going back to Harvard in the fall of 1940, Motherwell went to Columbia to study art history. There he met Meyer Schapiro, a young instructor who encouraged Motherwell to drop out and start painting. Schapiro introduced him to some of the European surrealists who had come to New York, including Kurt Seligmann, with whom Motherwell studied engraving. Soon Motherwell had befriended Matta, Duchamp, Ernst, Lam, Masson, Tanguy, and Breton. With his interest in psychoanalysis and strong intellectual background, he fitted in well with the cerebral surrealists. They shared an appreciation of the romantic and symbolist traditions, especially in poetry, and Motherwell became fascinated with their technique of automatism.

The problem for the artists of his generation, as Motherwell saw it, was "to bring American art up to the level of European modernism without being derivative."[47] Automatism seemed to him a viable means of accomplishing that, because it offered "a creative principle that did not impose a style."[48] Instead it brought out only what was native to the individual, and the aesthetic of the New York School came to center on precisely that point.

Whereas the surrealists used automatism to explore the workings of the unconscious mind and then turned to more conventional means to describe what they found, Motherwell and the other artists of the New York School saw automatism as a means for generating a form that would directly embody their existential struggle for self-definition. "Every artist's problem is to invent himself," Motherwell wrote in 1949.[49] Automatism provided the ideal tool for the painter in search of self who wanted to retain the vitality of each moment of discovery as it unfolded. Because of his fine education, Motherwell probably understood

3.26 Robert Motherwell, *Tobacco Roth-Händle*, 1974. Four-color lithograph and screenprint on HMP handmade paper, 41 × 31in (102.9 × 77.8cm).

Published by Tyler Graphics Ltd. Walker Art Center, Minneapolis, Tyler Graphics Archive, 1983.

the implications of automatism for his contemporaries' aspirations sooner and in greater depth than anyone and played an important role in communicating its possibilities to Pollock and others.

Shortly after Motherwell met Krasner, Pollock, and Baziotes in 1942, he experimented with writing automatist poems with them. The following year Peggy Guggenheim told him that she would be having a show of collages by various European moderns; she suggested that if he and Pollock wanted to try making some, and if they were good, she would include them. So in 1943 Motherwell and Pollock made their first collages [fig. 2.13] side by side in Pollock's studio and showed them at Peggy Guggenheim's gallery the same year.

Motherwell took to collage so naturally that for him it provided the expressive freedom that the automatist gesture gave Pollock. Yet the difference in their approach to modernism is also characterized by the contrast between Motherwell's affinity for, in effect, revolutionizing an established vocabulary with the introduction of an American sensibility and Pollock's wish simply to disregard that vocabulary (although he always struggled with the impossibility of doing so) [figs. 2.11 and 2.13]. Motherwell's admiration for the analytical and formal traditions of French art—embodied in cubist collage and in the painting of Picasso and Matisse—stood for him in perpetual counterpoint to the immediacy of emotional experience, and this opposition provided a central theme in his art.

Motherwell's fluency in the language of collage derived from his ongoing dialog with the European moderns. In 1951 he explained: "Every intelligent painter carries the whole culture of modern painting in his head. It is his real subject, of which everything he paints is both an homage and a critique, and everything he says a gloss."[50] This speaks to only one side of Motherwell's aesthetic and yet the formal traditions of European modernism had a degree of importance for Motherwell that differentiates him from the other major artists of the New York School. It also accounts for his success as the outstanding printmaker of his generation [fig. 3.26],[51] although it was only after his retrospective at the Museum of Modern Art in 1965 that he became deeply involved in printmaking.

Recurring Themes in Motherwell's Work

Unlike printmaking, collage was a mainstay of Motherwell's development from the outset. *Pancho Villa, Dead and Alive* [fig. 2.13], one of his first collages, was purchased for the Museum of Modern Art out of Peggy Guggenheim's 1943 show. He later talked about the immediate inspiration for the work, a trip to Mexico with Matta in the summer of 1941, and he noted: "I was fascinated . . . with Anita Brenner's fabulous book of photographs of the Mexican Revolution, called *The Wind Swept Over Mexico*. One picture showed Pancho Villa after he was shot, spread out—sprawled out, really—in a Model T, covered with blood."[52] The dead man in this collage is bullet-ridden and wholly

bereft of the sexual organs evident in the vital figure on the active backdrop to the right.

In this early collage Motherwell had already set out the most important and prevalent themes of his career: life and death, violence, and revolution. He also instigated a formal opposition between the intensely felt emotional elements (in the eccentrically drawn ovals, the painterly areas, and the brilliant touches of color—both pigment and collage) and the schematic, controlled structure of verticals and horizontals in a shallow cubist space (holding the emotions in check). The formal opposition of ovals and vertical stripes anticipates Motherwell's most famous series, the "Elegies," which he began in 1948. In some form, this opposition between the formal and the emotional defined virtually all Motherwell's future work. Finally the implicit reference to the refinement of European art and culture—here symbolized in the collage technique itself, with its allusions to Picasso and Matisse—would also be a recurrent preoccupation with Motherwell.

Teaching, Writing, and Editing in Motherwell's Early Career

However much Motherwell felt intellectually at home among the surrealists, he did not identify with their paintings. Instead his sensibility gravitated toward abstraction. A look at the interior of his studio in 1943 [fig. 3.27], with a photograph of Baudelaire pinned to the wall, shows the depth of his roots in a broader European tradition. He admired

3.27 Robert Motherwell
in his Greenwich Village studio, 1943 with *Collage in Beige and Black* (left) and *Wall Painting with Stripes* (right).
Photograph by Peter A. Juley.

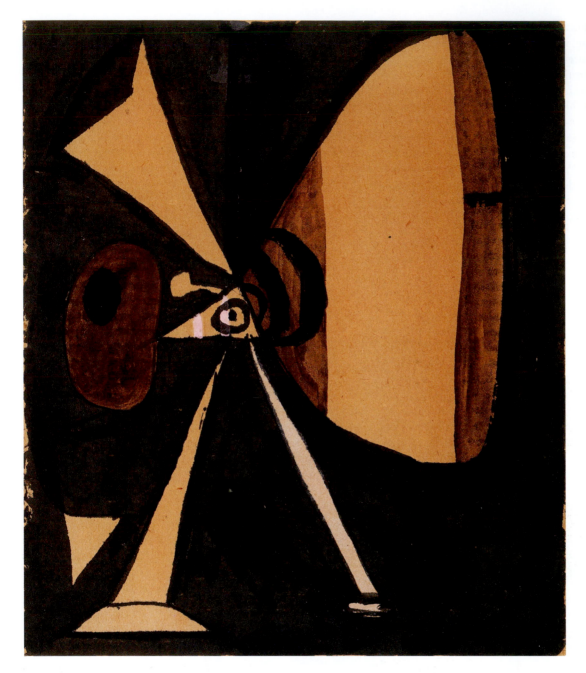

3.28 Robert Motherwell, *Untitled*, 1945. Gouache and ink on cardboard, 9¾ × 8¼in (24.8 × 21cm). Private collection, Illinois.

Mondrian as the painter of pure intelligence; he was drawn to Arp, Klee, and of course Picasso, Miró, and Matisse, who were in the mainstream of classical modernism. Thus in 1941 he not only sought out the surrealists in New York but he met Mondrian, Chagall, Léger, Lipchitz, Calder, Ozenfant, Zadkine, and Noguchi as well.

Peggy Guggenheim gave Motherwell his first one-person show in 1944 at the Art of This Century gallery, and in 1945 he signed a contract with the dealer Sam Kootz, which gave him some steady income. He also taught. In the summer of 1945 and again in 1951 Motherwell gave classes at Black Mountain College, the progressive school in North Carolina through which Willem de Kooning, Josef Albers, Merce Cunningham, John Cage, Robert Rauschenberg, and so many other interesting artistic and literary personalities

passed in the decade after World War II. Motherwell collaborated with David Hare, William Baziotes, Mark Rothko, and initially Clyfford Still in 1948 and 1949 to organize a school in Greenwich Village called Subjects of the Artist, so named to stress their concern with content despite their commitment to abstraction.

The public meetings and discussions held at the Subjects of the Artist school provided a focus for some of the vitality of the Greenwich Village art scene. Immediately after the school opened Still quit and Barnett Newman took his place on the staff. The next year Tony Smith took over the organization, closing the school but keeping up the program of lectures and meetings. Subjects of the Artist transformed into Studio 35 (the address was 35 East 8th Street) and then merged with The Club, which continued to host interesting meetings; but by this time Motherwell and his contemporaries had only an occasional involvement.

In addition to teaching, Motherwell's intellectual inclinations led him into an active schedule of lecturing, writing, and editing in the forties. In 1942 he wrote for the first issue of the surrealist journal *VVV* and then in 1944 took on the editorship of the *Documents of Modern Art* series for the publisher and book dealer George Wittenborn. The *Documents* series provided translations of major primary texts of modern art and had a crucial role in making the art theory of European modernism available to young American artists.

Motherwell's Painting

Motherwell spent the summers of 1945 and 1946 in East Hampton, which had become the summer outpost of the New York School. There he painted a number of metamorphic birds [fig. 3.28] and figures influenced by Picasso [fig. 5.17] and Miró. In 1947 Motherwell built a house in East Hampton, and in 1948 he began the "Elegy to the Spanish Republic" series with a little pen-and-ink drawing that he made to go with a poem by Harold Rosenberg called "A Bird for Every Bird" for the planned second issue of *Possibilities*, a new little magazine optimistically started by Robert Motherwell, Pierre Chareau, Harold Rosenberg and John Cage. The issue never materialized and Motherwell stuck the sheet in a drawer, forgetting about it for the better part of a year. In 1949 he rediscovered the sketch and inspired a small painting which he called *At Five in the Afternoon* [fig. 3.29], after the refrain in García Lorca's poem "Lament for Ignacio Sánchez Mejías."

In this painting the austerity of the monochrome palette and the regimentation of the composition into regular bars and ovals provide a dramatic foil for the spontaneous

3.29 Robert Motherwell, *At Five in the Afternoon*, 1949. Casein on composition board, 15 × 20in (38.1 × 50.8cm). Collection, Helen Frankenthaler, New York.

emotive elements, such as the loose gestural brushwork, the paint drips, and the free irregularity of the artist's rebellion against the self-imposed compositional order of alternating bars and ovals. The resistance to order embodied in the personal eccentricities of the work stands for resistance to order on wider fronts—psychologically, politically, and culturally. It has a complex layering of metaphorical meaning that is specific in its associations on several levels, despite its abstract vocabulary.[53]

The specificity of the subject matter in the abstractions of Motherwell and of the other New York School artists has been stressed by all of them. When Motherwell recalled painting this enlarged version of the drawing, he spoke about metaphors of "abandonment, desperation, and helplessness."[54] In the act of painting he transformed these emotions into a poetic vision on a tragic and universal scale. As he remembered it, "when I painted the larger version—*At Five in the Afternoon*—it was as if I discovered it was a temple, where Harold's [the small version he had made for *Possibilities*] was a gazebo, so to speak. And when I recognized this, I looked around for . . . what the temple should be consecrated to, and that was represented in the work of Lorca."[55]

The execution of the Spanish poet García Lorca by the Fascists in the Spanish Civil War of the thirties became a symbol of injustice. For many artists and intellectuals the Spanish Civil War embodied the modernist confrontation with established cultural values. As Motherwell once remarked, the theme of all the "Elegies" is the "insistence that a terrible death happened that should not be forgot."[56] The term "elegy" itself means a funeral dirge or lament. Lorca's poem concerns a heroic bullfighter who is gored in the ring, and three symbolic colors create auras around the key images of the poem—the red blood, the bleaching white light of the sun, and the blackness of death and shadows.

After painting *At Five in the Afternoon* Motherwell did a number of other works on the same compositional principle of black alternating bars and ovals over a white ground, and named them after various Spanish cities. He then went back and entitled the whole series "Elegy to the Spanish Republic" and began numbering them; this theme persisted for the remaining forty years of the artist's career [fig. 3.30]. Generally Motherwell painted the "Elegies" on a large, mural scale and worked by composing the major forms and then, later, filling them in. The contours and drips were modulated at the end of the painting process, and it is these areas that carry the most intense expressive content in the compositions.[57]

The "Elegies" constituted the first of several major thematic structures in Motherwell's work. The second to emerge was the "Je t'aime" series [fig. 3.31], most of which he painted between 1953 and 1957 during the latter half of his second marriage (1950–7). Motherwell's two daughters were born in these years; his friendship with David Smith also dates from this time (1950), as did his shift from summering in the Hamptons to summering in Provincetown

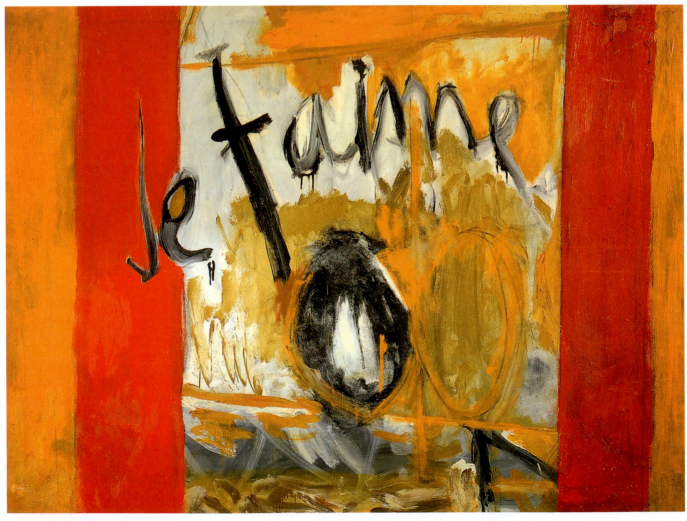

3.30 (opposite top) **Robert Motherwell**, *Elegy to the Spanish Republic, No. 78*, 1962. Oil and plastic on canvas, 5ft 11in × 11ft ¼in (1.8 × 3.36m).
Yale University Art Gallery, New Haven, Conn. Gift of the artist.

3.31 (opposite bottom) **Robert Motherwell**, *Je t'aime, No. 2*, 1955. Oil on canvas, 4ft 6in × 6ft (1.37 × 1.83m).
Collection, Mr. and Mrs. Gilbert Harrison, New York.

(as of 1956). The "Je t'aime" series is characterized by the French phrase (meaning "I love you") written across the canvas. The inscription is redolent of the elegance of Mediterranean culture and is usually surrounded by tempestuous color and raw brushwork.

Motherwell based the third major series, the "Opens," on a compositional device. He began them in 1967–8, just after his marriage to the painter Helen Frankenthaler ended. These works involve a geometric division, usually

3.32 Robert Motherwell, *The Blue Painting Lesson: A Study in Painterly Logic, Number One of Five*, April 20, 1973. Acrylic on canvas, 5ft 1in × 3ft 8in (1.55 × 1.12m).
Collection, Dedalus Foundation Inc. © Dedalus Foundation Inc./VAGA, New York, 1994.

a three-sided window or box motif coming down from the top of the canvas. The austere clarity of their structural architecture seems to equate to the emphasis on analysis promoted by formalist critics of the sixties (notably by Greenberg, who was close to Frankenthaler). Nevertheless, the proportion and often even the drawing of the "Opens" rely on an instantaneous gesture which is as spontaneous as the gestural elements in an "Elegy." Despite the limiting parameters of the format, the "Opens" have a broad expressive range. *The Blue Painting Lesson* [fig. 3.32], a five-painting sequence, has a rich, warm blue that evokes the refreshing sensuality of the seaside.

In the seventies and eighties Motherwell began generating more and more distinct series and subthemes within series. The subtlety of his work and his range continued to grow with increasing formal self-assurance. It seems as though every new work generated fresh and unresolved issues for him, while at the same time fitting precisely into the complex totality of his aesthetic project. For Motherwell, more than any other major figure of the New York School, painting was a process of philosophical elaboration.

WILLEM DE KOONING

Willem de Kooning's *Woman and Bicycle* [fig. 3.33] is a dozen different paintings superimposed on one another. Patches of raw canvas lie at the bottom edge of the composition adjacent to geometric forms in flat green, resembling the backgrounds to his seated women of the early forties [fig. 3.35]. As the viewer looks up from the lower edge of *Woman and Bicycle*, the anatomy of the feet and calves disintegrates into the turbulent cross-layering of brushwork. Strokes of many colors and speeds erupt in all directions, the intensity of each one canceling out the one below it. Light wisps dance over thickly applied masses of pigment; forceful vectors of contrasting colors collide in skirmishes of the brush that appear and then disappear again under the quick smear of a palette knife.

Here and there a sense of the figure comes into focus and quickly out again. "Content is a glimpse of something, an encounter like a flash,"[58] the artist explained. The enormous fleshy breasts bulge forward, then at second glance they seem flat, like a cutout that clings to the surface of the picture plane. A second grinning mouth hangs around the neck like a glittering necklace; it remains from a previous position of the head, an earlier composition, now largely crossed out. This is a painting in a perpetual state of redefinition. No passage is more than a temporary point *en route* to a new approximation. The inherently "unfinished," always "in process" character of de Kooning's work makes this canvas seem as freshly painted today as it did when the artist made it more than half a century ago.

De Kooning's inability to "finish" a canvas was already legendary in the early forties.[59] In fact, the characteristic "unfinished" quality of de Kooning's work expresses his

underlying aesthetic. He once described one of the large "Woman" pictures by saying: "It's not finished but it's a very good painting."[60] If it were finished, one imagines, it surely would not look so good.

De Kooning cultivated the inherent ambiguities in every situation. In *Woman and Bicycle* he created extreme spatial oppositions: the breasts read alternately as a flat pattern and as fully rounded forms; the energetic brushwork creates an expansive surface plane that provides a background for the figure while at the same time absorbing it; this active surface in turn seems to hover in front of yet another plane of flat background implied at the bottom edge. De Kooning heightened the disconcerting effect of the figure–ground relationships by constantly dissolving and reformulating contours and forms. All these expressive oppositions serve to create a figure that is simultaneously menacing and sensuous. Even the bold and authoritative handling is undercut by a frenetic, nervous, and tentative flipside.

Woman and Bicycle belongs to de Kooning's famous series of slightly over-life-sized women, painted in the early fifties. The style itself is an attack on closed systems, finality, and any fixed way of looking at things. "There is no plot in painting," de Kooning told Harold Rosenberg. "It's an occurrence which I discover by, and it has no message."[61] So de Kooning used the act of painting to examine things around him, keeping all possibilities open and maintaining an atmosphere of uncertainty. He had "slipping glimpses,"[62] as he called them, of things as they glanced in and out of apprehension. In pursuing a thought, he might obliterate the preceding idea or direction completely. This open-ended working process embodied Rosenberg's idea of the action painter, and it is a fundamental assertion of existence, of being alive, of resisting dissolution in the chaos of modern life.

De Kooning read widely in philosophy and literature, and he particularly liked Kierkegaard's idea that everything necessarily contains its opposite. "That's what fascinates me," he told Rosenberg; "to make something that you will never be sure of, and no one else will . . . That's the way art is."[63] Yet de Kooning did not have the distinctively American consciousness of Pollock or Newman, for example, who promoted the idea that they started from scratch each time they began to paint. De Kooning referred to that notion as "making art out of John Brown's body . . . standing all alone in the wilderness."[64] Instead de Kooning celebrated his deep engagement with the painting of the old masters, and felt more akin to Titian and Rembrandt than to Mondrian, Kandinsky, or the surrealists.

Nevertheless, de Kooning lived entirely in the present; he did not look back to a golden age or forward to a more perfect future. In this respect he and his fellow painters of the New York School differed from such modernist precursors as Mondrian or Kandinsky, who had sought to lead the way to utopia through their art. "Art never seems to make me peaceful or pure," de Kooning observed. "I always seem to be wrapped in the melodrama of vulgarity."[65]

De Kooning's Training and Early Career

De Kooning was born in Rotterdam, the Netherlands, on April 24, 1904. His early training at the Rotterdam Academy of Fine Arts and Techniques stressed craftsmanship, and there he studied foreshortening, modeling, and the rendering of light and shadow. His *Still Life: Bowl, Pitcher, and Jug* [fig. 3.34], drawn at the age of seventeen, demonstrates his prodigious skill at rendering. Made with little dots of conté crayon (a type of compressed charcoal stick), it rivals a photograph in its realism.

De Kooning arrived in the United States in 1926 at the age of twenty-two, moved into a Dutch seaman's home, and took work as a house painter in Hoboken, New Jersey, for $9 a day. He came to New York aspiring to a career as a commercial artist, but when he finally found a job in the field, he discovered that it paid no more than house painting. At this point de Kooning decided to start thinking of himself as a fine artist,[66] and in 1927 he moved into a loft on Manhattan's 42nd Street, still supporting himself with odd jobs, including commercial art, department store displays, sign painting, and carpentry.

In 1935 de Kooning signed on to the Federal Art Project. But the government barred aliens at the end of 1936, so he had only one year on the F.A.P. Like everyone else on the Project he earned the now famous $23.86 a week, and by de Kooning's unique style of reasoning, the fact that this salary was what the government paid an artist led him to conclude that it therefore cost only $23.86 a week to be an artist full time and that seemed like a bargain! Curiously the Depression was a good time for many young artists and writers. While older people lost businesses or their life's savings, young people had a special opportunity

3.34 Willem de Kooning, *Still Life: Bowl, Pitcher, and Jug*, c. 1921. Conté crayon and charcoal on paper, 18½ × 24¼in (47 × 61.6cm).
Collection, Metropolitan Museum of Art, New York. Van Day Treux Fund, 1983, 1984.436.

through the Works Progress Administration (W.P.A.). There was an excitement about social and intellectual ideas, people had time to talk, and money didn't matter; it could not get in the way since no one had any. There were no picture sales, no exhibitions, no careers to worry about. Although de Kooning had a great underground reputation among artists, he exhibited very little before the end of the forties and sold virtually nothing.

De Kooning met Arshile Gorky and Edwin Denby around 1927, and they became his closest friends. He also spent time with John Graham and Stuart Davis, from around 1929. By 1936 his circle included David Smith, Clement Greenberg, Fairfield Porter, Rudi Burckhardt, and Harold Rosenberg. John Graham enlisted de Kooning's participation in a 1942 exhibition, through which he met Pollock. But when Peggy Guggenheim invited de Kooning to show at the Art of This Century gallery, he refused. Not only was he reluctant to show his work when he had only just begun to find his own stylistic voice, he also disliked the

surrealists in Guggenheim's circle,[67] as did Graham. It was not until after his first one-person show at the Egan Gallery in 1948 that de Kooning began exhibiting actively.

The dominant influence on de Kooning's work of the thirties was that of his friend Gorky, through whose eyes he saw Miró, cubism, and abstract surrealism. De Kooning and Gorky associated with a circle of chiefly abstract artists, even though they were both painting the figure; as a consequence, the public still regards them both as abstract artists, even though neither ever abandoned figurative imagery. De Kooning, in particular, nearly always worked in both abstract and figurative modes simultaneously and in relation to one another.

The permanent trademarks of de Kooning's style emerged around 1939 or 1940 in such works as *Seated Woman* [fig. 3.35]. In particular, the painting nakedly shows the artist's method of working, a process which gives the canvas its characteristic unfinished look. Here the artist stopped at a point where one still senses the ongoing struggle for resolution. In addition, he intensified the color and radically fragmented the figure. De Kooning talked of how a "frozen glimpse" would come to him[68] in the process of painting, and one can see that here, in the independent identity of the anatomical parts as abstract forms.

The various altered positions of the crossed leg in *Seated Woman* have more affinity with the *pentimenti* (visible changes of mind) in Picasso's drawings for *Guernica* than with the automatic drawing of the surrealists. However, in de Kooning's painting, this appearance of work-in-progress lacks the elegance of the Picassos. In general, painters of the New York School in the forties rejected the refinement in composition and touch of the School of Paris. Moreover, *Seated Woman* shows de Kooning's discomfort with foreshortening, which he largely avoided, and despite some indication of a space behind the figure, the whole composition seems to be flattened against the picture plane, as in cubism [fig. 3.22].

The Dissolution of Anatomy into Abstraction

In 1944 and 1945 the anatomical fragments, with their multiplicity of drawn and redrawn lines, began taking over de Kooning's abstraction like a speculative commentary on his concurrent paintings of women. The compositions of 1944 began to convey the tension of de Kooning's investigative process much more vividly than his preceding works had done. The drawing in *Pink Angels* [fig. 3.36], for example, reveals a continuing trial-and-error process in the plethora of transparent overlappings. Meanwhile the forms in the picture hint at a figurative reference.

Most of the shapes in de Kooning's abstractions of the forties seem to have evolved from human anatomical parts. De Kooning pointed out that "even abstract shapes must have a likeness,"[69] a kind of meaningful familiarity that their derivation from the figure provides. At about this time de Kooning also seems to have begun tracing forms and reusing

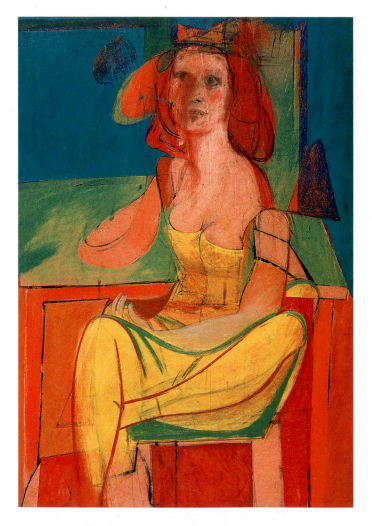

3.35 Willem de Kooning, *Seated Woman*, c. 1940.
Oil on charcoal on masonite, 54¼ × 36in (137.8 × 91.4cm).
Philadelphia Museum of Art. Albert M. Greenfield and Elizabeth M. Greenfield Collection.

them in other compositions, thereby further heightening their familiarity by linking them to other pictures as well as to objects and events. In the abstractions of 1946 the anatomical fragments woven together by the abundant linear *pentimenti* began to disperse themselves into an all over composition, as in the contemporaneous works of Pollock, and they created a curtain of flat forms that asserts the surface of the picture plane.

At this point de Kooning embarked on a powerful series of predominantly white on black paintings that climaxed in 1948 and 1949 with such works as the large *Painting* [fig. 3.37]. This composition relies on the same vocabulary of flat-patterned anatomical parts as de Kooning's other abstractions around this time. But because of its limited palette it creates an even greater ambiguity of space and volume than his more colorful compositions by establishing a more continuous surface of interpenetrating planes. De Kooning included some of the black paintings in his first one-person show at the Egan Gallery in 1948—the same year that Pollock first showed his groundbreaking drip pictures.

In 1948 de Kooning and several of his friends organized what came to be known as "The Club." De Kooning said he wanted a social club like the storefront parlors in the working-class Italian and Greek neighborhoods nearby. "We didn't want to have anything to do with art; we just wanted to get a loft, instead of sitting in those god-damned cafeterias."[70] So they pitched in and rented a loft on 8th Street, where the artists could just relax together. In the

3.36 (above) **Willem de Kooning**, *Pink Angels*, 1945. Oil on canvas, 4ft 4in × 3ft 4in (1.32 × 1.02m). Frederick Weisman Company, Los Angeles.

3.37 (right) **Willem de Kooning**, *Painting*, 1948. Enamel and oil on canvas, 3ft 6⅝in × 4ft 8⅛in (1.08 × 1.42m). The Museum of Modern Art, New York. Purchase.

summer of 1948 de Kooning taught at Black Mountain College in North Carolina with Josef Albers, John Cage, and Buckminster Fuller. He also visited East Hampton for the first time in April 1948 when he and his wife, Elaine, went out with Charles Egan to see the Pollocks.

During 1947 and 1948 de Kooning continued to paint the seated women alongside the great abstractions. In some pictures he also added yet another syntactical level by painting in letters and numbers. *Attic*, *Asheville*, and *Excavation* [fig. 3.38] come the closest of de Kooning's major compositions to the "all over" style of Pollock's contemporary drip paintings [figs. 4.1 and 4.5–4.9]. De Kooning achieved this effect by building up such a density of forms that the overabundance of images fills every available space within the confining edges of the frame. This results in an even

dispersal of the anatomically suggestive elements across the entire surface. The all over compositions of both Pollock and de Kooning brim over with energy, but where Pollock is assertive, de Kooning is quizzical. Another difference is that de Kooning packed his compositions so tightly that they seem to collapse in on themselves like black holes, whereas the Pollocks seem to expand outward.

A close look at *Excavation* and at any number of other de Kooning pictures from the late forties onward reveals what look to be fragments of newsprint buried under the surface. De Kooning frequently used sheets of newspaper to slow up the drying of the paint, and if he did not rework an area it retained a ghost of the photographs or columns of type. He liked this effect for its added complexity, but he did not construct a systematic iconography around such elements in the way Picasso did in his collages of 1912–14. For de Kooning the complexity of the individual's experience, especially in the urban environment, was central. The ubiquitous impressions of newsprint enhance the effect of the random overload of sensory information and anticipate the arbitrary

3.38 Willem de Kooning, *Excavation*, 1950. Oil on canvas, 6ft 9in × 8ft 4¼in (2.05 × 2.54m).

Art Institute of Chicago. Mr. and Mrs. Frank G. Logan Purchase Prize Fund, restricted gifts of Edgar J. Kaufmann, Jr. and Mr. and Mrs. Noah Goldowsky, Jr., 1952.1.

accumulations of Robert Rauschenberg's "combine paintings" of the mid-fifties.

In *Excavation* de Kooning fragmented anatomy into abstract parts and distributed them within a decentralized composition. But he seems also to have been conscious of developing a greater richness of symbolic meaning within each form. For this reason the work is more intellectually sophisticated than anything de Kooning had done before it. The painting appears to originate with impressions of a city's excavation site, with a backhoe and steam shovel represented in geometric forms at the lower right. Architectural supports (perhaps beams or piers) stand in a cadence of verticals across the bottom, and midway up on the left one can see a small block of older buildings, including a yellow-roofed tower. But the scale of these buildings does not match that of the earth-moving equipment; despite the possible unity of theme, then, there is a continuing transformation of the mental context as we move up the composition.

The metamorphosis of scale and forms in *Excavation* occurred through the complex and arbitrary layering of impressions in the busy "no environment," as de Kooning called it,[71] of New York City. He filled the upper three-quarters of this painting with an ongoing sequence of forms, each suggesting the next in an increasingly abstract train of thought. Here nothing remains legible except in a fragmentary way. The clearly delineated nipple on a breast mutates into an eye, as in the metamorphic expressionism of Picasso [fig. 5.17]. And to whom do the grinning teeth belong? The nude, the painter, or *Alice in Wonderland*'s Cheshire Cat?

Excavation is not a perspective space but a mental map of an interlocking chain of thoughts and experiences over time. It is a large canvas—roughly 6½ by 8½ feet—but it remains an easel picture made up of emotionally charged details rather than a mural to be read at a distance. "The squarish aspect," de Kooning explained, "gives me the feeling of an ordinary size. I like a big painting to get so involved that it becomes intimate . . . looks smaller."[72] Some of this intimacy also derives from de Kooning's brushwork, which started to take on a life of its own in *Excavation*.

The Anatomical Forms Dissolve into Brushstrokes

Immediately after the completion of *Excavation* in the late spring of 1950 de Kooning embarked on a series of monumental paintings of women [fig. 3.33]—the most celebrated works of his career. "It's really absurd to make an image, like a human image, with paint, today, when you think about it," he told David Sylvester in 1960. ". . . But then all of a sudden it was even more absurd not to do it."[73] Unlike the planar seated women of the early forties, these women are sensuous, full-figured Aphrodites of vulgar warmth, like the paleolithic *Venus of Willendorf*, which he cited as an inspiration for the series.[74]

De Kooning not only looked at Stone Age Venuses in books but also went to study Cycladic and Sumerian figures [fig. 3.39] in the Metropolitan Museum. The huge-eyed expressions of the Sumerian idols made them seem to de Kooning "like they were just astonished about the forces of nature."[75] Likewise, the 1948 exhibition of Giacometti's new figural sculpture [figs. 5.12–5.14] at Pierre Matisse[76] conveyed a sense of the fragile and fleeting existence of the individual in relation to "the forces of nature." According to Elaine, the show "knocked him out—it was crucial; it looked like the work of a civilization—not one man."[77] The primitive sexuality and raw textural handling of Dubuffet's monumental frontal nudes [fig. 5.5] (shown at Pierre Matisse in January 1951) also have a strong resonance with de Kooning's monumental women.

The explicit subject of de Kooning's "Woman" paintings is obvious, but there has been much speculation as to their

3.39 Ancient Sumerian standing male figure, Tell Asmar, c. 3000 B.C.
Collection, Metropolitan Museum of Art, Fletcher Fund, 1940, 40.156.

specific inspiration. Thomas Hess thought that de Kooning's mother, who had been a tough, demanding, and utterly unmaternal woman, provided the prototype for the "monstrous" females;[78] others suggested that Elaine was the subject, an assertion that she found so preposterous that on August 23, 1953 she asked Hans Namuth to photograph her in front of one of them [fig. 3.40] to "establish once and for all that I did not pose for these ferocious women. I was taken aback to discover in Hans' photograph that I and the painted lady seemed like . . . mother and daughter. We're even smiling the same way."[79]

If intimations of Elaine provided a starting-point for these paintings, then feelings about the artist's mother, about the comical variety of costumes and mannerisms among the ladies shopping on 14th Street, and the pretty pin-ups on his studio wall all entered into the complex sequence of thoughts that led gradually to the final compositions. "The *Women*," de Kooning mused, "had to do with the female painted through all the ages . . . I look at them now [in 1960] and they seem vociferous and ferocious. I think it had to do with the idea of the idol, the oracle, and above all the hilariousness of it."[80] As he told an interviewer in the fifties, "I *like* beautiful women. In the flesh, even the models in magazines."[81]

Ultimately these "Women" of the fifties, like all of de Kooning's paintings, had to do with testing and mastering his immediate personal experience. They represent the subjective "reality" of the artist. Harold Rosenberg challenged de Kooning on this point:

> R: The way you see something doesn't mean necessarily that that's the way it is. Putting a stick in water so that it looks as if it's broken . . .
> de K: Well it is. That's the way you see it.
> R: What do you mean, it is broken? If you pull it out of the water it's not broken.
> de K: I know. But it's broken while it's in the water.
> R: The break is an illusion . . .
> de K: That's what I am saying. All painting is an illusion.[82]

The painter must, in de Kooning's view, entertain any hypothesis: "In art one idea is as good as another";[83] at issue is what the artist does with an idea. Since all art is a matter of ideas to begin with, it made no sense to de Kooning even to distinguish abstract from representational painting.[84]

3.40 Willem and Elaine de Kooning, 1953.

Photograph by Hans Namuth. Courtesy Center for Creative Photography, The University of Arizona.

During the fifties de Kooning increasingly emphasized painterly gestures, muscular brushwork, and rich color. The central image of the figure, as an organizing principle for the composition, permitted greater freedom in the process of painting than did the anatomical segments, which needed a separate structural scheme. The "Women" also showed more clearly than previous paintings all the artist's creative struggles. They convey the sense not of a finished painting but of an arrested moment in the defining of a problem. "I never was interested in how to make a good painting," de Kooning remarked. ". . . I didn't work on it with the idea of perfection, but to see how far one could go—but not with the idea of really doing it."[85]

For the academic year of 1950–1, de Kooning taught at the Yale Art School, where his friend Josef Albers had become dean after leaving Black Mountain College. Teaching was a draining experience that de Kooning never repeated, but he still was not selling much and remained very poor. Thomas Hess recalled that "he ate in dingy cafeterias; he ducked landlords; once he received a message to telephone the Museum of Modern Art and found that he did not have the nickel for the pay phone."[86] De Kooning joked with Rosenberg: "[Sidney] Janis wants me to paint some abstractions and says he can sell any number of black and whites. But he can't move the women. I need the money. So if I were an *honest* man, I'd paint abstractions. But I have no integrity! So I keep painting the women."[87]

Nevertheless, in January 1950 de Kooning had a painting in the prestigious Whitney Annual; in June he had one of the six one-person shows in the American section of the Venice Biennale; in 1951 the Museum of Modern Art put him into its important "Abstract Painting and Sculpture in America" exhibition; and in April of the same year Egan gave him his second one-person gallery show. The Egan show consisted of abstractions, confirming the art world's impression of de Kooning as an abstract artist. Sidney Janis signed up de Kooning for the artist's third one-person show in March 1953, in which he presented the monumental "Women" (five of them) for the first time.

The "Women" scandalized many people, even some of de Kooning's friends who found it hard to accept the unavoidable fact that the paintings were not abstract. The Museum of Modern Art bought *Woman I* from the show but in general collectors did not respond to the work—de Kooning had to continue living on a shoestring. When Greenberg delivered the Olympian pronouncement to de Kooning that "it is impossible today to paint a face," de Kooning came back with: "That's right, and it's impossible not to."[88] In the sixties Greenberg had begun openly attacking de Kooning.

By 1954 deliciously sensuous figures in the Marilyn Monroe mold had begun to supplant the earlier, more grotesque and ferocious females. De Kooning even titled one of these new works *Marilyn Monroe*, and when Selden Rodman asked him why he painted her he said: "I don't know. I was painting a picture, and one day—there she was."

"Subconscious desire?" Rodman asked. "Subconscious hell!" the artist laughed.[89] The "Women" of the early fifties all inhabit the "no-environment" of the city, where one cannot tell what is indoors or outdoors; an architectural detail could be in the lobby of Rockefeller Center or outside on the façade of a building. This setting extends the simultaneously disturbing and enticing ambiguity of the figures themselves.

De Kooning's Abstractions of the Fifties

Around 1955 de Kooning turned away from the figure toward complex, urban abstractions, filled with the bustle of 14th Street; in works such as *Gotham News* [fig. 3.41] de Kooning portrayed the "no-environment" in itself. As mentioned earlier, de Kooning put sheets of newspaper on the surface of his pictures to keep the paint workable, and the traces of type, the pin-ups, and advertisements are especially prevalent in this group of abstractions. Newsprint artifacts of commercial America belong to the complexity of the city. At one point early in the genesis of the large "Women," de Kooning cut out numerous mouths from pictures of women in magazines and glued them on to his compositions;[90] thus advertising and the media already figured as an underlying theme of the series.

Where the abstractions of the late forties and early fifties are centripetal, the abstractions of the late fifties and early sixties are more expansive compositions, featuring broader strokes and flatter, more lyrical color. A feeling of countryside pervades these paintings. They are impressionistic in comparison to *Excavation* or even *Gotham News*, which require detailed and lengthy scrutiny. According to de Kooning, "they're emotions, most of them . . . landscapes and highways and sensations of that [i.e. of landscapes and highways], outside the city."[91]

De Kooning's 1956 show of abstractions at the Sidney Janis Gallery sold well, and he started to make some money. He moved in with Joan Ward when she gave birth to his daughter Lisa in 1956, although Elaine remained very much part of his daily life. In 1958 and again in 1959–60 he visited Italy, and after his highly successful 1959 exhibition of large abstractions at Janis he retreated from the scene, spending less and less time in the city, rarely attending parties, and never answering his telephone. De Kooning's growing numbers of imitators were a real psychological burden to him. In order to discourage people from bothering him, he even stopped his landlord at 831 Broadway from installing an elevator. In 1954 the de Koonings had rented a house in Bridgehampton, Long Island, with Franz Kline, Ludwig Sander, and Nancy Ward. Then in 1955 Elaine successfully encouraged her brother Peter to buy a house next to the Rosenbergs on Acabonic Road in East Hampton. In 1963 de Kooning built a new studio in The Springs (part of East Hampton), vacated his Manhattan loft, and moved out to Long Island permanently.

3.41 Willem de Kooning, *Gotham News*, 1955.
Oil on canvas, 5ft 11in × 6ft 10in (1.81 × 2.08m).
Collection, Albright-Knox Art Gallery, Buffalo, New York. Gift of Seymour
H. Knox, Jr., 1955.

The "Women" of the Sixties and the Late Works

The paintings of women that de Kooning began in 1961 have the same loose, sensuous handling as the abstractions of the same period, though he saturated the figures with richer color and a greater build-up of smaller brushstrokes. Even the simplest of pencil drawings from this time [fig. 3.42] have a fleshy voluptuousness. The "Women" of the sixties are more relaxed and more frankly sexual; increasingly, too,

the contours of the figure open out with a lateral sweep into expansive surrounding landscapes. These nudes belong to the tradition of Rubens, although their bodily functions and appetites are more explicitly revealed.

Two Figures [fig. 3.43] portrays women on the beach, with the sea in the background, in a landscape bathed in brilliant sunlight. Typically de Kooning used the colors suggested by the environment—a natural palette, in contrast to Léger or Mondrian, whose primary colors indicated the prevalence of theory and system over nature. From the beginning de Kooning's "Women" had always in some way originated in nature. Each figure had a specific and individual—if imaginary—character that seemed entirely real. About the 1966 *Woman Acabonic*, for example, he speculated: "I think she maybe is a woman who makes hats. She's kind of funny-looking; she's here for the weekend . . . well, she's turning into her forties, I guess . . . She's sweet and friendly. Don't you think so? People say I make such monsters. I don't think so at all."[92]

The loose, authoritative brushwork of de Kooning's figure paintings of the late sixties has a self-assurance that announces a late style as boldly distinctive as the late styles of Rembrandt or Matisse. *Two Figures* lacks the probative anxiety of the monumental "Women" of the fifties or the density of major abstract compositions like *Excavation*. Here the artist seems to enjoy the certainty of his hand as he savors the soft flesh, the rich light, and the fresh smells of the sea air. These late-sixties women express a joy of life in their tactile pleasure and in their appreciative portrayal of the human comedy.

In the early seventies the figures in de Kooning's paintings grew looser and more disembodied. In works of the mid-seventies they disappeared completely into a new kind of "all over" abstraction made up of saturated strokes of

3.43 Willem de Kooning, *Two Figures*, 1967. Oil on paper, mounted on canvas, 35¾ × 23¾in (90.8 × 60.3cm).

Collection, Toyota City Museum of Art, Nagoya, Japan. Photograph courtesy Grete Meilman Fine Art, New York.

3.42 Willem de Kooning, *Woman*, 1961. Pencil on paper, 11 × 8½in (27.9 × 21.6cm). Private collection, Illinois.

color as highly defined as the anatomical segments of the forties. These compositions are diffused with a disconcertingly unanchored energy, like an electric force field. Then around 1980 the color thinned out into paler washes shot through with powerful wide strokes of black. Even at the age of eighty, painting continued to provide de Kooning with a means of exploring his relation to the perpetually changing conditions of his existence. He could not avoid it. "Your individuality," he said, "is like having a rat in the room always walking around. You can't escape it," and, "at the end you take a walk in your *own* landscape. It's simple, feels good."[93]

4.1 Jackson Pollock, *Cathedral*, 1947. Enamel and aluminum paint on canvas, 71½ × 35⅛in (181.6 × 89.1cm). Dallas Museum of Art. Gift of Mr. and Mrs. Bernard J. Reis.

4 EXISTENTIALISM COMES TO THE FORE

JACKSON POLLOCK

In 1956 Willem de Kooning pointed out that "every so often, a painter has to destroy painting. Cézanne did it, Picasso did it with cubism. Then Pollock did it. He busted our idea of a picture all to hell. Then there could be new paintings again."[1] As early as 1942 Jackson Pollock was working at the defining edge of new painting. The painter Lee Krasner, with whom he lived from 1942 until the end of his life, reported that "in front of a very good painting [of his own] . . . he asked me, 'Is this a painting?' Not is this a good painting, or a bad one, but *a painting!* The degree of doubt was unbelievable at times. And then, again, at other times, he knew the painter he was."[2]

Pollock's *Male and Female* [fig. 2.11] relied on the surrealist device of automatism to yield the irrationally juxtaposed and associated anatomical fragments, numbers, and geometric shapes as well as the loose autographic brushwork. The frontality and the shallowness of the space in the work reveal the influence of cubism and of Picasso's interwar expressionism, particularly his *Guernica* [fig. 2.10]. For the totemic figures, Pollock drew inspiration from African and Native American art and from the work of the Mexican muralists.

Yet whatever Pollock's indebtedness to preceding styles, the directness with which he permitted his unconscious to determine the form of this painting had no art historical precedent. The picture's "reality" lies not in any reference to the phenomenal world but in the truth of the unconscious mind. Beginning in 1947 Pollock further refined the language of this radical content with the technical innovation of pouring or dripping his paint [figs. 4.1 and 4.5–4.9]. In addition he dissolved the customary compositional focus on a central image and broke down the illusion of objects in space, arriving at an "all over" composition in which the seemingly limitless intricacy of surface texture creates a vast, pulsating environment of intense energy, completely engulfing the viewer.

Although many of the writings on Pollock have overplayed the myth of tragic heroism, the artist did affect a tough exterior—he was isolated and independent—and he gradually self-destructed in a downward spiral of emotional turmoil during his early forties, after a dozen prolific years of majestic painting. Pollock lived and worked with relentless drive. As Lee Krasner explained: "Whatever Jackson felt, he felt more intensely than anyone I've known. When he was angry, he was angrier; when he was happy, he was happier; when he was quiet, he was quieter."[3]

Pollock's Early Life and Influences

Paul Jackson Pollock, born in Cody, Wyoming, on January 28, 1912, was the youngest of five sons in a working-class family. His mother had artistic aspirations and conveyed this sufficiently to her children that all five sons wanted to become painters. Pollock's father failed in one truck farm after another, causing an economic instability that forced the family to relocate seven times in Jackson's first twelve years. In the summer of 1927 he and his eighteen-year-old brother, Sanford, worked on a survey team, roughing it on the North Rim of the Grand Canyon. Pollock discovered alcohol at this time and also dropped the name "Paul," which he thought less manly than "Jackson."

Pollock went to high school in Los Angeles with Philip Guston, who also became a major painter of the New York School. They were both rebellious and intellectual. After being expelled twice in two years, Pollock headed to New York, where he joined his eldest brother, Charles, in the classes of Thomas Hart Benton at the Art Students League. Pollock met Stuart Davis, who taught there, and Arshile

Gorky, who was often to be found in the school cafeteria. Benton's influence continued to dominate both the younger artist's subject matter and style until around 1938.

Benton attempted to formulate a uniquely "American" style through the exploration of the country's historical subject matter and its contemporary life. His adulation of "American" frontier masculinity [fig. 2.6] must have appealed to Pollock. Benton's work, reinforced by the example of the Mexican muralists [fig. 2.8], sowed the seeds for the emergence of a grand scale and an epic quality in Pollock's painting of the forties. But large size also suited Pollock's grand subject matter, which concerned universals in the human psyche, and the powerful instinctual forces that acted on his consciousness.

Like so many others at the time, the Mexicans held a Marxist view of historical evolution, and they hoped to incite their countrymen to social change by educating them about their heritage and about the relentless progress of history. As a high school student Pollock had encountered Rivera's work through some communist meetings he attended. In 1936 Pollock took a job in Siqueiros's Union Square workshop in New York, where he experimented with unorthodox materials and novel techniques of application, including the spraying, splattering, and dripping of paint.

As Pollock moved away from Benton's influence and from representation as a whole, he focused increasingly on inner content. He found encouragement for this approach in a 1937 article by John Graham called "Primitive Art and Picasso," in which Graham wrote that primitives

> satisfied their particular totemism and exteriorized their prohibitions (taboos) in order to understand them better and consequently to deal with them successfully. Therefore the art of the primitive races has a highly evocative quality which allows it to bring to our consciousness the clarities of the unconscious mind, stored with all the individual and collective wisdom of past generations and forms. In other words, an evocative art is the means and the result of getting in touch with the powers of our unconscious.[4]

Graham's belief that the unconscious mind provided essential knowledge and creative powers for the artist, and that primitive art offered more direct access to this material, impressed Pollock so profoundly that he wrote to Graham. The ensuing friendship greatly emboldened Pollock in his search for universal mythic images in his own unconscious, while at the same time enlarging his understanding of recent European art.

The Europeans who arrived in New York around 1940 further sharpened Pollock's focus on unconscious imagery. "I accept the fact that the important painting of the last hundred years was done in France," he acknowledged in 1944. ". . . The fact that good European moderns are now here is very important, for they bring with them an understanding of the problems of modern painting. I am particularly impressed with their concept of the source of art being the unconscious."[5]

But Pollock was quick to add that the most important Europeans were Picasso and Miró, who did not come to the United States. It was to Picasso above all that Pollock returned again and again in his art. *Guernica* [fig. 2.10], which arrived in New York in 1939, was especially significant. This period of Picasso's work inspired the fragmentation of expressionist images in the shallow space of Pollock's drawings of the late thirties, and it also provided Pollock and his contemporaries with a profoundly moving example of painting with a social conscience that was at the same time at the forefront of formal innovation. The social imperative— already inherent in American art and greatly heightened by the two world wars and by the Depression—weighed heavily on Pollock and his contemporaries.

In 1935 Pollock went on to the easel-painting division of the Federal Art Project, which provided him with a modicum of financial stability. The Works Progress Administration (W.P.A.) also put Pollock into a community of painters, who were all trying to digest the same disparate influences of the Mexican muralists, abstract cubism, abstract surrealism, and Picasso's expressionist painting of the thirties, especially *Guernica*.

Pollock's Breakthrough of the Early Forties

Pollock struggled with acute depression and alcoholism in the late thirties and in 1939 he entered into Jungian psychoanalysis. In addition to whatever the treatment did for his emotional state, it profoundly affected his art by encouraging his search for totemic images with universal, unconscious meaning. Between 1942 and 1948 Pollock gave many of his compositions (including some of the early drip pictures) mythic titles with overtones of primitive forces: *Guardians of the Secret, Male and Female, Moon Woman, Totem Lesson, Night Ceremony, The She-Wolf,* and *Enchanted Forest.* Many of the early action paintings, such as *Galaxy* and *Cathedral* [fig. 4.1], were also given titles that evoked a sense of spirituality or the sublime in nature. From 1948 through 1952 Pollock mostly numbered, rather than titled, his paintings, but totemic associations still lingered on. Indeed, by not naming his pictures, Pollock sought to make their spiritual content more universal. Nevertheless, in 1951 Pollock reintroduced legible totemic figures and in 1953 he resumed the mythic titles.

In November 1941 John Graham put together works by Krasner and Pollock for a joint show. From this, Krasner discovered that Pollock lived around the corner from her, so she looked him up. The following fall they moved in together, and through Krasner Pollock greatly widened his circle of artistic friends; in particular she introduced him to de Kooning, Hofmann, Harold Rosenberg, and Clement Greenberg. Krasner also appears to have been more successful than the psychotherapists in stabilizing Pollock, who entered the most innovative and productive decade of his life.

In *Male and Female* [fig. 2.11], one of Pollock's first great pictures, the totemic quality and the stabilizing symmetry remained from the works of the previous two years, but the images poured forth in a freer, more disconnected way. The eyes at top left, the numbers, the impulsive gestures and spills come together, as if randomly, out of a dense chaos of active elements. The totemic figures superimposed on the two black vertical strips reinforce the geometry and stabilize the otherwise free play of gestures and small images.

In the works of the early forties Pollock transformed the influence of Benton's dramatic compositions and of the Mexicans' Marxist faith in the relentless evolution of history into the idea of a dynamic and inevitable unfolding of the content of the unconscious mind. Over the next four years this idea increasingly dominated not only the content of Pollock's work but the evolution of his style; as the gestures grew more genuinely automatic, it became necessary to devise some new means of balancing the composition. In *Male and Female* the geometry serves that purpose; later, Pollock developed the "all over" composition to solve this structural problem.

Although the surrealists helped to legitimize the unconscious as a subject for Pollock, as early as 1942 he already seems to have begun using psychic automatism in a wholly different way. The surrealist maintained an experimental distance, analyzing his or her automatist expressions, discovering their content through free association, and then going back into the picture to enhance these discoveries. Pollock worked impulsively and directly on the canvas to capture the unconscious images as they tumbled out. In *Male and Female* the occasional areas of dripped and splattered paint were not springboards for free association, as in surrealism, but an effort to record the spontaneity of his unconscious thought processes. As such this technique proved the ideological precursor for Pollock's great stylistic breakthrough in the "all over" drip pictures of 1946–7, such as *Cathedral*.

In addition, the paramount concern with immediacy among Pollock and his friends led them to reject sketches as not "modern," differentiating them from Picasso and Miró as well as from Gorky. Important painting, by definition, addressed the issues of its time, they believed, and this meant that you had to work spontaneously on the canvas. "My opinion is that new needs need new techniques," Pollock explained. "[T]he modern painter cannot express his age, the airplane, the atom bomb, the radio in the old forms of the Renaissance . . . the modern artist is . . . expressing the energy, the motion, and other inner forces."[6]

From the beginning of his career, Pollock also exhibits an anti-aesthetic awkwardness in the way he juxtaposes the forms, stabilizes the composition, and lays on the paint, as in *Male and Female*, which differs fundamentally from the elegance of works by a European artist like André Masson. For all the spontaneity, the coarseness of the sand, and the thickness of the bloodlike red drip in Masson's 1926 *Battle of Fishes* [fig. 2.1] for example, there is nevertheless an aestheticized elegance that Pollock's *Male and Female* lacks. That essential ungainliness makes the Pollock even more

emotionally "real," almost disconcertingly so, by breaking the easy passage into the illusionary space of painting.

In 1942 Motherwell and Baziotes introduced Pollock to Peggy Guggenheim, who asked him to participate in a group show of collages at her new Art of This Century gallery. Pollock, Motherwell, and Baziotes all made their first collages in preparation for that show and wrote automatist poetry together. Then in November 1943 Pollock had a one-person show at Art of This Century, for which James Johnson Sweeney (an important curator at the Museum of Modern Art) wrote the catalog. Alfred Barr bought *The She-Wolf* for the Museum of Modern Art out of the exhibition, and the San Francisco Museum bought *Guardians of the Secret*. In a review of the show, Clement Greenberg championed Pollock as the greatest painter of his time, and shortly after that Peggy Guggenheim put Pollock on a retainer. This provided him with a regular income just as the Federal Art Project was shutting down.

In the early forties Pollock balanced the scattered automatist doodles in his work against a persistent totemic imagery. The totemic figures were carried over from his expressionistic work, which had been heavily influenced by Orozco and Picasso. The looser automatist brushwork and the freer issuing forth of small spontaneous forms and symbols represented the newer influence of surrealism. In these works Pollock began to reconcile the two, using automatism to break down the formal isolation of the totemic images. The dissolution of these images as discrete entities enabled them to interact more fluidly with the free associations in a style of painting that was becoming increasingly oriented toward process.

Some critics have argued that a programmatic Jungian symbolism underlies the images, but no one has succeeded in providing a consistent reading of any such iconography.[7] Pollock did believe in the collective unconscious, and in the course of free association he may have called up and used individual images from material he read or heard about during his Jungian analysis. In the same way Pollock occasionally referred to specific myths in his titles, as in *Pasiphaë* of 1943, but they were never more than a means of enriching or deepening the associations. By his own account, Pollock created out of his unconscious, using automatism to transform his psychic experience into gestures and forms. In some instances he then found affirming similarities in known legends, but he avoided systematic referents, much less an iconography, from external sources.

Pollock's Transition to a Pure Gestural Style

Peggy Guggenheim commissioned Pollock to paint the 8-by-20-foot *Mural* for her home in July 1943. In this work the gesture itself carried the expressive content and yet certain specific associations persevere. In particular, the dark curving verticals in *Mural* appear to have a figural reference influenced by Native American pictographs.[8] Demonstrations of Indian sand painting, which the artist saw in 1941 at the

Natural History Museum in New York, also seem to have later encouraged the free gestural pouring technique that Pollock developed at the beginning of 1947. The grand scale of the picture, like the large works of Benton and the Mexicans, transforms the canvas into an engulfing environment. In this way it set a precedent for the scale of Pollock's celebrated drip paintings. It also forced the artist to work on the floor (like the Navajo sand painters he saw in New York) so that he could move around all sides of the picture and reach every part of it.

The even distribution of compositional interest across the entire surface of *Mural* was its most revolutionary feature. This anticipated the idea of the "all over" composition as a solution to the problem of how to organize a picture generated by automatist gesturing. As each of Pollock's painterly brushstrokes grew increasingly unique and individually formed, they became more and more adequate as replacements for the totemic images. At the end of 1946, Pollock finally abandoned imagery and structural systems for an "all over" composition and a completely gestural style. In this respect he went even further than Mondrian or Miró, who always maintained an underlying compositional structure though both had painted evenly dispersed compositions.

Pollock and Krasner spent the summer of 1944 in Provincetown and in 1945 they went to The Springs in East Hampton, Long Island, where they bought a farmhouse and 5 acres of land. As unceremoniously as possible they married in late October and moved out to The Springs permanently (albeit with frequent trips to New York). "It was hell on Long Island" in the beginning, Krasner later recalled.[9] Pollock's studio had no heat or electric light, they had no hot water at first, and they couldn't afford fuel to heat the house, much less to run an automobile. Yet Pollock did begin having annual exhibitions at this time—at Art of This Century, then at the Betty Parsons Gallery—and finally by 1949 he began selling enough to afford some modest comforts.

In 1946, Pollock's first full year on Long Island, his work underwent another dramatic change. During the first half of the year a mixture of gestural and totemic images dominated his painting, as in *The Key* [fig. 4.2]. In the latter part of the year he abandoned the overt images entirely and embarked on the "Sounds in the Grass" series, which culminated in

4.2 Jackson Pollock, *The Key*, 1946. Oil on canvas, 4ft 11in × 6ft 10in (1.5 × 2.08m).

Collection, Art Institute of Chicago, through prior gift of Mr. and Mrs. Edward Morris, 1987.216.

4.3 Jackson Pollock, *Shimmering Substance*, from the "Sounds in the Grass" series, 1946. Oil on canvas, 30⅛ × 24¼in (76.5 × 61.6cm).

The Museum of Modern Art, New York. Mr. and Mrs. Albert Lewin and Mrs. Sam A. Lewisohn Funds.

such extraordinary canvases as *Shimmering Substance* [fig. 4.3]. In these works the artist handled the entire surface as an even field of gestural strokes—sensuously applied, rich in color, and devoid of any overt imagery.

In *The Key* one may read some elements as figures or objects in space. *Shimmering Substance* has only the actual depth of the heavily sculptured paint surface and a subtle illusion of shallow space behind the woven plane of surface texture. The freedom of the gesturing in *Shimmering Substance* is made possible by the evenness of the distribution of visual activity (Pollock's "all over" structure), which avoids compositional anarchy.

The Dripped and Poured Canvases

Pollock's drip paintings, which followed immediately after the "Sounds in the Grass" series at the end of 1946 or early 1947, have still more gestural freedom than *Shimmering Substance*. In creating works like *Cathedral* [fig. 4.1] and *Number 1, 1948* [fig. 4.4], Pollock laid his canvas on the floor and used his brushes like sticks, hovering just above the surface, but never touching it. This permitted an easier, more spontaneous movement of the arm and body than he could achieve while still having to press the paint on to the canvas with a brush or knife, as in *Shimmering Substance*.

4.4 Jackson Pollock, *Number 1, 1948*, 1948. Oil and enamel on unprimed canvas, 5ft 8in × 8ft 8in (1.73 × 2.64m).
The Museum of Modern Art, New York. Purchase, 77.1950.

Pollock also generally made his drip paintings bigger. Thus by working directly on the floor he was not only able to use gravity to facilitate his method of application but he was also able to walk around the compositions, reaching every part by literally stepping into them [fig. 4.5].

In the dripped and poured canvases Pollock eliminated all symbols and signs; only the gesture itself remained as a mythic metaphor. This summed up what was radically new about Pollock's application of automatism: he used the technique to express rather than to excavate; he translated the act of painting itself into an adventure of self-realization. When Pollock told Hofmann in 1942 "I *am* nature,"[10] he meant that to him the central subject matter of painting derived from this direct, introspective exploration rather than from the external world.

Intuitively the viewer can feel the process by which Pollock made the drip compositions and imagine the sensation of moving freely across the canvas along with the gestures of paint. Indeed, the viewer must re-create the feeling of this process in order to experience the deeper meaning of the work, because the painting is "about" the introspective content recorded in those gestures. Pollock's drip paintings demand that the viewer surrender intellectual control while freely empathizing with the movement and the energetic color. One "should not look *for* [my italics]," Pollock explained, "but look passively—and try to receive what the painting has to offer."[11] This state of willing suspension of control is the only possible point of embarkation to the awe-inspiring emotions which the painter was recording.

As compositions, each of Pollock's drip pictures simultaneously dissolves into a chaotic jumble of individual lines while also coming together as a structurally uniform, whole field. They have no "correct" viewing position as do Renaissance paintings; indeed, the viewer must move across them. They draw their audience in to inspect the details closely, passage by passage, and at the same time overwhelm the viewer with their size [figs. 4.6 and 4.7]. Their coloristic and textural richness emphasizes the expansive surface, yet the elaborate and totally visible overlay of multiple layers of paint (and sand, cigarette butts, glass, and other materials) creates a very real, but literal, depth and space.

The transparency of the process—the way in which the viewer can so readily reconstruct the act of creation—gives the drip paintings an extraordinary immediacy. This highlights the present as the fixed reference point in the painting, and that emphasis is one of the hallmarks of modernism. The brilliance of its fulfillment in these pictures accounts in part for why so many of Pollock's contemporaries saw the drip paintings as an art historical watershed.

The painters of the New York School were exceptionally conscious of wanting to carry on the legacy of modernism. The collapse of time into the present is a central issue in modernism; the past exists only in its bearing on the present. Thus for many of Pollock's contemporaries the writings of James Joyce provided a paradigm in the way Joyce subverted sequential or historical time. Looking back, the New York School painter James Brooks remarked that Joyce "influenced me more than any painter . . . Joyce had a non-narrative style. What you were reading was right there.

You're not waiting for something to come."[12] Ibram Lassaw, a sculptor of the New York School, added: "It occurs to me about James Joyce, there is this overall feeling in Joyce's work,"[13] as there is in Pollock's painting. In 1950 Pollock himself commented on "a reviewer a while back who wrote that my pictures didn't have any beginning or any end. He didn't mean it as a compliment, but it was."[14]

In painting, Kandinsky pioneered the disintegration of narrative time, and his work must have encouraged Pollock to paint in a manner that seems to swallow up the viewer, physically and temporally. To Pollock's generation, Kandinsky's work stood for spontaneity and spiritual content in abstract

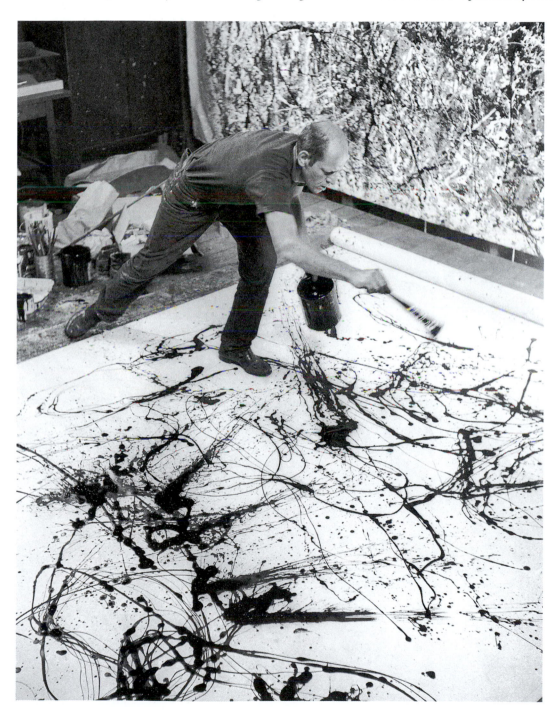

4.5 Jackson Pollock
at work, 1950.

Photograph by Hans Namuth.
Courtesy Center for Creative
Photography, University of Arizona.

4.6 (above) **Jackson Pollock**, *Number 27*, 1950. Oil on canvas, 4ft 1in × 8ft 10in (1.24 × 2.69m). Whitney Museum of American Art, New York. Purchase, 53.12.

4.7 (right) **Jackson Pollock**, *Number 27* (detail), 1950. See fig. 4.6.

art. In May 1943 Pollock worked as a janitor in the Museum of Non-Objective Painting, which had the world's greatest collection of Kandinsky paintings, and he undoubtedly saw the museum's 1945 Kandinsky memorial exhibition.

In one passage of his *Text Artista* (which Pollock owned) Kandinsky wrote about learning, "not to look at a picture only from the outside, but to 'enter' it, to move around in it, and mingle with its very life."[15] Pollock may have had this passage in the back of his mind—along with the Native American sand painters—when he talked about his new painting process, in 1947:

> On the floor I am more at ease. I feel nearer, more a part of the painting, since this way I can walk around it, work from all four sides and literally be in the painting. This is akin to the Indian sand painters of the West. I continue to get further away from the usual painter's tools such as easel, palette, brushes, etc. I prefer sticks, trowels, knives, and dripping fluid paint or a heavy impasto with sand, broken glass and other foreign matter added. When I am in my painting, I'm not aware of what I'm doing. It is only after a sort of "get acquainted" period that I see what I have been about . . . the painting has a life of its own. I try to let it come through.[16]

The genius of Pollock's drip style is not a technical discovery; Siqueiros and Hofmann had experimented with the technique before. As early as the mid-twenties the surrealists experimented with pouring and spattering paint, and Pollock certainly knew these works. The important point is not that Pollock invented the technique but rather that he started using it when it became relevant for exploring the implications of certain works of the mid-forties, and it was *how* he used it and the ideas that drove that decision which revolutionized painting.

One of the remarkable aspects of the drip pictures is the unerring control that Pollock maintained over the gestural marks, the color, and the overall visual evenness of the field using this freer technique of application. It seems that having physically to apply the paint to the canvas in Pollock's earlier work actually obstructed the continuity of the gestures; by contrast, dripping and pouring gave the artist more control, not less. In this sense the new technique offered a greater accuracy of rendering.

In his essay "The American Action Painters," written in 1952, Harold Rosenberg provided the definitive description of Pollock's position:

> At a certain moment the canvas began to appear to one American painter after another as an arena in which to act— rather than a space in which to reproduce, redesign, analyze, or "express" an object, actual or imagined. What was to go on the canvas was not a picture but an event . . . What matters always is the revelation contained in the act . . . A painting that is an act is inseparable from the biography of the artist.[17]

Just as this account is heavily influenced by existentialism, Pollock's emphasis on the unpremeditated act of painting derives at least in part from the existentialist idea of affirming being through action (to "realize" one's condition, as Sartre phrased it in *Being and Nothingness*).[18] The "action painter" examines him- or herself in the language of paint. When an interviewer asked Pollock in 1950, "Then, you don't actually have a preconceived image of a canvas in your mind?" he answered, "Well, not exactly—no—because it hasn't been created, you see . . . I do have a general notion of what I'm about and what the results will be."[19]

Pollock transformed the obligation for social relevance, a pervasive current between the wars, into an unrelenting moral commitment to a search for the "self." The multiple impressions of the artist's own hand in the upper right corner of *Number 1, 1948* stress the visceral immediacy of the artist's personal presence and, by contrast, emphasize the vastness of the canvas as measured against them. A number of painters of the New York School used handprints in this way [fig. 3.16].

Perhaps Pollock took some cues from jazz. According to Lee Krasner, he thought jazz "was the only other really creative thing happening in this country."[20] Like the bebop improvisations of Dizzy Gillespie or Charlie Parker, the style of each of Pollock's drip pictures was invented in the process of painting. What he was trying to convey preceded the ability to do so. By visibly recording the history of their own making, the drip paintings render form and content inseparable. Nevertheless, in bebop Parker rehearsed certain riffs repeatedly until they could be played as though he were collaging preformed elements together in the process of his spontaneous inventing. He even included themes from classical composers and from pop music. The same is true for Pollock.

In 1947 Peggy Guggenheim closed her gallery and returned to Europe. Betty Parsons agreed to take on Pollock, although she could not afford the monthly stipend that Guggenheim had been paying. The latter continued that herself for a short time until Pollock's sales became sufficiently buoyant to make him a meager living. He premiered his drip pictures in his first Betty Parsons exhibition of January 1948. They were widely ridiculed and continued to be so until his death, even though the recognition of his genius within the art world grew rapidly.

Pollock in the Fifties

With the help of a local physician, Pollock stayed completely away from alcohol between 1948 and 1950, and the work of these years is calmer and freer. He got national attention in the press after 1948, even if it was often unsympathetic; in 1949 *Life* ran an article entitled, "Is Jackson Pollock the Greatest Living Painter in the United States?"[21] and in 1950 the photographer Hans Namuth made a short film of Pollock working.

Pollock's drip pictures of 1950, like *Number 27* [figs. 4.6 and 4.7], are less anxious, larger, and more elegiac. They tend to have a more open weave of lines and seem more contained within themselves as they reach the outer edges of the canvas.

4.8 (above) **Jackson Pollock**, *Echo (Number 25, 1951)*, 1951. Enamel on unprimed canvas, 7ft 7⅞in × 7ft 2in (2.33 × 2.18m).

The Museum of Modern Art, New York. Acquired through the Lillie P. Bliss Bequest and the Mr. and Mrs. David Rockefeller Fund, 241.1969.

4.9 (below) **Jackson Pollock**, *Blue Poles*, 1952. Oil, enamel, and aluminum paint, glass on canvas, 6ft 11½in × 15ft 12½in (2.12 × 4.89m).

Collection, National Gallery of Australia, Canberra. Purchase, 1973.

By contrast, the denser works of 1949 continue at the same level of intensity edge to edge. The most monumental works of 1950 also have a soft, diffuse light, like the late paintings of Monet. These large compositions represent at once a summation of this phase of Pollock's development and a creative dead end.

In late 1950 Pollock started drinking again, and his creativity took a sharp turn toward purely black-and-white pictures, many with figures or totemic images, as in *Echo (Number 25, 1951)* [fig. 4.8]. He did a few drip pictures, too, but his productivity trailed off and he seemed to have lost confidence in the direction of his development. Several of the paintings from 1951 to 1953 are still of a majestically high quality, such as *Echo* and *Blue Poles* [fig. 4.9], but they also have a more anxious feeling.

In *Blue Poles* Pollock introduced the cadence of strong blue diagonals (painted against the edge of a two-by-four) as if he were seeking more stability. It may also imply a yearning to return to the security of his roots, since the idea of the poles resembles the compositional device that Benton taught Pollock in the early 1930s and that Pollock used in 1943 for *Mural* (though Benton meant for such poles to be hypothetical, not visible).

In 1954 and 1955 Pollock's painting nearly ground to a halt as his drinking got heavier and his depression deeper. The public still joked about his work: In 1956 *Time* magazine called him "Jack the Dripper."[22] By this time he had stopped painting entirely and, on the night of August 10th, he drove his car off the road, killing himself and one of the two young women he had with him.

Pollock's legacy to subsequent artists is profound but often not readily visible. His drip style did not inspire imitators precisely because it was so strikingly unique; whereas the gestural painters of the fifties could try out the autographic brushwork of de Kooning, Kline, and Guston without necessarily producing a baldly derivative work, no one could paint a drip composition that did not look like a weak Pollock. Yet Pollock's radical reorientation of time in painting—his concentration on the instant at which the paint hit the canvas, purging references to past time or previous painting—was the central inspiration for the immediacy in the gestural painting of the fifties as well as in the "happenings" that began at the end of the decade. The directness with which the materials are expressed in the minimal and process art of the sixties is also indebted to Pollock.

BARNETT NEWMAN

Style, in modern art, is the result of an artist's effort to find a successful, visual embodiment of his or her thinking. Whereas de Kooning and Pollock worked out their ideas on the canvas surface, Barnett Newman thought everything through in advance. His painting confronts us with such an uncompromisingly metaphysical idea that his work still leaves many seasoned art viewers bewildered.

Newman was a highly articulate intellectual, who fought against any kind of artistic subject matter that was tied down to an object. Yet, as Richard Shiff has pointed out, his art is by no means nonobjective in the usual sense; rather it is an attempt to distill and universalize individual experience of the most profound and personal kind.[23] In particular, Newman's painting has to do with the notion of the sublime, which he contrasted with what he called "the Greek, plastic achievement,"[24] namely the concept of the beautiful. The sublime comes through the direct intuition of universal experience; it consists of pure spirituality. By contrast, Newman viewed the Greek aesthetic as expressing the personal and depending on the physical beauty of the object.

Newman sought a direct embodiment of the experience of the sublime, appropriate to the middle of the twentieth century, and this quest preoccupied him throughout the forties. He expressed this concern first in writings such as his essay for the catalog of "The Ideographic Picture" exhibition (1947), which he organized at the Betty Parsons Gallery; in the show he included works by Hans Hofmann, Clyfford Still, Theodoros Stamos, Ad Reinhardt, Mark Rothko, and himself. An ideograph is a written symbol that communicates an idea directly, rather than through language or through the mediation of any symbolic form.

In his essay Newman wrote of seeking a modern equivalent to "primitive" art, in which the abstract shape itself is, he said,

> a living thing, a vehicle for an abstract thought-complex, a carrier of the awesome feelings that he [the Kwakiutl Indian] felt before the terror of the unknowable. The abstract shape was, therefore, real rather than a formal "abstraction" of a visual fact with its overtone of an already known nature. Nor was it a purist illusion with its overload of pseudo-scientific truths.[25]

Newman wanted to distinguish himself and his friends from the other types of abstraction then prevalent: on the one hand from that which was predominantly formal rather than emanating from content (this seemed to him a form of trivial decoration); and on the other hand from abstraction like Mondrian's, which, although steeped in metaphysics, seemed to Newman too impersonal and utopian.

Newman saw the artist as a revolutionary in search of universal truths, discovered by way of the personal and immediate. In addition, he regarded the search as heroic in the manner of Greek tragedy, even though he did not want to produce works that had anything to do with classical form or beauty. He wrote:

> The question that now arises is how, if we are living in a time without a legend or a mythos that can be called sublime, if we refuse to admit any exaltation in pure relations, if we refuse to live in the abstract, how can we be creating a sublime art? We are reasserting man's natural desire for the exalted, for a concern with our relationships to the absolute emotions. We do not need the obsolete props of an outmoded and antiquated legend ... We are freeing ourselves of the impediments of memory, association, nostalgia, legend, myth, or what have you, that have been the devices of Western European painting. Instead of making cathedrals out of Christ, man, or "life," we are making them out of ourselves, out of our own feelings. The image we produce is the self-evident one of revelation, real and concrete, that can be understood by anyone who will look at it without the nostalgic glasses of history.[26]

Newman was born in 1905 in New York City; at home he received a substantial education in religious philosophy from a steady stream of Jewish immigrants that his father housed on arrival from Europe. Newman always wanted to be an artist. He discovered the Metropolitan Museum as a teenager and took classes at the Art Students League in his last year of high school and while attending City College, from which he graduated in 1927. He then agreed to work for two years in his father's menswear manufacturing business in the hope of saving some money to help him through a career as a painter.

The 1929 stock-market crash derailed this plan and the thirties were bleak for Newman. He taught art in high school, while continuing to work for his father until 1937. Unlike most of his fellow artists, Newman was not on the Federal Art Project; he could not have produced the requisite amount of work at that time, and in addition he earned enough income as a teacher to make him ineligible. As a result Newman felt left out, particularly years later when so many people looked back at having worked on the Project as a mark of serious participation in the artistic developments of that era. In 1936 Newman married a young teacher named Annalee Greenhouse, who stuck by him devotedly, defending his art and encouraging him to persevere.

Although deeply reflective, Newman was also colorful and affable. The battles in which he fervently engaged, in "letters to the editor" or verbally with fellow artists, like his decision to run for mayor of New York in 1933, sometimes went to comic extremes in their vehemence and sincerity. In his mayoral platform, for example, he insisted: "We must spread culture through society. Only a society entirely composed of artists would be really worth living in. That is our aim, which is not dictated by expediency."[27]

Newman made little progress as a painter in the thirties and from the end of the decade until the mid-forties he stopped painting altogether. He could not find a satisfactory place to begin in existing styles of painting. Newman and his friends generally admired the spirit of surrealism, but they felt that one could not deal with an unconscious content and universal subjects in an antiquated illusionist style. Dada objects, although more radical in style, seemed to Newman to be too quickly consumed as precious objects of *petit bourgeois* taste. He did not want to make something that a collector could acquire as an object without engaging its content. So he wrote about art and encouraged his friends until he could figure out how to proceed with his own painting.

Between 1939 and 1941 Newman pursued a long-standing interest in science, studying botany and ornithology. In particular, he wanted to know about the beginnings of life— how it emerged and how its orders developed. He was always looking for an analog to the genesis of thought and the evolution of the human mind. In some ways this provided the philosophical basis for his successful resumption of painting. In the mid-forties Newman recommended painting with works that derived from surrealist automatism and free association, like the contemporary works of his friend Rothko [fig. 4.20]. But unlike the surrealists, Newman did not focus on psychological introspection; rather he looked to cosmic themes, as his titles indicate. In 1946, for example, he used such titles as *Pagan Void*, *The Beginning*, *The Command*, *The Euclidean Abyss*, *The Slaying of Osiris*, and *The Blessing*, evoking themes of rebirth from the chaos, Genesis, and evolution. In an essay of the period (1943–5) called "The Plasmic Image" Newman explained:

> All artists, whether primitive or sophisticated, have been involved in the handling of chaos. The painter of the new movement [i.e. Gottlieb, Rothko, Pollock and himself] . . . is therefore not concerned with geometric forms per se but in creating forms which by their abstract nature carry some abstract intellectual content. There is an attempt being made to assign a Surrealist explanation to the use these painters make of abstract forms . . . [but] Surrealism is interested in a dream world that will penetrate the human psyche. To that extent it is a mundane expression . . . The present painter is concerned, not with his own feelings or with the mystery of his own personality, but with the penetration into the world mystery. His imagination is therefore attempting to dig into metaphysical secrets. To that extent his art is concerned with the sublime. It is a religious art which through symbols will catch the basic truth of life which is its sense of tragedy . . . the artist tries to wrest truth from the void.[28]

The Revelation of Newman's *Onement I*

In a little painting he called *Onement I* [fig. 4.10] Newman finally found a visual expression for these ideas that "looked right" to him, and this painting established the direction for the rest of Newman's career. He reported that he had begun the canvas as a background for another painting, but that it sat unfinished in his studio for about three-quarters of a year—through the fall of 1948. He kept finding himself looking at it, wondering why it moved him so deeply and felt so resonant with his state of mind. He puzzled over it for months, trying to assess its significance. Newman referred to the line straight down the middle as the "zip." The structural symmetry provided by the zip wipes out the problem of composition. By reducing the composition to zero, Newman killed the preciousness of the painting as an art object and forced the viewer to apprehend the work more strictly in terms of ideas. Thus *Onement I* provided a brilliant visual analog for certain of Newman's key ideas, and he employed the zip (though most often not in the middle) in almost all his subsequent paintings.

The title "Onement" has a number of significant meanings. It is a component of "atonement," an important concept for Jews, which they mark during Yom Kippur. The Cabbalists regard this holy day as a time to reflect on the mystery of creation. Spinoza, the philosopher whose writings Newman studied along with the texts of the Cabbala, ranked knowledge into three levels: (1) data and rules learned by rote; (2) things learned by logic; and (3) immediate knowledge (the highest order), obtained through a direct intuition to the essence of things, an insight that went beyond reason. This last level resembled what Newman called "the sublime."

Newman was after an epiphany, a simultaneously terrifying and exalting moment of total reality. For him, as for Spinoza, this came from a oneness with God. Spinoza looked at man as an extension of the "all" of God, who is omnipresent. But he saw God as always growing and the layers of meaning as infinite. Newman tried to paint the fullness of this experience, not the void. The solid color fields, in *Onement I* and subsequent pictures, are this pervasive fullness. Newman's interest in Jewish mysticism might seem at odds with his scientific and intellectual side, but Newman used the science—as he used philosophy— to open another point of access into the mysteries of creation.

Once Newman began thinking in these terms, the existing styles of painting seemed anachronistic. He was left with only one option: to undertake an act of origination, starting from scratch, like Genesis itself. *Onement I* is an act of creation and of division. The zip down the middle evokes God's separation of light and darkness, a line drawn in the void. Like the Old Testament God, the artist starts with chaos, with the void; Newman begins with blank color—no texture, no form, no details. The zip is a primal act.

The colors in *Onement I* also refer to Genesis. The red-brown field of the background is the color of earth, Adam is the man created by God, and the Hebrew word for earth is *adamah*. So Adam is made from the earth, from clay. In addition, humans are the only animals that walk upright; the vertical gesture down the middle of the canvas stands for humankind, whose first incarnation is Adam. The sensuous edges of the painter's gesture give it an individual and human character in contrast to the impersonal and limitless field of color. The zip resembles Giacometti's figures, which despite their heavily modeled surfaces are so thin as to be fragile, fleeting moments in existence [figs. 5.12–5.14]— Giacometti exhibited his postwar figural work in New York for the first time in February 1948, just when Newman was painting *Onement I*.

"Onement" also carries a reference to Eve. The Talmud says: "It is only when he is complete that man is called 'one'

. . . When he is male together with female."[29] So "onement" has its roots in the Cabbala and in Talmudic literature, which pervade Newman's education. "Onement" is the Genetic moment; it is Adam and Eve conjoined; it celebrates human creativity, especially the creativity of the artist.

In October 1948 Newman painted a second version of the painting. In *Onement I* he painted the zip over a strip of tape that he left on the surface; this time he painted over tape then peeled it off to leave a clean-edged, unmodeled zip down the middle. This switch from the soft zip to the hard, unmodulated one recurs for the next two or three years in many pairs of paintings and has a female–male complementarity. Newman painted seven "Onement" pictures over half a decade. The fact that the zip is centered is their crucial trademark. This symmetry stands for perfection in man's oneness with the all of God.

The Paintings of the Late Forties

All of the painters of the New York School were moving toward a larger scale at this time. As Robert Motherwell said:

> the large format, at one blow, destroyed the century long tendency of the French to domesticize modern painting, to make it intimate. We replaced the nude girl and the French door with a modern Stonehenge, with a sense of the sublime and the tragic . . . One of the great images [of New York School painting] should be the house-painter's brush, in the employ of a grand vision dominated by an ethical sensibility that makes the usual painter's brush indeed picayune.[30]

Looking back to the late forties, Newman spoke in 1967 of the motives of the painters in his circle:

> Twenty years ago we felt the moral crisis of a world in shambles, a world devastated by a great depression and a fierce World War, and it was impossible at that time to paint the kind of painting that we were doing—flowers, reclining nudes, and people playing the cello [the subjects of such modern painters as Cézanne, Picasso, and Matisse]. At the same time we could not move into the situation of a pure world of unorganized shapes and forms, or color relations, a world of sensation. And I would say that, for some of us, this was our moral crisis in relation to what to paint. So that we actually began, so to speak, from scratch, as if painting were not only dead but had never existed.[31]

Newman had his first one-person show at the Betty Parsons Gallery in early 1950. *Be I*, the largest picture in the show, had barely fit into Newman's studio on 19th Street (he had had to carry it out on to the sidewalk and back in order to turn the picture around),[32] and this is important in understanding these works. He meant the viewer to see them very close up, just as he saw them as he worked on them in the studio. He even tacked a statement to the gallery wall, instructing visitors to stand close in order to feel the expansiveness of the color field.[33]

4.10 Barnett Newman, *Onement I*, 1948. Oil on canvas and oil on masking tape, 27¼ × 16¼in (69.2 × 41.3cm).
The Museum of Modern Art, New York. Gift of Annalee Newman. 390.1992.

4.11 Barnett Newman, *Abraham*, 1949. Oil on canvas, 6ft 10¾in × 34½in (210.2 × 87.7cm).

The Museum of Modern Art, New York. Philip Johnson Fund, 651.1959.

Newman painted *Abraham* [fig. 4.11] on a large scale, too, but instead of the fine metaphysical white zip and the earthbound cadmium red background in *Be I*, he conceived this picture in a somber mood, using a dark palette and a heavy stripe. The existential despair evident in this black-on-black painting has partly to do with the death in 1947 of the artist's father, who was named Abraham, though it also refers to the biblical Abraham. The relation of the stripe to the center still persists in *Abraham*—he encoded a secret symmetry, placing the right edge of the stripe on the centerline of the canvas. He divided the whole composition mathematically so that the width of the stripe was half the width of the left-hand section, in a 2:1:3 proportion. Newman's sketch for such a painting would have been a scrap of paper with calculations for the numerical proportions of the divisions. He made a few drawings that seem to relate to *Onement I* and one drawing of 1949 related to *Achilles*, which he painted three years later. Otherwise he did no drawings for paintings between 1947 and 1959.

Vir Heroicus Sublimis and Other Works of the Fifties

In 1950 Newman moved to a larger studio on Wall Street and began to paint even bigger pictures. But the move as well as his 1950 show briefly interrupted his work and seems to have precipitated a shift in his painting. Newman's monumental *Vir Heroicus Sublimis* [fig. 4.12] projects a metaphysical absoluteness; it is the antithesis of the precious object. The Latin title means "man, heroic and sublime."[34] The hidden square in the middle—described by the two zips—emphasizes the perfection of the center, around which he ordered the canvas. The color field evokes the universe, the infinite, and completely lacks any texture or sense of human intervention. The zips, on the other hand, convey the painter's presence and spatially establish the relation of the individual to the wider order of things. Pollock's first 16-foot canvas, *Number 1 of 1949*, must have encouraged Newman to experiment with a huge scale, which made the 18-foot-long *Vir Heroicus* and other pictures of this time practically impossible for all but a few collectors or galleries to hang, much less buy. As such they proclaim Newman's freedom to attempt the impossible.

Newman wanted to rid the painting of its physicality as an object in order to emphasize its meaning. But many have misread his work as a formalist statement, because of his concern with measurement and placement. In the fifties Newman embarked on a whole series of paintings such as *Untitled 4* [fig. 4.13] that consisted only of the zips. In these Newman concerned himself with the placement of the zips in a total space, rather than merely within the space defined by a color field. These paintings have so much sculptural physicality in real space that the leap to sculpture was not great and in *Here I (To Marcia)* [fig. 4.14] Newman turned a pair of zips—a textured one and a precise metaphysical one—into three-dimensional forms, in which one can sense a human presence.

4.12 Barnett Newman, *Vir Heroicus Sublimis*, 1950–1.
Oil on canvas, 7ft 11⅜in × 17ft 9¼in (2.42 × 5.41m).
The Museum of Modern Art, New York. Gift of Mr. and Mrs. Ben Heller, 240.1969.

In August 1949 the Newmans visited Annalee's family in Akron, Ohio, and went to see the nearby Miamisburg Indian mounds. Newman later described that experience to Thomas Hess as "a sense of place, a holy place. Looking at the site, you feel 'here I am, *here*' . . . and out beyond there [that is, beyond the limits of the site] there is chaos, nature, rivers, landscape . . . but here you get a sense of your own presence . . . I became involved with the idea of making the viewer present: the idea that 'man is present.'"[35] Newman built the sculpture *Here I* on a mound. It does not convey a sense of *space*, but of *place*. It has to do with a place in which one can "be," in a primal sense. Newman meant to epitomize a revelatory experience, like that of Joseph Smith selecting the Mormon Zion in a vision or of the Jewish Zionists' spiritual feeling for Palestine as the Jewish homeland.

The biblical subjects and the concern with the absolute persist in the works of 1951 and 1952. In *The Day One* the zips hover at the edges and in *The Day Before One* they do not yet exist at all. Neither of these works shows any paint texture: the canvas has absorbed the paint, in a way that heightens its immateriality. As in this case, Newman often made canvases in pairs of identically measured stretchers, though he sometimes painted them as much as a year apart. *Vir Heroicus Sublimis* has a dark mate called *Cathedral*, which could not be more different in character. But they undoubtedly have an iconographic connection, as in the case of *The Day Before One* and *The Day One*, which deal with the moment of the beginning in Genesis. Befitting the grandeur of the theme, *The Day Before One* and *The Day One* each stand 11 feet tall. When Betty Parsons gave Newman his second exhibition in 1951, she could not include them because they would not fit into the gallery. One can only assume that he knew perfectly well that they could not be shown and chose this course of action as a gesture of confrontation with the restraints of the known and the possible.

In the early fifties Newman painted a number of pictures titled for Greek mythological heroes. He was not intending to invoke Freud in an exploration of individual psychology, as in surrealism, but rather to continue his heroic quest for art. Such works as *Achilles*, *Ulysses*, and *L'Errance* ("The Odyssey") use the metaphor of the epic hero to portray Newman's own odyssey in the thirties and forties to find a means of artistic expression. But on the whole Newman's journey was not understood, even by his friends. Pollock encouraged him, Kline and some of the others expressed sympathy for him, but some, even among his fellow artists, thought Newman was a phony (even thirty years later, Motherwell still felt that way), and the Museum of Modern Art left him out of the 1952 "15 Americans" show which included so many of his colleagues.

The "Stations of the Cross"

Newman suffered feelings of failure in the mid-to-late fifties, and in 1957 he did no painting at all. Then he had a heart attack, which seemed to work like instant psychoanalysis.[36] He immediately went back to painting in 1958 and completed a series of stunning compositions based on the Stations of the Cross. As in the earlier works that deal with God or biblical subjects, Newman did not seek to represent the subject, but rather to deal with the abstract and universal experience which each of the stations evoked: "Lema Sabachthani—Why? Why did you forsake me? Why forsake me? To what purpose? Why? This is the passion, this is the outcry of Jesus. Not the terrible walk up the Via Dolorosa, but the question that has no answer . . . Lema?

4.13 (left) **Barnett Newman**, *Untitled 4*, 1950. Oil on canvas, 74 × 6in (188 × 15.2cm). Collection, Mr. and Mrs. I. M. Pei, New York.

4.14 (right) **Barnett Newman**, *Here I (To Marcia)*, 1950/1962 (cast: sculpture 1962, base 1971). Bronze with black patina, overall dimensions 107¼ × 28¼ × 27¼in (272.4 × 71.8 × 69.2cm). Collection, Moderna Museet, Stockholm, Sweden.

4.15 Barnett Newman, *The Stations of the Cross: Lema Sabachthani, First Station*, 1958. Magna on canvas, 6ft 5⅞in × 5ft ½in (1.98 × 1.54m).
Robert and Jane Meyerhoff Collection, National Gallery of Art, Washington, D.C., 1986.65.1.

of men, of nature, of the hard black chaos that is death, or the grayer softer chaos that is tragedy. For it is only the pure idea that has meaning."[39]

MARK ROTHKO

In 1949 Mark Rothko developed a pictorial format of softly defined, rectangular clouds of color, which he stacked symmetrically on top of one another [fig. 4.16]. These rectangles of uniform width fill the canvas almost edge to edge; at the top and bottom the forms also press close to the perimeter. This is a rudimentary visual language conceived to evoke elemental emotions with maximum poignancy. Rothko regarded this format as an inexhaustible structure for, in his words, "dealing with human emotion, with the human drama as much as I can possibly experience it,"[40] and except for his three late mural cycles, he worked exclusively in this format until his death in 1970.

The monumentality and static simplicity of these compositions express the workings of a complex, subtle, and

to what purpose—is the unanswerable question of human suffering."[37] In the biblical text, the first station concerns the condemnation of Christ. The hard black stripe at the left in *The Stations of the Cross: Lema Sabachthani, First Station* [fig. 4.15] has an absolute ring of spirituality coming through the blackness and across the white field toward the right edge, where the more clouded human doubts about death and the condemnation seem to reside. In most of the "Stations of the Cross," one may speculate that the left edge seems to address the eternal question "why?" whereas the right edge of the canvas suggests earthbound associations, human concerns—there is a constant dialog between right and left.

This moving series of paintings—which ended with *Fourteenth Station* (the entombment) in 1966—seems also to have been an autobiographical exploration,[38] confronting the artist's brush with death in his heart attack, his relation to his colleagues, and his rejection by the art world. But Newman always generalizes such specific experiences, giving a transcendental value to his philosophical and spiritual searchings. As he wrote in 1947, "The basis of an aesthetic act is the pure idea . . . that makes contact with the mystery—of life,

4.16 Mark Rothko, *Green and Tangerine on Red*, 1956.
Oil on canvas, 7ft 9⅝in × 5ft 9¼in (2.37 × 1.75m).
The Phillips Collection, Washington, D.C.

turbulent mind, plagued by depression but also by an over-whelming sense of urgent responsibility for the exploration of profound human content in painting. The critic Dore Ashton, who met Rothko in the fifties, portrayed him as a man disposed to causes—always ready to storm the barri-cades whether in the name of his leftist politics, his radical views on art education for children, or his concept of the mission of abstract art.[41] Robert Motherwell described him as a cauldron of "seething anger [that] would sometimes blow up, completely irrationally."[42]

Underneath the meditative reserve of his paintings and their deliberate reduction of vocabulary lies a passionate ethical and psychological fundamentalism. The very simplic-ity of the structure sets a moral tone that places matters of value in high relief. Rothko's work has a frightening sense of the absolute that resembles the primitive force of Old Testament justice. As William Rubin (a curator at the Museum of Modern Art) remarked, Rothko's "pictures sometimes rumbled and threatened like a live volcano."[43] Sometime around 1956, the artist told Dore Ashton that he was making the most violent paintings in America.[44] For Dominique de Menil, the patron of his last murals, Rothko's paintings evoked "the tragic mystery of our perishable con-dition. The silence of God, the unbearable silence of God."[45]

Rothko's Formative Years

Marcus Rothkowitz (he simplified the name to "Mark Rothko" around 1940) was born in 1903 in the Lithuanian town of Dvinsk. His childhood was marked by a terrible period of mob violence against Jews in Russia, and for the rest of his life he harbored memories of that. In August 1913 the ten-year-old Marcus, his older sister, and his mother left to join his father and two brothers in Portland, Oregon. Seven months later his father died.

The young Rothko had learned self-discipline memoriz-ing the Talmud in the Jewish school of Dvinsk and he excelled academically in Portland. In 1921 he won a full scholarship to Yale. Although he studied drawing in high school, he gave the larger share of his energy to radical politics. At Yale Rothko explored music, drama, literature, philosophy, and mathematics (at which he was particularly brilliant), but his radicalism still remained the focus of his intellectual life. In his second year at Yale the scholarship evaporated and after struggling along for the year he headed for New York.

In the city Rothko started taking courses at the Art Students League and briefly did some acting. Studying under Max Weber at the League, Rothko learned about cubism, Cézanne, the color harmonies of Matisse, and the primi-tivism of the German expressionists. The recently opened New Art Circle gallery of J. B. Neumann introduced Rothko to a variety of German expressionist works and he began his career painting uninspired figure compositions of an expressionistic character.

The 1938 *Subway Scene* [fig. 4.17] is the last and most accomplished work in a series that grew out of Rothko's expressionist style. The painterly handling, the generality of the forms, the symmetry and planar frontality of the composition, and the subject itself—the somber atmosphere

4.17 Mark Rothko, *Subway Scene*, 1938. Oil on canvas, 24 × 34in (61 × 86.4cm). Collection of The Rothko Estate.

of the New York subway—anticipated aspects of Rothko's mature work.[46] This painting also shows the influence of Milton Avery's quiet lyricism in the staid composition, the hints of rich but subdued color harmonies, and the large flat color areas, although the mood of frozen anxiety that hangs over the Rothko contrasts markedly with the calm sensuality of Avery's work.

Rothko's history in the thirties resembled that of other painters of his generation. He was struggling simultaneously with economic survival, his social conscience, and the stylistic influences of the European moderns. He was aided by the support of an artists' group called "The Ten," which he and Adolph Gottlieb helped to organize in 1935, and by close relationships with Gottlieb, Edith Sachar (whom he married in 1932), and Milton and Sally Avery. It was around the Averys' vacation house near Gloucester, Massachusetts, that the Gottliebs and Rothkos spent their summers in the mid-thirties. Rothko also met David Smith and Barnett Newman at that time, and in 1936–7 he worked in the easel-painting division of the Federal Art Project.

Political activism and a concern for social justice characterized the intellectual climate of New York in the late thirties. When John D. Rockefeller had Diego Rivera forcibly removed from the scaffold at Rockefeller Center in 1934 (and then destroyed the mural) for including a portrait of Lenin in his painting, the outcry from artists created a focus for political organizing. The event catalyzed the founding of the Artists' Union in 1934 with a journal called *Art Front*, edited by Stuart Davis.[47]

Rothko participated in the Artists' Union, in the American Artists' Congress, and in the Federation of American Painters and Sculptors. He was always drawn to leftist politics, characterizing himself as "still an anarchist"[48] as late as 1970. But in the interwar period the climate of ethical concern arising from the Depression, the looming specter of fascism in Europe, and then the war gave Rothko's social and political agenda particular urgency. For Rothko, Gottlieb, Newman, and many of their contemporaries this made conventional painting seem irrelevant and consequently immoral; they sought subjects that addressed the timeless ethical and ontological questions of the human condition.

Turning to Classical Myth

In 1938 Rothko and Gottlieb turned to classical myth to find themes of an elevated order of magnitude and universality. In 1943 Rothko explained:

> the known myths of antiquity . . . are the eternal symbols upon which we must fall back to express basic psychological ideas . . . And modern psychology finds them persisting still in our dreams, our vernacular, and our art, for all the changes in the outward conditions of life . . . The myth holds us, therefore, not thru [sic] the possibilities of fantasy, but because it expresses to us something real and existing in ourselves.[49]

Rothko and Gottlieb explored not only Greek tragedy but also the writings of Nietzsche and Jung, the mechanisms of the unconscious mind, and, for Rothko, classical music, especially Mozart operas.

Rothko's first mythic painting, *Antigone* [fig. 4.18], has an overall gray tone, like an archaic stone frieze. The layering of the forms in registers of shallow relief reinforces this association to antiquity, while the frontality of the composition gives it an emblematic character, stressing its distance from representation. The classical profiles and curly hair of the heads, as well as the part-animal, part-human feet in the lower stratum, refer in a general way to prototypes in Greek sculpture and painting. Rothko also infused this and other mythical pictures with quotations from architectural ornament on the buildings of New York that link his work to the material reality of the present. In addition, he included crucifixion imagery such as the outspread arms that separate the top two layers of forms in *Antigone* (extending the mythic content beyond the Greek pantheon). In his drawings Rothko even showed the hands of these outstretched arms pierced with nails. The Passion of Christ represented for Rothko, as it did for Newman, an embodiment of the eternal tragedy of the human condition and not a uniquely Christian subject—any more than *Antigone* was a uniquely Greek one. This mixture of iconographic elements broadened the base of Rothko's subject matter into a foundation for universal tragedy.

The stratification, which characterizes Rothko's mythic works from roughly 1938 through 1942, echoes the implicit collapse of time by which the artist brought the ancient past into the relevant present. The archaeological metaphor, centered on the idea of a cumulative memory of the past acting upon the present, permeates the theories of Freud as well as the writings of such literary modernists as T. S. Eliot and James Joyce, with whose works Rothko was conversant. For Rothko, history verified the universality of ancient themes. In a commentary to his 1942 painting *Omen of the Eagle* he explained: "The theme here is derived from the Agamemnon Trilogy of Aeschylus. The picture deals not with the particular anecdote, but rather with the Spirit of Myth, which is generic to all myths at all times. It involves a pantheism in which man, bird, beast and tree—the known as well as the knowable—merge into a single tragic idea."[50]

Stylistically the works of 1942 and 1943 owe a certain amount to the formal vocabulary of surrealism, particularly: the frottage techniques, birdlike forms, and dreamscapes of Max Ernst; Masson's metamorphic vocabulary of man and animal; the poetic structure of Miró's work; and the transformative vocabulary of biomorphic abstraction, as in Rothko's *The Entombment* [fig. 4.19]. But Rothko and Gottlieb concerned themselves above all else with content, as they took pains to assert in a now famous letter to the *New York Times*. "It is a widely accepted notion among painters," they wrote, "that it does not matter what one paints as long as it is well painted. This is the essence of academicism. There is no such thing as good painting about nothing."[51]

4.18 (above) **Mark Rothko**, *Antigone*, c. 1941. Oil and charcoal on canvas, 34 × 45¾in (86.4 × 116.2cm).

National Gallery of Art, Washington, D.C., Inc., 1986.43.119.

4.19 (left) **Mark Rothko**, *The Entombment*, c. 1946. Oil on canvas, 23 × 40in (58.4 × 101.6cm).

Collection, Edith Ferber.

Surrealism, Psychoanalysis, and "the Spirit of Myth"

In retrospect the letter to the *New York Times* also anticipated the development of Rothko's mature style. "We favor the simple expression of the complex thought," they proclaimed. "We are for the large shape because it has the impact of the unequivocal. We wish to reassert the picture plane. We are for flat forms because they destroy illusion and reveal truth."[52] If this proclamation sounds like Barnett Newman's art theory of the forties, that is not accidental. Newman worked closely with Gottlieb and Rothko on the letter, and in thanks for his publicly unacknowledged, but obviously substantial help, each artist gave Newman a painting in 1943.

In the theory of surrealism Rothko saw a passage through the specific anecdote toward the mechanisms of the unconscious mind. He had experimented with automatic drawing as early as 1938[53] and taken an interest in the Oedipus myth. The careful preparatory drawings for his mythic pictures clearly indicate that he did not conceive them in an automatist manner, but from 1944 through 1946 Rothko did experiment with automatism to produce loose, linear doodles that dominate the foregrounds of his compositions. He painted the backgrounds of these works in luminous, "all over" washes of color, often dividing them into wide horizontal bands. In several canvases of 1945 he also began to increase the scale. The paintings of this three-year period are uneven in quality, despite notable successes like *Baptismal Scene* [fig. 4.20], but they provided a crucial transition to Rothko's "multiforms" of 1947–9, where the doodles melted into soft color forms and then gradually coalesced, in 1949, into the softly defined color blocks of Rothko's mature style [fig. 4.21].

Freud's theories provided the surrealists with a link between the world of dreams (the unconscious mind) and the everyday world. Rothko's search for "the Spirit of Myth," encouraged by Jung's interest in universal myths, followed this path one step further. In 1945 Rothko described it this way:

> I adhere to the material reality of the world and the substance of things. I merely enlarge the extent of this reality . . . I insist upon the equal existence of the world engendered in the mind and the world engendered by God outside of it . . . The surrealist has uncovered the glossary of the myth and has established a congruity between the phantasmagoria of the unconscious and the objects of everyday life. The congruity constitutes the exhilarated tragic experience which for me is the only source book for art.[54]

The reviewers of Rothko's January 1945 show at Art of This Century immediately saw the connection to surrealism, but also noted that Rothko's work was at the same time different. While the meaning, according to *Art News*, for example, "derived from the unconscious . . . he does not

4.20 Mark Rothko, *Baptismal Scene*, 1945. Watercolor and graphite on paper, 20½ × 14½in (52.1 × 36.8cm).
Collection, Whitney Museum of American Art, New York. Purchase, 46.12.

use orthodox surrealist symbols."[55] During the early forties Rothko and a number of other New York painters had shifted their focus past that continuum stressed by Freud and the surrealists toward the universal orders of myth discussed by Jung. The deliberate planning of the structure in Rothko's "automatist" works of 1944–6, as evidenced in the numerous studies for them on paper, underscores this difference in emphasis between Rothko and the surrealists.

Clyfford Still, whom Rothko greatly admired,[56] referred disparagingly to the automatists as "scribblers";[57] he also rejected surrealism's link to the particularities of the individual psyche and the historical moment. Instead Still sought to embody the sublime and the absolute independence of the individual by rejecting all the conventions of painting; his crusty application, tenebrous palette, and his flat, anti-illusionistic forms [fig. 2.17] deliberately oppose traditions of sophisticated paint handling, coloristic harmony, and compositional structure.

Rothko met Still on a trip to California in 1943. Two years later Still began to show up occasionally in New York and East Hampton. In the summer of 1947 he taught

4.21 Mark Rothko, *Number 22*, 1949. Oil on canvas, 9ft 9in × 8ft 11⅛in (2.97 × 2.72m). The Museum of Modern Art, New York. Gift of the artist.

with Rothko at the California School of the Arts in San Francisco. During 1946—the high point of their relationship—Rothko's work suggested the impact of Still's compositional ideas. Rothko's automatist drawing dissolved into indistinctly defined color forms, moving among one another at a glacial pace over a flat plane. This shift in style to a more purified color abstraction gave way between 1947 and 1949 to larger shapes, frequently more geometric in character, and then an increasingly regular, horizontal layering of forms in 1949.

Between 1947 and 1950 Rothko made few sketches. He worked out his ideas directly on the canvas, and painted in thin washes of color that seem to dematerialize into the weave of the fabric. This identity of the paint with the surface, as well as the increasingly simplified order of the compositions, creates a meditative mood, stressing immateriality and universality while playing down the artist's presence, as expressed in the autographic gesture of an artist like de Kooning or Pollock.

The thin handling in Rothko's oils after 1945 derived from his watercolors of the mid-forties but they also took inspiration from Miró, who thinned his paint into washes to heighten their ethereal, poetic quality. Matisse's *The Red Studio* also influenced Rothko's approach. *The Red Studio* consists of a delicately traced map of insubstantial objects and architecture drawn over a large, flat, evenly washed expanse of red canvas and Rothko spent many hours in front of this painting after it went on display at the Museum of Modern Art in New York in February 1949.[58]

"Heroifying" the Ineffable

During 1949 Rothko finally arrived at a style that seemed to promise "the elimination of all obstacles between the painter and the idea, and between the idea and the observer," as he explained in an article for the journal *The Tiger's Eye* of that year. "As examples of such obstacles, I give (among others) memory, history, or geometry, which are swamps of generalization."[59] Rothko rejected memory in so far as it concerned forms that evoke an already known content, thus narrowing the experience and trivializing the universality of his painting. History, including identifiable myths like that of Antigone, also deflects the viewer's attention from a confrontation with the unknown, which was central to Rothko's vision by the late forties. "Geometry" refers to the ubiquitous geometric abstraction and other styles that derived from formal notions rather than from a compelling content.

In order to achieve "the simple expression of the complex thought . . . the impact of the unequivocal,"[60] as Rothko had expressed it in his 1943 letter to the *New York Times*, he relied on the large scale of the color blocks in the works of 1949 and after to create an overpowering material presence; yet it was the presence of something undefinable. Children's art may have been instrumental in Rothko's formulation. He taught art to children at the Center Academy of the Brooklyn Jewish Center from 1929 until 1952 and took a keen interest in their formal ideas. In a notebook from the late thirties Rothko observed that "the scale conception involves the relationships of objects to their surroundings—the emphasis of things *or* space. It definitely involves a *space* emotion. A child may limit space arbitrarily and then heroify his objects. Or he may infinitize space, dwarfing the importance of objects."[61]

Beginning in paintings of 1949, Rothko "heroified" the central color forms in the same manner as he described children doing it. Yet the lack of particularizing features in Rothko's forms creates an immediacy that is free from the secondary influence of narrative and overt cultural interpretation. He thus achieved a vivid sense of an ineffable presence. In the writings of Sartre existence precedes essence; in Rothko's work the subjective experience of the viewer's encounter with the indescribable painted object provides a foundation for the defining of object and self, and how they relate. The infinite variations of color, distribution, proportion, and handling—from canvas to canvas and even within a single work—manifest the artist's range of speculation on these unresolvable issues.

De Kooning's large women of the early fifties also fill the composition and create a powerful presence like Rothko's massive rectangular color clouds. However, the fact that de Kooning's work is figurative and his brushwork prominent gives his paintings a more earthbound focus. It is interesting that in 1951 Pollock also reintroduced figurative elements, derived from the mythic images of his work of the early forties [figs. 2.11 and 4.8]; and David Smith built several works in the fifties and sixties using geometric parts, arranged around a figurative structure [figs. 4.30 and 4.34]. For Newman no remnant of the figure is conceivable, because his work originated in a metaphysical thought, a pure abstract idea attained through the eidetic image (the ideograph) and concepts of placement in space. But Rothko reached for the universal content of human experience through an individual exploration of grand themes,

and this allows for the theoretical possibility of a lingering figurative content.

The stratification in Rothko's paintings of the late thirties and early forties into bands of symbols [fig. 4.19] prefigures the compositional order of the rectangular color blocks. This suggests not only a formal predisposition for such shapes but that, through association, the mythic content may still persevere indirectly in the abstract work. Rothko's interest in the entombment and other aspects of the Passion of Christ also lingers in these later works. The art historian Anna Chave has suggested that the horizontal band of red with incised lines across the center of *Number 22* [fig. 4.21] is literally derived from earlier depictions of horizontal dead figures lying across the laps of maternal figures—as in the many medieval and Renaissance paintings of scenes from the Passion of Christ, first reinterpreted by Rothko in works such as his *Entombment* [fig. 4.19] of around 1946.[62]

Yet "it was with the utmost reluctance," Rothko explained in 1958, that "I found the figure could not serve my purposes."[63] Rothko may well have struggled with the figure as late as 1949, although there is neither visual evidence nor any room in Rothko's art theory to demonstrate the perseverance of conscious imagery in more than a few works in 1948 and 1949. On the contrary, the presence of disguised figures would directly contradict the artist's statement that the "shapes . . . have no direct association with any particular visible experience, but in them one recognizes the principle and passion of organisms."[64] Such specific underlying subject matter would also run in opposition to his intention "to destroy the finite associations with which our society increasingly enshrouds every aspect of our environment."[65]

On the other hand, to the extent that a "clear preoccupation with death," as he phrased it, permeated his work and that he believed that "all art deals with intimations of mortality,"[66] Rothko's abstract painting continues to carry a spiritual link to entombment and *pietà* themes as well as to Greek tragedy. Such subjects persist as metaphysical content, associated to figural works from earlier periods but not literally derived from them.

Formally Rothko's luminous color structures are something genuinely new in the history of art; they have no antecedent, even though they draw on many sources. Rothko admired Mondrian for the way his forms hold the picture plane. Medieval religious pictures share the iconic symmetry that conveys an elemental religious feeling in Rothko's work. The mysteriously hidden source of his glowing light heightens this feeling; the same effect exists in the works of Rembrandt and Fra Angelico, whose handling of light he greatly admired. Like Pollock, Rothko also saw how the richness of color and surface in impressionism, especially in the late works of Monet, was more important than the representational subject matter.

Rothko looked shrewdly at work in museums and books to glean visual ideas, he read philosophy and literature, and he may even have taken formal inspiration from music.

For example, the composer Edgard Varèse (whose work Rothko knew) would separate a single timbre or tone in his most celebrated compositions, playing it off against various orchestrations and rhythms to bring out the nuances of its individuality. This has a parallel in Rothko's isolated clouds of individual hues. Rothko's painting is an art of perpetual and meticulous refinement. It is directly sensual and relies on great subtlety and variety in the color, application, and even the structure of the forms. Within his limited format, Rothko developed a remarkably wide emotional range, from exuberance to contemplation and foreboding.

The Murals and Other Late Work

By the late fifties the public had begun to appreciate the originality and subtlety of Rothko's work, and his reputation grew considerably. In 1958 Philip Johnson commissioned him to paint a monumental mural for the Four Seasons Restaurant in the new Seagram Building. This was Rothko's first mural commission and his first series. The idea of painting a permanent cycle of murals for a specific space appealed enormously to Rothko because it meant that he could finally have control over the way a group of canvases were viewed.

In the spring of 1959 Rothko set up a studio on the Bowery to paint the commission, and over the next two years he made three sets of murals. The first group—which he immediately either dispersed or destroyed—were in his usual format of stacked rectangles. Then he broke away and used open rectangles. He also abandoned this second set of murals; one can only speculate as to the reasons. Rothko completed the third and final sequence in a horizontal format of rectangles with open centers. But instead of delivering the paintings he returned the money and a decade later gave them to the Tate Gallery in London, where they were installed precisely according to his wishes. There may be some truth in the belief, which he evidently encouraged, that he rejected the Seagram commission because he found it distasteful that the restaurant catered to the rich, but the large scale of the room in relation to the murals and the lack of a meditative mood in the busy restaurant seem more likely as the precipitating causes.

Two years later the Nobel Prize-winning economist Wassily Leontief asked Rothko to execute a mural for the private dining-room of Harvard's prestigious Society of Fellows, which Leontief chaired. Rothko began the Harvard murals in December 1961 and completed them within a year. These murals loomed over the relatively small room, and the reddish backgrounds with dark forms over them created an air of somber silence. The orange rectangles in the left panel have a mysterious iridescence. The murals commanded the space quietly, even passively at first, and set a contemplative tone. But below the surface stillness they seem to vibrate with anxiety and elemental force.

The scale of the Harvard murals in relation to the room follows from a development, initiated by Rothko around 1950, toward larger, more monumental pictures.

I realize that historically the function of painting large pictures is painting something very grandiose and pompous. The reason I paint them, however—I think this applies to other painters I know—is precisely because I want to be very intimate and human. To paint a small picture is to place yourself outside your experience, to look upon an experience as a stereopticon view or with a reducing glass . . . However you paint the larger picture, you are in it. It isn't something you command.[67]

Like Newman, Rothko wanted his paintings to be seen from close up, to fill the environment and engulf the spectator. Rothko's concern with controlling the viewer's position in relation to the work had long been an issue; indeed, he had been generally unwilling to participate in group shows for some time because he could not control the space around his work.

A religious metaphor resurfaces persistently in connection with Rothko's paintings, particularly when seen in groups. He himself remarked that "the people who weep before my pictures are having the same religious experience I had when I painted them."[68] The Harvard murals create the atmosphere of a cathedral; but Rothko literally conceived his last mural commission for a Catholic chapel in Houston. In addition, the texts and art of early Christianity attracted Rothko because they embodied a simplicity of faith. Typically, early religious paintings seem to use the same symmetry, lack of motion, shallow depth, and richness of surface to evoke meditation on a spiritual realm that transcends earthly thoughts. One may find oneself transported by staring into the rich nuances of shadow and hue in the deep ultramarine robes of a medieval Virgin, just as one can in Rothko's subtle oscillating fields of color. But Rothko cleared away all reverberations of objects to create a grand, tragic silence.

In the late spring of 1964 Rothko received the commission from John and Dominique de Menil to paint a set of murals for an octagonal chapel in Houston. Here he had even greater control over the setting for the paintings than at Harvard. Inscriptions of the Stations of the Cross were planned for the outside walls of the chapel, and this set the tone for Rothko's concept of the murals. In the winter of 1964 he laid a parachute over the skylight of his studio to create a sacral light. Then he began work on the paintings, using a single, nearly black rectangle on a background of dark maroon. The purplish-red of the murals, which deepened by the time he finished them to an almost black on black palette, was, as Dominique de Menil wrote, "the color elected to bring his paintings to their 'maximum poignancy' as he said . . . as if he were bringing us on the threshold of transcendence."[69] Working incessantly, he completed the mural cycle in 1967, though the installation didn't take place until February 1971, a year after his death.

By the sixties Rothko had achieved financial security and a prodigious reputation. Presidents Kennedy and Johnson invited him to their inauguration festivities and to dinner at the White House; in 1961 the Museum of Modern Art gave him a major retrospective; and in the fall of 1963 the prestigious Marlborough Gallery took him on. Still he felt trapped and restless. In the spring of 1967 he sunk into a deep melancholy and a year later he had an aneurism of the aorta. His mood was black. During his last years he did many brilliantly colored works, though the somber tone of the Houston murals prevailed [fig. 4.22], and after his heart attack in 1968 he started painting predominantly with acrylic on paper. Rothko's marriage and emotional life steadily deteriorated during this period and finally on February 25, 1970 he took his own life.

In *The Birth of Tragedy* (a key work for Rothko)[70] Friedrich Nietzsche noted that the Greeks "developed their mystical doctrines of art through plausible *embodiments*, not through purely conceptual means."[71] Nietzsche chose the Greek deities Apollo and Dionysos to "embody" his postulate of an inherent dualism in the human psyche—on the one side chaos, dissolution, and excess (the "Dionysian"), in perpetual tension with the perfection of harmony, individuation, and restraint (the "Apollonian") on the other. Greek tragedy, he argued, merged the two in an eternally conflicted whole.

In Rothko's work from 1949 to 1970 the very simplicity of the radically pared-down structure provides an awe-inspiring material embodiment of "a single tragic idea." His compositional format maintains a tense equilibrium between the forces of disintegration and precise definition. He unified these drives into a single stylistic system, but deliberately avoided reconciling them. The obstinate, immovable presence of Rothko's paintings pushes the viewer out on his or her own, face to face with fundamental, unresolved, ontological questions. Free of "the familiar," he wrote, "transcendental experiences become possible . . . Pictures must be miraculous . . . a revelation, an unexpected and unprecedented resolution of an eternally familiar need."[72]

DAVID SMITH AND THE SCULPTURE OF THE NEW YORK SCHOOL

Like the painters of the New York School, the sculptors also shifted their focus in the late forties to the implications of surrealist automatism and to existentialism. Theodore Roszak, for example, abandoned his machine-age constructivism for expressionistically handled abstractions in bronze, stressing subjectivity. Ibram Lassaw began building up nubby accretions of surface texture on intuitively assembled linear structures of welding rods. The dreamlike mutations of figures in the surrealist bronzes of Max Ernst [fig. 4.23] informed the sculpture of the young American David Hare and may linger behind the figural presence of Herbert Ferber's welded, gestural abstractions as well [fig. 4.24].

David Smith was the outstanding sculptor to emerge in this shift and in the two decades after 1940 he successfully realized the gestural spontaneity of the action painters in an extensive body of welded sculpture [figs. 4.25–4.34]. Through the free association of forms, his work from 1952 until his untimely death in 1965 defined itself in the process of construction. Welding made this technically possible, by permitting the artist to fabricate his pieces quickly and to work in an improvisational manner. "I do not work with a conscious and specific conviction about a piece of sculpture," he explained in 1952. "It is always open to change and new association. It should be a celebration, one of surprise, not one rehearsed."[73]

In addition, the directness of fabricated sculpture—unlike bronze casting—retained the dominance of the "artist's hand" in all aspects of the work. Like automatist spontaneity, the personal gesture of the artist had become an important issue to artists of this generation, for whom it signaled authenticity. "The sculpture work is a statement of my identity," Smith said. "It is part of my work stream, related to my past works, the three or four in process and the work yet to come. In a sense it is never finished. Only the essence is stated, the key presented to the beholder for further travel."[74]

Like Pollock and others in their circle, Smith sought the particular truth of encountering himself at the most primitive level of his being. He saw it as a pioneering, existentialist odyssey that evoked for him the American frontier myth. "Art," he said, "is the raw stuff which comes

4.22 Mark Rothko, *Untitled*, 1969. Acrylic on canvas, 7ft 4in × 6ft 7in (2.34 × 2.01m).
Collection of Christopher Rothko

4.23 Max Ernst, *The King Playing with the Queen*, 1944.
Bronze (cast 1954, from original plaster), 38½in (97.8cm) high,
at base 18¾in × 20½in (47.6 × 54cm).
The Museum of Modern Art, New York. Gift of D. and J. de Menil, 330.1955.

from . . . aggressiveness by men who got that way fighting
for survival."[75] He even saw the materials as emblematic of
masculinity and of the machine age—"the metal itself possesses . . . associations . . . of this century: power, structure,
movement, progress, suspension, brutality"[76]—and he felt
that art had to engage this language of the machine in order
to express an authentic experience of the present.

Smith was characterized by his friend Herman Cherry as
"a sensual man with vast appetites [who] held to the rigors
of a monastic life in his work."[77] Typically Smith would work
in isolation on his farm in upstate New York for months at
a time and then, according to Robert Motherwell, he would
come down to New York City for a few days to have a
rousing good time.[78] Smith's farm gave him both the physical
and psychic space to work, but the loneliness could also

4.24 (right) **Herbert Ferber**, *The Flame*, 1949. Brass, lead,
and soft solder, 5ft 4¾in × 25½in × 19¼in (164.47 ×
64.77 × 48.9cm).
Whitney Museum of American Art, New York. Purchase, 51.30.

become overpowering. "Aloneness," he once complained, "is the condition of the artist's creative life."[79]

Smith's Initiation into the Art World

David Smith was born in 1906 in Decatur, Indiana. His father managed the local independent telephone company. The artist remembered him as a weekend inventor, and indeed Smith had the impression from childhood that everyone in town seemed to be inventing cars and other machines and devices. Smith's mother was an austere Methodist schoolteacher, obsessed with respectability and instilling discipline. In consequence Smith rebelled violently against authority all his life. His grandmother provided a refuge from home and the illustrations in the Bible that she gave him seem to have fostered his wish from an early age to be an artist.

At the age of twenty-one Smith went to New York. He studied at the Art Students League from 1927 to 1932, and on Christmas Eve of that first year married Dorothy Dehner, a fellow student. Smith discovered the works of Picasso, Kandinsky, Mondrian, and the Russian constructivists in classes with Jan Matulka, who had studied with Hofmann. Although Smith was a painting student, not a sculptor, Matulka encouraged him to experiment with textures and

relief. Through friends at the League, Smith met John Graham, who in turn introduced him to a wider circle of artists, including Stuart Davis, Arshile Gorky, Willem de Kooning, and Milton Avery, and provided a conduit of information about advanced art.

It was around 1930 that Smith saw reproductions of welded sculpture by Picasso and González in issues of *Cahiers d'Art* belonging to Graham. "I learned that art was being made with steel—the material and machines that had previously meant only labor and earning power,"[80] he recalled. It was the sculpture of Julio González that inspired Smith to buy welding equipment in 1932. But working in a Brooklyn apartment, he kept setting fire to the curtains and to drawings on the walls. Then one day by the docks he ran across a run-down structure called the Terminal Iron Works, inhabited by two Irish blacksmiths. Smith arranged to rent space from them and made his first series of welded heads there in 1933. He felt so much at home in this environment that he continued to call his studio the Terminal Iron Works even after he abandoned the docks and moved permanently up to his farm at Bolton Landing.

Like so many of his contemporaries in New York, Smith struggled to assimilate the formal languages of cubism and, beginning in 1937, biomorphic surrealism. In *Construction on a Fulcrum* [fig. 4.25] the flat abstract shapes and the manner in which the composition maintains reference to a picture plane—with a fixed viewing position and a deliberate ambiguity between two- and three-dimensional space—come directly from cubist constructions of 1912–14. *Construction on a Fulcrum* teases the viewer by making the sphere at the apex appear flat in the context of the planar

4.25 David Smith, *Construction on a Fulcrum*, 1936. Steel, 14 × 17in (35.6 × 43.2cm). Collection, Willard Gallery, New York.

and linear elements—and Smith's sculpture rarely lost this connection to the picture plane.

The Museum of Modern Art's stunning "Fantastic Art, Dada, and Surrealism" exhibition of December 1936 and January 1937 turned the heads of nearly everyone in the New York art world. In addition, many of the artists with whom Smith associated in the late thirties—not least Pollock, whom he met in 1937—were increasingly involved in psychological introspection and issues of presence and self-discovery. The death of Smith's father in August 1939 may also have heightened the emergence of more inwardly reflective content in his work. Early in 1938 Marian Willard gave Smith his first one-person show at her East River Gallery. This provides a rough benchmark after which Smith entered nearly six years of preoccupation with ideas inspired by the surrealists and the surrealist-influenced work of Picasso [fig. 5.17], González, Giacometti, and Miró, who were all represented in that show at the Museum of Modern Art.

The Aesthetic of Machines and the Unconscious

At the end of the thirties Smith began to integrate real tools—pliers, wrenches, washers—into his abstract sculptures. The tools had an evocative significance as emblems of the industrial world. Yet their presence only exacerbated the critics' hostility toward welding as a new fine art technique. The critic for *Cue* snidely referred to Smith's 1940 show as

4.26 David Smith,
Helmholtzian Landscape, 1946.
Steel, painted blue, red, yellow, and green, 15⅞ × 17⅝ × 7⅛in
(40.3 × 44.8 × 18cm).
Kreeger Museum, Washington, D.C.

"Sewer Pipe Sculpture,"[81] while a writer for *Time* described it as "plumbing that has survived a conflagration" in an article entitled "Screw Ball Art."[82]

In the early forties Smith experimented with metamorphic abstraction, indebted to Picasso's and Miró's figures of 1927–33 [fig. 5.17]. Like them, Smith preserved a clear connection to sources in the external world. Yet he used the unconscious as a tool to transform the subject, and the impact of surrealist dream imagery is evident. Smith referred to Freud as "the greatest single influence on the theoretical side of art, providing an analytical system for establishing the reality of the unconscious . . . from which the artist derives his inspiration."[83] What seemed important was the subject matter of the unconscious, which Smith recognized as part of the identity of the artist.

In the spring of 1940 the Smiths moved permanently to the farm in Bolton Landing, despite its rudimentary amenities. Anxious about being drafted, Smith took a deferrable job in 1942 on the all-night shift at the American Locomotive Company in Schenectady, where he built locomotives and M-7 tanks. This not only isolated him from the New York scene, he also had almost no time for sculpture. Metal was hard to find anyway, but he continued to draw. In 1944 he found he was medically unfit for service and he immediately quit the factory.

Marian Willard gave Smith regular shows in the forties and his reputation grew, although he sold very little. In a 1943 review for the *Nation*, Clement Greenberg wrote that Smith would become one of America's greatest artists if he kept up the pace of his development.[84] In 1945 Smith moved away from surrealism toward an almost pictorial naturalism with flat forms in a shallow cubist space, inspired by Picasso's sculpture of the late twenties.

Smith titled *Helmholtzian Landscape* [fig. 4.26] for the nineteenth-century German scientist who wrote a pioneering treatise on the physiology of perception. In this work Smith set a string of freely defined abstract forms in a frame, separating them into an illusionistic pictorial space apart from the real space around them. At the same time he defined the border in flat planes and organic contours that give the impression of a drawing on a two-dimensional surface. This also connects the frame visually to the imaginary world it surrounds. He further heightened the richness of the reality within the frame by painting the steel free-forms in bright colors.

In *Helmholtzian Landscape* Smith created a deliberate sequence of visual puns: three-dimensional forms in real space create an illusion of flat forms in a pictorial space; the illusion of a pictorial space in turn refers to a picture, which attempts to create the opposite illusion of real space on a two-dimensional canvas. Even the mechanism which separates the worlds of real and depicted space—the frame— is itself ambivalently defined as both a real object (the frame) and part of the imaginary landscape (as a drawing). The complexity of the perceptual ambiguities are what make this a proper homage to Helmholtz.

4.27 David Smith in his Bolton Landing studio with *Detroit Queen*, c. 1962.

Photographer unknown.

In 1946 and 1947 Smith sold a few sculptures, and in September 1948 he began his first teaching job at Sarah Lawrence College, then an exclusive women's school in New York City. He taught there for two years while also struggling to finish building his house at Bolton Landing. This left little time for sculpture, and he produced only three works in 1948 and seven in 1949. Then two sequential Guggenheim awards in 1950 and 1951 enabled him to work in the studio full time again and to buy the materials he needed [fig. 4.27].

The Pictograms and *Hudson River Landscape*

Smith turned almost exclusively to welding after 1950 and he increased the scale of his work dramatically. His work of 1950 and 1951 is dominated by several large pieces that look like "drawings" in steel lines. *Hudson River Landscape* [fig. 4.28], measuring over 6 feet across, captures the feeling of a rolling northeastern landscape. It is flat, narrative, and has a weightless lack of sculptural volume; instead it evokes a pictorial illusion in a shallow cubist space. Seen from the side, *Hudson River Landscape* disappears. Smith conceived the piece with a single viewing position in mind and little actual depth. He persistently played with the idea of three-dimensional forms that demanded to be read in two-dimensional (or "pictorial") terms, thus emphasizing "seeing" over engaging the sculpture physically, either by touching or walking around or into it. This trait characterizes a majority of Smith's works right to the end of his career.

To the extent that *Hudson River Landscape* looks like the contours of a Stuart Davis painting [fig. 3.12], it also reflects Smith's persevering connection to cubism. But instead of changing the picture plane into sculptured relief, he inverted the equation and changed the real volume of sculpture into a picture space. By this time Smith knew that precisely this fusion of "American machine techniques [his preoccupation with tools and welding] and European cubist tradition" was not only "accountable for the new freedom in sculpture making," as he put it, but that it constituted the stylistic core of his identity as an artist. "I am talking about direct metal constructions," he went on; "the new method is assemble the whole by adding its unit parts . . . an industrial concept, the basis of automobile and machine assembly."[85]

Looking out of the train window, Smith made hundreds of drawings of the Hudson Valley while commuting between Bolton Landing and Sarah Lawrence College in 1948 and 1949; *Hudson River Landscape* synthesizes the feeling of that picturesque journey. The vastness and romance of the American landscape, and in particular *this* landscape with its obvious association to the nineteenth-century painters of the Hudson River School, are themes that show Smith to have been part of a classic American tradition. The "sublime"— as evoked in the breathtaking visions of the Hudson River School and earnestly debated by Newman, Rothko, and Gottlieb a hundred years later—was indeed an underlying theme in this sculpture by Smith. As an expression of his willingness to take on the big themes, it is also a measure of his artistic self-confidence by 1951.

Around 1950 Smith had begun to look for timeless, grander themes. Gottlieb got him interested in pictograms, with which Smith experimented in various works of 1950 and 1951. Smith's interest in the origins of language and by 1952 in totems came out of the search for a universal content. The notion of pure visibility and of communication through visual forms that precede language may have been connected

4.28 David Smith, *Hudson River Landscape*, 1951. Welded steel, 49½ × 75 × 16¾in (125.7 × 190.5 × 42.5cm). Whitney Museum of American Art, New York. Purchase, 54.14.

4.29 David Smith, *Tanktotem I*, 1952. Steel, 89¾ × 39 × 16½in (228 × 99 × 41.9cm).

Art Institute of Chicago. Gift of Jay and Muriel Kallis Steinberg in memory of her father, Maurice Kallis, 1953.193.

to the transition in Smith's sculpture from the pictographic letters in sculptures of 1950 and 1951, through the pictorialism of *Hudson River Landscape*, to the more direct totemic figures of 1952 like the sculptures of the "Agricola" and "Tanktotem" series [fig. 4.29].

An Existential Encounter with the Materials at Hand

In the works of 1952 Smith became preoccupied with totemic figures—an interest to which Pollock had then also returned. In realizing these works, Smith employed more found objects and made few preparatory drawings. These sculptures involved an increase in improvisation with the materials at hand, because they evolved through free

association. Here Smith attempted a kind of sculptural collage in found machine parts and industrial materials that is indebted to the formal traditions of cubist collage and construction.

In these compositions Smith achieved a total harmony of personal identity and style. Each piece centers on an exploration of the artist's identity, as in the contemporary works of de Kooning, Pollock, or Rothko. "My problem is to be able to look every day and to press my limitations beyond their endurance," he told Katherine Kuh in 1960. "What are these limitations?" she asked. "They're me."[85]

The "Tanktotem" and "Agricola" pieces are the first of the more than fifteen different numbered series in which Smith began to work in 1952; nearly all of his sculptures from this point onward have series titles. For Smith a series was not a progressive or systematic exploration of a single theme, but rather a single mood. He nearly always worked on pieces in several series at one time and most often the collective titles relate to the materials: in the "Tanktotem" pieces he used steel tank heads, which he ordered from a standard catalog; "Agricola," which is Latin for "farmer," designates a group of works built with fragments of farm implements; the "Albanys" incorporate heavy steel plate purchased from the Albany Steel and Iron Supply.

Career Success and Personal Sacrifices

Smith completed 250 sculptures between 1950 and 1960, two-and-a-half times the number he made over the preceding decade. He drove himself as if he had to live up to Greenberg's prediction of 1943, that he would be the greatest sculptor in the United States. But the personal sacrifices were great. His ambition had made him increasingly difficult to live with, his uncontrollable temper had gotten worse, and he had been having an affair with a student from Sarah Lawrence when Dorothy left him on Thanksgiving Day of 1950.

Jean Freas, the woman Smith had begun to see at Sarah Lawrence in 1949, was twenty when they met, Smith was forty-three. They married on April 6, 1953 and had two daughters (in 1954 and 1955); in 1958 this marriage too came apart. By this time the momentum of Smith's work and career had accelerated, despite his reputation for being difficult to deal with. In 1957 the Museum of Modern Art gave him a one-person show of thirty-four sculptures, and by the end of the year his income had quadrupled.

The Figural Presence and the Work of the Last Decade

In 1954, while Smith was a visiting professor at the University of Indiana in Bloomington, he found an iron works called Seward and Company where they let him work on a power forge. The "Forgings," made at this foundry in early 1955, are all anthropomorphic with a wispy verticality reminiscent of the attenuated figures of Giacometti [figs. 5.12–5.14].[87]

4.30 David Smith, *Construction with Forged Neck*, 1955. Steel, 76¼ × 13 × 8⅝in (193.7 × 33 × 21.9cm).

Collection, Estate of David Smith. Photograph courtesy M. Knoedler & Co., New York.

Some of the "Forgings" have a totemic presence—they are "the savage idols of basic patterns,"[88] to use Smith's own words—and they follow from works like the "Tanktotems." Others seem more explicitly lifelike. *Construction with Forged Neck* [fig. 4.30], for example, has the appealing awkwardness of a young girl, perhaps a dancer. After Smith's death in 1965 the executors of his estate found and allegedly destroyed a stack of nude photographs he had taken of girls, probably from nearby Bennington College. Smith's executors leapt to the conclusion that he had taken the pictures for entertainment, but one wonders whether he might instead have been using the photographs as a source for these figurative sculptures of the fifties and sixties.[89] The latter conclusion is also suggested by Smith's *Running Daughter*, a figural piece from the later fifties, for which the source is well known to have been a photograph of his three- or four-year-old daughter.

Construction with Forged Neck is built humorously around the large orifice at the midsection. With its long skinny leg, tall neck, and tiny head, it seems to stand there in self-consciousness embarrassment. The subject of this work appears to be its youthful sensuality. Smith's remark that he did "girl sculptures"[90] and his involvement with the Bennington girls in the fifties and sixties seem pertinent to the character of such works.

The relation of Smith's sculpture to his life is part of what gives his work after 1951 such total conviction. "Art before my time," he remarked, ". . . is history explaining past behavior, but not necessarily offering solutions to my problems. Art is not divorced from life. It is dialectic."[91] This sense of continuity between art and life is reflected formally in Smith's increasing effort to eliminate the base from his sculpture or to incorporate it into the composition, as well as fusing "real" tools into the works. In several of the "Tanktotems" Smith set the figures directly on the ground. By placing the piece in the viewer's real space instead of visually creating a space apart by using a base (which serves like a frame in painting), the artist attacked the separation between art and viewer.

Smith started the "Cubi" series in 1961 [figs. 4.32 and 4.34], and despite their geometry many of them also retain a figurative character. He made this series in stainless steel partly to avoid the need to paint and laboriously maintain outdoor work that was otherwise prone to rust. Nevertheless, Smith also painted some sculptures to keep them from rusting, and to some extent the burnishing of the stainless steel in the "Cubis" gave them a brushed-on look which, like painting the pieces, pictorialized them. Although Smith could weld stainless steel, he did not have the equipment to cut it; consequently he had to order the volumes prefabricated and since irregular shapes were not readily available from the commercial suppliers Smith's stainless steel sculptures tend to be geometric.

As early as 1946 Smith had been purchasing leftover scraps from steel-fabricating plants so that he could have stockpiles of random forms on hand to work with. Although

Smith's work got larger after 1950, he still did not construct it from sketches. Instead he developed the practice of laying pieces out on the floor or on a white table and collaging them directly. He would weld the components in place and then work on other elements of the composition after he got the structure upright. This technique further reinforced the pictorialism of his sculpture by initially developing it in one view against a two-dimensional backdrop. In 1958 and 1959 Smith also made paintings by laying out forms on the floor and spray-painting over them to produce a composition of negative forms.

In 1962 the composer Gian-Carlo Menotti asked a reluctant Smith to participate in the upcoming summer festival of the arts in Spoleto, Italy, of which Menotti was the director. Once there, he was given an abandoned steel factory in Voltri, near Genoa, with all its contents and a crew of assistants for a month. The place unexpectedly struck a deep chord of nostalgia. Smith later commented that "these factories . . . were like Sundays in Brooklyn in 1934 at the Terminal Iron Works, except that here I could use anything I found."[92] He had an incredibly productive stay, completing twenty-seven sculptures—among the greatest of his career—in one month.

Smith built *Voltri XIII* [fig. 4.31] around what he called "chopped clouds"[93]—the freeforms that are cut off the end of a sheet of steel to square it off after rolling it out. The space, the limitless material, and the numbers of workers at his disposal in Italy got Smith interested in greater size. The flatcars that trundled among the railroad tracks into the old factory complex spawned the idea for the large

pieces on wheels; they must have evoked memories of the train engines that fascinated Smith in his youth. In addition, Smith had probably seen the figures on wheels by Giacometti in the Museum of Modern Art or the Pierre Matisse Gallery. Smith was so moved by the Voltri experience that he had a large quantity of the materials from the factory shipped home and he constructed the "Voltri-Bolton" or "Volton" compositions at Bolton Landing using materials from the factory in Italy.

Smith created all but one of the twenty-eight works in the "Cubi" series—the most celebrated series of his career—during the last three years of his life. By and large the "Cubis," like much of Smith's work, imply one viewing position. *Cubi XVII* [fig. 4.32], for example, loses its dynamism when seen from the side. The "Cubis" also toy with the viewer's perception by creating ambiguities that encourage a reading of the actual volumes as two-dimensional depictions. The highly reflective surface exaggerates the contrast between the lighted areas and those in shadow, creating the effect of a two-dimensional rendering of volumes with black shading rather than one involving real objects in space. In addition, the shimmering light pattern calls attention to the surface, flattening out the forms still more.

Smith liked the way in which stainless steel was able to reflect the light and atmosphere of the surroundings. But the hand-worked quality of the surface also attracted him and relates to the brushwork that can be seen in the painted sculpture of the period, such as *Zig VIII* [fig. 4.33]. Meanwhile, the rough finish of the welds in the "Cubis" conveys a sense of forms coming together quickly, as if with

4.31 David Smith, *Voltri XIII*, 1962. Steel, 64⅛ × 103¾ × 26in (162.9 × 236.5 × 66cm).
University Art Museum, University of California at Berkeley. Gift of Mr. and Mrs. Eugene E. Trefethen, Jr.

the spontaneity of action painting. However, the necessity for prefabricating the stainless steel components made improvisation more difficult; he was forced to plan them at least in so far as he had to order parts. So, in addition to the spray paintings, Smith devised the procedure of using empty liquor boxes to make three-dimensional studies for the "Cubis" and he also kept a stock of forty to fifty prefabricated cubes on hand to allow for spontaneous modifications.

Smith wrote an intriguing note in a sketchbook of 1952 about "reducing the human form to cubes—exploited by Cambiaso,"[94] referring to Luca Cambiaso, a sixteenth-century Italian mannerist, who made drawings of figures segmented into geometric volumes. Indeed many of the works in the "Cubi" series evoke figural associations. Even the horizontal *Cubi XXIII* [fig. 4.34], for example, seems to portray the same

4.32 (below left) **David Smith**, *Cubi XVII*, 1963. Polished stainless steel, 107¾ × 64⅜ × 38⅛in (273.7 × 163.5 × 96.8cm). Dallas Museum of Art. The Eugene and Margaret McDermott Fund.

4.33 (below right) **David Smith**, *Zig VIII*, 1964. Steel, painted red, white, and black, 8ft 4¾in × 7ft 7½in × 6ft 11in (2.55 × 2.32 × 2.1m). Museum of Fine Arts, Boston. Centennial Purchase Fund, 68.279.

classical subject as Henry Moore's *Reclining Figure* [fig. 4.35]. Yet, in others, if the figure provided the initial gesture from which Smith's process of formal association began, he left it buried beyond recognition under the final form.

In the last fifteen years of his life David Smith successfully transformed the automatist principle of the New York School painters into a major body of sculpture that has the immediacy of a series of charcoal sketches. The idea was antithetical to the traditional techniques of sculpture. Moreover, Smith's materials and technique were novel in that they came from the world of labor and industry; in this way he integrated his real experience of the world with the fundamental nature of his psyche. He believed that "from the artist's point of view he deals with truths, statements of reality,"[95] and also felt that "since impressionism the realities from which art has come have all been the properties of ordinary men."[96]

Nevertheless, "art is poetic," Smith insisted. "It is poetically irrational. The irrational is the major force in man's nature. And as such the artist still deals with nature."[97] Within the terms of the artistic metaphor, each new

sculptural synthesis—if only by virtue of its own entrance into the totality of experience—changes the world and is in turn outdated by events as soon as it comes into being. Thus in making sculpture an embodiment of identity, Smith kept his work and his sense of self poised on the edge of the unknown.

4.34 David Smith, *Cubi XXIII*, 1964. Stainless steel, 6ft 4¼in × 14ft 4⅞in (1.94 × 4.39m).
Los Angeles County Museum of Art. Modern and Contemporary Art Council Fund.

4.35 Henry Moore, *Reclining Figure*, 1935–6. Elmwood, 19 × 36¾ × 17½in (48.3 × 93.4 × 44.5cm).
Albright-Knox Art Gallery, Buffalo, New York. Room of Contemporary Art Fund, 1939.

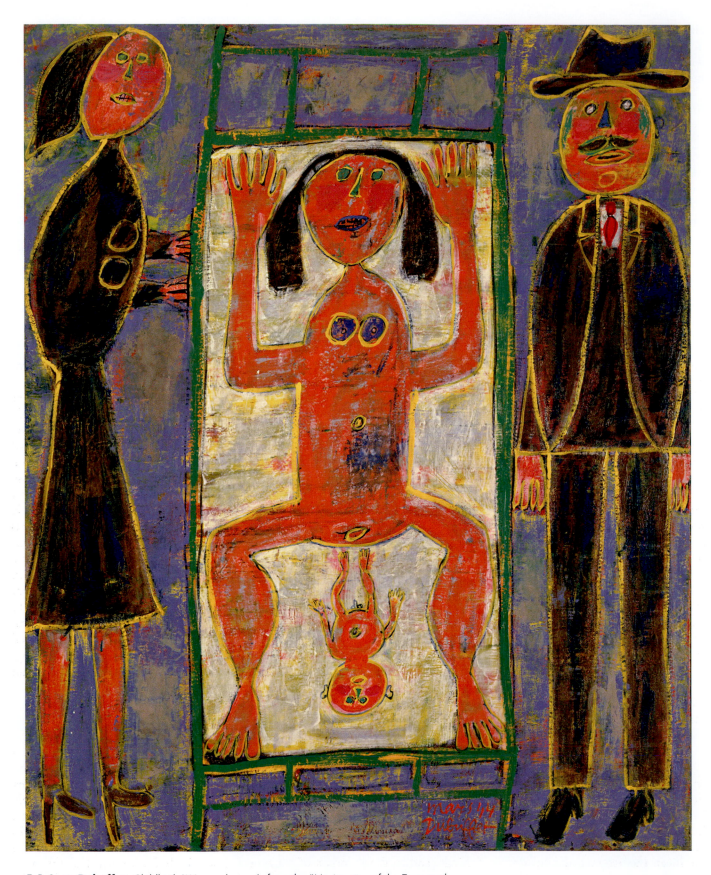

5.1 Jean Dubuffet, *Childbirth* (*L'Accouchement*), from the "Marionettes of the Town and the Country" series, 1944. Oil on canvas, 39⅜ × 31¾in (99.8 × 80.8cm).

The Museum of Modern Art, New York. Gift of Pierre Matisse in memory of Patricia Kane Matisse, 101.1982.

5 THE NEW EUROPEAN MASTERS OF THE LATE FORTIES

JEAN DUBUFFET AND POSTWAR PARIS

Although the surviving masters of prewar modernism—in particular Picasso, Matisse, Léger, Ernst, and Miró—continued to generate important new work after 1945, an entirely different set of issues informed and motivated the generation that emerged in Europe after the war. Meanwhile, the Depression and the war had also undermined the ideological credibility of abstraction. Painters such as Mondrian and Kandinsky had seen abstract art as a vehicle for bringing about a new spiritual awakening in society at large. But by the end of World War II this social metaphysics no longer seemed believable.

Surrealist automatism, which was essentially amoral, still provided a vital creating tool, yet after 1945 only Matta managed to produce a major new body of surrealist work [fig. 2.3]. Postwar artists felt they had to construct an authentic new foundation for art in response to the pressing social and ethical issues which had come to the fore in the thirties and early forties. Surrealism, with its exploration of the unconscious mind, indicated a possible route, but it was existentialism that provided the ideological context for a more emotionally immediate approach.

The pessimism of European intellectual life after World War I had deepened into despair during the thirties, and postwar existentialism grew out of that despair. If the existence of God still seemed credible at all, it had to be a harsh, incomprehensible God in a reasonless universe. By reasserting subjective individualism, existentialism responded to the moral failure of the Hegelian emphasis on the ideal, the abstract, the "essence" of things, and to the depersonalization of modern life. However, tortured by doubt, the individual could at least experience his or her own existence with integrity. "Read only your own life,"

Nietzsche had advised, "and from this understand the hieroglyphs of universal life."[1]

Jean-Paul Sartre, an atheist and the oracle of postwar existentialism, believed that the world was irreducibly irrational. He nevertheless imposed a moral imperative, a sober sense of "good faith" in facing the "truth" of one's condition. This underlies both the art of the New York School and the innovative new figurative art that arose in Europe at the end of World War II. In Europe Jean Dubuffet, Alberto Giacometti, and Francis Bacon (like de Kooning, Pollock, Rothko, and Newman in New York) returned to first principles and reinvented art for themselves. They were driven by a need to explore questions about the meaning of their own lives, and they directed their attention to immediate experience as the only knowable truth from which to proceed. Dubuffet in particular looked back to the French writer Georges Bataille, who coined the term "*l'informe*" in 1929 to imply an aesthetic that he hoped would undermine all definitions, all hierarchies in thinking, to "un-form all categories because he found them false to an underlying formlessness in all matter."[2]

Dubuffet's Painting of the Forties

Jean Dubuffet decided to leave his wine business and start painting in 1942, during perhaps the grimmest period of Hitler's occupation of Paris. At first glance his art [figs. 5.1–5.4] seems entirely detached from such worldly events. He depicted the most ordinary views of daily life in an ungainly style that was influenced directly by graffiti and the art of children. But deeply affected by the moral crises of wartime Europe, Dubuffet returned to the rudimentary origins of art at that point in history when the logic of civilized values had been twisted into a horrific conclusion.

The outlines of the figures in *Childbirth* [fig. 5.1] appear to have been scratched into the surface, like graffiti. Slogans and caricatures on walls are a time-honored vehicle of anonymous dissent and Dubuffet intended this allusion. His crude and impulsive style invokes the aesthetic of the uncultivated common man and prefigures the shift in art after 1960 from a romantic emphasis on the exceptional to ordinary life and popular culture. In 1946 Dubuffet remarked: "It is the man in the street that I'm after, whom I feel closest to, with whom I want to make friends and enter into confidence and connivance, and *he* is the one I want to please and enchant by means of my work."[3]

Childbirth also lacks perspective; the artist stacked up the bed and the stiff figures parallel to the picture plane and crudely rendered them in the manner of a child. Dubuffet deliberately constructed a style that was primitive by conventional standards of beauty. Like Barnett Newman, he rejected what he regarded as a Greek canon of beauty in order to elude the prejudices of culture; he wanted to make a fresh, unconventional exploration of such grand philosophical themes as the origins of thought and the fleeting existence of the individual.

"The values celebrated by our culture do not strike me as corresponding to the true dynamics of our mind,"[4] he explained.

> What to me seems interesting is to recover in the representation of an object the whole complex set of impressions we receive as we see it normally in everyday life, the manner in which it has touched our sensibility, and the forms it assumes in our memory . . . my persistent curiosity about children's drawings, and those of anyone who has never learned to draw, is due to my hope of finding . . . the affective reactions that link each individual to the things that surround him and happen to catch his eye.[5]

Dubuffet had a complex metaphysics. In his scheme the emotional connection between the individual and the objects around him provided a central clue to the underlying continuity of all things. Although rooted in the ideas of romanticism, Nietzsche, and Freud, Dubuffet went beyond them in speaking of man's primal unity with nature and opened a different perspective on his conflict with the strictures of civilization. For Dubuffet, everything around the object became part of its definition, and as a result the definition remained in a state of constant flux. In *Childbirth*, for example, there is a sameness in the general manner of rendering each person or thing that suggests a kind of slippage in which one form could begin to look more and more like another, perhaps to become something else or even dissolve completely. The implicit threat of disintegration into the environment and ultimately into a universe of undifferentiated matter is a pervasive theme in his art and thought.

Dubuffet studied the mental state in which one perceives an object before consciously focusing on it. In assimilating the object, the mind brings forth clusters of feelings and associations, transforming the perception in terms of the mind's own unconscious purposes. In attempting to "transcribe all the processes and mechanisms resulting from the sight (or evocation in the mind) of a certain object,"[6] Dubuffet looked to the art of children and others, whose rendering of experience is less dominated by cultural norms; there the raw evidence of these processes is more visible.

The primitive life of the mind is one of Dubuffet's central subjects. His sophisticated analysis made manifest the erudition of a well-read intellectual, but he systematically shed all traces of this in his artistic style. Instead he sought the revelation of the raw, psychic content of the most ordinary experience, which can "transform our daily life into a marvelous feast . . . I am speaking of celebrations of the mind . . . Art addresses itself to the mind, not the eyes."[7]

In the background of Dubuffet's assertion is an echo of Marcel Duchamp's aspiration to put "painting once again at the service of the mind"[8] and Breton's admonition that "painting . . . should not have for its end the pleasure of the eyes . . . a picture or sculpture is justifiable only insofar as it is capable of advancing our abstract knowledge."[9] Yet Dubuffet concerned himself with the physicality of painting more than either Duchamp or Breton did. He regarded art as "a language, an instrument of cognition and communication,"[10] but he believed that the material itself held an expressive power and constituted, by virtue of its materiality, a closer, more direct and precise language than words. "Art makes no sense if it is not a means of seeing and knowing through which man forces himself to perceive reality."[11] But: "I see no great difference (metaphysically, that is) between the paste I spread and a cat, a trout or a bull. My paste is a being as these are. Less circumscribed, to be sure, and more emulsified . . . foreign to us humans, who are so very circumscribed, so far from the formless (or, at least, think ourselves to be)."[12]

Dubuffet's working method resembled surrealist automatism. In the process of painting he recounted that "a larger part is given to facts that unroll themselves inside the mind of the painter as he works."[13] Margit Rowell, who was curator of an important Dubuffet show in 1973, pointed out that although Dubuffet never aligned himself with the surrealists, they "similarly considered categorical thought an impoverished aspect of the true workings of the mind," and she cited the "Second Surrealist Manifesto" of 1929 in which Breton declared: "There is every reason to believe that there exists a point in the mind where life and death, the real and the imaginary, the past and the future, the communicable and the non-communicable, the above and the below, cease to be perceived as contradictions."[14]

Jean Dubuffet was born in Le Havre on the north coast of France in 1901. After graduating from the *lycée* in 1918 he studied painting to some extent, but he felt ill at ease in his studies and he associated mostly with writers. However, toward the end of the forties the critic Michel Tapié began to associate Dubuffet and Fautrier with such artists as Wols [fig. 6.1] under the rubric of *informel*. An

5.2 Jean Fautrier, *Nude*, 1943. Oil on paper, 21½ × 15in (54.6 × 38.1cm).
Museum of Contemporary Art, Los Angeles. The Panza Collection.

existential alternative to both realism and geometric abstraction, *informel* was based on a principle of free expressive gesture.[15] Although derived from Bataille's concept of *l'informe* (meaning "anti-form"), *informel* was nevertheless assertive of identity in a way that Dubuffet and Fautrier abhorred, and they both dissociated themselves from *informel* at this time. Jean Fautrier's *Nude* [fig. 5.2] typifies the heavy, almost sculptured surfaces of their canvases. The densely modeled paint used to depict a representational subject had to do with the existentialists' shift of emphasis onto the individual's subjective experience of external reality. Fautrier's painting conveys the sensual, uncultivated, emotional content of the experience rather than a detached visual report on the subject.

Dubuffet's Philosophical Premises

Dubuffet had his first one-person show in October 1944, just a little more than a month after the Liberation of Paris. Those early compositions of 1942–4 have the dark outlines, crude brushwork, and flat, unmodeled color areas of child art. Soon the artist also began mixing the pigment with a variety of unconventional materials to create a dense, mortar-like paste. The technique, the style, and the raw sexuality of the imagery shocked the French public, and at Dubuffet's second show, in 1946, outraged viewers even slashed some of the paintings.

Although the work had an iconoclastic intent, it also had profoundly philosophical origins. As in child art and most tribal art, Dubuffet treated the subjects as a matter of subjective rather than psychological fact. A "psychological" portrayal would imply the distance of a detached observer. Instead, Dubuffet sought direct extensions of the observing mind itself. The artist's remarks about his *Large Sooty Nude* of 1944 [fig. 5.3] are telling:

5.3 Jean Dubuffet, *Large Sooty Nude*, August 1944.
Oil on canvas, 63¾ × 38¼in (162 × 97.2cm).
Private collection, New York. Courtesy PaceWildenstein Gallery, New York.

5.4 Jean Dubuffet, *Landscape with Drunkards*, 1949. Oil, sand, and granular filler on canvas, 35 × 45¾in (88.9 × 116.2cm). Menil Collection, Houston.

I've recently been scrutinizing anthracite. Thinking about anthracite—ecstatically. I almost felt as if I'd changed into anthracite. But as I was painting the ravishing body of a naked woman, my obsession made me paint her in the color and nature of anthracite . . . Was this valid for no reason? There is a continuity from any object to any other object . . . And would you have found it more logical of me, with my obsessive passion for anthracite, to paint an object, any object, in exactly the same mood and with exactly the same hand as someone who had never seen anthracite or who at the moment was obsessed with, say, an egg yolk, or bread, or sand?[16]

Instead of seeing the material as something neutral and inert, Dubuffet regarded it as a reality with which he collaborated. In his mind the preoccupation with the coal dust became inextricably merged with the reality of the nude.

In 1945 Dubuffet began collecting what he called *art brut*, or "raw art." This consisted of art made by untrained individuals, including psychotics, amateurs, and children, who were thus largely uninfluenced by cultural conventions of making art. The savage purity of *art brut* confirmed Dubuffet's repudiation of cultural values after the war. He was drawn to the authenticity with which *art brut* communicated the creative mental processes involved in forming a cohesive picture of an individual's reality. "Those who are predisposed toward physiological explanations," Hans Prinzhorn had written in his famous book on the *Artistry of the Mentally Ill*, "always start with the fallacy (one which is hard to overcome) that all well meaning people could agree on one conception of reality, as we might agree on the results of research."[17] But each being has its own version of reality according to Prinzhorn and Dubuffet, who had discovered the former's book in 1923.

Dubuffet painted several compositionally packed, graffiti-like landscapes in 1949. They tend to have a bird's-eye view of the ground while showing figures and buildings in profile, as in his *Landscape with Drunkards* [fig. 5.4]. Dubuffet dug the forms into the thick paste with the back of a brush or some other pointed object. The stony, monochrome surface recalls Brassaï's photographs of graffiti, which Dubuffet had known since the thirties. The two main figures seem to perch on the road, completely out of scale to other elements in the picture. In addition, the artist has drawn everything with the stiff, schematic quality of a six-year-old. Even the way in which he had conceived each form in isolation characterizes the art of young children.

A Focus on Matter in the Fifties

In the paintings of 1950 Dubuffet began expanding the figure—and later tables, stones, and beards—to fill the whole composition. *Le Metafisyx* [fig. 5.5] belongs to a series of magnificent, monumental nudes painted in 1950 and 1951; its vulgar sexuality and the masklike grimace on the face are characteristic. In such works the definition of the figure became marginal as its internal texture was pushed out toward the edges of the canvas. These compositions, Dubuffet explained, are no longer—or almost no longer—descriptive of external sites, but rather . . . the immaterial world which dwells in the mind of man: disorder of images, of beginnings of images, of fading images, where they cross and mingle, in a turmoil, tatters borrowed from memories of the outside world, and facts purely cerebral and internal—visceral perhaps. The transfer of these mental sites on the same plane as that of the real concrete landscapes, and in such a way that an uncomfortable incongruity is the result . . . the discovery that they are perhaps not so foreign [to one another] as one had believed, attracts me very strongly.[18]

In *Le Metafisyx* the unusual texture takes on a life of its own, freely setting off in directions independent of the explicit subject matter. The artist later used unexpected materials, like butterfly wings [fig. 5.6] or leaves, for the same liberating effect. In *Le Metafisyx* Dubuffet encountered the chaos of the unconscious mind in the disorder and detail of a concentrated focus on texture.

In 1951 Dubuffet began literally to cut up canvases and reassemble them on a new surface. He also drew figures on paper or newspaper and then cut them out for collage. Over a decade he assembled images out of a whole range

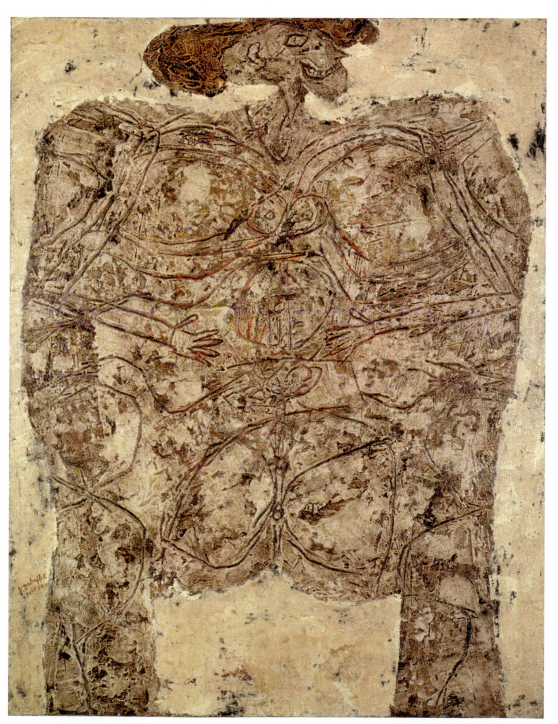

5.5 Jean Dubuffet,
Le Metafisyx, August 1950.
Oil on canvas, 45⅝ ×
35¼in (116 × 89.5cm).
Musée National d'Art Moderne,
Centre Georges Pompidou, Paris.

of "inartistic," or at least unconventional, materials, from driftwood to sponge. Dubuffet deliberately made use of novel techniques and materials to create perceptual obstacles to the recognition of subject matter; thus when the figure appears it has the surprising freshness of revelation, as in *The Squinter* [fig. 5.6]. Yet despite the newness of the material, the conception of the form and subject remain consistent with his other work.

A pervasive theme of figures emerging from and dissolving back into amorphous fields of texture embodies an existential sense of the absurdity of the individual's efforts to establish and assert an identity; it also expresses the hopeless resistance against an inevitable reabsorption into the nonbeing of universal time and matter. The recognition that, with only slight alterations in handling or context, a form in painting can represent a variety of objectively dissimilar things implied to Dubuffet that at some level—revealed to him only in painting—*all* things are reducible to a common denominator.

The most varied things are taken into my net ... But very often—and it is then that the game takes on its full significance—the facts are more ambiguous, susceptible to

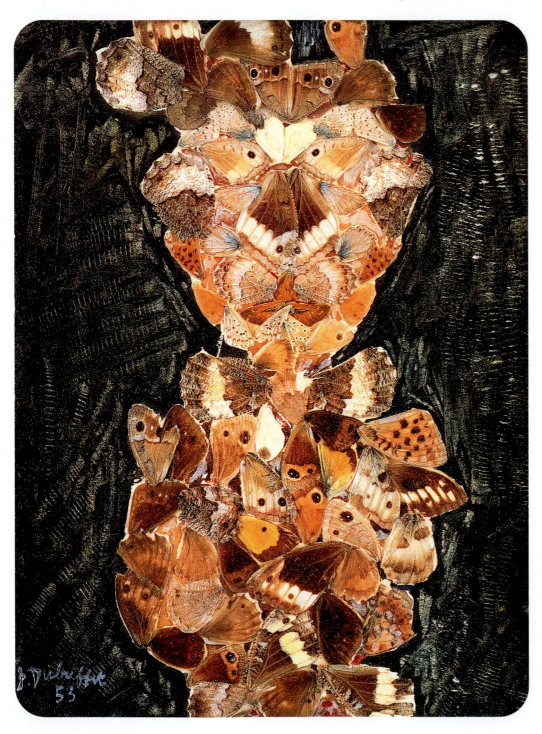

5.6 Jean Dubuffet,
The Squinter, October 1953.
Butterfly wing collage, 9¾ × 7in
(24.8 × 17.8cm).
Private collection. Courtesy
PaceWildenstein Gallery, New York.

5.7 Jean Dubuffet, *Place for Awakenings* (*Site aux éveils*), from the "Matériologies" series, 1960. Pebbles, sand, and plastic paste on composition board, 34⅞ × 45⅜in (88.6 × 115.2cm).
The Museum of Modern Art, New York. Gift of the artist in honor of Mr. and Mrs. Ralph F. Colin.

belonging to any one of these different registers, explicitly demonstrating, in a very troubling manner, what these registers have in common, how accidental their specificity, how fragile and ready to change. Such an image seems equally eager to transcribe a ravine or a complex, tormenting sky, or a storm, or the reverie of someone contemplating it . . . a thing with a strongly marked physical character . . . and . . . the course of a dream, or an emotion.[19]

In this existentialist aesthetic what matters most is the artist's conscious and explicit struggle to realize his condition. Sartre believed that the individual attained freedom from convention, became a law unto himself, in confronting death. In Dubuffet's art the implied evanescence of the individual in the perpetual metamorphosis and ambiguity of all things evokes precisely this confrontation.

Place for Awakenings [fig. 5.7] belongs to a series of paintings done around 1960 in which the explicit subject became the amorphous field itself. It is not an abstract picture in the usual sense but a perpendicular view of a small segment of ground. As such, it celebrates the most prosaic of all things in an attempt to bring what we most take for granted into conscious focus. But on another level this series evokes, more poignantly than anything else in Dubuffet's *oeuvre*, the artist's morbid preoccupation with the idea that man and his perceptual world both emanate from and will momentarily be reabsorbed into the infinite chaos of undifferentiated matter. As was the case with Pollock, the physicality of the material made the existential experience of the painting more real.

A new intensity of color entered Dubuffet's work in 1961 along with a shift in subject to complex urban landscapes. People sit trapped in boxlike cars and buses or line up on

5.8 Jean Dubuffet, *Business Prospers*, from the "Paris Circus" series, 1961. Oil on canvas, 5ft 5in × 7ft 2⅜in (1.65 × 2.2m). The Museum of Modern Art, New York. Mrs. Simon Guggenheim Fund, 15.1962.

crowded walks in *Business Prospers* [fig. 5.8]; in many of the canvases of this time they stand sideways and upside down in a new centrally oriented gravitational scheme. The surface patchwork of satirical shop signs, vehicles, and people conveys the vitality of Paris life. Yet at the same time the identity of each individual element dissolves into the general hum of visual activity. In the works of 1961 Dubuffet seems to transform the overabundance of stimuli into another kind of undifferentiated energy.

A Grand Style of Entropy

In July 1962, while doodling by the telephone with a ballpoint pen, Dubuffet made a pattern of interlocking forms. The quality of the ballpoint's unmodulated line eliminated all gestural individuality, and the principle of interlocking forms suggested to Dubuffet an infinitely expandable system of patterning. This became the guiding motif of the "*hourloupe*"[20] series, and he experimented with it for roughly a decade.

At this point the artist's concentration on the elemental matter of nature receded as he turned even more to the mechanisms of thought. The obsessive cellularity and repetitive patterning of works like *Erre et Aberre* [fig. 5.9] resemble traits in the art of psychotics and may have something to do with the retrieval at this time of Dubuffet's collection of *art brut* from years of storage in the United States. Stylistically these works also recast the theme of dissolution. As he explained: "This consistently uniform script indifferently applied to all things . . . will reduce them all to the lowest common denominator and restitute a continuous undifferentiated universe."[21] Dubuffet made up the term "*hourloupe*" for this new style and explained that he "invented [it] just for the sound of it. In French it calls to mind some object or personage of fairytale-like and grotesque state and at the same time also something tragically growling and menacing."[22]

In the mid-sixties Dubuffet carved out freeform, volumetric objects and covered their surfaces with the *hourloupe* script in a manner that made recognizable allusions to real objects. He designated these works "*simulacres*," because

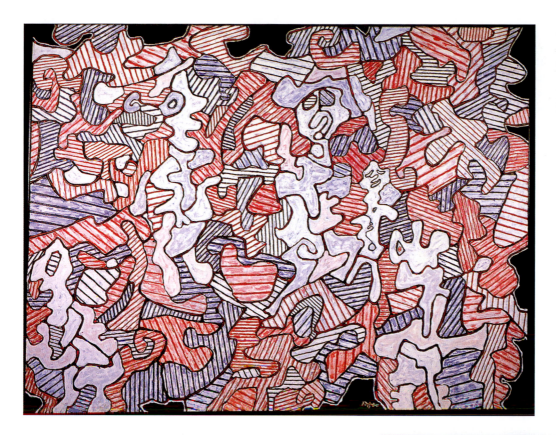

5.9 Jean Dubuffet, *Erre et Aberre*, 1963. Oil on canvas, 4ft 10⅝in × 6ft 4⅝in (1.49 × 1.95m).

Private collection. Photograph courtesy PaceWildenstein Gallery, New York.

they constituted a physical reality which signified an illusion, thus reversing the usual case in art of an illusion signifying a reality. Like doodles, they embody a mental process as a physical presence in which we then attempt to find recognizable form. In the late sixties Dubuffet enlarged this idea onto an architectural scale with the large "trees" and then expanded the *hourloupe* script into whole environments such as the *Cabinet Logo-Logique* and the *Villa Falbala*. "The effect I was after," he said, "was to achieve a feeling of *penetration* into the drawing by causing the matter to develop from a flat piece of household furniture to be looked at on the wall into *a creation of the mind fit to be physically inhabited.*"[23]

In the "Non-Lieux" paintings of 1978–85, his last series, Dubuffet eliminated the concept of a ground altogether. As their name suggests, they offer no sense of place. They extend the idea of penetration into the drawing and further "challenge the objective nature of Being";[24] this challenge had been the persevering core of Dubuffet's subject matter since the beginning of his career.

THE EXISTENTIALIST FIGURATION OF ALBERTO GIACOMETTI

Alberto Giacometti [fig. 5.10] was born in 1901 to a family of avant-garde artists. His godfather, Cuno Amiet, and his uncle, Augusto Giacometti, were important symbolist painters; his father, Giovanni Giacometti, was a well-known Swiss postimpressionist and a strong influence in the adolescent

5.10 Henri Cartier-Bresson, *Alberto Giacometti*, 1961. Black-and-white photograph.

Alberto's artistic development. At the age of seventeen, following in his father's footsteps, he attended the School of Arts and Crafts in Geneva, and at nineteen he accompanied the elder Giacometti to the Biennale in Venice where Giovanni's work was on show. In Italy Alberto studied Tintoretto, Giotto, and Cimabue with passionate dedication; the Egyptian and primitive art and the works of Cézanne in the Biennale also profoundly impressed him; then he stayed on for nine months among the art treasures of Rome. In January 1922 Giacometti enrolled for three years in the atelier of the highly acclaimed Parisian sculptor Antoine Bourdelle.

Giacometti later recalled that while studying antique sculpture in the galleries of Rome and again before the model in Bourdelle's class, "I was lost, everything escaped me, the head of the model before me became like a cloud, vague and undefined."[25] Thus in the early twenties he already seems to have experienced the existential anxiety that dominated his work after 1940. Giacometti made his first important sculptures in a simplified, cubist style reminiscent of Constantin Brancusi and Alexander Archipenko (whose work he had seen at the Biennale in 1920). He produced a few of these objects in 1926, but he created most of them in the little studio below Montparnasse that he took in 1927 with his younger brother Diego, and in which they both remained until Alberto's death in 1966.

Giacometti encountered the surrealists around 1928 and became especially close to Miró, Masson, Calder, and the painter/dealer Michel Leiris. Soon he also met Breton, Aragon, and Dalí, and began making surrealist sculpture in 1929. The cages [fig. 5.11] mostly date from the early thirties, although he came back to the idea twenty years later as a setting for some of his postwar figures. Giacometti nearly always maintained a connection to the figure in his work. Nevertheless, he saw a conflict between his experience of reality and the inherently abstract character of sculpture, which he sought to resolve in the dreamlike transformations of nature epitomized by his surrealistic experiments of the early thirties.

The Palace at 4 a.m. [fig. 5.11] crystallizes Giacometti's relationship with surrealism. This "fragile palace of match-sticks"[26]—to use the words with which he then characterized his existence—centers on an act of self-definition in the overlapping space of reality and the dream. The armature creates a stage set for a fantasy in which all living things seem to have undergone a metamorphosis into objects. He described the sculpture to Pierre Matisse as:

> a palace with a skeleton bird and a spinal column in a cage and a woman at the other end . . . It related without any doubt to a period of my life that had come to an end a year before, when for six whole months hour after hour was passed in the company of a woman who, concentrating all life in herself, magically transformed my every moment. We used to construct a fantastic palace at night . . . [In] the statue of a woman . . . I recognize my mother, just as she appears in my earliest memories. The mystery of her long black dress

5.11 Alberto Giacometti, *The Palace at 4 a.m.*, 1932–3. Construction in wood, glass, wire, and string, 25 × 28¼ × 15¾in (63.5 × 71.8 × 40cm). The Museum of Modern Art, New York. Purchase 90.1936.

troubled me; it seemed to me like a part of her body, and aroused in me a feeling of fear and confusion . . . I can't say anything about the red object in front of the board; I identify it with myself.[27]

As early as 1932 Giacometti began some nearly classical figure studies, which suggest that he probably started working from life again. He began to find ordinary reality more fertile for his imagination than dreams, and this precipitated a rift with the surrealists, who officially expelled him from the movement in 1935 when he began working from the model every day. Nevertheless, five years of consistent work from life failed to yield any finished sculpture, because he was never satisfied with his ability to portray what he saw in front of him. So from 1940 to 1945 he retreated to working from memory again.

In 1942 Giacometti went for a brief trip to Switzerland but was refused reentry into France and had to remain in Geneva until the end of the war. He finished almost nothing there either. *Woman with Chariot I*, one of the few sculptures from the period, adumbrates his later work in its narrow frozen posture and heavily worked surface. It also has wheels on a blocklike base, which the art historian Reinhold Hohl has suggested have to do with the idea of moving the object further from or closer to the viewer to change "its phenomenological size."[28] In this sense it expresses a concern with the role played by the viewer's perception in defining the scale of the work, and by implication asserts subjective experience as a basis for defining reality.

From this work Giacometti moved to a series of tiny sculptures (ranging from a mere half-inch in height) on massive bases [fig. 5.12]. The thin insubstantiality of the form in relation to the huge pedestal creates a sense of vast distance, as if the figure was disappearing. "Wanting to create from memory what I have seen," he wrote, "to my terror the sculptures became smaller and smaller, they had a likeness only when they were small, yet their dimensions revolted me, and tirelessly I began again, only to end several months later at the same point. All this changed a little in 1945 through drawing. This led me to want to make larger figures, but then to my surprise, they achieved a likeness only when tall and slender."[29]

Giacometti exhibited the tall, thin figures [fig. 5.13] in 1948 at the Pierre Matisse Gallery in New York, his first one-person show in fourteen years. Sartre, with whom Giacometti had become friendly in 1940, wrote the introduction to the catalog. The title of Sartre's famous book *Being and Nothingness* could equally have described the fragile presence of these figures, which first shrunk into near-nonexistence and then elongated to a pencil line in space. Existentialism stresses a radical return to the beginning of things. In *Being and Time* Martin Heidegger wanted to start over in order to penetrate being itself. Giacometti's sculpture after 1940, like the work of Pollock and de Kooning, was not driven by an envisioned, finished composition, but by a need to discover "reality" in the process of working.

5.12 Alberto Giacometti, *Figure I*, c. 1945. Plaster and metal, 3½in (8.9cm) high, with plaster base 3½ × 2 × 2⅛in (8.9 × 5.08 × 5.4cm). The Museum of Modern Art, New York. Gift of Mr. and Mrs. Thomas B. Hess.

Giacometti attempted to cut away all training in order to see what stood in front of him and to portray it. At the same time he repeatedly asserted that this was impossible. So every day he would destroy what he had done the day before and start over again until someone took the work away for a show. According to the accounts of those who sat for him, his efforts to render reality seemed to go inexorably from bad to worse, and he blamed himself for this perceived failure. "This is what I deserve for thirty-five years of dishonesty," he told his friend James Lord. "All these years I've exhibited things that weren't finished and never even should have been started. But on the other hand, if I hadn't exhibited at all, it would have seemed cowardly, as though I didn't dare to show what I'd done."[30]

The artist underlined the existentialist character of this anxiety-ridden, introspective exploration when he stated

5.13 (right) **Alberto Giacometti**, *Man Pointing*, 1947. Bronze, 70½ × 40¾ × 16⅜in (179 × 103.4 × 41.58cm), at base 12 × 13¼in (30.5 × 33.7cm). The Museum of Modern Art, New York. Gift of Mrs. John D. Rockefeller 3rd, 678.1954.

that "it's impossible ever really to finish anything."[31] Because the artist defined his identity and presence in the world through his work, he could never achieve a satisfactory self-affirmation. The Giacometti figures express this in their fragility—as if, in a moment, these narrow wraiths could slip through a crack in existence. The sculptures of disembodied anatomical parts, like those of just the hand or the head by themselves, also express this sense of dissolution.

Giacometti's biographers have demon-strated his art-historical self-consciousness. *Man Pointing* [fig. 5.13], for example, makes reference to the ancient Greek *Poseidon of Cape Artemision* and to Auguste Rodin's *St. John the Baptist*.[32] He also drew on the simplified abstractions of Archipenko as well as on Egyptian and ancient Near Eastern figures. Yet this does not contradict Giacometti's approach to the reality of his subject through sudden, transcendental glimpses of the unexpected. Indeed, these classical models gave him a place in time and tradition, all the more important for an artist plagued by such a strong sense of estrangement from nature, society, and even existence itself.

As in action painting, the thickly modeled surface of Giacometti's figures asserts the intimate presence of the artist. The cages and platformlike bases that first emerged in his surrealist work of the early thirties reappeared in the late forties as a device for defining the scale of the figures and creating a spatial context in which to explore the issue

5.14 (right) **Alberto Giacometti**, *The City Square*, 1948–9. Bronze, 9½ × 25½ × 17⅛in (24.1 × 64.8 × 43.5cm). Collection, National Gallery of Art, Washington, D.C. Gift of Enid A. Haupt.

of the figural presence. The cages, frames, the heavy bases, and the walking figures with their feet mired as though stuck in tar seem to function as holding devices to keep things from disappearing. In 1958 Giacometti enlarged the concept created in *The City Square* of a decade earlier [fig. 5.14] into a project for a monumental figure composition for the plaza in front of the Chase Manhattan Bank in New York. In this never-realized work the towering figures would have mingled among the pedestrians, creating a disquieting comment on the alienation of city life.

Although Giacometti's circumstances were modest, he never experienced any hardship of the sort that Picasso or, later, Pollock and Franz Kline did. He depicted the most familiar people and things around him and lived an uneventful life. Yet this very stability provided him with a silent theater in which the artist struggled to affirm his feeling of existence. James Lord, in his account of Giacometti at work painting his portrait, described any number of exchanges that revealed the artist's relentless anxiety: "Presently he started gasping aloud, with his mouth open, and stamping his foot, 'Your head's going away!' he exclaimed. 'It's going away completely.' 'It will come back again,' I said. He shook his head. 'Not necessarily. Maybe the canvas will become completely empty. And then what will become of me?'"[33]

FRANCIS BACON

The British painter Francis Bacon [fig. 5.15] emerged at the end of World War II painting figures that were frighteningly transformed by the imagery of the unconscious. He would begin with a familiar subject and, like Giacometti, paint it as it actually appeared to him. But the appearance that he sought to portray was a vision that was transformed by the uses and threats perceived in the object by the primitive drives of his uncensored, unconscious mind. "You're not only remaking the look of the image," he told the art critic David Sylvester, "you're remaking all the areas of feeling which you yourself have apprehensions of."[34]

In the fifties Bacon turned increasingly to ordinary models and, after 1959, to images of his friends. Yet as the overt subject became more unremarkable the visible evidence of the repressed, instinctual perception grew. The nakedness of the expression and the immanent reality of the sitter distinguish these paintings from surrealism. But the artist used an adaptation of surrealist automatism to work his way, in the process of painting, closer and closer to the immediate subjective truth. "I don't think one can explain it," he said; "if you could explain your painting, you would be explaining your instincts."[35]

Bacon's shockingly direct revelation of this primal aspect, hidden below the surface of everyday life, evokes the chaotic forces that civilization has repressed in us and captures a loss of control, a sense of helplessness and terror. In his *Study After Velázquez's Portrait of Pope Innocent X* [fig. 5.19] the claustrophobic space and the pressure of the vertical

5.15 Francis Bacon in his studio, 1959.
Photograph by Cecil Beaton.

strokes close in uncomfortably, while the figure blurs into anonymity. Bacon's 1969 *Self-Portrait* [fig. 5.20] shows the artist imprisoned behind a twisted, monstrous mask. The eyes look out piteously but make no contact; there is no escape. The portrait at once expresses a terror in what it has revealed, and yet fused with this fear and vulnerability there is an opulent, painterly beauty.

Francis Bacon was born into an aristocratic English family in Ireland in 1909. His father went to work in the War Office in London in 1914, shuttling the family back and forth between London and Ireland. Bacon also lived intermittently with his grandmother, who had married the Commissioner of Police for County Kildare. With the civil war against British rule then raging, Bacon remembered his grandmother's sandbagged house, snipers' traps in the roads, British military maneuvers in the grounds of his father's home, and a generalized sense of danger permeating his childhood.

In 1929 Bacon was designing furniture and interiors in London, and in August 1930 *Studio Magazine* published an article on his work; years later he incorporated the tubular furniture he had made into his paintings [fig. 5.19]. Bacon began painting at the end of the twenties, constructing a style from a synthesis of illusionistic surrealism and contemporary cubism. He destroyed most of his pre-World War II work, but the pictures which survive foreshadow certain lifelong preoccupations. In *The Crucifixion* of 1933, a fleshy human head—derived from an X-ray of the head of a collector—sits on a table beside a crucified figure. The body is proportioned like a flayed carcass of beef hung in a butcher's shop and the scene seems to take place in a simply divided, sparse interior.

5.16 Francis Bacon, *Three Studies for Figures at the Base of a Crucifixion*, c. 1944. Oil on board support, triptych, each panel 37 × 29in (94 × 73.7cm).
© Tate, London 2009.

In *Wound for a Crucifixion* of the same year a mass of flesh, which Bacon described as "a very beautiful wound,"[36] sits on a sculpture armature; this study was derived from color plates of wounds and rare skin diseases that he had seen in medical books.

Bacon exhibited his triptych *Three Studies for Figures at the Base of a Crucifixion* [fig. 5.16] at the Lefevre Gallery in London in April 1945. He had conceived these panels as "sketches for the Eumenides which I intended to use as the base of a large crucifixion."[37] In Greek *eumenides* literally means "kindly ones," but it euphemistically refers to the furies, because according to myth the truth of their nature was too terrible to utter. "The reek of human blood smiles out at me,"[38] they say in a line from *The Oresteia* of Aeschylus, a line which Bacon particularly admired. For him, the furies embodied repressed forces in the human psyche, and crucifixion was an emblem of sadistic inhumanity. Bacon's inspiration for the shocking vocabulary of *Three Studies (Crucifixion)* came from Picasso's metamorphic figures of the late twenties and early thirties [fig. 5.17].

In *Painting* [fig. 5.18], the figure with slabs of meat angled in toward him on the glass-topped table was inspired through free association in the process of painting by news photographs of Hitler or Mussolini speaking from a rostrum and hemmed in by microphones. The image of the dictator fascinated Bacon, yet its presence here does not indicate an iconography in the usual sense, as is clear in Bacon's description of the picture's evolution: "I was attempting to make a bird alighting on a field. And . . . suddenly the lines that I'd drawn suggested something totally different, and

out of this suggestion arose this picture . . . It was like one continuous accident."[39]

Nevertheless, a number of the images in *Painting* recur frequently in Bacon's work: the tubular frame table; the flayed beef hanging as though crucified; closed blinds with dangling cords in a stark and claustrophobic room; an umbrella darkly obliterating the eyes of the suited figure and setting off the row of teeth in his open mouth; slabs of raw meat on the table; and a deep red oriental carpet on the floor. The reemergence of these objects in other paintings by Bacon suggests that their presence is more than "accidental."

I've always been very moved by pictures about slaughter-houses and meat, and to me they belong very much to the whole thing of the Crucifixion. There've been extraordinary photographs which have been done of animals just being

5.17 Pablo Picasso, *Figures by the Sea*, January 12, 1931. Oil on canvas, 4ft 3⅜in × 6ft 5in (1.31 × 1.96m).
Musée Picasso, Paris.

taken up before they were slaughtered; and the smell of death. We don't know, of course, but it appears by these photographs that they're so aware of what is going to happen to them, they do everything to attempt to escape. I think these pictures were very much based on that kind of thing, which to me is very, very near this whole thing of the Crucifixion.[40]

The image of the black figure with hidden eyes and menacing teeth, inspired by wartime news clippings, the raw meat, and the sense of entrapment in these close interiors also have to do with the cruelty of existence, experienced by the artist in the most intimate terms. "When you go into a butcher's shop," he noted, "and see how beautiful meat can be and then you think about it, you can think of the whole horror of life—of one thing living off another."[41]

Although Bacon did not use a preordained symbolism, he began *Painting* with a conscious subject and explored his feelings about it by way of free association. Each new pictorial element that was suggested by what was already there revealed another aspect of the subject's emotional meaning—hidden from consciousness until brought forth. By permitting one image to suggest another, the artist gradually discovered the emotional reality of his subject matter. This technique derives from surrealism, which in turn borrowed the method from Freudian psychoanalysis. But Bacon's approach goes beyond surrealism in its adherence to the overt subject matter, and in this respect comes closer to Freud.

In 1949 Bacon inaugurated a series of some two dozen compositions based directly on a reproduction of Velázquez's *Pope Innocent X* in combination with a film still of the screaming nurse on the Odessa steps in Sergei Eisenstein's 1925 film *The Battleship Potemkin*.[42] The film shows a close-up of the nurse's face with her mouth wide open and blood streaming from her eye. In *Study After Velázquez's Portrait of Pope Innocent X* [fig. 5.19] he also used a contemporary photograph of Pope Pius XII for such details as the glasses.

The shower of vertical brushstrokes and the gold rails (derived from his tubular furniture) trap the figures; in some versions Bacon put the pope in a linear cage. The sense of confinement narrows the focus of the composition to a detailed examination, as if it were a clinical study of a specimen in a jar. The effect is anxious, searching, disquieting, and at the same time sensuous. "I'd bought that very beautiful hand-colored book on diseases of the mouth," he reported, "and, when I made the Pope screaming, I didn't want to do it in the way that I did it—I wanted to make the mouth, with the beauty of its colour and everything, look like one of the sunsets . . . of Monet."[43]

On the surface the reproduction of a seventeenth-century papal portrait seems a relatively low-key subject, unlike a crucifixion or a theme inspired by Greek tragedy. Yet the frightening sense of loss of control evoked in these works far surpasses that of his earlier paintings. Indeed, the safe historical neutrality of the subject works as

a counterpoint to the artist's highly charged transformation. In versions of this theme and in other works painted after 1960, such as *Self-Portrait* [fig. 5.20], the artist introduced cubist overlays of perspective—showing more than one angle at a time on a face or figure. The richly detailed and painterly handling, set off against the starkness of the backgrounds, makes the disturbing deformations uncomfortably close.

From the late forties until his death in 1992 Bacon worked largely from his memory of real motifs and from photographs or reproductions. In addition to snapshots of friends and news photographs, he made extensive use of such books as *The Human Figure in Motion*, a late-nineteenth-century collection of photographic studies by Eadweard Muybridge. He also made frequent recourse to a technical book by K. C. Clark entitled *Positioning in Radiography*[44] which influenced his use of arrows in some images, as did, according to the curator Hugh Davies, a golfing instruction book; in both cases he wanted the arrows to recreate the neutrality of a textbook.[45]

5.18 Francis Bacon, *Painting*, 1946. Oil and pastel on linen, 6ft 5⅞in × 4ft 4in (1.97 × 1.32m). The Museum of Modern Art, New York. Purchase, 229.1948.

5.19 (opposite) **Francis Bacon**, *Study After Velázquez's Portrait of Pope Innocent X*, 1953. Oil on canvas, 5ft ¼in × 3ft 10½in (1.53 × 1.18m).

Des Moines Art Center. Purchased with funds from the Coffin Fine Arts Trust, Nathan Emory Coffin Collection of the Des Moines Art Center, 1980.1.

5.20 (right) **Francis Bacon**, *Self-Portrait*, 1969. Oil on canvas, 14 × 12in (35.6 × 30.5cm).

Private collection.

Devices that promote this kind of clinical detachment seem almost mandatory to counterbalance the highly charged nature of Bacon's subject matter. Indeed, the whole enterprise of his style is delicately poised—trying to press on, to search for feelings of the most intimate kind, and at the same time maintaining enough distance to paint them. Bacon described achieving a likeness in a portrait, for example, but then when "I tried to take it further and tried to make it more poignant, more near . . . I lost the image completely."[46]

After 1960 Bacon also used chance in a more systematic way to loosen up his associative process as he continued to focus with unyielding discipline on his unconscious vision of his subjects. "I want a very ordered image," he said, "but I want it to come about by chance."[47] Increasingly, one

starting-point was literally to throw paint at the canvas. "In the better things," according to Bacon, "that paint has an immediacy, although I don't think it looks like thrown-about paint."[48]

What distinguishes Bacon from the surrealists in his use of chance is that the surrealist exploits chance to elaborate on dream material or provoke a glimpse of the irrational. Bacon, by contrast, remains focused on a real subject and uses the associations stimulated by chance to bring out still more of his underlying feeling about his subject matter. Bacon painted his models over and over again, continually refining their appearance to attain a more and more precise psychic likeness. "One wants a thing to be as factual as possible," he explained, "and at the same time as deeply suggestive or deeply unlocking of areas of sensation."[49]

6.1 Wols (Wolfgang Schulze), *Painting*, 1946–7.
Oil on canvas, 31½ × 31½in (80 × 80cm).
Nationalgalerie Staatliche Museen zu Berlin.

6 SOME INTERNATIONAL TENDENCIES OF THE FIFTIES

PURIFIED ABSTRACTION

Life seemed simpler in the fifties. Communism had replaced Hitler as the arch-danger in the mind of the American public, and although Europeans were less simplistic in their views they were more focused on their own domestic issues. The 1947 Truman Doctrine disbursed American economic and military aid to anyone who was against communism; the Western democracies founded NATO in 1949 to counter the growing Soviet threat in Europe; and in June 1950 the United States embarked on the Korean War to hold the line against communism in Asia.

The Eisenhower era (1953–60) was a period of unprecedented American prosperity and world dominance. Business was booming and the mainstream middle class were beaming with economic confidence, even though there was widespread paranoia about signing anything or "getting involved" lest one be hauled before Senator Joseph McCarthy's hysterically anti-communist House Un-American Activities Committee. In addition, there persisted an undercurrent of fear that the Soviets might attack (particularly after the Russian nuclear tests in 1949). But after the Depression, World War II, and then the onset of the Cold War "the people" had had enough of the nation's worries. "I like Ike!" was the winning slogan in the election of 1952. With his reliable paternalism, the general who won World War Two promised to be the "father" who could lift the world's affairs off everybody's backs so that people could get on with the American dream of the suburban home, two children, a station wagon, and a family dog.

An Encounter with the Physicality of the Materials in Europe

In the fifties Europeans continued to undergo rationing amid a context of major postwar reconstruction. Many envied the prosperity of the United States and somewhat resented its accompanying international influence. At the same time they appreciated American help in financing the European recovery. In fact, the Old World's chief preoccupation was the same as that of the New: achieving middle-class prosperity. Much of the new art of the fifties reflected this, veering away from the introspective focus of the New York School and Dubuffet's existentialism, and concentrating instead on tangible things; figurative subject matter experienced a revival, and the gestural richness of abstract expressionist painting was taken up in both representational and abstract art for its sensuality and painterliness, rather than for its underlying metaphysics.

In France Hans Hartung, Pierre Soulages, and Nicholas de Staël continued the tradition of painterly abstraction. Wols (Wolfgang Schulze) [fig. 6.1], developed a highly original automatist style, founded in existentialism, in 1945–6; but his gestural painting emphasized the identity of the artist over the base materialism that concerned Dubuffet and Fautrier. Wols, Georges Mathieu [fig. 6.2]—who also evolved in direct response to American action painting—and, after 1950, the American expatriate Sam Francis are among the best known of the Parisian artists who came to be known as *tâchistes*. "*Tâche*" means a splash or stain and, as this implies, the movement emphasized expressive paint handling. But they too seemed more concerned with the beauty of the surface—or, in the case of Mathieu, the performative act of painting—than with metaphysics.

The most interesting European painting in the early fifties came out of ideas related to the concept of *l'informe*. Antoni Tàpies, a Catalan painter, worked in an abstract style after 1952, influenced (as Dubuffet was) by his concern with the vital—indeed, spiritual—physicality of his materials. For the Italian painters Alberto Burri [fig. 6.3] in Rome and Lucio Fontana [fig. 6.4] in Milan an experience of

6.4 Lucio Fontana, *Spatial Concept, 60 0 48*, 1960. Oil on perforated canvas, 4ft 11in × 4ft 11in (1.5 × 1.5m). Kunstsammlung Nordrhein-Westfalen, Düsseldorf.

the material itself also constituted a more direct encounter with reality than representation. Burri had begun painting during 1943 as a prisoner of war interned in Marfa, Texas. He worked with various unconventional materials—even mixing tar, rags, and living molds with his pigments. But his best-known works are the burlap "Sacks" of the fifties. Burri's expressive manipulation of these earthy materials shifted the emphasis in painting from representation to the physical reality of the object itself.

Lucio Fontana sought "an art in which our idea of art cannot intervene,"[1] as he asserted in his 1946 *White Manifesto*. Like Burri, he wanted to stress the total reality of the canvas as a material object to be experienced directly and without formal preconceptions. But Fontana also sought to transcend the object, entering a metaphysical space; in effect, he used the vivid reality of the material object to set off an even more immanently "real," but at the same time immaterial, spatial concept.

At the end of the forties, Fontana began puncturing holes in the canvas, and in the fifties he slashed through it as a way of heightening the intensity of his interaction with its physicality. Fontana called nearly all of his paintings of the

fifties and sixties "spatial concepts" (*concetti spaziali*). He also experimented with "spatial environments" (*ambienti spaziali*) in 1949—neon installations in which he attempted to extend his ideas into a specific space. But Fontana's epiphany of space–time had to do with a flash of insight into cosmic order rather than with existential concerns.

In 1957 the American Cy Twombly settled in Rome and began painting his so-called "writings" [fig. 6.5]—a calligraphic style of marking the canvas (often configuring letters, words, or even fleeting images) in a dispersed "anti-compositional" order that has a cunningly random appearance, like a wall of graffiti. The sense of his stylistic origins in writing (especially in the anonymity of graffiti), rather than in the directly autographic gesture of the action painters, underscores Twombly's difference from abstract expressionism.

Twombly's line is not assertively focused like a Pollock or a de Kooning. Instead his sensibility more closely resembles that of John Cage and the earlier work of Jasper Johns (see Chapter 7). Twombly's work has a richly layered ambiguity that resists closure. Yet despite its seeming openness to the chance occurrence of future accretions it firmly asserts its

6.5 Cy Twombly, *Untitled*, 1960. Oil, crayon, and pencil on canvas, 38¼ × 55⅛in (97.2 × 140cm). Collection, Ralph and Helyn Goldenberg, Chicago.

place within the grand narrative of the classical tradition; Twombly diminishes rather than enhances the importance of individual identity, subsuming it into the collective and much larger history of Western culture. He used literature and myth, rather than a search for existential identity, as the touchstones of his style.

A Material Reading of Action Painting in New York

During the Depression and war years the largely self-educated community of vanguard artists in New York lived meagerly, with little hope of making a living by painting. The familial sense of a small artistic community, centered on Tenth Street and Broadway in Greenwich Village, survived as late as the mid-fifties. The continuing presence of such established figures as Harold Rosenberg, Willem de Kooning, and Philip Guston dominated the neighborhood. The Club on East 8th Street maintained a weekly program of speeches and discussions, and a number of cooperative galleries opened with the work of younger artists who emulated the first generation of the New York School, and among them were some prominent women, such as Joan Mitchell [fig. 6.6].

The audience for these gallery shows and discussions consisted chiefly of other artists, interspersed with a few dealers, critics, and friends. While the psychological and confessional tenor of the conversation persisted, there was a more narrow focus on style *per se*. The rapidly growing opportunities for teaching jobs and sales increasingly entered into artists' discussions. "Honesty" endured as a criterion in painting, but social or political "relevance" faded away.

By the end of the fifties the art world had vastly expanded, ushering in a new influx of university-educated artists who did not appear to have the "moral crisis in relation to what to paint,"[2] which Barnett Newman described. Reflecting the mood of the country at large, artists in the fifties were remarkably apolitical. University education, it seems, had actually made them less interested in discussing intellectual, social, and political issues and had instead taught them about careers.

Stylistically, Hofmann, Kline, and de Kooning were the leading models for young painters in the fifties. Emerging

6.6 Joan Mitchell, *August, Rue Daguerre*, 1957.
Oil on canvas, 6ft 10in × 5ft 9in (2.08 × 1.75m).
The Phillips Collection, Washington, D.C.

6.7 Philip Guston, *Oasis*, 1957. Oil on canvas, 5ft 1½in × 5ft 8in (1.56 × 1.73m).

Hirshhorn Museum and Sculpture Garden, Smithsonian Institution, Washington, D.C. Gift of Joseph H. Hirshhorn Foundation, 1966.

artists admired Pollock, but they could not emulate him without looking "derivative" (another catchword of the decade), and the rejection of "masterful" brushwork by Newman and Rothko was still too radical to inspire imitators. But instead of the existential crisis embodied in the autographic mark, the new gestural painters of the fifties talked of "polyreferential" marks, sought "lyrical beauty," and stressed the sensuous pleasure of laying on paint for its own sake. In 1955 a large, late *Waterlilies* composition by Monet went on display at the Museum of Modern Art, further heightening these younger painters' interest in surface richness and light.

Philip Guston's lush, painterly abstraction of the fifties [fig. 6.7] also became a leading influence in what Elaine de Kooning dubbed "abstract impressionism."[3] Despite Guston's own commitment to an existentially probative subject matter, he unwittingly encouraged a number of younger artists in the mid-fifties toward a more superficial, "lyrical" or decorative style. But most preferred what they regarded as the raw honesty of de Kooning, evidenced by his tendency to leave a painting unfinished, without disguising the marks of his creative struggle.

"Difficult" painting had credibility; elegant painting was seen as merely "decorative." But to select a model at all contradicted the premise of an existential approach and raised the question with which Irving Sandler provoked a two-part series of artists' statements for *Art News* in 1959: "Is There a New Academy?" One of the respondents summed up the feeling by asking: "Why is it that after an evening of openings on Tenth Street, I come away feeling exhausted from the spectacle of boredom?"[4] There was a widespread feeling that gestural painting had become a collection of tired conventions.

Greenberg's Definition of Modernism

The critic Clement Greenberg stepped into the disarray of second-generation gesture painting and decided he could single-handedly revitalize painting by laying down rules for painters to follow. It is "a law of modernism," he wrote in 1955, "that applies to almost all art that remains truly alive in our time—that the conventions not essential to the viability of a medium be discarded as soon as they are recognized." This "process of self-purification"[5] evolved, in linear progression, from Pollock to Still, Rothko, and Newman—whose flat expanses of color went beyond the shading and illusionistic depth still remaining in cubist-influenced painters such as de Kooning, according to Greenberg. From them the baton of vanguardism passed to the "color field" or "stain" painters Helen Frankenthaler and Morris Louis, and in the sixties to Kenneth Noland and Jules Olitski. The problem, as Barbara Rose pointed out, was that

> Clement Greenberg, quoting Matthew Arnold, saw the task of the critic as defining the mainstream tradition . . . But at any given time the mainstream is only part of the total activity . . . [Greenberg's] argument is that since modernist art emancipated itself from the demands of society, the history of forms has been self-referential and has evolved independently of the history of events.[6]

"This argument," she concluded, "is demonstrably false." Nevertheless, a number of influential people in the art world enthusiastically embraced the clarity and logic of Greenberg's monolithic "mainstream"; in 1960 William Rubin, for example, remarked that painterly painting was even "a losing proposition for de Kooning himself."[7]

Greenberg felt confident in his ability to spot the "next move." Moreover, he was certain there would be only *one* next move at a time and that it necessarily had to follow in a logical manner from his belief that

> the essence of Modernism lies . . . in the use of the characteristic methods of a discipline to criticize the discipline itself . . . The task of self criticism became to eliminate from the effects of each art any and every effect that might conceivably be borrowed from or by the medium of any other art. Thereby each art would be rendered "pure," and in its "purity" find the guarantee of its standards of quality as well as of its independence.[8]

In Greenberg's modernism color, for example, is "optical" and therefore belongs to painting; the same is true of the picture plane. Consequently sculpture that involved color or made reference to the picture plane would not qualify as an "important" next step. Similarly narrative (a literary device), figural representation, and certainly illusionism were strictly proscribed.

The Greenberg School

People love simple answers to complex questions, and by 1960 Greenberg had a prodigious network of influence that dominated the public debate on art. The school of young critics surrounding him included, notably, Michael Fried and Rosalind Krauss. There were a number of young museum curators and critics who took their cues from Greenberg, and for a full decade after the 1964 exhibition in Los Angeles called "Post Painterly Abstraction" (which set the canon of Greenberg's taste) Greenberg's followers also took over *Artforum* magazine.

Greenberg and Fried singled out David Smith and Anthony Caro as the leading innovators in sculpture. But Irving Sandler rightly wondered "if, as Greenberg maintained, each of the arts was turning in on its own medium, why had he opted for welded construction, which he claimed aspired toward the 'pictorial,' rather than sculpture that approached the object [i.e. minimalism], which was the nature of sculpture?"[9] Minimalism, as Sandler implied, focused on precisely these literal qualities of the object (see Chapter 10), but it didn't appeal to Greenberg.

John Cage's book *Silence*—which stood for inclusiveness and was consequently impure by Greenberg's standards—appeared in 1961, at precisely the same time as Greenberg's influential collection of essays *Art and Culture*. To the followers of Greenberg, Cage and Duchamp, Rauschenberg, Johns, Oldenburg, and all pop artists were the corrupting antichrists of kitsch. As late as 1974 the Greenbergian critic Kenworth Moffett called Oldenburg a "feeble" artist and chided: "The lack of the slightest formal integrity prevents his droopy painterly objects from being more than archly cute."[10] Michael Fried went even further, saying "if someone likes *that* stuff . . . I simply can't believe his claim that he is *also* moved or convinced or flattened by the work of Noland, say, or Olitski or Caro," and that anyone who sincerely makes such a claim is "in the grip of the *wrong* experience"[11] (my italics).

Subject matter was irrelevant, illusion forbidden, and anything that did not fit Greenberg's logic was dropped from his definition of modernism as if it had never existed. Fried described the inevitable march to purity in an equally affectless and narrow manner: "Once a painter who accepts the basic premises of modernism becomes aware of a particular problem thrown up by the art of the recent past, his action is no longer gratuitous but imposed."[12] The artist had to follow a more or less predetermined path.

Rosalind Krauss wrote that art history "was like a series of rooms *en filade* ['one after another']. Within each room the individual artist explored, to the limits of his experience and his formal intelligence, the separate constituents of his medium. The effect of his pictorial act was to open simultaneously the door to the next space and close out access to the one behind him."[13] In Krauss's formalist decathlon of opening and closing doors squeaky hinges were disqualified.

The best artists do not follow rules made up by critics, but invent their own. Moreover, art does not develop logically or in a linear progression; and if one could predict the next move in art, that art would be uninteresting precisely because it *is* predictable. At the outset Greenberg was reacting against the form of criticism practiced by Harold Rosenberg, whose chief interest was in ideas implicit in a work. What Rosenberg liked about art was its unpredictability—the entry of fresh ideas into the conversation; for him, art opened the eyes of the participants to new perspectives, particularly social and political issues. Greenberg, on the other hand, felt that such "expressionistic" criticism lacked rigor. But as the logical positivists have pointed out, the only absolutely provable truths are tautological: what Greenberg, Fried, and their friends gained in rigor they lost in significance.

One of the great ironies in this formalist episode is that all of Greenberg's judgments ultimately relied on taste to determine quality, and there were no objective criteria given for taste. Sandler justifiably complained about Fried, who "would allow only one *correct* formalist art at any moment. And he did not make clear why any one option should be any more modernist than any other . . . Fried chose to single out a few artists, notably Noland, Olitski, Stella, and Caro, and accept whatever they made as truly modernist, only because they made it."[14]

Increasingly people began taking issue not only with Greenberg's opinions but also with the manner in which he imposed them on others. In one widely discussed case Greenberg appears to have decided, after David Smith's death, how he thought Smith should have finished certain pieces. So, as an executor of Smith's estate, he reportedly had the colors, which the artist himself had painted on, removed and replaced with an entirely different type of surface.[15] Morris Louis, unlike Smith, evidently followed directions in the first place. The painter made a note on the edge of a 1958 canvas that he planned to fold out of sight: "1 inch of white on each side as per Clem."[16] By around 1970 the art and theory on which Greenberg and Fried had built their reputations began to look as dated and unconvincing as their claims of historical inevitability.

Formalist Painting

Greenberg tried to rejuvenate "decorativeness" as an alternative to expressionism, and he singled out the work of Helen Frankenthaler because she achieved an identity of the surface and color—making them inseparable. By literally soaking the color into the canvas, she made it textureless and thus more "optical" than tangible. Frankenthaler worked in an abstract style derived from Hans Hofmann with impetus from the work of Kandinsky and Gorky. Like Hofmann, she took inspiration from nature, but unlike him, she and several other "abstract impressionists" of the fifties were attracted to the decorative surface qualities of the late Monet.

In April 1953 Kenneth Noland (who came from Washington, D.C.) brought his friend Morris Louis to New York to meet Greenberg and look at art. They visited Frankenthaler's studio, and her painting *Mountains and Sea* [fig. 6.8] had a galvanizing effect on Louis. Immediately on their return to Washington, Louis and Noland began to experiment together with staining [figs. 6.9 and 6.10]. Louis abandoned the brush completely and began pouring viscous lines of paint that soaked into the surface. By the beginning of 1954 he had devised a new style based on the technique of staining unsized white cotton with a liquid acrylic medium.

Louis succeeded in getting a different effect from staining than Pollock or Rothko had achieved with the technique. Louis's colors blended into one another, leaving rich spectral layerings that revealed themselves with particular *élan* at the edges. Greenberg and his followers applauded Louis for his "honesty" in making explicit the real flatness of the canvas. Fried particularly praised the disappearance of "all suggestion of the gestural, manifestly spontaneous hand-writing of abstract expressionism."[17] For them Louis had surpassed Frankenthaler in pure opticality by establishing a uniformly

6.8 Helen Frankenthaler, *Mountains and Sea*, 1952.
Oil on canvas, 7ft 2⅜in × 9ft 9¼in (2.2 × 2.98m).
Collection, the artist, on extended loan to National Gallery of Art, Washington, D.C.

6.9 (opposite) **Morris Louis**, *Tet*, 1958. Synthetic polymer on canvas, 7ft 11in × 12ft 9in (2.41 × 3.89m).
Whitney Museum of American Art, New York. Purchase, with funds from the Friends of Whitney Museum of American Art, New York, 65.9.

textured "field" and dissipating any sense of depth or color substance. Even if others saw paintings like *Tet* [fig. 6.9] not as flat but diaphanous, conveying an illusion of depth in and behind the washes of color, Greenberg continued to delight in a feeling of "openness" in "pure painting," derived from the "identity of color and surface."

Taking off from the targets that Jasper Johns showed at the Leo Castelli Gallery in 1958, Kenneth Noland began a series of target paintings [fig. 6.10] late in 1958. The banality of the format was intentional, for the artist wanted to stress instead the interaction of colors—just as Noland's teacher, Josef Albers, had done in his compositions of nested color squares [fig. 6.11]. According to Fried, Noland sought a "strictly logical relation between the painted image and the framing edge."[18] Fried found precisely the same aspiration in the contemporary works of Frank Stella [figs. 10.1,

6.10 Kenneth Noland, *And Half*, 1959. Acrylic on canvas, 5ft 9in × 5ft 9in (1.75 × 1.75m).

Collection unknown. Photograph by Geoffrey Clements, New York. © Kenneth Noland/VAGA, New York, 1994.

6.11 Josef Albers, *Homage to the Square: "Ascending,"* 1953. Oil on composition board, 3ft 7½in × 3ft 7½in (1.11 × 1.11m).

Collection, Whitney Museum of American Art, New York. Purchase, 54.34.

10.3, and 10.4]. Noland moved from a Rothko-like softness in the definition of the outer edge to "hard-edged" circles by 1961. From there the stripes developed into chevrons and then into continuous horizontals.

The stain or color-field painting of such artists as Frankenthaler and Louis derived from a formalist analysis of the gesture painting of the New York School. A geometrically based formalist painting had already evolved, in large part out of a literal reading of Mondrian. Ad Reinhardt, its leading exponent, was a contemporary of Pollock and Motherwell but he loathed subjectivity and became increasingly engaged with the more self-negating kind of contemplation in Zen aesthetics. By 1960 his work moved toward a reduction so radical that the typical painting consisted only of a black rectangle inscribed with nearly invisible vertical and horizontal black trisections [fig. 6.12]. He concluded that this was the final solution to painting; and as further progress was therefore impossible, he announced that he intended to repeat this same painting from then on.

Josef Albers, the former Bauhaus master whom Noland had encountered at Black Mountain College in North Carolina, had a great effect on postwar painting through his teaching. Albers taught at Black Mountain from 1933 through the forties and then moved in 1950 to the Yale School of Art. He argued for an experimental attitude concerning materials and a technological rigor in the study of color and design. In his own work he focused narrowly on optical interactions and the expressive dimension is

suppressed to a whisper. "Angst is dead," he once wrote on a scrap of paper that he handed to Harold Rosenberg at a party.[19] The fixed compositional format of his "Homage to the Square" series preoccupied him for the last twenty-five years of his life. Albers's painting and writing were equally systematic, orderly, experimental. In 1963 he published a book of color theory called *The Interaction of Color*, and during that decade he enjoyed a considerable following as interest in a detached and theoretical style of art became more widespread.

In 1965 the Museum of Modern Art opened a widely discussed exhibition called "The Responsive Eye." William Seitz, the curator, wanted to bring together a survey of current artists who manipulated perceptual effects in a formalist—as opposed to an expressionistic—mode. The exhibition brought together "op art" (from "optical"), as in the paintings of Victor Vasarely [fig. 6.13], and kinetic art (having to do with actual motion), as in the delicately engineered works of George Rickey [fig. 6.14], where a light breeze will set all the finely hinged and balanced parts in motion. The popular media loved the show. But the art establishment detested it as a display of vulgar and empty visual gimmicks, and to the chagrin of Greenberg's circle Seitz also included color-field canvases by Morris Louis, Kenneth Noland, and Walter Darby Bannard; as well as works by Frank Stella, Larry Poons, Ellsworth Kelly, Larry Bell, and Agnes Martin (who were associated with minimalism); and by Josef Albers, Ad Reinhardt, and the interwar geometric abstractionist Leon Polk Smith. Greenberg and his

6.12 Ad Reinhardt, *Abstract Painting*, 1960–6.
Oil on canvas, 5 × 5ft (1.52 × 1.52m).
Photograph courtesy PaceWildenstein Gallery, New York.

6.13 Victor Vasarely, *VEGA PER*, 1969.
Oil on canvas, 5ft 3in × 5ft 3in (1.6 × 1.6m).
Honolulu Academy of Arts. Gift of the Honorable Clare Boothe Luce, 1984.

circle vigorously argued that the color-field painters practiced a "high" formalist aesthetics, whereas the others, they felt, were only a form of "visual entertainment." In retrospect, however, Seitz's premise for the show held up pretty well.

"NEW IMAGES OF MAN" IN EUROPE AND AMERICA

The Cobra

The drive toward liberated subjectivity in the figurative styles of Dubuffet, Giacometti, and Bacon led a wider tendency in postwar European and American art. The "Cobra" group—comprising artists from Copenhagen, Brussels, and Amsterdam—is the outstanding example of this broader phenomenon. At the end of 1948 the Belgian poet Christian Dotremont and the Danish painter Asger Jorn gave initial shape to Cobra as a movement. Over the next three years they and their collaborators produced ten issues of a journal entitled *Cobra* and numerous exhibitions. They also instigated artistic exchanges that aimed to give some coherence to this otherwise loose affiliation of northern European artists. Their unifying stylistic bond was a free, organic expressiveness in paint handling and an emphasis on imagery defined in the individual imagination. The major artists of the Cobra group were Asger Jorn from Denmark [fig. 6.15]; Karel Appel [fig. 6.16], Corneille (Cornelis van Beverloo), and Constant (Constant A. Nieuwenhuys) from Amsterdam; and Pierre Alechinsky [fig. 6.17] from Brussels.

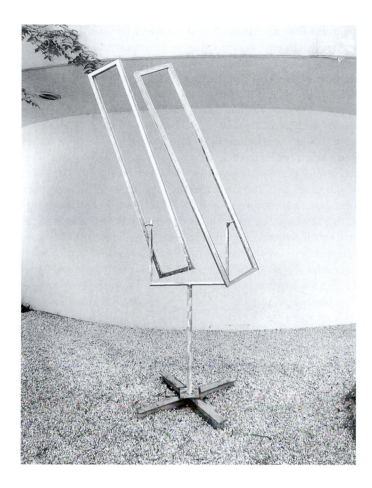

6.14 George Rickey, *Two Open Rectangles Excentric VI, Square Section*, 1976–7. Stainless steel, 144 × 36in (365.8 × 91.4cm).

Solomon R. Guggenheim Museum, New York. Purchased with the aid of funds from the National Endowment for the Arts in Washington, D.C., a Federal Agency; matching funds donated by Evelyn Sharp and anonymous donors, 1979.

6.15 (right) **Asger Jorn**, *A Soul for Sale*, 1958–9. Oil on canvas, 6ft 7in × 8ft 2¾in (2 × 2.5m).

Solomon R. Guggenheim Museum, New York. Purchased with funds contributed by the Evelyn Sharp Foundation, 1983.

Like Dubuffet, Giacometti, Bacon, and the artists of the New York School, the Cobra artists had roots in surrealist automatism, Freudian psychology, and existentialism. With Dubuffet, whom the Cobra members knew and admired, they also shared an interest in anonymous, untutored art and in the everyday experience of the common man. Jorn praised popular culture, celebrated inartistic materials, and emulated graffiti. Constant, in a statement that reflected the views of most of the group, remarked that "we consider the stimulation of the creative impulse as art's main task" and asserted that "truly living art makes no distinction between the beautiful and the ugly."[20]

The artists associated with Cobra also turned to children's art, as Dubuffet had, for an expression of the unconscious that circumvented the inhibitions of culture. However, as Alechinsky explained, "Cobra is a form of art which heads toward childhood, tries to recover folk art and child art for itself with the means available to adults, non-naïve means."[21] In this respect they differed from the surrealists. The Cobras' call for "spontaneity" acknowledged the full range of experiences that impinged on the processes of the developed mind, whereas Breton retained idealistic aspirations for a "pure" expression of the unconscious through automatism. Where Breton had hoped to prompt revelations of the unconscious, these artists sought a fuller encounter with reality through the marshalling of unconscious forces.

Consequently, Cobra's style stressed the act of creation and harked back formally to early-twentieth-century expressionism. Alechinsky's proclamation that "it is through action alone that the thought can intercede in matter"[22] not only suggests a parallel with Dubuffet's notion of "collaborating" with materials but underlines the dialectic between subjective intuition and empirical reality. From this point of view, imagination could mitigate man's alienation.

Although Cobra disintegrated as a cohesive movement in the early fifties, its leading artists continued to evolve, developing separately its principles of spontaneity and its existential concerns. Alechinsky's 1967 *Death and the Maiden* [fig. 6.17], for example, still relates to the ideas of Dotremont and Cobra, but it also breaks new ground. Here, the painter transformed the framing edge into a detailed commentary on the center. This black-and-white sequence of notations developed frame by frame in an implicitly ongoing interaction, unfolding through spontaneous responses, repetitions, and transformations of suggestions from the center. At this time Alechinsky painted an extensive series of works on this principle of surrounding the central image with a disparate set of images in the margins that challenge the emphasis on a central set of forms. These works resonate richly with contemporary French poststructuralism, which questioned the authority of the author over the reader in literature and the hegemony of the mainstream (the normative center) in social and intellectual structures.

The Figurative Revival of the Fifties

Figurative imagery in general underwent a revival in the fifties, both in Europe and America. In sculpture artists ranging from Reg Butler in Britain, Germaine Richier in France, the Italians Marino Marini [fig. 6.18] and Giacomo Manzú, as well as Americans like Leonard Baskin, treated the human figure in an expressionistic manner that is at once contemporary in sensibility and consonant with classical traditions of bronze casting. In Europe perhaps the outstanding traditional figure painter of the period was the Englishman Lucian Freud [fig. 6.19].

Though directly engaged in the outward appearance of things, Freud wanted his "portraits to be *of* the people, not *like* them. Not having the look of the sitter, *being* them."[23] This powerful sense of the reality beyond the picture creates an uncomfortable intimacy between the viewer and the sitter. On the one hand the viewer feels a formal distance in not being able to divine the enigmatic relations between the figures (where there are more than one) or to know

6.16 Karel Appel, *Questioning Children*, 1949. Gouache on wood, 34⅜ × 23½ × 6¼in (87.3 × 59.8 × 15.8cm).
© Tate, London 2009.

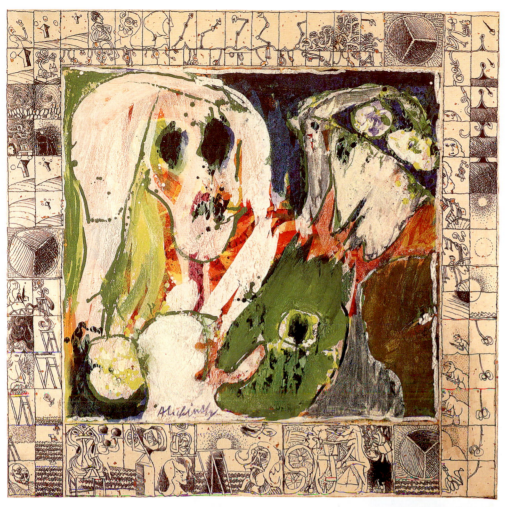

6.17 (left) **Pierre Alechinsky**, *Death and the Maiden*, 1967. Acrylic on paper mounted on canvas, 4ft 6in × 4ft 6in (1.37 × 1.37m). Collection, Marion Lefebre, Los Angeles.

6.19 (below) **Lucian Freud**, *Naked Girl*, 1966. Oil on canvas, 24 × 24in (61 × 61cm). Collection, Steve Martin.

6.18 Marino Marini, *Horseman*, 1947. Bronze, 64½ × 61 × 26½in (163.8 × 154.9 × 67.3cm). © Tate, London 2009.

6.20 Grace Hartigan, *River Bathers*, 1953. Oil on canvas,
5ft 9⅜in × 7ft 4¾in (1.76 × 2.25m).
The Museum of Modern Art, New York. Given anonymously. Courtesy ACA Galleries.

the true identity of the solitary subject. Yet the artist presses the viewer to intrude on an excruciatingly private scene. As the critic Robert Hughes pointed out, Freud "has seen everything with such evenness, while conveying the utter disjuncture between the artist's gaze and the sitter's lack of response."[24]

In New York the admiration for abstract expressionism produced not only a school of second-generation abstract gesture painters in the fifties but also figurative artists working in a painterly style. These include Grace Hartigan [fig. 6.20], Fairfield Porter [fig. 6.21], Alex Katz [fig. 6.23], and Philip Pearlstein [fig. 6.24]. Yet not even the return of de Kooning and Pollock to the figure in the early fifties could convince some artists of the ongoing viability of figurative art. For Greenberg and Ad Reinhardt, "going back"

to realist subjects constituted a betrayal of modernism. Greenberg claimed that "any painter today not working abstractedly is working in a minor mode," and Reinhardt quipped, "Enter nature, exit art."[25]

Larry Rivers, one of the outstanding gestural realists to emerge in New York during the fifties, had studied with Baziotes and Hofmann. Rivers treated the canvas as a field of random activity; rather than focusing on a single image, he scattered several centers of interest across the painting. In most cases these disparate areas cohere around a compositional center, but in some works, like *The Studio* [fig. 6.22], they approach the "all over" structure of de Kooning's *Excavation* [fig. 3.38].

6.21 (opposite) **Fairfield Porter**, *Katie and Anne*, 1955.
Oil on canvas, 6ft 8⅛in × 5ft 2⅛in (2.03 × 1.57m).
Hirshhorn Museum and Sculpture Garden, Smithsonian Institution,
Washington, D.C. Gift of Joseph H. Hirshhorn, 1966.

6.22 Larry Rivers, *The Studio*, 1956. Oil on canvas, 6ft 10½in × 16ft 1¼in (2.09 × 4.91m).
Collection, Minneapolis Institute of Art. The John R. Van Derlip Fund.

The starkness of the lighting and the banality of the subject matter, however, set Pearlstein's work apart from theirs, compelling the viewer to focus narrowly on the technique.

Rivers handled his subject matter with a perverse irony. His frontal, full-length portrait of *Frank O'Hara* wearing nothing but black military boots, for example, snidely stereotypes the poet as a gay pin-up. The many nude depictions of the artist's mother-in-law, Birdie, likewise accentuate her sexuality in a way that makes her appear vulgar and awkward, as in *The Studio*. The detachment with which Rivers related to his subject matter also manifested itself in his self-consciously "virtuoso" technique, displaying his fine gestural touch and superb draftsmanship at the expense of the subjects.

Unlike Rivers, who manipulated his subjects to stress the uniqueness of his vision and technique, Porter, Katz, and Pearlstein modestly painted what was in front of them; all the details are legible, and there is no pretense of theory. Alex Katz had a sharply simplified subject matter, focusing on individual objects or sitters that he kept isolated in his compositions [fig. 6.23]. This spare treatment of the individual form as a single image, rather than interacting with other figures inside the frame, made Katz's compositions seem more abstract.

Philip Pearlstein [fig. 6.24] concentrated on an indifferently objective representation of nude models posed in the studio. But Pearlstein made none of the concessions that Katz did to impact and scale. His factual, unidealized style leaves nothing to the imagination and gives no quarter to introspection. It is a visual discipline, unemotionally fixed on the material substance of things. The objectivity of description to which he aspired recalls such earlier American painters as Thomas Eakins and Eastman Johnson.

6.23 Alex Katz, *Ada (in Black Sweater)*, 1957. Oil on masonite, 24 × 18in (61 × 45.7cm).
Collection, the artist, on long-term loan to the Colby College Museum of Art, Waterville, Maine.

6.24 Philip Pearlstein, *Two Female Models with Drawing Table*,
1973. Oil on canvas, 6 × 5ft (1.83 × 1.52m).
Philadelphia Museum of Art. Purchased through a grant from the National Endowment
for the Arts and contributions from private donors.

Figurative Painting in the Bay Area

The impetus of abstract expressionist handling also produced an exceptional group of gestural painters in California. In particular David Park [fig. 6.25] and his students at the California School of Fine Arts in San Francisco, Elmer Bischoff [fig. 6.26] and Richard Diebenkorn [fig. 6.27], turned from painterly abstraction to a gestural style of figuration between 1950 and 1955. Diebenkorn studied with Still and Rothko as well as Park during the mid-forties. Attracted to abstract painting by reproductions of the work of Motherwell and Baziotes, he painted abstractly until late 1955. He worked in New Mexico, Illinois, and New York, and in 1964 he traveled to Russia, where the great collections of work by Matisse overwhelmed him. After his return he moved to Santa Monica, on the ocean side of Los Angeles and in 1967 began his "Ocean Park" series [fig. 6.28], stirred by the beauty of the coastal light. These paintings announced the artist's return to abstraction. Their sensuality and the tension between the classical elements of drawing and geometric composition against the lush color and light demonstrate his debt to Matisse.

6.25 David Park,
Standing Couple, 1958.
Oil on canvas, 6ft 3in ×
4ft 8¾in (1.91 × 1.44m).
Krannert Art Museum and Kinkead Pavilion, University of Illinois, Urbana-Champaign. Purchased out of the "Illinois Biennial" exhibition of 1961.

6.26 Elmer Bischoff, *Two Figures at the Seashore*, 1957. Oil on canvas, 4ft 8in × 4ft 8¾in (1.42 × 1.44m). Newport Harbor Art Museum. Museum Purchase with a matching grant from the National Endowment for the Arts.

6.27 Richard Diebenkorn, *Girl Looking at Landscape*, 1957. Oil on canvas, 4ft 11in × 5ft ⅜in (1.5 × 1.53m). Whitney Museum of American Art, New York. Gift of Mr. and Mrs. Alan H. Temple, 61.49.

6.28 Richard Diebenkorn, *Ocean Park No. 107*, 1978.
Oil on canvas, 7ft 9in × 6ft 4in (2.36 × 1.93m).
Oakland Museum. Gift of the Women's Board, Oakland Museum Association.

Wayne Thiebaud's rich painterly style also derives from the Bay Area abstract expressionists. Yet unlike them, he did not subordinate his subject matter to the handling. Thiebaud is often mistakenly associated with pop art because of his brilliantly lit and colored images of ordinary objects. The *Five Hot Dogs* [fig. 6.29]—each isolated in stark contrast against the white background and rhythmically repeated to create tense intervals in between—conveys a detachment toward the subject combined with a strong, graphic bravado. Yet the real motives behind Thiebaud's work are the direct pleasures of looking at things, of analyzing them into patterns, and above all of handling paint.

Chicago's Existential Imagists

Young Chicago artists of the fifties, like their peers in New York, looked to de Kooning, Hofmann, and Kline as models. But Chicago also enthusiastically embraced the new existential figuration from Europe as well as early-twentieth-century German expressionism—a combination of influences which prompted the emergence of a distinctive school of existential imagists. For the opening of an exhibition of his work at the legendary Arts Club of Chicago on December 20, 1951 Dubuffet delivered his now famous lecture entitled "Anticultural Positions." A typescript of the talk circulated in Chicago and made an enormous impression on artists and collectors there.

Even before artists like Cosmo Campoli [fig. 6.30] and Leon Golub of the so-called "Chicago Monster Roster" had read or heard firsthand Dubuffet's 1951 lecture, they were

6.29 Wayne Thiebaud, *Five Hot Dogs*, 1961. Oil on canvas, 18 × 24in (45.7 × 61cm).
Private collection, San Francisco.

6.30 Cosmo Campoli, *Birth of Death*, 1950. Bronze, rock, wax, and steel, 70 × 18¾ × 24½in (177.8 × 47.6 × 62.2cm). Museum of Contemporary Art, Chicago. Gift of Joseph and Jory Shapiro, 92.55.

predisposed toward his ideas by their exposure to German expressionism, to psychoanalysis, and to existentialism. Paul Tillich, the foremost American existentialist, was then a highly visible professor of theology at the University of Chicago, and the city's Institute for Psychoanalysis (the country's first) was already nearly twenty years old. In 1959 Golub used psychoanalytic terminology in describing his paintings as an "attempt to reinstate a contemporary catharsis, that measure of man which is related to an existential knowledge of the human condition."[26]

If Golub and other artists of the Monster Roster inaugurated a Chicago School of imagists, H. C. Westermann was the artist who defined its most distinctive form [figs. 9.32–9.37], anticipating the eccentric involvement with popular culture and psychotic art that ten years later pushed Chicago artists into international prominence. Yet by the sixties action painting and the existentialist figuration of the previous two decades looked like ideas from the distant past, the swansong of romanticism. By the end of the fifties it had already become clear that Robert Rauschenberg's idea of "collaborating with materials"[27] (so different from Dubuffet's) expressed an entirely new concept of the artist as a mediator between the world and the viewer. The new works of Jasper Johns also downplayed the existential "self," heralding the new definition of individuality that came to prevail in the art of the sixties.

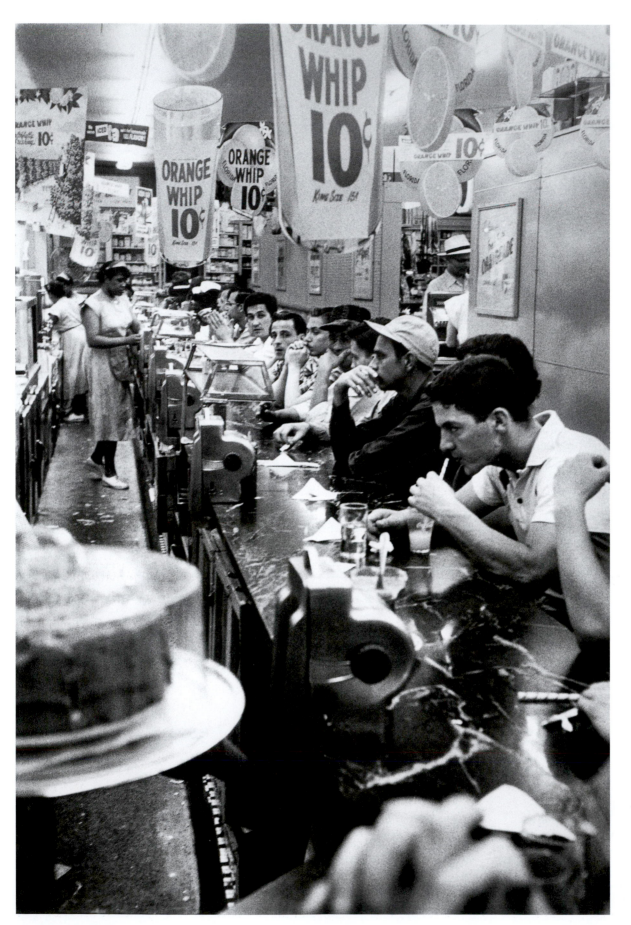

7.1 Robert Frank, *Drug Store—Detroit*, 1955–6, from *The Americans* (New York, 1959). National Gallery of Art, Washington, D.C. Gift of Christopher and Alexandra Middendorf in honor of the 50th Anniversary of the National Gallery of Art.

7 THE BEAT GENERATION

"A CONEY ISLAND OF THE MIND"

"I saw the best minds of my generation destroyed by madness, starving hysterical naked," Allen Ginsberg wrote in *Howl*, his landmark poem of 1955. They "were burned alive in their innocent flannel suits on Madison Avenue . . . or run down by the drunken taxicabs of Absolute Reality."[1] Ginsberg's America was a dehumanized prison of mainstream values, in which drug addicts, homosexuals, and the poor were defined out of existence in the common consciousness.

The alienated "beat" counterculture of the period revolved around Ginsberg and fellow writers Jack Kerouac and Lawrence Ferlinghetti, but also embraced John Ashbery, William Burroughs, Norman Mailer, Henry Miller, and Kenneth Rexroth. They lived in this limbo of nonexistence, raging against the complacent duplicity of fifties mass culture. The "beats," aided by alcohol, drugs, "cool" jazz, and the inspiration of Zen Buddhism, dropped out of the America celebrated by the *Saturday Evening Post*, the weekly magazine that embodied the homespun American culture of the 1950s perhaps better than any other single source. In the process they created their own "hip" vocabulary to reappropriate the American experience—*their* experience—of the struggle against conformity, mechanization, and materialism.

"The dog trots freely in the street and sees reality," Ferlinghetti wrote, as though speaking of the poet. "He will not be muzzled."[2] The gritty self-absorbed alienation of the beats evolved from the distinctive existentialism of the New York School painters and writers of the forties. No subject was too prosaic for beat poetry, precisely because immediate experience attacked the myths of consumer culture. Similarly, Robert Frank's photographs of the fifties [fig. 7.1] looked at the simple, unglamorized reality of ordinary life in America using a style that deliberately avoided aestheticizing it. As Harold Rosenberg wrote in 1948, "the anonymous

human being to whom [the makers of mass culture] bring their messages has at least the metaphysical advantage of being forced to deal daily with material things and real situations—tools, working conditions, personal passions."[3]

John Cage

For the New York artists of Rothko's and Pollock's generation, the purveyors of mass culture seemed to be aiming, as Marshall McLuhan wrote in 1951, "to get inside the collective public mind . . . in order to manipulate, exploit, control" it; the New York School painters expressed their rejection of commercialization by retreating into subjective experience. But McLuhan also suggested that "the very considerable currents and pressures set up around us today by the mechanical agencies of the press, radio, movies, and advertising . . . [are] full, not only of destructiveness but also of promises of rich new developments."[4] He pointed out that "discontinuity is in different ways a basic concept of both quantum and relativity physics. It is the way in which a Toynbee looks at civilizations, or a Margaret Mead at human cultures. Notoriously, it is the visual technique of a Picasso, the literary technique of James Joyce."[5] John Cage and Robert Rauschenberg also preached an aesthetic of inclusiveness, consciously embracing discontinuity, change, the arbitrary and unpredictable. They reveled in the complex reality of what Ferlinghetti called the "Coney Island of the Mind."[6]

John Cage, born in Los Angeles in 1912, studied with the composer Arnold Schoenberg. Schoenberg revolutionized modern music by breaking with harmony and with the teleological implications of tonality, in which the composer laid down a key and theme and then fulfilled the direction prescribed. Instead, he sought to construct what he viewed as a neutral vehicle for musical expression. Cage's invention in 1938 of the "prepared piano," together with his early role in the evolution of taped and electronic music, established his vanguard reputation in New York. Yet he realized from reading the reviews of his performances that his compositions failed to communicate the emotions he himself experienced in them. The turning point came after the performance of *Perilous Night*, written by Cage in 1945 about "the loneliness and terror that comes to one when love becomes unhappy."[7] The utter failure of the critics to understand the feeling in the piece led Cage to change direction completely; he gave up on the idea of trying to communicate in art and instead redirected himself to focus on the idea of opening up the listener's ears to what existed in the environment—unpredetermined experience, detached from artistic intention.

By avoiding the imposition of aesthetic hierarchies or systems designed to express order, Cage hoped to allow each element to present itself on its own. His discovery of Zen Buddhism in the mid-forties seems to have prompted the form of this radical change. Whereas the artists of the New York School generated art from personal introspection, Cage's study of Zen fostered a detachment from expressive intention and encouraged the idea that art originates in the noninterpretive contemplation of nature. "One may give up the desire to control sound, clear his mind of music, and set about discovering means to let sounds be themselves rather than vehicles for manmade theories or expressions of human sentiments," he explained. "Hearing sounds which are just sounds immediately sets the theorizing mind to theorizing, and the emotions of human beings are continually aroused by encounters with nature."[8]

Inspired by Duchamp's readymades (everyday objects which Duchamp presented, unaltered, as works of art) [fig. 7.2], Cage regarded the everyday world as the source of art. Like Duchamp, whom he befriended in 1941, he undercut the heroic myth underlying the New York School and opposed psychology as a foundation for art. "There is no room for emotion in a work of art,"[9] he later remarked. Cage looked to the senses as Duchamp had looked to the intellect; both rejected expressionism. In 1950 Cage even began to use chance, which he saw as nature's central operating principle.

Rather than using chance to bypass surface consciousness, as in dada and surrealism, Cage hoped to use it to avoid personal determination. This attempt to annihilate the artistic ego as well as the distinction between art and everyday experience was unprecedented and in direct contrast to the posture of his contemporaries in the New York School. Yet Cage resembled them in his emphasis on spontaneity and process.

By 1950 Cage's tenement apartment on the Lower East Side had become a meeting place for a group of friends interested in new music and dance. Christian Wolff (then a high school student) dropped by one day with the *I Ching* or *Book of Changes*, which Pantheon had just published. The book came to Cage at just the right moment, and he used the *I Ching* coins and charts to compose his 1951 *Music of Changes*. Cage tossed three coins six times, matching the results against a chart, which in turn determined the pitch

of each note. Then he went through a similar procedure for timbre and duration. He followed this elaborate process to avoid letting personal choice interfere with the chance procedures. Since the piece lasts for forty-five minutes, Cage had to make an extraordinary number of tosses.

In his theory of a "total soundspace" Cage asserted that music involves all sound, including nonmusical sound and the absence of sound. Whereas sound has pitch, timbre, loudness, and duration, Cage observed, silence has only duration. In his 1952 silent piece, entitled *4 minutes 33 seconds (4'33")*, the performer makes no sound for this exact period of time. Influenced by Rauschenberg's blank "White Paintings" of 1951, Cage eliminated everything but time (the shared feature of sound and silence) and the random sounds of the environment.

The chance operations of the *Music of Changes* produced results which, once Cage set them down, remained fixed. But in the silent piece Cage's antipathy to willful patterns took him still further, into indeterminacy, which assumes continual flux. He embraced the true arbitrariness of ambient sounds in order to get the listener to hear in a neutral way. *0'00"* of 1962 took this idea one more step in specifying that it could be performed by anyone in any manner. Although Cage credited Morton Feldman with leading the way into indeterminacy, Cage's chance (or "aleatory") music and ideas of ambient ("concrete") sound also influenced Feldman's music as well as that of Earle Brown, Christian Wolff, and La Monte Young.

7.2 Marcel Duchamp, *In Advance of the Broken Arm*, 1945. Replica of 1915 "original" readymade, wood and metal, 47¾ × 18in (121.3 × 45.7cm). Yale University Art Gallery. Gift of Katherine S. Dreier for the Collection Société Anonyme.

Merce Cunningham

Cage also had a close artistic exchange with the dancer/choreographer Merce Cunningham. Cage and Cunningham began working together in 1943, the year before Cunningham's first solo recital in New York (while he was still dancing with the Martha Graham Company). Their collaboration broke sharply with choreographic tradition in permitting the individual dancer any movement meaningful to her or him and relieving the performer of any obligation to tell a story, symbolize anything, or find equivalents for the music. The music, the sets, and the individual dancers all functioned independently but simultaneously. Cage and Cunningham created systems, overlaid them, and then watched what happened when they collided. As Cunningham explained: "We have chosen to have the music and the dance act as separate identities . . . one not dependent upon the other, but they coexist, as sight and sound do in our daily lives . . . as an opening out to the complexity we live in, even to the possible enjoyment of it."[10]

Merce Cunningham changed the language of dance. For him, any movement, no matter how ordinary—walking, falling, jumping—could constitute dance. Furthermore, no action in dance carried any significance beyond what it was in itself, he insisted; like Cage, Cunningham chiefly wanted to engage the viewer's senses. He also wanted to lay bare the sheer physicality of dance. With all six dancers in Cunningham's troupe moving independently, they would cover the whole stage at once, as in a Pollock or de Kooning "all over" painting. Cunningham created assemblages of unpremeditated gestures from real life just as Rauschenberg and the fifties junk sculptors did with found objects.

The high point of Cunningham's tours with Cage in the forties was their (unpaid) visit to Black Mountain College in 1948. Their presentation of Erik Satie's *Ruse of the Medusa*, directed by Arthur Penn (who later directed major Hollywood films), with performances by, among others, Willem and Elaine de Kooning, Richard Lippold, Buckminster Fuller, and Beaumont Newhall, was an electrifying event. Through this performance Cage established a friendship with Josef Albers, the art master of the school. However, when Cage later began working with chance and indeterminacy, Albers declaimed that Cage had "renounced his responsibility as an artist" and broke off relations.[11]

The Cage "Event" of 1952

It was John Cage's *Theater Piece #1* (often simply referred to as "the event"), performed at Black Mountain College in 1952, that became legendary as the first "happening" and the beginning of aleatory music and dance (even though Cage had already written the *Music of Changes* in 1951). M. C. Richards, a member of the Black Mountain faculty, had just finished translating Antonin Artaud's *The Theater and Its Double*—a book which encouraged Cage to think of theater as a time and space filled with coexisting but unrelated events, instead of as a narrative. Artaud's "theater of cruelty" proposed a primitive, ritualistic spectacle stirring a violent exchange with the audience. Cage's theater was more emotionally neutral but no less perplexing and enigmatic.

In the 1952 "event" M. C. Richards and the poet Charles Olson read poetry from ladders; Robert Rauschenberg's "White Paintings" hung overhead while the artist played Edith Piaf records on an old phonograph; David Tudor performed on the piano; Merce Cunningham danced in and around the audience (chased by a barking dog); coffee was served by four boys dressed in white; and Cage sat on a stepladder for two hours—sometimes reading a lecture on the relation of music to Zen Buddhism, sometimes silently listening.[12] Everyone did whatever they chose to do during certain assigned intervals of time, and the entire experience was so full of sensory input that no two accounts of it sound much alike. Indeed the individuality of each observer's experience was central to Cage's aspiration. Cage created his outline and organization for the "event" using chance operations, and yet the style is unmistakably his.

ROBERT RAUSCHENBERG

The Self as a Mirror of Life

In his 1959 novel *Naked Lunch* William Burroughs asserted that "there is only one thing a writer can write about: *what is in front of his senses at the moment of writing* . . . I am a recording instrument . . . I do not presume to impose 'story' 'plot' 'continuity.'"[13] Robert Rauschenberg [fig. 7.3] pioneered an art style that also ceased to rely on "'story' 'plot' 'continuity'"—elements still lingering in the action painter's arsenal of focused introspection; instead Rauschenberg promoted an unfocused openness to external events. Beginning with his "White Paintings" of 1951, Rauschenberg, like Cage, tried to redirect the viewer's attention from the psyche of the painter onto the outside world. The relative lack of surface detail in these flat white canvases provided a neutral backdrop for random shadows and for the reflection of the colors of the environment. Gradually found objects (and, later, found images) replaced the neutral surfaces as reflections of the experiential world.

Rauschenberg's art recast the existentialist discovery of the self as a discovery of the environment from which the self takes its form. Where de Kooning and Pollock pursued the refinement of a known artistic identity through introspection, Rauschenberg denied that there was a fixed core to identity at all. He tried to push his artistic persona into continual flux, so that he could perpetually reinvent himself through an acutely sensitive response to the prevailing situation. "I don't want my personality to come out through the piece," Rauschenberg explained. "I want my paintings to be reflections of life . . . your self-visualization is a reflection of your surroundings."[14]

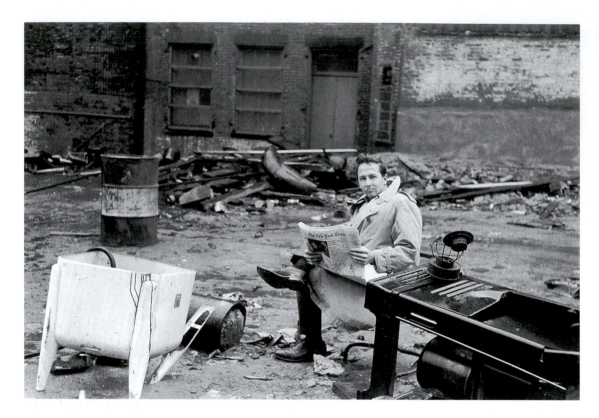

7.3 Robert Rauschenberg seated in an empty lot next to his loft on Water Street, New York, January 15, 1961.

Photograph © by Fred W. McDarrah.

Rauschenberg's "combine" paintings (his term for the arrangement of miscellaneous objects and materials, more broadly known as "assemblage") began tentatively around 1951 with the application of printed matter and other flat materials to the canvas. By 1953 he had begun to incorporate all manner of materials and actual objects into the compositions. *Bed*, for example [fig. 7.4], includes striped toothpaste and fingernail polish[15] as well as a pillow and quilt.

The Bauhaus-influenced exercises assigned by Josef Albers, his teacher at Black Mountain College, fostered Rauschenberg's openness to the inherent character of found materials. His extensive conversations with John Cage in the late forties and early fifties taught him in part to assimilate visual information in a receptive, unfocused way. With objects like the quilt and pillow in *Bed* or the stuffed bird, the flattened can, and the nostalgic family photographs in *Canyon* [fig. 7.5], Rauschenberg extended the action painter's stress on self-actualization through the spontaneous act of painting by exploiting the vividness of the associations attached to real things. Instead of discovering oneself in the act of painting, one perpetually reconstructs oneself in the process of adapting to one's encounters with the world.

In this association to real experience the images in Rauschenberg's work refer to specific meanings. They do not, however, constitute a systematic iconography.[16] The multiplicity of possible associations to each image in Rauschenberg's work permit one to "read" the individual elements in any number of ways at the same time. Though some art historians have tried, no one has convincingly "decoded" these works into a decipherable iconography. Indeed, the artist's stated aims consistently contradict the notion of a systematic iconography: "If you do work with known quantities—making puns or dealing symbolically with your material," he explained, "—you are shortening the life of the work."[17]

Rauschenberg's Early Career

Born in 1925, Robert Rauschenberg grew up in a working-class family in the Gulf Coast refinery town of Port Arthur, Texas. He abandoned his fundamentalist Christian training in the early fifties, but he continued to allude obliquely to Christian themes throughout his career.[18] After the Navy and a brief sojourn at the Kansas City Art Institute, Rauschenberg went to study with Albers at Black Mountain College in the fall of 1948. Albers found the young Texan frivolous and told him he "had nothing to teach him."[19] Nevertheless, the endless demonstrations by Albers on the relativity of color in the contexts of different surrounding colors provided the formal foundation for Rauschenberg's "White Paintings." The white panels are hypersensitive to the light around them and are thus affected by events in the environment beyond the artist's control.

From the start of his career Rauschenberg displayed a remarkably free, experimental approach to techniques and materials. In 1949 he made striking figure compositions by having a model lie face down on light-sensitive blueprint paper and bathing her in floodlight. In another work he directed John Cage to drive his Model A Ford with an inked tire down a 22-foot strip of pasted-together paper sheets, producing the disarmingly delicate *Automobile Tire Print*. His *Dirt Painting: For John Cage* sprouted real plants and

7.4 Robert Rauschenberg, *Bed*, 1955. Combine painting: oil and pencil on pillow, quilt, and sheet on wood supports, 75¼ × 31½ × 8in (191.1 × 80 × 20.3cm).

The Museum of Modern Art, New York. Gift of Leo Castelli in honor of Alfred H. Barr, Jr., 79.1989.

had to be watered—perhaps a response to Cage's idea that art should emulate natural processes.

In the fall of 1949 Rauschenberg moved to New York and began taking classes at the Art Students League. He married shortly thereafter and in July 1951 had a son, but in the meantime he began to develop a relationship with Cy Twombly which soon eclipsed the marriage. While in New York Rauschenberg had associated with abstract expressionists at "The Club" on 8th Street, and got to know most of the important artists. He participated in the "event" orchestrated by Cage and Cunningham at Black Mountain College in the summer of 1952 and in the fall of 1952 he and Twombly left on an extended trip to Europe and North Africa.

By the time Rauschenberg returned in 1953, he had clearly renounced the psychological introspection of the New York School.

> There was something about the self-confession and self-confusion of abstract expressionism—as though the man and the work were the same—that personally always put me off because at that time my focus was in the opposite direction. I was busy trying to find ways where the imagery, the material and the meaning of the painting would be, not an illustration of my will, but more like an unbiased documentation of what I observed, letting the area of feeling and meaning take care of itself.[20]

In his black paintings of 1952, Rauschenberg explained that he "was interested in getting complexity without revealing much."[21] He made them by laying down torn and crumpled newspaper and painting over it so that "even the first stroke in the painting would have its position in a gray map of words," he said.[22] In the red paintings that followed, Rauschenberg included increasing amounts of urban debris in his compositions.

In 1954 Rauschenberg met Jasper Johns and moved into a loft in his building. Although exceedingly different in temperament and style, they became close and deeply affected one another's work. Rauschenberg did not read much but absorbed an enormous amount talking with friends like Cage and Johns about what they were reading. Johns, by contrast, was highly intellectual and read a great deal.

Johns and Rauschenberg both had an ambivalent relation to introspective content in art. On the one hand they admired the subtlety of abstract expressionist handling—Rauschenberg's sentimentality often brought him to the edge of romanticism—on the other hand they resisted the New York School's focus on revelations of personality. In 1957 Rauschenberg even attempted to make two identical gesture paintings (*Factum I* and *Factum II*). "The point was to see what the difference could be between the emotional content of one and the other," he explained. "I couldn't tell the difference after I painted them!"[23] Like Duchamp's readymades, his pair attempts to undermine the idea of the authenticity of the autographic gesture.

Even when a composition ultimately failed to work, the free-associative process offered the exhilaration of fully and

spontaneously experiencing everything while it happened. This openness, which comes from action painting, was also embraced in different ways both by the "beat" writers and by John Cage; they celebrated "the coexistence of dissimilars"[24] (Cage). Cage's inclination to let the audience hear all the sounds of the environment and discover their innate disorder encouraged Rauschenberg in developing an aesthetic of accumulation and randomness, although he never fully embraced chance in the way Cage did. As Rauschenberg explained: "I was never able to use it [chance], I would end up with something quite geometric or the spirit that I was interested in indulging in, was gone . . . I felt as though I was carrying out an idea rather than witnessing an unknown idea taking place."[25] Rauschenberg reveled in the bewildering complexity of life.

The Combine Paintings

In the late fifties the found objects and images asserted themselves with increasing clarity and independence. Unlike the surrealists, who used the random juxtaposition of such material to unleash free association as a key to their analysis of the unconscious mind, Rauschenberg sought an experience of assimilation—*without* analysis of any kind. He did not set out to find objects by going to a junk yard, for example; this would imply a predetermined theme. Instead he wanted to use objects and ideas that cropped up in the course of his activities.

Increasingly, what turned up came via the media, and a great deal of the advertising in the media had erotic overtones. *Life* magazine, for example, ran an advertisement for Old Gold cigarettes in 1953 [fig. 7.6], in which naked female legs, complete with high-heeled shoes, are shown kneeling on an exotic courtesan's cushion. A sleekly dressed man centers the crown (a large open hole) over the unmistakably phallic tubes which burst out of the box. Marshall McLuhan's book *The Mechanical Bride* had alerted Rauschenberg and Cage to read advertising on this subliminal level. In works such as *Odalisk* [fig. 7.7], which Rauschenberg began in 1955, he exploited just this kind of sexual symbolism, reinforced by collage elements drawn from popular culture. In *Odalisk* the phallic post presses into the cushion on one end and on the other supports a box with a light inside. This can be "turned on" or "turned off" and the box is covered with erotic images like a "dog—lust—barking at a pin-up nude,"[26] and topped, as one critic noted, with a "cock."

The objects in a work like *Odalisk* create an environment that aims to evoke the complexity of life experience—ranging

from the sexual symbolism used in advertising to the visual maelstrom of the street. "I like the history of objects. I like humanitarian reportage,"[27] the artist said. "I would like my pictures to be able to be taken apart as easily as they're put together—so you can recognize an object when you're looking at it."[28] This approach maintains the raw spontaneity of the gesture painting of de Kooning and Kline. "After you recognize that the canvas you're painting on is simply another rag then it doesn't matter whether you use stuffed chickens or electric light bulbs or pure form."[29]

Despite the fact that such works as *Odalisk* evolved spontaneously, the latter nevertheless took three years to complete. When Rauschenberg first exhibited works of this kind at the Leo Castelli Gallery in 1959, the show elicited considerable hostility. Some of the abstract expressionists who came to the opening laughed out loud and actually began kicking one of Rauschenberg's sculptures. Rauschenberg was upset by this response, all the more because he admired these older artists. But they evidently saw his work as a parody of their high aesthetic purposes.[30]

7.6 Old Gold cigarettes advertisement, *Life* magazine, April 27, 1953, p. 3.

7.7 (left) **Robert Rauschenberg**, *Odalisk*, 1955–8. Oil, watercolor, pencil, fabric, paper, photographs, metal, glass, electric light fixtures, dried grass, steel wool, necktie, on wood structure with four wheels, plus pillow and stuffed rooster, 83 × 25½ × 25⅛in (210.8 × 64.8 × 63.8cm). Collection, Museum Ludwig Köln.

The Drawings for Dante's *Inferno*

Rauschenberg's desire to be taken seriously almost certainly played a role in motivating him, at the beginning of 1959, to embark on a suite of drawings to accompany the thirty-four cantos of Dante's masterpiece, the *Inferno*. These drawings come as close as anything in Rauschenberg's *oeuvre* to following a consistent iconography,[31] but still don't. When he finished the series in early 1960, he exhibited them with the poem to help viewers appreciate the images.

Dore Ashton reported that the artist took the photograph representing Dante from a *Sports Illustrated* advertisement for golf clubs, which showed a man with a towel around his waist, standing stiffly in front of a chartlike grid, as if awaiting some type of medical examination. Rauschenberg wanted to make Dante a representative of the common man and therefore sought a neutral image. The artist portrayed Virgil variously as a diving figure blurred by a scrimlike overpainting that gives him the vague immateriality of a spirit, then as an intellectual—using a photograph of Adlai Stevenson, the great statesman and orator who ran against Eisenhower in the presidential elections of 1952 and 1956. Other images also appear from contemporary life and politics, such as a satanic Richard Nixon and racing cars (to evoke the whirring and wailing sounds of Hell).

Although the individual images seem to have taken form intuitively as the artist read each successive line of the narrative, the viewer can follow some images in the drawings, correlating them with the poem, generally in sequence from left to right, like reading. Nevertheless, despite some close connections between the visual and the poetic images, Rauschenberg's work is overlaid with other simultaneously functioning meanings—not least a comparison between Dante's peregrinations through Hell and the artist's own reflections on the deterioration of his relationship with Jasper Johns—his own "Hell" of 1959. Dead center in the drawing for *Canto XXXIII* [fig. 7.8], for example, is a bent arm and hand that resembles the plaster casts Johns had

7.8 (opposite) **Robert Rauschenberg**, *Canto XXXIII: Circle Nine, Cocytus, Compound Fraud: Round 2, Antenora, Treacherous to Country: Round 3, Ptolomea, Treacherous to Guests and Hosts*, from the series "Thirty-four Illustrations for Dante's *Inferno*," 1959–60. Transfer drawing, watercolor, and pencil, 14½ × 11½in (36.8 × 29.2cm). The Museum of Modern Art, New York. Given anonymously, 346.1963.33.

constructed since the early fifties and incorporated into his paintings [fig. 7.45]. Rauschenberg worked for a year and a half on the series, spending six months alone on a deserted wharf in Florida.

Before 1958 Rauschenberg drew very little. Then he discovered, in an irreverent experiment with materials, that if he soaked reproductions from magazines in lighter fluid he could transfer them on to paper by rubbing the back with an empty ballpoint pen. This technique provided the basis for the Dante drawings, which he built around juxtapositions of found images transferred from magazines and advertising.

Rauschenberg's drawings for Dante's *Inferno* involve the sense of time unfolding, despite the lack of a clear narrative sequence. The artist explained: "I realized that the details should not be taken in at one glance, that you should be able to look from place to place without feeling the bigger image. I had to make a surface which invited a constant change of focus and an examination of detail. Listening happens in time. Looking also had to happen in time."[32] *Reservoir* [fig. 7.9] of 1961 includes two clocks, addressing time explicitly. Rauschenberg set the first clock at the time when he began work and the other when he finished, but the viewer cannot

7.9 Robert Rauschenberg, *Reservoir*, 1961. Oil, graphite, fabric, wood, metal on canvas, plus two electric clocks, rubber tread wheel, and spoked wheel rim, 85½ × 62½ × 14¾in (217.2 × 158.8 × 37.5cm).

National Museum of American Art, Smithsonian Institution, Washington, D.C. Gift of S. C. Johnson and Son, Inc.

tell whether the work ended after five hours and fifty minutes or twelve or twenty-four or some other multiple of twelve hours later than that.

Like Cage's embrace of discontinuity, Rauschenberg's visual syntax emulated the rapid scan of the city dweller rather than the fixed stare of the traditional art viewer. He sought to capture "reality" in all its confusion as a collage of details. He pointedly preserved the identity of the individual found objects, leaving the viewer with a sense of their original context rather than letting them disappear into the aesthetic of the work. They are neither metaphors nor symbols but objects with specific associations for the artist.

The End of the Combines

Rauschenberg came to the end of his combine paintings toward the beginning of 1962 as he introduced the photo-silkscreen into his work. Images rather than objects began to predominate, as is prefigured in the transfer drawings of the late fifties, including those for Dante's *Inferno*. By eliminating visually dramatic objects and flattening out the literal surface of the canvas, Rauschenberg further dissipated the focus in his works. In contrast to painters like Pollock or de Kooning, who refined their styles around the declaration of their identities, Rauschenberg veered toward disintegration, defining himself anew in relation to the exigent details of each moment.

Rauschenberg's *Erased de Kooning Drawing* (1953) is emblematic of this distinction. He asked de Kooning to give him a drawing that was good enough to be missed and difficult to erase. He erased for two months, but in the end he could not eliminate the lingering presence of de Kooning on the paper. This attempt to obliterate the artistic presence mirrors Rauschenberg's stated effort to erase the assertion of individual identity from his own work, which ultimately he could not do either. In contrast to the action painter's concept of starting from scratch, Rauschenberg starts from something concrete and moves toward self-annihilation.

> I don't want a painting to be just an expression of my personality. I feel it ought to be much better than that. And I'm opposed to the whole idea of . . . getting an idea for a picture and then carrying it out. I've always felt as though, whatever I've used and whatever I've done, the method was always closer to a collaboration with materials than to any kind of conscious manipulation and control . . . I'd really like to think that the artist could be just another kind of material in the picture, working in collaboration with all the other materials. But of course I know this isn't possible, really.[33]

The flipside of Rauschenberg's readiness to encounter freshly the changing facts of life and art and to redefine himself in response to them is a profound lack of self-worth. "I think my religious experience has built into my ethic an irreversible sense of inferiority . . . When I go to work I have to feel invisible to get away from the inferiority."[34] This feeling reflects, however obliquely, the central importance of identity even in Rauschenberg's work.

In 1961 Rauschenberg moved to a huge fifth-floor loft in Greenwich Village and Johns started spending more and more time in his new house on an island off the coast of South Carolina. The friendship ended during the summer of 1962 in a bitter break-up. Thereafter Rauschenberg shifted much of his energy into performance; in 1962 he logged more hours as a stage manager and lighting director

7.10 Robert Rauschenberg performing in *Pelican*, New York, 1965, first performed in 1963.
Photograph by Peter Moore.

for Cunningham than as a painter. In 1963 he even choreographed his own dance piece, *Pelican* [fig. 7.10]. Rauschenberg also began to drink more and more heavily.

The Silkscreen Paintings

Meanwhile in the summer of 1962 Tatyana Grosman persuaded Rauschenberg to try lithography at Universal Limited Art Editions (U.L.A.E.), her Long Island print shop. The technique required close collaboration with a master printer and Rauschenberg liked collective efforts, though he generally ended up dominating them. In 1961 Andy Warhol started using photosilkscreens to replicate images repeatedly across a canvas, and in 1962 he introduced Rauschenberg and Johns to the medium. The photosilkscreen immediately became Rauschenberg's standard technique in painting. He also

successfully photosensitized a lithographic stone at U.L.A.E. The photographic found images replaced the real objects of the combines and permitted an even freer clash of associations in the prints and large photosilkscreened paintings.

These silkscreen paintings have a documentary flavor, like a television screen jumping from one channel to the next to produce a seemingly arbitrary jumble of images. The photosensitive canvas picks up reflections of the world, recalling the underlying ambition of the earlier white canvases. But here the larger subject is the overload of imagery itself. It involves the more stylistically complex idea of bringing old associations to bear directly on new experience in a stream-of-consciousness style appropriate to the media age. "I was bombarded with television sets and magazines, by the excess of the world," he said. "I thought an honest work should incorporate all of those elements."[35]

7.11 Robert Rauschenberg, *Skyway*, 1964. Oil and silkscreen on canvas, 18 × 16ft (5.49 × 4.88m) overall.

Dallas Museum of Art. Purchase, Roberta Coke Camp Fund, The 500, Inc., Mr. and Mrs. Mark Shepard, Jr., and the General Acquisition Fund.

In one sense these works of the early sixties are modern history paintings that comment on current events. Rauschenberg used President Kennedy more than any other public personality; the photograph of J.F.K. was a symbol of change because of his innovative agenda and Rauschenberg used the image as an expression of his own social conscience. He also used pictures of astronauts as well as banal material from his immediate environment: street signs, neighborhood buildings in demolition, a box of tomatoes. "I needed some very simple images . . . to dull the social implications, to neutralize the calamities that were going on in the outside world."[36]

In *Skyway* [fig. 7.11] the images of Venus looking into the mirror and then out of the picture—taken from *Venus at Her Toilet* by Rubens—extend the picture's space to include the viewer. Rauschenberg himself looks into the picture in order to see out; the painting thus mirrors both the world outside and the artist. The repetition and resonances between forms and the abundant particular references function like the subjective thought processes of memory. Rauschenberg's paintings are about who he is in relation to the events he depicts; they are, he said, "a vehicle that will report what you did and what happened to you."[37]

Rauschenberg's March 1963 retrospective at the Jewish Museum gave him credibility. The next year the Museum of Modern Art bought a work by him, he had a rousing success with an exhibition at the Whitechapel Gallery in London, and then won the Golden Lion in the Venice Biennale. Immediately after the award Rauschenberg called his assistant in New York and had him destroy all the silkscreens with which Rauschenberg had been printing the images on his silkscreen paintings of the past two years. This kept him from repeating himself but it also signaled his feeling that he had come to a dead end. He nearly stopped painting.

Performance and the Prints of the Later Sixties

Rauschenberg had long been involved in collaborations with performers from theater and dance. In the fall of 1965 he began an art and technology performance project, enlisting the help of Billy Klüver (a Swedish engineer from Bell Labs). Rauschenberg's *9 Evenings: Theater and Engineering* of 1966 involved over thirty engineers from Bell Labs in a complex event of performance, dance, and technologically inventive staging. He followed up with the founding of Experiments in Art and Technology (or E.A.T.).

The rest of Rauschenberg's time was taken up with fancy clothes, curled hairdos, heavy drinking, and a groupie scene to rival Warhol's; his work in the studio became increasingly inconsequential. "Rauschenberg was a natural dissipater," wrote the critic Robert Hughes. "The sight of him in his porcupine-quill jacket, erect but reeling slightly, marinated with Jack Daniel's, cackling like a Texas loon and trying to get his arm around everyone at once, was too familiar."[38]

The great graphic works of the late sixties, *Booster* [fig. 7.12] and *Autobiography*, signaled Rauschenberg's return.

Measuring 6 feet from top to bottom, *Booster* was the largest hand-pulled lithograph that had ever been made and Rauschenberg's first collaboration with the innovative Los Angeles-based print workshop, Gemini G.E.L. Rauschenberg composed it around a full-length sequence of X-rays of his own body, and it had to be printed with two stones on a

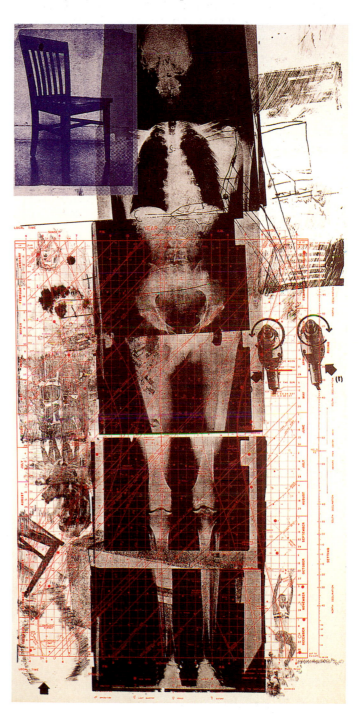

7.12 Robert Rauschenberg, *Booster*, 1967. Lithograph and serigraph, printed in color, composition: 71½ × 35⅛in (181.7 × 89.1cm). Publisher and Printer Gemini G.E.L., Los Angeles.

The Museum of Modern Art, New York. John B. Turner Fund, 2648.1967.

single sheet of paper made especially for the project. The work is a self-portrait, filtered through the distance of technological language—the X-ray, the astronomer's chart of celestial movement for the year 1967, and magazine images of drills with arrows diagramming their movement; it also contains the repetition of an empty chair, as though to suggest someone's absence.

The strength of *Booster*, like all of Rauschenberg's work, is that it reacted against the emotional distance of mass culture by appropriating it into an emphatically personal interaction with immediate experience. In this respect he continued the existentialist directness of action painting, but without its emphasis on the isolated identity of the artist. Rauschenberg's work, as John Cage said of his own compositions, is "an affirmation of life—not an attempt to bring order out of chaos nor to suggest improvements in creation, but simply a way of waking up to the very life we're living, which is so excellent once one gets one's mind and one's desires out of its way and lets it act of its own accord."[39]

REAL JUNK: ASSEMBLAGE AND HAPPENINGS

In a 1955 meeting at "The Club" on 8th Street Richard Stankiewicz [fig. 7.13] remarked that for an artist in New York to use junk in making sculpture was as natural as for a South Sea Islander to use shells.[40] The term "junk sculpture" refers to a specialized type of assemblage that involved the welding of discarded metal into sculpture. As such, it is a kind of urban realism, vividly evoking the environment of the city streets, where such debris is ubiquitous. David Smith and Stankiewicz pioneered junk sculpture around 1951–2, although there were notable precedents in the welded sculpture of Picasso and González and in the prewar accumulations of the German dadaist Kurt Schwitters.

John Chamberlain developed an entire *oeuvre* from crushed automobile body parts [fig. 7.14]. Mark di Suvero experimented with a variety of found materials, gravitating increasingly to industrially fabricated parts, such as I-beams [fig. 7.15]. Di Suvero's work of the sixties is particularly important for his success in translating the spontaneity of welded sculpture onto an architectural scale. Louise Nevelson [fig. 7.16] did not, strictly speaking, make sculpture out of junk; she mostly assembled monochromatically painted wood reliefs. Yet the character of her aesthetic is a fusion of junk assemblage and the insistence on the picture plane that she learned from her teacher, Hans Hofmann.

The term "assemblage" was coined in 1953 by Jean Dubuffet to refer to works that went beyond the pasted collages of the cubists.[41] By the time of the 1961 "Art of Assemblage" exhibition at the Museum of Modern Art the accepted use of the term in the art world embraced not only Dubuffet's work with "non-art" materials such as butterfly wings and industrial slag, but also junk sculpture and Rauschenberg's combines. All of this work challenged the

7.13 Richard Stankiewicz, *Diving to the Bottom of the Ocean*, 1958. Welded metal, 53⅜ × 33 × 37¾in (138 × 84 × 96cm).
Musée National d'Art Moderne–Centre Georges Pompidou, Paris.

7.14 John Chamberlain, *H.A.W.K.*, 1959. Welded steel, 4ft 1½in × 4ft 5in × 3ft 5in (1.31 × 1.35 × 1.04m).
Courtesy Leo Castelli Gallery, New York. © 2000 John Chamberlain/Artists Rights Society (ARS), New York.

7.15 Mark di Suvero, *Mohican*, 1967. Steel and wood, 15 × 9 × 30ft (4.57 × 2.74 × 9.14m). Collection, Federal Reserve Bank, Dada County, Florida.

7.16 Louise Nevelson, *Dawn's Wedding Chapel II*, 1959. White painted wood, 115⅞ × 83½ × 10½in (294.3 × 211 × 26.7cm). Whitney Museum of American Art, New York. Purchased with funds from the Howard and Jean Lipman Foundation, Inc., 7068a–m.

boundary between everyday objects and high art, reflecting a widespread concern in the art world of the fifties that was soon taken up in a different way by the pop artists of the 1960s.

UNDERGROUND FILM

As a corollary to the spontaneous collage aesthetic of assemblage and the free-flowing, collage-like texts by beat writers such as Burroughs, there was also a deliberately anti-professional, cut-up aesthetic in film that emerged in a subculture of, as it is still variously called, "avant-garde" or "expanded" cinema, or "underground," "independent," or "experimental" film. Many of the early innovators of experimental film saw it as an art medium rather than an extension of the world of the movies. The painters Marcel Duchamp, Fernand Léger, Hans Richter, and Salvador Dalí, and the photographers Man Ray and Paul Strand were among the earliest artists to work with film in this way. There were also a handful of poets experimenting with film, notably Jean Cocteau and the Italian futurist F. T. Marinetti. But there were also some early Russian filmmakers like Djiga Vertov and Sergei Eisenstein as well as surrealists like Luis Buñuel who made the boundary between avant-garde cinema and the movies difficult to delineate.

The story of American postwar experimental film begins with Maya Deren, a brilliant Russian émigré whose family, fleeing the persecution of Jews in the Ukraine in 1922, brought her to New York at the age of five. The influences of her psychoanalyst father, surrealist film, and French symbolist poetry flow together in her early masterpiece, *Meshes of the Afternoon*, a fourteen-minute silent film of 1943 [fig. 7.17]. Made during World War II, it has a nightmarish sense of paranoia, alienation, and intimations of violence that reflect the times. Deren casts herself as the central figure, doubling, tripling, and quadrupling herself in a surreal space and time, with rapid shifts in viewpoint transforming the images and sequences into a disjunctive state of poetic consciousness. A mysterious hooded figure with a mirror for a face implicitly reflects back the identity of the viewer, creating a disorienting estrangement, a sense of the uncanny.

Living a Bohemian existence in Greenwich Village in the 1940s, Deren dressed strikingly in handmade clothing, wrote on film and fashion, and developed a reputation as an intense and incisive intellect. After *Meshes of the Afternoon* she began but never finished a film with Marcel Duchamp called *Witch's Cradle*, and in 1944 released her second short film, *At Land*, followed by *Ritual in Transfigured Time* (with Anaïs Nin). In 1947 Deren was both the first American and the first woman to be awarded the *Grand Prix International* for amateur film at the Cannes Film Festival.

Deren provided a paradigm for American independent filmmakers in her insistence on the artist's control of the making, exhibition, and distribution of her films, as well as in her written commentary and framing of the reception of her own work. Deren went to Haiti on a Guggenheim fellowship in 1947 to record Voudoun rituals. On this and two subsequent trips she shot extensive footage and in 1953 she published *Divine Horsemen: The Living Gods of Haiti*, a landmark book on the subject. But the eponymous film was not compiled until after her death in 1961, at the age of forty-four from a massive cerebral hemorrhage (possibly precipitated by her long dependence on sleeping pills and amphetamines). In *Meshes of the Afternoon*, *At Land*, and *Ritual in Transfigured Time*, Deren emptied out and replaced her own character much as the spirits inhabit and possess the mind and body of a Voudoun celebrant. This elusive doubling of identities

7.17 Maya Deren, still from *Meshes of the Afternoon*, 1943. Fourteen-minute silent film.

7.18 (right) **Stan Brakhage**, strip of film from *Mothlight*, 1963.

throughout her films disturbingly erodes the boundaries of the self.[42]

Stan Brakhage is often seen as the successor to Deren. He radically revised her psychodramas into first-person lyrical films that centered more on the phenomenon of perception than on a poetic narrative. Brakhage made his first film, *Interim*, in 1952, influenced by the writings of Sergei Eisenstein, the films of Jean Cocteau, and Italian neorealism. He hung out in San Francisco in 1953 with the beat poets before moving to New York at the end of 1954, where he was close to Deren, Joseph Cornell, and John Cage. Brakhage's films flood the viewer with images in free-associative profusion, rapidly cut and montaged to create an abstract but charged experience. "Imagine an eye unruled by manmade laws of perspective, an eye unprejudiced by compositional logic, an eye which does not respond to the name of everything but which must know each object encountered in life through an adventure of perception," Brakhage wrote in his influential book *Metaphors on Vision*.[43]

Brakhage began working in 16mm but then moved to 8mm stock because 8mm projectors were more accessible to a home market and he intended his work to be viewed privately. His films are typically silent and range in length from a few seconds to several hours. He also experimented with the materials, hand painting the film, scratching images directly into the emulsion, and sometimes even using collage, as in the 1963 *Mothlight* [fig. 7.18], for which he literally taped moth wings, twigs, and leaves onto clear film stock and then made prints from it. *Anticipation of the Night*, a film of 1958, centers on the filmmaker's mind, making him the implied protagonist. The enigmatic sequences of expressive color, natural light, motion, rapid editing, and repetition strive to create the totality of the artist's inner experience without narrative, time, or an on-screen protagonist. In *Dog Star Man* (1961–4), his most famous work, he expands outward, beginning with a simple narrative idea of a man (himself) climbing a mountain to cut a tree but then expanding with a plethora of many image associations—the surface of the sun, childbirth, abstract bursts of light.

At the same time Bruce Conner was pioneering the use of found footage culled from extant movies, splicing them so densely that the viewer is constantly off balance trying to assimilate them. The images that pass across the screen in his famous *A Movie* of 1958 shift quickly from comedic to brutal: an image of a submarine captain looking through a periscope flashes to one of a scantily clad woman then back to that of the captain, then on to an image of a torpedo being launched, then to a giant mushroom cloud. The footage is often ruthlessly dark and reveals Conner's fascination with death: Mussolini and his dead wife's battered bodies hanging upside down, various accidents like a well-known shot of a collapsing suspension bridge, after which Conner cuts to an inspirational speech by Teddy Roosevelt. Conner carefully selects his stills and considers their sociopolitical content in such a way as to unveil the construction of culture through mass media, creating charged images that subvert

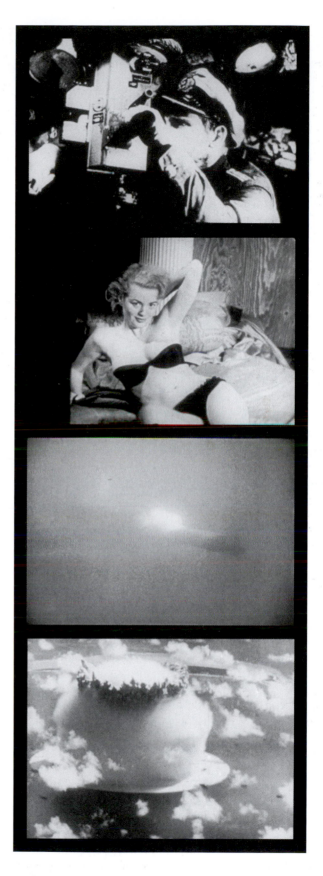

7.19 Bruce Connor, *A Movie*, 1958. Montage sequence of four stills. 16mm black-and-white film with sound. Twelve minutes. Courtesy of the Conner Family Trust.

our habits of thought and seeing [fig. 7.19]. Conner emerged in the San Francisco Bay area with the beat generation, innovating not only in avant-garde film but also in the visual arts with his "funk art" assemblages of the 1950s and 1960s [figs. 9.47 and 9.48]. The ripped nylon stockings stretched over an assemblage of objects, as in *Child* (1959), obscure the imagery from view, just as the rapid montage technique of his films adds mystery to the found footage by only allowing rapid glimpses.

Whereas by the 1940s commercial film (and soon thereafter television) were packaging a version of reality that viewers were all supposed to buy into, avant-garde cinema sought to undermine this tendency by making spectators aware of the literal techniques of a film. It is always difficult to see outside of our own representational structure, whether it be the norms of our language or our cultural habits of seeing. But causing us to see the structure itself has been the agenda of underground film from the beginning, and it is still the intention of the best artists working in video today.

The Genesis of the Happenings

Allan Kaprow, who inaugurated the happenings in New York in 1958, came out of this same counterculture perspective on assemblage. His sources were action painting, John Cage, junk art, and the work of Robert Rauschenberg. The last two, in particular, seemed to imply that the entire world was one big work of art, extending the urban aesthetic of the New York School to include literally everything on the street. The "happenings" of the late fifties evolved from a similar idea. In a Town Hall lecture of 1957 John Cage speculated: "Where do we go from here? Towards theater. That art more than music resembles nature. We have eyes as well as ears, and it is our business while we are alive to use them."[44] At the time Cage was teaching a class at the New School for Social Research which provided the germ for the first happenings in New York.

Allan Kaprow, who had studied with Hans Hofmann and was painting in an abstract expressionist style, signed up for Cage's course two years in a row. He had read about the radical dada events of the twenties in Robert Motherwell's 1951 anthology, *Dada Painters and Poets*. But Cage's discussion of the ideas of Zen, Duchamp, Artaud, and above all his description of the active participation of the audience in the 1952 "event" at Black Mountain College stimulated Kaprow to arrange his own happening in 1958. This took place on the New Jersey farm of the artist George Segal, at a picnic for members of the Hansa Gallery in New York.

Like many artists at this time Kaprow felt the need to go beyond the conventions of both gesture painting and junk sculpture. So he fused the urban realism of the latter with the spatial expressionism that he extrapolated from Pollock and set it in a real environment. He moved from the juxtaposition of found objects to the juxtaposition of "found events." In an article of 1958 entitled "The Legacy of Jackson Pollock" Kaprow reasoned as follows:

Pollock, as I see him, left us at the point where we must become preoccupied with and even dazzled by the space and objects of our everyday life ... Not satisfied with the suggestion through paint of our other senses, we shall utilize the specific substances of sight, sound, movements, people, odors, touch. Objects of every sort are materials for the new art: paint, chairs, food, electric and neon lights, smoke, water, old socks, a dog, movies, a thousand other things.[45]

Harold Rosenberg's idea of action painting also pressed Kaprow to pass beyond gesture into pure action [fig. 7.20]. In action painting the artist concerned him- or herself with a creative act of self-discovery, whose result was above all an artifact of the experience. Pollock, Rosenberg argued, was less preoccupied with image-making than the process, even though the finished work was spectacularly beautiful; indeed, the object's visual power relied on its ability to convey the energy of the process.

Kaprow had a "show" at the Hansa Gallery in 1958 that consisted of a complex, collaged environment with random sounds from a radio. He performed in the space, but his

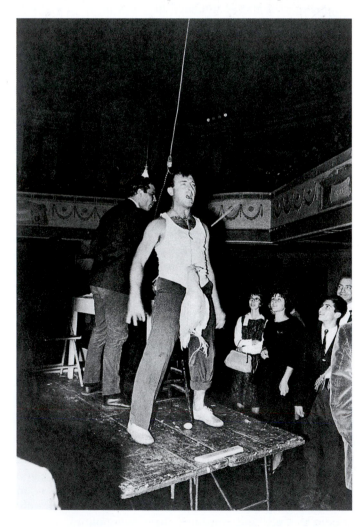

7.20 Allan Kaprow, *Chicken*, 1962. Happening.
Photograph by Edwin Sabol.

first full, public happening as such—called *18 Happenings in 6 Parts*—took place at the Reuben Gallery in October 1959. Here too the sources were not theater, but dada provocations, assemblage, and action painting. It therefore required the spontaneity of novices, rather than actors, as Kaprow explained: Actors "wanted to have stellar roles. They wanted to speak for the most part, and I utilized little verbiage in my work. And all the things which I suggested were quite contrary to their background . . . But my other friends, who were unaccustomed to acting, were quite capable because they sensed the origins of what they were doing in painting."[46]

Robert Whitman studied with Kaprow at Rutgers, the state university of New Jersey. He was the youngest of the first happenings artists, and his ideas tended to be more abstract. In general, happenings bombarded the viewer with sensations and the viewer had to make his or her own order out of them. Often the action included the viewers, and their participation added an unpredictability that dramatized its similarity with real life. Happenings were a kind of theater that took place in real, rather than staged, settings, and instead of plots they were structured in juxtaposed units as in an assemblage. The typical happening was nonverbal,

discontinuous, nonsequential, multifocused, and open-ended. According to Kaprow: "A Happening is *generated in action* by a headful of ideas or a flimsily-jotted-down score of 'root' directions."[47] Although some happenings engaged the audience extensively, others did not. Kaprow's *Fluids* of 1967, for example, involved tasks executed at various locations around a city, as determined by the performers; the only audience was that which serendipitously happened by, thus creating a true integration of art with life.

Inspired by Kaprow, Claes Oldenburg launched his Ray Gun Theater in January 1960. *The Street* [fig. 7.21] by Oldenburg and Jim Dine's *The House* were environments created at the Judson Gallery, a makeshift space in the basement of the Judson Memorial Church in Washington Square, and they emulated the squalor of the Lower East Side where the artists lived. Oldenburg characterized this kind of art as a "contemporary primitivism achieved through the exploitation of popular culture."[48] As Barbara Haskell has pointed out, by singling out everyday "unaesthetic" objects Oldenburg anticipated pop art.[49]

Red Grooms performed his first happening, *Play Called Fire*, in Provincetown, Massachusetts, on the tip of Cape

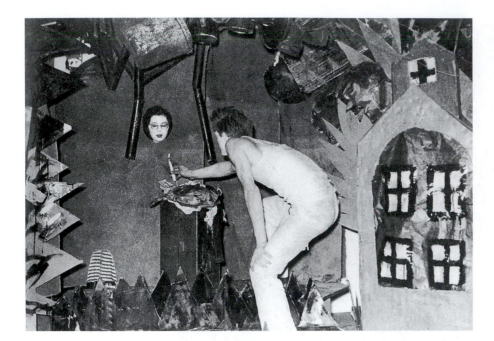

Cod, in the summer of 1958. He was less concerned than the early Kaprow with viewer participation, and like Oldenburg more involved in visual elaboration and improvisation. Grooms orchestrated his three major happenings—*The Walking Man*, *The Burning Building* [fig. 7.22], and *The Magic Train Ride*—between the summer of 1959 and January 1960. Jim Dine participated in several Oldenburg happenings but also devised his own, in which he played the principal role. Dine's happenings seemed like staged nightmares; he later wrote that "anyone could do anything and be liked," and that "the audiences were laughing at everything."[50]

Happenings were definitely the "in" thing for a period. Everyone sensed the excitement and vitality of a genuine revolution in the definition of art. Yet because they did not leave museum objects and their lifespan was short, the happenings may seem less important in retrospect than they actually were. However, by 1962 the whole phenomenon had grown too commercialized, according to Oldenburg: "People were arriving in Cadillacs."[51] So, except for Kaprow, the major artists all returned to painting and sculpture or went into video and film.

The Judson Dance Theater

As the Judson Gallery artists moved on to regular galleries, the Judson Dance Theater—including Yvonne Rainer, Steve Paxton, Simone Forti, Lucinda Childs, Judith Dunn, and Trisha Brown—took over the basement space, and with it the Judson Gallery's role as a focal point of the downtown scene. The artists of the Judson Dance Theater choreographed such commonplace movements as walking or sitting down. Yvonne Rainer invented the term "task movement," which characterized the general mood: the performances had no theatrical feel, they were anti-expressionistic (unlike the happenings), and they employed few if any objects or sets.

Like pop art and minimalism—which also emerged around 1962—these Judson Dance performances involved a deadpan delivery of charged subjects. In describing one section of Rainer's "love duet" *Terrain*, Barbara Haskell noted that "she delivered hackneyed expressions ('I love you,' 'I don't love you,' 'I've never loved you') in a flat monotone which one critic likened to the recitation of a grocery order."[52] By taking them out of context, Rainer and the others transformed everyday actions into abstract movement and encouraged the appreciation of accidental acts, just as Cage had in the realm of sound. Cunningham was of course the chief inspiration behind this minimalist dance.

Walk-in Paintings

Meanwhile in 1958—the same year in which Alan Kaprow organized his first happening on George Segal's New Jersey farm—Segal himself began making life-sized, three-dimensional figures out of wire, plaster, and burlap. "They looked to me as if they had stepped out of my paintings," he recalled, explaining that his "decision to enter literal space was determined by strong urges for total experience."[53] Soon he began constructing environments of real objects, as in *The Subway* [fig. 7.23], which has a real subway-car interior with lights that seem to flash by outside the darkened window. Marisol, a Venezuelan émigré in New York, also mixed real objects with wooden blocks—carved illusionistically and detailed with plaster and drawing or paint [fig. 7.24].

Red Grooms's painting style, as well as his reputation, was established with his happening *The Burning Building*, presented in the "Delancy Street Museum" (his loft) in December 1959. The expressionistically painted set and the evocative juxtaposition of events created a more controlled and unified structure for happenings than Kaprow's, and it was more interesting to watch. In the summer of 1957 the

7.23 (left) **George Segal**, *The Subway*, 1968. Plaster, metal, glass, rattan, electrical parts with light bulbs, and map, 7ft 4in × 9ft 5½in × 4ft 3in (2.25 × 2.88 × 1.30m).

7.24 (below) **Marisol**, *The Family*, 1963. Mixed-media assemblage, 6ft 7in (2.01m) high. Collection, Robert B. Mayer Family, Chicago, on loan to the Milwaukee Art Museum.

twenty-year-old Grooms had left his native Nashville for the Hans Hofmann School in Provincetown, and although Hofmann made little impression on him the community of younger artists there introduced him to the gestural styles of Lester Johnson and Alex Katz, which shaped his idea of painting. Grooms also painted what he called "stick-outs," which stand up independently in real space like stage flats. As with Segal's *tableaux* and the earlier cutout paintings of Katz, the "stick-outs" came from a desire for a total walk-in environment in order to enhance the "reality" of the painted experience.

Jim Dine began making junk accumulations and at the same time began to incorporate real articles of clothing into his paintings in 1959. Soon he moved on to fixing deliberately selected new hardware to his canvases [fig. 7.25]. In some works the gestural paint surface and the objects interact like distinct voices (as in the contemporary works of Jasper Johns); in other canvases Dine made expressive color or surface integral with the definition of the objects themselves; and in still other works he depicted the common objects as a subject matter. "When I use objects," he explained, "I see them as a vocabulary of feelings . . . my work is very autobiographical."[54] The tools had a particularly evocative quality for him because both his father and grandfather (who raised him) sold tools in their shops in his hometown of Cincinnati.

Lucas Samaras, another assemblagist, got to know Kaprow, Segal, and Whitman at Rutgers and he participated in many of Oldenburg's happenings of the early sixties. He began to construct abstract objects and boxes [fig. 7.26] in

the spring of 1960, having become obsessed by the evocative power of particular materials, including nails, pins, broken glass, and razor blades, set off by saturated rainbow colors, Day-Glo and silver paint, tin foil, and mirrors. His works, though sensual and opulent, frequently have a menacing aspect. His material accumulations are fetishistic and highly personal, like small, ecstatic relics of a bizarre, unidentified religious rite.

The "strong urges for total experience" that Segal spoke of when referring to his plaster figures were a defining feature of the happenings in New York. Their very theatricality provided a point of departure for the careers of not only Allan Kaprow but George Segal, Red Grooms, Jim Dine, Lucas Samaras, and Claes Oldenburg.

7.25 Jim Dine, *Five Feet of Colorful Tools*, 1962. Oil on unprimed canvas surmounted by a board on which thirty-two painted tools hang from hooks; overall, 55⅝ × 60¼ × 4⅜in (141.2 × 153 × 10.9cm). The Museum of Modern Art, New York. The Sidney and Harriet Janis Collection, 587.1967.a–g.

7.26 Lucas Samaras, *Untitled Box No. 3*, 1962–3. Wood, pins, rope, wire, and stuffed bird, 27 × 9 × 10in (68.6 × 22.9 × 25.4cm). Whitney Museum of American Art, New York. Gift of the Howard and Jean Lipman Foundation, Inc., 66.36.

CLAES OLDENBURG

Where Dine steadfastly retained the manufactured identity of objects, Claes Oldenburg persistently undermined them. He anthropomorphized them, eroticized them, changed them from organic to geometric and vice versa, or blew them up into architecture through formal associations that layered each object with alternative definitions. Oldenburg's work is also autobiographical, and as with Dine the happenings led Oldenburg to use objects as though they were stage props in a kind of introspective performance. Yet what interested Oldenburg above anything else was the power of his imagination to alter the shape and meaning of real things. His work, he said, "originates in actual experience however far my metamorphic capacities may carry it."[55]

Born in Stockholm in 1929 and raised in Chicago from the age of seven, Claes Oldenburg was the older of two sons of the Swedish Consul-General. As children and young teenagers, the Oldenburg boys collaborated on a highly detailed fantasy about an imaginary island country in the South Atlantic called "Neubern," which set some important themes for Oldenburg's mature work. They made scrapbooks with maps, diagrams, and drawings describing the island, its military and industries, and the events that took place there. Meanwhile Oldenburg's mother made collages from advertisements of consumer goods, which may have predisposed him to such subjects later. Oldenburg attended Yale and the School of the Art Institute of Chicago, and then in 1956 he went to New York.

Reading Allan Kaprow's article "The Legacy of Jackson Pollock" in *Artnews* and the *New York Times* piece on the Gutai artists (see Chapter 8) prompted Oldenburg to seek out Kaprow and Red Grooms in 1958. Through them, he met Samaras, Segal, and Whitman; his friendships with Jim Dine and Tom Wesselmann also date from this time. Oldenburg's art in 1958–9 followed a free-associative path. "My procedure was simply to find everything that meant something to me, but the logic of my self-development was to gradually find myself in my surroundings."[56] This sensitivity to those objects in the environment that resonated with his personality made Oldenburg a persistent collector of popular-culture trinkets and street debris—stiffened old gloves, flattened cans, bits of wood, and wrappers—that suggested significant meaning through his processes of aesthetic transformation. Rather than letting an object assert its own identity, as Rauschenberg did, Oldenburg redefined the found object in his own image: "What I see is not the thing itself but—myself—in its form."[57]

The "Cold Existentialism" of the Ray Gun and *The Street*

The phallic Ray Gun, in particular, became an increasingly prevalent icon for Oldenburg, not only in found objects but in his drawings and *papier-mâché* sculptures. "Ray Gun is ultimately the unknowable," Oldenburg noted in 1960, "pursued futilely through all its disguises."[58] His reading of Freud and his attempt at self-analysis in the fall of 1959 may well have prompted his reflections on the sexual drive, which was "unknowable" because sublimated, yet pervasive in the human unconscious. "If form in nature analyzes down to geometry," he observed, "content (or intent) analyzes down to erotic form."[59]

The Ray Gun, personified as Oldenburg's *alter ego*, made its appearance in 1960 on the bulletin board of the Judson Church during his show *The Street* [fig. 7.21]. *The Street* consisted of deliberately coarse figures made from ripped cardboard, burlap, and other shabby materials found on the streets of the run-down Lower East Side and fashioned into a continuous, drab environment of dark browns, black, and tan. Pieces hung from the walls and ceiling and lay across the floor, so that *The Street* resembled a dada event, except for its evident expressionism. "I sought a crudity in style," the artist said, "to match the crudity of my surroundings."[60]

Some of *The Street* figures had speech balloons, revealing the lingering influence of comic strips; but the dark outlines, the ephemeral "non-art" materials, and the formal crudeness made unmistakable reference to Dubuffet. "I don't come out of Matisse or the sunny concept of art," Oldenburg explained. "I come out of Goya, Rouault, parts of Dubuffet, Bacon, the humanistic and existentialist imagists, the Chicago bunch."[61] Moreover, Oldenburg's assertion that "dirt has depth and beauty. I love soot and scorching,"[62] his wish to make art of the "the impossible, the discredited, the different,"[63] and his description of himself as "an outsider"[64] breathe the cold existentialism of Dubuffet and the French *nouveau roman*.

The *Store* Days

After *The Street* Oldenburg began making a more vivacious style of object [fig. 7.27]. The raw, yet colorful textured surfaces of his new work were a departure from the somber squalor. As if looking up from the pavement and into the shop windows, he rendered the lively flurry of activity in crudely painted plaster forms. Yet this work too was indebted to Dubuffet—not to the graffiti-like monochromes but to his rich, elemental "pastes" [figs. 5.1 and 5.8].

In June 1961 Oldenburg rented a storefront at 107 East 2nd Street, on the Lower East Side, and in December he opened *The Store*. The sensuality, optimism, and humor of the work on display reflected an appreciation for the bustling, tactile, and visual variety of the neighborhood— the cheap clothing on Orchard Street, the arrays of food on Second Avenue, the boxes, wrappers, and signs, and all the energetic buying and selling. *The Store* was a friendly, over-filled room of hamburgers and tennis shoes, prepackaged shirt-and-tie combinations, and reliefs of Pepsi signs and sewing machines—all made of brightly enameled plaster— with a delicious vulgarity that celebrated what he called "the poetry of everywhere."[65]

The artist's manipulation of form took precedence over any inherent significance in the subject: "i wanted to see if i could make significant form out of a pair of ladys pantys

[sic]."[66] Indeed, Oldenburg used the banality of the subject matter to set off his aesthetic.

> I have made these things: a wrist watch, a piece of pie, hats, caps, pants, skirts, flags, 7 up, shoe-shine etc. etc., all violent and simple in form and color, just as they are. In showing them together, I have wanted to imitate my act of perceiving them, which is why they are shown as fragments (of the field of seeing), in different scale to one another, in a form sur-rounding me (and the spectator), and in accumulation rather than in some imposed design.[67]

The ragged edges on the reliefs and the fragmentation evoke the feeling that occurs when a multitude of disconnected perceptions are brought together.

People loved Oldenburg's work and yet he sold very little. *The Store* closed after two months with a net loss of $285, which Richard Bellamy (director of the Green Gallery on 57th Street) picked up when he offered Oldenburg a show for the fall of 1962. In February 1962 Oldenburg shifted his attention to developing the Ray Gun Theater, and for about five months he organized performances for capacity audiences in his tiny storefront. Like the objects in *The Store*, Oldenburg's happenings derived from an overriding interest in using his aesthetic thought processes to integrate his experience of the real environment. The Ray Gun Theater "seeks to present in events what *The Store* presents in objects," Oldenburg explained. "It is a theater of real events (a newsreel)."[68] In this theater of things, Oldenburg even used his actors like objects, rejecting dialog and plot. The artist's power to defamiliarize the objects he made, as well as the cathartic character of the performances, reflected a faith in the force of mind over matter that may have its roots in his Christian Science upbringing.

Oldenburg had gone several times to see *The Burning Building* by Red Grooms in December 1959, and he organized

7.27 Claes Oldenburg, *Pie à la Mode*, 1962. Muslin dipped in plaster over a frame of chickenwire, painted with enamel, 13 × 20 × 19in (33 × 50.8 × 48.3cm). Museum of Contemporary Art, Los Angeles. The Panza Collection.

7.28 Claes Oldenburg, *Floor Cake (Giant Piece of Cake)*, 1962. Synthetic polymer paint and latex on canvas filled with foam rubber and cardboard boxes, 4ft 10⅜in × 9ft 6¼in × 4ft 10⅜in (1.48 × 2.9 × 1.48m). The Museum of Modern Art, New York. Gift of Philip Johnson, 414.1975.

his own happening, *Snapshots from the City*, the next year. In *Snapshots* Oldenburg created a "living picture" of himself covered in rags and debris, literally and figuratively locating himself within the visual chaos of the street. The happening was a series of expressive but static *tableaux*, in which he used objects, or more properly "matter," as the stuff of an existential expressionism in the tradition of Pollock. The painterly handling which persisted in Oldenburg's sculpture, at least through the end of the sixties, also revealed his expressionistic approach.

Soft Sculpture

Oldenburg's Green Gallery show was scheduled to open in September 1962. The largest object in *The Store* had been 3 feet square, and now suddenly Oldenburg had a much bigger space to fill. Walking through midtown on the way to the gallery one day, he passed an auto showroom and admired the way the cars occupied the space. He decided that he wanted to fill the gallery in the same way, so he enlarged his objects to the size of cars, and at the same time he fabricated his first soft sculptures of canvas and later vinyl stuffed with foam rubber, cardboard, or kapok. The display included a 9-foot cake [fig. 7.28], an ice-cream cone over 10 feet long, and a hamburger that was 7 feet in diameter. The comparison to surrealism was inevitable, since the radical shift in scale and the metamorphosis of familiar objects into soft sculptures gave them a dreamlike aura. The show enjoyed commercial success but the established critics hated it. Not only was it figurative, and therefore—in Greenberg's relentless march toward abstract purity—reactionary, it had a sense of humor and that made it *ipso facto* insufficiently profound.

In November 1962 the Sidney Janis Gallery held the "New Realists" exhibition that scandalized many of the New York School artists whom Janis also represented; some quit the gallery as a result. Like "A Problem for Critics," held at Art of This Century almost twenty years earlier, the "New Realists" show attempted to encapsulate what nearly everyone recognized as a new movement. The title came from the French *nouveaux réalistes*, whom Janis included, and indeed the assemblage aesthetics of Oldenburg, Dine, Segal, Samaras, and probably even Grooms had more in common with the French *nouveaux réalistes* and with Rauschenberg than they did with Warhol, Rosenquist, and Lichtenstein, with whom they were eventually (and inappropriately) grouped under the heading of "pop."

At this point Oldenburg entered a period of reassessment. "I experienced a revulsion against my situation in New York, hating my *Store* (my studio and theater since 1961) on Second Street, my apartment, my body, my wife, everything."[69] In September 1963 he and his wife, Pat, fled New York and moved to Los Angeles. The abundance of vinyl and fake furs he found while rummaging through the area's surplus stores inspired him to try working in these materials, and since the cutting patterns for the soft sculptures came from "hard models" constructed in planes of wood or cardboard, the objects typically had "hard," "soft" (that is, vinyl), and "ghost" versions [figs. 7.29 and 7.30], the latter fabricated from canvas but lacking the "realistic" color or finish of the vinyl.

Oldenburg went back to New York in 1964, living in the Chelsea Hotel and working in a loft in SoHo (the post Civil War loft district *so*uth of *Ho*uston Street). At this time, he extended the corpus of soft sculptures begun in Los Angeles with a sequence of soft mechanical devices, including a giant fan, drainpipes, and the giant Dormeyer mixers. In 1965, he also inaugurated his studies of the *Airflow* (a special model of the 1935 Chrysler automobile), whole and in parts. For the most part he chose quaintly old-fashioned devices and exhaustively researched them on paper. Although they have a rich nuance of line quality, these drawings are often realized with the precision of a mechanical engineer [fig. 7.31].

Many of Oldenburg's objects are soft and fleshlike analogs to human anatomy. The artist's notebooks document many examples of their obsessive metamorphosis through visual free association [fig. 7.32], as with the ideas for the mixers, which evolve from a pair of pendulous breasts, to the collar on a prudish dress, to earrings, and then to the beaters on an electric mixer. There is, then, a wide variety of meanings underlying a form such as the *Soft Dormeyer Mixer* [fig. 7.29]—it is an extraordinary glimpse of an ordinary object, humorously eroticized into a *double entendre* with the human body. The *Soft Dormeyer Mixers—"Ghost" Version* makes yet another visual, anatomical pun, suggesting a penis and testicles [fig. 7.30].

Oldenburg's reading of Freud undoubtedly sharpened his sense of the sexual significance with which humans unconsciously imbue inanimate objects. "Basically, collectors want nudes," he remarked. "So I have supplied for them nude

7.29 (above) **Claes Oldenburg**, *Soft Dormeyer Mixer,* 1965. Vinyl, kapok wood, aluminum tubing, electric cord, and rubber, 32 × 20 × 12½in (81.2 × 50.8 × 31.8cm).
Collection, Whitney Museum of American Art, New York. Purchased with funds from the Howard and Jean Lipman Foundation, Inc., 66.55.

7.30 (right) **Claes Oldenburg**, *Soft Dormeyer Mixers—"Ghost" Version,* 1965. Canvas, kapok wood, sprayed enamel, and wood, 42 × 26 × 34in (106.7 × 66 × 86.4cm). Destroyed.
Courtesy Sidney Janis Gallery, New York.

7.32 Claes Oldenburg, unnumbered notebook page: *Dormeyer Mixer*, 1965. Ballpoint pen and collage on paper, 10⅝ × 8in (27 × 20.3cm).
Collection, the artist.

7.33 Claes Oldenburg, *Woman Figure with Medusa Ornaments of Nudes with Vacuum Cleaners*, 1967. Graphite with black chalk on cream wove paper, 2ft 6in × 1ft 10⅜in (76.2 × 56.8cm).
Art Institute of Chicago, restricted gift of Dr. Eugene A. Solow, 1968.38.

cars, nude telephones, nude electric plugs, nude switches, nude fans."[70] From the row of pale mixers with their limp handles and hanging "beaters" [fig. 7.30] to his overtly sexual drawings [fig. 7.33], eroticism is everywhere in Oldenburg's work. "The erotic or the sexual," he commented, "is the root of art."[71]

Proposals for Monuments

In 1965 Oldenburg also began to design fantastic proposals for monuments. "One day I combined landscapes and objects, only I didn't change the scale. I had a drawing of a vacuum cleaner and another of Manhattan—and I just super-imposed them. The result was automatically a "giant vacuum cleaner" because the city held its scale—it didn't become a miniature city. Somehow it worked."[72] An eighteenth-century folly shaped like a cow by the French visionary architect Lequeu inspired the *Proposed Colossal Monument for Central Park North, New York City: Teddy Bear* [fig. 7.34],[73] but the giant balloon figures in the Macy's Thanksgiving

Day Parades in New York also played a part. So too, perhaps, did the proposed projects of Christo [fig. 11.29], who was his neighbor in 1964 in the Chelsea Hotel. Like Christo, Oldenburg thought up his follies for real sites, such as the addition to the Art Museum at Oberlin College in Ohio, which he drew as a giant three-way plug, or the monumental fireplug intended to replace the Picasso sculpture on the Civic Center Plaza in Chicago. Oldenburg chose the objects based on his sense of the spirit of the place.

Realizing the Monuments and the Architectural Scale

In 1969 Oldenburg moved his studio to an old factory building in New Haven, Connecticut, close to a large-scale, steel fabricating plant called Lippincott and Company. Lippincott specialized in working with artists and began to construct monumental sculptures for Oldenburg, who had begun making models for monumental public sculptures as early as 1966. It was when a group of graduate students in the

7.34 Claes Oldenburg, *Proposed Colossal Monument for Central Park North, New York City: Teddy Bear*, 1965. Lithographic crayon and watercolor on paper, 23 × 17⅙in (58.4 × 43.7cm).
Collection, Mr. and Mrs. Richard Oldenburg, New York.

School of Architecture at Yale approached him to do a monument in May 1969 that the idea really took hold. He built a 24-foot-high *Lipstick (Ascending) on Caterpillar Tracks* and delivered it to the Beinecke Plaza in front of the Yale president's office in the midst of a student demonstration. It was an unsolicited gift, which the university was at first not certain it wanted. The appearance of the Yale monument had the quality of a happening, not only because of the dramatic and unpredictable circumstances of its arrival on the campus but because of the collaborative activity at Lippincott, where Oldenburg directed a team of men wielding heavy equipment to construct the piece. The improvisational procedure of testing ideas and reworking even in the final stage of fabrication gave the construction process a theatrical quality.

The formal idea for the monumental lipstick evolved from an early concept (on an altered postcard) to replace the Eros fountain in London's Piccadilly Circus with a cluster of giant lipsticks (clipped from a cosmetics advertisement). In its first incarnation the Yale monument had a collapsing, soft tip that would alternately blow up like a balloon and then deflate. At the height of the anti-war movement the sarcasm of the cosmetic/bullet/phallus was not lost on

7.35 Claes Oldenburg, *Clothespin*, 1976. Cor-Ten and stainless steel, 45ft 11⅜in (14m) high. Center Square, Philadelphia.

anyone, and after considerable vandalism the tip had to be reconstructed in steel.

In 1971 Oldenburg reestablished his studio in New York, moving down to Broome Street in SoHo, but he continued to direct the focus of his attention on large fabricated pieces. The work grew in ambition, and in the seventies he actually began to realize some of these ideas on an architectural scale. *Clothespin* in the center of downtown Philadelphia [fig. 7.35] is a particularly brilliant example. Coosje van Bruggen, a Dutch museum curator, whom Oldenburg married in the early seventies, became an increasingly important collaborator in the realization of such huge civic projects, and in the late eighties they entered into collaboration with the Los Angeles architect Frank Gehry to carry Oldenburg's monumental aspirations into functional architecture. For *Camp Good Times*, in the Santa Monica Hills, Oldenburg proposed a pavilion in the form of a giant milk can, and for the Chiat/Day Offices on Main Street in Venice, California, Oldenburg proposed an entrance in the form of a pair of giant binoculars. With Gehry's genius for integrating visual incongruity, these representational forms have in each case been seamlessly blended into the complex of buildings.

JASPER JOHNS

"Nature" Is How We Describe It

Advanced art, from Walt Whitman to Jackson Pollock, rested on the romantic assumption that meaningful subject matter emanates from within the individual. But the art of both Robert Rauschenberg and Jasper Johns called this notion into question. In an implicit attack on ontology they recast man as a nexus of information, reorienting input rather than originating content. By the end of the fifties the human mind began to seem to more and more artists and intellectuals like a complex circuit board for processing "nature." Meanwhile "nature" came increasingly to mean representations of things as well as the things in themselves. This radical shift in consciousness affected all quarters of the culture, with the explosive development in electronics and mass media being its major catalyst.

Marshall McLuhan, who became an intellectual celebrity after the publication of his book *Understanding Media* in 1964, pointed out that the electronic media (television, telephone, radio, and we might now add computers) had created a new environment, which altered the manner in which people experienced events. Moreover, this new way of apprehending information meant something, independent of the explicit subject matter. McLuhan's assertion that "the medium is the message"[74] stressed that meaning was vested in the very structure of advertising, say, over and above the particular product being advertised.

But McLuhan's books were only one focus of a wider cultural phenomenon. The title of an influential classroom textbook of 1959 by the literary critic John Ciardi posed the declarative question *How Does a Poem Mean?* Ciardi asserted that "the way *in which* it means is *what* it means."[75] Like McLuhan, he focused on the structure of the expressive vehicle (the poem) as a primary aspect of the "message"; he recognized that the "style" of the poem represented a point of view that was as important to the meaning as the explicit subject. In Europe intellectuals such as the French anthropologist Claude Lévi-Strauss and the literary critic Roland Barthes had begun to examine the way in which our understanding of the world is in part constructed by the language we use to describe it.

Painting as a Discourse on Language

In painting Jasper Johns formulated a pointedly nonintrospective style that stressed the complex semiotics of the art object (in other words, how it means what it means). For example, the painted targets by Johns [fig. 7.36] are so intractably literal that they *are* targets; at the same time the artist is ambiguously presenting them as painterly works of art, explicitly rendered in artistic materials. This substantially closed the gap between the thing and its representation. Moreover, the proximity of the target as a painting to the functional target brings to light the role of artistic intention in defining an object as a work of art. The detailed working of the surface and the restriction of the palette (in some of them) to the primary colors of red, yellow, and blue also foregrounds the artist's concern with analyzing the basic structural elements of the language of painting.

The visible newsprint that Johns used as a foundation for the thin layers of encaustic in a work like *Target with Plaster Casts* has prompted some writers to attempt to "decode" the texts.[76] However, as in the work of Rauschenberg, the evidence does not support an iconographic reading. Johns has said that "whatever printing shows has no significance to me. Sometimes I looked at the paper for different kinds of color, different sizes of type, of course, and perhaps some of the words went into my mind; I was not conscious of it."[77] Rather, the newsprint fragments attracted him because they convey the semiotic complexity (the sense of information overload) of media superimposition, as if one were watching two films running over one another.

The painted flag, as in *Three Flags* [fig. 7.37], is also an inherently flat subject, based on a readymade formal scheme rather than a unique physical object that exists in the world. Perhaps even more than a target, a painted flag is the thing in itself, regardless of the materials. By making the boundaries of the canvas identical with the image, Johns eliminated any

7.36 (opposite) **Jasper Johns**, *Target with Plaster Casts*, 1955. Encaustic and collage on canvas with objects, 51 × 44 × 3½in (129.5 × 111.8 × 8.9cm).
Collection, David Geffen. Courtesy Leo Castelli Gallery, New York.

7.37 Jasper Johns, *Three Flags*, 1958. Encaustic on canvas (three levels), 30⅞ × 45½ × 5in (78.4 × 115.6 × 12.7cm). Whitney Museum of American Art, New York. 50th Anniversary Gift of Gilman Foundation, Inc., The Lauder Foundation, A. Alfred Taubman, Laura-Lee Woods, and purchase, 80.32.

sense of composition, thereby leaving nothing but surface treatment as a basis for formal interpretation. In the same way the numbers and alphabets which Johns painted in the fifties cannot be representations, because by definition a number or letter is a concept with no unique material identity. Yet at the same time the prominence given to the handling of the paint seems to contradict this idea. In these paintings of targets, flags, letters, and numbers, Johns effectively posed a series of philosophical dilemmas concerning the language of art and the perception of reality. Moreover, the use of such prefabricated imagery tied art into mass production and popular consumerism in an unsettling way.

An Aesthetic of "Found" Expression

At first glance the brushwork in these Jasper Johns works seems at odds with the literalness of the imagery. Not only did the artist use a sensuously tactile, gestural style, but the

encaustic technique (heated wax mixed with pigment) further accentuates the individual identity of each brushstroke; since the molten wax solidifies almost instantly, it allows every touch of the brush to retain its identity without smearing under the pressure of the succeeding one. Nevertheless, the beautifully applied surfaces of these paintings do not convey the charged introspective mood of an abstract expressionist canvas. They have a surface sensuality, making the artist seem more receptive to the world around him; he is engaged in experiencing and understanding what is there rather than recording an act of introspection. In this respect the gestural handling also functions as an emblem of psychic expressivity rather than a vehicle for psychic expression. The handling reifies the gestural mark and thus normalizes action painting.

In one sense the general climate of painting in the fifties provided a foundation for such an approach. Rather than inventing a style "from scratch" in response to expressive needs, the second-generation gesture painters of the New York School were conscious of inheriting autographic brushwork as a stylistic given. Johns pushed the logic of this situation one step further in making style itself an overt subject in his painting.

Modern artists, from Gustave Courbet to the New York School, had sought to make their technique and medium increasingly transparent as a vehicle for their metaphysics.

Newman and Rothko wanted the viewer to experience an epiphany, a purely spiritual event that transcended the materials altogether, making them virtually disappear. Johns turned in the opposite direction. He stopped at what is literally there, enjoying the physical presence of the art object in all its concreteness. Johns was drawn to the rich ambiguity and uncertainty of meaning that exists in the object itself and in all the ways in which the object could be perceived. Each object seemed to offer multiple possibilities for interpretation, and he took pleasure in the sheer variety of that found environment, just as Cage did. "Do you use these letter types because you like them or because that's how the stencils come?" Leo Steinberg asked the artist in 1961. "But that's what I like about them, that they come that way."[78]

The work of Jasper Johns, then, is a way of seeing that is dominated neither by the tangible world outside the frame nor by the artist's intentions; it attempts to avoid imposing a hierarchy of meaning on events, and instead celebrates the full complexity of experience. "Intention involves such a small fragment of our consciousness and our mind and our life," Johns told David Sylvester. "I think painting should include more experience than simply intended statement." Painting, he said, should be a kind of "fact that one can experience individually as one pleases . . . so that experience of it is variable."[79]

Emotion and Distance

In 1959 Johns told *Time* magazine that people should be able to look at a painting in the same neutral way that they look at any ordinary object, "the same way you look at a radiator."[80] But he later elaborated on this statement, saying, "I mean that one shouldn't approach a work of art with a pre-existing attitude . . . [*laughing*]. But then someone pointed out to me that I had gone and boxed-in all my radiators, so you didn't see them!"[81] What you don't see in the work of Jasper Johns—the artist's own underlying emotions—is made poignant by its systematic absence.

Johns once remarked to one of his print publishers, Tatyana Grosman, that "when he was young he had so many desires and wishes, that he trained himself to think only of the present, and not of his wishes for the future."[82] By his own description, then, it seems that he has repressed a great deal of emotion. He is a shy person, nervous, remote, and impeccably polite. He speaks with controlled precision, often following on thoughtful silences. His intelligence is instantaneously obvious, and he focuses—whether on people in a conversation or on an idea in his work—with an unnerving precision.

Jasper Johns came to New York in 1952 at the age of twenty-two. But it was not until the spring of 1954, when he met John Cage and Robert Rauschenberg, that he became part of the art scene. What remains of his work from 1954 demonstrates his interest in the improvisational assemblage or junk-art aesthetic of the time. When someone pointed out the resemblance of his work to that of Kurt Schwitters—

with which he was not then familiar—Johns destroyed everything and started again. He saw this as the point of transition into his professional career. "I decided to do only what I meant to do, and not what other people did. When I could observe what others did, I tried to remove that from my work. My work became a constant negation of impulses . . . I had a wish to determine what I was . . . what I wanted to do was to find out what I did that other people didn't, what I was that other people weren't."[83]

Johns deliberately distanced himself from abstract expressionism with the flags, targets, letters, and numbers. Despite the sensuality of the surfaces, the targets and flags have a rigid order predetermined by definition and the others are grids. Even the individual brushstrokes in these works have a cool independence from one another, rather than a spontaneous interaction. "I didn't want my work to be an exposure of my feelings," he told Vivian Raynor. "Abstract expressionism was so lively—personal identity and painting were more or less the same . . . But I found I couldn't do anything that would be identical with my feelings. So I worked in such a way that I could say that it's not me."[84]

Yet on some level abstract expressionism did attract him, as one can see in his brushwork. He even told Roberta Bernstein that he used the title "Figure" for his paintings of numbers out of admiration for the figure paintings of de Kooning.[85] And as in the work of Rauschenberg, the persistent use of collage and found objects in Johns's work had to do with a desire for immediacy. Yet the artist's meticulous technical control, his detached analytical mind, and his masterful augmentation of the facticity of the art object itself distance him from direct experience. Indeed, underlying all of Johns's painting is a grand tragedy, in the sense of Greek theater, based on the artist's perpetual pursuit of an ultimately unattainable emotional immediacy that he denies.

Incorporating Objects: What One Sees and What One Knows

Across the top of *Target with Plaster Casts* [fig. 7.36] Johns recessed plaster casts of body parts into a row of little boxes with lids. One has to open the lids to uncover the "private" contents. The symbolism is a general evocation of the senses. Johns has always selected his motifs and devices with great deliberation and retained them indefinitely as part of an interconnecting repertoire of forms. He began making casts of body parts, for example, in 1953 and they have recurred intermittently in his work ever since, as in the 1964 *According to What* [fig. 7.45] and *Perilous Night* of 1982 [fig. 7.46].

In *Tango* of 1955 Johns included the literal presence of the title, stenciled on the surface as a tangible thing in itself, eliding the distinction between the object and the idea it expresses. He also attached a functioning music box to the back of the canvas which remains invisible and intangible except for the winding key projecting through the front of the painting and the sound. The incorporation of real objects by Johns drew on the assemblage styles of the fifties.

But rather than attempting to capture the chaos of subjective experience, as Rauschenberg did, Johns employed objects in a meticulously controlled manner, taking one thing at a time and thoroughly digesting its meanings.

The flags have spanned Johns's career, beginning with the most straightforward first *Flag* (1954–5) and the mono-chromatic *White Flag* (1955) through the representations of the flag paintings themselves in the autobiographical series "The Seasons" [fig. 7.47]. *Three Flags* [fig. 7.37] explores the conventions of pictorial space by making the smallest flag advance literally in space while it recedes perceptually in the sequence of diminishing sizes. The extreme thickness of the three layered canvases makes *Three Flags* more like an object than earlier flag paintings, and yet at the same time it emphasizes the flatness of the image even more.

Whereas the shimmering surface of *White Flag* has the impressionist delicacy of Monet's *Waterlilies* (which went on view at the Museum of Modern Art that year), *Three Flags* seems starkly cubist in its play on the illusion of the picture plane. It follows immediately on the display of Picasso's cubist works in the "Picasso: Seventy-fifth Anniversary" exhibition at MoMA in late 1957. One senses the struggle of the objects in early cubist Picasso to assert their full volumetric identity against the flattening and dematerializing pictorial system. The same tense conflict, between what one knows and what one sees, between the image and the rendering, and on the most fundamental level between the analytical detachment and the lingering traces of romanticism, can be found in Johns's *Three Flags* as well.

As an adjunct to the exploration of volume and solidity in paintings like *Three Flags* Johns also embarked on a series of small sculptures. Beginning with a *Light Bulb* and a *Flashlight*, he selected common objects from a hardware store and covered them with a hard-drying material called "Sculpmetal." In these works Johns turned real things into art. But the ironic pun on illumination, both in the sense of elucidating puzzling aspects of the world and as part of an ongoing discussion of the effects of light in art, seems distinctly Duchampian.

The Paintings of 1959

Leo Castelli opened his gallery in May 1957 with a group exhibition that included work by both Rauschenberg and Johns. He then gave them both one-person shows early in 1958. The Johns show was an overnight sensation. The Museum of Modern Art, along with a number of important collectors, bought work, and *Artnews* reproduced *Target with Four Faces* on its cover. The show made the artist an instant media celebrity.

In 1959 Johns veered even more directly into the meta-physics of painting. Images and objects ceased to determine his compositions, and instead he cultivated a more loosely brushed, "all over" style, sometimes swallowing up objects, as in *Thermometer* [fig. 7.39] (a homage to Barnett Newman with an object as the "zip" down the center). *Device Circle*

exemplifies this direct focus on the means of art, with its palette dominated by the primary colors (the fundamental colors from which all other colors can be mixed) and the incorporation of a stick, nailed at one end to the center of the canvas and used by the artist as the "device" for inscribing the central motif of the "circle." At the same time he painted over the device, camouflaging it and absorbing it into the composition. He then literally labeled the "device" and the "circle" in stenciled letters along the bottom edge. In one sense *Device Circle* is a schematic target, stressing the means of manufacture over the image. The brushwork is abstract expressionist in style, while the action painters' preoccupation with process is made more explicit and literal.

In *False Start* [fig. 7.38] Johns used oil rather than encaustic-over-newspaper, which he had been accustomed to using for the previous four years. The oil permitted a freer gestural style. Johns painted the surface as a weave of inter-penetrating patches of primary colors and folded in the names of colors in stenciled lettering—an allusion to the use of lettering in the cubism of 1912–14. But Johns pointedly incorporated the words for colors without rendering them in that color or even necessarily using the color in the area surrounding its name. Thus the painting highlights the dissonance between the name and the visual sensation (between what one knows and what one sees). In the mono-chromatic painting *Jubilee* (a nearly identical composition) Johns carried the idea one step further by completely elim-inating color visually, while retaining its presence in words.[86]

The way in which Johns carried through the implications of such ideas from one work to the next suggests a highly controlled approach to painting, and he denied the possibility of chance events in the process: "There are no accidents in my work. It sometimes happens that something unexpected occurs—the paint may run—but then I see that it has hap-pened, and I have the choice to paint it again or not. And if I don't, then the appearance of the element in the painting is no accident."[87] Yet the fact that Johns almost never drew studies for a painting—his drawings of a composition nearly always follow rather than precede it—indicates the degree to which he works by improvisation. The wish to be in control and yet open to discovery is one of the central, animating contradictions in his work.

Thermometer [fig. 7.39] has the same palette and starburst pattern of gestural application as *False Start*. But instead of the names of primary colors being woven into a shallow cubist grid, the artist has stenciled a scale of numbers flanking a real thermometer, fastened to the center of the composition. The thermometer effectively eliminates compositional movement, as in Barnett Newman's *Onement I* [fig. 4.13], with a perfectly symmetrical zip down the center. In the

7.38 (opposite) **Jasper Johns**, *False Start*, 1959.
Oil on canvas, 5ft 7½in × 4ft 5in (1.71 × 1.34m).
Collection Anne and Kenneth Griffin. Courtesy Jasper Johns.

flags, targets, letters, and numbers, Johns had already done away with perspective, foreshortening, and modeling (the devices of illusionism). In addition, Johns conceived each of these compositions to be seen as a totality, like a Newman, rather than as an amalgam of interacting parts. Johns admired the transcendental dimension of Newman's work and *Thermometer* is a kind of homage. Although the color-burst style of *Thermometer* and other works of 1959 is gestural, it is also formulaic rather than autographic like a de Kooning or Pollock. In this sense too it has an affinity with Newman's painting. Finally, the concern with measurement in *Thermometer* has a corollary in Newman's measurements for the placement of the zip in his compositions.

At the same time Johns makes fun of the legendary machismo of abstract expressionism in *Painting with Two Balls*. The seemingly improvisational act of forcing the steel balls between two stretcher bars was in fact achieved with a specially constructed, curved stretcher that kept the canvas from wrinkling. In other words it was not the impulsive act of the action artist.

7.39 Jasper Johns, *Thermometer*, 1959. Oil on canvas with object, 51¾ × 38½in (131.5 × 97.8cm). Seattle Art Museum.

In 1958 Johns discovered the work of Marcel Duchamp. He and Rauschenberg traveled to see the definitive collection of Duchamp's work in the Philadelphia Museum, and in 1959 the critic Nicholas Calas brought Duchamp himself to Johns's studio. For Johns and Rauschenberg, Duchamp's readymades, in particular, meant that every object could be art, just as for Cage every sound could be music and complete in itself. The measuring stick in *Device Circle* alludes to Duchamp's preoccupation with irrational and chance standards of measurement, as in Duchamp's *Three Standard Stoppages* of 1913–14.

The New Emotional Tone of the Early Sixties

Painted Bronze (ale cans) [fig. 7.40] provokes the viewer to wonder at first whether the ale cans are really what they seem to be. Are they works of art or common objects? "I like that there is the possibility that one might take one for the other," Johns explained, "but I also like that with a little examination, it's very clear that one is not the other."[88] He deliberately gave these sculptures a handcrafted look when viewed at close range, despite the initially effective *trompe-l'oeil*; he cast each ale can and the base as separate objects and rendered the labels in a largely illegible, painterly style.

The subject was in part chosen for its familiarity. Ballantine Ale was not only the beer Johns drank, but the bronze color of the can added an extra measure of ambiguity to the bronze casting.

I was doing at that time sculptures of small objects—flashlights and light bulbs. Then I heard a story about Willem de Kooning. He was annoyed with my dealer, Leo Castelli, for some reason, and said something like, "That son-of-a-bitch; you could give him two beer cans and he could sell them." I heard this and thought, "What a sculpture—two beer cans." It seemed to me to fit in perfectly with what I was doing, so I did them and Leo sold them.[89]

Johns put his thumbprint on the base of *Painted Bronze*. Like the painterly lettering, this emphasized the handmade character of the sculpture in contrast to the machine-made object (the real can). But it also revealed a new emotional intimacy that entered Johns's work at this time, an introspectiveness which may have gained its impetus from his personal life.

Rauschenberg had gone off to Florida in 1959. He and Johns still shared a place in New York through 1961, but they went their separate ways with increasing frequency. In the ale cans Johns portrayed himself and Rauschenberg—one open and light, the other solid, heavy, impenetrable. He painted the interlocking rings of the Ballantine symbol and lettered "Florida" on the top of the smaller, open can; he left the top of the closed can blank.

In 1961 Johns took a studio on Edisto Island, off the South Carolina coast. His fame in the art world had shattered his privacy in New York; but the deterioration of his relationship with Rauschenberg probably lay at the heart of

7.40 Jasper Johns, *Painted Bronze (ale cans)*, 1960. Painted bronze, two casts, 5½ × 8 × 4¾in (14 × 20.3 × 12.1cm). Museum Ludwig Köln.

his flight from the city. The words "Dead Man" appear in Johns's 1961 painting *In Memory of My Feelings*, and although he took both the title and the phrase from a poem by his friend Frank O'Hara, he obviously used them to express his own feelings of mourning for the death of his relationship with Rauschenberg. The hanging fork and spoon appeared for the first time in this work and suggest themes of nourishment and the senses, in contrast to the intellect, as Richard Field pointed out.[90]

The direct emotional engagement of *In Memory of My Feelings* characterizes the change of mood in the artist's work. Even the titles of that year—*In Memory of My Feelings*, *No*, *Water Freezes*, *Liar*, *Disappearance*, *Painting Bitten by a Man*, *Good Time Charley*—contrast markedly with the neutral, descriptive titles of the fifties. The frequently somber and searching paintings of 1962 and 1963 suggest anger and disappointment.

Like Rauschenberg, Johns became increasingly involved with performance in the sixties, and the objects in his paintings of the period take on a theatrical character. The cup hanging off the bottom of *Fool's House* [fig. 7.41] and the broom suspended from the top look like stage props. Johns had explored the idea of engaging the viewer's participation in *Tango* (where one needed to go up and wind the key to the hidden music box) and *Target with Plaster Casts* (which invited the viewer to open or close trap doors). In 1960 he even made a large-edition print of a blank target with an attached paint brush and three disks of watercolor paint, inviting the viewer to color in the target and sign his own name on the empty line to the left of the printed signature of Johns.

Explorations of Linguistic Philosophy

Where Rauschenberg selected and juxtaposed objects in his paintings in a spontaneous and improvisational manner, Johns did so with an unnerving deliberateness and focus. The cup suspended from *Fool's House* refers to the *trompe-l'oeil*

7.41 Jasper Johns, *Fool's House*, 1962. Oil on canvas with objects, 72 × 36in (182.9 × 91.4cm).

Collection, Jean-Christophe Castelli. Courtesy Leo Castelli Gallery, New York.

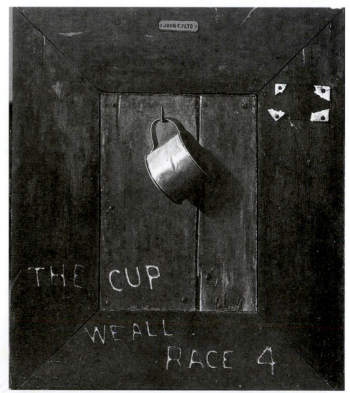

7.42 John Frederick Peto, *The Cup We All Race 4*, c. 1900. Oil on canvas on wood, 25½ × 21½in (64.8 × 54.6cm).

The Fine Arts Museums of San Francisco. Gift of Mr. and Mrs. John D. Rockefeller 3rd, 1979.7.80.

paintings of the nineteenth-century American artist John Frederick Peto. Johns inscribed "PETO" on another canvas entitled *The Cup We All Race 4*, after a composition of the same name painted by Peto from around 1900 [fig. 7.42]. In fooling the eye, the works of Peto question the relationship between truth and appearance. Johns reworked the idea by transforming all the familiar kitchen objects in *Fool's House* into tools of the studio: black paint in the cup, a broom as a paint brush, and a towel as a paint rag. The persisting importance of illusionism as an issue in the work of Jasper Johns, however obliquely presented, stems from his interest in the relativity of reality.

Johns also contrasted what we know with what we see by confronting images with their names, as the Belgian surrealist René Magritte had done in, for example, his famous painting *This Is Not a Pipe*, in which he presents a naturalistic rendering of a pipe on a white ground with the title inscribed in large letters below. In *Fool's House* Johns introduced handwritten labels, setting the word off against the depicted or real object. He also created a perceptual ambiguity in the pictorial space by lettering the title of the painting across the top as though we were reading around a cylinder: "USE FOOL'S HO."

Through the summer of 1961 Johns read substantially in the writings of the philosopher Ludwig Wittgenstein, who had a particular interest in the relation of thought and language to the world of things. Such questions began to attain particular currency among artists around 1960 as part of a growing anti-ontological mood. "You really get such a queer connexion," Wittgenstein remarked in his *Philosophical Investigations*, "when the philosopher tries to bring out the relation between name and thing ... For philosophical problems arise when language *goes on holiday*. And here we may indeed fancy naming to be some remarkable act of mind, as it were a baptism of an object."[91] In *The Blue and Brown Books* Wittgenstein remarked: "The use of the word *in practice* is its meaning. Imagine it were the usual thing that the objects around us carried labels with words."[92] This is precisely what Johns did to the objects in *Fool's House*—he literally realized Wittgenstein's remark. Moreover, the "use" of, for example, the kitchen broom as a paint brush transforms its meaning in a manner made all the more apparent by the label.

The ease with which such shifts of identity and definition take place in the work of Johns suggests a detached world in which things have no intrinsic identity. In this Johns anticipated the stress on the defining role of the linguistic or interpretive context by the French poststructuralists. "I think the object itself is a somewhat dubious concept," Johns reflected; "one wonders if one couldn't simply shift one's focus a bit in looking at a thing, and have the object be somewhere else, not be there at all."[93]

Diver of 1962

Johns attempted the mural scale of abstract expressionism for the first time in *Diver* [fig. 7.43], a 7½-by-14-foot painting

7.43 Jasper Johns, *Diver*, 1962. Oil on canvas with objects, 7ft 6in × 14ft 2in (2.29 × 4.32m) (five panels).

Collection, Irma and Norman Braman, Miami. Courtesy Leo Castelli Gallery, New York.

of 1962. The tape measure extending along the bottom of the third and fourth panels provides a literally "measured" commentary on the scale. Placed symmetrically along the adjoining borders of these two panels, Johns set two footprints and four handprints, the latter connected to planklike arms. He told the art historian Roberta Bernstein that the figure is making a swan dive and that the positions of the hands and feet indicated different stages of the action.[94] With small directional arrows he choreographed the diver's moves like those of a dancer. The diagrammatic and sequential schema indicates the artist's growing concern with time in painting, probably prompted by his concurrent work with the Merce Cunningham Dance Company.

In the upper left of the first panel of *Diver* Johns painted a multicolored "device circle." The second panel consists of a precisely drawn scale in gradations of gray, recalling the scale of color squares in Duchamp's painting *Tu'm* of 1919. In the lower corners of each panel Johns painted numbers that match up to the adjacent panel, making explicit the arrangement and the continuity across all five sections. In addition, the third and fourth panels relate to the fifth on the right by their loose brushwork and saturated palette. The right-hand panel has the stenciled names of the primary colors—as in *False Start*—and a vertical bundle of cutlery held in tension by two chains pulling horizontally from the bottom two sides. The painterliness and the tableware (recalling *In Memory of My Feelings*) link this panel to the emotional work of the preceding three years.

Johns connected the fifth panel of *Diver* with the panel to the left by a blocklike bar of paint toward the top, so that it crosses the break between the canvases. This geometric gesture, with paint dripping down, stands out as a stylistic oddity for Johns, though it seems identical with a consciously articulated, recurring element in the work of Rauschenberg (as in *Rebus*, where it appears as a single bar of color, or *Canyon* [fig. 7.5] where it appears as an "X"). The critics Cranshaw and Lewis noted in their essay on Rauschenberg that this "short stroke with calculated dribbles" had been singled out by Johns as a device Rauschenberg used to integrate objects into the surface visually and he referred to these strokes as Rauschenberg's "hinges."[95] Thus in *Diver* Johns glanced retrospectively over the preceding three years, and he must have intentionally included the bricklike, dripping stroke as a reference to Rauschenberg, who had so much to do with setting him on this period of probing self-examination.

Periscope (Hart Crane)

Johns also found a sympathetic echo of his emotions in the charged poetry of Hart Crane. In "Cape Hatteras" Crane wrote:

The captured fume of space foams in our ears—
What whisperings of far watches on the main
Relapsing into silence, while time clears

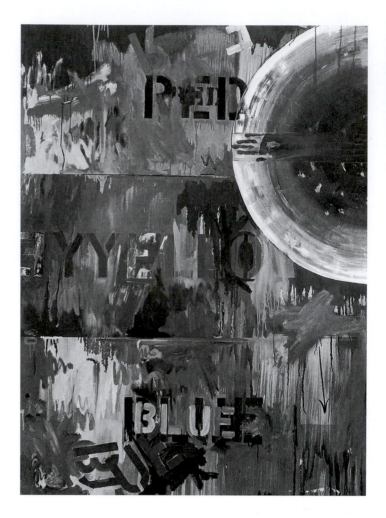

7.44 Jasper Johns, *Periscope (Hart Crane)*, 1963. Oil on canvas, 5ft 7in × 4ft (1.70 × 1.22m). Collection, the artist.

Our lenses, lifts a focus, resurrects
A periscope to glimpse what joys or pain
Our eyes can share or answer—then deflects
Us, shunting to a labyrinth submersed
Where each sees only his dim past reversed . . .[96]

John's painting *Periscope (Hart Crane)* [fig. 7.44] declares its relation to this poem, while elaborating on elements from earlier works: the "device circle" incorporating an arm and hand in place of the stick or ruler; and the division of the composition into three, with the names of the primaries lettered across each part in the manner of *Out the Window* (a painting of 1959 in which the "view" out the window is the words for the three primary colors instead of a direct view of nature). Rauschenberg's "hinge" also recurs here just under the "device circle." Cape Hatteras lies off the Carolina coast, where Johns had a studio. The back-to-front letters and perspective with the hands pressing out from within the canvas suggested the "dim past reversed."

The standard biography of Hart Crane, which Johns owned,[97] details the poet's suicide in 1932, when he dove into the ocean from a ship. The biographer described the vivid image of Crane's arm reaching up out of the sea as he disappeared. The disembodied hand and arm in *Periscope (Hart Crane)* reappeared as the "device circle" that marks the progression of life in the artist's autobiographical series of 1985–6 called "The Seasons" [fig. 7.47]. This transformation of the painter's hand into a mechanical device, as well as the fragmentation of the body, imparts a sense of personal dissolution. As Johns remarked about *Land's End*, a closely related painting of the same year, "I had the sense of arriving at a point where there was no place to stand."[98]

The Perceptual Complexity of Looking

According to What [fig. 7.45] is another major, mural-sized work. On the far left panel, Johns fastened a small canvas with the silhouette of Marcel Duchamp on the front, turned face down on the surface of this larger composition. This reveals the backside of the little canvas, on which Johns has inscribed the date, his signature, and the title "According to What." Above it, upside down, he has attached a cross-section of a real chair with a mold of a leg and buttock seated on it. "The shadows," he explained, "change according to what happens around the painting . . . Everything changes according to something, and I tried to make a situation that allows things to change."[99]

Johns sought out perceptual complexities and contradictions in the world of things and tried to capture the sheer multiplicity of it all in his work. Yet the consistency of his approach has given his work as a whole great coherence. As early as 1959 he articulated this idea in his "artist's statement"

for the Museum of Modern Art's "Sixteen Americans" exhibition catalog: "At every point in nature there is something to see. My work contains similar possibilities for the changing focus of the eye." He also discussed "Marcel Duchamp's suggestion 'to reach the Impossibility of sufficient visual memory to transfer from one like object to another the memory imprint,'" which fed into Johns's idea of communicating perceptual complexity. And he concluded: "Generally, I am opposed to painting which is concerned with conceptions of simplicity. Everything looks very busy to me."[100]

The idea of composing a painting around a "changing focus" places the viewer where he or she is in reality, looking around in different directions, instead of transporting the viewer into an illusionistic space with a contrived single perspective. Johns's work illuminates the fact that we look at the world in fragments, from different perspectives, and in constantly changing contexts over time.

> We look in a certain direction and we see one thing, we look in another way and we see another thing. So that what we call "thing" becomes very elusive and very flexible . . . It involves the way we focus . . . I tend, while setting one thing up, to move away from it to another possibility within the painting . . . the process of my working involves this indirect unanchored way of looking at what I am doing.[101]

In 1971 Johns executed a sequence of prints entitled "Fragments According to What," in which he systematically rethought individual parts of the painting. Johns has often

7.45 Jasper Johns, *According to What*, 1964. Oil on canvas with objects, 7ft 4in × 16ft (2.24 × 4.88m). Private collection. Courtesy Jasper Johns.

used printmaking in this way: "I like to repeat an image in another medium to observe the play between the two: the image and the medium."[102] Johns made his first lithograph in 1960 at Tatyana Grosman's Universal Limited Art Editions (U.L.A.E.) workshop on Long Island. In the course of the decade he made over 120 more, and he has continued to make prints at that pace. His prints provide a running, critical commentary on his painted *oeuvre*, while also forming a kind of technically innovative, aesthetic dialog among themselves.

Dropping the Reserve

In the far left panel of a major transitional work of 1972, known simply as *Untitled*, Johns introduced a pattern of hatch marks which went on to dominate his painting from the end of 1973 until 1981. Johns told David Sylvester that he discovered the hatching on the way to the Hamptons (Long Island) for the weekend; he saw the pattern for an instant on a car passing in the opposite direction.[103] Most of the hatch paintings involve predetermined maps of repeating and nonrepeating patterns that the viewer has to ferret out but that never lead to any deeper subject matter.

In 1978 Johns remarked: "In my early work I tried to hide my personality, my psychological state, my emotions . . . but eventually it seemed like a losing battle. Finally one must simply drop the reserve."[104] In the next group of works it seems that Johns attempted to do just that. After abandoning the hatch pattern style in 1982, he pursued a more charged and personal subject matter directly, through a new kind of realism. He once again used cast body parts and depicted objects from his home and studio that were not neutral. The stick that casts a shadow over the right edge of *Perilous Night* [fig. 7.46] is related to Newman's zip, and for the first time Johns seems to have been tentatively seeking the breathtaking confrontation in his art with what Newman called the "absolute emotions."

Inscribed, almost invisibly, into the left side of *Perilous Night* is a quotation from the Resurrection panel of Grünewald's early-sixteenth-century *Isenheim Altar*. It shows a detail, oriented sideways and backwards, of the sleeping guard with his sword. The same "found" image is repeated, in the correct orientation and on a smaller scale, in the right center of the right panel, portrayed this time as a reproduction tacked to the studio wall. In the top register of the right side are three casts of arms camouflaged with a flagstone pattern of shadows, and the top of each arm is painted in a different primary color. The arms grow progressively larger and more adult from left to right: the first one hangs over an unarticulated, dark backdrop; the second arm over a rendering of one of the more expressionistic and later hatch-mark drawings by Johns (pinned to the wall with *trompe-l'oeil* nails that recall the illusionistic devices of Peto); and the third over a score by John Cage for his 1945 composition *Perilous Night* (silkscreened directly on to the canvas). Below is an illusionistic handkerchief pinned to a horizontally paneled wall. The painting seems to concern the artist's personal

7.46 Jasper Johns, *Perilous Night*, 1982. Encaustic on canvas with objects, 67½ × 96 × 5½in (171.5 × 243.8 × 14cm). Collection, Robert and Jane Meyerhoff, Phoenix, Maryland.

7.47 Jasper Johns, *Summer*, from "The Seasons" series, 1985. Encaustic on canvas, 6ft 3in × 4ft 2in (1.91 × 1.27m). Collection, Philip Johnson. Courtesy Leo Castelli Gallery, New York.

confrontation with growing and aging and his accompanying emotional rites of passage.

From such paintings Johns launched into an explicitly autobiographical mode. In 1985 he decided to make an image for a volume of Wallace Stevens poems and painted *Summer* [fig. 7.47]. The seahorse marks the place in which he painted the work, his new studio on St. Maarten Island in the Caribbean; it also contains important motifs from other earlier paintings: George Ohr pottery (which he collects), the disguised "found" pattern from Grünewald, a *Mona Lisa* iron-on patch he acquired in the late sixties, the flags, and the device circle/arm from *Periscope* [fig. 7.44]. In addition, he included building blocks of the basic geometric shapes floating at the bottom.

Johns was inspired by a reproduction of Picasso's 1936 painting *The Minotaur Moves His House*,[105] showing the minotaur pulling a cart which holds a ladder, a painting, an olive branch, and a horse giving birth all tied in place with a

rope. The minotaur looks back at the cart full of symbols as he traverses the barren landscape under the expressionistic stars. The ladder, the painting, and the handprint from *Periscope* (which may stand for the birth of a new emotional frankness in Johns's paintings) are tied together with a rope in the right half of *Summer* under Picasso's stars. On the left is a shadow traced from Johns's own body. The curator Judith Goldman pointed out that Picasso's 1953 painting *The Shadow* provided a prototype for the artist's shadow in *Summer*. In this painting Picasso depicted himself, shortly after the departure of his long-time companion Françoise Gilot, as a shadow looking into the bedroom he had recently shared with her. Johns went on to paint three more panels to make up a series of "The Seasons" in 1986. All are either bisected in the middle or composed in some modular relation to the middle, like the paintings of Newman, and include the shadow of himself—surrounded by artifacts of his life as a painter—in the four seasons of life.

"I resent my continuing dependence on preexistent forms,"[106] Johns told an interviewer in 1987, and yet he continues to appropriate them. But there is a 1992 drawing called *Nothing At All Richard Dadd* in which Johns discards motifs from "The Seasons" onto a heap in the lower right corner: the ladder, the stick-figure hanged man, the *chute de glace* sign, the blocks and the silhouette of the child. Is this a way out of that dependence? The central image, half-hidden under a network of lines, is the floor plan of a house. "The plan," he told me, "is my attempt to remember the plan of my grandfather's house, where I lived for a number of years during my childhood."[107] But what of the title, evoking the nineteenth-century painter who murdered his own father? Did Johns discard the more removed "preexistent forms" of "The Seasons" in favor of the buried emotions of childhood?

From one perspective Johns's whole career is built on borrowed images and emotions (as though to keep his distance from his own emotions); this alienation is a helpless and terrifyingly empty feeling. This is, however, precisely what gives Johns's work such poignancy and universality. It throws one into confrontation with large philosophical questions of knowing and remembering, of integrity (in the sense of personal wholeness), as against the overpowering forces of dissolution. Through painting, Johns has seen the things around him and let one visual fact lead to another in an intuitive process that emphasizes the vital experience of looking *per se* and, in looking, of being alive. But in his work of the nineties he perhaps found another kind of vitality on a new level of intimacy. That has never been his intention, but as he said:

One has to work with everything and accept the kind of statement which results as unavoidable . . . one wants from painting a sense of life. The final suggestion, the final statement, has to be not a deliberate statement but a helpless statement. It has to be what you can't avoid saying, not what you set out to say . . . it should match what one is.[108]

8.1 Yves Klein, *Untitled Blue Monochrome (IKB)*, 1959. Dry pigment
in synthetic resin on paper, 8½ × 7⅛in (21.6 × 18.1cm).
Menil Collection, Houston.

8 ASIAN AND EUROPEAN VANGUARDS OF THE LATER FIFTIES

NOUVEAU RÉALISME

Yves Klein's Romanticism

The 1956 performance of the costumed Georges Mathieu making action paintings before an audience of 200 at the Théâtre Sarah Bernhardt in Paris had a catalyzing effect for French artists, just as Kaprow's first happenings did for artists in New York at the end of the fifties. Mathieu had already painted a work, *La Bataille de Bouvines* (*The Battle of the Bovines*), for *Life* magazine photographers in 1954. Together, these events made action painting the basis for greater direct engagement and a new theatricality in painting. Between 1958 and 1962 the art actions of Yves Klein fused this dramatic flair and the tendency toward a more directly physical expressionism with an aura of mysticism that tied them into the traditions of European romanticism. Klein sought a flash of spiritual insight for his viewers, in which he was the medium of revelation: unlike the American action painter's revelation of personal identity, Klein's work purported to evoke an intuition into the cosmic order.

In 1948 the twenty-year-old Yves Klein discovered a book by Max Heindel called *La Cosmogonie des Rose-Croix*. Heindel's book provided the key to the teachings of the Rosicrucianists, an esoteric Christian sect, which Klein studied obsessively for five years. According to Heindel, the world was approaching the end of the Age of Matter, when Spirit lies captive in solid bodies.[1]

Soon after coming to Paris in 1955, Klein began referring to himself as an "initiate," seeking to guide world into a new "Age of Space," in which "Spirit" would exist free of form, objects would levitate, and personalities would travel liberated from the body. Blue embodied Heindel's new age and also Klein's imagined freedom of the sky.

As self-appointed "Messenger of the Blue Void," Klein aspired to enter into the world of color, to exist as a color. Where form and line signaled separateness and limitation, color embodied spirit that had coagulated enough to be visible but not enough to precipitate into form. Color expressed unity, openness, enlightenment—the wholeness and infinity of space. "I espouse the cause of Pure Color, which has been invaded and occupied guilefully by the cowardly line and its manifestation, drawing in art," he proclaimed. "I will defend color, and I will deliver it, and I will lead it to final triumph."[2]

Klein had started painting seriously in Spain, where he had spent ten months prior to his arrival in Paris. His paintings each consisted of a single color, uniformly applied, edge to edge [fig. 8.1]. After the rejection of an orange "monochrome" from the 1955 "Salon des Réalités Nouvelles" in Paris, Klein sought out the young critic Pierre Restany to help him obtain a gallery show. According to Restany, they met in a café, and Klein explained to him the "diffusion of energy in space, its stabilization by pure color, and its impregnating effect on sensitivity."[3] Klein said he intended the monochrome painting to fix a focus for the cosmic energies traveling through space: it was to provide a locus of intuitions which could not be formulated. "The authentic quality of the picture, its very being," according to Klein, "lies beyond the visible, in pictorial sensitivity in the state of prime matter."[4]

"Yves the Monochrome," as he called himself, employed pure pigments, gold leaf, the female body, fire, and water in his art, and in 1958 turned to completely immaterial works in an ongoing effort to become conscious of and hold on to his revelation of the infinite. He persistently spoke of the "impregnation" of spiritual vibrations in a space or a thing (as in the Rosicrucian doctrine of Spirit impregnating solid objects).

At first Klein made his "monochrome propositions" (as Restany called them to emphasize their philosophical and immaterial nature) in a variety of colors. In 1956 he limited his palette to an ultramarine blue, then broadened the palette to blue, pink, and gold (the Rosicrucian trilogy of the colors of fire). Klein had a Paris gallery show in 1956. In January 1957 he launched *l'Epoca Blu* (*The Blue Epoch*) in the Galleria Apollinaire in Milan, where it irrevocably altered the career of the Italian artist Piero Manzoni. In May he had two Paris gallery shows simultaneously, in June he exhibited in Düsseldorf (the Zero Group came together in Cologne during 1957, influenced by Klein), and in late June he opened a one-person show in London. He successfully orchestrated his entrance onto the European art scene as though everywhere at once.

Le Vide

Klein went beyond the monochrome to pure immateriality in *Le Vide* (*The Void*) of April 1958. For this "exhibition" he cleaned out and whitewashed the Galerie Iris Clert, "impregnating" the empty space with his spirituality. By arranging to get a cabinet minister on the guest list, he succeeded in having Republican Guards in full regalia flanking the door at the opening and nearly 3,000 visitors turned up.[5] The streets were so crowded that police and fire trucks were called to the scene.

After some time Klein appeared at the door in formal dress and began guiding small groups into the vacant gallery. Many burst out laughing and walked right out, others found *Le Vide* deeply moving and stayed for hours. The writer Albert Camus wrote in the guest book: "with the void, full powers."[6] Meanwhile, glasses of a blue drink were offered to those waiting outside, as at a church sacrament. Klein had had the liquid specially concocted so that after the opening everyone who drank it had blue urine for a week.[7]

The "Living Brush"

A little more than a month later, on June 5, 1958, Klein performed his first "Living Brush" painting in a posh apartment on the Île Saint-Louis in Paris. In this performance a nude model applied blue paint to her torso and then pressed the paint onto the canvas on the floor, directed by the artist. As Klein explained:

I had rejected the brush long before. It was too psychological. I painted with the roller, more anonymous, hoping to create a "distance" between me and my canvases, which should be at least intellectual and unvarying. Now, like a miracle, the brush returned, but this time alive. At my direction, the flesh itself applied the color to the surface, and with perfect exactness. I could continue to maintain a precise distance from my creation and still dominate its execution. In this way I stayed clean. I no longer dirtied myself with color, not even the tips

8.2 Yves Klein, *Anthropométrie de l'époque bleue (ANT 82)*, 1960. Pigment in pure synthetic resin on paper mounted on canvas, 5ft 1⅜in × 9ft 3¼in (1.57 × 2.83m).
Musée National d'Art Moderne–Centre Georges Pompidou, Paris.

8.3 Yves Klein, *Performance: Anthropométries de l'époque bleue*, March 9, 1960, Galerie Internationale d'Art Contemporain, Paris. Photograph © by Harry Shunk.

of my fingers. The work finished itself there in front of me with the complete collaboration of the model. And I could salute its birth into the tangible world in a fitting manner, in evening dress. It was at this time that I noticed the "mark of the body" after each session.[8]

In February 1960 Klein began leaving the blue imprint of the models' bodies on the canvases, rather than covering the whole of each canvas in a monochrome field. He called the resulting series of paintings "Anthropométries" [fig. 8.2]. The most celebrated public performance of the "Living Brushes" was on March 9, 1960 [fig. 8.3]. Attired in blue formal wear and his ceremonial cross of the Order of St. Sebastian (an ancient fraternity of knights he had joined), Klein appeared before a seated audience at the Galerie Internationale d'Art Contemporain. He gestured to the orchestra, and they began to play his *Monotone Symphony*—a single chord held for twenty minutes, followed by twenty minutes of silence. He gestured again and three naked women came out, smeared themselves with blue paint, and, under his direction, pressed their bodies against sheets of white paper on the floor and wall. Klein never touched the work, remaining at a pure, "immaterial" distance.

Seeking Immateriality

Meanwhile in 1959 Klein pushed still further into the terrain of immateriality. At an exhibition in Antwerp he stood in the space allotted for his work and read a passage from the writings of Gaston Bachelard, impregnating the space with his spiritual vibrations. In August, when he decided to abandon Iris Clert for a more established dealer, he did not tell her directly but went into the gallery, picked up his work, and told Clert's assistant that his paintings were invisible and that prospective purchasers should simply write her a check. To her surprise, the very first person to whom she told this agreed to do it, so Klein devised his *Ritual for the Relinquishing of Immaterial Zones of Pictorial Sensibility*. On November 18, 1959 the buyer met the artist on the *quai* of the Seine, delivered a prescribed quantity of pure gold in exchange for an "immaterial zone of pictorial sensibility," and received a receipt which, following the terms of the agreement, the buyer solemnly burned. The artist then threw half the gold into the river. The entire transaction was recorded in photographs.

Despite this relentless drive toward the elimination of the object in art, the female form continued to demand Klein's attention. He made some of his "Anthropométries" by spraying paint around the form of the model to produce a negative imprint that has associations with the paleolithic handprints in the caves at Pech Merle and Lascaux [fig. 8.4]. He also sprayed models with water, had them press themselves onto the canvas, and then attacked the surface with a flame thrower to leave a haunting imprint which he likened to the human shadows left on the walls after the explosion in Hiroshima: "In the desert of the atomic catastrophe they were a terrible proof of the immaterial permanence of the flesh."[9]

In 1959 the Belgian artist Pol Bury published a volume of Klein's writings, which are filled with his visions of

8.4 Yves Klein, *Ant (hropométrie) 96. People Begin to Fly*, 1961.
Oil on paper mounted on canvas, 8ft 2½in × 13ft ½in (2.50 × 3.98m).
Menil Collection, Houston.

ushering in the new age of telepathy, levitation, and immateriality. This publication intensified Klein's commitment to live up to his proclamations. He not only sold invisible paintings, but to establish his credibility as the highest initiate and "Messenger of the Age of Levitation," he began planning a public demonstration of flying. "He was sure he could fly," his girlfriend Rotraut later reported. "He used to tell me that at one time monks knew how to levitate, and that he would get there too. It was an obsession. Like a little child, he really was convinced he could do it."[10]

Klein asked Pierre Restany to come to his apartment on January 12, 1960 for a matter of importance. Restany arrived late to find the artist on his way back from a demonstration of flying, limping slightly and in a state of ecstasy at having accomplished the feat of levitation! Restany was intended to have been a credible witness. Klein's girlfriend at the time, Bernadette Allain, did see the leap but later remarked that for a judo black belt, trained to fall without injuring himself, it was not spectacular.

When Klein reported his feat he was ridiculed, so in October he arranged another leap into the sky from the second story of a building in Paris. He selected a visually

unidentifiable spot across from a judo studio and arranged for a group of *judokas* whom he trusted to hold a tarpaulin to catch him. He then had the photographers alter the photograph to cut out the net and swore them to secrecy. On Sunday, November 27, 1960, the magnificent picture of Klein's *Leap into the Void* (captioned "The Painter of Space Hurling Himself into the Void") [fig. 8.5] appeared on the front page of a four-page newspaper called *Dimanche, le journal d'un seul jour* (*Sunday, the newspaper of a single day*), which Klein created and distributed to newsstands across Paris. However contrived the actual event, the realization of this gesture expressed magnificently Klein's aesthetic appropriation of all of space and its contents. It was a simultaneously frightening and exhilarating anticipation of dematerialization into the womb of infinite space, the void.

Klein's Demise

In 1959 Klein ceased teaching judo, by which means he had then been supporting himself. His "beautiful megalomania,"[11] as his friend Jean Tinguely called it, veered further out of control and even his relationship with Rotraut came under stress. Early in 1961 she and Klein went to New York for two months for a show of his work at the Leo Castelli Gallery but the critical reception was a disaster. His mood was darkening. Back in Paris he started to make

"Anthropométries" with blood; he was preoccupied with death and associated it with his progress toward dematerialization. Then he received news that a Japanese artist, influenced by him, had killed himself by leaping from a high building in Tokyo onto a canvas.[12] He was also still suffering from the humiliating portrayal in a film by Claude Chabrol of "an artist" making "Anthropométries": clearly the filmmaker did not see it as art.

Rotraut became pregnant at the end of the year, and on January 21, 1962 the pair had a magnificent church wedding attended by the Knights of St. Sebastian in full dress. But in the spring Klein suffered another stinging humiliation at the Cannes Film Festival when he went to see footage of himself making "Anthropométries" in the film *Mondo Cane* and found that he had been portrayed like a freak in a sideshow. In mid-May he suffered a heart attack after an agitated public exchange on a panel at the Museum of Decorative Arts in Paris and on June 6, 1962 his heart gave out, ending "The Monochrome Adventure."

The *Nouveaux Réalistes*

The critic Pierre Restany and the artists Arman, François Dufrêne, Raymond Hains, Yves Klein, Martial Raysse, Daniel Spoerri, Jean Tinguely, and Jacques de la Villeglé founded *le Nouveau Réalisme* (New Realism) in a manifesto of October 27, 1960, issued from Yves Klein's Paris apartment. César and Rotella were invited but not present, while Niki de Saint-Phalle, an American expatriate who later married Tinguely, and Gérard Deschamps were also associated with these artists, if not formally in the group. The young Christo was friendly with several of them and shared their inclination toward the appropriation of the real environment, but never joined the group.

Whereas Klein's aesthetic subsumed the entire cosmos, Arman created collections of trash, cast-off fragments of the most down-to-earth sort in his "Poubelles" ("Garbage Cans") [fig. 8.6]. For his famous exhibition "Le Plein" ("Full Up") at the Galerie Iris Clert in 1960, Arman filled the gallery

8.6 Arman, *Large Bourgeois Refuse*, 1960. Trash in a glass box with wooden base, 25¾ × 15¾ × 3¼in (65.4 × 40 × 8.3cm).

Collection, Jeanne-Claude Christo and Christo, New York.

8.7 Jacques de la Villeglé, *Rue de l'Electronique*, July 8, 1961. Torn posters mounted on canvas, 62¼ × 46in (158 × 117cm).

Courtesy Galerie Georges-Philippe et Nathalie Vallois, Paris.

from floor to ceiling with accumulated refuse. The title is a direct response to Klein's *Le Vide*.

César became famous for compressing whole automobiles into crushed blocks of supercondensed junk metal. Rotella, Dufrêne, de la Villeglé [fig. 8.7], and sometimes Hains made their compositions by tearing off layers of posters (*affiches* in French) that had accumulated on top of one another on city walls. The complex, arbitrary layering of fragmentary images and texts in the work of these *affichistes* has come to seem increasingly prescient of the information overload at the end of the century. Spoerri, Deschamps, and Hains assimilated other kinds of found materials, on occasion creating walk-in installations.

Christo's appropriations related to their work in so far as they involved wrapping and stacking collections of found objects. Niki de Saint-Phalle's work evolved from a kind of funk assemblage, resembling that of the early Dine, into a signature vocabulary of funky black female figures with brashly colored detailing. Martial Raysse increasingly used the vocabulary of pop commercial graphics with often ironic subjects from classical painting.

Jean Tinguely—after Klein, the most important signatory of the *Nouveau Réalisme* manifesto—evolved a junk-art aesthetic [fig. 8.8] from an interest in motion and impermanence, accident, and indeterminacy. With an ironic iconoclasm, his "meta-matics" were comically collaged machines that mechanically painted "abstract expressionist" pictures. Other works involved radios, lights, and motorized mechanisms that jerked this way and that in an energetic

8.8 (opposite) **Jean Tinguely**, *Baluba III*, 1961. Motor-driven scrap metal, with feather, wire, rubber belts, bells, and electric light on a wooden base, 4ft 8¾in (1.44m) high.

Collection, Museum Ludwig Köln.

display of pointless activity. Often he even invited the viewer to participate in his carnival-like contraptions.

His most celebrated triumph was his *Homage to New York* [fig. 8.9] which, after extensive negotiation, the Museum of Modern Art agreed to have inaugurated in its sculpture garden on March 17, 1960. *Homage* was a giant motorized junk assemblage which included a weather balloon, a klaxon horn, fifty bicycle wheels, a piano, chemicals that emitted horrible smells and smoke at some unpredictable moment, and motors. Tinguely painted the entire construction white because, as he confided to Peter Selz (the curator in charge), he wanted the *Homage* to be so beautiful that people would be dismayed when it began to destroy itself (which it was designed to do).[13]

The night of the inauguration was cold and drizzly. Watched by the Governor of New York along with various dignitaries and socialites in black tie, Tinguely started the machine. By accident he had attached the belt backwards on the paper roll for the painting machine; it immediately rolled the paper up and began flapping instead of making "automatic" drawings. From there the whole contraption took on an unpredictable life of its own, like all Tinguely machines. It created a tremendous din and flames began to emerge from the piano, where a can of gasoline had been set to overturn on a burning candle. Then, as Calvin Tomkins recounted it, a "small carriage suddenly shot out from under the piano, its klaxon shrieking, and smoke and flames pouring from its rear end. It headed straight for the audience, caromed off a photographer's bag, and rammed into a ladder on which a correspondent for *Paris-Match* was standing; he courageously descended, turned it around, and sent it scuttling into the NBC sound equipment."[14] Things got sufficiently out of control to frighten museum officials, who visualized the entire building on fire, and called in firemen to quench the blaze.

"I'll tell you what's going to happen," Marcel Duchamp explained. "The public will keep on buying more and more art, and husbands will start bringing home little paintings to their wives on the way home from work, and we're all going to drown in a sea of mediocrity. Maybe Tinguely and a few others sense this and are trying to destroy art before it's too late."[15]

GUTAI

The theatrical character of Tinguely's *Homage*, Mathieu's painting events, and Klein's art actions were part of a global tendency after World War II to focus on the performative in art.[16] John Cage's 1952 "event" and his subsequent class at the New School in New York played a seminal role. Fluxus, to which we will turn momentarily, was also centrally important. But contemporary with Cage and worth singling out among the different manifestations of this international tendency for its critical mass in its context is the Gutai Art Association in Japan whose members began staging art actions that were as radical as Cage's "event." When the war ended in Japan, General Douglas MacArthur (the commander of the occupying armies) began systematically dismantling the institutions of Imperial Japan in favor of a Western-style democracy. This destabilized conventions in cultural as well as civic realms, while economic matters were also in disarray. On the one hand this situation—which persevered through the 1950s—meant that there was no market for contemporary art. But on the other hand there was a new freedom to experiment.

8.9 Jean Tinguely, *Homage to New York*, 1960. Self-destructing installation in the garden of the Museum of Modern Art, New York. Photograph © by David Gahr.

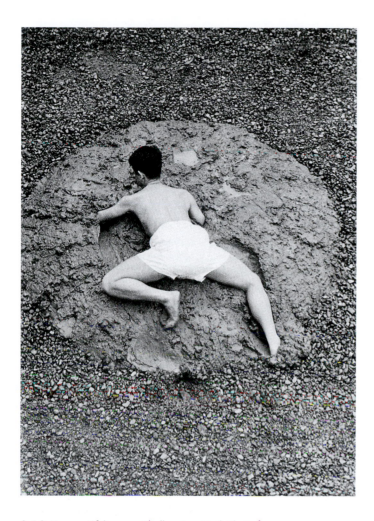

8.10 Kazuo Shiraga, *Challenging Mud*. Photo from "The First Gutai Art Exhibition" in 1955 at Ohara-Kaikan, Tokyo.
Courtesy Ashiya City Museum of Art and History.

the picture plane of layered paper in his piece. Shiraga in *Challenging Mud* enacted a free sequence of expressive bodily gestures while immersed in a circle of viscous mud. *Challenging Mud* both accented the visceral, bodily primitivism of the expressive act and attempted to go beyond the painterly gesture, still circumscribed in Western art by the canvas or sculpted object.

In 1954 the Gutai artists saw the *Life* magazine photos of Georges Mathieu, costumed and painting with great theatrical panache before television cameras; they in turn arranged their April 1956 Gutai exhibition primarily for the benefit of *Life* photographers, reenacting performance actions by various members.[17] Murakami's *Passing Through (21 Panels of 42 Papers)* [fig. 8.11] was an elaboration on *Paper Tearing*; the former was subsequently repeated and of course destroyed in each exhibition, but the artist gave precise instructions so that the paper panels could be reconstructed and the piece performed by others, making it clear that the authenticity inhered in the idea, embodied in the act, and that the physical object left over didn't matter. Atsuko Tanaka made an *Electric Dress* of colored (and very hot) illuminated electric light bulbs in which she performed. Just as *Passing Through* alluded to a long history of papermaking and painting, *Electric Dress* superimposed the traditional arts of the kimono on the one hand, and a reference to the bodily networks of nerves, ducts, arteries, and veins on the other, with a literally brilliant web of wiring and lights that flashed on and off while the artist wore it. In 1957

The Gutai artists from Ashiya, in the Kansai region near Osaka, were the first artists of the new Japan to capture the attention of the international art world. Jiro Yoshihara founded the group in 1954 and was quickly joined by a number of younger artists, who had already defined radical styles on their own: Kazuo Shiraga, for example, had exhibited paintings done with his feet in 1954, and in the same show Saburo Murakami had presented a painting made by throwing a ball soaked in paint at the canvas. The Gutai artists commenced publication of a journal in 1955 and arranged several important group exhibitions. "The First Gutai Art Exhibition," held in Tokyo in 1955, symbolized both a new formal freedom and an anarchistic critique of making and selling commodified objects by closing with a bonfire in which the artists destroyed all the works in the show.

The Gutai literally put the artist into the painting and, in retrospect, the two most famous works in "The First Gutai Art Exhibition" were Murakami's *Paper Tearing* and *Challenging Mud* by Shiraga [fig. 8.10]. With overtones of Japanese martial arts and shocking allusions to the traditional paper arts, Murakami took a running leap through

8.11 Saburo Murakami, *Passing Through (21 Panels of 42 Papers)*. Photo from "The Second Gutai Art Exhibition" in 1956 at Ohara-Kaikan, Tokyo.
Courtesy Ashiya City Museum of Art and History.

"The First Gutai On-Stage Art Show" seems to have been staged especially for the *New York Times* reporters who wrote it up in December of that year,[18] and the next year, in 1958, the Martha Jackson Gallery mounted a show of the Gutai's works in New York.

FLUXUS

The performative tendency in the art of the late fifties and early sixties followed a more metaphysical course among the Fluxus. In 1961 George Maciunas (an American) gave the name "Fluxus" to a very loosely connected group of artists that at times included Nam June Paik, Yoko Ono, Dick Higgins, Alison Knowles, Emmett Williams, Ben Patterson, and La Monte Young in New York, Josef Beuys and Wolf Vostell in Germany, and others. Some of these artists participated in a group performance festival in Wiesbaden, West Germany in 1962 that was probably the first "Fluxus Festival"—"Fluxus Internationale Festspiele Neuester Musik" (The Fluxus International Festival of the Newest Music). Maciunas had attended performances, some of them in Yoko Ono's loft on Chambers Street in New York, that encouraged his efforts and, in the spring of 1961, he opened the AG Gallery on Madison Avenue, on the Upper East Side. There he showed the early minimalist work of Walter De Maria and sponsored performances. Robert Morris and his then wife, the Judson dancer Simone Forti, had arrived in New York from San Francisco with De Maria in 1960; they were involved in some of the downtown loft performances that contributed to this performance scene as well.

In John Cage's now famous classes at the New School for Social Research (taught from 1956 to 1960), there were, in addition to Allan Kaprow, three artists who were central to the consolidation of Fluxus in New York: George Brecht, Al Hansen, and Dick Higgins. In an interview of 1965 Cage noted that "I wasn't concerned with a teaching situation that involved a body of material to be transmitted by me to them," but rather he "would show them what I was doing and why I was interested in it . . . After this basic introduction, the classes consisted simply in their showing what they had done."[19] The students experimented with chance, using objects and musical instruments at hand in a variety of forms, including musical ideas, performance, and poetry. These presentations set a paradigm for the two most characteristic devices of Fluxus: the event score and the Fluxkit. George Brecht's event score for his 1962 *Keyhole Event*, for example, consists of a card, handwritten as follows: "KEYHOLE through either side one event gb." The typical Fluxkit consists of a briefcase or box of small, seemingly trivial objects that don't obviously connect to one another.

Fluxus was formed as a Duchampian reaction against the expressionistic and symbolic aspects of happenings. The Fluxus events were minimal, as in the two performance scores that George Brecht submitted to a 1961 show at the Martha Jackson Gallery in New York; one of them consisted simply of the word "chair," whose realization was, in one instance, a white wicker rocker.[20] According to Robert Watts, "The most important thing about Fluxus is that nobody knows what it is. There should at least be something the experts don't understand. I see Fluxus wherever I go."[21] Al Hanson wrote that "Fluxus is everywhere at once, and nowhere."[22]

JOSEPH BEUYS

The center for advanced art in the divided postwar Germany evolved in the adjacent cities of Köln and Düsseldorf. French art dominated the German scene until well into the fifties. The expressionistic use of materials in *l'art informel* and the gestural individuality of *tâchisme* provided the context for the reception of Wols [fig. 6.1], the most admired new German artist of the period. Then American abstract expressionism arrived, profoundly influencing both abstract and figurative painting. In 1957 Yves Klein also became well known in Köln and Düsseldorf, where he inspired Heinz Mack, Günter Ücker [fig. 10.27], and Otto Piene to found the group "Zero" in 1958. But Joseph Beuys was the first postwar artist to achieve international celebrity based on the exploration of his indigenously German identity. Since Roman times, observers have consistently commented on the mysticism and the sense of closeness with nature in German culture. Both are central to the work of Beuys.

Born in 1921, Beuys grew up in the small town of Cleves, near the Dutch border. As an adolescent he ran away with the circus and learned to perform stunts. Then at nineteen he joined Hitler's *Luftwaffe*. Traumas associated with the war created an internal crisis for Beuys that remained at the thematic core of his artistic career. In particular, he often recounted the story of his plane crash in 1943 in a snowstorm over Crimea, between the Russian and German fronts. His compatriots gave him up for dead, but nomadic Tartars rescued him, covering him in animal fat and layers of felt to raise his body temperature. Whether true or not—and doubts have been raised—the story provides a key to the artist's iconography. But the doubts themselves also add to the mysterious leap of faith that all of Beuys's work evokes.

In 1947 Beuys enrolled in the Düsseldorf Art Academy, but it was not until 1949 that "the sense of trauma," according to the art historian Caroline Tisdall, "became a real illness, the season in hell through which every creative person must go." As Beuys explained to her: "The positive aspect of this is the start of a new life. The whole thing is a therapeutic process. For me it was a time when I realized the part the artist can play in indicating the traumas of a time and initiating a healing process."[23]

Germans lived an ascetic life after the war, which Beuys mirrored in the rudimentary methods and materials of his accumulations and sometimes by fasting before performing his art "actions." After a devastating studio explosion in

1954, Beuys's mental condition began to disintegrate[24] once again. In 1955 he disappeared from Düsseldorf to work in the country—toiling in the fields, shoveling manure in the stables, and (by his own description) doing "a lot of white-washing,"[25] symbolically cleansing away feelings of guilt and anxiety. The drawings with which Beuys reappeared at the end of the fifties described not objects but mental processes, a quality that became a characteristic of his art.

Revealing the Animism in Nature

Beuys's drawings are not "beautiful" in classically formal terms [fig. 8.12]. They strike the viewer as notations of an ongoing flow of ideas, fragments of a perpetual work-in-progress which was his life. By extension the art object no longer stands on its own but takes on its significance as an artifact of the artistic action that produced it. Each object by Beuys has an almost archaeological character, with a vague sense of familial connections to the Northern European mythology and folklore that had interested him since his schooldays.

For Beuys, animals had special significance, symbolizing a direct connection with the beyond (both literally and figuratively). He imagined the stag and the hare traversing the plains of Eurasia, unconscious of distance and conventional boundaries, linking Cleves to the far steppes of China. On another level, "the figures of the horse, the stag, the swan and the hare constantly come and go: figures which pass freely from one level of existence to another, which

8.12 Joseph Beuys, *Astral Chemical Goddess*, 1974.
Pencil on paper, 10 × 10½in (25.4 × 26.7cm).
Courtesy Anthony d'Offay Gallery, London.

represent the incarnation of the soul or the earthly form of spiritual beings with access to other regions."[26]

Beuys's rejection of materialism in favor of an essential spirituality stems from the German romantic tradition in art, as does his ponderous symbolism—both of which he passed on to Anselm Kiefer and Jörg Immendorff, two of his most gifted students. Beuys sought to bring to the surface the fundamental relationship of people to myth and magic. He believed that modern science and technology had obscured that connection with a narrow rationality, and he wanted to enrich scientific methods with a powerful atavistic knowledge. Beuys had a keen early interest in science and described a turning point in a lecture he attended at the University of Posen during the war, given by "a professor who had spent his whole life pondering a couple of fuzzy images of single cells somewhere between plant and animal structure . . . I'm still haunted by the image of those little amoebae on that blackboard."[27] The narrowness of the professor's focus shocked Beuys into the realization that he himself had not engaged life in a more meaningful way. Later, during his art actions of the sixties and seventies, he obsessively drew amoebaelike forms on blackboards [fig. 8.17], as though performing a homeopathic exorcism (healing like with like) of this traumatic revelation.

Nietzsche's description of modern society as hurtling into decline through its overzealous Socratism underlies the philosophy of Joseph Beuys. Beuys wanted his art actions to redress the imbalance Nietzsche pointed out between the intuitive, passionate, irrational soul of mankind (symbolized for Beuys in animals and represented in Nietzsche as the "Dionysian") and the powers of abstract thought and intellect, the Socratic mind (the "Apollonian" in Nietzsche's famous dichotomy).

Beuys's *Fat Chair* [fig. 8.13] offers metaphors for this process of redemption. The chair conforms to human anatomy and order. Fat signifies chaos because it undergoes radical metamorphoses with subtle shifts in temperature. For Beuys, "everything is in a *state of change*"[28] and the resulting "chaos can have a healing character."[29] He saw an analog for spirituality in the passage of fat from one state to another as suggesting the potential for spiritual transcendence in man. Some of Beuys's transcendentalism may come from his interest in the writings of the turn-of-the-century Christian mystic Rudolf Steiner.[30] Indeed, Beuys's woolen felt hat and fisherman's jacket (which he wore at all times) may both be Christian references, symbolizing the fish and the Lamb of God.[31]

In 1961 the Kunstakademie in Düsseldorf appointed Beuys professor of monumental sculpture. A decade later, amidst accusations of demagoguery, the Academy dismissed him. His controversial career as a teacher not only echoed the adventure of his art but also belonged inextricably to it. He did not maintain the conventional hierarchy of student and professor, nor did he teach art in the normal sense. Instead, he talked in an intimate way to his students about fundamental aesthetic and human problems.

8.13 Joseph Beuys, *Fat Chair*, 1963. Wooden chair with fat,
35⅜ × 11¾ × 11¾in (89.8 × 29.8 × 29.8cm).
Hessisches Londesmuseum, Darmstadt.

Each person must point out the way towards anthropological understanding through his field of work. That's what life is involved with—politics too. If one of my students should one day rear her children in a better way, then for me that is more important than just having taught a great artist . . . art and the perceptions gained through art can create an element of backflow into life.[32]

The Artist as Shaman

Beuys presented his first public performance in February 1963 as part of the "Festum Fluxorum Fluxus," for which he performed his *Siberian Symphony* at the Staatliche Kunstakademie in Düsseldorf. Performances, or, as he called them, "actions," instantly became his principal medium. The objects he made took on their meaning in relation to either proposed or realized actions. Beuys planned the objects and the sequence of the performances ahead of time in a "score," always involving sound in a central way. His deliberate use of the musical term *partitur* (or "score") instead of "script"

had to do with his attraction to Fluxus, and its origin in the new music of John Cage, La Monte Young, Yoko Ono, and Nam June Paik who had set the precedent for performances in a concert format. Yet Beuys's performances never had the emotional neutrality of a Fluxus event.

Beuys first performed *The Chief—Fluxus Chant* in Copenhagen in 1963 and then repeated it at the René Block Gallery in Berlin a year later [fig. 8.14]. This nine-hour event was an expressionistic ritual using the artist's body as a psychologically charged material for sculpture. The viewer entered by way of an adjacent room and looked in to see a roll of felt, which enshrouded a seemingly lifeless body (Beuys) lying on the floor. The stiff corpses of two dead hares extended from the roll at either end, and against the baseboard on one wall ran a long strip of fat. Fat was also methodically wedged into two corners of the room, and on one wall hung two fingernails and a tuft of hair. Two copper rods rolled in felt and various wires also lay about. Through a microphone inside the felt roll Beuys made sounds that related, in his mind, to the hares and the call of the stag; speakers broadcast the sounds in the gallery and out onto the street. In contrast to these animal calls, tapes of modern music played at irregular intervals.

In 1964 many parts of Berlin still had a primitive, bombed-out atmosphere, accentuated by the Wall (erected in 1961), which cut through the city like a crude gash. The primal disarray of this performance (and indeed all Beuys performances) has to do with a sense of profound injury as embodied in the face of postwar Berlin and in the memories of the artist's experience in Crimea. "There is certainly an echo of the nomads in *The Chief*," he reflected, continuing:

> and something Eurasian in the transmission of the sounds of the stag out on to the still-ruined streets of that part of Berlin . . . *The Chief* was above all an important sound piece. The most recurrent sound was deep in the throat and hoarse like the cry of the stag: öö. This is a primary sound, reaching far back . . . The sounds I make are taken consciously from animals. I see it as a way of coming into contact with other forms of existence, beyond the human . . . my presence there in the felt was like that of a carrier wave, attempting to switch off my own species' range of semantics.

The point was to reach some profound instinctual or atavistic level of experience, so fundamental as to precede language. He went on: "It takes a lot of discipline to avoid panicking in such a condition, floating empty and devoid of emotion and without specific feelings of claustrophobia or pain, for nine hours in the same position. Such an action, and indeed every action, changes me radically. In a way it's a death, a real action and not an interpretation." The action goes beyond metaphor into real experience, seeking to evoke transformative insights that prepare the individual for a genuine spiritual evolution. Beuys concluded:

> Transformations of the self must first take place in the potential of thought and mind . . . There is no other possibility in my understanding, and this was perhaps too little considered

8.14 (left) **Joseph Beuys**, *The Chief—Fluxus Chant*, December 1, 1964 (first performed Copenhagen, 1963). Action, approximately nine hours, René Block Gallery, Berlin, showing the artist wrapped in a roll of felt approximately 7ft 4½in (2.25m) long with two dead hares at either end and a microphone inside connected to external speakers; along the baseboard of the wall at left a strip of fat and above it hanging on the wall (out of photograph) a tuft of hair and two fingernails; in the corner a wedge of fat where two walls and the floor meet; next to Beuys on the floor a second roll of felt around a copper rod with another copper rod leaning against the wall.

by Marx, for instance. The idea of revolution coming from outer conditions, in the industrial field or the so-called reality of economic conditions, can never lead to a revolutionary step unless the transformation of soul, mind and will power has taken place.[33]

Art as the Creative Life of the Mind

On July 20, 1964—deliberately selected as the twentieth anniversary of the failed attempt to assassinate Hitler—Beuys performed an art action in the cathedral at Aachen. This performance involved filling a grand piano with various materials, melting blocks of fat, and then raising a felt-wrapped copper rod over his head. At that moment, before he could finish the action, right-wing students rushed the stage and attacked him. His nose bled dramatically and the police had to be called to stop a riot from ensuing.

After that incident Beuys became more directly political in his work. In particular, he campaigned for a genuine democracy in which the unaligned voter would have a real voice. This shift paralleled the move in Western society at large toward political activism and unrest in the late sixties, associated with growing protests against American involvement in Vietnam. Beuys founded the German Student Party in 1967 (the precursor to the Green Party); in 1970 he created the Organization for Direct Democracy; and after his dismissal from the Düsseldorf Kunstakademie in 1972 his art actions increasingly resembled eccentric lectures on social and political issues. At the international Documenta VI exhibition of 1977 he established a Free International University, with nonstop discussions on nuclear energy, equality for women, global politics, Northern Ireland, and other topical issues.

Beuys had his first one-person exhibition, as such, in 1965 at the Galerie Schmela in Düsseldorf, and for the opening he devised a performance entitled *How to Explain Pictures to a Dead Hare* [fig. 8.15]. He covered his head

8.15 Joseph Beuys, *How to Explain Pictures to a Dead Hare*, 1965. Performed at Galerie Schmela, Düsseldorf.
Photo © Ute Klophaus, Düsseldorf.

in honey and gold pigment, tied a steel sole onto his right shoe and a felt sole to his left (to represent hard reason and spiritual warmth), and then spent three hours silently mouthing explanations of his pictures to a dead hare that he held in one arm. The piece critiques the limits of painting in effecting social enlightenment. But it is also concerned with the irrelevance of explanations in art and with opening communication to the nonrational world of the soul. Honey embodies a life force and a metaphor for the products of creativity in Beuys's cosmology. The mysterious process by which the bees produce it evokes the idea of fecundity and transformation and provides a parallel to the creative mystery of the artist, not as object-maker but rather as a medium of esoteric knowledge.

For Beuys all creative thought was art. In the same way that the German romantic poet Novalis claimed that every man was a poet, Beuys wanted to counteract the overbalance of rationality in contemporary society by declaring "everyone an artist."[34] Since each individual can find the nature of existence within himself or herself by introspection—an idea Beuys took from the German philosopher Arthur Schopenhauer—each is therefore also capable of creating a revolutionary dialog between art (creative thought) and real events. Thus art serves as a politically liberating force—perhaps, as writers from Herbert Marcuse to Harold Rosenberg have suggested, one of the only viable ones left in a media-dominated society.

Beuys made a felt-covered piano for a performance of 1966 entitled *Infiltration-Homogen for Grand Piano, the Greatest Contemporary Composer Is the Thalidomide Child*. The felt skin trapped the sound of the piano inside, and the red crosses which Beuys placed on the flanks were to indicate an emergency. Whereas fat infiltrates other materials—in the installations where Beuys placed fat up against the wall one can readily see it soaked up into the plaster—felt absorbs everything—fat, dirt, water, and sound. For Beuys, the sound, symbolically held in the piano by the felt, offered a metaphor for the much-discussed tragedy of the children who suffered birth defects caused by the drug thalidomide, used widely in Europe in the fifties to alleviate morning

8.16 Joseph Beuys,
The Pack, 1969. Volkswagen bus with twenty sleds, each carrying felt, fat, and a flashlight, dimensions vary.
Neue Gallery, Staatliche Museen, Kassell.

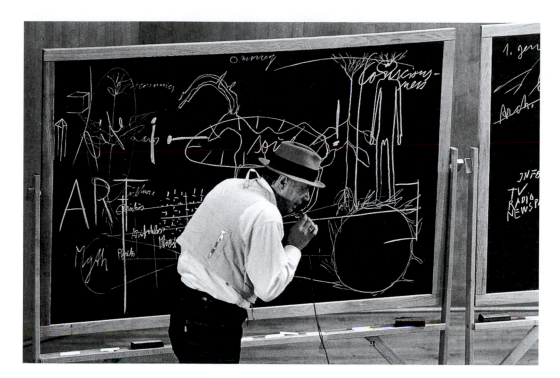

sickness in pregnancy. Their inability to lead normal lives gave rise to the inner turmoil that Beuys believed necessary for creativity. Thus the felt objects imply warmth, protection from outside disturbances, and silence, but also isolation, an inability to communicate, and powerlessness. As with his deliberate evocation of the Nazis, here again Beuys took on a subject so emotionally charged that the mere mention of it upset his audiences.

The Pack of 1969 [fig. 8.16]—with twenty sleds issuing out of the back of a Volkswagen bus—also has a sense of urgency about it, implying part invasion, part escape to survival. Each sled carries a roll of felt for warmth, fat for nourishment, and a flashlight to find the way. It is not only one of the artist's most evocative works but a market landmark as well: it sold in 1969 for over 100,000 marks, comparable in price to a major work by Rauschenberg or Johns.

In February 1976, after a grave illness in the preceding summer, Beuys assembled one of his most tragic and disturbing installations, *Show Your Wound*. He set the piece in a barren concrete passageway under a street in Munich. *Show Your Wound* relates, as he said in reference to an earlier work, to "the wound or trauma experienced by every person as they come into contact with the hard material conditions of the world through birth,"[35] or, it might be added, through any profound psychic injury. The objects—mortuary tables, filters and glass jars, batteries, fat, and a pair of old three-pronged pitchforks with the center prong broken out—create a sulfurous atmosphere. The presentation of everything in pairs (except the skull of a thrush emerging from a test tube) and the precision of their implied ritual use enhance the piercing, irrational, and unconscious realism of the work. *Show Your Wound* goes back to a proposal in 1958 for a monument at Auschwitz. Guilt for the Nazi atrocities preoccupied

Germans of Beuys's generation, and through his art Beuys sought to heal the trauma by reopening the wound. Once again the wound of Christ may be a subtextual reference in this work.

After 1973 Beuys did more and more lecturing. He prompted intense sessions of political consciousness-raising (almost like group-therapy sessions), drawing diagrams and notations on blackboards to punctuate his impassioned delivery [fig. 8.17]. This shift from actions to lectures did not constitute a break with sculpture, but rather a further evolution toward an encompassing "social sculpture." Beuys died in January 1986 at the age of sixty-four.

NAM JUNE PAIK'S ELECTRONIC "NATURE"

Although the Korean-American artist Nam June Paik was more than a decade younger than Beuys, they both emerged on the art scene at about the same time. Paik had come to Germany to study with the composer Karlheinz Stockhausen, who was the center of avant-garde music in Germany. Stockhausen's wife, the painter Mary Bauermeister, had events in her loft in Düsseldorf and Paik performed his first widely celebrated work there in 1960: *Etude for Pianoforte*. The piece consisted of Paik performing a Chopin *Etude*, breaking off in tears, and leaping from the stage into the audience, cutting off John Cage's tie with scissors, and dousing Cage and David Tudor with shampoo. He did not assault the formidable Stockhausen, who sat next to Cage, but he left a motorcycle running on the stage, filling the space with carbon monoxide, ran out, and then telephoned from downstairs to say that the piece was over.

Paik met Cage while studying new music composition in Germany and Cage introduced Paik to Zen. After exploring the extension of music into visual form and theater, Paik then turned to video, pioneering the formal exploration of television in his art of the early sixties. "We are moving in tv away from high fidelity pictures to low fidelity, the same as in painting," he explained, looking back in 1970. "From Giotto to Rembrandt the aim was fidelity to nature. Monet changed all that. I am doing the same."[36] Paik's work is revolutionary precisely because of this shift from "content-level perception" to "process-level perception." His emphasis is on both how we see and what we see, simultaneously; his work is a collage of overlapping information structures that cut across media from atonal music and performance to sculpture. At the same time that pop art was rendering the experience of nature as a perceptual screen of images, Paik juxtaposed vivid sensations of the body in real time (especially sexuality, one of the most vivid body experiences) with the remove and the collapsed and recombinant time of television (time that can be reconfigured at will). Paik came to art from a background in Western music, acquired in Japan, and worked with the fundamentally immaterial medium of electronics in the field of sculpture, which traditionally concerns palpable volumes in real space.

Paik had his first video exhibition at the Galerie Parnass in Wuppertal (near Düsseldorf) in 1963. His *Exposition of Music—Electronic Television* included thirteen "prepared" televisions, three prepared pianos, and noisemakers. He experimented with distortions of broadcast test patterns and in 1965 (when Sony introduced it) began using portable video equipment to make art, having immediately recognized the revolutionary potential of decentralizing control over media with the new availability of inexpensive equipment and the possibility of virtually limitless numbers of laser channels.

While performing in Japan in the early sixties, Paik met Shuya Abe, an electronics engineer, with whom he collaborated on ways to transform the video image and on *Robot K-456*, a remote-control robot that walked, talked, and defecated beans. In 1964, after spending a year in Japan, he went to New York, where George Maciunas and Dick Higgins—Fluxus artists whom he had met in 1961 in Europe—introduced him to Charlotte Moorman. Moorman, a cellist, then became the principal actor for his performances, as in *TV Bra for Living Sculpture* of 1969 [fig. 8.18].

In an effort to integrate sex into music, a theme that Paik felt had not been sufficiently developed, he included instructions for incorporating sexual acts into several of his compositions from the late sixties. In *Opera Sextronique*, for

8.18 Nam June Paik,
TV Bra for Living Sculpture, with Charlotte Moorman, 1969.
Collection Walker Art Center, Minneapolis.
T.B. Walker Acquisition Fund, 1991.
Photograph by Peter Moore.

8.19 Nam June Paik, *Video Fish*, 1975–9. Video installation: five aquariums, five monitors, two video tapes, live fish, 26 × 110¼ × 29½in (66 × 280 × 75cm). Musée National d'Art Moderne–Centre Georges Pompidou, Paris.

example, Charlotte Moorman had to do a striptease while playing the cello, and in *Young Penis Symphony* ten young men behind a paper curtain stuck their penises in sequence through the paper at the audience. In 1968 Moorman was arrested for indecent exposure during her topless performance of *Opera Sextronique* at the New York Film-Makers' Cinemathèque.

In *Video Fish* of 1975-9 [fig. 8.19] tanks of live fish stand in front of television monitors with videotape loops of fish swimming around. This seems to turn the real tanks into monitors and the monitors into fish tanks, as if equating representation and reality. Paik also subverted concepts of time and space, as in *TV Buddha* (1974), where the live monitor is continuously regenerating the image of a motionless statue of the Buddha.

Paik's *The Moon Is the Oldest TV* (1965) consists of twelve black-and-white monitors, each showing a partially eclipsed circle of light that looks like a phase of the moon. In *TV Clock* (1963) he compressed the image on each of the twenty-four sets to a line, like hands on a clock. These works all allude to time and yet he uses television, a medium of moving pictures and temporal events, for static images. For Paik, all time collapses into the present as he juxtaposes multiple, anti-narrative sequences of images. One needn't see a whole sequence on the tape loops he composes for the television sets in his sculptures to get the mind-bending effect of their simultaneous contrast and conflation between immediate experience and the artificiality of images and media time.

This radical simultaneity of multiple cross-tracking systems of thought and experience was both intrinsic to the form of Paik's work and at the same time it was also the content; his exploration of television and video laid a foundation for understanding the still-unanticipated development of computers and the Internet on how we think about the world.

YOKO ONO

Yoko Ono described her practice as one of "fabricating consciousness,"[37] rather than making art. "After unblocking one's mind, by dispensing with visual, auditory, and kinetic perceptions, what will come out of us?" she asked in an essay of 1966. "Would there be anything? I wonder. And my Events are mostly spent in wonderment."[38]

Born into one of the most elite mercantile families of Japan, Ono spent her childhood between San Francisco and Tokyo. She had a privileged education, including training in classical music, and entered the aristocratic Gakushuin University to study philosophy in 1952. After a year she moved to New York with her father, who ran the Bank of Tokyo in New York, and attended Sarah Lawrence College for a year before eloping with a young Japanese pianist/composer and moving into Manhattan.

Ono's work draws on both Eastern and Western metaphysical thought but Zen Buddhism had particular importance both for its radical empiricism and its "embrace of spontaneous, unmediated experience,"[39] as Alexandra Monroe pointed out. D. T. Suzuki, an important influence on Cage and others in New York through his books and his lectures on Zen at Columbia in the mid-fifties, wrote that the Dao "is no more than one's everyday experience . . . when you begin to think, you miss the point."[40] In this, Ono was of like mind both with Suzuki and with Cage, whom she met in the mid-fifties at one of Suzuki's lectures.

In 1960 Ono rented a coldwater loft at 112 Chambers Street, in which she and La Monte Young ran a "Chamber Street Series" of performances through June of 1961. Her works of this period were like Zen *koans*, instructions that confound reason but evoke insight through intuition, transcending the intellect. In July 1961 she exhibited "Instruction Paintings" done in sumi ink on canvas at George Maciunas's AG Gallery on upper Madison Avenue after first showing some in her loft on Chambers Street; she invited viewers to walk on *Painting to Be Stepped On* (1961), a torn piece of canvas lying on the floor.[41] She wrote these instructions for *SUN PIECE*: "Watch the sun until it becomes square. 1962 winter."

These highly conceptual pieces aspire to a kind of poetry, opening the mind to experience; they are an affirmation of the imagination. While they resemble the work of Cage in some ways—Cage's "score" for his 1952 *Water Music*, for example, contains enigmatic instructions such as:

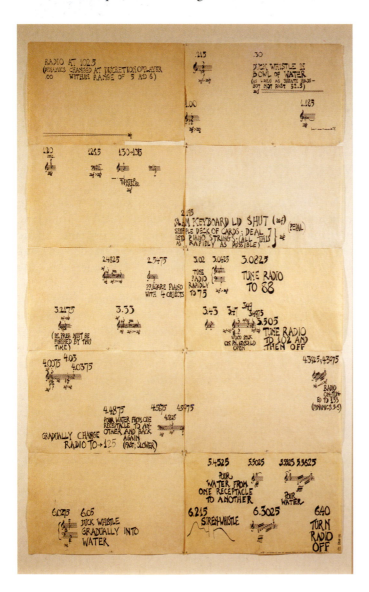

"Radio at 102.5; (dynamics changed at discretion of player .00 within range of 5 and 6); slam keyboard lid shut; shuffle deck of cards; deal 7 into piano strings. Call this as rapidly as possible) Pour water from one receptacle to another" [fig. 8.20]—they also differ from Cage's work in that Ono's pieces are far less structured, more abstract.

In March 1962 Ono returned to Tokyo after a decade. Though she had become estranged from her family, her husband, the composer Ichiyanagi Toshi, was by then famous in Tokyo and helped her connect with avant-garde groups such as Hi Red Center, the musicians Yasunao Tone, Kosugi Takehisa, and Shigeko Kubota of Group Ongaku, and Team Random (the first computer artists in Japan). But the Japanese avant-garde also already knew about Ono from the work she had done in New York. Then her circle was further expanded by the arrival of her friend Paik.

After an emotional crisis that overwhelmed Ono for the better part of a year, she fell in love with an American artist and had a child in 1963. She also began to pull herself back together by compiling her scores, instructions, and poems for the 1964 publication of *Grapefruit*. *Morning Piece*, done in May of that year. It consisted of thirty-three shards of broken milk bottles, tagged with a random future morning date, such as "December 27, 1999 after sunrise." She offered her collection of "Mornings" for sale, first in a gallery and then on her Tokyo apartment rooftop, keeping a detailed list of the sales (mostly to well-known people in the Tokyo avant-garde).[42]

One of the last works Ono did before returning to New York in the fall of 1964 was her radical and influential *Cut Piece*, which she performed for the first time in Yamaichi Hall in Kyoto in July of that year [fig. 8.21]. In the performance Ono walked onto the stage, scissors in hand, and invited the audience to cut off pieces of her clothes. She sat, legs tucked under her, motionless and silent as individuals from the audience cut away nearly all traces of her clothing. She performed *Cut Piece* again in Carnegie Recital Hall in New York in 1965 and again when she arrived in London in September 1966. The piece provokes an uneasy explicitness to the underlying sexuality and violence in everyday social relations. It also announces a new sensuality and expressionism in Ono's work.

In November 1966 Ono had a one-person show at Indica Gallery and at the opening she met John Lennon, whom she married in March 1969. Although Ono was now embarked on some of her most interesting work, her relationship to Lennon overshadowed her career in the minds of the public. In *Fly*, a film of 1970 [fig. 8.22], for example, she filmed a fly walking across the landscape of a naked woman's body.

8.20 John Cage, *Water Music*, 1952. India ink on paper, ten sheets, 11 × 17in (25.4 × 43.2cm); colophone sheet, 9½ × 6in (24.1 × 15.2cm).
Whitney Museum of American Art, New York. Purchase with funds from an anonymous donor 82.38a-k. Courtesy of the John Cage Trust.

8.21 Yoko Ono, *Cut Piece*, Yamaichi Hall, Kyoto, 1964. Performance.

We watch in close-ups as the fly slowly crawls across her stomach, onto her breast, over her face, and we feel ourselves twitching, we can hardly stay still, while the soundtrack plays what Alexandra Monroe described as "a continuous rhythm of the organic sounds of elemental womanhood—from the whimpers and groans of rapture to the cries of deep dread."[43]

It is a matter of social history that John Lennon was murdered on December 8, 1980. By then Yoko Ono had been collaborating consistently with Lennon on music and on social and political actions for many years. In the late eighties she turned to bronze to reinterpret some of her works of the sixties, contrasting the latter's lightness with the solidity of these heavy, intentionally commodified objects that reflected the reification of the revolutionary times of the sixties twenty-five years later. But she also continues still, in poetry, performance, music, and installation, to celebrate the potential of the creative imagination.

8.22 Yoko Ono, frame from the film *Fly*, 1970. Nineteen minutes.

9.1 Quang Duc, a seventy-three-year-old Buddhist monk, soaked himself in gasoline and set himself on fire, burning to death in front of thousands of onlookers at a main highway intersection in Saigon, Vietnam on June 11, 1963. He was protesting against the American-backed government's discrimination against Buddhists. A group of nuns and monks circled the burning martyr with banners that read "A Buddhist Priest Burns Himself for Five Requests."

Photograph by Malcolm W. Browne.

9 THE LANDSCAPE OF SIGNS: POP ART

THE ELECTRONIC CONSCIOUSNESS

The shift away from existentialism to a focus on semiotics (from expressions of identity to a concern with the language of art) in the art of the sixties was inseparable from the bewildering new social and political realities of the decade, particularly in America. Things changed radically as the fifties drew to a close, and foremost among the new conditions was the quantity and vividness of information about the world at large that began invading the private domains of the individual. In the ten years after 1947 the number of televisions in the United States jumped from ten thousand to forty million,[1] putting Selma, Alabama and Saigon, Vietnam right there in everyone's living room [fig. 9.1]. We had moved into Marshall McLuhan's "Global Village," playing Buckminster Fuller's "World Game."

On the political front, great concern had arisen among Americans in 1957 about a supposed "missile gap" when the Soviets launched *Sputnik*, the first manmade satellite, and then in 1961 put the first man in space. Meanwhile Fidel Castro overthrew an American-backed dictator in Cuba in 1959, and invited the Kremlin to begin setting up an armed camp there, well inside the American early warning missile defense system. The CIA failed miserably in its Bay of Pigs invasion—designed to oust Castro—and finally, in June 1961, the entire world held its breath as President Kennedy brought the nation to the brink of armed confrontation with the Soviet Union by ordering a naval blockade to stop the deployment of the Russian missiles. The construction of the Berlin Wall in 1961 summed up the tone of East–West relations.

For a brief time John F. Kennedy raised the spirits of America and Europe. He was the first television President, and the public identified with the young, glamorous, and dynamic First Family whom they came to know in an illusively "personal" way through television and magazines. However, the mood of involvement he engendered also mobilized movements against social injustices of which the expanded media had suddenly made everyone aware; the Civil Rights movement blossomed during the sixties, as did a consciousness of American adventurism in Vietnam. The effect of Kennedy's style on the conscience and activism of the era demonstrated the power of television. But the fact that Americans reacted with shock in October 1959 to the revelation that Carl Van Doren had been set up to give the right answers on the popular TV quiz show *The Sixty-Four Thousand Dollar Question* points to the late date of the nation's loss of innocence about the media; people had to admit to themselves that not everything on television was as it appeared, and America's faith in the honesty of the common man seemed shaken.

In Kennedy's "New Frontier," culture became a popular priority. The Metropolitan Museum's purchase of Jackson Pollock's *Autumn Rhythm* for $30,000 in 1957 had already given contemporary artists a new prestige, and in 1959 the de Kooning show at the Sidney Janis Gallery sold out on the first day for $150,000—an unheard-of amount of money at the time. In the sixties newly rich collectors were keen to be first in picking up on the latest trends, and some of the biggest (like Robert Scull and the Italian Count Panza di Buomo) began buying in quantity. Art openings became the "in" place for rich socialites to be seen, and before long a class of celebrity artists developed whom the collectors collected almost as much as the art.

Not only were growing numbers of people attending openings at local museums and art centers; they also took courses on contemporary art, subscribed to art magazines, and for the first time the demand for avant-garde art went mainstream. In 1962 even Sears Roebuck—the middlebrow catalog merchandising giant—launched an art-selling plan under the aegis of the Hollywood movie star Vincent Price. Assisted by the careful promotion of a few key dealers, the price of work by the most fashionable younger artists of the sixties escalated as much as 4,000 percent over the decade.

In the forties and early fifties the galleries of Samuel Kootz, Sidney Janis, Betty Parsons, Martha Jackson, and Charles Egan had a great deal to do with shaping the image of the artists and with associating them together as a movement. But in the sixties the role that dealers such as Janis and Leo Castelli played in making a name for their artists—carefully directing the work into important collections and exhibitions and controlling the market supply—set an (albeit restrained) precedent for the coarse manipulation of the contemporary art market by speculators in the late seventies and since. More and more artists organized their social life with their careers in mind. As money and fashion came onto the scene, the intellectual tone of the art world declined. In 1964 Allan Kaprow quipped that "if the artist was in hell in 1946, now he is in business."[2] American pop art came along at the beginning of the sixties, just as mass advertising and television took their quantum leap. It celebrated stars and consumer culture and it provided the most deliberately exploitable art form that had ever been offered to the media.

A Turning Point in Theory

The influence that television and other mass-cultural outlets exerted on the way in which increasing numbers of people viewed the world around them became the profound subject matter for the American pop artists of the early sixties. Predicated on the nonselective openness to experience in the work of John Cage and Jasper Johns, pop art detached the pervasive images of the media from any specific location in time and place. Images suddenly floated freely in the mind, becoming interchangeable parts of the puzzle that made up the new reality of the era. Pop art took images of things, rather than the things in themselves, as the reference to nature and fundamentally redefined the concept of iconography.

The parallels between pop art and structuralist theory, with which it was contemporary, help clarify what is revolutionary about them both in altering the way in which we were beginning to look at events. Structuralism was the cultural theory pioneered by the French anthropologist Claude Lévi-Strauss. Lévi-Strauss focused on the structure of a myth rather than on the individual version of it, encountered in a particular context. He argued, for example, that Freud's writings on the Oedipus Complex constituted not an analysis but merely a restatement of the Oedipus myth in terms that contemporary culture could understand.[3] In the same way pop artists began to treat images as signs that existed independently of any particular context in nature; thus they might be reconfigured (and redefined) at will. Images became nature—equal, in terms of how we perceive them, to a tree or a cloud seen in the landscape. Language, the structuralists argued, defined perception.

By the seventies this new definition of nature as a landscape of signs had evolved into what came to be known as "postmodernism." Postmodernism (and its corollary, "post-structuralist theory") went beyond detaching the image from a fixed time and place to relieving images of a stable meaning and creating a more complex and multidirectional way of seeing. With the emergence of the personal computer and the video cassette recorder (VCR) around 1980, the electronic consciousness of pop art took a jump in magnitude so vast that thirty years later we are only just beginning to understand its implications.

BRITISH POP: FROM THE INDEPENDENT GROUP TO DAVID HOCKNEY

The aesthetic forerunner to these events in America took place nearly a decade earlier in England. The Institute of Contemporary Arts (I.C.A.) in London opened in 1946 with the aim of providing focus and encouragement for new artistic developments in postwar England. Sir Herbert Read, its president, belonged to a liberal upper-class art establishment which saw the embodiment of its values in the conservative heirs to classic prewar styles. In 1952 some younger members of the I.C.A. formed the Independent Group, and from the start their enthusiasm for popular culture and technology set them on a collision course with the mainline modernism of the Institute's founders. The Independent Group attacked the modernist concept of self-referential and "timeless" high art; they opened up the discourse on art to ideas from areas as diverse as cybernetics, game theory, semiotics, science fiction, and the mass media (especially American advertising). They wanted art to be of the moment rather than above it, democratic instead of elitist, and linked to the forward edge of new technology.

Key Figures of the Independent Group

Peter Reyner Banham, a doctoral student in architectural and design history, emerged as the leader of the Independent Group in September 1952 and the group's lecture series of that season reflected his interest in the machine aesthetic. The imagery of science and engineering also fascinated the other leading members: Richard Hamilton, Eduardo Paolozzi, Peter and Alison Smithson, Lawrence Alloway, John McHale, Nigel Henderson, and James Stirling. Hamilton's dynamic installations for the exhibitions "Growth and Form" (1951), "Man, Machine, and Motion" (1955), and "This Is Tomorrow" (1956) demonstrated a brilliant design sense. Ironically, its principal source was in constructivism—one of those classic prewar styles against which the group rebelled.

Since the mid-forties Paolozzi had made collages using images of consumer goods, technology, and popular culture culled from books and mass-market magazines [figs. 9.2 and 9.3]. For many of these he drew on science fiction, which has always had a close relationship to the forefront of technology. One of the galvanizing events early in the Independent Group's first season was a "lecture" in which Paolozzi showed images from popular media, especially American sources such as *Life* magazine. The images ranged from advertisements for home appliances to automobiles, comics, pin-ups, and illustrations for science fiction. The presentation lasted for several hours, *without commentary*!

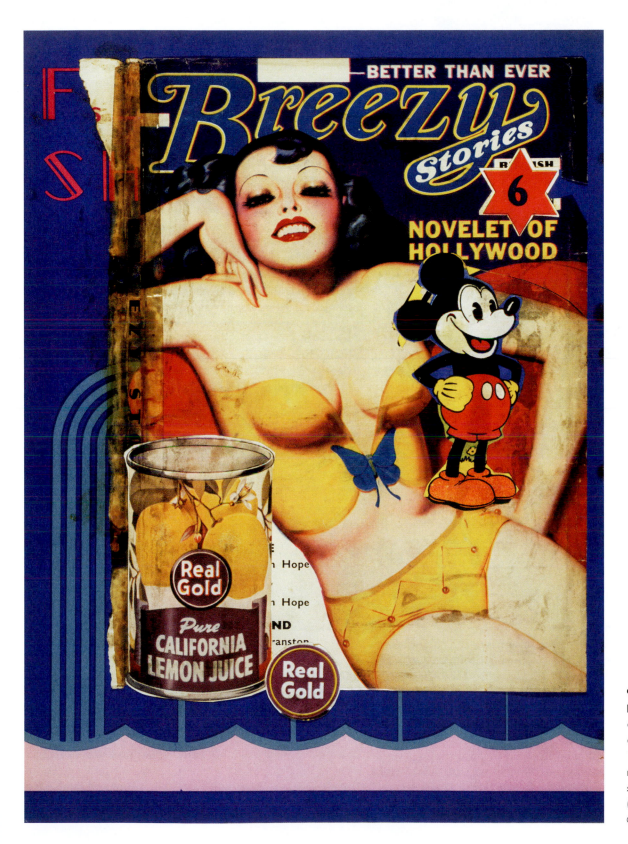

9.2 Eduardo Paolozzi, *Real Gold*, from *10 Collages from BUNK*, 1950. Collage mounted on card support, 14 × 9¼in (35.7 × 23.5cm). © Tate, London 2009.

appreciation for the imagery of the commercial environment and a rejection of the distinction between highbrow and popular culture.

Though the Independent Group officially disbanded in 1955, the most important group manifestation of their ideas was an exhibition in 1956 at the Whitechapel Gallery in London. The exhibition, called "This Is Tomorrow," consisted of individual pavilions, each designed by a team—generally a painter, an architect, and a sculptor. The different sections of the show represented a wide variety of aesthetic perspectives, but as a whole they evolved from an underlying concept of collaborative design as a vehicle for ideas and an overall stress on popular culture and technology in place of romantic individuality. As in the group's earlier exhibitions, "This Is Tomorrow" relied on reproductions, often enlarged to a cinematic scale and configured into total environments.

Richard Hamilton, John McHale, and John Voelcker built a pop-culture fun house inside the show's front door [fig. 9.4]; they included films, a live microphone (to prompt an interactive relationship with the viewer), and a working jukebox that successfully attracted working-class patrons from the neighborhood around the gallery. This section also included a 14-foot-high blow-up of Robby the Robot carrying off a voluptuous woman—a still from the film *Forbidden Planet*—and in the shadows they superimposed the famous photograph of Marilyn Monroe standing over an air vent in *The Seven Year Itch*. Meanwhile, Paolozzi, the Smithsons, and the photographer Nigel Henderson designed a rudimentary

9.3 Eduardo Paolozzi, *It's a Psychological Fact Pleasure Helps Your Disposition*, from *10 Collages from BUNK*, 1948. Mixed media on paper, 14¼ × 9⅝in (36.2 × 24.4cm). © Tate, London 2009.

The Exhibitions

After a year of meetings the Independent Group organized an inexpensive and accessible exhibition called "Parallel of Art and Life." Inspired by the variety of source material illustrated in such classic texts of design theory as Ozenfant's *Foundations of Modern Art*, Le Corbusier's *Towards a New Architecture*, Sigfried Gideon's *Mechanization Takes Command*, and *The New Vision* by Làszló Moholy-Nagy, they displayed sheets of Pollock-like automatist drawings as well as blown-up photographs of paintings, children's drawings, primitive art, machines, X-rays, microphotographs, athletes, pilots, hieroglyphics, scientific illustrations, and diagrams. They hung these reproductions freely in space with no labels. During the second and third seasons (1953–5) the group increasingly concentrated on popular imagery, for which they began to use the term "pop art." This implied a genuine

9.4 Richard Hamilton, John McHale, and John Voelcker, Pavilion for the 1956 "This Is Tomorrow" exhibition at the Whitechapel Gallery, London.

shack of pointedly cheap materials, littered with found objects and images.

Behind the activities of the Independent Group lay a serious concern for the direction in which the world was headed. "We still have no formulated intellectual attitudes for living in a throw-away economy,"[4] Reyner Banham worried in 1955. In an essay of 1956 entitled "But Today We Collect Ads," Alison and Peter Smithson observed that: "The student designer is taught to respect his job, to be interested in the form of the object for its own sake as a solution to a given engineering and design problem—but he must soon learn that . . . this is a reversal of the real values of present-day society." They concluded with a quotation from Arthur Drexler, the design curator of the Museum of Modern Art: "What is important is to sustain production and consumption."[5] Hamilton took a Duchampian delight in the idea that advertising could actually shape the desires of the consumer rather than merely responding to them.

Paolozzi and Hamilton as Artists

Paolozzi, the son of Italian immigrants, grew up around the docks of Edinburgh during the Depression of the 1930s. He attended art schools in Edinburgh and London, and then, at the age of twenty-three, moved to Paris for two years. There he met many of the older modern masters, including Léger, who arranged for Paolozzi to see his *Ballet mécanique* (a film that Léger had made in 1924 celebrating the machine aesthetic). To Paolozzi, the work of Dubuffet and Giacometti, like that of Pollock, represented freedom from established conventions. Paolozzi's collages, beginning in the late forties, are indebted to the German dada artist Kurt Schwitters, but Paolozzi's unique way of packing his compositions with whole images clipped from magazines displays a newer, McLuhanesque consciousness of semiotics.

Richard Hamilton, who left the Slade School of Art in London in 1951, had worked in advertising during the forties. Stylistically, his art came together in 1956, influenced by Paolozzi's collages. His own small collage *Just what is it that makes today's homes so different, so appealing?* [fig. 9.5] marked the turning point. Using commercial graphic-design techniques and imagery from popular media, he undertook a sophisticated exploration of the language of visual signs.

Hamilton described this collage as "'Instant' art from the magazines. The collage (made for the catalog of the 'This is Tomorrow' exhibition) is a representation of a list of items considered relevant to the question of the title. The image should, therefore, be thought of as tabular as well as

9.5 Richard Hamilton, *Just what is it that makes today's homes so different, so appealing?*, 1956. Collage on paper, 10¼ × 9¾in (26 × 24.8cm). Kunsthalle Tübingen, Sammlung Zundel.

pictorial."[6] Thus he meant the work to be read like a text cataloguing the concerns of the exhibition. In a later commentary on the work he listed these subjects as: "Journalism, Cinema, Advertising, Television, Styling, Sex symbolism, Randomization, Audience participation, Photographic image, Multiple image, Mechanical conversion of the imagery, Diagram, Coding, Technical drawing."[7] For the ceiling of the room in his collage Hamilton used a telescopic photo of the surface of the moon; the nubbly carpet was made by blowing up a Weegee photograph of people on the beach at Coney Island (randomization perhaps?); and with the movie marquee advertising Al Jolson in *The Jazz Singer* Hamilton provided a charged metaphor for his entire semiotic endeavor, for *The Jazz Singer* was the first film to synchronize spoken words and cinematic images.

Popular Imagery into High Art

The use of popular imagery implied an attack on the traditional division of "high" and "low" art, which in turn embodied an assault on the social hierarchy in Britain. The use of American popular imagery carried a consciously radical, social message. The prominence of black people in American popular music particularly struck these Europeans, who then still lived in a more racially and culturally homogeneous environment with little social mobility.

In addition, pop music had a special connection with pop art and with the British art schools, which offered one of the few mechanisms for lower-class students to cross over the usual social divisions. Many important English pop musicians of the sixties—including John Lennon, Eric Clapton, Cat Stevens (an American expatriate in England), Pete Townshend, and Keith Richards—went to art schools on government grants.[8]

Artistic self-consciousness, and the high-art seriousness that it engendered, was perhaps the leading contribution of the British bands to the pop music scene of the sixties, which was otherwise dominated by African-Americans. As a corollary to this increased intellectual aspiration, British pop musicians cultivated their connection with fine artists. The Beatles, for example, commissioned Peter Blake to design the cover for their 1967 album *Sgt. Pepper's Lonely Hearts Club Band* and Richard Hamilton to create the cover and insert for the so-called *White Album* of 1968.

The Independent Group broke away from the introspective and expressionistic model of artists like Bacon and de Kooning. Around 1960 their attraction to mass culture was picked up and reintegrated into a fine art context by two successive groups of students and former students from the Royal College of Art in London. This development paralleled the virtually simultaneous events in New York between 1959 and 1963, beginning with the work of Jasper Johns in the mid-fifties and followed by the emergence of the American pop artists Andy Warhol, Roy Lichtenstein, and James Rosenquist.

The revolutionary aspect of pop art transpired on a level so fundamental that not even the principals successfully articulated it in words. What the Independent Group (and concurrently Jasper Johns in New York) had set in motion, and then left for the artists of the early sixties to pursue, centered on the idea of using culture (ranging from comic books, instruction manuals, and advertising to art history and literature), instead of the direct experience of nature (including one's own human nature, as in de Kooning and Pollock), as the source of art. Indeed, the only meaningful definition of pop art derives from this concept of culture as mediating the terms in which one experiences the world.

David Hockney

David Hockney, the most gifted painter among the British pop artists, was influenced by the gesture painting of the fifties. However, he differed from the gesture painters in his semiotic sophistication, which younger artists learned from the new consciousness of images generated by the media around 1960. Born in 1937, Hockney came from a working-class family in Yorkshire and in 1959 he began graduate study at the Royal College of Art in London. Since 1964 Hockney has lived principally in Los Angeles and paints in a lush, coloristic style indebted to Picasso and Matisse.

Despite the prevailing pressure to paint abstractly at the time, Hockney abandoned abstraction for narrative painting in 1960. Nevertheless, the gestural handling of Hockney's work of the early sixties still reflects the influence of abstract expressionism, as well as Bacon and Dubuffet. Hockney also broke ranks with convention in his frankly homosexual subject matter, asserted by such paintings as *Adhesiveness*, *Doll Boy*, and *Queer* of 1960. That summer Hockney read the complete works of Walt Whitman, who also openly expressed his homosexuality in his work. Hockney took the title for *Adhesiveness* from Whitman as well as the idea of correlating numbers with the alphabet as a code for someone's initials. The two sexually engaged figures in *Adhesiveness* are labeled "4.8" ("D.H." for David Hockney) and "23.23" (for Walt Whitman).

Hockney made his first trip to New York in 1961, when he was twenty-four. He returned sporting stunning costumes, with his hair dyed platinum blond. He had come to the realization that he could consciously invent his artistic persona along with his style in painting, and this consciousness of style came to the fore in his work at that time. The marriage of styles is the theme of several paintings of 1961 and 1962, including *A Grand Procession of Dignitaries in the Semi-Egyptian Style*, *Figures in a Flat Style*, *Tea Painting in an Illusionistic Style*, and *The First Marriage (A Marriage of Styles)*. "I deliberately set out to prove I could do four entirely different sorts of pictures like Picasso," he told Larry Rivers in 1965.[9] Hockney treated the styles in these works like elements in a still life. The captions and the recurrent curtains indicate the artist's orientation toward the world as a landscape of signs.

The vocabularies of pop art and gesture painting collided head-on in Hockney's early work. In *Picture Emphasizing*

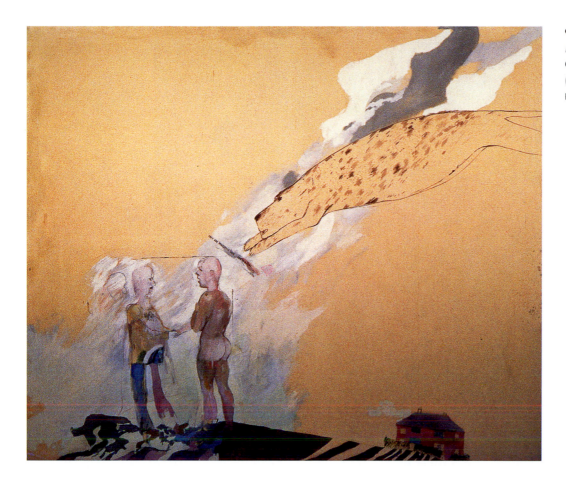

9.6 David Hockney, *Picture Emphasizing Stillness*, 1962. Oil on canvas, 6ft × 5ft 2in (1.83 × 1.58m). Private collection.

Stillness [fig. 9.6] the armature of lines around the painterly figures suggests his debt to Francis Bacon, while the introduction of lettering into a gestural style of figurative painting—in small print just in front of the leopard's forepaws—shows the influence of Larry Rivers. The caption, "They are perfectly safe. This is a still," implies that the linguistic context of the picture as a picture (rather than any referent in nature) defines the reality it describes. "I realized that what was odd and attractive about it was that, although it looks as though it's full of action, it's a still; a painting cannot have any action. It was the incongruity of it that attracted me to it as a subject."[10]

Hockney made his first trip to Los Angeles at the end of 1963, attracted by homoerotic magazines like *Physique Pictorial*, which originated there.[11] In January 1964 he moved to Los Angeles and his work took a turn toward greater realism. He also switched to acrylic paint at this time, a medium that made the surface of his painting flatter. In addition, Hockney bought a 35mm camera in 1967 and began taking pictures incessantly, using many of them as notes for paintings, as in the portrait of *Henry Geldzahler and Christopher Scott* [fig. 9.7]. This magnificent painting has a stark classicism in the precision of its drawing, in the hard-edge application of the paint, and in the orderliness of its composition and one-point perspective. Nevertheless, Hockney felt that photographs distort the way we see by taking in too much at once, so in 1972 he joined multiple close-up and fragmentary

photographs of his friend Peter Schlesinger. From this came a sequence of so-called "joiners"—composites of several separate photographs into a unified image. "I realized that this sort of picture came closer to how we actually see, which is to say, not all-at-once but rather in discrete, separate glimpses which we then build up into our continuous experience of the world,"[12] he explained.

These photograph collages as well as Hockney's paintings of the eighties have a moving focus in which the eye follows a path from point to point rather than holding to a conventional one-point perspective. As the art historian Gert Schiff pointed out, the eye also wanders through a cubist painting in this way and Hockney's idea may have derived from his ongoing dialog with Picasso.[13] Shifts in technique often signal jumps in style for Hockney and in the mid-seventies he went back to oil paint as he turned away from naturalism. Hockney's intense involvement in designing sets and costumes for opera between 1975 and 1978 and again in the eighties seems to have brought out this expressionistic tendency.

It was five years before Hockney returned to Los Angeles, but not without a final detour. Ken Tyler, the master printer who left Gemini G.E.L. in Los Angeles in 1973 for Bedford Village, thirty-five miles north of New York City, had been pressing Hockney to make lithographs with him. In the fall of 1978 Hockney went to see Tyler, with the intention of telling him he did not want to start making any prints—but when Tyler showed him the colors possible in a new technique of painting with dye in wet paper pulp Hockney decided to stay for three days to try it. Forty-five days later he had completed a spectacular series of twenty-nine "Paper Pools," by "painting" in vats of liquid pulp. *A Diver* [fig. 9.8] has a Matisse-like simplicity and richness of color, suggested to some extent by the technique. The fauvist sensuality anticipates Hockney's stage sets for the Metropolitan Opera in 1980 as well as the saturated hues of eighties paintings such as *Nichol's Canyon* [fig. 9.9].

9.7 (above) **David Hockney**, *Henry Geldzahler and Christopher Scott*, 1969. Acrylic on canvas, 7 × 10ft (2.13 × 3.05m). Private collection.

9.8 (below) **David Hockney**, *A Diver*, Paper Pool 17, 1978. Colored, pressed paper pulp, twelve sheets, 6ft × 14ft 3in (1.83 × 4.34m) overall, each sheet 36 × 28in (91.4 × 71.1cm). Private collection. Produced and published by Tyler Graphics, Ltd.

Collaging Reality on Pop Art's Neutral Screen of Images

For the members of the Independent Group in London, the elimination of distinctions between high art and popular culture was a vanguard political statement—they wanted to democratize art and anticipate a more egalitarian future. The work of American pop artists, on the other hand, was largely apolitical. Andy Warhol, Roy Lichtenstein, and James Rosenquist (the central figures of pop art in New York) intuitively recognized that something fundamental was changing in the way we see, that images, rather than a direct encounter with nature, were increasingly defining the norms of experience and that shift was their real subject.

The flux of free-floating impressions in beat poetry and in the combines of Rauschenberg foreshadowed the passive detachment with which the pop artists treated what came into their view. But they, along with Rauschenberg himself in the sixties, replaced found objects with the found images of magazine culture. This laid the groundwork for reality as it came to be seen in the eighties and beyond. The pop-culture producer John Carlin characterized it as "reality . . . homogenized on the level of the sign," and he pointed out that "the exchange of images has become the symbolic structure through which our seemingly entropic social, cultural, and economic existence is unified."[14]

On this level plane of images, *TV Guide* [fig. 9.10] could market the "girls" in the *Charlie's Angels* detective show just like Arby's roast beef sandwiches. The New York pop artists addressed this aspect of advertising in the neutrality with

9.9 (above) **David Hockney**, *Nichol's Canyon*, 1980. Acrylic on canvas, 7 × 12ft (1.52 × 2.13m). Private collection.

9.10 (right) Advertisements for the ABC television series *Charlie's Angels* and Arby's roast beef sandwiches in *TV Guide*, vol. 26, no. 37 (September 16, 1978), pp. A-104 and A-107.

which they handled their motifs; the utterly nonintrospective character of their work was radical with respect to the art that preceded it, although the deadpan representation of commonplace subjects by Jasper Johns in the fifties anticipated this cool attitude, and the stunning semiotic shifts in the work of H. C. Westermann [fig. 9.33] prefigured the structure of its language. The pop artists cultivated impersonality and drew on commercial art techniques; Warhol used photosilkscreening, Lichtenstein's replicated the printing of flat color areas in dots as in newspapers, and Rosenquist painted in the style of billboards.

New York pop art evolved in the studios during 1959 and 1960, the artists saw one another's work for the first time in 1961, and it burst onto the art scene in 1962, when Rosenquist, Lichtenstein, and Warhol all had major one-person shows in New York. Toward the end of 1962 Sidney

9.11 Tom Wesselmann, *Still Life #12*, 1962. Acrylic and collage on fabric, 4 × 4ft (1.22 × 1.22m).
National Museum of American Art, Smithsonian Institution, Washington, D.C. Photograph courtesy Art Resource, New York.

9.12 **Tom Wesselmann**, *Great American Nude #57*, 1964. Synthetic polymer and paper collage on composition board, 4ft × 5ft 5in (1.22 × 1.65m).

Whitney Museum of American Art, New York. Purchase, with funds from the Friends of the Whitney Museum of American Art.

Janis opened the "New Realists" exhibition which linked the New York pop artists with others in New York as well as with the French *nouveaux réalistes*. The show also connected (and thereby validated) them by association with the blue-chip moderns, for which the Janis Gallery was known. Pop art outraged the abstract expressionists and infuriated the established critics, but it instantly swept the worlds of mass media and fashion.

Tom Wesselmann was in the "New Realists" show. He began making collages of found materials in 1959–60 and by 1962 he had extended his paintings off the flat surface with three-dimensional objects. In this sense his work is indebted to environments and happenings. But Wesselmann's art did not have the gestural surface or expressionist tone of works by Oldenburg, Segal, or Dine. Instead he explored the world of the popular imagination with an analytical detachment, appropriating images from contemporary advertising and actual objects of consumer culture. On the other hand his art did not suggest the same leveling of images that characterizes the work of Warhol, Lichtenstein, and Rosenquist.

In *Still Life #12* of 1962 [fig. 9.11] Wesselmann screwed a metal sign depicting two Coke bottles in shallow relief right onto the canvas alongside magazine illustrations of food and a camera. The clear geometry of the composition sets off the slightly jarring shifts in scale among the objects as well as the syntactical jumps from the painted fruit to the magazine ads to the real metal sign, which is at the same time a found representation of Coke bottles. "One thing I like about collage," he told Gene Swenson, "is that you can use anything, which gives you that kind of variety; it sets up reverberations in a picture from one kind of reality to another."[15]

In 1960 Wesselmann inaugurated a series of "Great American Nudes," drawing from life but evoking an often literally faceless, mass-consumer eroticism. In *Great American Nude #57* of 1964 [fig. 9.12] the figure is a simply outlined, flat, flesh-colored shape; instead of rendering the face, Wesselmann provided pointedly detailed glimpses of just the most sexually charged features—the lips, nipples, and pubic

9.13 Richard Artschwager, *Table and Chair*, 1963–4, Formica on wood, table 29¾ × 52 × 37⅜in (75.7 × 132.1 × 95.9cm), chair 45¼ × 21 × 17¼in (114.9 × 53.3 × 43.8cm).
Courtesy Leo Castelli Gallery, New York.

hair—which he deliberately quoted in the vase of flowers. Wesselmann depicted the American woman as commodity, seductive and depersonalized, like a page of advertising.

Richard Artschwager is another important artist who doesn't quite fit the look of pop, but who nevertheless focuses on the popular taste for the ersatz, which comes down to a reading of the world as symbols or images. His *Table and Chair* of 1963–4 [fig. 9.13] inverts the customary representational transformation of a flat surface into an illusion of objects in space by rendering the clearly recognizable objects as flat, caricature-like pictures of furniture on the sides of a lifeless but nevertheless fully volumetric cube. His rigorous simplification of prosaic images into geometric objects with coolly impersonal surfaces suggests an ironic crossover between the vocabularies of pop art and minimalism, as does his characteristic use of Formica (a durable plastic replica of natural materials), which at the same time expresses an interest in industrial materials. The Formica and the synthetic, pretextured board he has used for his paintings attracted him precisely because they make such an unconvincing attempt to simulate wood or a hand painted surface.

Making the representation of a thing the reality in itself—as Artschwager's Formica cube does in relation to a table—implies the variety of simultaneous levels on which any definition of reality exists. This destabilizes fixed notions of what is real, making reality contingent on any number of fluctuating conditions. In 1962 *Time* reported that the average American was exposed to about 1,600 advertisements per day.[16] There was a comparably vast expansion in the presence of other kinds of images as well. Pop art largely concerned the way in which these pictures from television, magazines, and movies had become reality in their own terms.

ANDY WARHOL

Andy Warhol's devotion to the aesthetic of television, society columns, and fan magazines was opposed to the European model of the struggling avant-garde artist which the abstract expressionists had emulated. Warhol wanted wealth and fame, and he found anybody who had them fascinating. In addition, his "lipstick-and-peroxide palette" is, as Adam Gopnik pointed out, "a completely original sense of color . . . [which] makes all previous American palettes look European."[17] The originality of Warhol's denial of originality defined his artistic persona, and the fresh look of his paintings validated it.

Part of Warhol's genius lay in his recognition that a persona could be communicated via the media better than an art object, and he attempted to define his existence entirely on the shallow plane of representation (in reproducible images). "If you want to know all about Andy Warhol, just look at the surface of my paintings and films and me, and there I am," he said. "There's nothing behind it."[18]

9.14 Andy Warhol, *Dick Tracy*, 1960. Casein and crayon on canvas, 48 × 33⅞in (121.9 × 86cm).
Private collection, New York.

From the early sixties until his death in 1987 Warhol cunningly exploited both style and the media, and in doing so he exposed the values of contemporary society with a subversive frankness. He demonstrated that all fame is equal and essentially meaningless in the world of interchangeable images; his own public persona was irresistibly glamorous, yet its shallowness also tapped into a disquieting emotional void.

Warhol's Background

Andy Warhol was born outside Pittsburgh in 1928 to working-class Czech immigrants. After graduating in graphic design from Carnegie Tech in 1949, he moved into an apartment in New York with his classmate Philip Pearlstein and quickly achieved success as a commercial artist. Warhol's delicate drawings of shoes for I. Miller and Company in the *New York Times* brought him particular acclaim, and by 1959 he was one of the highest-paid commercial artists in the city, earning nearly $65,000 a year (equivalent to about $525,000 in 2010).[19] Warhol continued to make his living in advertising until the end of 1962, but from the beginning he also had aspirations as a fine artist.

Stylistically, Warhol's attempts at art in the fifties closely resembled his work for advertising, and several of the techniques from his graphic design practice anticipated aspects of his later art as well. For example, he organized "coloring parties" to produce his advertisements and delegated signa-

tures and lettering to his mother, presaging his extensive use of assistants in painting after 1962. Similarly, his technique of drawing—or tracing images from magazines—on nonabsorbent paper and then transferring the lines in wet ink by pressing them onto a prepared background set a precedent for the way he subsequently used silkscreens.

Selecting Nonselectivity

Even though some of Warhol's studio practices of the fifties persisted in his later work, they can scarcely be said to have led up to the shocking directness with which he suddenly began to apply a commercial art style to painting at the end of 1959. Nor was there any precedent for his radical appropriation of subject matter straight out of the pulp media for his large canvases of comic book images and newspaper ads [figs. 9.14–9.16]. Warhol used an opaque projector to transcribe and enlarge his sources with mechanical accuracy[20] in the early sixties, and in his statements about his work he made a point of dismissing any originality in it. Nevertheless, he abandoned the comics as a subject from the moment he saw Lichtenstein's paintings of comics at the Castelli Gallery in 1961, demonstrating a keen instinct for constructing and marketing an original style.

9.15 Andy Warhol, *Storm Door*, 1960. Synthetic polymer paint on canvas, 3ft 10in × 3ft 6⅛in (1.17 × 1.07m).
Courtesy Thomas Ammann, Zurich.

9.16 Andy Warhol, *Storm Door*, 1961. Synthetic polymer paint on canvas, 6 × 5ft (1.83 × 1.52m).
Private collection, New York.

As he settled on a subject matter—comics, cheap ads, and headlines from the pulp tabloids—Warhol also experimented with style between 1960 and 1962. In some compositions he transcribed his sources in a loose, brushy manner with deliberate paint drips to give them an expressive character, as if in a parody of gesture painting. At the same time he rendered other pictures with hard, precise edges. Eventually he decided he preferred these coldly handled, "no comment" paintings, as he called them;[21] indeed, he favored the most mechanical look he could render, just as he had sought out precisely the kind of subject matter that went most dramatically against the prevailing prescriptions of high art as individual and expressive.

Warhol made an aesthetic of the nonselectivity encouraged by media advertising. Henry Geldzahler characterized Warhol's "new attitude toward the media" as "not being selective, just letting everything in at once."[22] Warhol took pains to exaggerate the numbing effect of simultaneously bombarding himself with so many sensations that they canceled each other out. "The music blasting cleared my head out and left me working on instinct alone. In fact, it wasn't only rock and roll that I used that way—I'd also have the radio blasting opera, and the TV picture on (but not the sound)—and if all that didn't clear enough out of my mind, I'd open a magazine, put it beside me, and half read an article while I painted."[23]

Warhol's work celebrated the sameness of mass culture that intellectuals of the abstract-expressionist generation abhorred. "What's great about this country," Warhol remarked, "is America started the tradition where the richest consumers buy essentially the same things as the poorest. You can be watching TV and see Coca-Cola, and you can know that the president drinks Coke, Liz Taylor drinks Coke, and just think, you can drink Coke, too . . . All the Cokes are the same and all the Cokes are good."[24]

Nevertheless, Warhol's choice of subjects was not arbitrary. As Kynaston McShine has pointed out, for example, many of the early images—*Wigs, Where Is Your Rupture?, Before and After, Advertisement*—suggest the artist's aspirations for his own metamorphosis: "Promoting devices and products promising improved posture and silhouette, fuller hair, broader shoulders, and bigger arms, these ads touch the core of Warhol's physical insecurities."[25] Even Popeye and Superman, whom he painted in 1960 and 1961, are characters that undergo instant, physical transformations. McShine's speculation is further confirmed by Warhol's attempts to remake himself in the fifties, wearing a silver wig and having cosmetic surgery to refine his nose in 1957.

Warhol did not have a show of his pop paintings in New York until Eleanor Ward exhibited them at the Stable Gallery in the fall of 1962, though he did hang some of

9.17 Andy Warhol, *32 Campbell's Soup Cans*, 1961–2.
Acrylic on canvas, thirty-two works, each 20 × 16in (50.8 × 40.6cm).
The Museum of Modern Art, New York. Gift of Irving Blum. Nelson A. Rockefeller Bequest, gift of Mr. and Mrs. A. M. Burden, Abby Aldrich Rockefeller.

9.18 Andy Warhol, *Marilyn Monroe's Lips*, 1962. Synthetic polymer paint, silkscreened, and pencil on canvas, two panels, 6ft 10¾in × 6ft 8¾in (2.10 × 2.05m) and 6ft 10¾in × 6ft 10⅝in (2.18 × 2.11m). Hirshhorn Museum and Sculpture Garden, Smithsonian Institution, Washington, D.C. Gift of Joseph H. Hirshhorn, 1972.

them—*Advertisement, Little King, Superman, Before and After,* and *Saturday's Popeye*—as a backdrop to the mannequins in a department store window display he arranged for Bonwit Teller in April 1961. It was Irving Blum of the Ferus Gallery in Los Angeles who gave Warhol his first gallery show, in the fall of 1962: an installation of *32 Campbell's Soup Cans* [fig. 9.17], measuring a uniform 20 × 16 inches each.[26] Warhol, always alert to the latest trend, may have painted them in response to the *Painted Bronze (ale cans)* of 1960 [fig. 7.40] by Jasper Johns, but they surpassed the Johns sculpture in the inexpressive literalness with which they were presented. The soup cans are so intractably what they *are*; they are not cans of soup but images, divorcing the signifier from the signified (to use a term from semiotics) more radically than perhaps any painting up to that time had done. While some of Warhol's drawings of soup cans retain a delicate, gestural quality as late as 1962, these canvases have no trace of expressive gesture or individuality.

Eliminating the Artist's Touch

Warhol painted the soup cans and newspaper headlines of 1961–2 by hand, but toward the end of 1962 he discovered how to transfer a picture photographically onto a silkscreen and immediately switched over to this technique, eliminating all vestiges of the artist's touch and creating a more mechanically detached image. Moreover, he increasingly relied on assistants to make his paintings. In June 1963 he hired Gerard Malanga to work full time on the silkscreen paintings, and gradually others joined the payroll too—in addition to the occasional help that he always had around. Warhol would manage his assistants as if they were staff in a

graphic design sutdio, using them as his tools. "When I first knew Andy they were working on the Marilyn Monroes," one regular reported. "Malanga and Billy Name did most of the work. Cutting things. Placing the screens. Andy would walk along the rows and ask, 'What color do you think would be nice?'"[27]

Warhol made a style of his noninvolvement. "Somebody should be able to do all my paintings for me," he remarked in 1963. "The reason I'm painting this way is because I want to be a machine. Whatever I do, and do machine-like is because it is what I want to do. I think it would be terrific if everybody was alike."[28] Nevertheless, Warhol could have contracted the works out if he had really wanted a perfectly commercial look. Instead, he preferred the human error reflected in the misregistration of the screens, the uneven inking, and the occasional smears.

Marilyn Monroe's Lips [fig. 9.18] looks like an imperfect print run, in which the black line and the color screen do not quite match up and the inking varies widely. The invasive banality created by the mechanisms of consumer culture seems to be at odds with an (albeit passive) individual presence in paintings like this and *Gold Marilyn Monroe* [fig. 9.19]. The repetition forces the images into an anonymous, decorative pattern while particularizing features in each imperfectly fabricated unit continue to assert themselves, creating an expressive dissonance between the machine-like façade and the sense of the individual buried within it. This overwhelming barrage of surface glitter reduces the observer (and the artist) to a helpless voyeur, passively experiencing life as an assembly line of images.

A Terrifying Emptiness

On the one hand the proliferation of portraits of Marilyn Monroe, Liz Taylor, Troy Donahue, and other movie stars had to do with Warhol's enthusiasm for the glamour of Hollywood. "I love Los Angeles. I love Hollywood," he said. "They're beautiful. Everybody's plastic ... I want to be

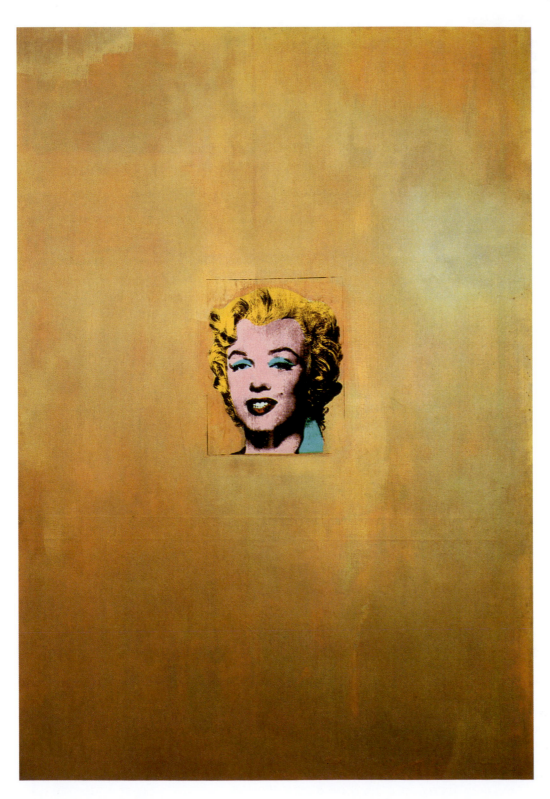

9.19 Andy Warhol, *Gold Marilyn Monroe*, 1962. Synthetic polymer paint, silkscreened, and oil on canvas, 6ft 11¼in × 4ft 9in (2.12 × 1.45m).
The Museum of Modern Art. Gift of Philip Johnson, 316.1962.

plastic."[29] He was the ultimate fan, acting as though consuming it all vicariously made him a part of it. Yet the "Marilyns" also have a dark side. The series followed Monroe's suicide in August 1962. Moreover, the mechanical repetition of her portrait makes her seem paper-thin, robbing her of any sense of existence beneath the superficial image. It is a frighteningly annihilating depersonalization and echoes an anxiety that underlies the artist's image of himself. As late as 1975 he wrote: "I'm still obsessed with the idea of looking into the mirror and seeing no one, nothing."[30]

In the television coverage of a national tragedy like the death of Marilyn Monroe or the Kennedy funeral (which Warhol also painted obsessively) the same film loops play over and over for days on end. Warhol's "Marilyns," especially the double canvas of *Marilyn Monroe's Lips*, have that same anaesthetizing repetition; they have the focus of a Tibetan mantra, an incantatory reiteration of the charged event.

In 1963 Warhol embarked on a disaster series [fig. 9.20] that amplified the morbid preoccupations of the "Marilyns." He based the series on gruesome tabloid photographs of mutilated accident victims, the atomic bomb, and the electric chair. He multiplied the images in decorative patterns and brilliant colors. "The more you look at the same exact thing," he said, "the more the meaning goes away, and the better and emptier you feel."[31] These images not only disturb us because of their horrifying explicitness, but also because Warhol's detachment suggests a depersonalization that is in itself terrifyingly death like.

In 1962 and 1963 Warhol also made several portraits of Robert Rauschenberg, whom he admired greatly for having risen from poverty to fame. Warhol named one of the Rauschenberg portraits *Let Us Now Praise Famous Men*, appropriating the title of a book by James Agee with photographs by Walker Evans of poor people from the rural South (from which Rauschenberg also came). The book embodied Warhol's fantasy that "in the future everybody will be world famous for fifteen minutes,"[32] in the sense that these anonymous country people became arbitrarily and fleetingly famous. Warhol liked the notion of celebrity as a kind of consumer good that anybody can have.

The Factory Scene

At the end of 1963 Warhol moved his studio to an old factory building on East 47th Street. "The Factory," as it came to be called, evolved into an environment lined in silver foil and filled with drag queens, listless "beautiful people," chic fashion personalities, and the rock music underground, many of them wasted on drugs or engaged in bizarre behavior. Warhol seemed to need this circus around him. As his friend Henry Geldzahler recalled, "Andy can't be alone . . . . Sometimes he would say that he was scared of dying if he went to sleep."[33]

By 1965 Warhol's celebrity was attracting the rich and famous, who wanted to see and be seen at The Factory. The press hounded Warhol too and everyone vied for his attention. Edie Sedgewick, a rich and pretty young socialite

who self-destructed on drugs at the age of twenty-eight, symbolized The Factory of the mid-sixties; she was a personification of "mod" style, and for a time she was Andy's constant escort. In the fall of 1965, when Andy and Edie went to his opening at the Institute of Contemporary Art in Philadelphia, nearly four thousand people crushed into the two small rooms and the staff had to take the paintings off the walls for security. It became an art opening *without art!*

"I wondered what it was that had made all those people scream," Warhol later recalled. "I'd seen kids scream over Elvis and the Beatles and the Stones—rock idols and movie stars—but it was incredible to think of it happening at an *art* opening . . . . But then, we weren't just *at* the art exhibit—we *were* the art exhibit, we were the art incarnate and the sixties were really about people, not about what they did."[34] In the same way "The Factory" wasn't a place where products

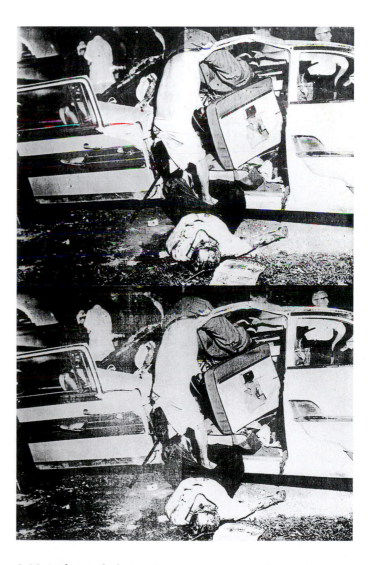

9.20 Andy Warhol, *Saturday Disaster*, 1964. Synthetic polymer paint, silkscreened, on canvas, 9ft 10⅞in × 6ft 9⅞in (3.02 × 2.08m). Collection, Rose Art Museum, Brandeis University, Waltham, Mass. Gervitz-Mnuchin Purchase Fund, by exchange.

were manufactured either; it *was* the product, a prescient symbol of the transformation into what ten years later Daniel Bell would call the "post industrial society."[35]

Warhol had wanted to get into Leo Castelli's gallery—it was the most talked about—and Castelli took him on in 1964. His first show, in November, was of the "Flowers," in which he broke further away from naturalism in his palette—not that one could call his earlier works naturalistic,

but up until 1964 Warhol had tended either to print the screens in monochrome, so that the scale of values corresponded to nature, or to find more artificial-looking versions

9.21 Andy Warhol, *Self-Portrait*, 1967. Synthetic polymer paint, silkscreened, on canvas, 6 × 6ft (1.83 × 1.83m). Pinakothek der Moderne, Munich.

of naturalistic colors. In 1964 and 1965 he painted pink and turquoise "Campbell's Soup Cans" instead of red and white ones and made multi-tone "Self-Portraits" with a blue face and yellow hair, for example, changing the values of the photograph and dissociating the colors from any reference in nature at all [fig. 9.21].

Having become the decade's leading art star, with an exhibition in the most fashionable gallery, Warhol publicly announced his retirement from painting in May 1965. It was an outrageous gesture, capped by a show at Castelli the following season in which he covered the walls of one room with his *Cow Wallpaper* and filled the other space with helium-inflated silver pillows designed to float at head level. It seemed the logical next step to turn art into wallpaper and then say farewell to painting by making "paintings" that would literally float away.

In 1966 film and the celebrity scene completely captivated Warhol. He got bored with painting and virtually stopped, instead promoting and touring with a psychedelic, multimedia performance called "The Exploding Plastic Inevitable," featuring the rock band Velvet Underground. He also made *The Chelsea Girls*, the first financially successful underground film, which Calvin Tomkins described as a "three-hour, twin-screen examination of assorted freaks, drug addicts, and transvestites," adding that "Warhol had removed the artist from art through the use of commercial techniques; he went on to subtract movement, incident, and narrative interest from movies, grinding out epically boring, technically awful films that failed signally to live up to their sex-and-perversion billings."[36]

Business Art and the "Shadows" That Linger Behind It

In 1967 Andy moved The Factory to 33 Union Square West and the scene got more and more bizarre until one day in June 1968 when a groupie walked in and shot Warhol. The sideshow atmosphere abruptly ended. Warhol was pronounced dead on the operating table but revived. After spending two months in the hospital he returned to The Factory very frightened. His assistants started limiting access to The Factory, despite Warhol's anxiety that he would lose his creativity without the carnival around him. The Factory became a place for the mass-production of art that would sell: commercial souvenirs of the avant-garde that Warhol called "Business Art."[37] To some extent Warhol's work had been an assembly-line product since 1963—in the mid-sixties The Factory produced as many as eighty silkscreen paintings a day and at one point a movie every week.[38] At that time, however, the overproduction was part of the tease that gave him celebrity in the first place, and it succeeded so well because it forced into the open the growing sense of alienation that people felt as mass culture came into its ascendancy.

By 1969, however, the point had been made. Looking back over the decade, many critics still feel that Warhol's important work dates from 1960 through 1964. In 1969 the national press carried a quote from one of Andy's studio hangers-on that reinforced this opinion. She said: "Andy? I've been doing it all for the last year and a half. . . . Andy doesn't do art anymore. He's bored with it. I did all his new soup cans."[39] But the idea that his staff was producing paintings without him was part of his ongoing effort to strike a shocking pose. "I really worked on all of them," he later admitted.[40]

In the early seventies Warhol rediscovered his interest in painting with a series of society portraits and pictures of Mao Tse-tung. Who else could make a portrait in 1978 that could claim to be avant-garde? And that, of course, is also what made them so marketable. By this time Warhol had become a household word, the most famous artist after Picasso, and a regular on elite guest lists from Halston's to the White House. The last and most painful phase of the Vietnam War and Watergate dominated the press in the early seventies, and more than ever both the very rich and the counterculture of political protests alike concerned themselves with images and symbols.

Warhol's paintings of Chairman Mao provided a little ideological pornography. They titillated the wealthy collector while at the same time confirming the triumph of money by transforming the great hero of the anti-capitalist world revolution into a consumer good for the rich. The photograph came from the front of *Quotations from Chairman Mao Tse-tung* (the "Little Red Book"), published in 1966 and carried around by campus radicals of the late sixties.

Warhol took on more advertising and design commissions in the seventies and eighties. The 1986 Christmas catalog for the Neiman-Marcus department stores advertised a portrait session with Warhol for $35,000, tempting customers to "Become a legend with Andy Warhol."[41] Warhol's intensifying involvement with social status and money played on the superficialities of American culture in the seventies and eighties. The materialism of those decades left people feeling increasingly alienated from one another, from American society, and finally from themselves. Identity dissolved into the nonbeing of the voyeur. As Warhol said, "When things really do happen to you, it's like watching television—you don't feel anything."[42]

"Before media," Warhol reflected, "there used to be a physical limit on how much space one person could take up by themselves. People, I think, are the only things that know how to take up more space than the space they're actually in, because with media you can sit back and still let yourself fill up space on records, in the movies, most exclusively on the telephone and least exclusively on television."[43] But inextricably linked to this materialistic vanity is a dissolution of self, and while doing his ingratiating society portraits Warhol also embarked on a series of "Skulls" [fig. 9.22] that did *not* sell so well, and then "Shadows," which showed only the indirect evidence that "something" was there. "Everything I do," Warhol observed in 1978, "is connected with death."[44]

9.22 Andy Warhol, *Skulls*, 1976. Synthetic polymer paint, silkscreened, on canvas, two canvases, 15 × 19in (38.1 × 48.3cm) each.

ROY LICHTENSTEIN

Like Warhol, Roy Lichtenstein wanted his art "to look programmed or impersonal," mirroring the impersonality of mass culture as America entered the sixties. Unlike Warhol, however, he added: "I don't really believe I'm being impersonal when I do it."[45] Lichtenstein sought to use painting as a self-contained arena in which to investigate and respond to this subject matter, and he had a probative interaction with his materials, as in action painting. "I was brought up on abstract expressionism," he said, "and its concern with forming and interaction is, I think, extremely important, even though . . . it's very had to tell where I have interacted with the developing work because the tracks are not there."[46] That lack of any physical evidence of the process in the finished work suggests the more formal nature of Lichtenstein's interests. Rather than a concern with asserting his identity in the work, he seems focused on exploring the imagery and style.

"In abstract expressionism," Lichtenstein explained, "the paintings symbolize the idea of ground-directedness as opposed to object-directedness. You put something down, react to it, put something else down, and the painting itself becomes a symbol of this. The difference is that rather than symbolize this ground-directedness I do an object-directed appearing thing. There is humour here. The work is still ground-directed."[47] By "ground-directed" he meant that the work centers on the internal, aesthetic unity of the painting and the internal dialectic between the formal elements that generated it, rather than on the subject matter. As a metaphor for Lichtenstein's worldview, this more detached perspective with regard to subject matter unambiguously separates him from abstract expressionism.

"The turning point was probably the influence of Happenings," he reflected. "In Happenings, there was the gas station culture and the 'objectness,' with the object not connected to its ground by cubist composition."[48] In Lichtenstein's paintings of single objects, like *Standing Rib* [fig. 9.23], the object hangs as though self-contained in a vacuum—it does not relate to the visual ground nor have a spatial context. In addition, he simplified the object and—through the object's frontality—he also simplified the space into a nearly abstract formal composition. This style of rendering resembles the simple linear sketches in inexpensive product catalogs and back-page advertisements in the newspapers because the subject is these images of objects, not the objects themselves. Like the comics, the advertisements had "a bigness and brashness that is important," he pointed out, "and it is industrial. It stands for the actual world we are in."[49]

Born in 1923, Roy Lichtenstein grew up in Manhattan and studied briefly with Reginald Marsh at the Art Students League before going off to college at Ohio State. The sentimentality and concern with common culture and life in the paintings of Marsh left an enduring impact on Lichtenstein's choice of a subject matter from popular culture. The happenings had a similar mixture of expressionism, detached humor, and objectivity—the objectivity of assimilating found objects from the urban environment without alteration.

During 1960 Lichtenstein painted an abstract-expressionistic picture related stylistically to the de Kooning "Women," but with Mickey Mouse in it. Then in 1961 he began painting enlarged frames of comics and images out of advertisements [figs. 9.23–9.26], improving on them slightly in the composition and details. After 1961 he abandoned easily identifiable cartoon characters like Popeye and Mickey Mouse in favor of anonymous strips, most often with soap-opera romance or action themes. With this kind of imagery, the subject matter comes already translated into the highly conventionalized language of commercial line drawing. Thus Lichtenstein was not painting things but

9.23 Roy Lichtenstein, *Standing Rib*, 1962. Oil on canvas, 21¾ × 25¾in (55.2 × 65.4cm). Collection, Museum of Contemporary Art, Los Angeles. The Panza Collection.

signs of things. His true subject is not the embracing couple, a rib roast, or jets in a dogfight, but rather the terms of their translation into the language of media and the implications of that metamorphosis.

By turning everything into a form that can be reproduced in newspapers or on television, the media homogenizes experience. One image can readily substitute for another on this flat screen of events. Lichtenstein explored this situation in a cool style that he consistently described in terms of its formal qualities, as if he had little interest in the subject matter. "One of the things a cartoon does," the artist told Gene Swenson in 1963, "is to express violent emotion and passion in a completely mechanical and removed style."[50]

Lichtenstein painted the single objects from 1961 through 1963 and the comics from 1961 through 1965. From the first paintings of the comics, he increasingly used tight rows of small dots to create the color planes.

Lichtenstein made stencils to imitate the commercial printing technique of screening flat color areas into regular patterns of what are called Ben-Day dots. However, with small holes and heavy pigment Lichtenstein's screens frequently clogged up, so that he had to touch up sections of the painting by hand to enhance the mechanical look! In addition, he often contrasted these dot-patterned areas with flatly painted patches to achieve the crass, visual punch of popular media imagery, as in *Drowning Girl* [figs. 9.25 and 9.26].

The paintings of 1961 and early 1962 tend to have a patchy application of dots, but by the end of 1962

9.24 Roy Lichtenstein, *Blam*, 1962. Oil on canvas, 5ft 8in × 6ft 8in (1.72 × 2.03cm).
Yale University Art Gallery. Gift of Richard Brown Baker.

9.25 (right) **Roy Lichtenstein**, *Drowning Girl*, 1963. Oil and synthetic polymer paint on canvas, 67⅝ × 66¾in (171.6 × 169.5cm). The Museum of Modern Art, New York. Philip Johnson Fund and gift of Mr. and Mrs. Bagley Wright, 685.1971.

9.26 (below) **Roy Lichtenstein**, *Drowning Girl* (detail), 1963. See fig. 9.25. The Museum of Modern Art, New York.

Lichtenstein had perfected his technique, getting more even results. By 1963 the primitive outlines and hatchings had also receded into a more refined style of drawing in which each line seems controlled and consciously shaped. Lichtenstein painted *Drowning Girl* in a remarkably impassive style. He also shaped the individual forms with studied

elegance—the waves recall the prints of Hokusai. Once Lichtenstein had planned his subject, he focused his attention on the formal refinement of the composition and details. "I think of it as an abstraction. Half the time they are upside-down anyway, when I work," he said.[51]

JAMES ROSENQUIST

Since 1960 James Rosenquist has painted large-scale compositions of fragmentary images, mostly from magazines, juxtaposed in a style that Judith Goldman characterized as "noisy, fast, vulgar, overlapping, public, visible."[52] The complex layerings of images evolve from free association rather than from conscious themes, and draw on the formal devices of cubist collage and Pollock's "all over" composition. But if the inexplicable shifts in the scale and context of Rosenquist's images invite comparison with surrealism, they are not introspective like surrealism, nor did the artist subject the objects to the dreamlike metamorphoses of surrealism. Instead the images create a flat screen of impressions that resembles the fast cuts of magazine layouts, television, and film. "I'm amazed and excited and fascinated about the way things are thrust at us," Rosenquist explained. We are "attacked by radio and television and visual communications . . . at such a speed and with such a force that painting . . . now seem[s] very old-fashioned . . . why shouldn't it be done with that power and gusto [of advertising], with that impact."[53]

Despite Rosenquist's externally directed gaze, his paintings are autobiographical in that they draw upon his memory and associations. Yet they do not attempt to define the identity of the artist, as in abstract expressionism. "I want to avoid the romantic quality of paint,"[54] he said. Rosenquist

9.27 James Rosenquist, *White Cigarette*, 1961.
Oil on canvas, 60½ × 35¾in (153.7 × 90.8cm).
Museum of Contemporary Art, Los Angeles. The Panza Collection.

relives his experience through his associations to the things and images he paints, yet he only reluctantly reveals his feelings. "Painting," the artist reflected, "is the ability to put layers of feeling in a picture plane and then have those feelings seep out as slowly as possible, and those feelings, a lot of them, have to do with where you are from."[55]

Rosenquist was born on November 29, 1933 in Grand Forks, North Dakota. The solid technique he acquired in art classes at the University of Minnesota and the skills he learned doing summer work as a sign and billboard painter laid the technical foundation for his pop style. Rosenquist headed for New York in 1955 and shopped around in classes at the Art Students League for a while. By 1958 Rosenquist knew many of the most interesting younger artists and was painting, though he had not yet found his artistic voice. Meanwhile, he continued to earn a living painting billboards of movie characters over Times Square and giant salamis over Brooklyn. The huge, simple forms of the billboards looked abstract close up from the scaffolding; to him they resembled the sensuous abstractions from nature by his friend Ellsworth Kelly. He also admired the sheer pleasure of laying on pigment that he saw in the work of Jasper Johns, though he probably did not yet see its relation to the sweeping gestures of liquid paint he was laying on the billboards.

In 1960 the sense of scale that abstracted the images on the signs at close range, and the sure hand he had developed in making them, coalesced with his ambitions as a fine artist:

> I decided to make pictures of fragments, images that would spill off the canvas instead of recede into it . . . I thought each fragment would be identified at a different rate of speed, and that I would paint them as realistically as possible. Then I thought about the kind of imagery I'd use . . . I wanted to find images that were in a "nether-nether-land."[56]

He painted the 5-foot-high *White Cigarette* [fig. 9.27] on canvas, and he made the images in the composition all legible. But he used fragmenting, shifts in scale, and abrupt cuts to black and white to keep the imagery on a single perceptual plane in contrast to the varied contexts of the individual pictorial references. This style reduces the subjects to equivalent units of signage. In other works of 1961 Rosenquist sometimes oriented figures upside down or sideways in addition to fragmenting them and painting them in grisaille, and he created even more radical shifts in scale that made many of the images hard to decipher.

Rosenquist's style of enlarging forms does not provide more detail. Instead of a microscopic view of every pore in the skin, he rendered the blow-up vague at close range like a billboard, implying a hugely expanded space. "I wanted the space to be more important than the imagery," he said.[57] In *White Cigarette* the shaped canvas also emphasizes the literal presence of the work as an object at the expense of the natural reference in the subject matter. "Nature becomes increasingly modified by man until the natural and artificial blend into each other," Rosenquist explained.[58]

9.28 James Rosenquist, *Nomad*, 1963. Oil on canvas,
plastic, and wood, 7ft 6⅛in × 11ft 8in (2.29 × 3.56m).
Albright-Knox Art Gallery, Buffalo, New York. Gift of Seymour H. Knox, Jr., 1963.

This in turn precipitates a breakdown between the images and the meanings to which they refer.

The sexual metaphor of the burning, phallic cigarette thrust at the opening of the bottle, which is poised just above the top of a woman's legs, is a deliberate appropriation of the way in which advertising exploits subliminal sexual messages. The falling glass below echoes this theme with a symbol for the loss of virginity that dates back as far as ancient Greek pottery painting and confirms the consciousness with which the artist has manipulated the pictorial language. Rosenquist's control over the pictorial semiotics is sophisticated and subtle. But by 1962 the complex juxtapositions cohere only in extremely oblique ways, and it is rare that such a literal reading as this can be carried through.

In 1961 Allan Stone visited Rosenquist's studio, followed almost immediately by Ileana Sonnabend and Ivan Karp (all important dealers), Henry Geldzahler (the new associate curator for twentieth-century art at the Metropolitan Museum), and Richard Bellamy (who was just then organizing his Green Gallery). Stone offered Rosenquist a two-person show with Robert Indiana, whose work dealt more explicitly with signage, but the two artists discussed it and decided to decline. Bellamy started bringing collectors around who wanted to buy Rosenquist's work and even though Rosenquist needed the money, he did not want to part with these paintings just yet because he was still thinking about them. He nevertheless did sell a few but in February 1962 his first show, at the Green Gallery, sold out before it even opened.

The real objects which Rosenquist had intermittently incorporated into his paintings of 1961 and 1962 took on greater importance in compositions of 1963, such as *Nomad* [fig. 9.28]. The work includes a flimsy, transparent funnel with paint drips suspended from the top of the canvas over a pile of paint-splattered wood on the floor. Rosenquist also pushed his experiments with found objects into independent sculptural assemblages in 1963, and although the objects did heighten the flatness of the depicted images, they never held their own against his self-assured rendering and composition.

Political, and especially anti-war, imagery became prominent in Rosenquist's painting after the assassination of John F. Kennedy in November 1963. Lyndon Johnson had taken over the Presidency and was elected the following year. Rosenquist found new impetus for his painting in his mounting feelings against the Vietnam War. The military allusions in works like *Silo* and *Pad* of 1964 anticipated the

9.29 James Rosenquist, *F-111*, 1965. Oil on canvas with aluminum, 10 × 86ft (3.05 × 26.21m).
Private collection.

imagery of *F-111* [fig. 9.29], Rosenquist's ambitious masterpiece of 1965. Designed to cover all four walls in the main room of the Castelli Gallery, where he had begun showing, this 86-foot-long panopticon of American mass culture immersed the viewer in a gaudy Day-Glo stream of consciousness: the sharp treads of a Firestone tire, a premixed cake staked-out like a minefield with little pennants listing the vitamins, a light bulb, an enlarged field of spaghetti in artificial orange as if from a can, a nuclear explosion under a multicolored beach umbrella, and a picture-perfect little girl under a hairdryer that looks like the nose cone of a missile.

The imposing profile of the newly deployed F-111 fighter-bomber runs the entire length of the mural. It underlies everything, just as the public's concerns over the war did in 1965, when the United States began the bombing of North Vietnam. The reflective aluminum panels follow by association from the cold, metallic plane. "I'm interested in contemporary vision—the flick of chrome, reflections, rapid associations, quick flashes of light. Bing-bang! Bing-bang! I don't do anecdotes; I accumulate experiences," Rosenquist explained.[59]

Rosenquist led a highly active and success-filled life in the early sixties. But on February 12, 1971 a car accident in Florida left his son John unconscious for five weeks and his wife Mary Lou in a coma for four months. Rosenquist himself had a punctured lung and some broken ribs, but the worst of his agony was the worry over his family, exacerbated by the mounting medical expenses. *Paper Clip*, a monumental

9.30 James Rosenquist, *Paper Clip*, 1973. Oil and acrylic on canvas, four panels, 8ft 6in × 18ft 7½in (2.59 × 5.68m).
Dallas Museum of Art. Gift of The 500, Inc., Mrs. Elizabeth B. Blake, Mr. and Mrs. James H. W. Jacks, Mr. and Mrs. Robert M. Meltzer, Mr. Joshua Muss, Mrs. John W. O'Boyle, Mrs. R. T. Shalom, and Dr. Joanne Stroud in honor of Robert M. Murdock.

masterpiece of nearly 20 feet in width [fig. 9.30], sums up, as it says, "This is Love in 1971": a roll of adding machine tape, a worn billfold, and nostalgic memories from the late thirties of his father's Mobil station in Atwater, Minnesota (the flying red horse was Mobil's corporate symbol), all tenuously held together with a paper clip.

In the mid-seventies Rosenquist settled permanently in Florida, near Tampa, and began a major commission for the state capitol in Tallahassee. A new self-confidence and renewed productivity burgeoned in his work, and an escalated level of ambition also emerged as the scale of some works increased over the next decade to extraordinary dimensions. *Through the Eye of the Needle to the Anvil* [fig. 9.31], a work of the late eighties, measures 46 feet in width. An increasing number of high-tech allusions appeared in Rosenquist's painting at this time along with cosmic themes and a more exaggerated manipulation of the images into a dream of common objects gone wild. *Through the Eye* seems to be shot through with charged fields that operate on

multiple levels of experience simultaneously. The red lipstick and flesh tones of a woman's face seem to slice across alternating wavelengths in and around the x-ray-like images of the brain in its cradle, portrayed as a kind of nexus of information and agency.

CHICAGO AND POINTS WEST

H. C. Westermann

H. C. ("Cliff") Westermann inaugurated a tendency in Chicago in the mid-fifties to turn away from the psycho logical introspection of the Monster Roster toward the complex simultaneity of popular culture. Contemporary with Rauschenberg and Johns in New York and with the Independent Group in London, Westermann combined an assemblage aesthetic with an intuitive sophistication about visual language that rivaled that of Johns. But Westermann did not aestheticize the objects he assimilated; instead he permitted their original, often vulgar, context to survive their incorporation into his work. This makes the viewer acutely aware of the multiplicity of contexts and semantic levels that coexist in Westermann's work.

9.31 James Rosenquist, *Through the Eye of the Needle to the Anvil*, 1988. Oil on canvas, 17 × 46ft (5.18 × 14m). Collection of the artist.

9.32 (right) **H. C. Westermann**, *Memorial to the Idea of Man, If He Was an Idea*, 1958. Pine, bottle caps, cast-tin toys, glass, metal, brass, ebony, and enamel, 56½ × 38 × 14¼in (143.5 × 96.5 × 36.2cm). Museum of Contemporary Art, Chicago. Susan and Lewis Manilow, Collection of Chicago Artists, PG 86.2.

9.33 (below) **H. C. Westermann**, *Memorial to the Idea of Man, If He Was an Idea* (detail), 1958. Center with open door. See fig. 9.32. Museum of Contemporary Art, Chicago.

The methods and materials, not just the images, are what make works such as Westermann's *Memorial to the Idea of Man, If He Was an Idea* [figs. 9.32 and 9.33] genuinely subversive. Rising from the center of the head of *Memorial* is a tiny dime-store globe atop a carved, red-nailed finger. The boxlike head and the larger box-torso seem an indefinable hybrid of architecture, cabinetry, and knick-knack shelf in a dream-state of human animation. Meanwhile, the meticulous carpentry, with its beautiful brass hardware and screws, asserts yet another, completely self-sufficient level on which the viewer encounters the work—as handcrafted cabinetry.

Westermann lined the lower box with the then-ubiquitous bottle caps [fig. 9.33], using shifts in context to redefine them onto five separate semantic levels: writing his initials with them on the inside of the door, using them as the backdrop for narrative scenes of a sinking ship in a bottle-cap sea, and above that as background for two athletes at play, while a pop-top on this background also stands in visually for the head of the batter. Yet neither the bottle caps, nor the cheap little toys (the globe, the acrobat, the batter), nor the rustically simple wooden model of a ship ever lose their identities as pop-tops, toys, or models. This continuing connection of the incorporated objects to their real origins effectively integrates the rude reality of popular culture into the representation, thus compromising the usual boundary that set "high" culture apart. Yet Westermann appropriated the pop materials and images because he felt a genuine affinity for them.

The title, *Memorial to the Idea of Man, If He Was an Idea*, suggests the death of existential metaphysics about man in the same way that the components of the assemblage—prefabricated elements, such as toys and bottle caps—undermine the abstract expressionist idea of the autographic gesture. *Memorial* commemorates the dissolution of identity itself into the enigmatic relativity of cultural context. The sudden shift of the batter's head into a bottle cap (behind it) and back again, or the box itself, which is now a cabinet, now a human torso, are both analogies for the instability of things. The wry comment "A MAD CABINETMAKER MIGHT" (inscribed on the edge of the inner shelf) seems to consign even the artist's intentions to the inexplicable realm of madness while also suggesting the idea of open-ended possibility in this destabilized field of image and meaning.

Like *Memorial*, Westermann's *Brinkmanship* (fig. 9.34) relies on a kind of wisecracker's humor to talk about serious things. As David McCarthy has shown, the title of *Brinkmanship* refers to the Cold War policy of John Foster Dulles (President Eisenhower's Secretary of State), enforced by General Curtis LeMay, the cigar-smoking chief of the Strategic Air Command, which deployed the American nuclear arsenal. *Life* magazine pictured LeMay in a profile feature of 1954 entitled "Toughest Cop of the Western World,"[60] and it seems as though Westermann may have used those photos as his source. Westermann, a decorated war hero of both World War II and Korea, adamantly opposed the U.S. policy of repeatedly taking the nation to "the brink" of nuclear confrontation in the fight against Communism.

Here Westermann portrays LeMay's plump face as a metal toilet float. The rim at the seam divides the top off as a helmet (surmounted by an American eagle), and the artist uses grommets for the eyes and mouth (one of LeMay's popular nicknames was "the grommet"). The Pepsi bottle top stands in for the star on the front of the general's helmet. He has a metal stogy in his mouth (like the one Westermann often smoked) with a flat cutout puff of smoke, and—miniature by comparison to the cigar—his penis sticks out from the lower part of the pole of his torso.

Meanwhile, the "ground troops," so to speak, are Westermann himself with his wooden profile (labeled with his military "dog tag" number) laid down on the platform. The door of the ramshackle outhouse, with the tin smoke stack at the back, is framed by the legs of a humble little smiling figure with the number "25" (Westermann's address on East Division Street in Chicago) across the face. On the façade is a much more robust-looking organ than the general's, pointing off to the right, and the inscription "Sail on, old bird" over the door. Here the reference to Longfellow's famous poem "Sail on, Oh Ship of State!" is turned into a bawdy joke.

In Westermann's *Death Ship Run Over by a '66 Lincoln Continental* [fig. 9.35] the menacing shark fin circles, endlessly waiting, in a sea of dollar bills. The fin has a strong illusionistic presence on the gray-green water, despite one's awareness of the money as money. In the same way the fast cut from the narrative of the death ship surrounded by predators to the idea of inking the tires of the family car and literally driving over the piece has a slapstick absurdity. The extreme conceptual distance from the narrative of the boat and shark to the bills to the car is simultaneously disturbing and ridiculous. As in *Memorial to the Idea of Man, If He Was an Idea*, part of the humor of the work derives from the dizzying jumps from one mental context to another.

Westermann made a number of lonely "Death Ships" followed by an ominous shark fin in dangerous waters and the subject has a specific autobiographical source. In 1942 the twenty-year-old Westermann enlisted in the marines and went to sea in the Pacific on the aircraft carrier U.S.S. *Enterprise*. On March 20, 1945 he experienced a terrifying *kamikaze* attack.

9.34 H. C. Westermann, *Brinkmanship*, 1959. Assemblage of plywood, electroplated and welded metal, bottle caps, and string on plywood base, 23¼ × 24 × 19⅜in (59 × 60.8 × 49.2cm).

Hirshhorn Museum and Sculpture Garden, Smithsonian Institution, Washington D.C. Gift of Allan Frumkin, 1984.

> I was the gunner there of that time. One morning early a lone Japanese kamikaze attacked u . . . I saw my tracers going into the god-damned thing but he kept coming . . . Well it was a terrific explosion + many people up forward were killed + wounded + there was a terrific fire up there . . . I looked down on the fantail of the ship + they had all the dead people stacked there like cordwood. It was a pretty ungodly sight.[61]

9.35 H. C. Westermann, *Death Ship Run Over by a '66 Lincoln Continental*, 1966. Pine, plate glass, ink, and currency, 15½ × 32 × 11¾in (39.4 × 81.3 × 29.9cm).

Collection, Ann Janss. Courtesy George Adams Gallery, New York.

One can already see the first phase of Westermann's fully developed narrative drawing style in letters he sent home from the war, but his sculpture didn't emerge until the mid-fifties. As a student at the School of the Art Institute of Chicago in 1952 he began studying carpentry from manuals, seeking a way to support himself while in school. By 1954 his interest in carpentry had developed into an obsession that drew him into sculpture and soon his craftsmanship became too exacting to take on household building projects for clients who wanted quick and simple results. In 1958 Westermann began showing at the Allan Frumkin Gallery in Chicago, and the sale of his sculpture brought in a modest income. In 1959 Frumkin opened a gallery in New York, giving Westermann regular exposure there, and Westermann was finally able to stop hiring out to do carpentry. In the fall of 1961 he left Chicago for his wife's family farm in Connecticut [fig. 9.36], where he stayed (except for a year in San Francisco) until his death in 1981.

The untransformed character of the materials that Westermann assimilated into his sculpture of the fifties gives that work a vernacular overtone of folk art. His work of the sixties and seventies on the other hand had an increasing indebtedness to the spirit of comics, not only in his cartoon-like self-caricatures as Mr. Swami, The Human Fly, Champion of Justice, and the aging Romeo with slicked-back hair in *High Swan Dive: The Sea of Cortez* [fig. 9.37], but also

9.36 H. C. Westermann building his studio at Brookfield Center, Connecticut, 1969.

Photograph by Joanna Beall Westermann, courtesy Martha W. Renner.

in the comic book's methods of representation. In comics, as in Westermann's works, the images refer to concepts, not to the actual appearance of things. This point of reference in ideas rather than directly in the physical world results in a revolutionary concept of figuration in which a recognizable abstract symbol—like Popeye's anchor tattoo, which Westermann used for his signature—functions on the same level as an image with a direct reference in nature. This involved a radical rethinking of representation that profoundly influenced such artists as William Wiley and the young Chicagoans of the nascent Hairy Who in the sixties, and (more or less directly) many important figurative artists in New York in the seventies and eighties, especially David Salle and Keith Haring.

Peter Saul

Like Westermann, Peter Saul drew heavily on pop culture and had a profound influence on Chicago artists of the sixties, who became familiar with his work through regular shows at the Allan Frumkin Gallery, even though Saul never actually lived in Chicago. Peter Saul's packed compositions of the early sixties have a pop art layering of common images (as distinct from objects) in arbitrary profusion, manipulated in the manner of *Mad* magazine's satirical, adolescent fantasies. In *Mickey Mouse vs. the Japs* [fig. 9.38] Saul sends a vicious-looking Mickey Mouse with teeth to fight Japanese war machines in a sequence of disconnected actions. Neither rational space nor proportional scale apply. A comic strip

9.37 (above) **H. C. Westermann**, *High Swan Dive: The Sea of Cortez*, 1973. Ink and watercolor on paper, 30 × 22¼in (76.2 × 56.5cm). Private collection, New York.

9.38 (right) **Peter Saul**, *Mickey Mouse vs. the Japs*, 1961–2. Oil on canvas, 4ft 11in × 5ft 11in (1.50 × 1.80m). Collection, Susan Wexler, Chicago.

9.39 Peter Saul, *Typical Saigon*, 1968. Oil, enamel, acrylic on canvas, 7ft 9in × 12ft (2.36 × 3.66m).

Krannert Art Museum and Kinkead Pavilion, University of Illinois, Urbana-Champaign. Purchased out of the "Illinois Biennial" exhibition of 1969.

thought bubble saying "Banzai" emanates from a Japanese fighter plane, a large Mickey Mouse on the graph paper grid leers to the right while the left half of his torso metamorphoses into a solid mass with a hole through the middle. A hammer grows out of this left side of the torso and smacks a war plane on the nose and off the side of the hammer an arm and hand come out thrusting a knife into a disembodied penis that happens to be floating by. These permutations reflect a free train of thought that goes from one idea to the next without looking back, modeled on the kind of doodle one might find in the margins of a high school notebook. "I'm guarding very carefully against any loss of vulgarity," Saul insisted.[62]

Saul was born in San Francisco in 1934. From 1952 to 1956 he studied painting at Washington University in St. Louis, where he began painting from pictures in *National Geographic*. While in St. Louis he also discovered the complex political compositions of Max Beckmann and developed an admiration for Francis Bacon's "'adults only' psychology," as he described it.[63] He then lived in Europe for eight years, until 1964. Matta "discovered" him in Paris and introduced him to Allan Frumkin who started showing his paintings in 1960. "The years 1959–61 were pretty much used in reconciling

specific drawings from *Mad Comics* [*sic*] with my need to resemble de Kooning," Saul wrote to Frumkin some years later.[64] Indeed, such early works as *Mickey Mouse vs. the Japs* have rich, gestural passages with an eccentric pop iconography. Perhaps the most widely discussed work in Saul's 1962 show depicted Superman on the toilet.

Saul finally returned to San Francisco in 1964 and stayed there through the ten stormiest years of protest against the war in Vietnam. During this period he shifted his attention to that and other political subjects, increasingly rendered in a crass, Day-Glo palette. The war is "a filthy pervert game," he told Frumkin and noted that his "work is an accusation."[65] Adamantly iconoclastic and hardcore in its description, a painting like the monumental *Typical Saigon* [fig. 9.39] indicts the cruelty of the American soldiers as well as the enterprise that brought them to Indochina.

In an orientalized script Saul wrote "Start Praying You Bastards" down the left side of *Typical Saigon* and lettered the title down the right. While the lurid Day-Glo palette and the slippery plastic surface are hard to look at, they pale compared to the violence with which he portrayed the American GIs sodomizing, assaulting, and crucifying Vietnamese women, whose bodies distort and metamorphose (especially in their sexual anatomy) like comic book superheroes to deflect the bullets and attack the soldiers. The painting makes its political statement by its deliberate attack on good taste. "My pictures always give me a hard time psychologically," he said. "[They] are meant as a kind of 'cold shower.'"[66] Toward the end of the sixties Saul began depicting recognizable public figures in this shocking manner, explaining to Frumkin that he hoped to read in the press: "'Upper Classes of Chicago Terrified by Mad-dog Sex Pervert at Art Gallery. Hundreds Faint.'"[67]

Saul's work directly influenced R. Crumb [fig. 9.54] and S. Clay Wilson, the originators of *Zap Comix*, who first saw his paintings in an exhibition at the University of Nebraska in 1965. He also had a profound impact on William Wiley. But Saul is more strongly associated with Chicago than with San Francisco, because his work was shown principally by Allan Frumkin and had an important influence on Chicago artists.

The Hairy Who

In Gladys Nilsson's *Enterprize Encounterized by the Spydar People* [fig. 9.40] the particular manner of the surrealistic distortion and the complex, energetic composition seem indebted to Peter Saul. Nevertheless, the strange, elongated appendages, intertwining with what Whitney Halstead has called a "madcap sense of abandon,"[68] contribute to the uniqueness of the style. The title, inspired by the TV series

Star Trek, evokes a vivid science-fiction fantasy. As in the narratives of Saul and Westermann, each vignette in Nilsson's composition evolves as a complete thought in itself, a sort of mini-adventure, before going on to the next idea. They proceed along a train of association that builds the whole of the composition in a cumulative fashion, unlike a work of the pop art mainstream—a Warhol or a Rosenquist—in which the details are subsumed by the overall design.

The same sequential composition characterizes the work of Jim Nutt and Karl Wirsum as well as much psychotic art, adolescent doodling, and naive or unschooled art—the so-called "outsider" art which the Chicago artists long admired. Nilsson, Nutt, Wirsum, James Falconer, Art Green, and Suellen Rocca all finished school at the Art Institute of Chicago in the early or middle sixties and banded together for a sequence of five exhibitions under the collective banner of the Hairy Who. While no ideological program united them, they shared certain predominant interests, including

9.40 Gladys Nilsson, *The Enterprize Encounterized by the Spydar People*, 1969. Watercolor on paper, 22¼ × 30in (56.5 × 76.2cm). Collection, the artist.

9.41 James Falconer, Art Green, Gladys Nilsson, Jim Nutt, Suellen Rocca, and Karl Wirsum, *Hairy Who (Cat-a-log)*, 1968. Exhibition catalog cover in paper, printed in color, 11 × 14in (27.9 × 35.6cm) (open).

Private collection, courtesy Phyllis Kind Galleries, Chicago and New York.

an attraction to funky popular kitsch, comic books, and toys (which they presented alongside their work), and a propensity to play with language (using puns or having fun with spelling as in "Encounterized" and "Spydar"). Perhaps most importantly, they tended to view popular culture and outsider art not only as a source but as art in its own right.

The Hairy Who existed as a group for four years. They had three shows in 1966, 1967, and 1968 at the Hyde Park Art Center in Chicago, a fourth in 1968 at the Gallery of the San Francisco Art Institute, and a final one in 1969 at the Corcoran Gallery of Art in Washington, D.C. In the third show the artists covered the walls with gaudy flowered linoleum and hung bright yellow tags off each work with a bargain price in dollars and odd cents. The style of the exhibition, like the different styles of the six artists, accentuated that which upper-class "good taste" had left out.

For each exhibition except the one in San Francisco, the Hairy Who produced a collaborative catalog in the form of a comic book. The sci-fi he-man figures on the front and back covers of the Corcoran catalog [fig. 9.41] are joined with stitches at the shoulder, playfully responding to the way figures are pulled apart when the covers are folded around the booklet. In the other direction the figures tear apart a pair of boxer shorts with "Hairy Who" written across the front as the booklet is opened. The label on the waistband of the putty-headed creature on the back reads "Hairy but true!" while the inscription from the tight lips of the weightlifter on the front with the surrealistically deformed limbs says "g?'-me. (one dollar)" using a phonetic spelling and diacritical marks. Above, to the right, "cat-a-log" is written as a rebus with the visual symbols of a cat and a log. These and other details make clear the intellectual sensitivity of these artists to the way in which language frames both reality and art in the human mind.

9.42 Karl Wirsum, *Screamin' J. Hawkins*, 1968. Acrylic on canvas, 48 × 36in (122.1 × 91.4cm).

Collection, Art Institute of Chicago. Mr. and Mrs. Frank G. Logan Prize Fund, 1969.248.

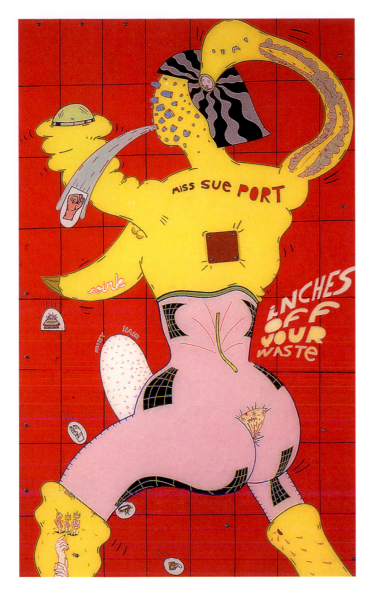

9.43 Jim Nutt, *Miss Sue Port*, 1967–8. Acrylic on Plexiglas and enamel on wood, blue screws and red rubber, 61 × 37in (154.9 × 94cm). Collection, the artist, courtesy Phyllis Kind Galleries, Chicago and New York.

The Corcoran catalog consists only of images—there is no text, though many of the compositions incorporate phrases or words. A version of Karl Wirsum's 1968 painting *Screamin' J. Hawkins* [fig. 9.42] (the title refers to a well-known blues singer) fills one page with its jarring clash of patterns and brilliant colors, influenced by the folk art Wirsum saw on a trip to Mexico in 1961. However complex the forms, they nevertheless have a comic book clarity of definition and flatness against the simple background color.

Jim Nutt also uses notational devices from the comics, such as motion marks and narrative frames within frames. He indicates spatial relations through overlapping rather than perspective, and completely eliminates all surface texture by painting on the back of Plexiglas and then reversing it so that the viewer looks at the images through it, as in

Miss Sue Port [fig. 9.43]. The glassy surface with bright colors evokes pinball machines, yet there is nothing mechanical in the genesis of these paintings.

Despite the stylistic individuality of each of the Hairy Who artists, they all built their vocabularies from blends of surrealism and expressionism. Nutt, in particular, found inspiration in Miró's metamorphosis of anatomy, especially his exaggeration of sexual parts. In *Miss Sue Port* (a pun on "support"), for example, Nutt distended the pubic area and annotated it with the words "shiny hair." The hardware and the rubber square in the center of *Miss Sue Port* derive from Westermann's assemblage aesthetic. In addition, Westermann's cartoon-like drawings, as in the mechanomorphic head on the side of *Angry Young Machine* [fig. 9.44], are a primary influence for Nutt and the other artists of the Hairy Who.

9.44 H. C. Westermann, *Angry Young Machine*, 1960. Painted wood and metal on casters, 6ft 5in × 3ft 4in × 3ft 4in (2.26 × 1.02 × 1.02m). Art Institute of Chicago. Restricted gift of Mr. and Mrs. Edwin A. Bergman, 1975.132.

9.45 Ed Paschke, *Ramrod*, 1969. Oil on canvas, 44 × 26in (111.8 × 66cm).

Jones/Faulkner Collection, Chicago. Courtesy Phyllis Kind Galleries, Chicago and New York.

9.46 Roger Brown, *Tropical Storm*, 1972. Oil on canvas, 6ft ⅛in × 4ft ⅛in (1.83 × 1.22m).

Collection, Marlene and Gene Siskel, Chicago. Courtesy Phyllis Kind Galleries, Chicago and New York.

Ed Paschke and Roger Brown were the most important Chicago imagists apart from (but contemporary with) the Hairy Who, and they share many of the same interests, although Paschke and Brown were less language-oriented. Paschke, a native Chicagoan, injected the most perverse imagery of marginal subcultures into the language of high culture. He portrays the truly popular culture of pimps, sideshow freaks, hookers, transvestites, and wrestlers, all with a bizarre sexual ambiguity. In *Ramrod* of 1969 [fig. 9.45] he transitions visually through the facial and body tattoos to the cartoon image of Mighty Mouse.

Roger Brown [fig. 9.46] came from Alabama and Nashville to the School of the Art Institute of Chicago in 1962. His first important show was with a group of artists who called themselves False Image (modeled on the pattern of the Hairy Who). He credits Ray Yoshida, one of his Art Institute teachers, with helping him, as he said, to "put myself into my art."[69] Although his work has more variety of paint surface than that of Nutt or Wirsum, it nevertheless retains a comic book narrative (sometimes literally inscribed under the images on the painting), with a cartoon like description and flatness. Brown typically painted fantastic, anecdotal scenes filled with amazing, little dramatic details in luminous color, often located in familiar Chicago landmarks.

WEST COAST POP

Far Eastern culture—particularly Zen Buddhism and Taosim—has long influenced the intellectual climate of California and the Pacific Northwest. The contemplative spiritualism of Mark Tobey [fig. 2.20] and his student Morris Graves was reflected in their meditative response to nature, while in the fifties the familiarity with Eastern philosophy contributed to the receptive climate for the meditative Dynaton painters in Los Angeles—Wolfgang Paalen (who began the journal *Dyn* in Mexico City in 1942), Lee Mullican, and Gordon Onslow-Ford. Zen also had a formative impact on the beats, who sought their escape from the mainstream by retreating into their own consciousness.

Funk Art

Alienation was at the core of beat culture. For writers such as Jack Kerouac, Allen Ginsberg, J. D. Salinger and William Burroughs, Samuel Beckett's sense of the absurd had replaced Sartre's existentialist "responsibility" in each of their consuming journeys inward. Whereas the New York art world spotlights what is "in," the artists of San Francisco have, since the fifties, cultivated a tradition of being out—"far out" to use a phrase from "hip" (the language of jazz and the beats). The beat counterculture of San Francisco centered on the coffee houses and jazz clubs of North Beach—places with names like the Coffee Gallery, the Co-Existence Bagel Shop, and the Jazz Cellar—where poets, musicians, and artists gathered for readings, often to a background of cool jazz.

Bruce Conner's assemblages *THE CHILD* and *SENORITA* embody this beat sensibility [figs. 9.47 and 9.48], conveying the priority of improvisation with whatever material was at hand. The intuitive process of making the object takes precedence over any preconception of a final product. Conner shunned conventional art materials and craftsmanship precisely to celebrate the triumph of spontaneous

9.47 Bruce Conner, *THE CHILD*, 1959–60. Assemblage: wax figure with nylon, cloth, metal, and twine in a high chair, 34⅝ × 17 × 16½in (88 × 43.2 × 41.9cm).

The Museum of Modern Art, New York. Gift of Philip Johnson. Courtesy the artist.

9.48 Bruce Conner, *SENORITA*, 1962. Assemblage on wood, 34 × 21 × 5in (86.4 × 53.3 × 12.7cm).

Museum of Contemporary Art, Los Angeles. Purchased with funds provided by LLWW Foundation. Courtesy the artists.

9.49 Robert Hudson, *Double Time*, 1963. Painted steel and aluminum, 58¾ × 50 × 35in (149.2 × 127 × 88.9cm). Oakland Museum. Gift of the Women's Board of the Oakland Museum Association.

creativity over the grimy reality of the material world; he emphasized living for the moment. Borrowing from the parlance of hip, this art came to be known as "funk," meaning something visceral and earthy, often so powerful and primitive as to threaten "good taste."[70]

Conner, who arrived in San Francisco in 1957, belongs to a group of funk assemblagists and collage makers in California that also included Joan Brown, Wally Hedrick, Jess Collins, Wallace Berman, and Ed Kienholz. Funk assemblages not only attacked the boundaries between one art form and another—Conner, for example, also collaged together underground films, such as *A Movie* of 1958 [fig. 7.19], from discarded Hollywood film clips—but also the separation of art from life. The humorously awkward, improvisational compositions and the bright polychromy that came to be associated with California sculptors such as Robert Hudson [fig. 9.49] in the sixties was one major offshoot of this assemblagist style, influenced by surrealist abstraction and pop color.

Jess Collins, one of the most gifted of the Bay Area assemblagists, cut up and reassembled Dick Tracy comic strips in seven "Tricky Cad" compositions (1953–9). By scrambling both words and images, he subverted the clarity of communication that normally characterizes comics. Jess, who went only by his first name, trained as a scientist, worked on the Manhattan and Hanford Projects, and then left the field in 1949 in response to the horrifying implications of the atomic bomb. He sought to create "an antidote to the scientific method."[71] In his photocollage *The Face in the Abyss* [fig. 9.50] the crown of the Statue of Liberty rests on top of a menacing machine, flanked by another enigmatic device that shoots out a jet of steam. They seem to have harnessed the forces of the scenic landscape into a frightful science fiction.

9.50 Jess Collins, *The Face in the Abyss*, 1955. Paste-up, 30 × 40in (76.2 × 101.6cm). First National Bank of Chicago.

9.51 Joan Brown, *Portrait of Bob for Bingo*, 1960. Oil on canvas, 29 × 29in (73.7 × 73.7cm).

Collection, Dr. Jay Cooper, Phoenix, Arizona.

The funky paint surfaces of Joan Brown's expressionism around 1960 is another development out of the beat assemblage aesthetic. Brown discovered the classes of Elmer Bischoff [fig. 6.26] in the summer of 1956, when she was eighteen. His influence proved decisive. In 1958 and 1959 Brown made crude, fetish-like figures (often animals), wrapped and tied in crumpled fabric, cardboard, and wire. Her heavily painted canvases of the early sixties, such as *Portrait of Bob for Bingo* [fig. 9.51], show more clearly the influence of Bischoff, as well as of Francis Bacon and Willem de Kooning, whose work she had seen in San Francisco. Over the summer of 1965 Brown left these densely painted, expressionistic surfaces and shifted her attention to an increasingly eccentric and original subject matter, including a magnificent series of self-portraits on imaginary voyages and another group of self-portraits with fantastic accouterments [fig. 9.52].

Peter Voulkos

Peter Voulkos had an important effect on a number of the Bay Area funk artists, particularly the sculptors. As early as 1950–2, while still a graduate student, Voulkos began pushing the limits of clay in both scale and form. He worked in a center for ceramic artists in Montana over the summer of 1952 and there a Zen-inspired Japanese potter named Shoji Hamada taught him about the "courting of the accidental."[72] This encouraged Voulkos to move away from the symmetry of the potter's wheel. Further inspired by his encounter with abstract expressionism in New York the following year, he developed an abstract expressionist style of ceramic sculpture between 1954 and 1958 while he was teaching at the Otis Art Institute in Los Angeles.

This stylistic breakthrough in ceramics had a particularly direct effect on Voulkos's students at Otis, who included Ken Price, John Mason, and Billy Al Bengston. In 1959

9.52 Joan Brown, *Self-Portrait with Fish*, 1970. Enamel on masonite, 8 × 4ft (2.43 × 1.21m).

Courtesy George Adams Gallery, New York.

Movement in Berkeley started in 1964, using mass demonstrations to disrupt "business as usual" and make the voice of young people heard on matters of national policy. Folk music and the Beatles replaced cool jazz, and the emphasis in everything was on youth. Radical revolutionaries rose up on university campuses and in city centers side by side with hippies, who turned the Zen introversion of the hip beatniks into a popular pastime of the young with the discovery that psychedelic drugs let you "tune in" to yourself.

"Doing your own thing" was one of many new buzzwords heard at "love-ins," psychedelic light shows, and mass-audience rock concerts, and rising from the smoke of marijuana "joints" from college dorm rooms and public parks all across America. An aggressive scrutiny of public policy on every level, coupled with an unprecedented openness to a complex variety of opinion, also characterized the ranks of this youth culture. Poster-making flourished as a natural corollary to this highly politicized atmosphere, and

9.53 Peter Voulkos, *Sevillanas*, 1959. Glazed stoneware, 56¾ × 28 × 16⅞in (144.1 × 71.1 × 43cm). San Francisco Museum of Modern Art. Albert M. Bender Collection. Albert M. Bender Bequest Fund Purchase. Work no long extant due to 1989 earthquake.

Voulkos went on to Berkeley, where he built a foundry (the Garbanzo Iron Works), and by 1960 he had shifted largely to using metal. Robert Hudson and Manuel Neri worked with him in the foundry and he also influenced the young ceramicists Ron Nagle and Stephen De Staebler.

Voulkos pierced and sliced his clay forms in a loose, improvisational way. His organic response to the material suggests his affinity with the expressionism of Japanese Zen pottery. In works of the later fifties, such as *Sevillanas* [fig. 9.53], he achieved the freedom and gestural boldness of abstract expressionist painting. Yet, even though Voulkos followed Picasso and Miró in making ceramic sculpture, he still had to overcome the conventional notion that anything made in ceramic is necessarily craft rather than art.

The Politicized Cultural Climate of the Sixties

In the mid-sixties the cultural climate changed abruptly with the escalation of the Vietnam War, and the protest in the Bay Area set the pace for the nation. The Free Speech

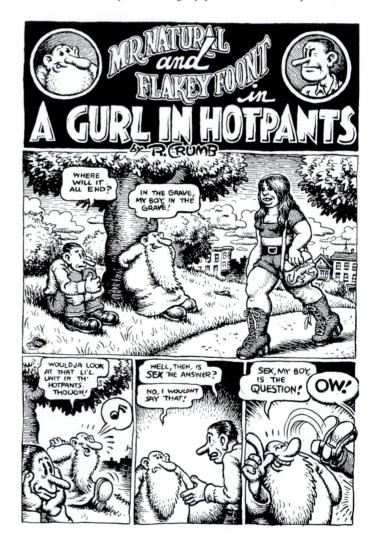

9.54 R. Crumb, *"Mr. Natural and Flakey Foont in 'A Gurl in Hotpants,'"* front panel of comic strip from *Mr. Natural*, no. 2 (1971), p. 1, 9¾ × 6¾in (24.8 × 17.2cm).

out of the widespread interest in posters came the underground comics, originated by R. Crumb [fig. 9.54], S. Clay Wilson, Rick Griffin, and Victor Moscoso of *Zap Comix*. For a few brief years it seemed as if the counterculture would rival the mainstream.

William Wiley

Thank You Hide by William Wiley [fig. 9.55] emerged from this polarized context of intellectual activism on the one hand and an increasing retreat into complex, personal reference on the other.

I picked up the hide at a rummage sale—it was already there, so I felt absolved of any responsibility for killing *[the animal]*. Then Brenda *[Richardson, a curator in Berkeley]* gave me Nietzsche's *Beyond Good and Evil* to read. One day on the can, I just opened it to the middle and read a statement. I can't remember what it was, but it made me think, and I said "thank you" to myself. Then I saw the words cut out on the hide. The hide seemed like a perfect net for a whole lot of things, in terms of the history of objects—Indian artifacts, for example; I used to sift the ground for them when I was growing up in Washington. The broken bottle, a friend brought by one day.[73]

9.55 William T. Wiley, *Thank You Hide*, 1970. Wood, leather, ink, charcoal, cowhide, pickaxe, found objects, and watercolors, 6ft 2in × 13ft 4½in (1.88 × 4.08m).

Des Moines Art Center. Purchased with funds from the Coffin Fine Arts Trust, Nathan Emory Coffin Collection of the Des Moines Art Center, 1977.9.

To the hide itself Wiley attached a rusted spike, a broken bottle, an arrowhead, an iguana skin from his son's collection, and a piece of petrified wood surrounded by wavy lines. He inscribed "Nomad is an Island," punning on the famous line by the seventeenth-century poet John Donne, "No man is an island."[74] On the shelf above he set bottles, forked branches, a jar labeled "Fresh Bait" and a copy of *Beyond Good and Evil*. A fishing pole arches over the shelf and around with a line to a pickaxe resting on the floor. Wiley's aesthetic involves an openness to every object one encounters as the embodiment of an association, in a free, experiential juxtaposition. It is highly intellectual in the puns and in the deliberateness with which he selects and places each object, and freely eclectic both in the use of materials and in the references to other artists. The iconography seems almost, but not quite, decipherable. Influenced by Duchamp and Johns, Wiley's work has the enigmatic anti-rationalism of a Zen *koan*.

Inspired by Duchamp's *alter egos* and by H. C. Westermann's puns and personas, Wiley has several invented personas for himself in his paintings. Mr. Unnatural, with the false nose and dunce cap, usually appears in a kimono

9.56 Ed Kienholz, *The Wait*, 1964–5. Wood, fabric, polyester resin, flock, metal, bones, glass, paper, leather, varnish, black-and-white photographs, taxidermied cat, live parakeet, wicker, and plastic, 6ft 8in × 13ft 4in × 7ft (2.03 × 4.06 × 2.13m).
Whitney Museum of American Art, New York. Gift of the Howard and Jean Lipman Foundation, Inc., 66.49a–m.

and high *geta* sandals. The name is a take-off on R. Crumb's short, balding, pop guru "Mr. Natural," but Wiley's lanky character is also a befuddled and absent-minded version of himself in a borrowed bathrobe.

Ed Kienholz

Ed Kienholz was the most visible figure on the Los Angeles scene in the late fifties, and his Ferus Gallery was the closest Los Angeles got to having a focus of artistic activity. The city had no center, physically or ideologically. The cosmological abstraction of Dynaton had nothing to do with the funk aesthetic of Kienholz; likewise, the Southern California strain of abstract expressionist ceramics had more to do with Bay Area figurative painting than with anything going on in L.A.

Ed Kienholz moved to Los Angeles in 1953 from his native Washington state. During the fifties he made funk assemblages that evoked the squalor of the urban environment, stressing its psychological and social dimensions. Like the Bay Area assemblagists, he found inspiration in beat poetry and in surrealist juxtapositions of images and materials. He began making the full-scale, walk-in *tableaux* for which he is best known in 1961. He constructed the aged lady in *The Wait* [fig. 9.56] mostly out of desiccated animal bones. Her head is a plastic-encased photo of a young woman's face, as if the woman of her youth still lives on in her mind. She sits patiently waiting in her heavy, dark, antique chair, dressed in brittle, yellowed garments.

9.57 Ed Ruscha, *Large Trademark with Eight Spotlights*, 1962.
Oil on canvas, 5ft 6¾in × 11ft 1¼in (1.69 × 3.38m).
Whitney Museum of American Art, New York. Purchase, with funds from the Mrs. Percy Uris Purchase Fund.

A necklace of jars around her neck seems to contain tokens of memories. The old lady's knitting and shawl lie at her feet and a nostalgic display of old photographs rests on the table beside her. Her immobility is set off by a live canary chirping in a cage that stands to one side.

L.A. Pop

By 1962, when Warhol showed his soup cans at the Ferus Gallery, Ed Ruscha and his boyhood friend Joe Goode had already pioneered indigenous pop styles in Los Angeles. Signage is a particularly omnipresent aspect of the landscape in L.A. Ruscha's trademark and word paintings make an equivalence between words, signs, and objects feel like a matter of course. He rendered the *Large Trademark with Eight Spotlights* of 1962 [fig. 9.57], for example, with the convincing three-dimensionality of objects in a landscape, yet the objects are the letters of a sign for Twentieth Century-Fox and the landscape has the hard edges and simplicity of a cartoon. The reality in the picture hovers uneasily between abstraction and representation, undermining the conventional distinction between them. As with New York pop art, Ruscha's painting also attacks aesthetic and semiotic hierarchies by setting advertising and commercial art devices in a fine art context.

In 1963 Ruscha published a book of photographs of *Twenty-six Gasoline Stations* between Oklahoma City and Los Angeles on Route 66 [fig. 9.58]. Like his sign and word paintings, the book concerns the interchangeability of images—the uniformity of the gas stations transforms the road into a conveyor belt of mass-produced and therefore reproducible images. It is as if the experience related to the image is not tied to a geographical reality but to the mobile

9.58 Ed Ruscha, *Standard Station, Amarillo, Texas*,
from the book *Twenty-six Gasoline Stations*, first edition 1963.
Collection, the artist.

9.59 (above) **Vija Celmins**, *Hot Plate*, 1964.
Oil on canvas, 25 × 35in (63.5 × 88.9cm).
Collection Renee and David McKee, New York. Courtesy
of McKee Gallery, New York.

9.60 (left) **Vija Celmins**, *Untitled*, 1988.
Oil on canvas, 15¾ × 18½in (40 × 46.9cm).
The National Gallery of Art, Washington, D.C. Gift of
Edward R. Broida. Courtesy of McKee Gallery, New York.

reality of the reproduction. Ruscha also made photo books of *Some Los Angeles Apartments* (1965), *Every Building on Sunset Strip* (1966), and *Thirty-four Parking Lots in Los Angeles* (1967), anticipating some of the issues raised by the conceptual artists in the later sixties.

Vija Celmins, a young artist at the beginning of her career in Los Angeles in the sixties, could hardly be called a pop artist. But she did have a very focused aesthetic on single, often common, utilitarian objects like her 1964 *Hot Plate* [fig. 9.59], which resonates interestingly not only with Ruscha but with the beginnings of minimalism. Like them, her work has a detached objectivity about it; it makes you want to look at something long and hard to see nuances in it that aren't about an outpouring of artistic emotion but rather a kind of wonder about familiar things. Finally, the degree of focus makes them unfamiliar and that is what is so interesting about them. The cord for the *Hot Plate* heads right for the viewer, making the object seem to be part of the viewer's space; and in this rather spare setting the red glow of the hot coils seems so important. A drama of some uncertain kind is implied. It also introduces a sense of time that is at odds with the timelessness of the presentation of the object. Celmins often takes a dramatic subject but looks at it with an eerily steady calm, sometimes representing it as a picture within a picture—making an almost photorealist rendering of a newspaper clipping, as she did with the atomic bomb blast on Bikini Atoll.

Beginning in the late sixties, she began making graphite images and paintings of the moon's surface, segments of oceans, and the night sky [fig. 9.60]. In these images the Zen-like wonder at what was seen or imagined to be seen was aptly characterized by Stuart Morgan in this way: "For Celmins, art depends on slowness of making, slowness so extreme it resembles a belief."[75]

ROBERT ARNESON

Robert Arneson was the most influential figure on the Bay Area arts scene in the seventies and eighties, though he emerged at the beginning of the sixties as a key figure in California "funk art" with his outrageous sculpture in clay. As with Manuel Neri and Robert Hudson, Arneson's encounter with the fifties work of Peter Voulkos was pivotal. Arneson first laid eyes on a Voulkos pot in 1957 and was simultaneously impressed and intimidated. "At that time," he recalled, "I never thought I'd be an artist. Just being a good potter would be enough. And then I saw Voulkos's piece."[76] Arneson had acquired a solid technical mastery by then but he was still reactionary in his ideas about ceramics.

Within two years, however, he was experimenting with rough, nonfunctional pots and by 1960 he had begun breaking through to his own organic, abstract expressionism.

Arneson's Break with Conventional Ceramics

In September 1961, while manning a demonstration booth at the State Fair, Arneson threw a pot on the wheel that reminded him of a quart beer bottle; so he put a ceramic cap on it and lettered it "No Deposit, No Return." Although he had had no thought of making a statement with this beer bottle, it nevertheless brought commercial culture into a fine art context, just as the pop artists in New York were beginning to do, and heralded a major transformation in Arneson's work. However, like Newman's first *Onement* or the initial sketch for Motherwell's "Elegy" series, the full implications of *No Deposit, No Return* for Arneson needed some time to germinate.

The beer bottle's sarcastic jab at the tradition of elegant vases and at the pottery establishment that maintained the compartmentalizing of clay as craft signaled Arneson's radical departure from that kind of work. In the summer of 1961 he had already begun making primitive, gestural sculptures in clay, drawing inspiration from Miró's ceramics and Asian works on display in the Avery Brundage Collection in San Francisco. In the fall of 1962 Arneson was brought in to establish a ceramic sculpture program at the University of California at Davis. Wayne Thiebaud [fig. 6.29], William Wiley, Manuel Neri, and Roy De Forest [fig. 9.61] all joined the Davis art faculty around that time, making it a very exciting place to be. The remarkable list of graduates from that program included not only important clay artists such as David Gilhooly and Richard Shaw [fig. 9.62] but sculptors such as Deborah Butterfield and the conceptualist Bruce Nauman, both of whose experimental approaches to natural materials and process owe something to the physical directness of Arneson's example.

The Toilets

In the summer of 1963 Arneson received an invitation to exhibit alongside Voulkos and John Mason in an important show at the Kaiser Center in Oakland called "California Sculpture." With his own style still somewhat unformed and feeling in awe of these celebrated clay artists, Arneson concluded that the occasion called for a personal manifesto. "I really thought about the ultimate ceramics in western culture... so I made a toilet,"[77] Arneson explained. He attributed sexual anatomy to the flush handle, the seat, and the opening of the bowl, put fingernails on one end of the

9.61 Roy De Forest, *Wise Horse's Dream*, 1972. Synthetic polymer on canvas, 5ft × 5ft 6¼in (1.52 × 1.68m).
Whitney Museum of American Art, New York. Purchase with funds from the National Endowment for the Arts, 73.29.

horseshoe seat and, as in *John with Art* of 1964 [figs. 9.63 and 9.64], he even installed a pile of ceramic excrement inside. Then he inscribed the piece with scatological jokes.

"I wasn't transforming anything," Arneson said. "I was looking at a toilet like someone would look at a figure, you know, a very traditional kind of art, and then I started to talk about it, putting the graffiti on."[78] The director of the Kaiser Center insisted that Arneson remove *Toilet* from the exhibition, causing the artist to realize that although it

was offensive, shocking, and in bad taste, he had succeeded in making something original. "This produced a presence of the artist," he explained, ". . . I had finally arrived at a piece of work that stood firmly on its ground. It was vulgar, I was vulgar."[79]

With *Toilet* and *John with Art* Arneson aimed a vulgar satire at the abstract expressionist aspiration of letting everything within the artist spill out freely in the work. The heavy, monochromatic stoneware of *Toilet* resembled the ceramic sculpture of Voulkos. In addition, Arneson treated the surface with an abstract expressionist touch. Despite his satirical irreverence, Arneson's outrageousness stems from and even pays homage to the iconoclasm of abstract expressionism.

9.62 Richard Shaw, *Seated Figure with Grey Head*, 1985. Glazed porcelain, 33 × 19 × 11¾in (83 × 48.2 × 30cm). Courtesy George Adams Gallery, New York.

9.63 Robert Arneson, *John with Art*, 1964. Stoneware with glaze, 34½ × 18 × 25½in (87.6 × 45.7 × 64.8cm). Seattle Art Museum. Gift of Manuel Neri.

A Technical Breakthrough

Arneson worked for the whole of the summer of 1965 on an academic self-portrait to get away from "the silly stuff,"[80] as he described it, and was very upset when the bust cracked in the kiln. On an impulse he glued some marbles into the crack to look as if they were spilling out. Retaining cracked pieces and assembling elements with glue were procedures that ceramicists never used, but from this point forward Arneson did so without inhibition. In effect, the accident liberated him technically and later Arneson would regularly insist that his students build something, destroy it, and then rework it in order to free them from a sense of preciousness about the materials.

9.64 Robert Arneson, *John with Art* (detail), 1964. See fig. 9.63. Seattle Art Museum.

Objects of the Mid-Sixties

Around 1965 Arneson began working in the low-fired bright colors on white earthenware that James Melchert and Ron Nagle were using at the San Francisco Art Institute. Nagle had learned the technique from Ken Price, who started working with it in Los Angeles around 1959. Arneson concentrated increasingly on the expressive possibilities of glazing as a kind of painting and soon had an extraordinary mastery of the techniques. This interest in painting also belongs to Arneson's ongoing dialog with abstract expressionism, a recurrent theme in his career from the sarcasm of *Toilet* and this painterly glazing through his explicit investigations of Philip Guston and Jackson Pollock in the 1980s.

Toaster, created in 1965, has a surrealist tone, with the toasted fingers reaching out of the slot. But Arneson deliberately pushed the idea too far, scratching a small swastika on the side to turn the piece into a pun on the Nazi ovens, a joke in shockingly bad taste. Yet that startling offensiveness is precisely what raises everyone's emotions to maximum poignancy, prompting serious thought on the subject. No artist has ever been simultaneously so objectionable and so endearing and that combination is Arneson's signature. His preoccupation with common objects in the mid-sixties has neither the cool, dry cynicism of New York pop nor its tastefulness. Instead, his black, Brechtian humor rests on an outraged morality founded on a fundamental warmth toward his fellow man.

The Self-Portraits

In 1971 Arneson embarked on a concentrated series of self-portraits with works such as *Smorgi-Bob, the Cook* [fig. 9.65]. He turned to his own face [fig. 9.66] not out of an introspective urge but, on the contrary, as an infinitely malleable, neutral vehicle through which to explore ideas. In *Smorgi-Bob, the Cook* he used the pictorial device of one-point perspective to give an illusion of greater depth. He deliberately made the scheme explicit by forming the elements into a perfect receding triangle and then humorously put a portrait of himself at the apex. This ironic underlining of the formal device to point to himself deliberately parodies all the talk about flatness, illusionism, and the framing edge in the pretentious formalist art jargon of the late sixties. It also demonstrates the artist's ongoing dialog with painting. "My work," he noted in 1974, "is not about sculpture in the traditional sense, volumes and planes . . . I am making drawings and paintings in space."[81] Moreover, the finish of *Smorgi-Bob, the Cook* looks like shiny porcelain dinnerware, which is what potters are expected to make anyway, and since the potter cooks his art in a kiln, Arneson sarcastically celebrates his achievement as a master chef.

Like plumbing fixtures and place settings, bricks also belong to the historic concerns of the ceramic craft that beckoned Arneson in the late sixties. He did a numbered edition of them, made surrealist transformations of them with ears and wings, set one in ceramic flames, and even finished

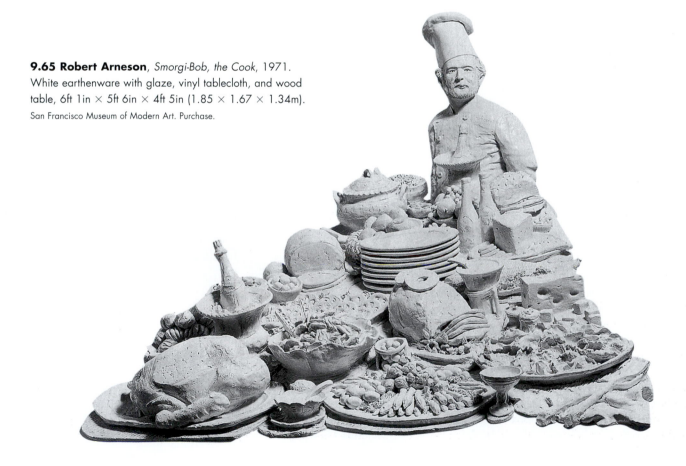

9.65 Robert Arneson, *Smorgi-Bob, the Cook*, 1971.
White earthenware with glaze, vinyl tablecloth, and wood table, 6ft 1in × 5ft 6in × 4ft 5in (1.85 × 1.67 × 1.34m).
San Francisco Museum of Modern Art. Purchase.

9.66 Robert Arneson in his studio in Benicia, California, 1978.

Photograph by James Woodson.

one with a delicate celadon glaze as in classic Chinese pottery. There is also a brick *tableau* called *Fragment of Western Civilization*, which resembles the antique ruins of a colossal self-portrait wall, inspired by pictures in *National Geographic* of ancient sites in Mexico with magnificent, monumental heads lying about on the ground.[82] In this piece he wanted to break away from the singular object and make a scatter work of the kind that Barry Le Va or Robert Morris were doing in the late sixties [figs. 10.13 and 10.14].

It was in part to avoid offending anyone that Arneson so frequently used his own face as a vehicle in the seventies. In *Klown* [fig. 9.67] he poked fun at himself in the best comic tradition, and yet the lifelike mask also appears to trap the artist underneath. In this work Arneson seems to have been more focused on the disconcerting "second skin" than on the internal character. The physical distortions of a self-portrait sketch by the seventeenth-century Flemish artist Adrian Brouwer, in which he is pulling faces in a mirror, and the psychologically impenetrable sculptures of the eighteenth-century psychotic sculptor F. X. Messerschmidt both informed the train of association that led up to *Klown*.[83] The graffiti scrawled all over the base are Arneson's rendition of the satirical humor of the *vox populi*, the anonymous voice of the people.[84]

In 1975 Jack Lemon of the Landfall Press in Chicago persuaded Arneson to make some prints and that exercise refocused his attention upon drawing. From that point until the end of his career, Arneson continued to make large, finished drawings in a loose, Pollock-like, color gesture that reflects his ongoing preoccupation with action painting. *Klown* and other sculptures of the late seventies have some Pollock-like splashes of color on the base that also subtly

9.67 Robert Arneson, *Klown*, 1978. Glazed ceramic, 37 × 19 × 19in (94 × 48.3 × 48.3cm).

Des Moines Art Center. Purchase, with funds from the Gardner and Florence Call Cowles Foundation, Des Moines Art Center permanent collection, 1980.4.

express this discourse, but it was not until 1983 that Arneson took up Jackson Pollock explicitly as a subject. The juxtaposition of Pollock's extreme emotional anguish and the lush, sensual beauty of his surfaces attracted Arneson in part because Arneson had identified this same conflict in his own work. *The Eye of the Beholder*, for example [fig. 9.68], is both exquisitely beautiful and cruel and the same time.

Discovering a Political Voice

Arneson had hit a stride in his work by early 1981, when he was asked by the San Francisco Art Commission to make a monumental portrait bust of the late mayor George Moscone for the new Convention Center. The head captured Moscone's likeness to everyone's satisfaction, but the inscriptions on the pedestal—that sarcastic voice of the people—caused a national scandal.

Dan White, a former San Francisco city official, had lost his position to an openly homosexual politician named Harvey Milk. On November 17, 1978 White walked into Mayor Moscone's office and shot him four times. White then reloaded, went down the hall to the office of Harvey Milk, and shot him five times. Six months later a jury convicted White of voluntary manslaughter rather than first-degree murder on the basis that he had hypoglycemia and had consumed a large quantity of Hostess Twinkies before the shooting spree, making him temporarily insane. This outrageous verdict caused the "White Night" riot at City Hall, which left 119 people injured (half of them police officers) and over a million dollars in damage.

On the base of the Moscone portrait Arneson portrayed a Twinkie and five bloody bullet holes as well as numerous inscriptions related to Moscone's career, including the headline "and Feinstein becomes mayor." Mayor Feinstein asked the artist to replace the pedestal, but he refused because it was part of the conception of the piece. So the mayor draped the pedestal for the dedication of the building on December 2, after which Arneson returned the money and withdrew the sculpture.

The publicity over the Moscone piece made Arneson realize that he had a platform from which to take up a cause,[85] so toward the end of 1982 he turned to a theme so sober it shocked even those who knew his work well. In *Ass to Ash* of late 1982 Arneson used his own head as ground zero for a nuclear holocaust. On the base of the charred and deformed *Holy War Head* [fig. 9.69] he inscribed a lengthy passage from John Hersey's *Hiroshima*, describing the horrific effects of radiation exposure on people. In 1983 Arneson began focusing on nuclear weapons, radiation poisoning, and above all on the terrifyingly detached attitude with which nuclear materials are handled and discussed.

Introspection Via Pollock

In 1984 and 1985 Arneson turned even more directly on the military establishment, portraying it as a savage martial court presiding over total annihilation. Then he looked to Jackson Pollock as a subject through which he could investigate his own psyche. Donald Kuspit described Arneson's growing interest in Pollock during the eighties as an identification with the artist as the brutalized and isolated victim and survivor.[86] But Pollock self-destructed, whereas Arneson overcame the odds. Far from being a hapless victim, Arneson externalized momentous rage and a corresponding terror in the anti-nuclear works and faced them head-on in his works on Jackson Pollock.

This exploration of Pollock seems to have contributed to the emergence of a late style in Arneson's work, with the loose gesture of his red conté crayon drawings of 1991 and a series of sculptures in 1991 and 1992 (the year of his death) that transcend the ephemeral emotions of present situations. Whereas the eccentricity of Arneson's wry humor had always represented rebellion against convention, these late works no longer concern themselves with external standards at all. Instead, a work such as *Head Eater* of 1991 (a double self-portrait mask of one self-image taking a bloody bite out of the head of the other) foregrounds the unruly forces of the unconscious mind as the norms against which to measure both experience and form.

9.69 Robert Arneson, *Holy War Head*, 1982. Glazed ceramic, 72 × 28 × 28in (182.9 × 71.1 × 71.1cm). Collection, Rita and Irwin Blitt. Courtesy the Estate of the artist.

10.1 Frank Stella, *The Marriage of Reason and Squalor*, 1959.
Enamel on canvas, 7ft 6⅝in × 10ft 11¾in (2.3 × 3.34m).

Saint Louis Art Museum. Museum purchase and gift of Mr. and Mrs. Joseph A. Helman,
Mr. and Mrs. Ronald K. Greenberg, 23.1969.

10 IN THE NATURE OF MATERIALS: THE LATER SIXTIES

BACK TO FIRST PRINCIPLES— MINIMAL ART

In an important essay of 1965 entitled "ABC Art," Barbara Rose wrote about the recent emergence of "an art whose blank, neutral, mechanical impersonality contrasts so violently with the romantic, biographical abstract expressionist style which preceded it that spectators are chilled by its apparent lack of feeling or content."[1] This new art asserted an overtly unsymbolic physicality as opposed to the abstract expressionist idea of the object as a vehicle for dramatic, emotional introspection. "Minimal art," as this work came to be known, gravitated toward regular, geometric forms or modular sequences with uninflected surfaces, especially in sculpture which was placed not on pedestals but directly on the floor or wall to stress its continuity with real space. Donald Judd, whose clear prose style made him an unofficial spokesman for this new art, coined the term "specific object"[2] in 1965 to refer to the literalness with which this new sculpture and painting revealed itself to the observer as precisely what it was in the physical sense rather than as a metaphor or representation.

The reductive appearance of minimal art shocked viewers accustomed to the visual complexity of gesture painting. Indeed, Lucy Lippard (a critic close to these artists) felt compelled to argue in 1966 that the monotony of minimal sculpture (her choice of words) was, in itself, an avant-garde gesture: "The exciting thing about . . . the 'cool' artists," she said, "is their daring challenge of the concepts of boredom, monotony and repetition."[3] The antagonism to minimal art, however, involved more than a response to its boredom: minimalism came to be seen by some as aggressively authoritarian, a "displaced will to power,"[4] in particular white male power, in the art world.

Inspired by the work of Ad Reinhardt [fig. 6.12], Frank Stella's schematic, monochrome paintings of 1959–61 [fig. 10.1] launched minimalism. During the mid-sixties Donald Judd, Tony Smith, Carl Andre, and Dan Flavin gave definition to it as a movement, with Robert Morris pushing it out in the direction of "process art" (so-called for its focus on procedures interacting with materials), and later in the decade Sol LeWitt using minimalist ideas as the foundation for "conceptual art"—an art which struck out for independence from the physical object altogether. These artists were united above all in their attempt to treat works of art literally as objects instead of as vehicles for metaphysical ideas or introspective emotions, and yet, as we shall see, a hint of romanticism (see page 288) perseveres.

Ironically, minimalism depended upon a prodigious amount of polemic—written largely by the artists themselves—to reveal the motives behind these apparently simple works. As in Clement Greenberg's formalism, the simplest object might generate the most complex, theoretical *raison d'être*. Morris, for example, wrote that where painting was optical, sculpture was tactile, literal, and had a monolithic physicality. Judd concurred on "the lesser position of painting";[5] sculpture as sculpture, in Greenberg's modernist reduction too, had made it the most current stage of modernist art. Yet Morris rejected Judd's relief sculpture [fig. 10.2]:

> Relief cannot be accepted today as legitimate. The autonomous and literal nature of sculpture demands that it have its own, equally literal space—not a surface shared with painting. Furthermore, an object hung on the wall does not confront gravity; it timidly resists it. One of the conditions of knowing an object is supplied by the sensing of the gravitational force acting upon it in actual space.[6]

Even though Stella and his friends largely fulfilled Greenberg's theoretical prescriptions for modernism, Greenberg discounted minimalism as contrived, "something deduced instead of felt or discovered,"[7] while Michael Fried attacked the minimalists—but not his friend Stella—in a virulent and personal tone, threatening to "break the fingers of their grip." Fried argued that "the entire history of painting since Manet could be understood . . . as consisting in the progressive . . . revelation of its essential objecthood,"[8] but, exempting Stella from the movement, he admonished minimal artists for going too far, making objects so literal they directed the viewer to external relationships, which Fried called "theatrical," thereby detracting from their aesthetic purity.

10.2 Donald Judd, *Untitled*, 1967. Galvanized iron with green lacquer on front and sides, twelve units 9 × 40 × 31 in (22.9 × 191.6 × 78.7 cm), each with 9 in (22.9 cm) intervals.
The Helman Collection, New York.

Minimal art made the reductive geometry and theory of Ad Reinhardt newly relevant in the sixties. "The one object of fifty years of abstract art," Reinhardt wrote in 1963, "is to present art-as-art and as nothing else, to make it into the one thing it is only, separating and defining it more and more, making it purer and emptier." He sought an "art preoccupied with its own process and means."[9] Reinhardt attacked any suggestion of external references in art and championed a psychological emptiness that rivaled Warhol's. In his "Twelve Rules for a New Academy," Reinhardt proclaimed that: "The laying bare of oneself . . . is obscene."[10] The "Twelve Rules" were: no texture, no brushwork, no drawing, no forms, no design, no color, no light, no space, no time, no size or scale, no movement, and finally no object.

Reinhardt, an articulate and ardent formalist, remained principally committed to the exploration of the epistemological potential of painting. He had become increasingly interested in Zen after the war, and from 1954 until his death in 1967 he worked at version after version of one painting. The "black paintings" [fig. 6.12] which comprise this final series produce the initial effect of a uniform black field until one's eyes acclimatize to see the subtle division into nine squares and even some trace of brushwork.

Frank Stella

In the flag paintings of Jasper Johns the objects themselves are the image. This made a powerful impression on Frank Stella when, as a senior in college at Princeton, he saw the 1958 Johns show at the Leo Castelli Gallery.[11] Indeed, the thickness of the stretcher made a Johns flag more object-like than a real flag. Johns thus furthered a development—inaugurated in symbolism at the turn of the last century and inflected by Picasso's collage—toward transforming the painting from an illusion into an object. In addition, the flags provided an example of making a painting from clearly set out, preconceived ideas: "The thing that struck me most," Stella later explained, "was the way he [Johns] stuck to the motif . . . the idea of stripes—rhythm and the interval—the idea of repetition. I began to think a lot about repetition."[12]

Stella singled out abstract formal ideas from Johns one by one, and then followed them to a logical extreme. In this distillation he eliminated not only the subject but the painterly touch (both of which Johns had retained precisely for their provocative ambiguity). Stella also enlarged his pictures to a greater scale than those of Johns, yet one nevertheless sees the Stellas all at once rather than dwelling on details. The idea of eliminating foreground and background by painting a single motif, identical with the form of the canvas (as in the flags), led directly to Stella's most important innovation—the shaped canvas [figs. 10.3 and 10.4].

Such paintings as *The Marriage of Reason and Squalor* (which Dorothy Miller exhibited in the Museum of Modern Art's "Sixteen Americans" show in 1959) and *Lake City* married the influences of Reinhardt and Johns. Stella asked

10.3 (left) **Frank Stella**, *Lake City*, 1962. Copper paint on canvas, 22⅝ × 30in (57.5 × 76.2cm).
Menil Collection, Houston.

10.4 (below) **Frank Stella**, *Hatra I*, 1967. Acrylic on canvas, 10 × 20ft (3.04 × 6.09m).
Art Institute of Chicago. Major Acquisitions Fund, 1970.842.

Carl Andre to write his artist's statement for the "Sixteen Americans" catalog, thus keeping himself at an expressive remove. In it Andre wrote:

> Art excludes the unnecessary. Frank Stella has found it necessary to paint stripes. There is nothing else in his painting. Frank Stella is not interested in expression or sensitivity. He is interested in the necessities of painting . . . Frank Stella's painting is not symbolic. His stripes are the paths of brush on canvas. These paths lead only into painting.[13]

Despite this avowed neutrality of expression, Stella endowed many of his early pictures with emotionally charged titles. As Brenda Richardson observed, "death and especially suicide are prevalent references," along with allusions to Nazi Germany, as in *Arbeit Macht Frei* from the inscription over the gates of the Auschwitz concentration camp.[14] It almost seems as if Stella segregated the expressive aspects of his work into discretely contained and controllable areas just as he separated out the formal issues, one at a time.

In Stella's black paintings there was still a discernible brushwork—visible paths of the brush that make every aspect of the process entirely clear. Unlike Reinhardt's black on black squares, Stella made the edges of the stripes completely visible too (leaving a gap of exposed canvas and showing a pencil line between them). He also cut notches in the edges and holes into the centers, or altered the shape of his canvases (as in *Lake City*) to conform to the patterns of his geometric designs. In this way he avoided an illusion of spatial recession and enhanced the object's presence as an object, making a flatter and less referential canvas than anybody had painted up to that time. Michael Fried claimed that in doing this Stella had posed and solved the central formal problem in modern art since impressionism—namely, asserting the painting's presence as an object (its "objecthood").[15]

Stella delineated a radical posture by systematically inverting the assumptions of abstract expressionism. His friend Walter Darby Bannard explained: "Abstract expressionism was repudiated point by point: painting within the drawing replaced drawing with paint; overt regularity replaced apparent randomness; symmetry replaced asymmetric balancing; flat, depersonalized brushing or open, stained color replaced the smudge, smear and spatter . . . The entire visible esthetic of abstract expressionism was brutally revised."[16] Above all, Stella attacked the introspective motive in abstract expressionism: "My painting is based on the fact that only what can be seen there is there," he said. "It really is an object . . . you can see the whole idea without any confusion . . . what you see is what you see."[17] Like Greenberg's "Post Painterly" painting, Stella's work is an attack on transcendence. Thus even though Stella's large scale, lack of gesture, and definition of the surface as an overall field are indebted to Barnett Newman, he couldn't have been less interested in Newman's subject matter.

Stella went from single colors to industrial Day-Glo in the mid-sixties [fig. 10.4], probably under the influence of Warhol, though it would have been unthinkable to say so.

Shape, configuration, and pattern all continued to refer to one another in a closed—if increasingly complex—system that asserted the work as an object. As studio assistants increasingly did the painting for him, Stella's work also lost its painterly edges.

Stella's denial of expressive content—"what you see is what you see"—echoes Warhol's famous maxim: "If you want to know all about Andy Warhol, just look at the surface of my paintings and my films and me, and there I am. There's nothing behind it."[18] But Stella's persistent recourse to the logic of formal structure *for* the content, rather than as a vehicle *of* content, made it clear that "what you see" is not in fact "what you see" but rather an illustration of all that theory about flatness and objecthood, and after the mid-sixties that began to seem less and less interesting.

Donald Judd

Meanwhile, Donald Judd's antipathy toward illusionism led him to abandon painting in 1961 in favor of sculpture. He attempted to fulfill Tatlin's machine-age prescription for "real materials in real space," but, unlike Tatlin, Judd had no social message. Judd insisted that his objects lacked any significance beyond what was literally there. If an image suggested three dimensions, the three dimensions existed; they were not illusions or representations.

Barbara Haskell pointed out that Judd's training in philosophy as an undergraduate at Columbia and in particular his affinity with the writings of the eighteenth-century Scottish empiricist David Hume confirmed an intuitive disposition toward concrete experience.[19] Judd's rejection of abstract expressionism derived in part from his belief in the dialectical progress of ideas in art (making abstract expressionism outmoded) and from his insistence on experientially verifiable truth (which excluded existential introspection). In a 1962 review for *Arts Magazine*, Judd wrote:

> Frank Stella's new paintings are one of the recent facts. They show the extent of what can be done now. The further coherence supersedes older forms. It is not only new but better, not necessarily on an onlooker's scale of profundity which can measure Pollock against Stella, but on the scale . . . of development. The absence of illusionistic space in Stella, for example, makes abstract expressionism seem now an inadequate style, makes it appear a compromise with representational art and its meaning.[20]

Judd's red sculptures of 1963 consist of enclosed volumes with visible interiors: open frames, boxes, and constructions of wood and pipe. He was interested in clarifying all aspects of the structure and materials. In the works of the mid-sixties [fig. 10.2] be began exploring forms with patterned variations or modular units, spaced equidistantly, symmetrically, or in mathematically determined intervals, which the viewer would immediately recognize as a pattern instead of as compositional elements in balance. Indeed, these arrangements eliminated the conventional idea of composition while at the same time allowing a more complex form. However, "the series doesn't mean anything to me as mathematics,"[21] Judd said.

For Judd, even the use of pure geometry implied its opposite in the wildness of nature and it was that idea—which he found in the work of Stella—that compelled him. "Geometry," Judd said, "could be used in a non-Neo-Plastic way, an impure way, without the purity that geometric art seemed to have. Mondrian, though really great, is too ideal and clean. In another way, Reinhardt is too. That was not a believable quality for me. Stella's painting had a possibility that became evident of an impure geometric art."[22]

By 1964 Judd had begun making enough money to have his work fabricated commercially instead of handcrafting it himself. Whereas he made the red boxes of the early sixties out of wood, by 1964 he was working in metal and Plexiglas. Judd's reliefs of galvanized metal boxes cantilevered from the wall and given automobile lacquer finishes express an aesthetic affinity for the detachment of industrial materials and processes. Although David Smith anticipated their geometric modularity and Jasper Johns their semantic fundamentalism, Judd's floor boxes [fig. 10.5] and box reliefs achieved a singleness of focus on the literal object that was genuinely new.

Tony Smith

Tony Smith, born in 1912, was of the abstract expressionist generation and taught several of the minimalists. His greatest contribution involved the delicacy with which he calibrated the scale of his works in relation to their sites, undercutting the conventional notion of monumentality and making his sculptures remarkably responsive to their architectural or natural setting. "Why didn't you make it larger so that it would loom over the observer?" someone asked Smith about

Die, the 6-foot-high black steel cube of 1962 [fig. 10.6]. "I was not making a monument," he replied. "Then why didn't you make it smaller so that the observer could see over the top?" "I was not making an object."[23]

Smith took his cue from Barnett Newman, who had been exploring the idea of the holistic image as a spatial concept. (The holistic image is an image seen all at once as a single form, rather than as parts making up a whole.) Smith conceived his forms as whole, unified (holistic) images and suppressed the intimacy of details and relations among parts that might promote a detachment from the central concept. He even eliminated all signs of the fabrication process so as not to detract from the unitary gestalt; for *Die* he merely gave the specifications to a fabricator over the telephone, thus separating himself completely from the physical object.

Carl Andre

By the mid-sixties the minimal artist's predilection for certain types of materials and generative systems—like Carl Andre's stacks of timber—began to look as individual as the abstract expressionist splash of paint. Andre met Frank Stella in 1958 and worked in his studio while Stella was making the black paintings of 1959. It was under this influence that Andre arrived at the basic principle of anaxial symmetry in

10.7 Carl Andre, *Pyre (Element Series)*, constructed 1971, Minneapolis, from a 1960 plan. Wood, eight units, 12 × 12 × 36in (30.5 × 30.5 × 91.4cm) each, 48 × 36 × 36in (121.9 × 91.4 × 91.4cm) overall.

Gilman Collection, Texas. Courtesy Paula Cooper Gallery, New York.

which any part of a work can replace any other part, as in *Pyre (Element Series)* [fig. 10.7]. Over the next three years he gradually abandoned carving and the assemblage of found materials in favor of arranging his sculptures from modular units. The rigidly arranged scheme of *Pyre* or *Steel Magnesium Plain* [fig. 10.8] sets off the natural eccentricities of the materials. The clear geometry relates to Frank Stella's early shaped canvases, while the overall structure implies infinite continuation as in Brancusi's modular series of "Endless Columns." Andre explained:

> Brancusi to me is the great link into the earth and the Endless Column is, of course, the absolute culmination of that experience. They reach up and they drive down into the earth with a kind of verticality which is not terminal. Before, that verticality was always terminal: the top of the head and the bottom of the feet were the limits of sculpture.[24]

Brancusi also provided a precedent for the minimalists' interest in the inherent qualities of the materials.

In 1965 and 1966 Andre shifted from stacked wood—which had an object-like presence—to commercially prefabricated materials, disposed in a particular space. The specificity of the work for its site caused it to blend into the space, dissipating its object-like quality. *Lever* was Andre's first site-specific piece, consisting of 137 fire bricks laid side by side in a line on the floor at the "Primary Structures" exhibition of 1966. Then he went on to squares of metal which he placed directly on the floor for viewers to walk on and experience in a directly tactile way. Site-specificity in the sense of *Lever* was not the central concern in these works—rather the focus was on their physicality.

"I severed matter from depiction, in the way Turner severed light and color from depiction," Andre explained. "My work is about critical mass. The flat squares let you see the mass and form rather than the same mass in a cube where you would see only a little."[25] This underscores the

10.8 Carl Andre, *Steel Magnesium Plain*, 1969. Steel and magnesium, thirty-six units, 12 × 12in (30.5 × 30.5cm) each, 6 × 6ft (1.82 × 1.82m) overall.

Private collection, Switzerland. Courtesy Paula Cooper Gallery, New York.

10.9 (above) **Carl Andre**, *Stone Field Sculpture*, 1977.
Thirty-six glacial boulders, Hartford, Connecticut.
Courtesy Paula Cooper Gallery, New York.

literal presence of the material, its hardness, color, and
weight. On the one hand the raw presence of the materials
evokes a sense of nature—the artist's idea of positioning
himself in a lineage from Turner is quite to the point here.
On the other hand the plates are also materials in and of the
industrial world, fashioned into regular squares in a grid.

Andre experimented with the subversion of reasoned
order by chaos in several works of the mid-sixties and later.
He made wavy lines of nails and laid pieces of pipe end to end
on the floor; these materials resisted the regularity of their
placement by the sheer awkwardness of their form. In *Spill* of
1966, the artist scattered 800 small plastic blocks randomly
across a gallery floor. Andre also took his systems out of
doors, arranging units in nature, as in *Joint* of 1968, where
he arranged bales of hay; in the *Stone Field Sculpture* of 1977
[fig. 10.9] he conceived a monumental work that exists at the
interface between natural matter and the rational ordering
systems of the human mind.

Dan Flavin

Dan Flavin's work emerged out of a mixture of influences,
from Kaprow's happenings and junk sculpture to his struggles
with the spirituality of his Catholic upbringing that he
rejected and yet somehow could not eliminate. In 1961–2 he
made a series of "Icons" combining flat color planes, simple

10.10 (right) **Dan Flavin**, *Untitled*, 1963. Green fluorescent
light, 8ft (2.44m) high. Edition of five.
Private collection. Courtesy Leo Castelli Gallery, New York.

geometric forms, and light bulbs (both incandescent and fluorescent). Then, in 1963, he began working exclusively with new, industrially prefabricated fluorescent tubes and fixtures. He merely arranged the parts and any hardware-store patron could reproduce them indistinguishably from the originals. Thus Flavin's works tease the viewer's definition of art as dependent on an original object. They also assert the continuity with the real world of everyday things. Both inclinations are influenced by Duchamp's readymades.

Choreographing the light from the tubes, Flavin investigated the idea of sculpture as space rather than form. The light articulates the space in a way that makes each piece particularly interdependent with its site. *Untitled* of 1963 [fig. 10.10], for example, fills a confined alcove with green light, marking off an area (as it was originally displayed at the Castelli Gallery) even when the tubes themselves remained hidden around the corner. The series of "monuments" in homage to Vladimir Tatlin [fig. 10.11], the Russian constructivist who embraced industry and insisted on the continuum of art and life, involves multiple permutations in the arrangement of the same set of plain white, fluorescent tubes. The boundlessness of the light implied the sublime for Flavin and it still carried an association of spirituality—the unlikely fusion of the industrial and the transcendental made these works what he called "a modern technological fetish."[26] This romantic aspect is more pronounced in the work of Flavin and Andre than in that of Stella, Judd, and Morris, whereas they all shared an affinity for industrial materials, simplified forms, systems, permutations, and a concern with focusing on real materials and space.

10.11 (above) **Dan Flavin**,
Monument for V. Tatlin, 1968.
Cool white fluorescent light,
8ft (2.44m) high.
Private collection. Courtesy Leo Castelli Gallery, New York.

10.12 (right) **Robert Morris**,
Untitled ("L" Beams), 1965 and 1967.
Painted plywood, three pieces, 96 × 96 × 24in (243.8 × 243.8 × 61cm).
Original destroyed.

Robert Morris

Robert Morris followed a less formally focused set of protocols than Judd or Flavin but his approach was no less anti-illusionistic. He consistently worked with an experimental objectivity in his investigations of process, materials, and actions. In 1961 he made *Box With the Sound of Its Own Making*, enclosing a three-hour tape loop playing a recording of himself in the process of constructing the box. In 1963 he completed *Cardfile* by alphabetically indexing all decisions related to transforming the found object into a work of art, including how long it took to find the thing, all the different kinds of files he looked at, interruptions, and so on. He also had an electroencephalogram made while he thought about himself for the time it took to make a tape as long as he was tall and designated it a self-portrait.

In each of these instances Morris invented a task and then carried it out in a routine manner, leaving the details to chance as in the reductive dance pieces of the Judson Dance Theater and the Fluxus actions. The influence of Duchamp is also evident.[27] The idea of the "L" beams [fig. 10.12] was to take a given form and see how many different ways he could dispose it in the space. In another group of works of the mid-sixties he cut up a form and then reassembled it in a variety of ways to see what happened to its gestalt (its identifying mental image).

Anticipated by Carl Andre's 1966 *Spill* and the scatter pieces by Richard Serra and Barry Le Va [fig. 10.13], Morris began exploring the idea of sculpture without fixed form. In 1968 he randomly spread industrial threadwaste (the extra threads clipped off in garment manufacturing), along with other random materials, across the gallery floor [fig. 10.14]. To move the piece, Morris simply ordered another bale to be sent directly to the museum or collector with instructions to dump it on the floor themselves. In some he added double-sided mirrors that undermined the perception of finite form still more.

The threadwaste pieces extended Duchamp's attack on the concept of the aesthetic object and his assertion of the dominance of the idea in art. It also drew on the inspiration of Cage and Cunningham in the use of chance. In addition, these pieces prompted a fresh look at the boundary of order and chaos, emphasized the role of sculpture in defining space rather than form, and directed the viewer to the literal specificity of the context. "When you build something rigid you know what it's going to look like . . . I wanted a material that I could predict even less about," Morris explained. "The particular concrete situation in a given time. That's where the fascination is."[28] Morris's well-known industrial felt pieces [fig. 10.15] also arise from these concerns, exploring space and gravitational mass (like sculpture), as well as the idea of mutable form.

10.13 Barry Le Va, *Continuous and Related Activities: Discontinued by the Act of Dropping*, 1967 (reconstructed in 1990). Glass and maroon felt, 15 × 25ft (4.57 × 7.62m) in this view, but dimensions vary.

Whitney Museum of American Art, New York. Purchased with funds from the Painting and Sculpture Committee.

10.14 (right) **Robert Morris**, *Untitled*, 1968. Threadwaste, mirrors, asphalt, aluminum, lead, felt, copper, and steel, 30 × 30in (76.2 × 76.2cm).

Private collection. Courtesy Leo Castelli Gallery, New York.

10.15 (below) **Robert Morris**, *Untitled*, 1967–8. Felt, ⅜in (0.9cm) thick, dimensions variable.

Collection, Philip Johnson. Courtesy Leo Castelli Gallery, New York.

Sol LeWitt

Sol LeWitt applied the minimalists' systemic logic and literalness to the generative procedures in his work without sharing their interest in the literal object. Indeed, by the late sixties he had reasoned his way beyond the object into a conceptual art, consciously separating the abstract idea system that produces an object from the object itself. "The idea or the concept is the most important aspect of the work," he wrote in a seminal article for *Artforum* in 1967 entitled "Paragraphs on Conceptual Art." In it, he asserted:

> When an artist uses a conceptual form of art, it means that all of the planning and decisions are made beforehand and the execution is a perfunctory affair. The idea becomes a machine that makes the art. This kind of art is not theoretical or illustrative of theories; it is intuitive; it is involved with all types of mental processes, and it is purposeless. It is usually free from the dependence on the skill of the artist as a craftsman.[29]

In 1965 LeWitt began constructing modules of open cubes, first in black and then in white [fig. 10.16]. He arbitrarily decided on a ratio of 8.5:1 between the thickness of the structural members and the spaces between them. These visually complicated works embody simple structural systems that the viewer can extrapolate from their form. LeWitt referred to the underlying concept of these works as a "grammar."[30]

10.16 (left) **Sol LeWitt**, *Wall/Floor Piece #4*, 1976. Private collection. Courtesy John Weber Gallery, New York.

10.17 (below) **Sol LeWitt**, *Wall Drawing #1, Drawing Series II 18 A & B*, 1968. Black pencil, drawn directly on the wall of the Paula Cooper Gallery, New York. Private collection, San Francisco. Courtesy the artist.

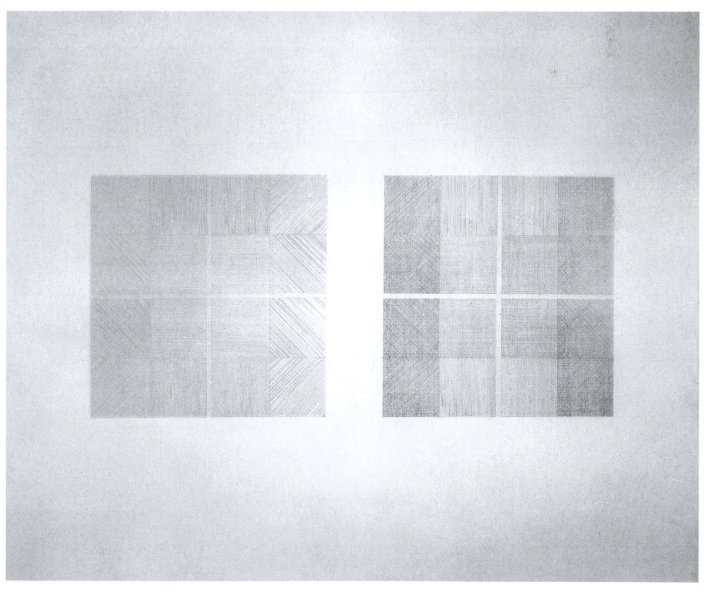

LeWitt's allusion to language derived from structuralism, which posited meaning as a decipherable, universal structure underlying the form. Moreover, LeWitt recognized that while the underlying logic in a work may be a simple scheme set on a predictable course, the object itself is experientially unpredictable. This establishes a dissonance between sensation and system that suggests the arbitrariness with which (according to structuralist theory) signifiers and signifieds (or words and the objects to which they refer) are linked.[31]

LeWitt's most radical formal innovation was his idea of drawing directly on the wall. He made his first wall drawings in 1968 in the Paula Cooper Gallery [fig. 10.17]. They involved a set of predetermined procedures carried out by assistants. These wall drawings further eroded conventional notions of the art object because they could be removed and re-created according to instruction without benefit of the artist's hand at all. If a museum wanted to borrow one, it could be painted out in one place and repainted in another. In several of the wall drawings the instruction that generated each line is written directly on the wall next to it.

The Los Angeles Light and Space Movement

Meanwhile, in Los Angeles, Robert Irwin and James Turrell formed the nexus of a "Light and Space" movement in the late sixties that had a literalness and an experimental tone resembling the approach of Robert Morris. The Light and Space movement centered on the exploration of visual perception itself in works so subtle in their visual calibration as to be near meaningless in reproduction. Irwin dematerialized objects, then space, while Turrell worked chiefly with light and space. By the mid-sixties Irwin was using principles of Gestalt psychology, manipulating different kinds of light, shadows, scrims, and controlled environments to fool the eye into seeing something other than what was actually there. Nevertheless, Irwin conceived such experiments

10.18 James Turrell, *Daygo*, 1990. Light into space, dimensions variable.
Courtesy Barbara Gladstone Gallery, New York.

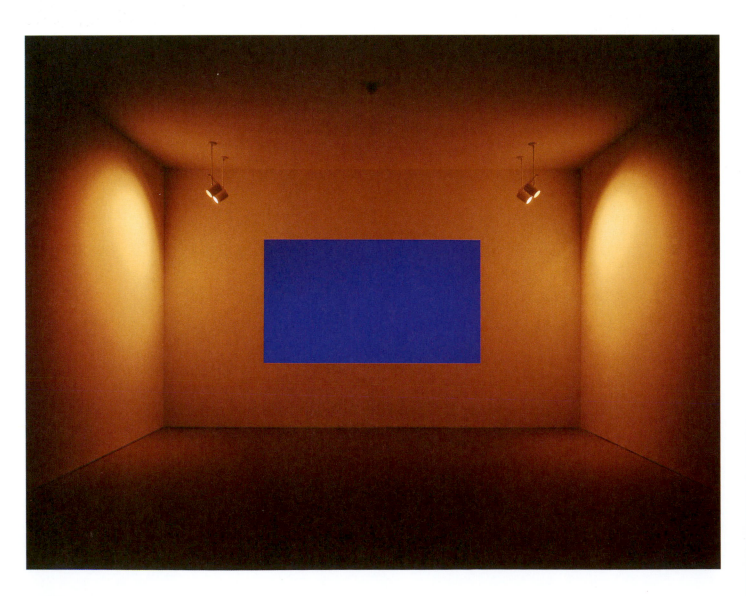

in the broader context of "a construction and ordering of individual reality."[32] Art, he said, is "the placing of your attention on the periphery of knowing. It is . . . a state of mind."[33]

Turrell had a more spiritual cast of mind, influenced by Eastern philosophy. In a work of 1967 entitled *Afrum* he created a visually "solid" cube in the corner of a room with projections of white light; this is a characteristic example of his work of the mid-sixties, in which he boldly confronts the viewer with a contradiction between what is there and what seems to be there. He went on to create other light forms and then rooms in which the viewer sees walls where there are none. In *Daygo* [fig. 10.18], for example, the viewer can walk right up to the blue rectangle and still be unable to discern whether it is a hole in the wall with blue light behind it, or a sharply delineated blue surface on the wall. "This is not minimalism and it is not conceptual work," Turrell explained, "it is *perceptual* work."[34] But it is also a kind of work that teases the viewer's perceptions into an unsteady reality. "The daydream," he explained,

> . . . is, I think, the space that we inhabit most of the time, much more than this conscious awake space that is called reality. It's this daydream space overlaid on the conscious awake reality that I like to work with . . . I'm interested in having a work confront you where you wouldn't ordinarily see it. When you have an experience like that in otherwise normal surroundings, it takes on the lucidity of a dream.[35]

In 1972 Turrell began thinking about constructing a monumental earthwork that would then provide a contemplative experience of light and space on a grand scale and in 1974 he selected a site—an extinct volcano called the Roden Crater, north of Flagstaff, Arizona. By carefully shaping the crater rim, Turrell attempted to control the viewer's perception of the open space above as seen from the bottom of the crater's bowl. Turrell also calculated movements of the celestial bodies in relation to this viewing point and made plans to shape different parts of the site to exploit them.

Many of Turrell's works of the seventies and eighties involved ideas related to this large work-in-progress. *Meeting* of 1983–6, for example, was a room for P.S.1 (then an alternative art space in New York) in which the ceiling is open to the sky. The viewers sit on benches that ring the featureless, square room and look up to a pure patch of blue (depending on the weather). The sky takes on a fascinating panoply of perceptual variations in color and space as the exterior light shifts and eventually fades, gradually bringing out the artificial lights around the perimeter of the opening. One seems to see what is there with a preternatural acuity but also to encounter the presence of one's own mind in the act of perceiving. *Meeting* has a resonance of Turrell's Quaker background; "the sites I like to use are ones that . . . are really inhabited by consciousness . . . generated not by the architecture of form but by the overlay of thought," Turrell said.[36]

Object/Concept/Illusion in Painting

By the end of the sixties a number of artists had begun methodically separating the work of art into overlays of distinct systems, like medical specialists isolating the vascular system or the network of endocrine glands for a focused evaluation. Mel Bochner began using mathematical formulas to derive the forms in his paintings, while Robert Mangold played off physical qualities of the object against pictorial concepts or illusions. In Mangold's *Four Color Frame Painting #1* (1983), for example [fig. 10.19], he juxtaposed the framing edges and seams of the canvases with drawn lines that allude to a continuous geometry. In some cases he deliberately created perceptual contradictions to underscore the incompatible realities of the different systems.

For Ellsworth Kelly, the whole picture had become the unit in a hard-edge style of painting as early as 1958. Unlike Mangold and Bochner, Kelly arrived at this in the more intuitive manner characteristic of the late fifties. At the beginning of that decade Kelly had already evolved a style of painting in large, flat, hard-edged forms juxtaposed (rather than interacting) on big rectilinear canvases. Nevertheless, his stress on dividing the entire space of a painting, juxtaposing flat forms on a plane rather than arranging them within a composition, resulted in an articulation of the surface as a single field of color which in turn became the form

10.19 Robert Mangold, *Four Color Frame Painting #1*, 1983. Acrylic and black pencil on four canvas panels, 9ft 3in × 12ft 6in (2.82 × 3.81m) overall.
Courtesy Pace Gallery, New York.

10.20 (above) **Ellsworth Kelly**, *Three Panels: Orange, Dark Gray, Green*, 1986. Oil on canvas, A: 8ft 8½in × 7ft 10in (2.65 × 2.38m), B: 7ft 4in × 8ft 2in (2.23 × 2.48m), C: 8ft 1½in × 9ft 11½in (2.47 × 3.03m).
Collection, Douglas S. Cramer Foundation, Los Angeles. Courtesy Blum Helman Gallery, New York.

10.21 (right) **Robert Ryman**, *Untitled*, 1963. Vinyl on unstretched linen glued onto stretched cotton canvas, 25¼ × 22¾in (64.1 × 57.8cm).
Private collection. Courtesy PaceWildenstein Gallery.

[fig. 10.20]. "By removing the content (brush marks, subject matter, etc.) from my work," Kelly remarked, "I shifted the visual reality of painting to include the space around it."[37] In avoiding the effect of figures on a field, Kelly's reduction asserted the painting as an object and that in turn undermined the convention of the rectangular format for Kelly, as it did for Stella.

A Focus on Surface in Painting

In a similar way Robert Ryman's concentrated focus on the nuances of the abstract mark seemed to open a whole new range of possibilities for him [fig. 10.21]. "Abstract painting is just beginning," he said in 1986. "All possibilities are open to it."[38] Restricting himself to an all-white palette since the beginning of the sixties, Ryman has heightened the pure visibility of each component of the painting—the gestural mark, the surface, even the mechanical support and the way it is fastened to the wall. For Ryman, the registration of the process of making the object becomes the content. These investigations come out of John Dewey's pragmatism—

learning by doing, as Suzanne Hudson has shown.[39] In an active exploration of the materials, the support, and the viewing context Ryman highlights the subtleties of seeing what is there rather than aspiring to a transcendental experience. Something similar takes place in the late-sixties and early-seventies work of Brice Marden [fig. 10.22], whose exquisitely refined sense of touch, gesture, and surface concerns the literal but sensuous experience of the paint itself. The same cool, experiential investigation of materials and process was also evident in what came to be called "structuralist film."[40] Michael Snow's forty-five-minute *Wavelength* (1966–7) and Hollis Frampton's slightly shorter *Nostalgia* (1971) exemplify this focusing of the viewer on a reduced set of actions and filmic devices rather than on a narrative or a fictive space.

10.22 Brice Marden, *D'après la marquise de la Solana*, 1969. Oil and wax on canvas, three panels, 6ft 5⅝in × 9ft 9⅜in (1.97 × 2.98m).
Solomon R. Guggenheim Museum, New York. Panza Collection, 91.3784 a–c.

EVA HESSE AND INVESTIGATIONS OF MATERIALS AND PROCESS

In the mid-sixties the somber, detached objectivity of minimalism and the emotional disengagement of pop art and formalism prompted some artists to seek a way back to the individual psyche. Corporate culture, like the cool aesthetic that had come out of the early sixties, was impersonal and alienating, and these artists wanted to reestablish a connection with subjective experience. Lynda Benglis recollected that when she came to New York in 1964 she felt the need for "something very tactile, something that related to the body."[41] So Benglis sought out the most visceral, physically engaging materials and procedures she could devise. Her solidified spills of brilliantly pigmented latex and her amorphous, poured mounds of foam or cast metal of 1969–70 [fig. 10.23] had a counterculture tone that echoed the rebellious political atmosphere. Most importantly, her work employed materials and processes in ways that centered on a sense of the artist's bodily identification with them.

Yayoi Kusama [fig. 10.24], Louise Bourgeois [fig. 10.25], and Lucas Samaras [fig. 7.26] had already pioneered an expressionism of organic forms and unusual materials at the beginning of the decade. Coming out of surrealist-inspired construction (in the case of Bourgeois) and out of the assemblage aesthetic and happenings of the late fifties (Samaras and Kusama), they made sculpture with an especially vivid sensation of touch. What made the new, radically expressionistic sculpture of Eva Hesse and the intensely personal explorations of Bruce Nauman, Richard Tuttle, and Richard

10.24 Yayoi Kusama, *Accumulation No.1*, 1962.
Sewn stuffed fabric, paint, fringe on chair frame,
37 × 39 × 43in (94 × 99 × 109cm).
Beatrice Perry Family Collection. Courtesy Gagosian Gallery.

10.23 (below) **Lynda Benglis**, *Untitled*, 1969–70.
Pigmented polyurethane foam, 15 × 48 × 36in
(38.1 × 121.9 × 91.4cm).
Collection of the artist. Courtesy Paula
Cooper Gallery, New York.

10.25 (above) **Louise Bourgeois**,
Double Negative, 1963. Latex over plaster,
19⅜ × 37½ × 31⅜in (49.2 × 95.3 ×
79.7cm).
Rijksmuseum Krökker-Müller, the Netherlands.
Courtesy Robert Miller Gallery, New York.

Serra different and exceptionally important was not only that they (in particular Hesse) succeeded against the prevailing trends of the art world (which favored reduction and impersonality), but that they created this personally engaged style in a manner that took the anti-illusionist preoccupation of minimalism as a foundation while at the same time remaining so palpably involved with their own intimate body experience. The need to make something that felt real called for the tactile experience that a sculpture of new materials provided.

Eva Hesse

In Hesse's case, her drive to find form (in whatever material seemed most evocative) for her profound emotional struggles presses the viewer irresistibly into identifying with her discovery of herself in the objects she created. Eva Hesse [fig. 10.26], a German-born Jew, narrowly escaped the concentration camps in 1939, when she fled with her sister to Amsterdam at the age of two. After two months in an

10.27 Günter Ücker, *Table*, 1963. Oak, nails, white spray paint, 31½ × 25½ × 25½in (80 × 64.8 × 64.8cm).
Kunstsammlung Nordrhein-Westfalen, Düsseldorf.

orphanage Hesse and her sister were reclaimed by their parents, who took them to New York. But shortly thereafter the parents divorced and in 1946 Hesse lost her mother to suicide. This early history left severe anxiety related to issues of intimacy, abandonment, and self-image that Hesse explored in her art.

Hesse studied art at the Cooper Union and then the Yale School of Art, from which she graduated in 1959. She met and married a sculptor named Tom Doyle and in 1964 they went off together to work in Germany for fourteen months. When she arrived, the twenty-eight-year-old Hesse still saw herself as a painter. It was a year filled with tensions and self-doubt: "I cannot be so many things," she confided to a notebook in 1964. ". . . Woman, beautiful, artist, wife, housekeeper, cook, saleslady, all these things. I cannot even be myself."[42]

Nevertheless, this year in Germany was the turning point in Hesse's development as an artist. She shifted into three-dimensional work and at the end of their stay she had her first one-person show at the prestigious Düsseldorf Kunstverein. Doyle and Hesse lived near Düsseldorf, where the influences of the city's two leading artists, Günter Ücker [fig. 10.27] and Joseph Beuys, seem to have had a formative effect on her stylistic transformation.[43]

Hesse created the twenty breastlike hemispheres (her association) in *Ishtar* of December 1965 [fig. 10.28] by painstakingly winding and gluing spirals of cord around the

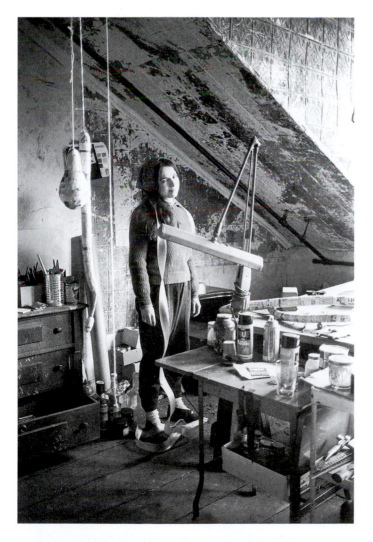

10.26 Eva Hesse in her New York studio, c. 1967.
Courtesy Robert Miller Gallery, New York.

10.28 (above) **Eva Hesse**, *Ishtar*, December 1965. Twenty
cord-bound and painted hemispheres, with black cords mounted
on heavy paper stapled and nailed on wood; paper gessoed and
painted with acrylic, 36 × 7½ × 2½in (91.4 × 19 × 6.3cm),
height with cords 3ft 6½in (1.07m).
Collection of Florette and Ronald B. Lynn, New Jersey.
Courtesy Robert Miller Gallery, New York.

forms, painting them, and fixing them to the evocatively
handled gesso surface. The black plastic strings, loosely
issuing from the centers of each mound, provide a sensual,
fragile connection to this ritualistically reiterated maternal
image. The erotic orbs in *Ishtar*, the dangling phallic shapes
in *Several* of November 1965 [fig. 10.29], and the other
overtly sexual forms that permeate Hesse's sculpture of
1965–70 have a fetishistic character not only in the obsessive
process of their manufacture but in their repetition. Indeed,
both the title and composition of *Ishtar* evoke the multi-
breasted ancient fetish *Diana of Ephesus*, a cognate of the

10.29 (right) **Eva Hesse**, *Several*, November 1965. Acrylic paint,
papier-mâché over seven balloons with rubber cord, 84 × 11 × 7in
(213.4 × 27.9 × 17.8cm).
Saatchi Collection, London.

Semitic goddess of love, fertility, and war for whom Hesse named her work.[44]

The serial structure of the breastlike forms in *Ishtar* also alludes directly to the systemic character of minimal sculpture, which Hess successfully appropriated and personalized in works such as this. She saw right through to the generally unacknowledged, expressive content of minimalism and was moved by it. To her, the highly structured systems of minimalism expressed confinement, as if the coolness expressed the repression of its opposite. "I feel very close to Carl Andre," she said. "I feel, let's say, emotionally connected to his work. It does something to my insides. His metal plates were the concentration camp for me."[45]

Soon after Hesse returned to New York at the end of 1965 her husband left her, and a year later her father died. Hesse was panic-stricken with a sense of abandonment. Yet at the same time influential exhibitions like "Eccentric Abstraction" (1966), "Nine at Leo Castelli" (the so-called "Warehouse Show" of 1968), and "Anti-Illusion: Procedure/Materials" (1969) created an escalating trajectory for Hesse's reputation as central to the emergence of a new kind of abstract sculpture. The increasingly positive public reception of her work and a group of exceptionally supportive friends—among them Mel Bochner, Lucy Lippard, Robert Smithson, and above all Sol LeWitt—fostered a growing artistic self-confidence that kept Hesse emotionally afloat.

The Direct Sensuality of Fiberglass and Latex

During 1967 Hesse's work shifted away from overtly erotic imagery toward a more direct sensuality that was immediately present in the materials themselves—"not symbols for something else," as she wrote in a note to herself of 1970.[46] Her decision to begin working in fiberglass and latex rubber early in 1968 had to do with their translucence and luminescence, the hands-on physicality of building up the body of the work in layers like a skin, and the sensitivity of both materials to the touch. The chainlike sequences of simple units that serve as the compositional principle of many of these late works deliberately echo the underlying structure of the polymers themselves—Hesse sought to relate, in a fundamental way, with the invisible nature of her materials.[47]

In the late spring of 1968 Hesse had begun working with a plastics fabricating company on Staten Island. Like so many artists in the sixties, she found that the help of outside fabricators and studio assistants could quicken the pace of

10.30 Eva Hesse, *Untitled*, 1970. Fiberglass over wire mesh, latex overcloth, and wire (four units), 7ft 6⅞in × 12ft 3⅜in × 3ft 6½in (2.31 × 3.75 × 1.08m) overall.
Des Moines Art Center. Purchased with funds from the Coffin Fine Arts Trust, Nathan Emory Coffin Collection of the Des Moines Art Center, 1988.6.

10.31 (left) **Eva Hesse**, *Untitled* (detail), 1970. See fig. 10.30.

Des Moines Art Center.

10.32 (below) **Eva Hesse**, *Untitled (Rope Piece)*, 1970. Latex over rope, string, and wire, two strands, dimensions variable.

Whitney Museum of American Art, New York. Purchase, with funds from Eli and Edythe L. Broad, the Mrs. Percy Uris Purchase Fund, and the Painting and Sculpture Committee, 88.17a–b.

production and the development of ideas as well as letting her increase the scale of her work. Doug Johns, one of the owners of the plastics company, became so absorbed in working with Hesse that he closed his business and devoted himself to her full time.

In works of 1969 such as *Expanded Expansion*, *Contingent*, and *Untitled (Ice Piece)*, Hesse explored the idea of infinite expansion. They "take a stand on absurdity,"[48] as she put it, by courting the incomprehensibility of infinite extension in space, the improbable transformation of repulsive surfaces into beautiful effects of light and form, and the contradiction between the strength of the fiberglass and the fragility of the latex. She even chose to build impermanence into the work (giving it a morbid evanescence) by using the latex in ways that disrupted its proper curing.[49]

"There isn't a thing in my life that has happened that hasn't been extreme—personal health, family, economic situations . . . absurdity is the key word," Hesse told Cindy Nemser. ". . . It has to do with contradictions and oppositions. In the forms I use in my work the contradictions are certainly there. I was always aware that I should take order versus chaos, stringy versus mass, huge versus small, and I would try to find the most absurd opposites or extreme opposites."[50] This attraction between polarities underlies both the eroticism and the conscious humor of Hesse's work. In *Untitled* ("Wall Piece") of 1970 [figs. 10.30 and 10.31] the four fiberglass boxes with tenuous strings dangling out clearly set an overall order. Yet the endearingly anthropomorphic eccentricity of each unit mocks the rigor of a serial regularity.

In early April 1969 Hesse collapsed from a brain tumor and underwent three operations before dying in May 1970 at the age of thirty-four. The fact that she had already developed a system of working with assistants made it possible for her to continue working right to the end, and indeed she produced her greatest work in that final year. *Untitled (Rope Piece)* of 1970 [fig. 10.32] undermines the notions of fixed form and scale. As with the gestural field of a Pollock, the detail in this work pulls the viewer in, yet disorients him or her with its unfamiliarity of material and form. "I wanted to totally throw myself into a vision that I would have to adjust to and learn to understand," she said. ". . . I want to extend my art perhaps into something that doesn't exist yet."[51]

BRUCE NAUMAN AND RICHARD SERRA

Bruce Nauman

Bruce Nauman's art is introverted without being psychological in the sense of Hesse's, and although he has focused on the literal presence of each work it may not necessarily yield an object at all. Nauman's curiosity about the nature of immediate experience—embodied in a unique style of

questioning—is what unifies his work. By 1965 it was already clear to Nauman that whereas minimalists like Judd wanted to be in control, he wanted precisely not to be—he was bent on the experience of discovery. Nauman said that as often as not "I was using my body as a piece of material and manipulating it. I think of it as going into the studio and being involved in some activity. Sometimes it works out that the activity involves making something, and sometimes the activity itself is the piece."[52]

Nauman's earliest surviving sculptures date from 1965 [fig. 10.33], made during his two years as a graduate student in art at the University of California at Davis. The eleven crudely finished fiberglass abstractions of 1965 announce Nauman's fully developed artistic character. Their forms relate to the body positions and gestures of the rudimentary performances that Nauman inaugurated that year; at the same time they emphasize the literal process of their fabrication, attacking any notion of transcendence.

10.33 Bruce Nauman, *Untitled*, 1965. Fiberglass, 96 × 5 × 10in (243.8 × 12.7 × 25.4cm). Courtesy Leo Castelli Gallery, New York.

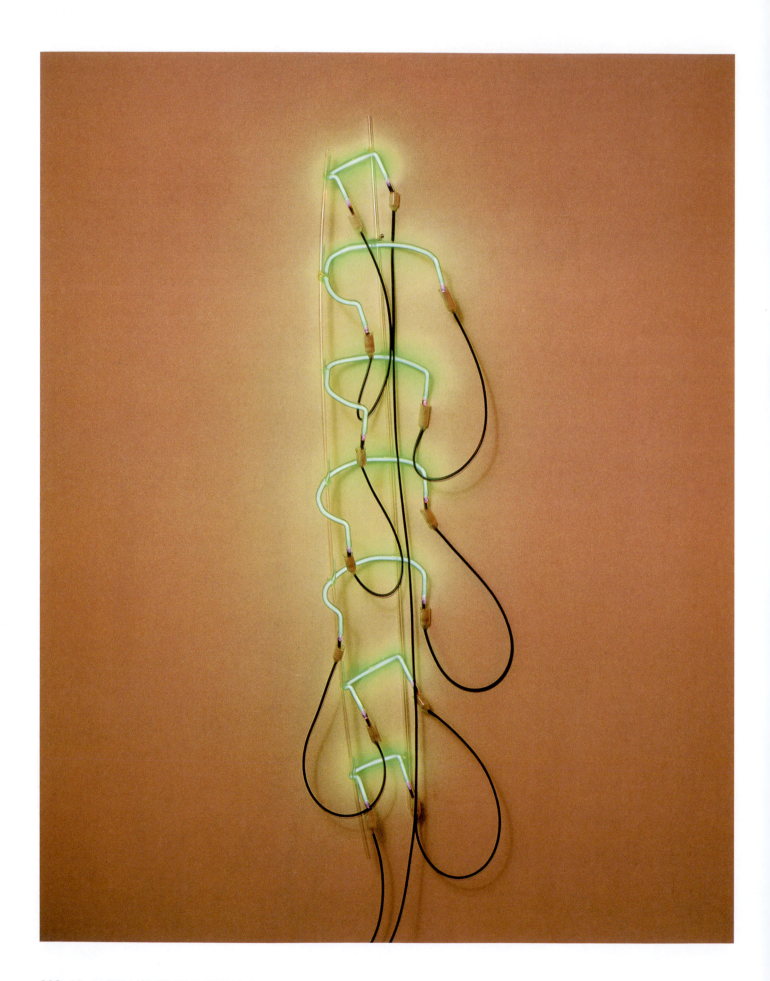

10.34 (opposite) **Bruce Nauman**, *Neon Templates of the Left Half of My Body, Taken at Ten-Inch Intervals*, 1966. Neon tubing on clear glass tubing frame, 70 × 9 × 6in (177.8 × 22.9 × 15.2cm). Collection, Philip Johnson. Courtesy Leo Castelli Gallery, New York.

These fiberglass pieces involved making a cast, then throwing away the object and constructing the sculpture from the hollowed halves of the mold. The lack of finish avoids a sense of preciousness or finality to the object, emphasizing instead an ongoing investigative process. Nauman set up tasks for himself "just to see what would happen."[53] In order "to find things out," he said, he would do "things that you don't particularly want to do . . . putting yourself in unfamiliar situations, following resistances to find out why you're resisting, like therapy."[54] He did anti-form pieces in latex and began making works in neon during 1965 and 1966. The pieces related in specific ways either to his body or to the spaces that it occupied. *Neon Templates of the Left Half of My Body, Taken at Ten-Inch Intervals* [fig. 10.34] precisely conveys the process of its origin in the title. Yet as Brenda Richardson pointed out, even the tubing, cords, and transformer have the elegance of an abstract expressionist drawing.[55]

In the fall of 1966, after Nauman finished his master's at Davis, he took a storefront studio in San Francisco. He described himself as having "the normal artist's paranoia . . . kind of cut off, just not knowing how to proceed at being an artist."[56] He made some performance pieces and films and then, in the late fall, saw a Man Ray retrospective in Los Angeles that prompted a series of photographic self-parodies, including *Self-Portrait as a Fountain* [fig. 10.35]. Although Arneson has said that Nauman "was already an artist" when he arrived at Davis,[57] the unflinching, ethical self-scrutiny of Arneson's work has an echo in the integrity of Nauman's self-examination and Nauman also shares with both Arneson and Wiley (two of his teachers at Davis) a passion for the kind of provocatively witty enigmas and word-plays transformed into visual puns that underlie *Self-Portrait as a Fountain*.

10.35 Bruce Nauman, *Self-Portrait as a Fountain*, 1966–7. Color photograph, 19⅞ × 23¾in (55.5 × 60.3cm). From eleven color photographs of 1970, edition of eight. Courtesy Sperone Westwater Gallery, New York.

Nauman read Wittgenstein's *Philosophical Investigations* in 1966 and the philosopher's examination of contradictory and nonsensical arguments that pushed logic to irrational extremes intrigued him. In his neons of 1967 Nauman began exploring semiotics and verbal propositions like "The true artist helps the world by revealing mystic truths," a sentence that spirals out in neon letters from the center in *Window or Wall Sign*. "It was a kind of test—like when you say something out loud to see if you believe it," Nauman explained. "[It] was on the one hand a totally silly idea and yet, on the other hand, I believed it."[58]

During the following year Nauman met the performance artist Meredith Monk in San Francisco. They talked about the work of Cage and Cunningham, and Nauman began to think of the simple task-oriented actions in his performance pieces as related to dance. He was also impressed with the new music of La Monte Young, Steve Reich, Philip Glass, and Terry Riley, and their work as well as Monk's inspired him to work more with sound. In his *Separate Touch and Sound* (1969) Nauman hid a microphone behind a wall

to pick up the friction of the viewer touching the surface. Speakers hidden in another wall, some 40 feet away, broadcast the sound, creating a time lag. The idea was to push the viewer into confronting him- or herself in the space. In the various video corridors that Nauman constructed between 1968 and 1970, he involved the viewer more actively in the work, enticing him or her to enter the space and then playing the viewer's image back on a video monitor.

In the seventies and eighties Nauman shifted to more overtly social and political concerns. In a disquieting installation of 1972 entitled *Get Out of My Mind Get Out of This Room* a tape with this message permeated the space, seemingly from all directions at once. Jacopo Timermans's accounts of his political imprisonment and torture as a political dissident in Argentina inspired a powerful series of sculptures built around empty chairs suspended by wires in a timeless isolation, cordoned off by raw steel girders. The theme of *Mean Clown*, a video installation, is of malevolence and libido under the sexless clown's traditionally happy façade. Yet on one level the anger, the frustration, the repetitive reworking,

10.36 Richard Tuttle, *Canvas Dark Blue*, 1967. Dyed and shaped unstretched canvas, 70 × 35⅞in (178 × 90cm). Courtesy Sperone Westwater Gallery, New York.

even the sense of entrapment and then exhilarating freedom in Nauman's works of this period are all aspects of the creative act itself. Josef Beuys asserted that everyone is an artist in the creative act of living. Nauman's work embodies the assertion that only in the creative act is one fully alive.

Richard Tuttle

Richard Tuttle's work is also very much engaged with the immediate experience of living. What might seem almost too subtle a detail for most people to even notice can engage him completely, like a Zen monk wrapped in the contemplation of a blade of grass. For many people walking into the Whitney Museum's Tuttle exhibition in 1975, it took a moment even to find some of the work. There was a tiny yellow triangle painted at the base of a large gallery wall, for example, and a square of fine wire wrapped around four nails—one could barely see it. *Canvas Dark Blue* of 1967 [fig. 10.36] seems so deceptively simple: after all, it is only a faded rectangle of wrinkled blue fabric with a hole cut in the middle. Well, it isn't quite a rectangle; there is a notch in the side, and the top and bottom edges are slightly curved.

Actually, the curve on the bottom comes to a point and the edges are hemmed. There seem to be so many little things that make it more complicated to describe than you think at first. Tuttle makes things that are so refreshingly simple that they leave you in a state of heightened sensitivity, noticing nuances everywhere you go for some time to come.

Richard Serra

Like Nauman and Tuttle, Richard Serra reconceived the anti-illusionism of minimal art as an aesthetic of direct physical experience. He concentrates on palpable qualities of the materials and on the improvisational process of making sculpture. "The significance of the work," he said, "is in its effort not in its intentions. And that effort is a state of mind, an activity, an interaction with the world."[59]

10.37 Richard Serra, *Belts*, 1966–7. Eleven vulcanized rubber belts and neon tubing, 6ft × 2ft × 20in (182.9 × 76.2 × 50.8cm). Solomon R. Guggenheim Museum, New York. Panza Collection, 1991, 91.3863. Photograph by Peter Moore, courtesy Leo Castelli Gallery, New York.

10.38 Keith Sonnier, *MM (Neon Wrapping Light Bulbs)*, 1968. Incandescent bulbs with porcelain fixtures wrapped in neon tubing, 45 × 40 × 12in (114.3 × 101.6 × 30.5cm).
Courtesy Leo Castelli Gallery, New York.

10.39 Richard Serra throwing lead, Castelli Warehouse, New York, 1969.
Photograph by Gianfranco Gorgoni.

10.40 Richard Serra, *Splashing*, 1968. Lead, 18 × 312in (45.7 × 792.5cm).
Installed Castelli Warehouse, New York, 1968, destroyed. Courtesy Leo Castelli Gallery, New York.

Serra derived the form for *Belts* [fig. 10.37] from, on the one hand, the intrinsic character of the vulcanized rubber strips (particularly as expressed in their response to gravity) and, on the other, from minimalist ideas of serial repetition, indeterminate form, and of creating a continuum with the real world of industrial or commercial materials. The neon contrasts so strikingly with the flaccid strips of rubber that the two materials each help to bring out a vivid sense of the physical nature of the other. As in Hesse's work, Serra's rubber and neon pieces project a moving personal presence, though the artist has always been reticent about this aspect of his work.

Serra did several neon and rubber works late in 1966 and early 1967, perhaps inspired by Nauman, whom he met when he moved to New York in 1966. Within two years Nauman's neons had become entirely concerned with writing and signage, and Serra had abandoned the medium altogether for more direct processes. However, several artists continued to work with neon, notably the Italian Mario Merz [figs. 10.55 and 10.56] and Keith Sonnier, a New Yorker whose poetic abstractions in a mixture of materials centering on incandescent fixtures and freely bent neon tubes celebrated the new formal freedom of the late sixties [fig. 10.38].

At about this time Serra made himself a now-celebrated list of verbs denoting activities one could undertake in relation to sculpture.[60] "To splash" is about a quarter of the way down the column and is the motive for his 1968 piece *Splashing* [figs. 10.39 and 10.40], in which Serra threw molten lead against the wall in Castelli's Upper West Side warehouse. *Splashing* literally splattered up and out from the angle where the floor and wall met, adhering fast to both surfaces; it could not be moved without completely destroying it. Other versions were made, including one in the studio of Jasper Johns, and occasionally the artist has repeated the process for retrospective exhibitions.

In works of 1969 the artist simply distributed the materials on the floor, emphasizing their literal weight and character. Similarly, Serra's drawing style—densely applied build-ups of thick oil crayon—highlights the physical process. Serra's propped lead pieces from 1968 and 1969 rivet the viewer's attention on the physical weight of the material and its manner of disposition in the space even more compellingly. In *One Ton Prop (House of Cards)* (1969) he leaned four 500-pound lead sheets into one another like a house of cards. In *Corner Prop* [fig. 10.41] he leaned a 2-foot cube of lead, balanced 6½ feet up in the air, between the wall and a soft lead pipe which holds the weight from below. The work is not fastened in any way, despite its weight. It seems—and is—dangerous.

"There is a difference between definite literal fixed relationships, i.e., joints, clips, gluing, welding, etc.," he noted in 1970, "and those which are provisional, non-fixed, 'clastic.' The former seem unnecessary and irrelevant and tend to function as interposed elements." So in works such as these propped lead pieces he has eliminated any such imposition that might falsify the impression of the real balance and

10.41 Richard Serra, *Corner Prop*, 1969. Lead antimony, box 25 × 25 × 25in (63.5 × 63.5 × 63.5cm), pole 6ft 8in (2.03m). Gilman Paper Company Collection, New York. Photograph by Peter Moore, courtesy Leo Castelli Gallery, New York.

weight of the materials. By way of analogy he went on to remark: "A shift in interest in recent films is from subject matter, qua literature which utilizes a narrative time, to that of those films in which time can be equated with 'live time' or with procedural time: the time of the film in its making."[61]

Films of the late sixties, such as Warhol's *Empire* (which focuses fixedly on a still object, the Empire State Building, for eight hours) or Yvonne Rainer's *Hand Movie*, which merely shows her hand as she does finger exercises, inspired Serra's own foray into films. His *Hand Catching Lead* (1968) shows a block of lead dropping through the frame as his hand attempts to catch it. Here too the emphasis is on an action in real time. Serra has denied the existence of any kind of expressionism in his work: "My works do not signify any esoteric self-referentiality. Their construction leads you into their structure and does not refer to the artist's persona."[62] And yet in his best work, like the prop pieces and *Splashing*, Serra achieves a threatening presence.

10.42 Richard Serra, *Tilted Arc*, 1981. Cor-Ten steel, 12ft × 120ft × 2½in (3.66 × 36.58 × 0.06m).

Installed Federal Plaza, New York. General Services Administration, Washington, D.C. Photograph by Glenn Steigelman, Inc., courtesy Leo Castelli Gallery, New York.

In the seventies Serra began using hot rolled steel, which allowed him to increase the scale. The work is tough; there is a defensive brutality to the reduction. Serra's best outdoor pieces also force themselves uncomfortably on the viewer. Their high steel walls loom over the viewer, dictating the paths of movement among and around them; they feel frightening, even dangerous, as though the massive walls of steel might crush you. It is a painfully backhanded compliment that in the notorious case of his *Tilted Arc* [fig. 10.42] this disturbing quality ultimately caused the Federal Government, which had commissioned the piece, to have it removed from Federal Plaza in New York. As it was a site-specific work (namely one designed and scaled precisely to this location) removing it destroyed it. In the nineties Serra embarked on a group of "Torqued Ellipses" into which the viewer walks, enclosed in rusted Cor-Ten steel walls looking up to the open sky above. These works exploit the frightening sense of crushing weight and enclosure to evoke a powerful sense of the openness of the sky, like the simultaneous freedom and vulnerability one feels in the vast landscapes of the American West.

ARTISTS WORKING IN THE LANDSCAPE

Michael Heizer

The issue of site-specificity and the evocation of the vastness of the western landscape reached their most dramatic expression in the work of Michael Heizer, who pioneered the new genre of site-specific art (art that defines itself in its precise interaction with the particular place for which it was conceived). Heizer had come from a family of geologists and archaeologists and grew up in Northern California and Nevada where he developed a great affinity for the landscape of the West. In 1966, at the age of twenty-one, he came to New York for a year and a half and then went out to the Nevada desert to begin doing "dirtwork"[63] projects. He began with temporary works such as trenches, "drawing" with his motorcycle tracks, and dispersals of pigment and soil. In *Displaced–Replaced Mass* of 1969 [fig. 10.43] Heizer transported three 30- to 68-ton granite boulders a distance of 60 miles from the High Sierras down to the Nevada desert and placed them in cement-walled depressions that he had cut into the ground. The work had to do with exploring the large forces of nature—bringing rocks from the Sierras back down to their original elevation in the desert reversed the mountain building processes of geological evolution.

Later in 1969 Heizer disappeared into the desert again, procured another site, earthmoving equipment, and a crew,

10.43 Michael Heizer, *Displaced–Replaced Mass, #1/3*, 1969. Granite and concrete in playa surface, 100ft × 800ft × 9ft 6in (30.48 × 243.84 × 2.89m). Silver Springs, Nevada (dismantled). Commissioned by Robert Scull.

10.44 Michael Heizer, *Double Negative*, 1969–70. 240,000-ton displacement in rhyolite and sandstone, 1,500 × 50 × 30ft (457.2 × 15.24 × 9.14m). Mormon Mesa, Overton, Nevada.

and at the end of the year returned to New York with photographs of an even more massive site-specific work called *Double Negative* [fig. 10.44]. He had gouged 240,000 tons of rhyolite and sandstone out of the landscape of the Virgin River Mesa in Nevada to create a huge excavation 30 feet wide, 50 feet top to bottom, and 1,500 feet long. A small canyon intersects this cut in the landscape, splitting it into two sections of a straight line facing each other across the gap.

Heizer's line in the desert recalls Newman's Genetic moment (see page 101)—an existential assertion of man's place in the chaos. "In the desert," Heizer explained, "I can find that kind of unraped peaceful religious space artists have always tried to put in their work."[64] Heizer's desert works attack the idea of art as a portable object. Instead, they are about space and an experience of the landscape, of geologic time and of the ancient past. If they echoed the radical political climate of the late sixties by rejecting the established institutions of museum and gallery (making work which they could neither exhibit nor sell); this too was a by-product rather than the central focus of his project. In 1969 Heizer

wrote in a rough-edged, telegraphic prose: "the position art as malleable barter-exchange item falters as the cumulative economic structure gluts. The museums and collections are stuffed, the floors are sagging, but the real space still exists."[65]

Walter De Maria

Walter De Maria and Heizer shared an interest in the western landscape, but De Maria's work was consistently more concerned with systems of ordering and measurement rather than with geological time and the experience of the landscape itself. In 1968, perhaps stirred by Heizer's work in the open land, De Maria filled the Heiner Friedrich Gallery in Munich with 3 feet of dirt. Eventually, he re-created this *Earth Room* as a permanent installation on the second floor of a New York loft owned by the Dia Art Foundation. *The New York Earth Room* of 1977 [fig. 10.45] consists of 250 cubic yards of black soil, 22 inches deep. It covers the floor of a 3,600-square-foot loft and weighs 280,000 pounds. The presence of the work is critical—one cannot successfully reproduce it in pictures or by description. As visitors ascend the stairs they slowly begin to feel the moisture and smell the rich humus. The soil also has a distinctive effect on the sounds in the space.

10.45 (left) **Walter De Maria**, *The New York Earth Room*, 1977. 250cu. yd (191.25cu. m) of black soil in a 3,600sq. ft (334.44sq. m) loft. Long-term installation at Dia Art Foundation, New York.

10.46 (below) **Walter De Maria**, *The Lightning Field*, 1977. Stainless steel poles, average height 20ft 7½in (6.29m), overall 5,280 × 3,300ft (1,609.34 × 1,005.84m). Near Quemado, New Mexico. Dia Art Foundation, New York.

The *Earth Room* evokes a romantic apprehension of landscape in an enclosed urban space—which is antithetical to the experience of nature. In this sense it relates to Serra's disposition of his materials in ways that test their natural weight or strength, a practice that both relies on and brings out an acute sensitivity to the nature of the materials. But the *Earth Room* also reflects the influence of John Cage in the way it emphasizes the ambient experience over the expression of the artist's personality and creates an interesting discourse with the pop art disjunction of image and experience.

De Maria had come to New York in 1960, gotten involved with the Judson dancers and Fluxus, played drums with the rock group Velvet Underground in 1964, and in 1968 began working with specific sites using real landscape as an artistic material. Heizer, De Maria, and (in his late, large-scale earthworks) Robert Smithson all sited their most important work in remote areas of the southwestern desert, making it as literally inaccessible as it was difficult conceptually. Indeed, the pilgrimage through the lost landscape to the site was an important aspect of the experience of the work. John Weber, then director of the Dwan Gallery, once took a collector out to see De Maria's 1969 *Las Vegas* piece and could not even find it. By setting the work so far out in the middle of nowhere, the artists made visitors to these works feel acutely vulnerable to the elements. If your car broke down, Weber later remarked, you might die of dehydration before anyone could find you.[66]

De Maria's *Lightning Field* [fig. 10.46] sits in a flat, semi-arid basin of southern New Mexico with awe-inspiring vistas of distant mountains all around. Here the artist constructed a 1 mile-by-1 kilometer grid of 400 stainless steel poles, arranged in sixteen rows of twenty-five, 220 feet apart. The 2-inch diameter poles have an average height of 20 feet 7½ inches and they are set so that the tops all terminate on a unified, level plane whatever the variations in the terrain. When they are viewed from a distance the bleaching sun makes the grid nearly invisible except in the reflected light of dawn and dusk. The desolate beauty of the site seems to exist beyond time, with the power of nature brought home most dramatically by the play of lightning in the sky behind the grid.

Robert Smithson

Where Heizer is in romantic communication with nature and De Maria engaged in a cerebral encounter with it, Robert Smithson explored the sublimity of nature with a darker, more melodramatic tone. Questions of personal identity, struggles of good and evil, and Catholic mysticism figured importantly in his abstract expressionist beginnings, but science fiction and geology provided the vocabulary for him to move beyond those issues by 1964. Smithson's interest in crystals in particular allowed him to begin dealing with nature without the biological metaphor.[67]

In a 1966 essay called "Entropy and the New Monuments,"[68] Smithson expanded upon the Second Law of Thermodynamics—the idea that energy dissipates toward a disintegrated homogeneity of matter. Entropy negates the concept of progress on the scale of geological time. Consequently, Smithson regarded monuments to disintegration as the most valid form of art and attacked the idea of an art centered on human beings.

An interview with Tony Smith, published by *Artforum* in 1966, acted as a catalyst for Smithson's idea of the entropic monument as realized in manmade sites. Smith said an experience of driving at night on an unfinished section of the New Jersey turnpike had opened his eyes to the aesthetic possibilities of an "artificial landscape without cultural precedent." For Smith, "this drive . . . couldn't be called a work of art. On the other hand, it did something for me that art had never done . . . It seemed that there had been a reality there that had not had any expression in art . . . Most painting looks pretty pictorial after that."[69]

Smithson began making regular trips to abandoned industrial sites and quarries in New Jersey during 1966, and the following year he wrote about them in an article for *Artforum* called "Tour of the Monuments of Passaic." Smith's remarks had encouraged Smithson to think about the manmade environment as part of nature, and he developed a morbid aesthetic based on an appreciation of sludge heaps, tailings ponds, and the ubiquitous commercial strips of American suburbia. This apotheosis of the ordinary had something in common with the assimilationist aesthetic of Oldenburg and Rauschenberg and the non-hierarchical appreciation for American vernacular in pop art, except for Smithson's profoundly pessimistic emphasis on the irreversible destruction of the universe. John Cage's suppression of self-expression and his abrogation of control came full circle with Smithson, who determined that man's willful acts were minor events in this larger trend toward cosmic disintegration.

Smithson conceived the idea of his "Nonsites" in 1967 [fig. 10.47]. These consisted of topographical maps or aerial photographs of a particular site mounted on the wall with earth, rocks, or gravel from the actual place in trapezoidal bins on the floor. The bins looked like minimal sculpture and typically echoed the shape of the map or the plot of land. Smithson described the "Nonsites" as a "dialog . . . between indoors and outdoors . . . The site, in a sense, is the physical, raw reality—the earth or the ground that we are really not aware of when we are in an interior room . . . [whereas] the Nonsite . . . is an abstract container."[70]

10.47 (opposite) **Robert Smithson**, *A Nonsite (Franklin, N.J.)*, 1968. Two parts: five painted wooden bins and limestone; gelatin silver prints and typescript on paper with graphite and transfer letters, mounted on mat framed sheet. Bins installed: 16½ × 82¼ × 103in (41.9 × 208.9 × 261.6cm), board: 40¾ × 30¾in (103.5 × 78.1cm). Museum of Contemporary Art, Chicago. Gift of Susan and Lewis Manilow.

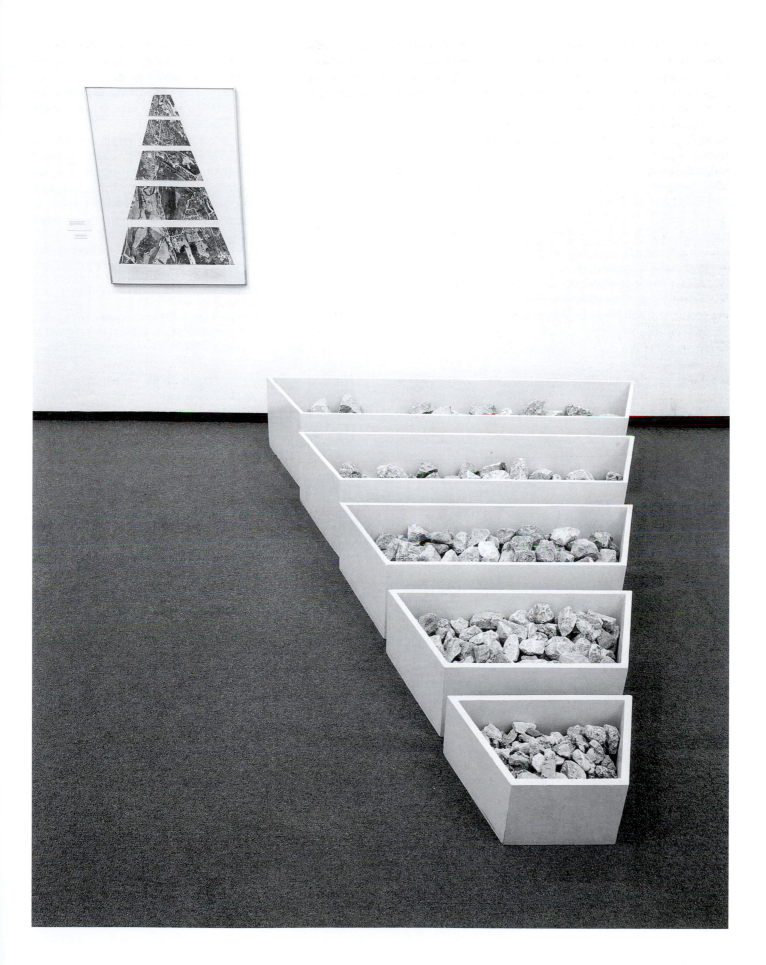

On the most direct level Smithson's "Nonsites" concern space, mental projection, mapping, and the gap between the reality of a site and its representation. Standing in a site, one recognizes the material from the "Nonsite" but one cannot see from where it was extracted. In this way it subverts one's sense of boundaries and definition. Smithson used the metaphor of the enantiomorph—a pair of crystals that are mirror images of one another—to describe the relation of his "Nonsites" to the actual sites. The "Dialectic of Site and Nonsite," as he elaborated it, consists of a series of inversions such as: open limits versus closed limits, subtraction (from the site) versus addition (to the "Nonsite"), indeterminate certainty versus the determinate uncertainty (of the "Nonsite"), some place (physical) versus no place (abstract).[71]

In the mirror and salt pieces, such as *Rock Salt and Mirror Square* [fig. 10.48] from the "Cayuga Salt Mine Project," the salt gradually dissipates with exposure to the air, conveying the hopelessness of ordering something that will ultimately disorganize itself into randomness. The mirrors involve a minimalist concern with measurement, in effect mapping the

forms by reproducing them in reflection. In addition to the spatial displacement of images in the mirrors, these works involve the displacement of the salt from the earth to the gallery, and a metaphorical displacement of Smithson's formal concept for the "Nonsite" by surrounding the geometrically fixed forms of the mirrors with the amorphous piles of salt instead of containing the salt in rigid bins. Yet on a molecular level the salt, which appears random, has a clearly defined crystalline structure while the overtly regular glass mirrors are actually in a liquid state, creating one more conceptual displacement within the work.[72] This compounding series of displacements within the piece keeps repeating the same structural principle, as in the growth of a crystal.

In another series of 1969 Smithson poured flows of viscous material, such as glue, cement, and asphalt. These works

10.48 Robert Smithson, *Rock Salt and Mirror Square*, 1969.
Rock salt and mirrors, 10 × 78 × 78in (25.4 × 198.1 × 198.1cm).
Courtesy John Weber Gallery, New York.

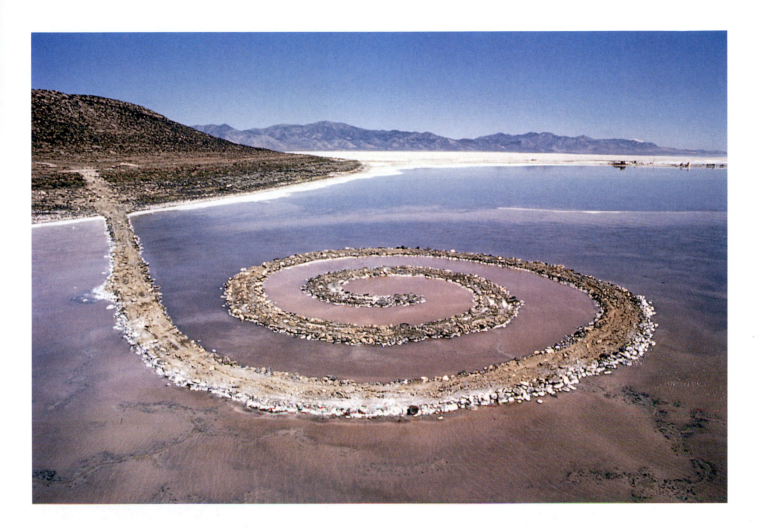

10.49 Robert Smithson, *Spiral Jetty*, April 1970. Black basalt, limestone rocks, and earth, length 1,500ft (457.2m). Great Salt Lake, Utah.

Photograph by Gianfranco Gorgoni, courtesy John Weber Gallery, New York.

took place in locations which few viewers would witness firsthand and, recognizing that his work would largely be seen in photographs or experienced through his increasingly influential essays written between 1966 and 1973, Smithson exaggerated this effect of displacing the museum or gallery with the art journals.

In April 1970 Smithson began constructing his best-known work, the *Spiral Jetty* [fig. 10.49], in an abandoned industrial site on a remote corner of the Great Salt Lake in Utah. Virtually no one ever saw the work in actuality before it was destroyed by the natural fluctuations in the lake, but it was widely viewed in the art press and Smithson carefully framed the *Jetty* to seem much larger in photographs than it actually was. In an eponymous film of *Sprial Jetty*, Smithson cleverly used the possibilities of cinematic time and space to set the work in the context of its underlying ideas. The film opens with an overlay of the site on a map of the geography of the Jurassic Period, contrasting the precise calculations of the map with geologic time, in which whole continents appear and disappear.

Eugenie Tsai has pointed out that Smithson's entropic landscapes took inspiration not only from science writing but from the desolate landscapes of science fiction.[73] In the case of *Spiral Jetty* the site attracted Smithson precisely because it seemed like a strange, futuristic wasteland. The microorganisms in the water colored it an eerie red and the shoreline was littered with abandoned earthmoving machinery and vehicles from the time when it was used by the military in World War II as a gunnery range. Smithson noted that "a great pleasure arose from seeing all those incoherent structures. This site gave evidence of a succession of man-made systems mired in abandoned hopes."[74]

Here, the artist bulldozed 6,650 tons of material into a coil of rocks and earth 1,500 feet long and 15 feet wide, swirling out into the water. Salt crystals precipitated all around the edges of the jetty and, Smithson noted, "each cubic salt crystal echoes the Spiral Jetty in terms of the crystal's molecular lattice."[75] The "matter collapsing into the lake" was also "mirrored in the shape of the spiral,"[76] according to the artist, as was the giant mythological whirlpool in the middle of the lake under which, legend had it, a channel existed to the ocean.

Smithson died in 1973 in a plane crash while making an aerial survey of a site in Texas. His last work centered on (unrealized) proposals for reclaiming abandoned industrial sites as entropic monuments (parks structured according to his aesthetic of disintegration). In 1971 he transformed an exhausted sand quarry in Emmen, Holland, building a black, cone-shaped hill with a white sand path spiraling up it and describing a broken circle, 140 feet in diameter, with a 12-foot-wide, semicircular canal and a half-circle jetty. This work, called *Spiral Hill and Broken Circle*, suggests a romantic exaltation in the morbidity of man's industrial processes laying waste to the earth. Even the underlying contradictions of Smithson's attempt to order the world while simultaneously acknowledging its inevitable tendency toward entropic disorder express his aesthetic of existential hopelessness. "A bleached and fractured world surrounds the artist," he wrote. "To organize this mess of corrosion into patterns, grids, and subdivisions is an esthetic process that has scarcely been touched."[77]

An Accidental Rubric

The works of Heizer and the large outdoor projects of De Maria and Smithson have in common their allusion to geologic time and prehistory. In addition, these artists all relate to minimalism in their concern with the literal presence of the materials and in the extent to which they derived their works from preconceived systemic ideas. All saw associations with the sublime in the frightening vastness and desolation of the American West. They even played up the ethos of virility celebrated in myths of the West—De Maria's movie *Hardcore* (filmed in the desert with Heizer in 1969) tellingly opens with cowboy music, horses, and the imagery of the range hand and the harsh roar of the desert wind.

In 1968 Heizer took Smithson out to the western desert to work on the former's *Isolated Mass/Circumflex*. Inspired by the experience of the desert landscape, Smithson organized an exhibition at the Dwan Gallery in New York in October 1968 called "Earthworks," a title that has ever since linked these fundamentally different artists. Walter De Maria's contribution to the exhibition was an expansive (20-foot-wide), chrome-yellow painting with a brass plate embedded in the center, bearing the inscription "the color men choose when they attack the land." The show also included Smithson's *Nonsite, Franklin, New Jersey*, a 6-foot-high, backlit transparency of a vast tract of the Nevada desert where Heizer had dug a series of trenches in the earth, and works by several friends experimenting with site-specific ideas, including Carl Andre, Herbert Beyer, Steven Kaltenbach, Sol LeWitt, Robert Morris, Claes Oldenburg, and Dennis Oppenheim [fig. 10.50].

Yet whatever Smithson, De Maria, and Heizer may have had in common, only Heizer was centrally concerned with the experience of the site and its real geological matter. "Anything is only part where it is," he insisted.[78] Moreover, Heizer's earthworks were too big to be seen at once like a

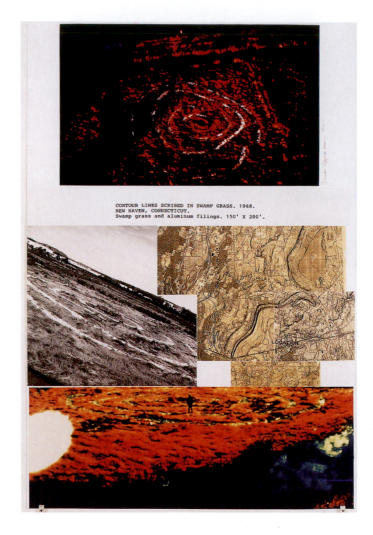

10.50 Dennis Oppenheim, *Contour Lines Inscribed in Swamp Grass*, 1968, New Haven, Connecticut. Inscribed with the title and "swamp grass and aluminum filings," 150 × 200ft (45.72 × 60.96m). Black-and-white and color photographs, handstamped collage map dry-mounted on rag board, 4ft 11in × 3ft 3⅛in (1.50 × 1.00m). Collection Fundação de Serralves, Oporto. Photograph courtesy Fundação de Serralves.

sculpture, whereas *Spiral Jetty* and *The Lightning Field* do have defining gestalts. Indeed, Heizer's work centers on the idea of sculpture as place rather than object, invoking the precedents not only of Barnett Newman but of such prehistoric sites as the Great Serpent Mound constructed by the Hopewell culture of the ancient Ohio Valley.

ARTE POVERA AND A PERSEVERING RAPPORT WITH NATURE IN EUROPE

As in the rest of Europe and North America, the late sixties was a period of social upheaval in Italy. The unbroken power of the Christian Democrats over the twenty-five years since World War II had led to massive corruption and inefficiency as well as the imposition of repressive public policies tailored to suit big business interests and conservative Catholic mores. The workers' revolution of 1968 began in the universities, but the government's insensitivity to widespread poverty—especially in the less industrialized South—resulted in massive migrations northward and a climate of instability and disaffection. This lasted to the end of the seventies, culminating in the abduction and murder of Prime Minister Aldo Moro by the leftist Red Brigades in 1979.

Artists took a radical stance at the end of the sixties too, attacking the values of established institutions of government, industry, and culture and even questioning whether art as the private expression of the individual still had an ethical reason to exist. The critic Germano Celant organized two exhibitions in 1967 and 1968, followed by an influential book called *Arte Povera*, promoting the notion of a revolutionary art, free of convention, the power structure, and the marketplace. Although Celant attempted to encompass the radical elements of the entire international scene, the term properly centered on a group of Italian artists[79] who attacked the corporate mentality with an art of unconventional materials and style.

Michelangelo Pistoletto began painting on mirrors in 1962, connecting painting with the constantly changing realities in which the work finds itself. In the later sixties he began bringing together rags with casts of the omnipresent classical statuary of Italy to break down the hierarchies of "art" and common things. An art of impoverished materials is certainly one aspect of the definition of *arte povera*. In his 1967 *Rag Wall* [fig. 10.51] Pistoletto makes an exotic and opulent tapestry wrapping common bricks in discarded scraps of fabric.

Building on the work of Burri, Fontana, and Manzoni, artists such as Jannis Kounellis and Mario Merz attempted to make the experience of art more immediately real while also more closely connecting the individual to nature. In 1969 Kounellis tethered eleven live horses to the walls of the Galleria L'Attico in Rome, lined up equidistantly like paintings [fig. 10.52]. He implied in this exhibition that a

10.51 Michelangelo Pistoletto, *Muretto di stracci (Rag Wall)*, 1967. Fabric-covered bricks, dimensions variable.

Collection Fundação de Serralves, Oporto. Photograph courtesy Sperone Westwater Gallery, New York.

work of art is not transcendent but rather just like any other form of life: an identity that contains an idea.

Kounellis often incorporated fire into his works, along with the scorch marks and the apparatus of the process [fig. 10.53]. "Fire, in medieval legend," he explained, "goes with punishment and purification."[80] It suggests the entropic dissolution of matter which is, perhaps, the final form of purification. Gilberto Zorio, another *arte povera* sculptor, also invokes alchemical allusions with evaporating alcohol or acid in glass crucibles or with other unusual materials that often remain visible only faintly and by implication, as with the traces of chartreuse left by the evaporated liquid in *Serpentine* [fig. 10.54].

10.52 Jannis Kounellis, *Cavalli*, shown at the Galleria L'Attico, Rome, 1969.

10.53 Jannis Kounellis, *Untitled*, 1984. Steel, iron, and wood,
9ft 8in × 18ft (2.95 × 5.5m).

Kunstmuseum, Düsseldorf.

The work of Mario Merz [figs. 10.55 and 10.56] brings about a fusion of natural elements with fragments of urban society in a way that also seems to suggest the idea of nature overwhelming culture from within. For Merz, the artist is like a nomad using humble materials from everyday life, both from culture and from the organic world, mediating between the two. Merz began making his "Igloos" in 1968, covering segmented metal armatures in nets, wax, mud, glass, and bundles of twigs. These small hemispherical dwellings use the materials indigenous to the sites at which the exhibitions take place; Merz thus creates a hypothetical artist who is at home everywhere. The "Igloo" is architecture, shelter, and an abstract idea associated with the nomad. It is a skin that embodies the receptivity of the artist to nature and to culture.

Merz described his working method in this account of a drawing:

I had spent all day drawing that endlessly convoluted line, . . . following my thoughts and everything happening around me—for example, the twittering birds, the falling leaves, the distant rumble of a van. All these things entered the drawing not in a natural way, of course, but as time, as a recording, as if the pencil lead were the point of certain instruments registering on a sheet of paper.[81]

Merz often used neon to inscribe political and literary references in his installations, as in *Giap Igloo* [fig. 10.55], named after a North Vietnamese general and bearing his maxim: "If the enemy masses his forces, he loses ground; if he scatters, he loses strength." The recurring stuffed iguanas and alligators in Merz's installations evoke the primitive, prehistory, and geologic time balanced by the "reproduction of words and thoughts"[82] in the stacks of newspapers that also recur in Merz's work. In addition, many works include sequences of numbers illuminated in neon. These refer to the arithmetic progression discovered by a thirteenth-century monk known as Leonardo of Pisa, or Fibonacci.

The Fibonacci series—in which each number is the sum of the preceding two (1, 1, 2, 3, 5, 8, 13, 21, 34, and so on)—corresponds to the rate of simple growth in nature. As the number in the series increases, the ratio of each number to the last one approaches the "divine proportion," also known as the ratio of the "golden section." This is the ratio between two sides of a rectangle or two halves of a bisected

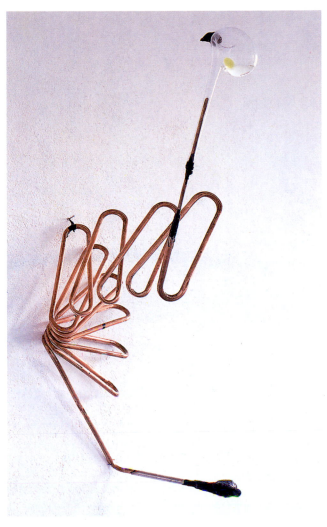

10.54 Gilberto Zorio, *Serpentine*, 1989. Copper, glass, wax, and alcohol, 63 × 32 × 48in (160 × 81.3 × 121.9cm). Collection of Anne and William J. Hokin, Chicago.

10.55 Mario Merz, *Giap Igloo*, 1968. Metal tubes, wire mesh, neon tubes, and dirt, 9ft 10⅛in (3m) diameter.

10.56 Mario Merz, *Double Igloo*, 1979 (showing *Alligator with Fibonacci Numbers to 377* on the ceiling). Outer structure: metal tubes, clamps, glass, and hat; inner structure: metal tubes, wire mesh, dried mud, neon tubes; 9ft 10in (3m) high × 19ft 8¼in (6m) diameter overall. Installation at Sperone Westwater Gallery, New York.

line such that the smaller side is to the larger as the larger is to the sum of the two. Fibonacci based his discovery on the reproductive rate of rabbits, but there are countless growth patterns in nature that correspond miraculously to the Fibonacci series and the golden ratio, including the rate of increase in the radius of the spiral cross-section of a nautilus shell, the growth of trees and leaves, the scales on an iguana's skin, deer antlers, and pine cones. For this reason the golden section has fascinated artists since ancient times. Merz incorporated many of these natural objects, as well as individual numbers from the Fibonacci series itself, into his work to refer to this arithmetic discovery. To Merz, the series symbolizes constant, open-ended change, infinity, and integration with nature. "This parabolic, deep breathing whole," he said, "is the real subject of art."[83]

The romantic tradition runs deeper in Europe than in the United States, and the relationship of European artists to nature has tended to be more profoundly spiritual. Richard Long and Hamish Fulton, who studied at St. Martin's School of Art in London, both independently introduced walking in nature as their principal medium. In 1967, while still a student, Long began treading paths in grass and arranging stones on a Somerset beach. For Long, the walk was the work of art, but for Fulton the walk was a reverent encounter with nature, and the photographs he took, together with the matter-of-fact texts framed with them [fig. 10.57], were the art. Fulton touched nothing and left no trace of his romantic rambles in nature beyond his footprint. Long also made photographic records of his incursions into nature, but unlike Fulton, he stopped to arrange stones or twigs into a pattern and then photographed the site.

Long also arranged materials he encountered on walks into geometrically composed collections on the floor in an

10.57 Hamish Fulton, *Grims Ditch* (ancient pathways, Hertfordshire), 1969–70. Photograph, 22⅝ × 37in (57.5 × 94cm). Collection Fundação de Serralves, Oporto. Courtesy John Weber Gallery, New York.

art gallery or museum [fig. 10.58]. These may consist of pieces of wood or stone quarried from a particular location in which Long walked, and sometimes he splashed mud from the site on the gallery wall or made handprints in it. From low to the ground or floor, the view across the circles or lines of stone even in the controlled space of the gallery evokes the vastness and sublime irregularity of the landscape itself. The precision of these installations in circles and lines laid down within a penciled circumference on the floor brings home the interaction of reason, in the Enlightenment sense, with raw nature and recalls the planned "randomness" of the eighteenth-century English garden.

10.58 Richard Long, *Red Slate Circle*, 1980. Red slate, 28ft (8.53m) diameter.

Solomon R. Guggenheim Museum, New York. Courtesy Sperone Westwater Gallery, New York.

11.1 Yayoi Kusama, *The Anatomic Explosion*, in front of the statue of George Washington across from the New York Stock Exchange (one of several sites around Manhattan), July 14, 1968.

Courtesy Gagosian Gallery New York/Ota Fine Arts, Tokyo.

11 POLITICS AND POSTMODERNISM

THE CRITICAL ATMOSPHERE AT THE END OF THE SIXTIES

As America left the uncomplicated innocence of sock-hops and Brylcreem for Bob Dylan and the burning of Detroit, art too assumed an increasingly political and critical tone in the latter half of the sixties. The escalating movement against the Vietnam War in particular caused heated debate that gave rise to a broad range of radical forces for change in virtually every aspect of American and West European culture. In art the self-consciously specialized focus in minimalist and process art on the literal presence of the materials and on the generative basis of a work, the excessive theorizing of formalist critics (largely on behalf of color-field painting), the emerging cross-currents of structuralist and post-structuralist theory from Europe, and the cool detachment of the painting of Jasper Johns and of pop art pointed many younger artists toward the idea of a purely "conceptual" form of art.

In addition, consumerism had careened out of control in the early sixties, and many artists reacted against that too. In the catalog for an exhibition matter-of-factly entitled "January 5–31, 1969," the conceptual artist Douglas Huebler noted: "The world is full of objects, more or less interesting: I do not wish to add any more."[1] The show, organized by Seth Sieglaub in New York, had a catalog, but no objects. In 1967 Terry Atkinson and Michael Baldwin, two artists from the English "Art+Language" group, held an "Air Show" by making a series of assertions about a theoretical column of air with a base of 1 square mile and an unspecified vertical dimension. No particular location was mentioned. Sol LeWitt defined his practice as a "conceptual art" that "is made to engage the mind of the viewer rather than his eye or emotions."[2]

What stood out was the sheer cacophony of all the different, often conflicting, voices in the art world. Postmodernism's embrace of simultaneously cross-tracking trajectories of ideas as the ground plane of cultural discourse had not yet been clearly articulated by 1970, even though many recognized what began to be called the "pluralism" of the seventies; for the most part, the art world was still looking for the next "leading movement" and the art market in particular had great difficulty with the widespread tendency that Lucy Lippard called the "dematerialization of the art object."[3] In addition to liberating art from the object, it seemed as though everybody wanted to liberate or be liberated in other ways too: First, just about everyone wanted to be liberated from the Vietnam War. Meanwhile, some artists wanted to liberate themselves from producing commodities, others wanted to be free of the convoluted language of contemporary art theory. In 1966 the English artist John Latham chewed up and spat out pages from Clement Greenberg's book *Art and Culture* in a visceral purge of formalist criticism.

John Baldessari wanted to rid himself of the clutter of old work in his studio, so he burned it, put the ashes behind a wall in a show at the Jewish Museum in New York, exhibited a label describing the deed, and then posted a notice of it in a San Diego newspaper. Finally, there were the ubiquitous liberations from inhibition, ranging from performance pieces such as Yayoi Kusama's *The Anatomic Explosion*, staged at various public sites around Manhattan in 1968 [fig. 11.1], to the August 1969 Woodstock Festival, where 450,000 rock-music devotees celebrated the peak of the youth counterculture in a field in upstate New York—many of them stoned, naked, and slathered in rain and mud.[4]

Language and Measure

Meanwhile, more and more artists began to write art theory in the sixties.[5] The effect on artists of the increasingly analytic atmosphere had already become apparent at the beginning of the decade. For example, the assertion by the Cambridge

11.2 (above) **Joseph Kosuth**, *One and Three Hammers (English Version)*, 1965. Hammer, photograph of a hammer, photostat of the definition of hammer, 24 × 53⅜in (61 × 135.6cm). Courtesy Leo Castelli Gallery, New York.

11.3 (left) **Walter De Maria**, *The Broken Kilometer*, 1979. 500 brass rods, 6ft 6¾in (2m) each, 45 × 125ft (13.71 × 38.1m) overall. Long-term installation at the Dia Art Foundation, New York.

philosopher Ludwig Wittgenstein that explanation obstructs one's perception of an object fed the minimalists' concern for the direct, literal experience of the material fact—Carl Andre quipped at the time that everyone had *The Blue and Brown Books* (Wittgenstein's published notes) in the bathroom! Wittgenstein's assertion also nurtured the personal detachment in the paintings of Jasper Johns after 1960.

Some conceptual artists (for whom there was frequently no object anyway) made explanation a work in its own right, as in Joseph Kosuth's "Art as Idea as Idea" (a title used by Kosuth for several works of the late sixties, including one consisting of a blow-up from the dictionary of the definition of the word "idea"). Kosuth examined verbal assumptions and definitions with disconcerting literalness. In *One and Three*

Hammers (English Version), for example [fig. 11.2], he juxtaposed three distinct but overlapping realities, with a hammer mounted on the wall next to a photograph of the hammer and a blow-up of a dictionary definition of a hammer. "The art I call conceptual," Kosuth wrote, "is . . . based on . . . *the understanding of the linguistic nature of all art propositions*."[6]

Amidst these hyperintellectual debates about theory, some artists of the late sixties began a cool analysis of the structure of language itself. Lawrence Wiener stopped painting in 1968 and began writing impenetrable verbal propositions directly on the gallery wall. "As I see it," he explained, "it's an imposition to impose my personal life on the art which attempts to present something to people that is not *just* about me. It is about materials, and about the world they live in, perhaps, but it is not about themselves, their own personal everyday lives, which is what I try to take out of my art."[7]

Detached analysis as an approach to art also fostered an interest in measurement. Mel Bochner, for example, used mathematical systems as a foundation for painting and Walter De Maria's *The Broken Kilometer* of 1979 [fig. 11.3] was an orgy of measurement, consisting of 500 highly polished, round, solid brass rods, each measuring precisely 2 meters in length and 5 centimeters in diameter. The 500 rods were placed in five parallel rows of 100 rods each. The sculpture weighs 17,000 kilograms (nearly 19 tons) and would measure 1 kilometer if all the elements were laid end to end. Each rod is placed so that the spaces between the rods increase by 5 millimeters with each consecutive space, from front to back; the first two rods of each row are placed 80 millimeters apart, the last two rods 580 millimeters apart. Metal halide stadium lights illuminate the work, which is 45 feet wide and 125 feet long overall. In 1977 De Maria drove a single brass rod of the same overall dimensions into the ground, leaving only the 2-centimeter end visible (*Vertical Earth Kilometer*, Kassel, Germany).

There was also an indexical tendency in the work of a number of artists at the time. The Japanese-American artist On Kawara, for example, painted an ongoing series of small, square black canvases consisting simply of the date meticulously painted on them in white, accompanied by a box containing a newspaper from the day the painting was made. He subtitled each work with a headline of the day in the language of the place in which the work was painted: Thus *July 29, 1969* is subtitled "Man Walking on Moon", which is the headline of the newspaper in the box. Robert Morris's *Cardfile* of 1962 (see page 289), the series of books made by Ed Ruscha (see pages 271–3), and Gerhard Richter's *Atlas* (begun in 1964; fig. 11.45) are all expressions of this interest in documentation in the late sixties and early seventies. Hans Haacke's 1971 *Shapolsky et al, Manhattan Real Estate Holdings, a Real-Time Social System, as of May 1, 1971* [fig. 11.4] included two maps and 142 typewritten data sheets attached to photographs giving each property's address along with other information such as the owner, the value, and six charts on business transactions related to the individual buildings. Like much of Haacke's work, this project used detailed

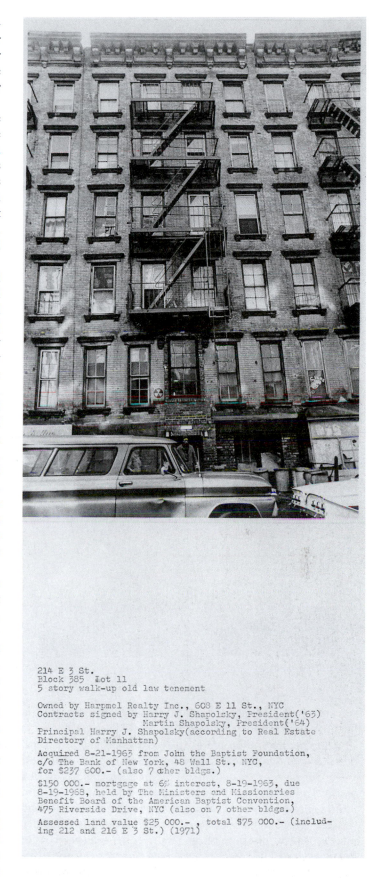

214 E 3 St.
Block 385 Lot 11
5 story walk-up old law tenement

Owned by Harpmel Realty Inc., 608 E 11 St., NYC
Contracts signed by Harry J. Shapolsky, President('63)
                    Martin Shapolsky, President('64)
Principal Harry J. Shapolsky(according to Real Estate
Directory of Manhattan)

Acquired 8-21-1963 from John the Baptist Foundation,
c/o The Bank of New York, 48 Wall St., NYC,
for $237 600.- (also 7 other bldgs.)

$150 000.- mortgage at 6% interest, 8-19-1963, due
8-19-1968, held by The Ministers and Missionaries
Benefit Board of the American Baptist Convention,
475 Riverside Drive, NYC (also on 7 other bldgs.)

Assessed land value $25 000.- , total $75 000.- (including 212 and 216 E 3 St.) (1971)

11.4 Hans Haacke, Shapolsky et al, *Manhattan Real Estate Holdings, a Real-Time Social System, as of May 1, 1971* (detail).

11.5 Bernhard and Hilla Becher, *Watertowers*, 1980. Nine black-and-white photographs, 20¼ × 16¼in (51.4 × 41.3cm) each. Courtesy Sonnabend Gallery, New York.

research to highlight sociopolitical issues—in this case the business practices of a prominent New York slum lord.

Documentary photography played a key role in this work by Haacke. In addition, many works of art produced around 1970 were either so ephemeral (as in performance art) or physically so inaccessible (as in the works of Heizer and Smithson) that the documentary "objectivity" of photography was reasserted in their service.[8] This in turn led to a wider interest in the photograph generally. The German couple Bernhard and Hilla Becher cataloged functionally and visually related architectural structures with a tone of detached neutrality [fig. 11.5]. Their collective authorship and the exclusion of any incident of light or atmosphere reinforced

this impression of neutrality. By stressing unintended visual relationships in the manmade environment, they caused such buildings to be seen as a form of "anonymous sculpture," created by social function and convention.

Recasting Photography

The work of the Bechers was as profoundly marked by the subjectivity of the artists as any other work of art. Freud's concept of the unconscious had long ago made clear the ineluctable subjectivity of all human acts, undermining any thought of photography as "objective" documentation, though it took the computer-manipulated photography of the 1980s to drive the point home. Until the early seventies one could still assert the "transparency" of photography, as though it were a medium that simply documented what was in front of the camera. As a result a Whitmanesque poetry of the ordinary persisted, especially in American photography from F.S.A. photographers like Dorothea Lange [fig. 2.9], Gordon Parks, and Walker Evans in the thirties and forties, through such great artists of the fifties and sixties as William Klein, Robert Frank [fig. 7.1], Gary Winogrand, Diane Arbus [fig. 11.6], and Lee Friedlander. The aesthetic uniqueness of Arbus's vision, perhaps more obviously than that of any other maker of unaltered (so-called "straight") photographs of the time, was undeniable; as she said, "I really believe there are things which nobody would see unless I photographed them."[9]

Nevertheless, the lingering aura of objectivity in photography kept photographers in a realm apart from the art world through the sixties, except as "documentation" in conceptual works or as an aspect of a predominantly painting or sculptural practice as in the *oeuvres* of Rauschenberg and Warhol which incorporate photography into painting. It wasn't until the large-format photography of the late 1970s by the Bechers and Cindy Sherman began appearing in major contemporary art galleries alongside large paintings that photography came out of a segregated art space.

11.6 Diane Arbus, *Child with a Toy Hand Grenade in Central Park, New York*, 1962.

Copyright © 1970 The Estate of Diane Arbus, LLC.

11.7 Seydou Keïta, *Untitled*, 1959.

Courtesy Association Seydou Keïta, Bamako, Sean Kelly Gallery, New York and JM Patras, Paris.

After that, more and more large-format photographers emerged and a number of earlier photographers began to be rediscovered as "artists"—not only those we already knew as "photographers," like Arbus and Evans, but also artists from previously ignored cultures such as Seydou Keïta, a portraitist from Mali, whose work of the 1950s [fig. 11.7] and after revealed a magnificent eye for both a formal aesthetics of patternation and for the social portrait of his cross-section of Mali.

Art and Nature

The critique of photography at the end of the sixties emerged as part of a systematic scrutiny of representation. This in turn belonged to a broader criticality with regard to all kinds of assumptions both within the art world and outside of it. Some artists applied this analytical style to a search for aesthetic structures in nature. The rows of colorful soil core samples in Alan Sonfist's *Earth Monument to Chicago*

(1965–74) and the moving patterns of live ants he created using chemical trails in his *Army Ants: Pattern and Structures* (1972) combine an artistic sensibility with scientific procedures and natural processes.

In 1961 the Italian artist Piero Manzoni declared the entire world a work of art by putting it on a sculpture pedestal labeled *Socle du Monde* (*Pedestal for the World*) [fig. 11.8]. Influenced by Yves Klein, Manzoni also made "living sculptures" in 1961 by signing the backs or arms of live models. For Manzoni, individuality itself became art in real time, expressing "being and living."[10] His most scandalous gesture was to produce ninety cans of *Artist's Shit*, to be sold at the same price per gram as gold. Making art out of his own blood and excrement verified the physicality of the work with an even more shocking reality than Lucio Fontana's assault on the canvas with a knife (see page 145).

Rauschenberg's extension of his aesthetic to the world and Warhol's "de-definition" of reality[11] into an aesthetic collage also prefigured such artists of the late sixties as Gilbert Proesch and George Passmore (known as "Gilbert and George"), who began collaborating as *Living Sculpture* in 1969. They reasoned that as artists they themselves constituted living art and that everything done by an artist is art as long as it is conceived in an aesthetically conscious way. In 1967 a fellow student at St. Martin's School of Art in London, Bruce McLean, made "Floataway Sculptures" by throwing scraps of board and linoleum into a river and "Splash Sculptures" by skipping stones on the water's surface. Like John Latham, McLean and Gilbert and George were reacting against the narrow aesthetic of their teachers—artists such as Anthony Caro whom they saw as too influenced by Clement Greenberg's formalism.

In their performance piece *The Singing Sculpture* ("*Underneath the Arches*") [fig. 11.9], Gilbert and George stood on a table dancing a sequence of highly controlled movements and poses while singing along with the popular old song "Underneath the Arches" coming from a tape

11.9 Gilbert and George, *The Singing Sculpture* ("*Underneath the Arches*"), 1969, performed at Sonnabend Gallery, October 1971. Photograph courtesy Sonnabend Gallery, New York.

player that was literally under their feet. Their props—a rubber glove, a walking stick, primly bourgeois, worsted suits, and bronze make-up for their faces and hands—attempted a leveling of individuality. By the glove these artists meant to imply that they were not those who form but those who have taken form, hollow and interchangeable. Every five minutes one of them would get down to restart the recording of the song of two tramps lost in fantasy as they sit under the arches of a bridge. The implication is of the all-encompassing totality of an artistic vision.

In the early seventies the San Diego artists Newton and Helen Mayer Harrison began to use scientific research to create an elaborate network of metaphors, as in their "Lagoon Cycle." The Harrisons' idea developed around their attempt to replicate the ecosystem of the Sri Lankan crab in a San Diego laboratory. Structured as a dialog between a "Lagoon Maker" and a "Witness," the evolving text is augmented by maps and images. The hubris of the Lagoon Maker's ambitious plans to re-create the habitat of a mangrove thicket in a tank in California is challenged by the Witness, who sees its artificiality and the narrowness of its ecological isolation from global systems. The discourse

11.8 Piero Manzoni, *Socle du Monde* (*Pedestal for the World*), 1961. Iron and bronze, 32¼ × 39⅜ × 39⅜in (81.9 × 100 × 100cm). Herning Kunstmuseum, Denmark.

11.10 (opposite) **Newton and Helen Mayer Harrison**, *Boulder—Underground/Overground Seep—a Wetlands Walk for Boulder Creek*, 1990. Photograph collage with mixed media, drawing and text, two panels 17⅛ × 30¾in (43.5 × 78.1cm) and 29 × 30¾in (73.7 × 78.1cm).

Courtesy Ronald Feldman Fine Arts Inc., New York.

becomes a confrontation of the romantic notion of the self-contained creative ego against the interactive model of global symbiosis. In a commentary to the *Third Lagoon* the artists wrote: "An estuarial lagoon is the place where fresh and salt waters meet and mix. It is a fragile meeting and mixing, not having the constancy of the oceans or the rivers. It is a collaborative adventure. Its existence is always at risk."[12]

In the nineties the Harrisons succeeded in pushing their ecological aesthetic into land projects, as in their *Boulder—Underground/Overground Seep—a Wetlands Walk for Boulder Creek* [fig. 11.10]. Here the artists intervene in the interaction between man and the ecology with a design that purifies the sewerage effluent and makes the walk a metaphor for the water's path to near-potability.

Vito Acconci: Defining a Conceptual *Oeuvre*

Much conceptual art focused on the artistic experience itself and its theoretical components, such that recourse to an object was superfluous. Vito Acconci, for example, explored the artist–viewer relationship in his *Following Piece* of 1969 [fig. 11.11] by randomly selecting individuals on the street in New York and following them until they went somewhere that wasn't public. "I was a passive receiver of someone's time and space," he explained. One episode lasted nine hours, ending when Acconci followed the person into a theater showing a film entitled *Paranoia*![13]

After this group of works Acconci decided that the next pieces ought to be about the person making them. He asked himself: "How do I prove I'm concentrating on myself? I do something to myself (attack myself)." In 1970 he sat in a

11.11 Vito Acconci, *Following Piece*, 1969. Black-and-white photographs with text and chalk, text on index cards, mounted on cardboard, 30¼ × 40¼in (76.8 × 102.2cm).

Courtesy Barbara Gladstone Gallery, New York.

FOLLOW DIFFERENT PERSON EVERY DAY UN-

TIL PERSON ENTERS PRIVATE PLACE

FOLLOWING PIECE
STREET WORKS IV, ARCHI-
TECTURAL LEAGUE OF NY
OCT 3-25. 1969

restaurant and rubbed his arm until it bled to see if viewers could more easily approach him if he made himself more vulnerable. This led to a group of actions designed to stress himself physically; like so much art of the time, these actions survived only as documentation on film and in photographs.

In 1971 Acconci became concerned that he had left the viewer out by being so self-obsessed, so he devised a group of psychologically charged works that directly engage the viewer. In one notorious action of 1972 called *Seedbed* he explored the distinction between public and private space by crawling under a ramp and masturbating while viewers walked on the ramp over him. The viewers could not see him, but they were informed that he was under the ramp masturbating, and they could hear him through a sound hook-up, which he used to invade their psychological space by making uncomfortably transgressive sounds and statements such as "I'm touching your ass."

Body Art

If these Acconci pieces seem invasively personal in their engagement with the body, they were actually as detached emotionally as the hyperintellectual and analytic side of conceptual art. The body became just another material. In Dennis Oppenheim's 1970 *Reading Position for Second Degree Burn*, the artist spent three hours on a Long Island beach "painting" his body by laying a leather-bound book entitled *Tactics* on his chest and getting a sunburn around it (documented in color photographs).

The best-known body artist in the United States, Chris Burden, went in for startling acts of self-mutilation. He dragged himself bare-chested through broken glass, shot a bullet through his arm, and performed a series of symbolic rituals such as those that resulted in the "relics" he showed at the Ronald Feldman Gallery in New York in 1976. *Trans-fixed* consisted of two bloodstained nails accompanied by a label that read:

> TRANS-FIXED, Venice, California, April 23, 1974. Inside a small garage on Speedway Avenue, I stood on the rear bumper of a Volkswagen. I lay on my back over the rear section of the car, stretching my arms onto the roof. Nails were driven through my palms into the roof of the car. The garage door was opened and the car was pushed halfway out into Speedway. Screaming for me, the engine was run at full speed for two minutes. After two minutes the engine was turned off, and the car pushed back into the garage. The door was closed.

Only the bloodstained nails and the description remained as artifacts of this machine-age crucifixion.

The pioneers of body art were the Viennese actionists. Hermann Nitsch made an expressionistic use of his own body in a series of bloody rituals that he began enacting in 1962 [fig. 11.12] and continued performing through the seventies. Inspired by action painting as well as by Freudian psychology, he sought a psychological catharsis through fear. If it was, in part, an exorcism of the legacy of National Socialism, it was as a history that symbolized more fundamental drives in the human psyche. In one characteristic Nitsch performance the artist's assistants brought in a slaughtered lamb, strung it up, and disemboweled it before the audience. Then they poured buckets of the blood over the artist, nude and tied upside down to a cross. The aim was to liberate the socially repressed but natural aggressive instincts of both artist and spectator. Nitsch confronted his own deep psychic drives in a critical confrontation with gesture painting.

Arnulf Rainer took this style of visceral expressionism onto the streets of Vienna. In once instance he was arrested when he appeared in public painted with dried blood in streaks down his face to attack the complacency of bourgeois society. However, Rainer is best known for his paintings (beginning around 1960), which he often made by smearing the paint on with his hands and feet, sometimes working on

them until his hands bled. The physical intensity of Rainer's involvement in the act of painting made these works extensions of body art rather than painting in the usual sense.

Valie Export was also directly influenced by Viennese actionism in conceiving some of the most talked-about feminist performances of the sixties. In *Tapp- und Tast-Kino* (*Touch Cinema*) of 1968–71 Export built a box with a "theater" curtain around her naked torso and invited people randomly in the street to reach in behind the curtain to touch her breasts. In her 1969 *Aktionshose: Genitalpanik* (*Action Pants: Genital Panic*) [fig. 11.13] Export walked through a porn

11.13 Valie Export,
Aktionshose: Genitalpanik
(*Action Pants: Genital Panic*),
1969. Black-and-white poster,
26⅜ × 19⅝in (67 × 49.8cm).
Courtesy Charim Galerie, Vienna.

11.14 Dieter Roth, main room in *Schimmelmuseum* (*Mold Museum*), Hamburg, early 1990s.

theater during a film screening, carrying a machine gun and wearing pants with the crotch removed, challenging the spectators to "look at the real thing." In contrast to the female body as packaged and sold by male directors and producers, she controlled and offered her own body freely on her own terms and in defiance of social rules. Export's groundbreaking *Facing a Family* (1971) was one of the first uses of commercial television as a medium. The video, broadcast on the Austrian television program "Kontakte," shows a bourgeois Austrian family watching TV while eating dinner. When viewed by middle-class families on TV, the piece played back the audience to itself.

Another much-talked-about manifestation of Viennese actionism was the "fatal" performance by Rudolf Schwartz-kogler, who cut off his own penis as an "art" action in 1969. In fact, he cunningly substituted a sausage that fooled the viewers, but he did commit suicide (by other means) soon

thereafter. The German-born artist Dieter Roth made a different kind of sausage by chopping up a book and pressing the shredded remains into a wurst—*Literaturwurst* (*Literature Sausage*) (1961). Though this preceded Nitsch's first *Aktion* (Otto Muehl splashing Nitsch with blood in 1962), Roth's work shares with the *Aktionistes* a visceral quality that cuts to a level of direct body experience.

The eccentric Roth is unclassifiable (as most great artists are). His physicality relates to Nitsch, but he is also connected to Beuys (in the transcendent use of natural materials), and to both Fluxus (in the diaristic integration of performance and life) and to Tinguely's countercultural sensibility. Though German, Roth spent much of his life in Switzerland and Iceland; his restless travels mirrored a restlessness in his work, never settling down to a style but rather constantly exploring unexpected materials and methods as part of a meticulously documented daily work stream.

Roth's diaries contain many sausage recipes, to be sure, but more central to his work is the ongoing interaction with natural materials and particularly with the processes of organic decay. In 1970 he filled a Los Angeles gallery with suitcases of rotting cheese—*Staple Cheese (A Race)*—until the city health authorities discovered it. In 1959 he transitioned out of a Bauhaus style of pattern painting into working with ephemeral, organic materials—painting with cheese and chocolate, doing monoprints with pressed bananas, creating photo documentation projects, videos, and extensive lists, books, and diaries. Roth's *Schimmelmuseum* (*Mold Museum*) [fig. 11.14], built in the early 1990s in Hamburg, is part of a private museum dedicated to his work. He constructed it in a disintegrating coach house with moldy walls and raw cut-throughs that he made and deliberately left unfinished. Among the contents of this installation—a *Gesamtkunstwerk* (total work of art) with precedence in the *Merzbau* structures of the German dadaist Kurt Schwitters—are towers of hundreds of self-portrait heads cast in different kinds of chocolate and others in sugar with different food colorings, all decaying from mildew and insects.

By contrast, the work of the Serbian body artist Marina Abramovic in the 1970s pushed intense body expressionism beyond metaphor into performances that genuinely put her at risk. In *Rhythm 10* (1973), for example, she lined up twenty sharp knives, spread her fingers out, and stabbed between her fingers one after another as quickly as possible. Each time she cut herself she changed knives until she had used them all. She tape-recorded the rhythm of this action and then played the tape back, following the rhythm as she repeated the action again. *Rhythm 0* (1974), performed in a gallery in Naples, consisted of her standing next to a table with seventy-two objects (including weapons) and inviting the visitors to use her and the implements as they saw fit. Her clothes were cut away and then she was forced to put a pistol in her mouth, at which point someone stopped the performance. This kind of work tested on a visceral level both her own and the viewer's sense of their own bodies, their boundaries, and the feelings of exposure and vulnerability increasingly inherent in human encounters.

Hannah Wilke, a New York performance artist, used her body as a medium for expressing her sexuality and addressing social constructions of her femininity. It was a feminist gesture that was out of step with the feminists of the seventies but came to be more admired later as subsequent generations of feminists began to value the celebration of sexual identity in a different way. Beginning in the 1960s, Wilke made obsessively repetitive vulva-like, folded forms in terra cotta, kneaded eraser (punning on "erase her"), and chewed gum, as well as anatomically suggestive latex forms. In 1974 she began doing live performances, with her debut in "Soup and Tart" at the Kitchen, a performance space in New York. Wilke titled her now legendary piece *Hannah Wilke: Super-T-Art*

(a play on the title of the evening of performances and on the then current Broadway musical *Jesus Christ Super Star*). In it she stripped down to a loincloth (and high heels), ending in a pose like the crucified Christ. *Intercourse with. . .*, a video of 1977, suggests more than it shows or says, playing the names of callers from her answering machine as she strips to reveal the names stenciled on her breasts. There is also an accompanying document that lists, day by day, all the people with whom she had intercourse (some several times a day) over a period of a few weeks; that a few of the names were of women (including her mother) leaves one to jump to conclusions but the particular *form* of "intercourse" is not specified. The photographs of her "S.O.S. Starification Object Series" [fig. 11.15] are perhaps her best-known works. In these, she struck seductive poses like a model in advertising with her body covered in small, vulva-shaped lumps of chewed gum: "I chose gum because it's the perfect metaphor for the American woman—chew her up, get what you want out of her, throw her out and pop in a new piece."[14]

11.15 Hannah Wilke, "S.O.S. Starification Object Series," 1974. Performalist self-portrait with Les Wollam, black-and-white photograph, 7 × 5in (17.8 × 12.7cm).

Scharlatt Family Collection. Courtesy Ronald Feldman Fine Arts, New York.

At the same time the New York artist Adrian Piper undertook art actions in public, non-art spaces that centered on the conventions of social interaction, especially with regard to the idea of difference or "otherness" (originating in her own experience as a black woman). In her "Catalysis" series of 1970–1 Piper appeared on the streets of New York deliberately doing something that would objectify herself in an exaggerated way as different from (and often disturbing to) other people, to see how it affected their interaction with her. In *Catalysis IV* [fig. 11.16], for example, she "dressed very conservatively but stuffed a large red bath towel in the side of my mouth until my cheeks bulged to about twice their normal size, letting the rest of it hang down my front, and riding the bus, subway, and Empire State Building elevator."[15] In these pieces she effectively made her own body a site of social discourse.

The German artist Rebecca Horn also experimented with body actions, beginning around 1970, but her work had more to do with examining her own bodily sensations. *Finger Gloves* [fig. 11.17], for example, extends the function of the hands as an interface between the inner self and the task of acting in the external world. Many of her works are costumes devised for performances (and increasingly films), as in the fabric and wood horn and straps for her *Unicorn* of

11.17 Rebecca Horn, *Finger Gloves*, 1972. Fabric and balsa wood, 27½in (70cm) long.
Appears in the film *Performances II* (1973). Courtesy Sean Kelly, New York.

1970–2, which she performed nude, outdoors in natural surroundings, and recorded on film. The artifacts of Horn's performances have developed an increasingly opulent visual presence as objects and her work, though directly engaged with the body, creates a sensuous and introspective rather than either a social or a psychologically cathartic experience.

Ana Mendieta

Ana Mendieta was another body artist working in the United States in the seventies. She inscribed herself into nature in a way that brought out both the sensuality of bodily experience and the opulence of nature. Mendieta came from a prominent Cuban family that was abruptly shattered by the Cuban Revolution and in 1961, at the age of twelve, she was sent by a Catholic relief agency to live in a foster home in Iowa. Underlying her work was always a longing to reconnect with her Cuban childhood.

Mendieta's "Tree of Life" series [fig. 11.18] and her "Siluetas" [fig. 11.19] were a celebratory assertion of the female body as a primal source of life and sexuality, like the paleolithic "Venuses" of Europe. But her insertion of her own body into these landscape settings covered in mud,

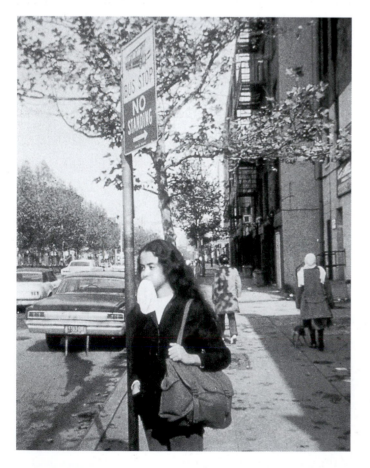

11.16 Adrian Piper, *Catalysis IV*, street performance, New York City, 1970–1.

11.18 Ana Mendieta, *Serie "arbol de la vida"* ("Tree of Life" series), 1977. Color photograph of earth-body work with tree and mud executed at Old Man's Creek, Iowa City, Iowa, 20 × 13¼in (50.8 × 33.7cm).
Collection, Ignacio C. Mendieta. Courtesy the Estate of Ana Mendieta and Galerie Lelong New York.

flowers, earth, sticks, and later into molded or carved forms that resembled prehistoric effigies (in place of the actual presence of her body) also returned to early childhood memories of stories overheard or told to her by the household servants in Cuba. These stories painted an animistic portrait of nature for her that was rooted in the Santería religion, a New World fusion of Catholicism with the magical personifications of nature and the occult practices that came to the Caribbean with the first Yoruba slaves in the early sixteenth century. For Mendieta, the organic materials that she used in her body *tableaux*, and even the places she invested with these constructions, had magical spirits in her mind connected to the world of her childhood memories, "a dialogue between the landscape and the female body (based on my own silhouette)," but, she added, it was also "a return to the maternal source."[16]

Mendieta studied art at the University of Iowa, where she began using her body as a medium in 1973. Among the first of her body works was a direct response to a rape that had occurred on the campus; people were invited to her apartment at an appointed hour, and when they entered they found her stretched out and bound, stripped from the waist down and smeared in blood. This shocking encounter brought home to the viewer the horror of rape with breathtaking immediacy. It also announced some fundamental

11.19 Ana Mendieta, *Untitled (Silueta Series, Mexico)*, 1976. Lifetime color photograph, 13¼ × 20in (33.7 × 50.8 cm). Original documentation 35mm color slide, red flowers and one dried cactus.
The Estate of Ana Mendieta Collection, Courtesy Galerie Lelong, New York.

characteristics of Mendieta's artistic vocabulary: the use of blood and other organic materials, the visceral immediacy achieved by the use of her own body, and the way in which the artist seized power over the subject through her control of the medium. Both in Mendieta's celebration of the female body and in her authority over the representation of her own body, her work was a consciously feminist statement.

Feminist issues continued to play an important role in her work. But so did other aspects of her rich exploration of her own identity and her unique sense of the materials in natural settings. Since most of Mendieta's work was impermanent and executed in remote areas of Iowa or during the summers in Mexico, photography played an important role in documenting and communicating her artistic vision. Mendieta died in 1985 at the age of thirty-six in a fall from an apartment window in New York, leaving behind her an influential *oeuvre* of more than 200 color photographs.

Lygia Clark

Between 1959 and 1961, almost a decade before conceptual and body art took hold in New York and Europe, artists of the "Neo-Concrete" movement in Brazil explored issues of social engagement and bodily sensation in a way that is prescient of the issues raised in the U.S. and Western Europe in the context of the anti-war movement of the late sixties. Although largely unknown in the United States until the 1990s and only slightly better known in Europe before that, Lygia Clark's work constantly undermined the boundaries between what is inside and outside the body, between the self and other, between individual and public space. In the 1959 "Neo-Concretist Manifesto" she wrote: "We neither consider the work of art a machine, nor an object, but rather an almost-body, which is to say, a being whose reality is not exhausted in the eternal relationships between its elements; a being which, even while not decomposable into parts through analysis, only delivers itself up wholly through a direct, phenomenological approach."[17] Her work is participatory and involved with immediate bodily sensation; it is not intended for a detached spectator. "The work, being the act of making the work," she pointed out, "you and it become wholly indissociable."[18]

In a sense there is no "viewer" of a Lygia Clark after 1963 because the "viewer" must physically interact with these "relational objects" to experience them. She made the *Six Sensorial Helmets* of 1967 [fig. 11.20], for example, to be worn by the "viewer" who would experience a variety of visual, olfactory, and auditory sensations in wearing one. Her works are very much centered in the moment of interacting with them; she had little concern for a residual life in a museum or even in pictures. As she noted in 1965:

> The instant of the act is not renewable. It exists by itself: to repeat it is to give it another meaning. It doesn't contain any trace of past perceptions. It's another moment. At the very moment in which it happens it is already a thing-in-itself. Only the instant of the act is life ... To become aware is already to be in the past. The raw perception of the act is the future in the process of making itself.[19]

Clark's work crosses the boundary with therapy, using a model based in the psychoanalytic theories of Melanie Klein and attempting to bring the unconscious into consciousness by articulating unconscious experience directly as body sensation.

11.20 Lygia Clark, *Six Sensorial Helmets*, 1967. Fabric masks of various colors and odors, and with different mechanisms to affect hearing, vision, and smell. Alvaro Clark collection, Brazil. Courtesy Fundació Antonio Tàpies, Barcelona.

Hélio Oiticica

The work of the Brazilian artist Hélio Oiticica also focuses on physical immediacy and on the catalyzing effect of the "viewer's" participation. But Oiticica's work is more explicitly political. With the 1964 military coup in Brazil, he moved to the *favelas* (the shanty town slums) of the Mangueira Hill in Rio de Janeiro. His incorporation of the samba and use of cheap construction materials, as in his 1967 installation *Tropicália* [fig. 11.21], refer to the marginalization of the poor and make a claim for freedom rather than romanticizing the poverty. His "*Parangolés*" (capes for dancers) are costumes for body actions, his installations are works into which the viewer enters and becomes immersed, even his objects elicit bodily apprehension (as in his "*Bólides*" which are containers—boxes, drawers, bottles—of pure color into which the viewer can immerse his or her hands). Bringing the capes (with slogans on them like: "we are hungry," "cape of freedom," and "from adversity we live") and the samba of the slums into the museum of modern art, as he did in 1964, shockingly foregrounded the social disparities and transgressed the distance between and hierarchy of high and low.

In *Tropicália*, he said that he wanted "to characterize a Brazilian condition . . . *Tropicália* is the very first conscious, objective attempt to impose an obviously Brazilian image upon the current context of the avant-garde."[20] The Brazilian image he had in mind was that of the marginal settlements of Rio, where people crowd into makeshift shanty towns. The viewer enters into a complete environment with flimsy shacks constructed of light wood and fabric walls. All around are lush tropical plants and a cage with beautiful, live parrots. You walk the dirt or gravel paths and step inside the curtained rooms, going from one to the next, and in a third chamber of the central structure is a television, perpetually switched on. Oiticica loved the art of the streets, samba music and dance, the interplay of Brazilian popular culture: "it is an image which then devours the participant, because it is more active than his sensory creating."[21]

The image of "devouring" is a legacy of the 1928 "Anthropophagite" manifesto of the poet Oswald de Andrade. The first modernist ideas came to Brazil in the 1920s when artists sought to apply international formal practices to a Brazilian subject matter. Andrade, by contrast, put forward the metaphor of cannibals eating outside influences to gain their power. Instead of the image of the well-behaved, noble, idealized Amerindian of nineteenth-century romanticism, he celebrated the cannibal, an embodiment of the Nietzschean irrational, repressed by Western high culture. Oiticica made his signature "*Parangolés*" (capes) for the performers of "the dionysic dance, which comes from a collective inner rhythm."[22] He used the power of the body to transgress the social hierarchy.

Anthropophagism lay at the foundation of Brazilian "Tropicalism." For Oiticica and the "Neo-Concrete" artists of Rio, this involved a dissolution of art into life (influenced by European constructivism). Andrade's paradigm of cannibalistic cultural encounters in the New World came to stand for not only transnational issues but also the mingling of different arts and different social strata within Brazilian society itself. Thus Oiticica's *Tropicália* underscores the violent domestic colonialism of the Brazilian inner city, but along with its poverty, he also reveals the mixture of races (black, Indian, white), the rich layerings of popular culture with different traditions, and the inherently anti-hieratic

11.21 Hélio Oiticica, *Tropicália* (detail), 1967. Installation, wood, plastic, canvas, sackcloth, eucatex, cotton fiber, sand, cracked stone, tropical plants and birds, television set; dimensions variable.
Hélio Oiticica project collection, Rio de Janeiro.

fluidity of the *favelas*. At the same time *Tropicália* has echoes of early European abstraction; in particular, Bauhaus and the constructivism of the twenties and thirties is evident here in the geometry and in the clear planes of flat color.

Oiticica's art demands that viewers share the space with the work of art, and he embraced dance (especially samba) as a way to viscerally affirm the continuum of art into the body. "I was feeling threatened by an excessive intellectualization. [Dance] would be the definite step in search of the myth, a reintroduction of myth in my art . . . an experience loaded with vitality, essential experience, mainly as a demolisher of prejudices, stereotypes."

Performance Art

Another impetus for the burgeoning of art actions and the performance scene in New York around 1970 came from vanguard dance and new music. These, in turn, fed into the momentum begun in the late fifties and early sixties by happenings, Fluxus, and the Judson Dance Theater. It was, for example, an innovative dancer-choreographer in New York, Trisha Brown, who in 1969 outfitted a man in mountaineering gear to stroll sideways down a seven-story building, in her matter-of-factly titled *Man Walking Down the Side of a Building*.

Robert Wilson's *The Life and Times of Sigmund Freud* (1969) and his *Einstein on the Beach* (1976) had a grander, almost Wagnerian scale and staging. These works, and those of Meredith Monk, also defied traditional boundaries between visual art, music, and theater to address the experience of perceptual abundance that came to dominate life in the late twentieth century (not only owing to the profusion of media but because of the dramatically new scale of the global cities). In *Einstein*, a five-hour extravaganza at the Metropolitan Opera House in New York, Wilson collaborated with the radical composer Philip Glass and engaged such avant-garde dancers as Lucinda Childs to perform in this theater of metaphysical dream images, projected onto minimalist structures on the stage. *Einstein on the Beach* was a magnificent hybrid of genres; it has no plot and is suffused with a postmodern profusion of disconnected symbols that relate to Einstein's life and thought. Wilson also plays with slowing down and speeding up time in his anti-teleological theater of images.

In 1967 Max Neuhaus also played with time and space, inaugurating an art practice of "sound installation"

11.22 Laurie Anderson, *United States Part I*, 1980, at the Orpheum Theater, presented by The Kitchen.

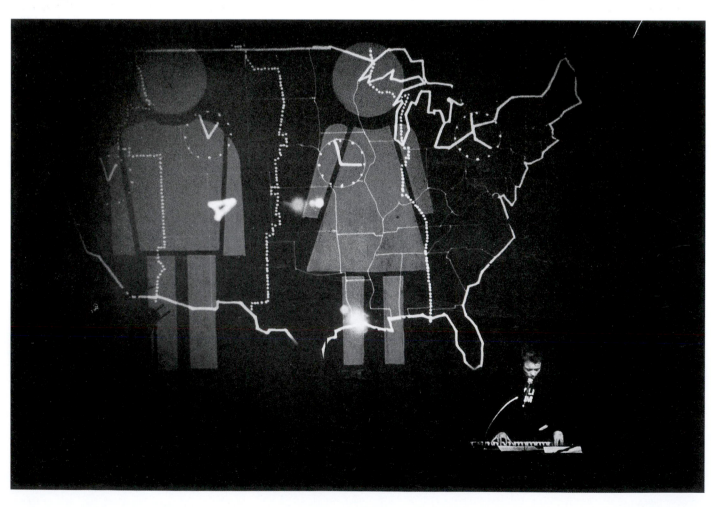

(prefigured by such radical composers as Edgard Varèse and John Cage). He made his first sound installation, called *Drive-in Music*, in Buffalo, New York. The composition consisted of a series of antennae placed over a road with transmitters that sent sound on a frequency one could receive at the end of the dial on a car radio. As one drove down the road and passed under them, each person had a private sound experience in the public space. Neuhaus had put sound in a place rather than in time.

In 1980 performance art crossed over into mainstream popular culture when Laurie Anderson's recording of "O Superman" made the charts. The following year Warner Brothers signed Anderson on for a six-record contract. "O Superman" alludes to a song written by Massenet, an appeal to God that begins "O Souverain" ("O Lord"). Rose Lee Goldberg, who wrote a survey of performance art, described Anderson's piece as "an appeal for help. About the media culture that controls, it appeals to a generation exhausted by its artifice."[23]

Anderson began doing performance works in 1972, often involving the violin, which she has played since the age of five. In *Duets on Ice* Anderson selected four locations in New York City during the summer of 1974 and stood by herself playing a Bach violin duet while wearing ice skates embedded in a block of ice. When the ice melted and the blades hit the pavement, the piece was over. Increasingly, Anderson altered her violin in various ways. In one piece, for example, she put a recording head on the violin and replaced the hair on the bow with a tape on which she had recorded the sentence "I dreamed I had to take a test in a Dairy Queen on another planet." By moving the bow across the head at different speeds she could distort the sound and pace of the voice. The intuitive collage of images—taking a test, a Dairy Queen, space adventure—has the familiarity of recollections from an American childhood of the fifties. At the same time the electronic manipulation disembodies the voice disturbingly. Janet Kardon characterized Anderson's performances as "a theatrical artifice, cross-fertilizing whimsical pyschodrama with the intimacy of the diary."[24]

By the time Anderson performed her monumental, four-part *United States* (the first part was performed in 1980 [fig. 11.22], and the full composition, divided into two long evenings of performance at the Brooklyn Academy of Music, in February 1983), the simple self-presentation of works like *Duets on Ice* had been superseded by a complex opera of light, sound, movement, and text on the order of *Einstein on the Beach*. In *United States* enigmatic narratives slip through one another in a disorienting subversion of time and space, as in a William Burroughs novel. The critic Michel Serres described the work as a discourse on the media as a "scramble system." Anderson's voice through a harmonizer shifts octaves back and forth from male to female. As Craig Owens, another critic, reported: "The woman repeatedly asks: 'Hello, excuse me, can you tell me where I am?' To which the [gas station] attendant responds over and over, 'You can read the signs.' . . . Communication grinds to a halt; messages miss their destinations, and drift aimlessly off into space."[25]

Political Comment

In the highly charged political atmosphere of the late sixties many artists wanted more than metaphors. Joseph Beuys started the Green Party in Germany in 1967. In 1968 the French artist Daniel Buren wrote: "Art is the safety valve of our repressive system. As long as it exists, and, better yet, the more prevalent it becomes, art will be the system's distracting mask. And a system has nothing to fear as long as its reality is masked, as long as its contradictions are hidden."[26] Buren painted a signatory pattern of regular stripes in public places as an act of political appropriation. He even appropriated art history, as in his 1977 *Forms: Painting Under "Composition" of Theo Van Doesburg, A Fabric of 136 × 86.4 cm. Black and White Vertical Stripes of 8.7 cm of Which the First White Band Is Recovered with White Acrylic*. He attached his stripe pattern to the wall behind the painting by Van Doesburg that hangs in the Musée National d'Art Moderne in Paris. All you would normally see is the label on the wall, but if you look closely behind the painting you can see that Buren's canvas is there.

Hans Haacke wanted the artist to engage in direct political critique, challenging the *status quo*. In the "Information" show at the Museum of Modern Art in New York in 1970 he installed a ballot box where visitors could express their opinion of then Governor Rockefeller's stand on President Nixon's Indo-China policy. The results came in two-to-one against the Governor, whose family were (not coincidentally) founding trustees of the museum. The Guggenheim Museum also invited Haacke to show his work *Shapolsky et al* [fig. 11.4], but when the director, Thomas Messer, discovered that Haacke wanted to put up photographs of slum real estate holdings owned by associates of the museum trustees, Messer canceled the show and fired the curator.[27]

Marcel Broodthaers

The Belgian artist Marcel Broodthaers also undertook a critique of museums, although in a more poetic fashion. Broodthaers was a poet, and like his compatriot René Magritte whom he greatly admired, he was deeply interested in the way in which language shapes experience. In 1962 he met Piero Manzoni, who signed Broodthaers's arm and gave him a certificate of authenticity as "a work of art." Broodthaers later described the event as very important in prompting him "to appreciate the distance which separates the poem from a physical work which implicates the space in fine arts."[28] In his brief, twelve-year career as a visual artist Broodthaers made a number of memorable poetic objects in assemblages of egg or mussel shells; following on a tradition from Magritte, he painted a number of "typographic" paintings playing on words, and created an ongoing series of installations, which are probably his best-known works.

The 1967–8 revolution on the streets of Paris seems to have led Broodthaers to his critique of the museum as the principal class of institution that mediated an artist's work. In September 1968 he transformed the ground floor of his Brussels apartment into the first of his "museums": *Le Musée d'Art Moderne, Département des Aigles, Section XIXéme Siècle* (*Museum of Modern Art, Department of Eagles, Nineteenth-Century Section*). Over the succeeding four years different "departments" came into existence as he was commissioned to do different exhibitions [fig. 11.23].

One of the critical themes of the work is the authority of systems of classification in museums—whether by period, function, nationality, or other categories—over the viewer's understanding of the meaning of an object. At this time the French cultural theorist Michel Foucault was writing about power relations in the modern state, concerned as he was with such issues of categorization and control of individuals in a society. Broodthaers created a museum of objects, all of which contained the representation of an eagle (a symbol of power and authority). The Musée Royal des Beaux-Arts, the main public museum space for contemporary art in Brussels, had a lion as its symbol and Broodthaers's eagle was in part a reference to that. *Le Musée* consisted of packing cases for works of art, postcards from museums from all over the world, some projected slides, and an empty, motionless transport truck. By the time Broodthaers reinstalled the work for a show in Düsseldorf a few years later, the presentation had more than three hundred different representations of the eagle. The concept is akin to the famous proposition of the French minister of culture André Malraux, who talked of the great possibilities in the age of mechanical reproduction of images, of an "imaginary museum" in which one could juxtapose objects in reproduction without regard to their location in the physical world; it was a discourse of objects as disembodied ideas.

11.23 Marcel Broodthaers, *Section Publicité Musée d'Art Moderne, Département des Aigles*, created Brussels 1968–72. Installation, mixed media, dimensions variable.

Courtesy Marian Goodman Gallery, New York.

Situationism

Another set of ideas connected to the 1968 student/worker revolution in Paris was "situationism." In 1957 the French writer Guy Debord founded a group called the "Situationist International," in which the Cobra artist Asger Jorn was involved until the group disavowed works of art in favor of street actions in the mid-sixties. Debord mockingly called the bureaucratized, media-saturated, postwar culture of Europe and the United States a "society of the spectacle."[29] He wanted to dislodge public passivity and prompt widespread critical engagement through a kind of guerrilla tactic of "situations" or street events that would shake passers-by out of their conventional habits of looking and thinking. The Situationist International developed a critique of Western capitalism that focused on how media spectacles serve to depoliticize citizens and replace public participation in urban environments with passive consumerism. In the book that served as the manifesto of "situationism" (*The Society of the Spectacle*, 1967) Debord wrote: "THE SPECTACLE IS NOT a collection of images; rather it is a social relationship between people that is mediated by images."[30] Like the constructs of other French cultural theorists of the period, such as Jean Baudrillard's "simulacra," Michel Foucault's "governmentality," and the "hegemony" that the underlying political agenda of Jacques Derrida's "deconstruction" is meant to supplant, the "spectacle," as Debord described it, "is the very heart of society's real unreality."[31] Like Foucault, he describes an evolution in this control of political relations: "An earlier stage in the economy's domination of social life entailed an obvious downgrading of being into having"; then, he says, "having" becomes "appearing."[32] As vision focuses on representation, it becomes more abstract and more easily deceived. The commodity itself becomes spectacle. For Debord, as for the Cobra artists, creativity mediates life and may undermine this "society of the spectacle."

The Potential for Broader Political Action

Throughout the twentieth century modern art has been associated with vanguard social ideology. In the politicized climate at the end of the sixties many artists wanted to substitute actions in real time for work in the more traditional media of painting and sculpture. In 1945 Jean Dubuffet had written of "the arts that have no name . . . the art of speaking, the art of walking, the art of blowing cigarette-smoke gracefully or in an off-hand manner. The art of seduction. The art of dancing the waltz, the art of roasting a chicken."[33] Dubuffet's remarks underscored the perennial concern of modern artists with the idea of art as a means of revising life. "Painting . . . is a way of living today," de Kooning explained in 1951;[34] Yves Klein declared a decade later that "life itself . . . is absolute art."[35] Another decade after that Joseph Beuys stated that "Man is only truly alive when he realizes he is a creative, artistic being," and that "even the act of peeling a potato can be considered a work of art if it is a conscious act."[36]

CHRISTO AND JEANNE-CLAUDE

When the revolt of May 1968 swept through Paris, the revolutionaries threw red paint on the decorative statues in the Tuileries [fig. 11.24] and hung nooses around the necks of the busts of Poussin and Puget on the gates of the Ecole des Beaux-Arts. The students correctly perceived that those harmless old sculptures symbolized the stability of the tradition-oriented governing aristocracy, an *ancien régime* that has remained remarkably intact over the two hundred and some years since the French Revolution. The point, which has been made with increasing frequency over the last forty years, is that the words and images with which a problem is described limit the range of possible solutions one can see.

The students in Paris intuited the power of those seemingly apolitical sculptures as part of a class of symbols which defined the context of the reigning discourse on social structure, so they used red paint to appropriate those visible signs into the language of their revolution. The paint on the statues, however crude and destructive, moved the debate forward by symbolically attacking the *status quo*. This act of appropriation made change—even in the royal gardens of the Louvre Palace—seem possible.

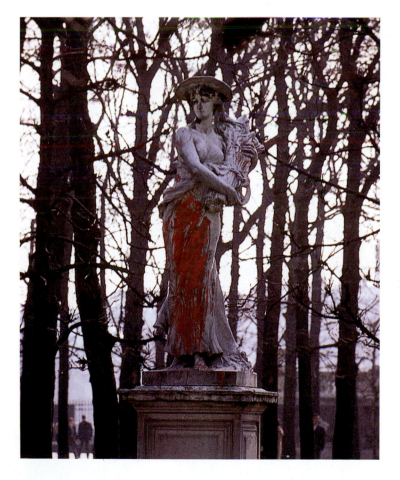

11.24 Classical statue in the Tuileries in Paris defaced by revolutionaries with red paint, May 1968.

Art in the Theater of Real Events

No artists have had a more sophisticated understanding of political appropriation than Christo and his wife, Jeanne-Claude. Their art relies on the use of their subtle political insight, empowered by the sheer visual beauty of the projects, to engage the public *en masse* in a critical debate on society. The political upheaval of the late sixties centered on the growing realization that those with wealth and power could control a democracy by shaping what people saw on television and read in the newspaper, that the "military-industrial complex" had indeed gained the "unwarranted influence" against which President Eisenhower had warned the American people in 1961.[37] The Christos were the first artists to communicate ideas successfully on a scale that enabled them to compete with big corporations in shaping the public's perception of events.

In September 1985 Christo and Jeanne-Claude wrapped the Pont Neuf, the oldest bridge in Paris, in a shimmering, sandstone-colored fabric for fourteen days [fig. 11.25]. The Pont Neuf, completed in 1606 under Henry IV, links the right and left banks of the River Seine to the Ile de la Cité (the heart of Paris for over two thousand years). This solidly proportioned historic monument—and indeed the perfectly preserved center of Paris as a whole—seems to embody the timeless identity of France. Yet, for the duration of their temporary *The Pont Neuf Wrapped, Paris, 1975–85*, Christo and Jeanne-Claude effectively transformed the context for viewing the bridge to underscore ephemerality and the power of an individual creative vision over the stable and anonymous monolith of social convention. They even maneuvered the conservative mayor of Paris into letting them do it!

It is part of the complexity of meaning in a Christo and Jeanne-Claude project that it sets in bold relief all the mechanisms within a society as each constituency attempts to appropriate the reality of their monumental, temporary work of art into its normal manner of functioning. The old man painting a touristic view of their wrapped bridge [fig. 11.26],

11.25 Christo and Jeanne-Claude, *The Pont Neuf Wrapped, Paris, 1975–85*, September 1985.

11.26 An old man making a painting of Christo and Jeanne-Claude's *The Pont Neuf Wrapped, Paris, 1975–85.*

photographs of the sites, engineering diagrams, and specifications—incorporated into the drawings and collages. One is left in no doubt of the artist's determination to construct these works, and this conviction, combined with the aesthetic attraction of the studies, makes it hard to resist imagining how the project might look. This, in turn, builds the reality of the idea in people's minds, and builds the momentum that may ultimately drive the project to be realized.

Christo Javacheff was born in Bulgaria in 1935. He grew up amidst the bombardments of World War II and then the country's brutal postwar Stalinization. He escaped through Czechoslovakia to Vienna in 1957, and within a year was in Paris, painting portraits for a living but meanwhile exploring the formal possibilities of wrapping and stacking as a visual language.

The employment of real objects—oil barrels, bottles, and the various other items he has wrapped—coincided with the interest of his contemporaries and friends, the *nouveaux réalistes*, in appropriating found materials at the end of the fifties. The loosely spilled paint on Christo's wrapped bottles and cans of 1958 and 1959 owes a debt to the legacy of gesture painting. Yet this work also has a quite new sense of continuity with the real environment, a trait that soon emerged as central to the artists' aesthetic.

In the *Dockside Packages* of 1961 [fig. 11.27] Christo and Jeanne-Claude stacked and draped oil barrels and industrial paper rolls on the docks outside a Cologne gallery where they were having a show of their work. The wrappings fitted so naturally into the normal setting that they seemed scarcely distinguishable from the goods that had been unloaded on the docks. The surprising discovery that they

as if it were no different from the unwrapped monument he had rendered for sale on countless canvases before, parallels the policemen directing traffic around the crowds, the factory worker sewing the fabric into patterns, the lawyers negotiating the permits, and Mayor Jacques Chirac himself triumphing in this public celebration of his "enlightened" patronage. Everyone finds themselves doing their usual job, but now in relation to something that has no practical purpose—a work of art. This idea has important parallels with Guy Debord's "situationist" aesthetics.

Taken together, the fundamental irrationality of these situations that Christo and Jeanne-Claude create, the startling scale and presence of the work in the theater of real events, and its disarming formal beauty prompt nearly everyone to look with fresh eyes at themselves and at the world around them. "The project is teasing society," Christo explained, "and society responds, in a way, as it responds in a very normal situation like building bridges, or roads, or highways. What we know is different is that all this energy is put to a fantastic irrational purpose, and that is the essence of the work."[38]

Christo and Jeanne-Claude embark on each project by talking to people about it and by showing them drawings and collages in which Christo has convincingly visualized it. While the large projects are a collaborative practice, only Christo works on the drawings, collages, and objects and his magnificent draftsmanship makes the concept seem entirely plausible; he further reinforces this credibility with technical data—maps,

11.27 Christo and Jeanne-Claude, *Dockside Packages*, Cologne Harbor, 1961. Rolls of paper, tarpaulin, and rope, 16 × 6 × 32ft (4.87 × 1.83 × 9.75m).

11.28 (above) **Christo and Jeanne Claude**, *Package on a Wheelbarrow*, 1963. Cloth, metal, wood, rope, and twine, 35⅛ × 59½ × 20¼in (89.2 × 151.1 × 51.4cm). The Museum of Modern Art, New York. Blanchette Rockefeller Fund.

11.29 (below) **Christo and Jeanne Claude**, *Two Lower Manhattan Wrapped Buildings, Project for #2 Broadway and #20 Exchange Place*, 1964–6. Photomontage, detail from collage, 20½ × 29½in (52.1 × 74.9cm). Collection, Horace and Holly Solomon, New York.

were a work of art caused the viewer to do a double-take, a device Christo and Jeanne-Claude developed to great effect in the large-scale projects of the seventies, eighties, and nineties: *Valley Curtain, Running Fence, Surrounded Islands, The Pont Neuf Wrapped,* and the *Wrapped Reichstag.*

During the early sixties Christo extended and refined his vocabulary of wrapping, elaborating on the variety of cords, knots, and fabrics like a language of autographic brush strokes. He also used photomontage to visualize his packages on an architectural scale, setting them on the site of such Parisian monuments as the Arc de Triomphe and the Ecole Militaire. Christo wrapped a range of objects from magazines to furniture to automobiles, though as often as not the contents of his packages remained unidentifiably mysterious, as in *Package on a Wheelbarrow* of 1963 [fig. 11.28]. When the Galleria del Leone in Venice exhibited this work in 1963, leaving the contents to the viewer's imagination, it caused the local bishop to order the exhibition closed on grounds of obscenity! We can only imagine what he *thought* it contained. The recognizable forms, from wrapped trees to the *Packed Girl* of 1963 (the temporary wrapping of a live nude model), have an even more sensuous allure. Like the drapery in classical statuary, the fabric makes the forms—whether recognizable or not—all the more enticing by suggesting, rather than revealing, them.

The Shift to an Architectural Scale

In 1964 Christo moved to New York with Jeanne-Claude and son Cyril. His fantastic projections of giant packages onto architectural sites continued to evolve in New York [fig. 11.29] until in 1968 he succeeded in obtaining a commission to wrap a real building for an art exhibition in Bern, Switzerland. The following summer, he and Jeanne-Claude erected a *5,600 Cubicmeter Package* [*sic*] (a package of air, inflated by a power fan) [fig. 11.30] for the Documenta art fair in Kassel, West Germany. Christo and Jeanne-Claude's monumental air packages and wrapped buildings of 1968 and 1969 forced them for the first time to employ machinery they could not operate themselves, as well as the services of professional engineers. This pushed them still further out of the insulated fine art context and into the realm of real events.

11.30 Christo and Jeanne-Claude, *5,600 Cubicmeter Package*, Kassel, 1967–8. Documenta IV, Kassel. Height 280ft (85.34m), diameter 33ft (10.06m), 22,000sq. ft (2,043.80sq. m) of fabric, 12,000ft (3,657.6m) of rope, weight 14,000lb (6,356kg).

In *Wrapped Coast—One Million Square Feet, Little Bay, Australia* (1969) the increased scale and the siting of the work in a non-art context added a new dimension to Christo and Jeanne-Claude's task—the necessity of handling public relations successfully. Christo wanted to cover a mile-long section of Australian coastline with fabric and rope. The land belonged to a private hospital and the nurses at the hospital thought that the institution was paying for the work at the expense of things they needed for the patients. In addition, they assumed that their recreational beachfront would be closed. In fact, Christo and Jeanne-Claude paid for the project themselves and designed the work so that people could walk and sunbathe on it, but they failed to communicate this and the nurses threatened a strike that nearly scuttled the project.

For *Valley Curtain* (1972) Christo and Jeanne-Claude hung an orange curtain across a mountain pass in Colorado. Here the engineering was still more complex, the cost greater (about $800,000), and instead of a familiar group of art enthusiasts with a few heavy-equipment operators and engineers, dozens of highly skilled (and organized) steelworkers, carpenters, and high-wire riggers were required. Christo and Jeanne-Claude entered a whole new arena, learning about union labor relations. In the summer of 1971, with the project halfway unfurled but unsecured, the foreman told the union workers to take their customary break when the shift ended, and the wind destroyed the curtain. Christo and Jeanne-Claude had to come back the following summer to start again. Forewarned, this time they succeeded.

Ever since *Wrapped Coast* Christo and Jeanne-Claude had professional photographers traveling with them, documenting possible locations as well as all the events leading up to the final realization of each project. Christo has also based drawings on the photographs or painted directly on them to study his formal concepts in relation to the sites. For example, Christo tried out his first ideas for *Running Fence* in 1972, painting on photographs of different sites. Once he and Jeanne-Claude chose the site, they commissioned careful engineering drawings as well as topographical maps and scale models. As early as 1967 Christo had included such documentation in their collages, setting a formal precedent for Smithson's "Nonsites."

The Logistics of the Projects

Christo and Jeanne-Claude's *Running Fence* [fig. 11.31] was an 18-foot-high, 24½-mile-long line of fabric panels that ran across Sonoma and Marin counties just north of San Francisco, traversing private ranches, intersecting fourteen roads and a highway, passing through the middle of a town and descending into the ocean at Bodega Bay. It was so large that one couldn't see the entire project even from the air. *Running Fence* took four years of negotiations with the fifty-nine private ranchers who owned the land, required a 450-page environmental-impact statement, prompted

eighteen public hearings (including three sessions of the Superior Court of California) to obtain the permits, and cost a total of $3.2 million ($12 million in 2010 dollars)— paid entirely from the sale of Christo's original drawings, wrapped objects, and collages.

Since Christo and Jeanne-Claude set all their huge temporary projects in public spaces, no one pays to see them. They have never accepted grants or sponsorship, nor do they profit from films or souvenirs. Christo stops making collages and drawings for a project once they have built it. In sum, there is no way in which Christo and Jeanne-Claude make money on their projects. Instead, they raise the extraordinary sums required by selling small sculptures and works on paper, and then they spend all the money (and more) to build the work, which they remove after a one- to three-week display period. Christo and Jeanne-Claude deliberately exploit all the mechanisms of capitalism, finding collectors to invest in their collages and drawings, contracting out the manufacturing tasks, managing public relations—then they negate capitalism's most distinctive feature, namely the accumulation of capital, and leave people incredulous.

Christo and Jeanne-Claude believe that their projects have their most poignant effect during a brief display period. After that they remove them because in their view their relevance diminishes with the passage of time. "I don't believe any work of art exists outside of its prime time," Christo explained, "when the artist likes to do it, when the social, political, economical times fit together."[39] Underlying the working process of Christo and Jeanne-Claude is their indefatigable optimism and a fundamental faith that everything is in a state of perpetual evolution. A work of art should, from this point of view, engage the issues of its time and place, and contribute to a constructive dialectic. This was as true for Fra Angelico, Christo argues, as it is today:

> To do valid work then, it was necessary to be profoundly religious . . . [whereas] we live in an essentially economical, social and political world. Our society is directed to social concerns of our fellow human beings . . . That, of course, is the issue of our time, and this is why I think any art that is less political, less economical, less social today, is simply less contemporary.[40]

This dialectical aspect of Christo's thinking has its roots in his Marxist education. AgitProp theater, as exemplified by Berthold Brecht, attempted to create a didactic continuum with reality rather than to take the viewer out of reality and into a realm apart (on the Aristotelian model). This training also predisposed Christo to work in the real environment, and to work collectively with teams of people. As a student at the Academy in Sofia, Bulgaria in the fifties, Christo was sent out with his fellow students on weekends to the farms that bordered the rail lines in order to arrange the equipment and produce. Westerners saw Bulgaria only from the windows of the international trains that passed through, and the government wanted the farms to look prosperous.

11.31 Christo and Jeanne-Claude, *Running Fence*, Sonoma and Marin Counties, California 1972–76, September 1976.

Surrounded Islands

After *Running Fence* Christo and Jeanne-Claude juggled several major projects but all of them were held up by frustrating political struggles. They had wanted to wrap the Reichstag in Berlin since 1972 [fig. 11.32] and the Pont Neuf in Paris since 1974. They had also proposed the installation of between 11,000 and 15,000 golden "gates" along the paths of Central Park in New York [fig. 11.36], but they hadn't gotten clearance on any of these projects. Thus, when they received an invitation in 1980 to do a major project for a community-sponsored festival of the arts in Miami, it seemed a welcome opportunity.

Christo and Jeanne-Claude dissociated themselves from the festival, but after looking around Miami they decided to go ahead on their own to surround eleven of the tiny "spoil" islands in Biscayne Bay with floating skirts of pink fabric. In 1936 the Army Corps of Engineers had dredged the bay to create a navigational channel for oceangoing ships and had dumped the excavated material in fourteen piles that formed a chain of islands. These islands sat, unnoticed for decades, between the cities of Miami and Miami Beach, in the midst of the heavy cross-bay traffic of boats and automobile causeways.

Over the next two-and-a-half years Christo and Jeanne-Claude painstakingly studied the environmental issues, as well as the engineering problems and logistics. They found that the shallow bay contained a plethora of protected wildlife—endangered birds, manatees, and a variety of seagrasses—and eliminated three of the fourteen islands from the project for environmental reasons. Different fabrics, anchors, and flotation booms were tested, scientific studies of everything from the micro-organisms in the sand to the nesting sites of the birds were commissioned, and the most up-to-date satellite calibrated instruments were used to position the anchors and create computer maps for the fabric patterns.

Christo and Jeanne-Claude also met endlessly with lawyers, government agencies, and public groups to present the idea, win support, and negotiate permits. After numerous lawsuits and cliffhanger hearings they finally won the permits,

11.32 Christo and Jeanne Claude, *Wrapped Reichstag, Project for Berlin*, 1979. Collage, pencil, fabric, twine, pastel, charcoal, crayon, photograph by Wolfgang Volz, and map, on photostat and paper, 28 × 22in (71.1 × 55.9cm).
Private collection.

11.33 Christo directing the work in May 1983 during the installation of the *Surrounded Islands*, Biscayne Bay, Greater Miami, Florida, 1980–83.

and installed the *Surrounded Islands* in May 1983 [figs. 11.33–11.35], the most expensive project they had so far undertaken. Though the project sat in the middle of a major city and stretched 11 miles from one end of the bay to the other, it nevertheless seemed oddly isolated and unreal. In addition, it so closely resembled the artist's renderings (as in all the projects) that when one saw the actual work one had a sense of *déjà-vu*, compounding the feeling of unreality. It was in every sense extraordinary. Another striking aspect of the *Surrounded Islands* project is that it blended so remarkably into the visual surroundings. Here the idea prefigured in *Dockside Packages* reached a glorious climax. Not only did the project pick up on the pastels of the local architecture in this beautiful Latin city, but it even echoed the pinks and blues of the indigenous flora. *Surrounded Islands* seemed more like a magnification of nature than an imposition upon it.

Unlike any of Christo and Jeanne-Claude's other projects, the best view of *Surrounded Islands* was either from a helicopter or on television. Most people experienced it through the media. Communicating an aesthetic idea to a mass audience is certainly one of the most important new

issues in the art of the late twentieth and early twenty-first centuries and Christo and Jeanne-Claude have been more successful than any other artists in developing the radical potential of media, including television. Not only have they sited nearly all of their projects in or near populous areas, but they have made all the preliminary planning for them public through the media, thereby forcing large and diverse populations to become involved in the making of the work over an extended period of time. Robert Arneson, who lived near *Running Fence*, observed, "When the *Fence* was up it

11.34 (opposite top) **Christo and Jeanne-Claude**, *Surrounded Islands*, Biscayne Bay, Greater Miami, Florida, 1980–83, May 1983.

11.35 (opposite bottom) **Christo and Jeanne-Claude**, *Surrounded Islands, Project for Biscayne Bay, Greater Miami, Florida*. Drawing, 1982, in two parts: pencil, charcoal, pastel, enamel paint, and aerial photograph, 15 × 96in (38.1 × 243.8cm) and 3ft 6in × 8ft (1.07 × 2.44m).
Collection, John Kaldor, New York.

was great! The checkout ladies in the supermarket were arguing about the definition of art!"[41]

This argument has been fundamental to almost all the opposition to Christo and Jeanne-Claude's projects, because in that challenge to conventional definitions of art lies a metaphor for the loosening of other definitions as well. Of *Surrounded Islands* Christo said:

> I think the project has some kind of subversive dimension and this is why we have so many problems. Probably all the opposition, all the criticism of the project is basically that issue. If we spend three million dollars for a movie-set there would be no opposition. They can even burn the islands to be filmed and there would be no problem. The great power of the project is because it is absolutely irrational. This is the idea of the project, that the project put in doubt all the values.[42]

Christo and Jeanne-Claude in the Nineties and Beyond

Christo and Jeanne-Claude's subsequent and even more ambitious project, *The Umbrellas, Japan–U.S.A. 1984–91*, opened simultaneously in Ibaraki prefecture and in California on October 9, 1991 for slightly less than three weeks. The project involved the seemingly random scattering of 3,100 specially designed umbrellas over 12- and 18-mile lengths respectively of the two inland valleys. The project took five years of preparation with a price tag of more than seven times the cost of *Surrounded Islands*.

For all of the escalation in logistics and cost, what was really breathtaking and new about *The Umbrellas* was its aesthetic. Here, for the first time, Christo and Jeanne-Claude

placed a collection of discrete objects into the landscape rather than using the fabric in a more receptive response to the forms of nature, as in *Running Fence* or *Surrounded Islands*. Compared to these earlier works, politics also seemed relatively less prominent than formal expression. One might almost say that *The Umbrellas* was unabashedly romantic in highlighting nature, using gold or blue accents to bring out the crest of a hill much as Constable dramatized his paintings of the English countryside with brilliant flecks of white.

In June of 1995 Christo and Jeanne-Claude wrapped the Reichstag in Berlin, and as of 2007 they had still not finished paying off the loans. But in the meantime they also constructed *The Gates, Central Park, New York City, 1979–2005*, consisting of 7,503 gates, standing 16 feet high and following the Olmsted-designed pathways of the park [fig. 11.36]. Even though the innovative protocols of their process had been set by earlier projects, this was in many respects a culmination because of New York's position in the art world and because it is their home. The project's saffron fabric panels accented the ribbons of walkway against the winter landscape and provided a much-loved sense of renewal for the people of the city still in the shadow of the terrorist attack of "9/11" in 2001.

Despite the death of Jeanne-Claude in November 2009, Christo continues work on two major new projects in process, *Over the River*, covering a 5.9-mile section of the Arkansas River in Colorado with a succession of fabric panels 8–25 feet above the water, and a project, first conceived in 1977, to build a mastaba larger than the Great Pyramid in Egypt near Abu Dhabi in the United Arab Emirates. The latter project is a substantial revision of the artists' practice

11.36 Christo and Jeanne-Claude, *The Gates, Central Park, New York City, 1979–2005.*

in large part because the projected cost is more than $400 million and if it succeeds it will have to be a permanent structure funded by the Emirates. But this fact is also part of revealing the economic structure of the political situation there and in this way follows the protocols of earlier Christo and Jeanne-Claude projects. In their seventies, Christo and Jeanne-Claude created a corporate and financial structure for realizing these projects even in the event of their deaths; this too engages the new social and economic realities of the present in a dynamic way.

POSTMODERNISM

The revolt against the normalizing functions of tradition is a defining feature of modernity, but while the classical modernist believed absolutely in the truth of what he or she thought of as an alternative to the prevailing mainstream, "postmodernism" questions the very concepts of objectivity, absolute truth, the monolithic authority of a mainstream, and the possibility of fixed meaning. The French cultural theorist Jean-François Lyotard understood modernity as a cultural condition founded on a belief in constant change in the pursuit of progress, and postmodernity as the culmination of this process, where constant change has become the *status quo* and the notion of progress, obsolete.

Postmodernism views both images and concepts as radically polyvalent. This permits a fluid reconfiguring of one's experience of the world, continually changing juxtapositions and sequences in a manner that fundamentally destabilizes their meaning. In late-twentieth-century science—from evolutionary biology to nuclear physics—we saw a revision in thinking that configured the natural world in terms of a dynamic of complex, sometimes contradictory, and multivalent tendencies. Duchamp's readymades set an important precedent for art because they established a dialog among everyday objects that pointedly does not refer to the everyday life from which they come.[43] John Cage and Jasper Johns reoriented art away from the vehement assertion of identity (as in abstract expressionism) toward the essential undecidability that underlies postmodernism and the social construction of identity as we have come to see it in the twenty-first century.

The dominant stylistic feature of postmodern art is the lack of stable referents, whether in the sense of detaching a snow shovel from its commonly understood function [fig. 7.2] or in the narrower fashion of cannibalizing advertising images or past styles in art without regard to their original intent [figs. 7.11 and fig. 12.40]. Postmodernism is an inclusive aesthetic that cultivates the variety of incoherence. But, as Neil Postman pointed out, this attitude had already permeated the popular media in the sixties, for instance in the randomness of the juxtaposed soundbites on the television news, where "all assumptions of coherence have vanished. And so, perforce, has contradiction. In the context of *no context*, so to speak, it simply disappears."[44]

Sigmar Polke

The sixties paintings of the German artist Sigmar Polke anticipated some of the key issues of the discourse on postmodernism in the seventies. For him, the enigmatic *oeuvre* of Marcel Duchamp and Francis Picabia's "Transparencies" (paintings of the late twenties in which seemingly unrelated images are superimposed) inspired a liberation from linear coherence and from the idea that art emanates from personality (the romantic core of German art for the past two hundred years). In 1963 Polke and two other young Düsseldorf artists, Gerhard Richter and Konrad Lueg (a.k.a. Konrad Fischer), founded "capitalist realism" (an ironic counterpart to socialist realism) in response to the realities of capitalist mass culture.

Polke, born in East Germany in 1941, crossed into the West on the Berlin subway in 1953 and by 1961 was studying at the Düsseldorf Kunstakademie with Josef Beuys. He drew *Würstchen* (*Little Sausage*) of 1963 [fig. 11.37] in ballpoint pen. The medium itself is a mass-market instrument

11.37 Sigmar Polke, *Würstchen* (*Little Sausage*), 1963.
Ballpoint pen on paper, 11¾ × 8¼in (30 × 21cm).
The San Francisco Museum of Modern Art. Fractional gift of Robin Quist Gates.

that permits none of the nuanced variation in line associated with a traditional fine artist's pen. The subject is not a woman eating a hot dog but *an image of* a woman eating a hot dog; the lettering suggests a cross between cheap newspaper ads and an adolescent doodle. The style too seems pointedly "artless" in its awkwardly unbalanced composition and deliberately "bad" drawing; the hand looks as though a child rendered it. This deliberate flirtation with anti-aesthetic values is both radical and prescient of the issues raised by the evolving mass culture of the sixties.

In the mid-sixties Polke painted a group of twelve canvases, collectively entitled *The Fifties* [fig. 11.38], in which he deliberately employed an incoherent selection of kitsch fifties styles. In this composite work he found himself absorbed into the vulgarity of popular taste. There is doubtless some cynicism in this work about the cultural level of the German economic miracle of the fifties and sixties, but it is at the same time mixed with genuine nostalgia. Rather than dwelling in depth on any one image in this series, the installation prompts the viewer to see a profusion of disparate images all at once, to see across the surface, as in pop art. However, the simultaneous multiplicity of styles in *The Fifties* differs from pop art, which also exploits kitsch or popular culture, because it attacks the very idea of stylistic coherence and the normalizing force of personality in art.

In 1963 Polke began simulating the dot patterns of commercial four-color printing (Raster dots) only months after Lichtenstein turned to this commercial metaphor (the Ben-Day dots) in New York [figs. 9.24–9.26]. For Polke, these patterns represented a dissolution of the self into commercial imagery—he cast himself as the involuntary transmitting instrument, very much in the sense that William Burroughs meant it. In the 1966 painting *Bunnies* [fig. 11.39] Polke played ironically on the subject of Playboy Club Bunnies (mass-market sex) by using a mass-media technique that breaks down in such a way that the viewer actually sees less the closer he or she looks. Indeed, when you look closely there is no substance at all. The difference in expression between the printer's dots, derived from the mechanical process of rendering half-tone images, and the clichéd sexuality of the subject matter creates a provocatively unresolvable interplay of meanings.

Polke painted *Alice in Wonderland* of 1971 [fig. 11.40] on a patchwork of preprinted fabrics with images of soccer players and polka-dot patterns, making an obvious wordplay on his own name with "polka" dots. In this work the artist superimposed a ghostly white, almost stencil-like rendering of a basketball player from a sports magazine, a transcription of Tenniel's illustration of the caterpillar and Alice from *Alice in Wonderland*, and a repeated outline stamp of the heads of a fifties-style man and woman over the preprinted images of the commercial fabrics that he used as a canvas. In this way he deliberately enhanced the dissonance between these appropriated images and the visual

11.38 Sigmar Polke, *The Fifties*, 1963–9. Mixed media on twelve canvases, installation dimensions variable.

Karl Stroeher Foundation, Hessisches Landesmuseum, Darmstadt.

11.39 Sigmar Polke, *Bunnies*, 1966. Acrylic on linen, 58¾ × 39⅛in (149.2 × 99.4cm).

Hirshhorn Museum and Sculpture Garden, Smithsonian Institution, Washington, D.C. Joseph H. Hirshhorn Bequest and Purchase Funds, 1992.

seductiveness of the color and patterning underneath. This creates multiple layers of conceptual "static" superimposed on one another. It is in this sense that Polke—more like Burroughs than Beuys—is the innocent transcriber, approaching only dead, secondhand or mediated forms to point up our entrapment within them. Things as they exist in images are the reality, a hallucinatory reality in which Polke plays out what Robert Storr described as an "enduring dynamic between reason and terror, expanded consciousness and derangement."[45]

In *Mrs. Autumn and Her Two Daughters* of 1991 [fig. 11.41] Polke has lifted the figures and landscape from mid-nineteenth-century engravings by the French illustrator Grandville[46] and rendered them in a precise technique that mimics the fine control of the original wood engravings, blown up in scale. The scene itself seems to be an allegory of the seasons, with "Mother Autumn" cutting up confetti which her daughters scatter in anticipation of the coming snows of winter. Yet the remaining three-quarters of the painting is a luminous abstraction, experimenting with the

11.40 (left) **Sigmar Polke**, *Alice in Wonderland*, 1971. Mixed media on fabric strips, 10ft 6in × 8ft 6⅜in (3.2 × 2.6m). Raschdorf Collection.

11.41 (below) **Sigmar Polke**, *Mrs. Autumn and Her Two Daughters*, 1991. Artificial resin and acrylic on synthetic fabric, 9ft 10⅛in × 16ft 4¾in (3 × 5m). Walker Art Center, Minneapolis. Gift of Ann and Barrie Birks, Joan and Gary Capen, Judy and Kenneth Dayton, Joanne and Philip Von Blon, and Penny and Mike Winton, with additional funds from the T.B. Walker Acquisition Fund, 1991.

chemistry of synthetic polymers and esoteric minerals. This chemical exploration invites chance effects as though seeking an entrance into the mystic dimension of alchemy. These wildly disparate voices in the work nevertheless make a grand, irrational, and inclusive whole.

In his paintings of the 1980s and since, Polke has continued to experiment with chemicals that change with time and environmental conditions. At the 1986 Venice Biennale Polke painted the front of the German pavilion with hydrosensitive paint that changed from blue to pink depending upon the humidity of the lagoon nearby. In 1988 he used a thermal-sensitive paint for a show in Paris and asked viewers to touch the paintings to see them change.

Gerhard Richter

The *oeuvre* of Gerhard Richter also has this oddly integral diversity that we see in Polke's work; for Richter, it is an attack on ideology (both political and aesthetic) and at the same time an expression of the state of postmodernity. "I pursue no objectives, no system, no tendency; I have no program, no style, no direction. I have no time for specialized concerns, working themes, or variations that lead to mastery. I steer clear of definitions. I don't know what I want. I am inconsistent, non-committal, passive; I like the indefinite, the boundless; I like continual uncertainty."[47]

Born in 1932, Richter moved to West Germany in 1961, just two months before the Berlin Wall was erected. He saw the work of Pollock and Fontana in 1959 at the Documenta II exhibition, and the unashamed formal radicalism of their work deeply affected him. His encounter with the anti-aesthetic attitudes of Fluxus and of pop art, which he saw after he came to the West, also shocked but at the same time liberated him.

Richter was in his late twenties when he left the East Bloc for Düsseldorf and had already mastered the skills of socialist realism. In his painting of the sixties he turned this training to account in rendering images that looked like out-of-focus, black-and-white snapshots of everyday subjects. He intuitively took a postmodern posture of trying to remain open to the full complexity of experience and made "reality" itself the main preoccupation of his painting in the 1960s, using photography—especially amateur snapshot photography and photojournalism—as his point of reference. "The photograph," he said,

> reproduces objects in a different way from the painted picture, because the camera does not apprehend objects: it sees them. In freehand drawing, the object is apprehended in all its parts, dimensions, proportions, geometric forms. These components are noted down as signs and can be read as a coherent whole. This is an abstraction that distorts reality and leads to stylization of a specific kind.[48]

It is for this reason that a photograph you take never really captures your experience.

The photograph takes in the incongruous multiplicity of reality, whereas the painting depicts a synthesized (and therefore interpreted) view, which has the undesirable effect (from Richter's perspective) of normalizing the reality into the already known. "A picture presents itself as the Unmanageable, the Illogical, the Meaningless. It demonstrates the endless multiplicity of aspects; it takes away our certainty, because it deprives a thing of its meaning and its name. It shows us the thing in all the manifold significance and infinite variety that precludes the emergence of any single meaning and view."[49]

Richter's 1966 *Eight Student Nurses* [fig. 11.42] looks, at first, like a row of blurry black-and-white photos of eight smiling girls from a high school yearbook. Then you discover that these are the victims of Richard Speck, who entered a random apartment on Chicago's South Side on July 14, 1966,

11.42 Gerhard Richter, *Eight Student Nurses*, 1966. Oil on canvas, 37½ × 27½in (95.3 × 69.9cm) each. Courtesy Marian Goodman Gallery, New York.

and strangled and stabbed these eight young women; it was the first highly publicized mass-murder case in America. The viewer's discovery of the subject matter sets in high relief the dissonances created in the mediation of experience; Richter effectively separates the signifier from the signified, as Andy Warhol did in his *Campbell's Soup Cans*. In a painting like *Woman with Umbrella* of 1964 Richter's blurring and general degradation of the image makes the subject (Jackie Kennedy shortly after the assassination of her husband) unrecognizable; the blurring in the photo-pictures of the sixties effectively undermines closure on the definition of the subject, leaving the viewer less rather than more clear about the state of the object. The unfocused technique undermines the boundary between photography and painting, challenging the truth claim of the photograph and the distinction between "reality" and "distorted reality."

The distortion of the image by blurring localizes the beholder's perception in the act of comprehension rather than in the identity of the subject. Richter's openness suggests his uncertainty, his reluctance to bring closure to the task of defining. In his 1986 interview with Benjamin Buchloh, Richter explained: "The only paradoxical thing is that I always set out with the intention of getting a closed picture, with a proper, composed motif—and then go to great lengths to destroy that intention, bit by bit, almost against my will. Until the picture is finished and has nothing left but openness."[50]

Like Warhol, Richter pointedly undercut charged subject matter with generalizing techniques and neutral titles; he painted most of the works of the sixties in grisaille: gray, he remarked, "like no other color is suitable for illustrating 'nothing.'"[51] Moreover, the photo from which he painted might in one instance be a banal snapshot of a kitchen chair and at the next moment a newsphoto of the arrest of a Red Brigade terrorist (blurred into generic and unrecognizable indistinctness), as though one was no more charged for him than the other. He especially liked images from the media because they were available in profusion and were artless:

> Suddenly, I saw it [the photograph] in a new way, as a picture that offered me a new view, free of all the conventional criteria I had always associated with art. It had no style, no composition, no judgement. It freed me from personal experience. For the first time, there was nothing to it: it was pure picture. That's why I wanted to have it, to show it—not use it as a means to painting but use painting as a means to photography.[52]

In 1988 Richter painted a portrait of his teenage daughter Betty [fig. 11.43] coolly turned away from the camera. It is done in a blank, photorealist style, from a photograph. Quite soon after that, he painted another innocent-looking girl in black and white, *Youth Portrait*. This young girl, looking straight into the camera, is Ulrike Meinhof, one of the leaders of the brutal Baader-Meinhof terrorist gang. One painting comments on and undermines the reading of the other. In the same way Richter also undermines

the coherence of his own style by painting broadly brushed, colorful abstractions [fig. 11.44] side by side with his photo-realist paintings; indeed, he subverts the distinction between abstraction and representation, painting both in a deliberately detached manner.

In 1964 Richter began compiling the source photos for all of his paintings on panels, and in December 1972 he showed them in Utrecht as the *Atlas of Photos and Sketches* in 343 sheets. By 1995–6, when he showed the *Atlas* at the Dia Center for the Arts in New York [fig. 11.45], it contained 583 sheets, all of them published in a complete book documenting the *Atlas*, so anyone could compare to see precisely how he altered his sources in the final composition. He also meticulously documented the sequence of all his works by numbering them in a published *oeuvre* catalog, reproduced accurately in relative scale with one another. In thus making all aspects of the process behind his work as transparent as possible, he both "condenses a much more complex reality into a grid,"[53] as Rainald Schumacher pointed out, and at the same time he also makes it clear how little the facts really tell us.

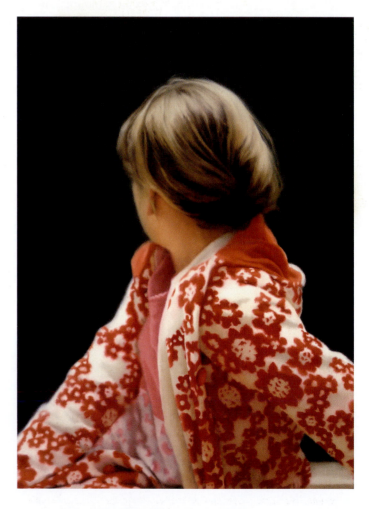

11.43 Gerhard Richter, *Betty (663–5)*, 1988.
Oil on canvas, 40¼ × 28½in (102.2 × 72.4cm).
Saint Louis Art Museum. Museum Purchase by exchange, 23:1992.

The most photorealistic paintings, like *Betty*, are perhaps the most unstable form of truth for Richter. Abstraction is at first seemingly more stable in that

11.44 Gerhard Richter, *Untitled (591–2)*, 1986. Oil on canvas, 38⅛ × 36¼in (96.8 × 92.1cm).
Courtesy Marian Goodman Gallery, New York.

abstract paintings . . . visualize a reality which we can neither see nor describe but which we may nevertheless conclude exists. We attach negative names to this reality; the unknown, the ungraspable, the infinite, and for thousands of years we have depicted it in terms of substitute images like heaven and hell, gods and devils. With abstract painting we create a better means of approaching what can be neither seen nor understood because abstract painting illustrates with the greatest clarity, that is to say, with all the means at the disposal of art, "nothing." . . . [In abstract paintings] we allow ourselves to see the un-seeable, that which has never before been seen and indeed is not visible.[54]

11.45 (left) **Gerhard Richter**, *Atlas*, 1962–95. Installation view, Dia Center for the Arts, New York, 1995–96.
Courtesy Dia Center for the Arts.

11.46 (opposite) **John Baldessari**, *Heel*, 1986. Black-and-white photograph, oil tint, oil stick, acrylic, 8ft 10½in × 7ft 3in (2.7 × 2.2m).
Los Angeles County Museum of Art, Modern and Contemporary Art Council Fund.

But even in the abstractions, Richter's lack of theoretical commitment and his sense of the elusiveness of meaning highlights a fundamental state of uncertainty. The gestural brushstroke (an emblem of personality and expression) is created by Richter in his abstractions with the same cold detachment that characterizes his photorealist works. This is especially true after he began, in the early eighties, to create his thickly painted "gestural" works by laying paint on a glass plate and then pressing it onto the canvas. This effectively conceals the real mark of the hand while teasingly alluding to it in gestural-looking daubs. Despite the detachment of this approach, the abstract paintings nevertheless often create an illusionistic space, like a romantic landscape. Everything about Richter's painting is riddled with contradictions: not least the contradiction that he never escapes from painting despite negating its premises in every way. His humanness is asserted through this fallibility.

John Baldessari

Since the early seventies the work of John Baldessari, a Southern California artist, has also centered on the barrage of informational input from daily life [fig. 11.46]. He sees in a kind of fast surface scan, picking up images that can be reconstituted at a distance and in the privacy of his imagination. As he told the art historian Coosje van Bruggen:

It's like when I am in an airplane cabin and overhear two conversations: one says something and another one says something else. I could not have thought up those phrases on my own, and I respond to it by connecting one to the other, taking both out of their own context and by making them a part of my imagination.[55]

In the mid-sixties Baldessari had a friend in an advertising agency where advertising posters would be cut up into regular squares before being discarded. Baldessari began collaging these small, arbitrarily cropped fragments, painting over some and in the others dealing with the abstract shapes created by the random fragmentation of the original images. Whether using snippets of unrelated conversation, recycled images, or the accidental forms left from chopped-up posters, Baldessari works by intuitively reinventing found images as meaningful symbols of his own thoughts.

Talking about a work of the mid-seventies, Baldessari explained that:

I wanted the work to be so layered and rich that you would have trouble synthesizing it. I wanted all the intellectual things gone, and at the same time I am asking you to believe the airplane has turned into a seagull and the sub into a mermaid during the time the motorboat is crossing. I am constantly playing the game of changing this or that, visually or verbally. As soon as I see a word, I spell it backwards in my mind. I break it up and put the parts back together to make a new word.[56]

Transition to the Seventies

Baldessari's implication is that each individual constitutes a separate reality. Christo is even more explicit about this idea when he talks about the unique way in which each individual viewer defines the reality of the artist's projects for him- or herself, from the perspective of his or her own life experience. Broadly speaking, the pluralism of the seventies grew out of a widespread late-sixties assault on hierarchies of authority, political as well as cultural, in favor of the uniqueness of each individual's experience as an equal (and mobile) component of the cultural whole. Globalization, brought on by innovations in communication, manufacturing, and transportation, has since 1970 driven our increasingly decentralized modern life, creating a culturally pluralistic and interconnected global society that lacks any single dominant center of political power, communication, or intellectual production. What was referred to as pluralism in the 1970s was in fact the burgeoning of what we now understand as postmodernism.

12.1 Rafael Ferrer, *Puerto Rican Sun (The Sunny Side)*, 1979.
Painted steel, 25ft (7.62m) high, Fix & 156th Street, South Bronx.
Courtesy Nancy Hoffman Gallery, New York.

12 CORPORATE CULTURE AND ITS ENEMIES

A "NEW" PLURALISM

To many critics, curators, and even artists at the time, the art world of the seventies seemed lacking in direction. No new movements dominated the scene in the way that pop art and minimalism had in the early and middle sixties respectively. Indeed, minimalism and conceptual art continued to prevail in the galleries, but both seemed to have lost their spark and a widespread feeling existed that painting had died somewhere along the way too. At the end of the decade the critic Calvin Tomkins stated categorically in *The New Yorker* that "no major new artists emerged in America during the 1970s,"[1] and in 1980 Barbara Rose, another New York critic, went so far as to launch a pre-emptive strike by organizing an exhibition entitled "American Painting: *The Eighties*"[2] in the hope of setting the terms for the approaching decade so that it would not go wrong too.

Yet, in retrospect, a number of "major new artists" clearly did emerge in the seventies, as radical changes took place not only in art but in Western culture as a whole. Foremost among those changes was the broadening recognition of a richer, pluralistic culture, signaled by the very same complex multiplicity of cross-tracking directions in the art world that so worried seasoned art-trackers. In essence, that lack of a single dominant discourse *was* the new movement, and it manifested itself in many ways, including the unprecedented numbers of women emerging at the forefront in the seventies and the challenge of artists from Europe, California, and elsewhere to the previously exclusive focus on New York in the art press and art market. The appearance of two European art magazines—*Flash Art* (from Italy) in 1979, and then *Parkett* (from Zurich) in 1984—reinforced this new variety of perspectives. Today it seems hard to imagine the degree to which people in 1970 still expected to see a dominant movement in art and a monolithic trajectory in

culture and how much the global art world still looked to New York. But the language in which we describe the world frames what we perceive it to be, and in 1970 people still thought in terms of an avant-garde and a resisting mainstream rather than of the often irreconcilable complexity that we have since come to expect.

The burst of social egalitarianism in the U.S. in the late sixties opened the door for Americans to reframe their picture of the world as a chorus of many voices. This and the enervation of the established art movements created a fresh opportunity for artists who did not conform to expectations; black and Hispanic minorities entered the institutions of high culture, while women and those outside of New York began to redefine the terms of cultural discourse. Rafael Ferrer, a Puerto Rican artist working in New York, recalled: "It was obvious to me that it was a very frenzied moment when suddenly there's an opening."[3] Ferrer's own success, beginning in the mid-seventies, relied not on his relation to pop, minimalism, or conceptual art, but precisely on his distance from them as a predominantly figurative artist, with an expressionistic style and Latin sensibility that was both fresh and authentic.

Largely a painter, Ferrer also made installations and objects in the 1970s, narrating imaginary voyages through visceral but haphazard accretions of colorfully painted found objects and primitively fashioned forms. *Art in America* featured his *Puerto Rican Sun* [fig. 12.1] on the cover of its March 1980 issue. This monumental steel sculpture, erected in a predominantly black and Puerto Rican neighborhood of the South Bronx, depicts the hot, orange orb of the Caribbean sun setting between two tropical palms. A cool blue moon appears on the flipside. The nostalgic Latin idiom contrasts with the work's blighted urban setting in the northern ghetto.

Likewise, the growing fascination in the seventies with the work of black artists such as Betye Saar and Faith Ringgold

12.2 Faith Ringgold, *Aunt Bessie and Aunt Edith*, from the "Family of Women Mask" series, 1974. Acrylic paint on canvas, fabric, yarn, beads, raffia, foam base, 65½ × 19 × 13in (166.4 × 48.3 × 33cm) and 64 × 19 × 13in (162.5 × 48.3 × 33cm). Collection, the artist.

reflected a widening understanding that America is—and has been all along—an ever-changing mixture of many cultures. The broad recognition that most Americans are varied mixtures of many ethnic backgrounds has taken another thirty-five years; today racial generalities seem meaningless. But in 1970 the assertion of a black identity was an important aspect of opening up the cultural mindset of the country. In Faith Ringgold's effigies of *Aunt Bessie and Aunt Edith* [fig. 12.2], the intense, contrasting patterns and the elegant abstraction of the facial expressions draw directly on West African textiles and sculpture. This is a deliberately political gesture, emphasizing the African roots of Ringgold's cultural

lineage. Similarly, the African-American "yard shows," which derive from Afro-Caribbean traditions, linger behind the work of the Los Angeles artist Betye Saar. One can still see these visionary yard shows—magical accumulations of found and fabricated objects—on front lawns from Port-au-Prince to Watts. Their influence resides side by side in Saar's work with a sophisticated understanding of pop art and cubist construction (in itself an example of cultural hybridity).[4] Saar used found emblems from popular advertising as points of embarkation into a transcendental spiritism, in tandem with a sociopolitical content, as in her 1972 assemblage *Is Jim Crow Really Dead?* [fig. 12.3], referring to the "Jim Crow" laws that enforced racial segregation in the American South from the Civil War to the 1960s. The African-American traditions on which the works of Ringgold and Saar drew began to be recognized by the art world of the seventies as offering something exciting and, in their very *difference* from Clement Greenberg's mainstream, central to a new understanding of the diversity that defines America.

ROMARE BEARDEN

Romare Bearden, an African-American master of the abstract expressionist generation, remarked in 1964: "What I've attempted to do, is establish a world through art in which the validity of my Negro experience could live and make its own logic."[5] The validity of Bearden's "Negro experience" was indeed what finally pushed his work after 1964 to a level of first importance, and in the more open atmosphere of the seventies it began to be widely recognized as such. Bearden enjoyed great success after his retrospective at the Museum of Modern Art in 1971. He had begun his artistic career as an undistinguished social realist during the W.P.A. and then painted in established idioms through the forties and fifties. In 1964 he turned to collages of African-American life and emerged as the most brilliant new collage maker of the decade. Two traits in particular made his post-1964 work so important and relevant to the changing cultural ethos of the seventies and eighties. First, he anticipated the collage aesthetic of postmodernism in his recontextualization of images into a perception of reality on the picture plane. Secondly, the way in which he brought his own Afro-Caribbean cultural heritage into a rich relation with the Eurocentric traditions in which he was formally educated provides a paradigm for the awakening of a broader multi-culturalism.

"I work out of a response and need to redefine the image of man in the terms of the Negro experience I know best," Bearden said.[6] Continuing until his death in 1988, he continued to apply his acute powers of observation to contemporary African-American life, in which he found variations on the timeless human concerns raised by writers of the Western classical tradition from Homer to Joyce, and by the more recent African-American writers, notably Ralph Ellison, Richard Wright, and James Baldwin. In addition, he drew

12.3 Betye Saar, *Is Jim Crow Really Dead?*, 1972. Mixed-media assemblage, 17 × 5¼ × 1in (43.2 × 13.3 × 2.54cm).

on a sophisticated understanding of art history (favoring styles of maximum complexity, such as the baroque and Picasso's early cubism) to describe the variety of street life in the Harlem of his childhood and his memories of black life in the rural South. The inherent prominence of improvisation and appropriation in collage made it the ideal form for such an aesthetic. The fact that Picasso had partly derived his language of cubist collage from the complex rhythms and analytical fragmentations of African art may have made it all the more attractive to Bearden. In adapting collage for his particular expressive synthesis, Bearden made a contribution that was significant not only in terms of its subject matter but in its approach to the medium.

Bearden was born in Charlotte, North Carolina, in 1912, and was reared in North Carolina, Pittsburgh, and Harlem. He earned a degree in mathematics at New York University in the early thirties and began to paint seriously around 1935. It was in that year that he attended a meeting of about fifty African-American artists at the Harlem YMCA, out of which the Harlem Artists Guild was formed.[7] Discovering the existence of a substantial community of black artists was important in helping Bearden to visualize himself as a professional painter. The "Harlem Renaissance" of the late twenties and early thirties (a great flowering of African-American art, celebrating African-American subjects) made this a particularly auspicious moment for Bearden to seek such models.

In the late thirties Bearden studied with George Grosz at the Art Students League. The work of this German expatriate provided Bearden with an example of direct social and political commentary in high art which ultimately encouraged him to see the possibilities of an African-American subject matter.[8]

Bearden served in the military during World War II, showed with the abstract expressionists at the Samuel Kootz Gallery in the late forties, and went to Paris on the GI Bill in 1950. It was the Civil Rights movement in the early sixties, together with his discovery of black Caribbean culture on the island of St. Martin in 1960, that seems to have galvanized him into focusing his artistic gifts on the complexity of the black experience, with all its heritage and adaptations, in mid-twentieth-century America.

Bearden's Collages of the Sixties

The Dove, a collage of 1964 [fig. 12.4], portrays contemporary Harlem overlaid with reminiscences of childhood. The busy scene, crowded into a shallow pictorial space, vibrates with activity. On the left a figure lifts his enlarged fist in a "Black Power" salute. A hunched-over pedestrian scurries from the left side toward the center as a young dandy struts across the picture from the opposite direction. A mysterious "conjur woman" with a half-veiled face reaches out and steps down into the right corner of the picture, leaning on a caduceus of intertwined stalks (a symbol of both the divine messenger Hermes and of the tribal healer). "Even in Pittsburgh, living in the house in back of my grandmother's," Bearden recalled, "there was an old woman much feared for her power to put spells on people."[9]

The unpopulated foreground in *The Dove* sets off the intensity of the street life, which seems overpopulated to the point of bursting, while the radical fragmentation and shifts in scale within each form keep the viewer constantly readjusting. In some details, such as the legs of the hunched-over walker, Bearden has cut forms from photographs of patterns

12.4 Romare Bearden, *The Dove*, 1964. Cut-and-pasted paper, gouache, pencil, and colored pencil on cardboard, 13⅜ × 18¾in (33.8 × 47.5cm). The Museum of Modern Art, New York. Blanchette Rockefeller Fund.

12.5 Romare Bearden, *Prevalence of Ritual: Baptism*, 1964.
Photomechanical reproductions, paint and graphite on paperboard,
9⅛ × 12in (23.2 × 30.5cm).
Hirshhorn Museum and Sculpture Garden, Smithsonian Institution, Washington, D.C.
Gift of Joseph H. Hirshhorn, 1966.

and textures that bear no relation in source or scale to the object they are called on to represent in the collage. Even more than in the contemporary works of Rosenquist, these semiotic breaks in the description of every detail increase the visual speed of the work, with the strong vertical and horizontal grid making the visual cacophony even more pronounced. *The Dove* pays homage to the cubist grid as a way of setting off the energetic fragmentation of the subject. The brick wall in the background, obstructing a long view into space, is directly inspired by seventeenth-century Dutch street scenes such as those by Pieter de Hooch. Meanwhile, the dove of the title, perched above the central doorway, suggests the presence of Christian faith, without, however, suggesting any systematic allegory.

Bearden's collages have some recurrent symbols, such as the train in the upper left corner of *Prevalence of Ritual: Baptism* [fig. 12.5]. "I use the train," he explained, "as a symbol of the other civilization—the white civilization and its encroachment upon the lives of blacks. The train was always something that could take you away and could also bring you to where you were. And in the little towns it's the black people who live near the trains."[10] Yet Bearden seems

always to stop short of confining himself within a deliberate iconography of any kind. Moreover, he collages the subject matter and forms in an additive manner that is at once Afro-Caribbean and postmodern.

In *Prevalence of Ritual: Baptism* Bearden consciously quotes historical styles of art in the four faces borrowed from West African masks, and in a general way he also quotes art history in the compositional structure, which takes inspiration from the paintings of Francisco de Zurbarán, as Sharon Patton has pointed out.[11] In *The Dove* the conjur woman with her mysterious knowledge of African spiritual powers is an alternative incarnation of the Greek oracle. In the same way the art historical appropriations in *Prevalence of Ritual: Baptism* are another means of filtering the events of life and memory through the myths of other eras and cultures.

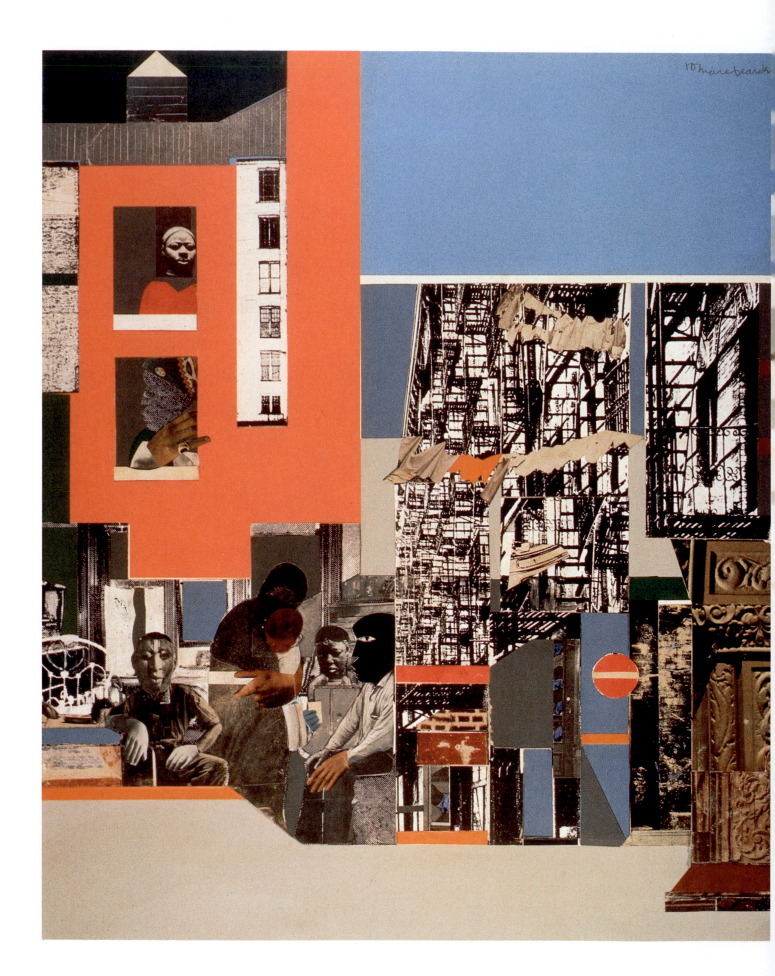

"I seek connections so that my paintings can't be only what they appear to represent," Bearden explained. "People in a baptism in a Virginia stream are linked to John the Baptist, to ancient purification rites, and to their African heritage."[12] This multiplication of voices makes clear Bearden's proprietary attitude toward all great traditions in art and literature.

At the end of the sixties Bearden augmented his innovations in collage composition—especially the speed of the informational breaks in the fragmentation of individual figures—with a unique color sense, involving large, flat areas of intense saturation and often contrasting hue. By juxtaposing complementary colors of the same value (brightness), like the orange and blue in *Black Manhattan* [fig. 12.6], for example, Bearden made the colors vibrate with the same frenetic intensity as the imagery while simultaneously using the blankness of the orange, gray, and blue fields to set off the busy collision of patterns and forms around them. Bearden was a one-time songwriter, whose love of jazz profoundly influenced the percussive contrasts of pattern, color, and subject matter that defined his collages. He created a harmony of inclusiveness in his style, a celebration of complexity rather than a modernist reduction that excludes "the extraneous." In this sense Bearden's collage work elucidated a central concern for the decade as a whole.

IDENTITY, CORPORATE CULTURE, AND PLURALISM

The pluralism of the seventies expressed a unifying concern with the radical potential of individuality. Artists, like everyone else, were alienated by the increasingly fractured experience of life in the era of electronic media and marketing; they were made hyperconscious of political and semiotic issues, supersaturated with visual stimuli, and overwhelmed by the anonymity of mass culture. For many, a more self-contained search for the integrity of one's individuality as against the colonization of identity by corporate culture superseded any interest in collective movements. Even the loose consensus of the minimalists and pop artists seemed anachronistic. Instead, a fierce nonalignment characterized the best artists to emerge in the seventies, and that vehement assertion of individuality in itself has radical implications for a society of mass markets and media.

Art and Feminism

Feminist criticism became particularly important in the seventies in directing the broad public toward a more openly inclusive approach and a deeper appreciation of what makes each of us who we are. In January 1975 Miriam Schapiro and Robert Zakanitch founded a "Pattern and Decorative Artists"

12.7 Joyce Kozloff, *Plaza Las Fuentes*, Pasadena, 1990. Glazed ceramic tiles; sculpture Michael Lucero, landscape architecture Lawrence Halprin.

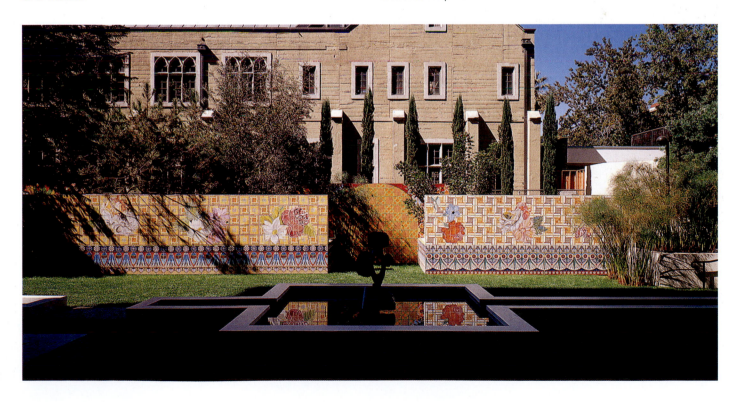

group, and the Holly Solomon Gallery, which opened that year in SoHo (the new artists' quarter *South* of *Houston* Street in New York), became the focus of a widely touted "pattern and decoration movement." A new dimension to the reassertion of patterning and decorativeness by artists such as Joyce Kozloff [fig. 12.7] was added by the concomitant attack on the modernist division of high art from the "minor arts" of decoration. Schapiro and Kozloff saw this as a gender-based distinction—for them, "decorative" connoted "women's work." In addition, they wanted to reverse the tendency toward a reduction of means (as in minimalism) in favor of an additive and inclusive aesthetic (as in Robert Venturi's rejection of the international style in architecture).

In the seventies feminist artists also focused on photography, which they perceived as a newer fine art medium and thus less hidebound by traditions of male dominance. Bea Nettles, a photographer who emerged at the beginning of the decade, combined a late-sixties irreverence for technical conventions with the "minor art" of sewing. Out of nostalgia for home when she went to graduate school in 1968, Nettles started sewing herself a quilt. This led to the idea of painting on quilted canvas, and by the summer of 1970

12.9 **Nancy Spero**, *Rifle/Female Victim*, 1966. Gouache and ink on paper, 24 × 19in (60.9 × 48.2cm).
Courtesy of the gallery.

she was experimenting with sewing paper photographs and then painting photo emulsion on fabrics, which she stitched into reliefs.

The rebellion against the pristine quality of the traditional photographic silver print demonstrated in the uneven brown-stained surface of *Suzanna . . . Surprised* [fig. 12.8] echoes the defiant subject matter. Nettles made this work at the height of the counterculture protest against American involvement in Vietnam. She stuffed this unmistakably confrontational nude self-portrait and sewed it around the edges, then fixed it onto a faint image of a formal garden. This version of "Susanna and the Elders" shows only the bather in her garden, forcing the viewer into the role of the elders, caught peering from the bushes. Nettles looks the viewer square in the eye; and instead of the passive embarrassment of Giorgone's or Rembrandt's Susanna, the gaze of this nude overpowers the spectator and assumes control.

The feminists of the late sixties and early seventies were among the first to identify the body as not only a social but also a political site. Nancy Spero, for example, made powerful anti-war images using sexual anatomy as metaphors. "I was so enraged. Coming back from Europe, I was shocked that our country, which had this wonderful idea of democracy, was doing this terrible thing in Vietnam. I wanted to make

12.8 **Bea Nettles**, *Suzanna . . . Surprised*, November 1970. Photoemulsion on muslin, photolinen, stitching, 28 × 35in (71.1 × 88.9cm).
The Phillips Collection, Washington, D.C.

images to express the obscenity of war."[13] In *Rifle/Female Victim* of 1966 [fig. 12.9] ferocious heads seem to fly out of a vertically aimed rifle to bite off the feet, hair, and one hand of a bleeding female nude, flung upside down in the skirmish. The victimization of the female body stood in as the locus of this broader cruelty and the penis/rifle became a surrogate for the war machine.

Martha Rosler's 1967–72 series *Bringing the War Home: House Beautiful (Balloons)* [fig. 12.10] takes place in a comfortable suburban home. A terrified Vietnamese woman—appropriated from a magazine piece on the Vietnam War—carries a dead baby up the living-room stairs, bringing the war home, as the title says. In the series to which this image belongs, Rosler clipped and disjunctively superimposed images of the war on affluent American interiors from mass-market magazines, especially those read by women, thus invading the domestic space in another way too. In this instance the balloons collide with the war victim in a powerful semiotic clash. Part of the feminist critiques of the seventies, this body of work nevertheless took twenty years to garner the attention it deserved. It may be that the style itself transgressed the expectations of what constituted a "high art" practice by veering too close to magazine layouts.

It wasn't until the 1970s that explicitly feminist concerns started to take the foreground in defining an important *oeuvre*, as in Ana Mendieta's exploration of the sexuality of the female body (her body) or Eleanor Antin's imaginary narratives in which she cast herself in different gendered

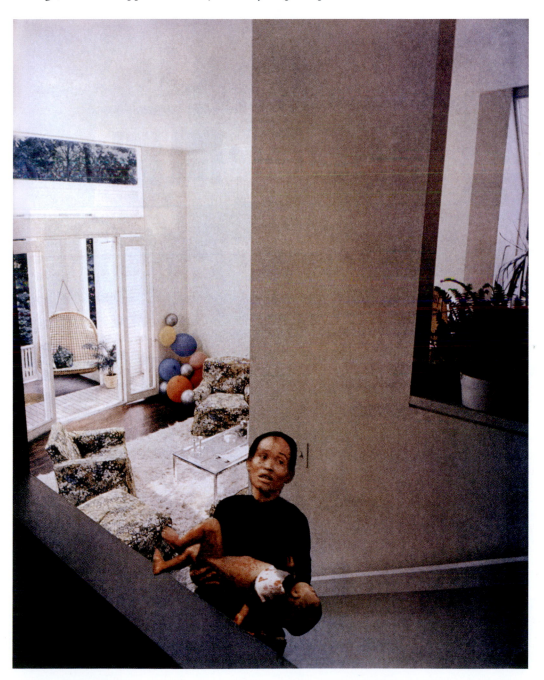

12.10 Martha Rosler,
Bringing the War Home: House Beautiful (Balloons), 1967–72. Photomontage printed as color photograph, 24 × 20in (60.9 × 50.8cm). Edition of ten.
Courtesy Martha Rosler and Mitchell-Innes and Nash, New York.

identities (both male and female). Carolee Schneemann is a notable precursor to this in groundbreaking performance works such as *Meat Joy* of 1964 and in her film *Fuses* of 1964–5, both visceral celebrations of sexuality and of the female body. Certainly artists before her focused on the joy of sexuality; what made Schneemann's contribution so important was that, as a woman, she took control over the production of the sexualized female image.

Schneemann's *Interior Scroll* [fig. 12.11], a performance piece of 1975, is one of the icons of seventies art. In this work, performed first for an entirely female audience and then two years later before a mixed group, the artist stroked the contours of her body with paint, tied an apron around her waist, and read from a book. At the end she dropped the book and the apron, and pulled a long, thin scroll of paper out of her vagina, reading from the scroll as she extracted it. The text narrates a male filmmaker's critique of the "the personal clutter/the persistence of feelings"[14] in a woman's film. The work addressed a critique of "woman's" work and the imposition of predetermined (gendered) criteria of quality, rather than standards developed in appropriate relation to the intentions of a particular work. A significant portion

12.11 Carolee Schneemann, *Interior Scroll*, 1975. Performance photograph.

12.12 Judy Chicago, *The Dinner Party*, 1974–9. Mixed media, 48 × 42 × 3ft (17.6 × 12.8 × 0.9m).

The Brooklyn Museum, New York. Gift of the Elizabeth A. Sackler Foundation. Courtesy The Dinner Party Trust.

of feminist writing in the seventies turned on precisely this point. Not only did feminists make clear that those criteria were often inappropriate to a woman's expression, but the power of the feminist critique also helped everyone to see the "hegemonic" criteria (as they have come to be called) that favored a range of established gendered, racial, national, and socioeconomic cultural practices over others less "privileged."

Another signal feminist work in the seventies was Judy Chicago's *Dinner Party* [fig. 12.12], a collaboration by more than four hundred women, completed between 1974 and 1979. The work is a symbolic history of women's achievements and struggles, with inscriptions of the names of important women on the ceramic floor and on the table runner below the thirty-nine place settings (thirteen on each side, with a vaginal form at the center of most of the plates). Anne Wagner criticized "Chicago's closure on the various possibilities [as] absolute and brook[ing] no contradiction,"[15]

but in the 1970s feminist art had to take a hard line against an equally inflexible male orientation in the art world. Feminism in the seventies was chiefly concerned with societal definitions of women's roles; with practices such as collaboration that undermined what was viewed as a patriarchal interest in the authorial role of the artist; with the body (both in respect to its cultural construction and its natural processes); with a broad questioning of authority; and with expressive directness, especially as carried out in installation and performance. These issues came up in debate over *The Dinner Party*, which continued to provide a lightning rod for discussion of social issues of gender for the next twenty years.

A Dazzling Photorealism

Another new and completely different development that emerged at the same time as all the conceptual and polemical work was a dazzling photorealism that focused on perfecting techniques of recording what we see with extraordinary precision. Painters such as Richard Estes and Chuck Close used opaque projectors, slides, and other mechanical aids to produce an image that seemed technically precise but had its

12.13 Richard Estes, *Telephone Booths*, 1968.
Fundación Colección Thyssen-Bornemisza.

point of reference in photographic reproduction rather than in nature. Here the photograph no longer simply fixed the subject, it became the subject in its intriguing intervention between the painter and the motif. This new "photorealism" fed on the detachment of sixties art—the work of Jasper Johns, minimalism, pop, and conceptual art. At first sight it may seem disconnected from other concerns of the decade, but whether wittingly or not it expresses another point of view on the way in which the language we use to describe the world also defines it.

Richard Estes [fig. 12.13] turned to photorealism in 1967, maintaining that he continued to be "an old-fashioned academic painter trying to paint what I see ... Nor do I have any verbal theories behind the work."[16] He painted nostalgic views of the old Upper West Side in a dazzling technique, using photographs as the source for his paintings. The photographs equalized the variety of textures and objects in the scene to a common denominator as formal elements, an effect the artist further enhanced by painting everything in a uniformly sharp focus (unlike photographs).

Many seventies realists specialized in particular subjects, such as Ralph Goings's concentration on old pick-up trucks, diners, and trailers [fig. 12.14]. Duane Hanson [fig. 12.15]

and John De Andrea perfected a fully lifelike style in sculpture; their figures have an unnervingly real presence. By focusing such detailed attention on the polyester homeliness of the average American, Hanson in particular illuminated the real popular culture of America and at the same time made us look twice at the people around us, wondering, as Andy Warhol famously remarked, "where the artificial stops and the real starts."

Chuck Close painted his 9-foot-high *Self-Portrait* [fig. 12.16] and the series of monumental portraits of friends that followed from photographs, using an airbrush (a commercial art technique). As in minimalism, Close set arbitrary rules for himself: the mugshot compositions, the restriction to black and white, the colossal scale. In each case he carefully prepared the surface with multiple layers of smoothly sanded gesso, laid on a light pencil grid for scaling up the photograph, roughed in the image with the airbrush, and then meticulously refined and finished the painting. When Close introduced color in 1970, he overlaid four monochrome

12.14 (above) **Ralph Goings**,
Moby Truck, 1970. Oil on canvas,
4ft × 5ft 8in (1.21 × 1.72m).
Private collection. Courtesy O.K. Harris
Works of Art, New York.

12.15 Duane Hanson, *Woman with Dog*, 1977. Cast polyvinyl,
polychromed in acrylic, with mixed media, life-size.
Whitney Museum of American Art. Purchase, with funds from Frances and Sydney Lewis, 78.6.

paintings (in the primary colors and black) as in the color separations made for color printing, again referencing commercial rather than "high" art practices. Close made many photographs of the people around him, and when he chose one to paint he has said that he based his selection on whether the forms in the photograph had interesting edges to paint. Once he selected the subject, his process was so methodical that he could accurately calculate the length of time it would take to finish a work by measuring the area left to be painted; he could also visualize exactly how the finished work would look.

Everyday Places

Pop art's attack on the boundary between high and low art, minimalism's sense of literal presence in real space, and the undermining of the aesthetic object *per se* in conceptual art prompted a number of artists in the seventies to enter their work into a non-art context. Scott Burton's functional sculpture [fig. 12.17] deliberately hovers over the ambiguous line between fine and applied art. Burton made functional objects (chairs and benches for the most part) but drew on an art tradition—Richard Artschwager, Donald Judd, Tony

12.16 Chuck Close, *Self-Portrait*, 1967–8. Acrylic on canvas, 8ft 11½in × 6ft 11½in (2.73 × 2.12m). Walker Art Center, Minneapolis. Art Center Acquisition Fund, 1969.

Smith—for his formal vocabulary, and the audience for his work was an art audience.

Populists like Terry Schoonhoven and Victor Henderson (who made up the "L.A. Fine Arts Squad") simply weren't concerned with the approbation of the art world. They painted startling illusionistic murals on blank walls in the workaday environment of the inner city. Often, these murals depicted topical themes, as in the precarious *Isle of California* [fig. 12.18], painted just after the earthquake of 1971. Murals sprang up in city neighborhoods all around the United States at the beginning of the decade. Perhaps the most celebrated of them was *The Great Wall of Los Angeles* (1976–84), for which the Mexican-American artist Judy Baca organized some four hundred teenagers over seven summers to paint a 2,500-foot mural on the retaining wall of the Tujunga Wash drainage canal dealing with the history of what she called "the ethnic peoples of California." Baca studied the great Mexican muralists (Siqueiros, Rivera, Orozco, and others) and her work helped spawn a widespread Chicano mural movement. In 1988 the city of Los Angeles began commissioning her to organize the production of murals across the city.

12.17 Scott Burton,
Two-Part Chairs' Obtuse Angle (A Pair), 1983–4.
Granite, 33 × 24 × 33in (83.8 × 61 × 83.8cm) each.
Walker Art Center, Minneapolis.
Gift of the Butler Family Fund 84.3.

12.18 Los Angeles Fine Arts Squad (Terry Schoonhoven and Victor Henderson),
Isle of California, 1972.
Enamel on stucco, 42 × 65ft (12.8 × 19.81m).
Los Angeles, California.

12.19 Boston Architectural Center before the painting by Haas.

Richard Haas also started painting the sides of buildings in the seventies [figs. 12.19 and 12.20], but he nostalgically delved into the real architectural past of his sites. "My work," Haas explained, "often involves, among other things, bringing back an aspect of a place that was somehow lost."[17] Haas adjusted this architectural past of the site, sometimes inventing an altogether imaginary one that effectively unhinged historical styles, using them in a postmodernist collage of architectural fantasies. In the dramatic cutaway-rendering on the west wall of the Boston Architectural Center (seen here both before and after its completion in 1977), Haas amalgamated Etienne-Louis Boullée's visionary project for a museum of the 1780s, the early-nineteenth-century Federal Hall in New York, and the profile of the dome on the Pantheon in Rome with echoes of the nearby Christian Science complex in the Boston Back Bay.[18]

Alison Sky, Michelle Stone, and James Wines chartered SITE Projects in 1970, addressing the singularly non-art audience that populates retail chain stores and shopping-mall parking lots—as in their 1978 *Ghost Parking Lot* in Hamden, Connecticut [fig. 12.21]. Theirs was a more genuinely "pop"ular art sensibility than that of Haas. But the collaborative nature of SITE's design process, as well as the brilliantly imaginative results, reflected the multiplicity of overlapping frames of reference that characterized the cultural climate of the seventies. A number of other talented artists began gravitating to civic and corporate design commissions, too, toward the end of the seventies and in the eighties, reintroducing a vitality that had largely disappeared from view in the subways, airports, parks, and sterile corporate structures of the fifties and sixties, when the best artists retreated into a more autonomous context for their work. Joyce Kozloff's 1990 ceramic tiles for the Plaza Las Fuentes in Pasadena, for example, provide an exuberant reprieve from the working milieu of the city [fig. 12.7].

Jackie Ferrara expanded from making meticulously planned objects to also collaborating with architects and working in public spaces at the end of the seventies. The most interesting aspect of her work has persistently been the injection of an eccentric individuality into highly schematic programs of construction, as in *A209 Zogg* [fig. 12.22]. Ferrara had been involved in the happenings of the late fifties and early sixties and made small sculptures during the sixties in funky materials. One series involved a batch of four hundred stuffed pigeons, which she acquired from a taxidermist's warehouse in 1964.[19] Ferrara's work of the early seventies hints at that background in the eccentricity of the form of works such as *Zogg*, set off by their meticulous planning and construction. The artist titled *Zogg* after the personality it took on, "awkward looking, pugnacious, even kind of ugly . . . And I confess I thought of Godzilla too."[20]

12.20 Boston Architectural Center with *trompe-l'oeil* painting by Haas, 1977.

12.21 James Wines, SITE, *Ghost Parking Lot*, 1978.
Plaza and environmental sculpture, Hamden, Connecticut.
Used automobiles, bloc bond, and asphalt.

The drawings for a Ferrara sculpture are integral to the meaning. In a work such as *Zogg* she attempted to visualize all aspects of the sculpture in drawings and in her head. Then she would figure out the measurements for each of the small wooden elements, list them (there could be a hundred or more), cut each of them precisely, and then, working from the plan, neatly construct the form. The drawings include the cutting list and various views—aerial perspectives, isometrics, side elevations, and particularly complex views which the studies on paper helped her visualize. The juxtaposition of the three-dimensional form with the various two-dimensional interpretations of it in the drawings intriguingly highlights the relation of an idea to the variety of possibilities for interpreting it in material form, and

12.22 Jackie Ferrara, *A209 Zogg*, 1980.
Pine, 112 × 46½ × 31½in (284.5 × 118.1 × 80cm).
Collection, Donald Sussman, Greenwich, Conn.

despite all the careful planning each work yields unexpected revelations when built.

The Japanese sculptor Tadashi Kawamata trained as a painter. Then, he said, "it seemed to me that the structural support of the canvas, i.e. the wooden frame, could itself become the basis of my work."[21] In 1979 he began constructing ever-more complex temporary installations of wood. As with the *Spui Project* [fig. 12.23], which he constructed over the spring and summer of 1986 in The Hague, most of his site projects involve an architectural space or structure.

The site projects of Mary Miss have an affinity to Isamu Noguchi's gardens in that they promote an individual and intimate encounter with nature. But where Noguchi looked to nature as an inspiration to create form, Miss created a more complex experience of sculpture as an orchestrated passage through space. "When I am looking at structures that interest me," she has noted, "I am focusing on the experience I am seeing contained within them."[22] Her work draws on early memories of the American West, particularly on prehistoric sites such as Mesa Verde, which she visited as a

12.24 Mary Miss, *Pool Complex: Orchard Valley*, 1985.
Curved walkway, wood, stone, concrete, 3-acre (1.21-ha) site.
Laumeier Sculpture Park, St. Louis, Missouri.

12.25 Mary Miss, *Pool Complex: Orchard Valley*, 1985.
Wood, stone, concrete, 3-acre (1.21-ha) site.
Laumeier Sculpture Park, St. Louis, Missouri.

child. When she came to New York from Colorado in 1968, she recaptured that experience of the extended landscape in the confined space of her New York studio by distributing the compositional elements in implicitly infinite sequences across the floor.[23] By the end of the seventies she had moved into ambitious excavation and construction projects in the natural landscape, as at Laumeier Sculpture Park in St. Louis [figs. 12.24 and 12.25].

Appropriated Sites: Charles Simonds

Charles Simonds came to be known on the Lower East Side of New York in the early seventies not for commissioned site works but for work in appropriated sites. Unsuspecting pedestrians would happen upon his miniature clay villages [fig. 12.26] under eaves, in cracked walls of condemned buildings, and on outdoor window ledges, where most were eventually lost to the elements or to the curious, who destroyed them in trying to take them home. These dwellings, which look like miniature ancient ruins, have to do with a sense of dynamic transition from the ephemeral present to a mysterious and undisclosed future. Simonds elaborated mythological civilizations of "Little People" that moved on, through organic growth and chance encounters, to perpetually evolving self-conceptions. Their cosmologies were reflected in their styles of building and they left a natural history in these artifacts as they migrated through different neighborhoods of New York, building and then abandoning sites.

The dwellings of Charles Simonds concern organic growth in architecture, culture, and civilization. The impermanence of the outdoor pieces—fragile and exposed in the most vulnerable settings—heightens a sense of the evanescence of things. They leave the viewer with the unsettling conviction that someone has lived there but has now mysteriously vanished—indeed, one might return tomorrow for another look to find even these small traces gone. For Simonds, this was a gesture against the materialism and conformity of the corporate culture of the seventies. "If you leave thoughts behind you that other people can develop," Simonds pointed out, "you've had an effect on how the world looks or how it's thought about. I don't see any reason to leave behind 'things' which lose their meaning in time, or even exist as a symbol of meaning at a given time past."[24]

Gordon Matta-Clark's Site Critiques

Like Simonds, Gordon Matta-Clark appropriated sites for a social critique, and as in the site projects of Mary Miss and Kawamata, his work involved a sense of place rather than form. But instead of constructing a site, Matta-Clark attacked the structural integrity of existing buildings, cutting gaping holes through the walls, ceilings, and floors as shown in the pair of photos entitled *Bronx Floors: Floor Above, Ceiling Below* [fig. 12.27]. "I wanted to alter the whole space to its very roots," he explained. "[This] meant a recognition of the building's total (semiotic) system, not in any idealized form, but using the actual ingredients of a place."[25]

Matta-Clark's "anarchitecture," as he called it—a play on words fusing anarchy and architecture—was a deliberate political expression. "By undoing a building," he said, "there are many aspects of the social conditions against which I am gesturing."[26] He saw the housing of the New York ghettos as akin to prison cellblocks, and the isolation of the suburban "box" as scarcely any better. Matta-Clark's aim was to destroy the barriers between people, literally and figuratively opening up these "non-u-mental"[27] structures, to use another of his acerbic puns. Matta-Clark's aggressive "destructuring" was designed to create a new biography for abandoned buildings, "to convert a place into a state of mind."[28]

The son of the surrealist painter Matta, Gordon Matta-Clark studied architecture at Cornell and the Sorbonne, returning to New York in 1969 to make sculpture. He died of cancer in 1978 at the age of only thirty-five, but his short career nevertheless had a profound effect on the tone of the New York art scene, undermining fixed ideas of art as a cohesive entity. He also figured importantly in fostering a sense of community among young artists in SoHo at the time, helping to organize a collective exhibition and work space at 112 Greene Street as well as an inexpensive cafeteria called "Food" run by and for artists in the neighborhood.

Matta-Clark courted danger on several fronts—gangs roamed the deserted neighborhoods in which he worked, he risked being caught by police (since he generally cut up these abandoned buildings without permission), and his assault on the support systems of the buildings made them vulnerable to structural collapse. This attitude manifested

12.26 Charles Simonds, *Dwelling* (detail), 1981. Unfired clay wall relief, 8 × 44ft (2.44 × 13.41m).
Museum of Contemporary Art, Chicago. Gift of Douglas and Carol Cohen, 81.19.

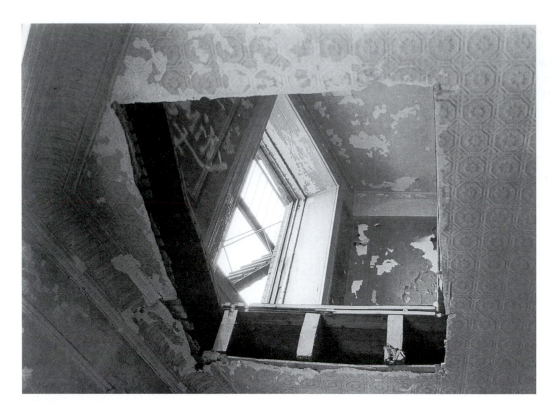

12.27 Gordon Matta-Clark,
*Bronx Floors: Floor Above,
Ceiling Below*, 1973.
Site project in a building in the Bronx,
New York.

12.28 Gordon Matta-Clark,
Splitting: Four Corners, exterior,
1974. Six black-and-white
photographs, two 12½ × 8¼in
(31.8 × 21cm) each and four
16 × 20in (40.6 × 50.8cm).

itself outside his work too—in 1976 he was invited to participate in an exhibition for artists and architects called "Idea as Model," but instead of submitting a proposal for new architecture he decided to exhibit photographs of the current state of some former "model buildings" in the South Bronx in which the occupants had smashed out the windows. On the eve of the show's opening he used Dennis Oppenheim's BB gun to shoot out the windows of the gallery to drive the point home. (They were repaired in time for the opening but the unhappy organizers removed Matta-Clark from the show.)

In 1974 Matta-Clark cut a suburban New Jersey house in half and chopped out the corners [fig. 12.28]. The house was scheduled for demolition and belonged to the art dealers Holly and Horace Solomon, who sponsored the project. Like all of Matta-Clark's work, *Splitting: Four Corners* was undocumentable. The artist exhibited fragments cut out of his various projects and struggled to find a way of collaging photographs to suggest the radical feeling of his idea, but nothing could recapture the sensation of actually entering the spaces he altered. As the painter Susan Rothenberg recalled: "From outside, the cut had a real formal look. The insides were like a chasm opening up the earth at your feet. Realizing that a house is home, shelter, safety . . . being in that house made you feel like you were entering another state. Schizophrenia, the earth's fragility, and full of wonder."[29]

ALICE AYCOCK

This disorienting spatial sense is one of the many competing logics assimilated into the work of Alice Aycock too. Her deep fascination with architecture and the complexity of her language of simultaneous, intertwining, and yet distinct trains of thought in spatially conceived constructions give her art a fantastic character. In a single work she may overlay ideas from a Babylonian diagram explaining the structure of the universe, the tumbler on a cement truck, the image of an angel floating on a yellow cloud in an obscure Renaissance painting, and a chart of the paths of particles in a nuclear accelerator. Each implies a system of ideas to her, and she visualizes such ideas into forms and even machines that function, not as symbols, but as incarnations of cross-tracking trains of thought; they are maps of the mind visualized in drawings and constructions in space. Aycock's art becomes a vehicle for living a plethora of different discoveries and ways of thinking all at once. In this sense her work epitomizes what was so new about the pluralism of the seventies—its complex simultaneity. She approaches sculpture as an interdisciplinary arena for exploring ideas, an open system which perpetually expands and, by definition, undermines all canons.

Aycock has generated her prodigious output of sculpture and drawings by weaving her sources into richly detailed stories. She scans across historical experiments in science, linguistic structures, and the magical fantasies of children; she may imagine herself as that particle traveling through an accelerator or see the drum of the cement truck as a whirling vortex that opens a hole in the universe with a stairway to Paradise. Curiosity overcomes fear in Aycock's work—a frightening whirring of blades or an awesome breakthrough in astrophysics will draw her in for a closer look and she masters the technology through projections of imagination.

> I want to crack it open. A machine is a tool and the tool is a mental extension of your body . . . it reflects on the structure of your mind. It's that that I'm interested in, the structure of the mind . . . my work is a very personal attempt to deal with the period that we are in . . . Duchamp[,] who really had one foot in the Middle Ages and the other in quantum mechanics . . . played very poetically with these ideas . . . I play with history. It's also necessary to play with science.[30]

At the very core of Aycock's self-realization as an artist is an early childhood memory of watching her father, an engineer and contractor, build a small model of a house. It was so small she could hold it in her hand.

> Night after night, I would watch him make this. Afterwards, he gave me the model to play with and he built the house. This was the house I grew up in. So I had an experience which I think was very important because I could mentally possess something, control it, see it as a whole, literally hold it in my hand and then later, I was inside of it, surrounded by a physical, large structure. I was given an early chance to conceptualize a space that I would live in. A space in which all sorts of emotional events took place. But it was a visual concept.[31]

In 1972 Aycock built a wooden maze on an isolated farm in Pennsylvania. She was fresh out of her master's degree at Hunter College, where she studied with Robert Morris. He had encouraged her interest in making sculptures as tools for exploring certain experiences. Bruce Nauman's video corridors also suggested to her this kind of psychological confrontation with oneself. Aycock got the idea for *Maze*—a twelve-sided wooden structure, 32 feet across, with 6-foot-high walls—from the circular plan for an Egyptian labyrinth which she came across in the *World Book Encyclopedia* while looking for a definition of magnetic north. "Originally, I had hoped to create a moment of absolute panic," she said, "when the only thing that mattered was to get out."[32]

Aycock's work through the mid-seventies centered on physical actions that led to a conflicting mixture of extreme psychological sensations. In her seminal *Low Building with Dirt Roof (For Mary)* (1973), the viewer had to crawl on all fours into the entrance of the 3-foot-high shack, under a roof laden with 7 tons of earth. One felt frightened and closed in by the weight overhead, and yet oddly secure as in a dream state. *Project Entitled "The Beginnings of a Complex . . ."* [figs. 12.29 and 12.30], an elaborate wooden complex which Aycock built for Documenta VI in Germany in 1977, consisted of five separate structures connected by a system of underground tunnels. The subterranean maze provided the only access to the interior ladder which in turn led up into an enclosed tower. When one finally did emerge from the dark, crushingly narrow tunnels of the labyrinth into the light, one was trapped in a well shaft or tower.

This work simultaneously evoked claustrophobia, euphoria in the sensation of heights, and vertigo. The narrow and low underground passages referred back to Aycock's trip in 1970 to the Egyptian pyramids and the Greek beehive tombs at Mycenae, when she fantasized about being buried alive at the heart of these great masses of stone and earth. Many of Aycock's works of the seventies and early eighties forced the viewer into seemingly dangerous situations, as in a frightening amusement-park ride.[33] In these works she courted disaster with obvious pleasure; the fear elicited by them has an almost erotic quality. "I like to scare myself for the pleasure of it,"[34] she explained.

12.29 (above) **Alice Aycock**, *Project Entitled "The Beginnings of a Complex . . .,"* 1977, Documenta, Kassel, Germany. Wood and concrete, wall façade: 40ft (12.19m) long, 8ft (2.43m), 12ft (3.66m), 16ft (4.88m), 20ft (6.1m), 24ft (7.32m) high respectively; square tower: 24ft (7.32m) high × 8ft (2.43m) square; tall tower group: 32ft (9.75m) high.

12.30 (below) **Alice Aycock**, *Project Entitled "The Beginnings of a Complex . . .,"* 1977, Documenta, Kassel, Germany. See fig. 12.29. Interior view looking down into shaft with ladder.

Seeing two thousand people climbing around the construction for Documenta VI undermined for Aycock the privacy of this psychologically complex experience, and in *The Angels Continue Turning the Wheels of the Universe*, her next major work, the viewer could enter in concept only. In 1979 Aycock moved from the wooden structures to apparatuses that resembled the laboratory in a vintage Frankenstein movie. She had read that when people first discovered electricity and magnetism they thought those phenomena were magical and could be used to conjure up ghosts. As her imagination went to work on this she concluded that ghosts probably come out of light, so she constructed *How to Catch and Manufacture Ghosts* (1979) with intense theater lights trained on a platform surrounded by various elements of steel, glass, and wire. A live woman was recruited to sit on a bench, blowing bubbles at a pan of water, in which there was a bottle with a little bird inside. Attached to the pan was a "lemon battery," taken from the instructions in a science book for children.

When the work was first shown, Aycock put a quotation on the wall beside it from a schizophrenic who had written down his dreams.

> This person really felt that he was the air, he thought that he had created Alaska, he felt speed moving through his body, he felt himself being pushed along the walls, and all the time he seemed to be experiencing sensations which we can only imagine. In one of his writings he said "sometimes I dream my mother dreaming me and that's how I travel home."[35]

What Aycock liked especially in this man's writings was that she could identify with the way he thought, "with the simultaneous insertion of multiple levels of diverse matter that I go through when I make a piece."[36] As an example: "He would talk about moving through space and time. At one moment he was fighting a battle with the archangel Michael in the sky and at the next moment, because he had eaten beef stew and was not supposed to, he caused World War I."[37]

Aycock's Work of the Eighties

From the Series Entitled How to Catch and Manufacture Ghosts, "Collected Ghost Stories from the Workhouse" [fig. 12.31] developed out of *How to Catch and Manufacture Ghosts*. To visualize the parts, the artist borrowed from early experiments in electricity, a Standard Oil refinery on the New Jersey Turnpike which resembles a futuristic city, the launch pad for the Montgolfier brothers' pioneering balloon ascent of 1783, and elements of Marcel Duchamp's *Bachelor Apparatus*. According to the artist, the galvanized drums—which resemble Duchamp's *Chocolate Grinder* (from the *Bachelor Apparatus*)—are "'agitation canisters.' When I was a child I thought that my soul looked like the inside of a washing machine . . . So I designed this with a movement like that."[38] The canisters and platform have multiple mechanized parts and originally she intended the work to include live birds in cages as well, though that proved too problematic.

Aycock's work from the late seventies through the mid-eighties re-creates the magic, the nostalgia, and the mysterious threatening forces of dreams. Often, individual works comprise only a small fragment of what initially seems like a convoluted narrative but which does not actually follow the sequential logic of a narrative at all. Her blade machine of 1984, *A Salutation to the Wonderful Pig of Knowledge (Jelly Fish, Water Spouter, . . . There's a Hole in My Bucket, There's a Hole*

12.31 Alice Aycock, *From the Series Entitled How to Catch and Manufacture Ghosts, "Collected Ghost Stories from the Workhouse,"* 1980. Cable, copper, galvanized steel, glass piping, steel, wire, wood, 30 × 75 × 120ft (9.14 × 22.86 × 36.58m). University of South Florida, Tampa.

in My Head, There's a Hole in My Dream) [fig. 12.32], has a disquieting presence, with moving glass blades and electrical parts that seem dangerous to approach. Yet at the same time the imaginative bravado of the title and the innocence with which Aycock manipulated these forbidding materials and devices suggests the transformative power of a child's fantasy.

The ambiguity of the title in this work mirrors the double-edged formal conception. The grand gesture implied in the "salutation" and the reference to the repetitious children's song "There's a Hole in My Bucket" evoke images of childhood. Casting knowledge as a pig and twisting the innocent song into an expression of existential disillusionment turns these sensations inside out. The title and the piece are childlike, vulnerable, and yet cruel. The poetry of the work lies in this juxtaposition of the delicately elaborated associations to childhood and the perversely threatening character of the physical components.

12.32 Alice Aycock, *A Salutation to the Wonderful Pig of Knowledge (Jelly Fish, Water Spouter, . . . There's a Hole in My Bucket, There's a Hole in My Head, There's a Hole in My Dream)*, 1984. Mixed media, 11ft 7in × 9ft 4in × 6ft 10in (3.53 × 2.85 × 2.08m). Courtesy the John Weber Gallery, New York.

Aycock stepped into a more abstract and philosophical mode during the mid-eighties, concentrating on esoteric diagrams of the universe and mystical languages. In a drawing of 1985 entitled *Circling 'Round the Ka'Ba: The Glass Bead Game* [figs. 12.33 and 12.34] Aycock rendered the universe as a board game. The swirling forms at the center derive in part from a Renaissance representation of the cosmos by the English mystic Robert Fludd (whose fanciful drawings also inspired the curving forms for many of Aycock's blade machines). Aycock metamorphosed these swirling curves into the idea of a small, disklike amphitheater, for which she found prototypes in the constructivist "Total Theater" designed by Walter Gropius in 1927. At the center is the secret edifice of the Ka'Ba, a Muslim shrine in Mecca that houses a black stone said to have been given by the archangel Gabriel to Abraham— the object toward which Muslims all over the world face to pray. Ka'Ba also means "box" in Arabic, and a "black box" is the term used in science for an "unknown" to be deduced by experiment. Here it embodies a cosmic mystery that one can't penetrate; it is also a shack, like the *Low Building with Dirt Roof (For Mary)* (1973). So the drawing combines architecture, nature, and the magic that is in so much of her work.

In *Tree of Life Fantasy: Synopsis of the Book of Questions Concerning the World Order and/or the Order of Worlds* [fig.

12.34 Alice Aycock drawing *Circling 'Round the Ka'Ba: The Glass Bead Game*, 1985.

12.35] of 1990–2 Aycock turned the stepped amphitheater upright, making it vertical "so that the steps are not steps that you can walk on . . . They're not quite of this world," she explained. In addition, she had for some time been working with bowls, inspired by ancient Indian observatories. The work also refers to the helices of DNA, to fragmentations of the Gropius theater, and to medieval and Renaissance illustrations of people walking off to Paradise through a whirling hole in the sky.[39] Here that ladder to Heaven has undergone a radical metamorphosis into a "loop-the-loop" rollercoaster surmounted by cosmograms, and on the trellis at the apex the artist imagines a live wisteria growing up from the back, a garden in Paradise and a tree of life. The white represents the purity that the real world lacks.

Aycock has, in one sense, always been preoccupied with objects in space, frequently realized in drawings that recall architectural plans. But her work is founded in a conceptual practice of using systems to generate form. In the early

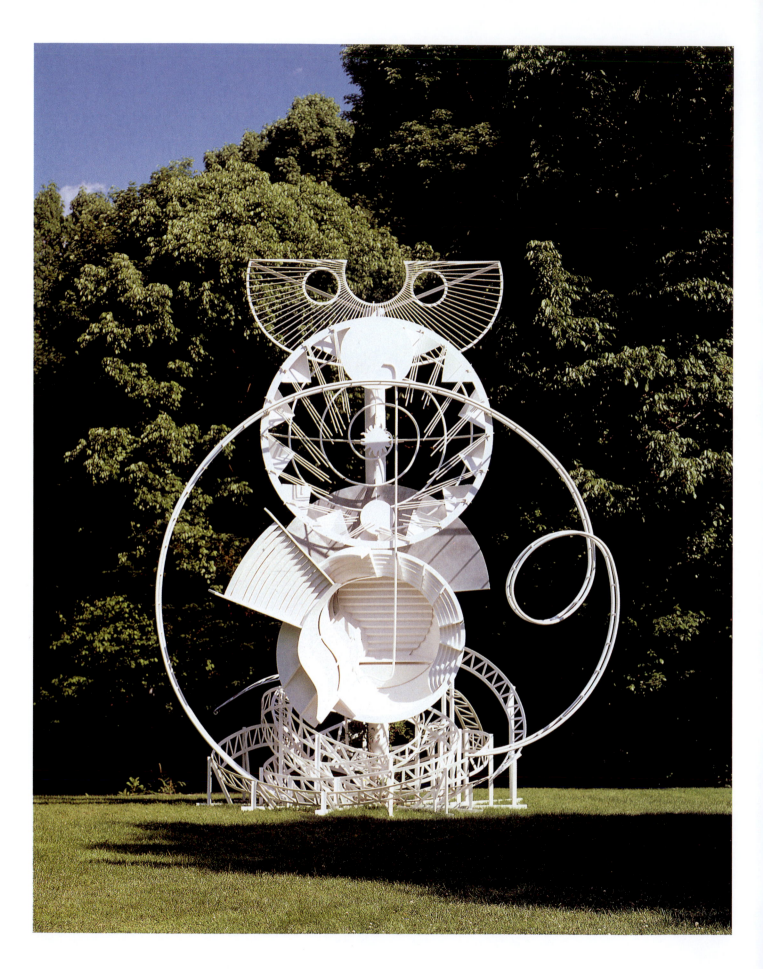

12.35 (opposite) **Alice Aycock**, *Tree of Life Fantasy: Synopsis of the Book of Questions Concerning the World Order and/or the Order of Worlds*, 1990–2. Painted steel, fiberglass, and wood, 20 × 15 × 8ft (6.1 × 4.57 × 2.44m). University of Illinois, Urbana-Champaign.

seventies her highly personal, complex vision was radical in relation to the minimalist cube, the pop icon, and the conceptual art action that dominated sculpture at that time. Her work is inclusive and maximal instead of exclusive and minimal—it is about everything at once, filtered through her perpetually expanding network of imagination. It is also a simultaneously feminist and postmodernist rejection of an authorial center. Each object has layer upon layer of unexpectedly intersecting stories and open-ended allusions that keep reappearing in her work as a way of bringing everything together into some complex whole, while at the same time undermining the fixed relations of a stable world view with a constant influx of new ideas. "I think that it's just simply the desire to push farther, to go beyond the known structures, and, in a sense, the work is a metaphor for that,"[40] she said.

CULTURAL COMPLEXITY

The seventies were about complexity and the most important art veered toward impurity—the opposite of Greenberg's formalist cleansing—though it took time for everyone to recognize what was happening. Artists like Matta-Clark, Christo and Jeanne-Claude, Smithson, and the conceptualists

challenged the conventions about artistic subject matter, the hierarchies of high and low art, and the protocols of how art can be made. Meanwhile such artists as Alice Aycock and Elizabeth Murray (see Chapter 13) pioneered styles in the seventies founded on overlays of different disconnected systems operating in a single work simultaneously. That complexity was mirrored in the variety of the art world and in the course of the seventies culture slowly began to be understood as a complicated layering of multiple different and simultaneous trajectories of thought that did not necessarily cohere. But what at first appeared simply as "pluralism" revealed itself as a fundamental shift in how we look at the world, embracing contradiction. "Appropriation" emerged from this situation as the new critical language of the last quarter of the century, because the act of taking images from advertising or mass media and assigning them new meaning reflected a world in which the meaning of things no longer seemed stable. The critical climate of the late sixties, the questioning of art in conceptualism, and Warhol's radical appropriation of media imagery to replace nature as a point of reference in his work set the stage for this shift to postmodern culture.

Media as a Medium

Dan Graham's *Homes for America* [fig. 12.36], a conceptual art piece that he first presented in 1966 as a slide show in the exhibition "Projected Art" at Finch College in New York, was an important harbinger of this shift. Graham had been shooting photographs of one-family suburban development homes in America since 1965, and the piece consisted of

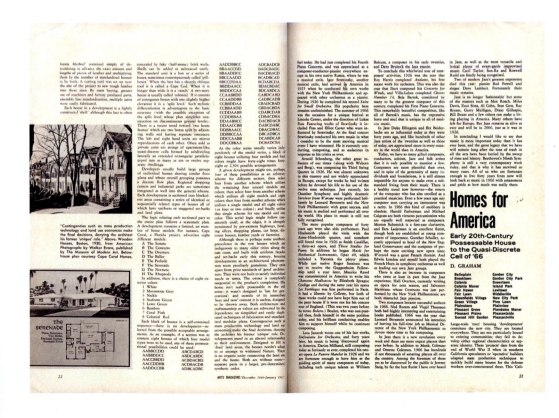

12.36 Dan Graham, *Homes for America*, page layout *Arts Magazine*, December 1966–January 1967.

pictures of tract housing, shown as though they were modular units of style and color, as in minimalist art. He originally intended to publish the work in a mass-circulation magazine like *Esquire*. Instead it appeared as an article in the December 1966–January 1967 issue of *Arts Magazine*, where the text took on more importance than Graham had originally intended, detracting from the impact of this radical idea of using the magazine itself as an art medium. This had the effect of casting prosaic reality as subjective representation.

APPROPRIATION

In an influential essay of 1967 entitled "The Death of the Author," the French literary critic Roland Barthes stated that "a text is not a line of words releasing a single 'theological' meaning (the 'message' of the Author-God), but a multi-dimensional space in which a variety of writings, none of them original, blend and clash," and he attacked traditional ways of reading in which "the *explanation* of a work is always sought in the man or woman who produced it, as if it were always in the end . . . the voice of a single person, the *author* 'confiding' in us."[41] Instead, Barthes argued, every sign (a word or, by extension, an image or a brushstroke) is a product of history and social convention.

By assigning a role to the reader and to culture (both of which are perpetually changing) in defining the content of a text, Barthes negated the possibility of finding a stable interpretation of any text (or image). Moreover, he denied the concept of originality: "The text is a tissue of quotations drawn from the innumerable centers of culture . . . The writer can only imitate a gesture that is always anterior, never original . . . Did he wish to *express himself*, he ought at least to know that the inner 'thing' he thinks to 'translate' is itself only a ready-formed dictionary."[42]

Following the lead of Polke and Baldessari, and often influenced by Barthes, many artists of the late seventies looked to readymade images or ideas as the data of personal experience as well as the raw material of one's own expressive work. This approach, which came to be known as "appropriation," grew out of collage, via pop art. Indeed, as John Carlin has written: "Pop art wasn't just a 60s phenomenon. It has become the dominant form of realism in the late 20th century." He pointed out that pop art replaced "the mimetic basis of realism . . . with a purely semiotic one. The primary artistic reference is no longer nature, but culture—the fabricated system of signs that has taken the place of things in our consciousness. In short, landscape has become signscape."[43]

The art world took up the issue of appropriation and the arbitrary overlay of ready-formed images in the later seventies as part of a reexamination of the possibility of originality and authenticity in the growing corporate mass culture. Thomas Lawson, for example, praised David Salle's paintings [fig. 12.37] for being "dead, inert representations of the impossibility of passion in a culture that has institutionalized

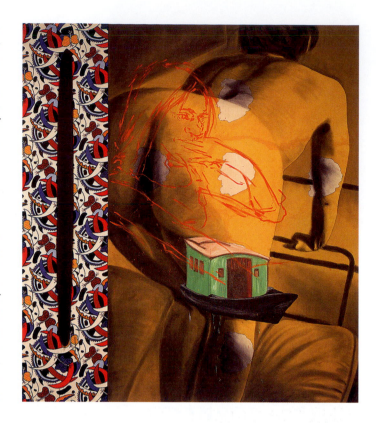

12.37 David Salle, *His Brain*, 1984. Oil and acrylic on canvas, acrylic on fabric, two panels, 9ft 9in × 8ft 9¾in (2.97 × 2.69m) overall.

Courtesy Gagosian Gallery, New York.

self-expression."[44] For this writer, the impassiveness of Salle's work was a new value in art precisely because it responded to the new cultural situation.

Sherrie Levine and Mike Bidlo attracted attention in New York by making look-alikes of celebrated works from the history of art. Bidlo painted a look-alike Jackson Pollock, for example, and Levine photographed a work by Walker Evans in a manner scarcely distinguishable from the original and presented it as her own work [fig. 12.38]. Their art explores the possibility of expressing oneself using the ready-made expressions of someone else, asking: can this method express authentic feeling? Is it original? Similarly, Richard Prince introduced the concept of "rephotography" in 1977, making photographs of pictures in magazine advertisements and then blowing them up, cropping, or rearranging them to take on new meanings by the new juxtapositions. His work underscored the postmodern emphasis on the surface of events, "scanning" experience as in the media and computers rather than penetrating its depth.

12.38 (opposite) **Sherrie Levine**, *After Walker Evans: 4*, 1981. Gelatin silver print, 10 × 8in (25.4 × 20.3cm).

Whitney Museum of American Art, New York. © Walker Evans Archive, The Metropolitan Museum of Art.

Salle, a student of Baldessari's, began overlaying images in 1979 and, as with Polke ten years earlier, the primary stimulus was the experiential complexity of a culture defined by images from advertising and media. "Everything in this world," he explained, "is simultaneously itself and a representation of the idea of itself. This was in a sense my big art epiphany . . . The pleasures and challenges of simultaneity continue to be one of the driving forces in my work."[45]

The visual busyness of the graphic design in Salle's paintings deflects emphasis away from considering the imagery as iconographically significant. Indeed, the artist has repeatedly downplayed any reference external to the paintings: "To focus on where the images come from," he has said, "distorts their life together *in a painting*."[46] Thus Salle encourages us to see the female nude, for example, as an image among images, part of the undifferentiated—and by implication ethically neutral—stuff of received experience. The fact that we cannot is one of the inherent contradictions that, for Lisa Phillips, made Salle's work poignant and relevant; she saw it as "embracing the intensity of empty value at the core of mass-media representation."[47]

Gary Panter [fig. 12.39], who began overlaying forms in Los Angeles in the mid-seventies, leaves the viewer with a more unsettling and thought-provoking ambiguity about where, conceptually, to place his images. One isn't sure whether to read them as appropriations from life or advertising, or as caricature from the underground comics (a genre in which Panter has a considerable reputation). Panter's famous comic character "Jimbo," a disconcerting fusion of man and automaton, roams the dehumanized fantasy city of Dal-Tokyo which is simultaneously futuristic and antiquated. Thus unhinged from rational time, even the setting of Panter's narratives undermines the conceptual hierarchies on which one's sense of orientation in the world relies.[48]

For Richard Prince, the mass media provides a stock catalog of contemporary desires (symbolized in advertising images, for example) which he can appropriate as vehicles for his own experience. He dislocates the images by projecting his own fantasies into them, superimposing and recoloring them. In *Untitled (Three Women Looking in the Same Direction)* [fig. 12.40] the similarities between the three images from different advertisements became the overt content, making a conceptual connection that is individual (and unintended by the advertisers). However, the act of manipulating found images and assigning them personal meaning is in itself an exploration of the experience of living in a world flooded with images. Prince is a kind of passive witness, yet he controls the camera, so he can manipulate the pictures in his own way. In this sense he reclaims authority over his own identity in the depersonalized world of the mass media, and that reassertion of self is at the heart of his work: "I have always found it difficult to talk about what it's like to rephotograph an image," he has said, "but 'what it's like' is what it's about."[49]

The threat of dissolution in mass culture is clear enough, and so is the solution proposed by Prince: "I think the audience has always been the author of an artist's work. What's different now is that the artist can become the author of someone else's work."[50] He acknowledges "the commonality of this information retrieval, the fact that we've shared it

12.39 Gary Panter, *Untitled*, 1988. Acrylic on canvas, 5ft 6in × 7ft 8in (1.67 × 2.34m). Private collection.

12.40 Richard Prince, *Untitled (Three Women Looking in the Same Direction)*, 1980. Set of three Ektacolor prints, edition of ten, 3ft 4in × 5ft (1.01 × 1.52m) each.
Collection of the Chase Manhattan Bank, New York.

and think it's somehow part of us, makes us think about the information as a genuine experience."[51] Thus Prince seeks a route into individual authenticity through media culture rather than against it.

A puzzling narrative fragment—very often literally written right over a collage of appropriated images—brings the experience of mass culture back to the level of individual anecdote in the installations, assemblages, and paintings of Vernon Fisher from Dallas. In Fisher's *Show and Tell* [fig. 12.41], for example, the artist has blown up what seems to be a snapshot of the catch by two men out for an afternoon's fishing and then punched the lettering through the surface for a long narrative text which has nothing explicitly to do with the image. Then next to that he has hung a school blackboard with white paint spattered across it, and to the right a cutout of a young woman dressed in a fancy hat and gloves and polka-dot blouse. The stenciled text is a poignant

story of a shy child so wrapped in the world of her creative imagination that her reality completely fails to connect with the reality of her classmates and teacher in school—a microcosm of the alienation of the individual in a mass culture.

One little girl never brought anything to sharing time. Other children might bring an authentic Indian headdress acquired on a vacation in Arizona, or a Civil War sword handed down from Great Granddad, but whenever the teacher asked: "Dori, do you have anything to share with us today?" she only stared at the top of her desk and shook her head firmly from side to side. Then one day, long after her turn had mercifully disappeared, Dori abruptly left her seat and walked to the front of the class. With everyone's startled attention she began: "Today on the way to school I found something that I want to share." She held her arm stiffly out in front of her and began slowly dropping tiny pieces of shredded Kleenex. "See?" she said. "Snow."

12.41 Vernon Fisher, *Show and Tell*, 1981. Photograph on laminated paper, blackboard, oil on wood, overall dimensions 60 × 174 × 6in (152.4 × 442 × 15.2cm).
Collection, Michael Krichman and Leslie Simon.

Raymond Pettibon had graduated college and begun teaching high school mathematics in Los Angeles when, at the end of the seventies, he decided to dedicate himself to drawing. His career is built around a feverish production of nothing but small pen and ink drawings; he had little career ambition and his work circulated chiefly among friends for nearly twenty years, until he found a wider public in the late nineties. Though generally influenced by comic book line drawings, he has never settled into a single style of rendering, but his drawings all depend upon sometimes lengthy inscriptions and there is a disjunctive manner of putting together image and text that is uniquely his own. In his *Untitled (Since You Can't)*, a drawing of 1983 [fig. 12.42], for example, the surreal vision of a distraught female nude inside a bottle is captioned "Since you can't get her out anyway, the thing to do is to throw out the whole thing." The text has such a matter-of-fact tone of common-sense advice, and yet, taken together, the situation, the tone, and the suggestion are so disconcertingly irrational! The intriguing oddness of it all—the way it simply won't hold together—creates a conceptual fragmentation that seems emblematic of the seventies and eighties.

12.42 Raymond Pettibon, *Untitled (Since You Can't)*, 1983.
Pen and ink on paper, 13 × 9in (33 × 22.8cm).
Courtesy Regen Projects, Los Angeles.

Cindy Sherman

Cindy Sherman [figs. 12.43 and 12.44] also creates dispersed narrative fragments to create multiple layers of open-ended, simultaneous readings of her work. She came to New York in 1977 and began photographing herself in campy fifties outfits and then in other costumes and settings. "These are pictures of emotions personified,"[52] she explained, and although she is the model in her entire *oeuvre*, none of the pictures are self-portraits in the ordinary sense. Instead, she creates imaginary narratives in which she acts, using the common faith in the truth of the photograph to explore a wide range of roles. She often turns to stereotypical roles for women, but her point of reference seems to have been the representation of the pre-fabricated roles in movies and media rather than the roles as they exist in daily life. This second degree of remove is especially intriguing since her work is so emotionally evocative.

"I was thinking of a young girl," she says of one of the photographs, "who may have been cleaning the kitchen for her mother and who ripped out of the newspaper something asking 'Are you lonely?' or 'Do you want to be friends?' or 'Do you want to go on a vacation?' She's cleaning the floor, she rips this out and is thinking about it."[53] Sherman challenges fixed identity by taking on so many guises. Yet the specificity of each image suggests how fully the artist throws herself into every character. In the seventies Sherman made only small black-and-white photographs, directly influenced by film and television, but not by specific films or shows. She shifted to a larger scale and to the use of a rich color technique around the end of 1980. Then she turned to increasingly bizarre, sometimes macabre themes, testing an ever-widening range of subjects and emotions.

Sherman's work has had a great impact in encouraging younger artists to use photography in this personal yet disconnected narrative way. Just as Robert Arneson's self-portraiture of the seventies and eighties explored the narcissistic self-reflection that unfolds in the culture of common human interaction (the way the world invades and shapes the self), Cindy Sherman's photographs allowed the viewer to look over her shoulder as she examined narcissistic self-projection into media types. In the hypothesis of living pre-existing identities from mass culture, one by one—whether inspired by Hollywood celebrity photos, as in her early work, or by horror-film stills as in her work of the late eighties—Sherman's photographs provide the collateral pleasures of erotic exhibitionism and tabloid drama while at the same time opening a window onto the emptiness of our narcissistic culture. "They're not at all autobiographical,"[54] she has said about her photos, and yet they "should trigger your memory so that you feel you have seen it before."[55] They do, and the reason for this sense of familiarity is not because any of the images come from a particular movie or advertisement (they don't), but because the types are so pervasive in shaping the fantasies and desires of our consumer culture. Sherman's work evokes an existential anxiety of personal dissolution into the clichés of contemporary mass-marketing.

12.43 Cindy Sherman, *Untitled Film Still #3*, 1977. Black-and-white photograph, 8 × 10in (20.3 × 25.4cm). Collection, the artist. Courtesy Metro Pictures, New York.

12.44 Cindy Sherman, *Untitled #119*, 1983. Color photograph, 3ft 9½in × 7ft 10in (1.16 × 2.39m). Collection, the artist. Courtesy Metro Pictures, New York.

13.1 Philip Guston, *The Studio*, 1969. Oil on canvas, 4ft × 3ft 6in (1.22 × 1.07m).
Private collection, New York. Courtesy David McKee Gallery, New York and the Estate of Philip Guston.

13 PAINTING IN THE SEVENTIES

PHILIP GUSTON'S LATE STYLE

"In the anti-historical position," Philip Guston insisted in a lecture of 1974, "each artist is . . . himself."[1] In contrast to postulates of historical inevitability or the social construction of meaning put forward in the latest "critical theory," to the impersonality of minimalism, and to the language-based signscape that preoccupied Johns, the pop artists, and many conceptualists, Philip Guston's reassertion of the self as the procreative nucleus of art in the seventies announced, and influenced, a rejuvenation of introspective painting in New York.

What made Guston's work after 1968 so important was not just its political dimension—its "imaginative grasp on the epoch," as Harold Rosenberg put it—even though that was there too, but also that the depth of its existential struggle made painting real again. To most of the art world, painting had become irrelevant as a response to the pressing concerns of the later sixties. Rosenberg hinted at Guston's role in reconnecting painting to the self when he wrote of his late work as a "liberation from detachment."[2] For Guston and other artists of the abstract expressionist generation, painting made concrete one's thoughts about the most important questions of ethics and identity—who one was in relation to events and to the painful dilemmas of the human condition. Their deliberations became palpably visible in their work and thus points of style engendered passionate exchanges.

The sheer courage of Guston's leap to a figurative style at the end of the sixties [fig. 13.1], as if willfully tossing out his "old master" status as an abstract expressionist [fig. 6.7], brought on a storm of rebuke from his established colleagues and former friends. For that very reason it also reaffirmed painting as an arena for radical ideas in so far as Guston, in the service of authenticity, felt he had no alternative. Guston was a painter perpetually beginning again, risking everything to follow an idea into the unknown, both seduced and tortured by doubt. "My whole life is *based* on *anxiety*," he wrote to his friend Dore Ashton, "where else does art come from, I ask you?"[3]

Ashton described Guston's character as one of "extreme nervous tension (he was a chainsmoker and a pacer) and the high irritability that existentialist philosophers regarded as the hallmark of the artist."[4] What particularly struck the critic Peter Schjeldahl about Guston's late work was that it "appeared to deal with a level of doubt that would paralyse anyone else."[5] Even in the early fifties, when the abstract expressionists all hung out at the Cedar Bar, Guston's friend Mercedes Matter recalled that "he'd come in one night in an absolute gloom. He'd say, 'I just scraped off months of work on the floor. I'm not a painter. It's no use.' And he'd have everybody down . . . And it never failed that the following week he would float in, not touching the ground, and say, 'I've just finished the first painting I've ever done!'"[6]

Guston's Early Career

Guston was born Philip Goldstein in 1913 to an impoverished Russian immigrant family. He grew up in Los Angeles and at the age of twelve started drawing seriously, encouraged by his mother. He loved the comics, especially *Krazy Kat* and *Mutt and Jeff*, and wanted to be a cartoonist. Guston attended the Manual Arts High School, where he established lifelong friendships with Reuben Kadish and Jackson Pollock, but he left without ever finishing high school. Instead, he hung out with a small and rebellious group of intellectual and artistic friends who educated themselves by reading literature and philosophy and vanguard art journals like *Transition*, *The Dial*, and *Cahiers d'Art*. At seventeen he got to see the magnificent collection of modern art that belonged to Walter and Louise Arensberg. This was a turning point, and

Guston later credited the de Chirico paintings in particular with helping to crystallize his ambition to become a painter.

Guston read avidly—especially in the fields of philosophy and literature—and he taught himself to paint. There wasn't much to see in the public collections in Los Angeles at the time, but he studied reproductions, especially of paintings by Picasso and the Renaissance masters. In 1932 the Mexican muralist David Siqueiros painted a wall at the Chouinard Institute in Los Angeles and then caused a political stir with an outdoor work for the Plaza Arts Center on Olvera Street. By this time Guston was already involved in leftist politics and keenly interested in the Mexican muralists. He and Pollock even went out to see Orozco at work on his *Prometheus* mural at Pomona College.

Guston painted some portable frescoes of his own in 1931, on the theme of the notorious racist trial of the Scottsboro Boys. In one painting of this subject he depicted

13.2 Philip Guston, *Conspirators*, 1932. Oil on canvas, 50 × 36in (127 × 91.4cm).

Location unknown. Courtesy David McKee Gallery, New York and the Estate of Philip Guston.

Ku Klux Klansmen whipping a roped black man; in another, hooded Klansmen armed with crude weapons huddle in front of a primitive gallows [fig. 13.2]. He showed the frescoes in a friend's bookstore shortly after painting them and a group of Klansmen and American Legionnaires brandishing lead pipes and guns broke in, smashed the space up, and shot the eyes and genitals out of the figures in the paintings. Because there was an eyewitness, the artist and his friend were able to sue. But the judge, who obviously disliked their leftist politics, dismissed the case, teaching Guston a lesson about "justice" in America he never forgot.

In 1934 Guston worked as an assistant on two mural painting commissions, one in Morelia, Mexico, and another in California, and then moved to New York where he stayed with Pollock until he got settled. In the late thirties he painted his own murals for the W.P.A. The federal projects brought together a real community of intellectuals and artists in New York. With the Pollock brothers and the painter James Brooks, for example, Guston would go to Orozco's lectures at the New School or to a play put on by the Federal Theater Project and stay up half the night talking about it with the others.

In 1941 Guston left this lively scene to teach at the University of Iowa and then at Washington University in St. Louis. Whereas Guston's painting *Conspirators* of 1932 [fig. 13.2] has not only the monumentality but the dramatic volumes and spatial recession of Renaissance and Mexican frescoes and of de Chirico, his painting *The Porch* (1946–7) [fig. 13.3] is squeezed into a shallow cubist space. The figures reveal Guston's late-thirties discovery of Max Beckmann, then in St. Louis, with their emblematic but undecipherable props: the flute, a crown, a child with a paper bag hat turned away playing the drum, a little girl covering her eyes with a handkerchief or paper hat, a masked harlequin in white with the sole of his shoe flattened against the picture plane, and a figure with one leg wrapped as though in the ribbons of a ballet slipper, holding cymbals that recall the garbage can lids used by the children at play in Guston's W.P.A. murals.

The powder blue sky and orange ground plane in the backdrop to *The Porch* suggest the continuing influence of Piero della Francesca's *Flagellation*, a kind of artistic beacon for Guston from the beginning of his career. In addition, the building in the left distance evokes an Italian piazza, but this (like the wide wooden floorboards) may have more to do with the Arensbergs' de Chiricos. Guston's interest in cubism, and specifically in Picasso's *Guernica* [fig. 2.10], emerged between the time he painted *Conspirators* and *The Porch*, inspiring him in the latter work to flatten the figures and use the wood frame porches of the houses in Iowa (as Piero della Francesca used the columns and beams on the left side of *The Flagellation*) to create a visual tension between the diagrammatic recession and the anti-illusionistic flattening of patterns on the picture plane. There is a classical rigor to this formal structuring that lends a timelessness to the composition. However, the uncomfortable compression also relates to newsreels the artist had recently seen of the piles of bodies in

Guston's Action Paintings of the Fifties

Guston's paintings from 1951 through the early sixties [fig. 6.7] evolve organically through the artist's interaction with the paint and surface. Guston's unique variation on the idea of action painting concerns "touch" more than "gesture"— the sensuality of the surface complements an increasingly rich spectrum of saturated color through the fifties. At first the artist constructed clouds of little vertical and horizontal strokes, like the "plus and minus" strokes in Mondrian's "Pier and Ocean" series. These paintings are all about openness and freedom—Guston largely dissolved solid form and yet the legacy of Piero and Cézanne still persists in the way he seems to locate the brushstrokes in a defined space. In 1957 the strokes became a little more aggressive, heavier and more irregular, with a deeper palette. At the same time the increasing specificity of the titles accompanied a gradual consolidation of the touches of color into forms.

The fifties was a period of masterful action paintings for Guston. He worked largely in a loft in Greenwich Village and was once again involved with the community of painters in New York, working off nervous energy on long walks in the streets, smoking and drinking heavily in bars with other artists or at the Friday night meetings of "The Club." In January 1952 he showed the light, calligraphic action paintings of 1951 at the Peridot Gallery, his first show in New York since 1945. The next year he joined the Egan Gallery, where his work prompted talk of "abstract impressionism," although the real ancestry of these works was not in *plein air* painting but in the psychologically charged glow that illuminated the paintings of Rembrandt.

The Re-emergence of the Figure

By the end of the fifties Guston began to feel that it had become "too easy to elicit a response"[8] with these sensuous abstractions. Thus his first major museum retrospective, at the Guggenheim Museum in 1962, marked another turning point. In that year he had not only drastically reduced the color—or rather painted it out with layers of broad gray and black brushstrokes—but in the process had begun to discover palpable forms in space. As he told Harold Rosenberg in 1966:

> To preconceive an image, or even to dwell on an image, and then to go ahead and paint it is an impossibility for me . . . it's intolerable—and also irrelevant— because . . . it's simply and only recognizable . . . Paul Valéry once said that a bad poem is one that vanishes into meaning. In a painting . . . it vanishes into recognition. The trouble with recognizable art is that it excludes too much. I want my work to include more. And "more" also comprises one's doubts about the object, plus the problem, the dilemma, of recognizing it.[9]

Thus in the sixties Guston's painting turned into a dialog about touch and form as a prolog to a more complex exploration of the tension between touch and image in the works

13.3 Philip Guston, *The Porch*, 1946–7. Oil on canvas, 56⅛ × 34in (142.6 × 86.4cm).

Krannert Art Museum and Kinkead Pavilion, University of Illinois, Urbana-Champaign. Purchased out of the "Illinois Biennial" exhibition of 1948. Courtesy David McKee Gallery, New York and the Estate of Philip Guston.

the Nazi concentration camps—he said he "was searching for the plastic condition, where the compressed forms and space themselves expressed my feelings about the holocaust."[7]

In 1947 Guston left teaching for a rustically appointed house in Woodstock, an old artists' colony in upstate New York. His painting was at another crossroads and he used the isolation to find his direction. In October 1948 he left for Europe on a Prix de Rome scholarship for a year, and of course went to see the Pieros, the Masaccios, and the Uccellos. In 1947–8 Guston began radically abstracting the shallow space and emblematic figures of paintings such as *The Porch*, while the palette carried the reduction even further toward just black, red, and some touches of brown. In 1950 he moved into a more purely improvisational dialog with the painted surface by itself.

of 1969–80, as in *Central Avenue* [figs. 13.4 and 13.5] where the same sensual touch and palette as in *Oasis* [fig. 6.7] still exist, but now with another layer of discourse about the subject matter superimposed on top. "Sometimes I know what [the forms] are," he said of his black-and-white compositions of the mid-sixties. "But if I think 'head' while I'm doing it, it becomes a mess . . . I want to end with something that will baffle me."[10]

In 1967 Guston retreated to the isolation of Woodstock again, even disconnecting his phone so no one could call in. It was an anxious period—his drinking ran out of control and his painting nearly ground to a halt for two years as he swung back and forth between drawings of just two or three bold black lines on a white ground and sketches of little objects around the studio.

I remember days of doing "pure" drawings immediately followed by days of doing the other—drawings of objects. It wasn't a transition in the way it was in 1948, when one feeling was fading away and a new one had not yet been born. It was two equally powerful impulses at loggerheads. I would one day tack up in the house a bunch of pure drawings, feel good about them . . . And that night go out to the studio to the drawings of objects—books, shoes, buildings, hands . . . The next day, or day after, back to doing the pure constructions and to attacking the other. And so it went, this tug-of-war, for about two years.[11]

It was the time of the intensifying protests against the war in Vietnam and a pointing finger emerged in Guston's work. As he grew more and more outraged by what he saw on television—the Democratic Convention of 1968, and assassinations of Bobby Kennedy, Martin Luther King, and Malcolm X; government violence against students; the Vietnam War—the rebellion of his youth came rushing back. First he painted dozens of blocky cartoon-like shoes, buildings, clocks, and books, and then in 1969 the hooded figures emerged in increasingly ambitious compositions [figs. 13.1

13.4 Philip Guston, *Central Avenue*, 1969. Oil on canvas, 4ft 9⅛in × 6ft 8in (1.45 × 2.03m).
University Art Museum, University of California at Berkeley. Gift of Mrs. Philip Guston and Musa Jane Mayer. Courtesy David McKee Gallery, New York and the Estate of Philip Guston.

and 13.4]. "This was the beginning. They are self-portraits. I perceive myself as being behind a hood."[12]

That these cigar-smoking hoods represent the artist himself is plain enough in paintings like *The Studio* [fig. 13.1], where the hood paints his own portrait in a closed-off room with a bare bulb hanging down from a wire. The scene itself goes back to Guston's childhood memories of hiding in a closet on Sundays when his relatives came to visit. A single light hung down on a cord in this closet so he could draw and read, and he would hear his mother telling the family that he wasn't home.

From 1969 through 1972 the hoods obsessed Guston. He issued a constant flow of notes to himself for paintings: "Have them playing poker, have them sitting around drinking beer and eating hamburgers."[13] He explained that his intent

was really not to illustrate, to do pictures of the Ku Klux Klan, as I had done earlier. The idea of evil fascinated me, rather like Isaac Babel who had joined the Cossacks, lived with them and written stories about them. I almost tried to imagine that I was living with the Klan. What would it be like to be evil? To plan, to plot.[14]

The hoods are the ambiguously frightening and lovable sides of the artist's own creativity. The dangling light bulb goes back not only to his boyhood closet but to Picasso's *Guernica* [fig. 2.10] and this Jekyll-and-Hyde view of the artist's creative force resembles Picasso's identification with the simultaneously sympathetic and frightening minotaur. In *Central Avenue* the hoods with their wooden cross are also artists with an easel and stretchers; the sensuous, "fat pink paint"[15] (as Guston described the kind of passages he used

for the tops of the highest background buildings in *Central Avenue*) revisits abstract works of the fifties like *Oasis*, but in *The Studio* it suffuses everything.

The idea of the *golem*, which fascinated Guston,[16] seems particularly germane to the hoods. Cabbalists (mystic Jews) of the Middle Ages would model a human figure (a *golem*) out of red clay (like the "fat pink" paint?) as a pious reenactment of the creation of Adam. But that was a double-edged blade, since Jewish law forbade graven images—only God had the right to make things in his own image. Likewise, Guston's reintroduction of graven images in his paintings transgressed the laws of abstract expressionism and was even more of an affront to Greenberg's "pure painting."

Guston showed his figurative work for the first time in October 1970 at the Marlborough Gallery. The critical response to his show was predictably withering and it took nearly a decade for even his friends to catch up with the total rethinking that these works represented. The Marlborough show was another watershed for Guston, marking the final phase of his work that lasted from 1972 until his death in 1980.

The black and gray paintings of the first half of the sixties simultaneously reveal form and cross it out, while the hoods mask the identity of the ambivalently endearing and menacing artist. In this new work of the middle and late seventies the painter is revealed everywhere. *Head and Bottle* [fig. 13.6] unmasks the painter's vision and his vice. The hoods began disappearing in 1972, replaced by raw images of the artist's disembodied eye and head as in this drawing, piles of legs and the soles of shoes as in *The Floor* [fig. 13.7], and paintbrushes, ugly bugs, and strange lunar landscapes as in *Moon* [fig. 13.8].

13.6 (above) **Philip Guston**, *Head and Bottle*, 1975. Ink on paper, 19 × 24in (48.3 × 61cm).

Collection, Armando and Gemma Testa. Courtesy David McKee Gallery, New York and the Estate of Philip Guston.

13.7 (below) **Philip Guston**, *The Floor*, 1976. Oil on canvas, 5ft 9in × 8ft 2in (1.75 × 2.5m).

Private collection, New York. Courtesy David McKee Gallery, New York and the Estate of Philip Guston.

13.8 Philip Guston, *Moon*, 1979. Oil on canvas, 5ft 9in × 6ft 11½in (1.75 × 2.12m).

Collection, Philip Johnson. Courtesy David McKee Gallery, New York and the Estate of Philip Guston.

Guston's late style is torn between Piero della Francesca and the comics, Rembrandt and Kafka. While on the one hand there is his exhilaration in discovery—"What you want is an experience of making something that you haven't seen before"[17]—there is also the anxiety: "Our whole lives (since I can remember) are made up of the most extreme cruelties of holocausts," he wrote Dore Ashton after the CIA coup in Chile. "We are the witnesses of the hell. When I think of the victims it is unbearable."[18] And yet it is the peculiar fate of such an artist to want to see everything.

NEW EXPRESSIONIST PAINTING IN EUROPE

Like Guston, the twenty-seven-year-old Düsseldorf artist Jörg Immendorff was, in 1972, rediscovering painting for himself in a series of poignantly soul-searching compositions. The increasingly politicized atmosphere of the sixties was reaching its climax, and Immendorff was seeking to reconcile his own strong commitment to political and social activism with his deep-seated desire to paint. His studies with Joseph Beuys (1964–70) had reinforced his dedication to a politically engaged art as he watched Beuys himself move increasingly in this direction.

In particular, the 1965 Beuys performance *How to Explain Pictures to a Dead Hare* [fig. 8.15] seems to have had a catalytic effect on Immendorff, bringing home the limitations of both pictures and words. Pamela Kort, in a catalog on Immendorff's work, has described how he turned to childhood in 1966 for a language that satirized what he regarded as the elitist bourgeois hierarchies of high art, the veneration of artistic genius, and the preciousness of the art object.[19] He issued "baby talk" manifestoes and painted works like *Teine Tunst Mache* or "top toing art" (an infantile speech rendering of *keine Kunst mache* or "stop doing art"). At the same time this work embodies Immendorff's ambivalence about his growing inability to justify "doing art"—which he saw as politically ineffective—and his nevertheless ineradicable attraction to painting. Beuys had taken a turn toward political engagement in 1964 and entreated his students to abandon painting. But the image of Beuys sweeping the Karl-Marx-Platz in East Berlin with a push broom as the 1972 May Day Parade went by also had particular significance for Immendorff; the red painted broom expressed solidarity with the revolutionary principle but the sweeping away protested adherence to any form of dogmatism.

Immendorff labeled his work between 1968 and 1970 "Lidl" (referring to the sound of a baby rattle). A child's universe of symbols—paintings of turtles, dogs, goldfish, and polar bears—populated the "Lidlraum" (his aesthetic space of child-sensibility), offering alternatives to the vocabulary of adult artists whose creativity Immendorff saw as confined by bourgeois convention and by the spiritual wounds still lingering from the Nazi period. The "Lidl" art stood for beginning again, free of history and convention, but it also brought back the accusation of childishness, used by the Nazis as a weapon against modernism. Nor could Immendorff keep his *fausse naïveté* pure of his unconscious ambitions—as Kort noted, Immendorff identified himself with the turtle outracing the hare (an emblem for his teacher Beuys).

Jörg Immendorff's Political Analysis of Painting in the Seventies

In an autobiography published in the early seventies entitled *Here and Now: To Do What Has to Be Done*,[20] Immendorff invoked Lenin's plan of 1905, *What Is to Be Done?* Yet, despite his dedication to leftist ideology, the artist analyzed himself, his political convictions, and the social relevance of painting with excruciating honesty in a series of didactic paintings of 1972, subtitled "Rechenschaftsbericht" ("Calling to Account"). "Can one change anything with these?" he wrote across one of them [fig. 13.9]. Centered on the white canvas like an illustration on a page, he depicted himself three times. In each pose he holds one of the painter's most basic materials, captioned with small yellow labels like a diagram in a technical manual: "This is a simple brush for 70 pfennigs. This is normal housepaint. This is a canvas stretched on a wooden frame. It is where the artist's ideas take shape."

Below the picture the artist hand printed a text in the improvised manner of a political placard. Here he speculates in response to his own question about whether painting can change anything: "Surely not," he writes, "but when ideas take shape we can investigate the conditions from which they develop. We can ask what aims motivate them. We can determine whether they superficially reflect social conditions, serve to decorate walls, or whether they contribute to revealing contradictions and enter into the struggle to resolve these contradictions."[21]

"I wanted to be an artist," Immendorff wrote above another painting in this series. The work shows him on the floor of a romantic artist's garret, staring at a blank canvas by candlelight while a gleaming full moon hangs in the window above him. The caption below explains: "I dreamed about seeing my name in the newspapers, having a lot of shows, and naturally I intended to do something 'new' in art. My guideline was egoism." In yet another work he reflected: "I was unable to put myself in the place of working people, I was unable to fight for their interests. This will not change until one begins to struggle, on a daily basis, against one's own egoism and against the philosophy of egoism and profit."

Immendorff simplified his style in these placard-like works for the sake of legibility, as in socialist realism. The purported egalitarianism of Maoism attracted him at this moment. But if the style attacks the preciousness of painting by invoking the syntax of illustration, the handmade character of everything from the lettering to the brushiness of the images asserts the perseverance of a romantic individualism. Moreover, the series is autobiographical. Beuys too struggled with the contradiction of personality as against the political imperative for a collective practice (as Marxist theory demanded). Beuys knew he needed his own biography, he even mythologized it as the ground plane for his charismatic authority. This contradiction both in Beuys's work and in Immendorff's did not escape the latter's draconian self-scrutiny, and the fact that he accomplished his self-analysis through his painting must also have been apparent to him. In 1976 he dropped the didactic style of the early seventies for a more introspective approach.

Identity on the Plane of Images

Immendorff began painting his "Café Deutschland" cycle in 1977. The café is the metaphor for the artist's own mind—a tumultuous swirl of current political figures, German national heroes, and the working class of Marxist theory in a thick soup of inherited symbols. In *Café Deutschland III* (1978) [fig. 13.10], for example, Immendorff created a crowded, tipped-up space that recalls the anxious compositional angularity of Kirchner. But unlike the classic German expressionists, Immendorff provides no stable grounding in nature. The hackneyed symbol of the German eagle, for example, comes to life and inhabits the same space as the artist's self-portrait; memory, perception, fantasy, and media imagery all interact on an equal footing.

Immendorff shows himself at the center of *Café Deutschland III* asleep, slumped over a round table, clutching a paintbrush. A mirrored column behind him reflects (in

13.9 Jörg Immendorff, *Can One Change Anything with These?*, 1972. Synthetic resin on canvas, 31½ × 35⅜in (80 × 90cm). Courtesy Galerie Michael Werner, New York and Cologne.

grisaille) the Brandenburg Gate in Berlin—the most visible interface of the totalitarian Eastern Bloc with the West in the still-divided Germany of the seventies. There are reliefs of menacing characters carved into the columns in the foreground—a shadowy figure encircles one of the columns in rope—and above the hall a bespectacled man (Erich Honecker, the East German party chief) hurls lit candles as though he were casting symbols lifted ready-formed from a painting by Max Beckmann. Brilliantly illuminated nudes in scenes of sexual abandon highlight the background while a fierce German eagle swoops down on the painter, who wields a club and falls back on the theater ropes in a scene to the upper left. The simultaneity of these self-portraits within a single, continuous space (as in the "Calling to Account" works of 1972) reflects a new kind of reality in which perceptions coexist on the same plane as abstract concepts and need not conform to the structure of sequential time. There is no simple story line or message here but rather a plethora of images and vignettes, charged with political and personal associations, cross-tracking in time and space as in a dream.

The animism of such symbols grew even more pronounced in Immendorff's paintings of the eighties and the anarchy that reigned in the theater of the *Café Deutschland* intensified. Then in the late eighties the focus shifted from chaotic simultaneity toward the depth of individual characters in the still complex compositions of the nineties. These ambitious pictures also frequently take place in theaters as well as a café, but now the café is the Parisian Café de Flore, where Immendorff set himself in dialog with an expanded,

13.10 Jörg Immendorff, *Café Deutschland III*, 1978.
Oil on canvas, 9ft 3in × 8ft 11½in (2.82 × 2.73m).
Private collection. Courtesy Galerie Michael Werner, New York and Cologne.

international circle of great artists and intellectuals from both the past and present.

Among these new interlocutors, the late-nineteenth-century French poet Arthur Rimbaud, the most radical of the major symbolist poets, takes on particular significance. Through Rimbaud, Immendorff addresses the structure of his own new language, pioneered in the "Café Deutschland"

series, where multiple semiotic levels coexist and interact. There, he had begun detaching symbols from their stable points of reference in nature, redefining them at will in the pictorial space. The famous declaration of Rimbaud "*Je est un autre*" ("the 'I' is an 'other'")[22] implied a fundamental alienation in which the self, too, detaches from natural meaning and functions symbolically (in a poem or painting) as a form to which the poet or painter can assign different meanings in different works. In the Café de Flore Immendorff also engages the artist Marcel Duchamp, the inventor of the "readymade."

13.11 Jörg Immendorff, *Untitled*, 1993. Pencil and gouache,
12¼ × 10in (31.1 × 25.5cm).

Private collection. Courtesy Galerie Michael Werner, New York and Cologne.

13.12 Jörg Immendorff, *Gyntiana*, 1992–3. Oil on canvas,
11ft 5¾in × 22ft 11½in (3.5 × 7m).
Courtesy Galerie Michael Werner, New York and Cologne.

At the same time, Immendorff turned to epic narratives, first *Peer Gynt* and then, in 1993, he received a commission to design sets for a production of Stravinsky's opera *The Rake's Progress*. These provided rich metaphors for his own utterly secular but nonetheless spiritual quest. The story of *The Rake's Progress* comes from a morality tale (told in eight engravings by the eighteenth-century English artist William Hogarth) in which the young Tom Rakewell, engaged to marry Anne Truelove, suddenly comes into an unexpected inheritance (presented by Nick Shadow, the devil). Tom goes to London, squanders his money, forsakes his fiancée, and ends up destitute in Bedlam (the dismal asylum of the insane) believing he is the Greek god Adonis. An entirely new cast of symbols entered Immendorff's painting with this commission, as he turned the travails of Rakewell into a parable of the artist, casting himself and his circle of Düsseldorf artists—especially Beuys, and Immendorff's contemporaries A. R. Penck and Markus Lüpertz—in the major roles.

Untitled [fig. 13.11], a beautiful drawing of 1993, shows Immendorff with his face in white stage make-up and lips painted bright red, sleeping on top of an airplane. The plane alludes to the legend of Joseph Beuys (cast as Truelove, Anne's father, in Immendorff's version of the *Rake's Progress*). Here, the plane (see chapter 8) stands for Beuys's invocation to abandon painting for a more politically engaged art, but it also represents the means by which Beuys wielded artistic power (by the invention of a charismatic artistic persona). The inscription in the lower right of this drawing reads "Vorbereitung für den 3. Wunsch" ("Preparation for the Third Wish"). Immendorff interpreted the story as being about three unfulfilled wishes, of which the third concerns the wish to do good for humanity. But the artist fails in this because he first has to be happy himself and he doesn't know how to achieve that. As he sleeps, in the drawing, Immendorff dreams of a cannon that refers back to his "Lidl" performances of the sixties in which he shot crumpled wads of paper into his audience inscribed with notes that said things like "I love you" or "Be happy." But in this dream the cannon has become a phallic object, self-critically suggesting that the artist's own narcissism is the real motive behind this supposed altruism. The cannon seems to be firing a loaf of bread, referring to a machine that Nick Shadow brings to Rakewell with the fraudulent claim that it turns stone into bread. Rakewell is so gullible he believes it.[23] So the artist, Immendorff seems to be saying, deludes himself into justifying what he wants for himself as "altruism."

Beuys, who had been a huge influence on Immendorff in the sixties, disappeared in Immendorff's didactic paintings of the early seventies and in the "Café Deutschland" paintings. But he came back with singular symbolic force for Immendorff in the nineties. As Immendorff became increasingly introspective and gave in to his overwhelming desire for the sensuality of paint, he came back to thinking about Beuys in new ways. Beuys himself was viscerally engaged with the physicality of his materials and used them to construct his powerful personal myth (which became his artistic medium). At the same time Duchamp's readymades (which only *became* works of art through the force of the artist's thought) symbolized the power of the mind for Immendorff. Beuys had criticized the readymades for what he saw as their failure to articulate a statement of the universal liberation of creativity: In 1964 he did a performance called *The Silence of Marcel Duchamp Is Overrated*.

In the late eighties Immendorff reappraises Duchamp's import; he titles a painting *Marcel's Redemption* (1988) and in 1989 he painted *A Meeting to Honor the Dogmatic Picture— The Words of Beuys Are Overrated*. Beuys was Immendorff's teacher and so, while he needed to displace Beuys as a dominant artistic father figure, Beuys and Duchamp both, in different ways, remained heroic symbols for him of the power of ideas in art. In a 1992–3 painting called *Gyntiana* (after Henrik Ibsen's *Peer Gynt* [fig. 13.12]) Immendorff shows Beuys and Duchamp riding a donkey together. Immendorff stands in front with his arm languorously over the donkey's neck, feeding it handfuls of color from a bucket [fig. 13.13]. He again struggles here with his dueling passions of mind and body, art as ideas and art as a visceral sensation of paint.

At the far left of *Gyntiana* Beuys seems to aim his broom at the woman giving birth to the onion. The Marxist critic Georg Lukács criticized Ibsen's play as an onion in which you peel away many layers and in the end find nothing. But for Immendorff the "layers of the onion stand for the various phases of our lives," as he explained. It's a positive image of complexity and Immendorff's onion-man is a self-portrait. The many other portraits in the painting—Heiner Müller, Berthold Brecht, Curzio Malaparte, Arthur Rimbaud, Jean-Paul Sartre, Georg Baselitz, as well as Beuys and Duchamp—stand for a world of intellectual positions with which Immendorff sees himself struggling. They are, he tells us, "a selection of stances which preoccupy me. *Gyntiana* is a new land which has to be shaped by us. Each observer that wants to enter this picture basically has to be prepared to use a spade … to delve into himself to understand the picture. It doesn't make any sense to merely recognize the figures. They're only a trigger or a signal."[24]

Peer Gynt is an exile who searches for an idealized country—Gyntiana—which is a metaphor, a longed-for land that doesn't exist, and "must be realized afresh every day,"[25] the artist tells us. Like Beuysland, the Lidlraum, the Café Deutschland, and the Café de Flore, hypothetical places which Immendorff had painted earlier, Gyntiana stands for

13.13 Jörg Immendorff, *Gyntiana* (detail). See fig. 13.12.

13.14 Jörg Immendorff, *Untitled*, 2007. Oil on canvas,
5ft 6⅞in × 6ft 6¾in (1.70 × 2.00m).
Courtesy Galerie Michael Werner, New York and Cologne.

the space of the artist's imagination and Immendorff, like Peer Gynt, is an endless seeker for unrealizable knowledge. In the lower right of this painting, which takes place in the Café de Flore, an art historian charts Immendorff's themes on the black floor. Encircling a Jewish star (his grandfather was half Jewish) are three empty bicycle forks—their wheels seemingly lost to Duchamp's first readymade (the *Bicycle Wheel*), which Immendorff also represents here and points to in this diagram with arrows. He also draws arrows to the onion, to a (working) bicycle, and to a chart listing the imaginary spaces of Beuysland, the Café Deutschland, the Café de Flore, and Gyntiana. A framed photo of Gertrude Stein—who hosted a famous *salon* in Paris where Picasso first met Matisse—stands on the floor overseeing the diagram, as though the patron saint of intellectual spaces.

In 1998 Immendorff contracted ALS (Lou Gehrig's Disease) which leads to increasingly grave stages of paralysis

and then death but the mind remains completely undiminished to the end. As Immendorff lost, first, the use of his painting hand, then both hands, he developed a way of working with a corps of trained assistants whose particular traits and skills he knew precisely. Some were especially skilled in graphic techniques to transfer images precisely from art books or from Immendorff's previous work. Others had special qualities in applying paint. Immendorff had become engaged with the aesthetics of reproduction techniques when he began working on *The Rake's Progress*, derived from Hogarth's engravings, and for some time had played with inkpad stamps in his works. Now, in these late works, Immendorff exactly directed his assistants from a wheelchair to select images, compose on a computer screen, and execute his work in paint, making work of astonishing visual power without ever touching the canvas himself. His aesthetic is so powerful in all aspects of the process that these paintings are unerringly of his "hand" in the smallest detail.

In 2005, at the opening of his great retrospective in the New National Gallery in Berlin, Immendorff commented on this new studio practice. "I wish I had begun doing this much earlier," he said, and he spoke of how Duchamp's readymades now took on an unexpected and even greater significance for him as a paradigm of great art without the artist's literal "touch."[26]

Immendorff died in May 2007. In the last year of his life he painted prolifically, often on a grand scale. In these last works [fig. 13.14] he takes postmodern painting to an entirely new place. The monkey men (his surrogates) are everywhere in these compositions (they seem to proliferate in parallel to his studio personnel) and as Immendorff's own past work becomes reified in these compositions into "art book reproductions" on loose sheets, the monkeys sweep them away: We see blackboard paintings from the "Lidl" series, placards of Mao, symbols from the Café Deutschland, renderings from the eighteenth-century engravings he used for his operas, even Immendorff's late, controversial, "official" portrait of German Chancellor Gerhard Schröder, all swept away by Time.

The theme of *Time Smoking a Painting* (by Hogarth) preoccupied Immendorff persistently from the 1990s. As increasingly he thought about the evanescence of his own life and his desire for immortality through art, Hogarth's reverie on the smoke of time obscuring meaning came more and more to the fore. The sweeping monkey itself alludes to the Beuys action of 1972 of sweeping away the dogmatism of the May Day parade from the Karl-Marx-Platz, but it also sweeps away the temporal presence of the artist in these magnificent untitled paintings of 2006 and 2007, for a timeless presence in art history's boundless ether of images and ideas.

Georg Baselitz and A. R. Penck

The power of symbols weighed heavily on Immendorff's generation of German artists. Some had formative childhood memories of the war and of the privations in its aftermath. Georg Baselitz and A. R. Penck, the oldest of the German neo-expressionists, had grown up just outside Dresden and as children had witnessed the firebombing of the city; Baselitz described it as the most riveting memory of his life.[27] Penck and Baselitz were just six and seven at the end of the war, and though this generation of German artists

13.15 Georg Baselitz, *Late Dinner in Dresden*, February 18, 1983. Oil on canvas, 9ft 2¼in × 14ft 9¼in (2.8 × 4.5m). Kunsthaus, Zurich. Courtesy Galerie Michael Werner, New York and Cologne.

13.16 A. R. Penck, *Standart*, 1971.
Acrylic on canvas, 9ft 6¼in × 9ft 6¼in
(2.9 × 2.9m).

Courtesy Galerie Michael Werner, New York
and Cologne.

bore no responsibility for the war or the atrocities of the Third Reich, they inherited them as part of the German national consciousness.

As the critic Donald Kuspit observed, this situation endowed abstract symbols with a particularly profound psychic force in the work of contemporary German painters.[28] By successfully giving form to such a powerful psychic experience, these artists elucidate it to a profound level. The vitality of the symbols—the fact that they hold their own with conventional figurative imagery in these artists' paintings—underscores the abstract distance with which everything began to be experienced in the late twentieth century. If nature is conspicuously absent in the work of the German neo-expressionists, it is also rarely encountered, unaltered by man, in the reality of modern urban life. Thus the preoccupation of many of these German painters with asserting a tactile immediacy—as in the viscosity of the paint in the work of Baselitz [fig. 13.15] or the use of straw and lead in Anselm Kiefer's compositions [figs. 13.17 and 13.18]—is as critical in coming to terms with contemporary experience as the more explicitly theory-driven postmodernism of other artists.

Georg Baselitz and A. R. Penck came to the fore of a group of outstanding gestural painters in Berlin in the sixties. Along with Eugen Schönebeck, K. H. Hödicke, Markus Lüpertz, and Bernd Koberling, Baselitz and Penck came

from East Germany. Baselitz studied at the West Berlin Hochschule für Bildende Künste from 1957 to 1962 and had his first show with the fledgling gallery of Michael Werner and Benjamin Katz the following year. He began isolating and then fragmenting the figures in his compositions in the mid-sixties; in 1969 he came upon the idea of turning the whole painting upside down in what has become a signature device to take the focus off the subject matter and redirect it toward the structure and expressive surface. The build-up of thick, bravura brushwork in the painting of Baselitz runs head on into the late-sixties denial by the theorists of the cultural establishment of heroic individuality (or romantic "genius") in painting.

A. R. Penck (the *nom de plume* for Ralf Winckler) worked in East Berlin until 1980 and, as in the case of Immendorff, his internal struggle with leftist ideology peaked around 1971. He wanted to make paintings that would communicate as clearly as the information signs that direct people in public places to escalators and bathrooms. His formulation in 1970 of the generic "standart"—a primitive stick figure with its arms thrown up submissively into the air [fig. 13.16]—was partly derived from the vocabulary of the signs and from his fascination with cybernetics (the science of regulating and controlling the relationship of humans and machines). Penck used the standart as a fixed organizing principle around which he varied the style to test a panoply of emotions. Both

Penck and Baselitz consciously cultivated the independence of their subject matter from the expressive manner in which they applied the paint and color. This not only anticipated the separation of subject matter and style by the new imagist painters in the United States in the seventies, it sharply distinguished Penck and Baselitz from their expressionist precursors of the early twentieth century.

Anselm Kiefer

Anselm Kiefer works unabashedly in the German romantic tradition. He conveys a heavy authorial presence and, like Beuys, his materials—lead, straw, and dense pastes of pigment [fig. 13.17]—seem at once linked to nature and to some esoteric mystery. Kiefer studied only briefly with Beuys, but Kiefer expanded upon the *physicality* of Beuys's work—its monumentality, the attention to materials, and its transcendence. Kiefer's search for parallels in world mythology—Nordic, Greek, Egyptian, Early Christian, Jewish (the Cabbala)—is a romantic trait, as is his morbid preoccupation with death, destruction, and renewal.

Kiefer's subject matter centers on his personal and cultural identity. In 1969, at the age of twenty-four, he made a book of photographs of himself giving the Hitler salute in front of monuments in Italy and France. Instead of traveling as the curious tourist, eager to explore another culture, he went to experience the sensation of the Nazi occupation force and to understand better this undiscussed facet of his heritage. For Kiefer, this acknowledgement of his own dark thoughts mirrors the idea that Satan belongs inextricably to the totality of God.

In 1974 Kiefer's attention shifted to the scorched landscapes on which he fantasized the battles of German history having taken place. In *Wayland's Song (with Wing)* of 1982 [fig. 13.17], an immense lead wing surmounts the burnt black field. The grand scale of Kiefer's painting—this work measures nearly 10 by 12 feet—and the density of the materials expresses the monumentality of his theme. The story of *Wayland's Song (with Wing)* derives from the anonymous Scandinavian poems (the Eddas) that tell the history of the Teutonic gods. Richard Wagner based the operas of *The Ring of the Nibelung* on these stories and thus Kiefer's choice of subject also carries the aura of this most romantic and histrionic of all German composers. Moreover, Wagner (like Nietzsche) was appropriated by

13.17 Anselm Kiefer, *Wayland's Song (with Wing)*, 1982.
Oil, emulsion, and straw on photograph, mounted on canvas, with lead, 9ft 2¼in × 12ft 5⅝in (2.8 × 3.8m).
Courtesy Anthony d'Offay Gallery, London.

Hitler in the latter's melodramatic celebrations of German nationalism. Kiefer deliberately courts such emotional and symbolic extremes.

The last part of the Eddas tells of "The Twilight of the Gods" (*Die Götterdämmerung*) in which the greed and deceitfulness of the gods lead to their own demise. The King of Sweden captures Wayland, the greatest of all metalsmiths, cripples him so he cannot flee, and places him on an island as a prisoner, thenceforth to forge treasures for the court. In revenge Wayland rapes the king's daughter and murders his two sons, presenting the king with drinking cups made from their skulls. He then fashions himself wings and flees.

The smith is an ancient metaphor for the artist. He is also the alchemist who magically fashions base metal (lead) into gold (in Christian symbolism, the smith offers redemption). Kiefer is, as it were, handing Germany the heads of its children on a plate. He incorporated straw into the painted surface of this and other paintings after 1980, intending the organic deterioration of the straw to mirror the natural cycle of life, devolving to death and dissolution. The straw is "transfigured" (to use the artist's term)[29] by fermentation, evoking not only the metaphors of alchemy and redemption but Kiefer's prognosis on the fate of Germany.

The self-destructing organic materials in Kiefer's work had precedents in Italian *arte povera*, which also brought home the proximity of nature. For the Italians, however, the resulting impermanence of the object also serves as an attack on the commodification of art—the commerce in "things" that transforms the spiritual act of making art into a saleable object. By contrast it is only the material presence and the symbolism that attract Kiefer to such materials. Kiefer emulated the materiality of Joseph Beuys's work and the physicality of the American minimalist and process artists of the sixties.

The pages of Kiefer's books are made of lead, and rely for their aesthetic impact on the changing effects of oxidation, chemical impurities, and the palpable weight and softness of the lead itself, as in the work of Carl Andre and Richard Serra. However, Kiefer also invests his works with historical allusions and mystic content, as in *Breaking of the Vessels* [fig. 13.18]. This work consists of 15,000 pounds of lead books, crammed into a 17-foot-high steel bookcase. The bookcase is positioned amid a field of shattered glass and has corroding copper wires trailing from part to part. The daunting material presence of the work resembles the large steel pieces made by Richard Serra, but the concept of the construction derives from the mystic Jewish *Zohar* which posits ten divine emanations—the attributes of god (*Ain Soph*)—contained in the *sefirot* (vessels or spheres). Kiefer inscribed "*Ain Soph*"

on the glass semicircle (the "dome of heaven") above the work, and the names of nine of the vessels on the sides and fronts of the shelves below, omitting the hidden *sefira— Daath*, or knowledge. The three shelves correspond to the three pillars—Mercy, Judgment, and Mildness.

Underlying Creation, according to the *Zohar*, is the act of *Zim Zum* in which the infinite (*Ain Soph*) contracted inside Himself to allow for the existence of something other than Himself. The vessels were created to catch the emanations that fell from primordial space but six of them shattered, releasing evil into the world. In the sculpture menacing spears of shattered glass jut out from the books and litter the floor. On one level *Breaking of the Vessels* encompasses the totality of good and evil, heaven and hell, resurrection and death. On another, the shattered glass—an allusion to the broken dome of the heavens—brought home Kiefer's persistent examination of German identity by also calling to mind *Kristallnacht* in 1938 when Nazis shattered the windows of Jewish-owned shops all over Germany, signaling what was to come.

Italian Neo-Expressionism

Italy also produced a dazzling group of neo-expressionist painters in the seventies, including Enzo Cucchi, Mimmo Paladino, and Francesco Clemente. Although they are sometimes grouped under the rubric of the *transavanguardia*, they were not a movement, despite important commonalities. Above all, they share the influence of *arte povera*, in their sense of the primal force of nature and of man's place in it as an animal among other animals. They are all figurative painters—painters of the visceral presence of the body (Clemente spoke of his admiration for "those who have 'thought' with their bodies")[30]—and all have an especially Italian sense of the living presence of the history of art. In addition, each of these artists conveys in their work a unique mixture of sensual proximity and an uncentered sense of individual identity.

Francesco Clemente

Clemente's *Myriads* [fig. 13.19] consists of nineteen small pastel drawings belonging to a larger group of eighty-five such works (the so-called "Pondicherry Pastels") done in Pondicherry and Madras, India. The drawings express a spirituality in the smallest detail of nature, an aspect of Clemente's work that is very much at home in the religions of India. Clemente read "the beats" (see Chapter 7) in translation during his youth and hung out with conceptual artists in the early seventies. These influences undoubtedly contributed to the eccentricity and the notational character respectively of these drawings. The "Pondicherry Pastels" vary widely in size, overt subject matter, and style, defining an aesthetic of open boundaries and orders.

Clemente explained, "My overall strategy or view as an artist is to accept fragmentation, and to see what comes of it—if anything . . . Technically, this means I do not arrange the mediums and images I work with in any hierarchy of value. One is as good as another for me." He views the multiplicity of the self in the same way: "I believe in the dignity of each of the different levels and parts of the self. I don't want to lose any of them. To me they each exist simultaneously, not hierarchically . . . One is not better than another.'[31]

The pastels in *Myriads* are conceived as a group within a group and introduce a way of seeing art in profusion and simultaneity. As a composition, *Myriads* has the same undecidability, open-endedness, and emphasis on seeing across the surface that we have discussed as a trait of postmodernism. Clemente emphasizes fragmentation and polarities, wandering from image to image, subverting control and

cohesion. Where Kiefer obsessively seeks to define his identity, Clemente seems determined to deconstruct his.

"I feel a lack of affinity, a dislocation that gives me room to work."[32] To balance this precarious dissolution, his sexuality provides an affirmation of his existence as part of the overwhelming and infinite processes of nature. The curator Kathy Halbreich called him "a voyeur of his own homelessness, and his sexuality gives him his portable dwelling, the shelter of identity. In Hindu fashion, he often portrays evanescent or out-of-body experiences reached (paradoxically, in Western terms) through the widening of orifices and erotic possibility. This opening of the senses to the world creates a visage alternatingly vulnerable, terrified, resigned, preterhuman."[33]

In the left-hand section of *He Teaches Emotions with Feelings*, a portable fresco painting [fig. 13.20], Clemente portrays himself as though helplessly bound while a shower of arms reach out from all directions, the fingers invading and

13.19 Francesco Clemente, *Myriads*, 1980. Nineteen drawings, ink, pastel, gouache, charcoal, and graphite on paper, 6⅜ × 3½in (16.2 × 8.9cm) to 13½ × 13in (34.3 × 33cm).
Courtesy Anthony d'Offay Gallery, London.

penetrating every orifice of his body. The individual forms in the three sections of the fresco not only have no explicit relation to one another, they also float in undefined space within each segment, like motifs in the Roman frescoes at Pompeii. The composition within each segment of this work, as in several of the drawings in *Myriads*, deliberately undermines conventional notions of pictorial balance. In this, one senses the influence of the even more notational drawings of Joseph Beuys and more proximately of Cy Twombly, who shares with Clemente a classical aesthetic elegance.

13.20 (above) **Francesco Clemente**, *He Teaches Emotions with Feelings*, 1980. Fresco, 9ft 10⅛ × 19ft 8¼in (3 × 6m). Private collection. Courtesy Galerie Bruno Bischofberger, Zurich.

13.21 (left) **Francesco Clemente**, *Name*, 1983. Oil on canvas, 6ft 6in × 7ft 9in (1.98 × 2.36m). Collection, Thomas Ammann, Zurich.

Clemente was born into the titled aristocracy of Naples in 1952 and had a privileged background of elegant surroundings and classical education.[34] He moved to Rome at the age of eighteen and traveled to India in 1973, when he was twenty-one. He returned there for longer and longer periods, as well as spending time in New York. Clemente's constant physical dislocations to Madras, Rome, and New York, as well as travels to Afghanistan, Japan, and elsewhere, mirror the dislocated sense of self in his paintings. He even displaces his sexuality in his paintings, often reinventing himself with an amorphous sexuality that is at once feminine and masculine.

Clemente seeks to achieve a kind of limbo in his work, making it possible to experience everything, even to become something else. This remarkable openness can only exist by suspending fixed identity. "The images are results," he remarked about a painting of 1981, ". . . of wandering from one idea to another without giving more weight to one or the other . . . you forget where you began. So what you see there, I don't know myself. I made a safe . . . and I lost the key. And losing the key . . . gives the work this autonomy."[35] Under these conditions it doesn't matter where one enters the composition—one begins wherever one engages it, like picking up a newspaper after months of not reading them and moving forward with current events without ever looking back.

It is part of the rich ambiguity of Clemente's work that an artist so dedicated to the suspension of self should also focus relentlessly on the self-portrait. He is an enchanting fabulist [fig. 13.21], reawakening the fantasy and sensual pleasure of art by placing an infinitely malleable self into constantly changing places in the imagination. In his receptivity to chance encounters he is mesmerized by the rituals that codify them.

NEW IMAGE PAINTING

Contemporary with the rediscovery of painting in the 1970s by these Europeans and following on the new paintings by Guston in New York, the Whitney Museum opened a show of "New Image Painting" in December 1978 that singled out ten younger American painters who used recognizable images in their work but whose execution was principally in dialog with abstraction rather than traditional figurative painting. These artists were consciously working with multiple, interacting but independent layers of discourse simultaneously in their works, carrying off this separation of style and imagery without subordinating one to the other.

"New Image Painting" included the work of Nicholas Africano, Jennifer Bartlett, Denise Green, Michael Hurson, Neil Jenney, Lois Lane, Robert Moskowitz, Susan Rothenberg, David True, and Joe Zucker. Apart from Moskowitz, these painters were still in their twenties during the late sixties, when rules of all kinds were thrown open to question, and they were raised on the more multidimensional world made available through television. In their work they freely selected ideas from abstract expressionism, minimalism, pop, and conceptual art without feeling constrained by the dogmas of any of them.

Jennifer Bartlett created a sensation among artists on the downtown scene in New York with three shows, each of which filled a whole gallery with a single work made up of hundreds of 1-foot-square steel plates, hung in regular rows. She had the plates commercially coated with a layer of baked-on white enamel like the signs in the New York subway (from which she got the idea in 1968).[36] The final show, held in 1976 at the Paula Cooper Gallery—a work entitled *Rhapsody* [fig. 13.22]— involved the installation of 988 plates. Bartlett had grand ambitions for the work to include "everything": figurative imagery (a house, a tree, a mountain, the ocean); geometric forms (a circle, a square, and a triangle); and a catalog of different styles of drawing (freehand, ruled, and dotted).

Bartlett painted on the plates with Testor's enamel, and the shapes and images could appear miniaturized on a single square or rendered large across multiple squares. She worked according to an elaborate set of self-imposed rules, even using a mathematical scheme to determine the precise placement of dots in some sections. Although Bartlett painted the circles freehand, dotted, and measured in small, medium, and large sizes in the first section of the mural, she forgot to do the same in subsequent sections for the square and triangle.[37] Thus she made rules but then lost interest in them as she went along, disregarding or modifying them. So while

13.22 Jennifer Bartlett, *Rhapsody*, 1975–6. Detail of installation, enamel silkscreen, baked enamel on steel plates, 988 plates, 12 × 12in (30.5 × 30.5cm) each, 7ft 6in × 153ft 9in (2.29 × 46.86m) overall. Installed in Paula Cooper Gallery, New York, May 8–June 16, 1976.
Private collection. Courtesy Paula Cooper Gallery, New York.

13.23 Michael Hurson, *Eyeglass Painting #1*, 1970.
Oil and silkscreen on canvas, 24 × 48in (61 × 121.9cm).
Private collection. Courtesy Paula Cooper Gallery, New York.

Rhapsody seems fastidiously procedure-oriented, like a LeWitt, modularized like an Andre, codified into various catalogs in its language like a conceptual work, Bartlett only used each of these stylistic ideas as one of several, overlaid for expressive purposes in the work. Finally, there is even an iconographic dimension in such works—for example, the individual names of the composite title *Falcon Avenue, Seaside Walk, Dwight Street, Jarvis Street, Greene Street* of the same year—each referring to one of her former addresses.

Michael Hurson could spin out elaborate soap operas around such intrinsically banal objects as a pair of eyeglasses [fig. 13.23]. He retreated from the complex macrocosm of the world and magnified the ordinary into the most incredible grid of event and emotion. The commonest details of life imply intricate melodramas filled with events "still to be explained . . . dramas that are inconclusive, absent of people, and missing the narrative itself . . . intimations of a dramatic situation, like a chair overturned, or a door left ajar."[38] Hurson's revelation of nuances that no one else notices is comic in its naivety and at the same time frightening in its acuity. He transformed everything into an anecdote, trivial in scale and yet somehow credibly important.

Hurson constructed beautiful miniature rooms in balsa wood during the early seventies, as if to imagine the space in which these dramas took place. At the end of the decade he wrote a play called *Red and Blue*, which opened at the Public Theater in New York in 1982. There were no actors on stage in his play, only an empty, miniature room with an overturned chair and a red and a blue light bulb conversing, exchanging fragments of gossip, and dimming on and off.

Despite the relaxed spontaneity of Hurson's drawing style and the witty informality of his subject matter, a formal underlying grid controls his compositions. The style and images in the drawings lead independent lives, and each detail, each brushstroke, each structural schema has its own highly developed and insular significance. Hurson remarked that the images in his *Eyeglass Painting #1* have nothing directly to do with what is happening expressively in the paint.[39] In this sense, the paintings are figurative and abstract at the same time.

Neil Jenney's paintings of 1969 and 1970, like *Girl and Doll* [fig. 13.24], have a viscerally gestural brushwork—in some he even seems to have used his hands to manipulate the paint directly. At the same time the imagery is presented in a strikingly neutral way. "I was more concerned with approaching the viewer with relationships," he explained in the "New Image Painting" catalog, "for instance, a crying girl and a broken vase, birds and jets, or trees and lumber . . . I'm not interested in a narrative . . . I wanted the objects to be stated emphatically with no psychological implications."[40] So if the brushwork has associations with abstract expressionism, the images—one or two objects, isolated in a visual field—seem like a minimalist reduction and the psychological remove of the subjects into neutral images like a work of pop art.

After 1971 Jenney took a stylistic jump into a meticulous naturalism of a seemingly nineteenth-century sort, and his use of exaggeratedly heavy black frames with the titles lettered on them emphasizes the nineteenth-century idea of painting as a "window onto nature," in contrast to the self-contained object put forward in formalist theory.

13.24 Neil Jenney, *Girl and Doll*, 1969. Acrylic on canvas, 4ft 10in × 6ft 4½in (1.47 × 1.93m).
Private collection. Courtesy Thomas Ammann, Zurich.

In 1964 Robert Moskowitz started teaching a seminar at the Maryland Institute in Baltimore in which he simply showed slides of works of art he liked in alphabetical order by artist.[41] There is a simple, Warhol-like deadpan to this that also characterizes Moskowitz's best paintings. Geometric blocks dominate the simplified silhouette of *Empire State* (1978) [fig. 13.25]; with the scarcely visible antenna, the outline fills the 9-foot-high canvas. It could be a minimalist painting but for the instant recognizability of the building. Naturally, once the viewer identifies it, what at first seemed like a minimalist abstraction changes completely for the viewer.

Susan Rothenberg exhibited six of her horse paintings in the "New Image Painting" show. She began the series in 1974, describing it as paintings about "placement in space" (a minimalist idea). The point, as she explained it, was to take the charged image of the horse and de-energize it (as Warhol did with his subjects) while at the same time putting the emotion (not a minimalist concern) into the field of brushwork.[42] She drew all the horses as flat outline figures, in left profile, more or less centered and filling the composition. She dealt with the paint surface (influenced by the bravura brushwork of Neil Jenney's canvases of 1969–70[43]) and the color (which had no relation to the color of an actual horse) as elements of an abstract gesture painting. The expressive use of materials in the work of Eva Hesse as well as the remarkable synthesis of abstract expressionist handling with an emotionally reserved, indeed ostensibly neutral, treatment of imagery in the work of Jasper Johns had an important impact on her thinking.

13.25 (right) **Robert Moskowitz**, *Empire State*, 1978.
Oil on canvas, 9ft × 3ft 2¾in (274.32 x 98.43cm).
Private collection. Courtesy of the artist and D'Amelio Terras Gallery, New York.

13.26 Susan Rothenberg, *Two Tone*, 1975. Acrylic and tempera on canvas, 5ft 9in × 9ft 5in (1.75 × 2.87m).
Albright-Knox Art Gallery, Buffalo. Gift of Mr. and Mrs. Armand J. Castellani, 1977.

For Rothenberg, the painting process is a corrective experience in which she starts with an idea, then keeps correcting all the things that she thinks are wrong with it until she gets it right. The antagonism between elements is crucial but the elements are also interdependent—in each case the field, for example, evolved in relation to the image.[44] In addition, Rothenberg in some manner cut the image with geometric divisions or lines or the bisection of the composition—as in *Two Tone* (1975) [fig. 13.26]—to emphasize the physicality of the canvas over the image.

Nevertheless, as Joan Simon pointed out, the horses tend toward a human scale, and their movement—even in some sense their anatomy—seems reminiscent of human beings too. The artist herself was aware of the connection and in 1974 photographed a friend in poses related to the horses (all in left profile) and then did three paintings of her that in every other way belong to this first series of horse compositions. But, she said, "I got more concerned with the articulation of the figure than painting and was having a hard time keeping them flat, silhouetted. Finally I had to stop it."[45]

Why horses? To be sure, the artist identified with the horses but at the same time also wanted to maintain a distance from herself in her subject matter. In *For the Light* (1978–9) [fig. 13.27] the horse has broken out of the controlled

13.27 Susan Rothenberg, *For the Light*, 1978–9. Synthetic polymer and vinyl paint on canvas, 8ft 9in × 7ft 3in (2.66 × 2m).
Whitney Museum of American Art, New York. Purchase, with funds from Peggy and Richard Danziger, 79.23.

silhouette and charges at the viewer. Rothenberg blocks this advance with a bonelike form hovering in front of the animal, on the picture plane. This device contradicts both the volume and the implied movement, locking the form into the space of the composition. The sheer sensuality of these paintings suggests an immediacy, a body presence (as in Hesse's work and in *arte povera*). As Simon suggested, this may be related not only to feminist issues in the air at the time but also to the physicality of the dance and body performances Rothenberg had been involved with over the preceding decade.[46]

Rothenberg was born in 1945 and lived a counterculture existence in the late sixties, finishing a B.A. at Cornell in 1967 and finally settling in New York in the fall of 1969.[47] There she reconnected with friends she had known at Cornell, including Gordon Matta-Clark and Alan Saret, who brought her in touch with the downtown art scene. She studied dance and performance with Deborah Hay and Joan Jonas and the direct bodily expressionism of this work came out in her subsequent paintings. Rothenberg made her first horse paintings of 1974 in a raw sienna color, like clay, relating to the earth, to the body, and to prehistoric cave paintings.

13.28 Susan Rothenberg, *Red*, 2008.
Oil on canvas, 55 × 57½in (140 × 146.1cm).
Courtesy Sperone Westwater Gallery, New York.

It was during a lonely fall semester at CalArts in 1977 that Rothenberg started taking the horses apart. As they become more volumetric, mobile, alive (and more human), she headed them off—as in *For the Light*—with surface forms, or dissected them into free-floating legs and heads. In 1979 Rothenberg made a painting called *My Bones* and with this her subject matter became more directly personal. The horse transformed itself, she recalled:

> It turned almost into a figure. And it turned up in the bare bones. No superfluous geometry dealing with the edges of the painting, but just the bare bones of the frontal horse, which suggested that a figure was appearing—that the horse was metamorphosing into a human figure. I realized that there weren't very many of those images left, that it had absolutely naturally reduced itself to a place where I was going to be forced to continue—differently.[48]

So "the horse just ran out," she said, and she was left "scared again."[49]

In 1980–1 Rothenberg painted a series of schematic faces and hands. In the summer she shifted to oil paints at the suggestion of her friend Elizabeth Murray, and that promoted a finer, longer, impressionistic brushstroke—a directional gesture with more color. This work of the mid-eighties was very different from what had come before. All of a sudden she found herself struggling with more complicated compositions and focusing on movement, painting dancers, jugglers, and spinning figures in cinematic motions. Then, at the end of the eighties, the horses returned in a calmer and more erotic form.

In 1989 Rothenberg married the artist Bruce Nauman and the next year they moved permanently to New Mexico. There the underlying separation of subject and paint has persevered in her painting, and although the imagery seems more often connected to the things in her life there—a man at a fence, the dogs, the horses' heads, snakes, and birds—the metaphysical self-portraits (often as masks) and the fragmentation of the body have also continued what seems like an existential and anxiety-ridden body of work, as in *Red* (2008) [fig. 13.28].

If the "New Image" show had not been restricted to painting, it might well have included the sculptor Joel Shapiro, who by the late seventies was making figurative sculpture driven by concepts and stylistic influences that went in different ways from the subject matter. In 1971 Shapiro was still experimenting with process works such as *One Hand Forming/Two Hands Forming*—two piles of modular forms in raw fired clay made into an oblong volume (with one hand) and a ball (with two hands), respectively. He made pieces concerned with physical weight and measurement, and simple, abstract, geometric forms. One of these "minimal" geometric forms turned out to be a bronze house, like a hotel from a "Monopoly"-style board game, and another a miniature bronze chair [fig. 13.29]. As in the work of Bartlett and Rothenberg, Shapiro rendered his house and chair in a manner more concerned with issues of abstraction—scale, how they occupied space, the sense of material weight— than with representation.

The 3-inch-high bronze chair (like the little house) sat on the floor in a large public space, raising peculiar issues of

13.29 Joel Shapiro, *Untitled*, 1973–4. Bronze, 3 × 1¼ × 1¼in (7.6 × 3.2 × 3.2cm). Edition of two.
Private collection.

13.30 Joel Shapiro, *Untitled*, 1980–1.
Bronze, 4ft 4⅞in × 5ft 4in × 3ft 9½in
(1.34 × 1.63 × 1.16m). Edition AP/3.
Private collection.

scale and perspective. It both disappeared and at the same time brought the viewer along. "I was insisting on an intimate experience in a public situation," he explained.[50] By the end of the decade Shapiro's simple geometric configurations (cast largely from constructions of wooden two-by-fours) became more and more overtly recognizable as active, mobile figures [fig. 13.30]. He contradicted the motility of the athletic poses with the relatively untransformed identity of the wooden blocks, which persevered as such, even when formally frozen into bronze. This set the character of the figure in tension with the overt expression of the materials and influences (largely from Russian interwar constructivism).

Elizabeth Murray

Alice Aycock once made the observation that the work of many women artists derived an interesting and particularizing eccentricity from an exceptional responsiveness to the realities of their lives.[51] According to Elizabeth Murray, one finds art "in the street. Or you find it at home, right in front of you. I paint about the things that surround me—things that I pick up and handle every day. That's what art is. Art is an epiphany in a coffee cup."[52] Murray paints the encounter of her inner life with the world and renders this collision of internal and external by superimposing several trains of thought over one another in her compositions without for a moment losing the independence or momentum of any of them. The figurative subject matter and narrative,

the abstract construction of forms in relief, the expressive brushwork, and the interplay of depicted abstract forms all maintain their own identities, development, and associations, while at the same time interacting with one another, with the artist's personal history, and with the history of art.

The Origins of Murray's Style

Elizabeth Murray's daily encounters with the great Cézannes in the Art Institute of Chicago while she was a student in the School there from 1958 to 1962 taught her to see the way pictorial structure, handling, and description could imbue a vital spirit into the simplest inanimate objects. She would also "go upstairs to de Kooning's *Excavation* to see how he manipulated the paint," she remembered.

> I had an idea of what it ought to feel like to make a painting. It's a very "inner" experience. When things go well, you stop thinking about what you're doing. I was in my last year of art school when I finally put it together and discovered how to get my feelings out. It's not that you learn how to paint—anybody can do that—but you learn how to be expressive with paint.[53]

Murray went to Mills College for an M.F.A. There she met Jennifer Bartlett, who, when Murray finally moved to New York City in 1967, introduced her to a group of like-minded artists. At that time Murray felt simultaneously connected to and also competitive with process art and minimalism, especially the work of Richard Serra, Keith Sonnier, and Brice Marden. The prevalent attitude "that painting was out . . . was unnerving," she recalled, "but then I didn't give a damn . . . For the first time in my life I was exactly where I wanted to be."[54]

Murray's unique vocabulary of biomorphic abstraction and expressive surface handling came together around 1975, and the Paula Cooper Gallery took her on. Cooper and Murray were a good match, both fiercely independent, dedicated to their work, and little interested in the fashions and careerism of the marketplace. In 1968 Paula Cooper had chosen to open her gallery in the run-down area where the artists were taking up residence rather than uptown near the collectors. Cooper's was the first commercial gallery in SoHo, and her first show was a benefit for Veterans Against the War in Vietnam. Joining Cooper's gallery allowed Murray to concentrate on painting.

If the title of *Tempest* [fig. 13.31], a canvas of 1979, suggests some turbulence in Murray's emotional life, the style provides a rejuvenating escape into the comics. The cartoon-like black outlines and clear, brilliant, and intensely contrasting color areas recall the drawings of Donald Duck, Little Orphan Annie, and Dick Tracy. "I remember writing to Walt Disney to ask if I could be his secretary," she said. ". . . I think cartoon drawing—the simplification, the universality, the diagrammatic quality of the marks, the breakdown of reality, its blatant, symbolic quality—has been an enormous influence on my work."[55] In *Tempest* the fine yellow line that connects and penetrates the figures seems almost narrative and at the same time like the emblematic signs used by cartoonists to indicate motion, surprise, or an aside that is not meant to be seen within the narrative frame.

Intimations of the figure increased steadily in Murray's abstraction at this time. Yet, like her contemporaries in the "New Image Painting" show, she had a paramount interest in the paint and structure. Indeed, Murray's focus on being *expressive* with paint connects her to abstract expressionism, while her use of figural references enhances the associational depth of the handling, rather than leading the viewer away from the abstract content toward a recognizable subject.

13.31 Elizabeth Murray, *Tempest*, 1979.
Oil on canvas, 10ft × 14ft 2in (3.05 × 4.32m).
Collection, Memphis Brooks Museum of Art, Memphis, Tenn.
Courtesy Paula Cooper Gallery, New York.

"I sort of know what they are," she remarked about the sometimes complex forms, "but I don't completely know what they are either."[56]

Formally, *Tempest* relates to pop art in its palette and in the reference to the comics. The shaped canvas, which she introduced in 1978, derives from Stella's paintings of the sixties, but instead of confirming the structural logic of the interior in the fashion of formalist painters, Murray (in a decidedly postmodern attitude) set the perimeters of the work off against the interior action. Similarly, she explored a variety of surface handling, from a delicately refined touch in monochromatic fields (inspired by the surfaces of Brice Marden's paintings of the late sixties) to flatly painted or improvisationally variegated passages. By 1981 she had developed this simultaneous variety of handling with sufficient deliberateness to remark that she "felt it was possible to paint all the ways I can paint in one painting."[57]

Pursuing the Logic of the Shaped Canvas

The shaped canvases of 1978–9 soon proliferated into composite paintings made up of multiple canvases, like puzzles that don't quite fit together. The transition took place in 1980 with a painting called *Breaking*. Murray had made four shaped panels, painted two, and then put the other two "down on the floor and looked at them together. It was an enormous step because it had never occurred to me to break up or use the shapes together . . . The beer glass [the central motif] is breaking in half in an illusionistic as well as in a physical way, and that's the first time I realized that I could do both at once."[58]

In *Painter's Progress* [fig. 13.32] Murray broke apart the central image of the artist's palette and brushes, scattering it across nineteen separate canvases, as though realizing in tangible form the shattered surface of facet planes in a cubist Picasso of the early teens. "I was imagining a whole thing—

13.32 Elizabeth Murray, *Painter's Progress*, 1981. Oil on canvas in nineteen parts, 9ft 8in × 7ft 9in (2.94 × 2.36m) overall.

The Museum of Modern Art, New York. Acquired through the Benhill Fund and Gift of Agnes Gund. Courtesy Paula Cooper Gallery, New York.

dropped or fallen and then shattered—on the ground, in the air, or perhaps in the body or mind. The image inside is trying to form the pieces whole again . . . The psychological meaning of the painting for me is my own conscious and unconscious efforts to bring disparate conflictive parts of [my] self together."[59]

A clearly discernible coffee cup emerged as the central motif in Murray's painting during the summer of 1981 and became the dominant theme in the paintings of the following year. Meanwhile, Murray also began constructing more complicated supports that literally overlap one another, building out toward the viewer and leading to such complex supports as in *Her Story* (1984) [fig. 13.33].

The subject of *Her Story* concerns, in part, the death of the artist's mother in 1983. In this painting Murray adopted an almost storytelling mode to deal with the subject. She explained, "I associated books with my mother. *Her Story* is really a portrait of her sitting with a book, holding a cup."[60] At the same time Cézanne's *Madame Cézanne in a Yellow Armchair*, which Murray studied closely in the Art Institute, also seems present as a lingering influence on this portrait of a seated woman.

In *Her Story* the blue figure (abstracted into simple angular forms) sits on a red chair with a pink book in her left hand and a coffee cup in her right. Under the book rests a freeform low table and, behind her, one sees the spines of the chair back. Murray painted these images right over the negative spaces and tiers of relief in the canvases, making unmistakable both the independence of the subject from the sculptural structure of the surface, and the rich dynamic of their juxtaposition. The artist has elaborated each object with the same degree of engaged emotional commitment as she has the abstract constructed elements.

Such oppositions even exist within the color, as in the way Murray plays off the refinement of the blue, red, and lavender against the rustic browns and greens and the gritty unfinished surface application. Murray experimented with a cruder, dryer, and less elegant style of application in the later part of 1982 just as she started to assemble her overlapping forms and build out toward the viewer with multivalent pictorial and constructed elements. The physical structure and depth refer to the evolution of the shaped and constructed canvas from Picasso through Stella. In addition, Murray turned the shaped canvases into another thread of literal

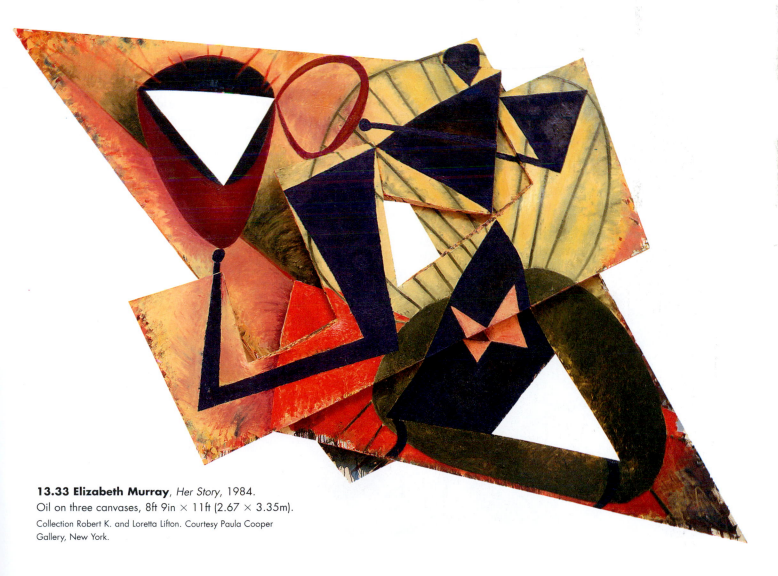

13.33 Elizabeth Murray, *Her Story*, 1984.
Oil on three canvases, 8ft 9in × 11ft (2.67 × 3.35m).
Collection Robert K. and Loretta Lifton. Courtesy Paula Cooper
Gallery, New York.

subject matter. The individual canvases of *Her Story* consist of two letter "A"s set bottom to bottom at the middle of the composition (the top of one points down to the lower right and the other to the upper left) and over them a backwards letter "E," playing with language as a tangible reality.

Her Story is a portrait of a woman, pulled in different directions yet cohesive and calm. The painting portrays simple, ordinary things—a chair, a book, a cup of coffee—yet it is layered with complexity in structure and allusion. It is a contemplative moment to do with reading, remembering, thinking about how all the pieces fit together (both literally and figuratively). It is at once a portrait of the artist's mother and a self-portrait.

Domestic subjects dominated the iconography of Murray's painting through 1985 as she awaited the birth of her second daughter, Daisy. She even "did two drawings right before Daisy was born about babies, spoons and organs," she noted.[61] In 1985 Murray also followed the sculptural implications of the layered canvases into more fully rounded protrusions where gigantic molded forms extend above and below and out from the center of the composition. Some paintings became almost fully rounded sculpture, as in *Tomorrow* of 1988 [fig. 13.34], where the relation to comic book description comes out in a witty exaggeration. Here Murray penetrated the soles of the giant shoes with openings that shift in cartoon fashion into knotholes in a plank of wood. These become eyes on faces in profile and orifices.

Whereas in the mid-eighties Murray could make paper templates for her studio assistants to translate into wooden stretchers, paintings like *Tomorrow* required small clay maquettes for their wood foundations. Even so, the artist still did not visualize the works completely in advance.

She made the forms by an intuitive process and then painted in an intuitive response to the forms, often modifying the structures in the course of painting.

One of the most remarkable aspects of Murray's work throughout is her courage in following a train of association wherever it leads, whether it be a formal development from the surface into three-dimensional space (as in *Tomorrow*) or in terms of the subject matter or expressive handling. In her last paintings she allows the compositional elements to scatter across the wall with breathtaking freedom. In a work like her 2006 painting *Morning Is Breaking* [fig. 13.35] she once again engages de Kooning's fragmentation of anatomy in *Excavation* [fig. 3.38]. The subject matter is clearer here with the sunbursts, the large green paintbrush dripping with blue paint, and the two figures arguing with one another face to face in the upper left. In this work the artist depicts both heads with the inoperable tumors that had been discovered in her own head at the time; she seems to be thinking about the elements of her world—the pleasures of nature and art and of the people around her as she also notes her mortality.

The Internationalization of Neo-Expressionism

"New Image Painting" encouraged attention to painting again, and at the end of the seventies the New York art world became excited about the new expressionist painting of Germany and Italy too. These events led to a broad revival of interest in expressionist tendencies in painting and a rapid internationalization of the art world. The Germans and Italians were shown widely in the eighties, and in the nineties artists from Japan, and then at the end of the decade artists from China, India, and Southeast Asia, began showing in

13.34 Elizabeth Murray, *Tomorrow*, January–February 1988. Oil on two canvases, 111½ × 132¾ × 21½in (283.2 × 337.2 × 54.6cm). Collection, Fukuo Sogo Bank, Ltd, Fukuoka, Japan. Courtesy Paula Cooper Gallery, New York.

13.35 Elizabeth Murray, *Morning Is Breaking*, 2006.
Oil on canvas on wood, 9ft 2½in × 10ft 1in × 2½in
(280.7 × 307.3 × 6.4cm).
Courtesy PaceWildenstein Gallery, New York.

prominent New York galleries and museums. The electronic communication and jet travel of the eighties and nineties made it possible for artists from anywhere to participate actively in the international discourse on art.

The Australian artist Mike Parr [fig. 13.36], for example, worked with the Viennese actionists in the mid-seventies in Europe and found inspiration in their stirring emotionalism. Well read in philosophy, linguistics, and psychology, he was drawn not simply to the arguments of major theoreticians in social science and the humanities but to the irrational that is masked behind their theories. In particular, he focused

on works such as the late writings of Antonin Artaud and those of the psychoanalyst Wilhelm Reich, when their language lost grammatical structure and devolved into a sequence of disjointed images. Parr's neo-expressionist style of drawing emerged in the early eighties, driven by his exploration of this hidden content in theoretical texts. Many

13.36 Mike Parr, *The Inertia of Night (Self-Portrait as a Slat)*, 1983. Charcoal and Girault on paper, 8ft 11⅞in × 6ft (2.74 × 1.83m). Private collection. Courtesy Roslyn Oxley9 Gallery, Sydney.

of these monumental drawings center on the artist's head, deformed by rendering a photograph twisted in perspective space. In counterpoint to the meticulous, if tormented, transcription of the head is a response to its deformity in a free gestural field of abstract line and color.

AMERICAN NEO-EXPRESSIONISM

In February 1979 the twenty-eight-year-old painter Julian Schnabel had a hotly debated first exhibition at the Mary Boone Gallery in SoHo in which he showed his plate paintings for the first time [fig. 13.37]. In these bombastically large, heavy, and crudely painted compositions he applied the paint thickly over fields of shattered crockery which was fastened to masonite grounds with automobile body repair bonding cement. Schnabel simultaneously infuriated and entranced the New York art world through the early eighties, focusing attention on the emergence of a new expressionist current in American painting. The new Mary Boone Gallery sold out his first one-person show before it even opened and then enticed Leo Castelli (the world's most famous dealer in contemporary art) to lend his imprimatur by joining in on a two-gallery show of Schnabel's work. Schnabel and Mary Boone orchestrated a media blitz that caused considerable resentment; to many, it symbolized the supercharged careerist tone of the New York art world of the eighties. This made it very difficult to look at the work objectively, and many of the critics were inclined to write Schnabel off as an arriviste.[62]

"All my images are subordinate to the notion of painting," Schnabel announced in 1983. What matters, he said, is "not what is painted, but how it's painted."[63] But in another statement he warned: "To those who think painting is just about itself, I'm saying the exact opposite. The concreteness of a painting can't help but allude to a world of associations that may have a completely different face other than that of the image you are looking at."[64] This kind of self-contradictory pronouncement, mixed with a baroque energy and ambition, characterized Schnabel's paintings as well as his public persona. What other painter would attempt a *Portrait of God*, as Schnabel did in 1981, or refer to himself (a Jewish artist from Brooklyn) as *St. Sebastian—Born in 1951* (1979)? Schnabel's work is an outrageous explosion of inarticulate energy, filled with contradiction, good passages and bad, all at maximum intensity. That very inconsistency is also its greatest strength. Schnabel takes formal risks and pursues grandiose ambitions that no cautious or deliberate artist would, and that had an immediate and profound effect on other important artists in the early eighties.

In *The Patient and the Doctors* [fig. 13.37] Schnabel cemented a field of broken dishes, cups, and other ceramic fragments to a disjointed construction of wooden planes as the support for the painting. The colorful relief of jagged edges and awkward lumps is so distracting that one can barely make out the images painted over them. Moreover, the various crudely painted figures and objects seem to have no more to do with one another than with the potshards or, for that matter, the title. "I wanted to make something that was exploding as much as I wanted to make something that was cohesive,"[65] he said of the plate paintings, which he began with this work in 1978 after seeing Antoni Gaudí's use of tile fragments in Barcelona.

Schnabel mixed multiple styles of drawing within a single composition and in the eighties would incorporate antlers, paint on velvet, and freely change styles altogether from one painting to the next. His strength was the ability to assimilate everything he saw into his compositions. Schnabel attempted to be as uncensored as possible. By way of explanation he offered the metaphor of an "incredible computer with all the information in the world on it. But it's going around so fast that it's too hot to be able to get the information. If they can ever figure out how to cool it off then we can get all that information. The simultaneity of it all is what interests me."[66]

13.37 Julian Schnabel, *The Patient and the Doctors*, 1978. Plaster, oil, plates, tiles on masonite, and Bondo on wood, 96 × 108 × 12in (243.8 × 274.3 × 30.5cm). Courtesy PaceWildenstein Gallery, New York.

Schnabel called the integration of painting and image as well as the premise of stylistic continuity into question. He painted a representational and an abstract picture at the same time. In addition, he said, "I want my life to be embedded in my work . . . crushed into my painting, like a pressed car."[67] However much Schnabel sought to carry forward the heroic individualism of the abstract expressionists, the world of the eighties was too full of confusing input to focus with that kind of certainty. Indeed, what distinguishes American neo-expressionist painting from classical forms of expressionism is precisely this diffuse sense of identity, together with a pervasive materialism.

Whereas Schnabel thrashed about in his compositions, filled with vitality, wanting to assert himself in the world no matter the odds, Robert Longo seemed deliberately to make his person disappear into the corporate woodwork. Longo started out drawing cool black-and-white figures in freeze-frame dramatic poses as though he were lifting stills from *film noir* detective stories (in which he had a considerable interest). He has an elegant formal finesse with minimalist form and pop art appropriation (including its arbitrary juxtaposition of images), while the theatricality with which he three-dimensionalizes pictorial concepts seems to feed, and to be fed by, set-building for his simultaneous work in film and performance.

In *National Trust* [fig. 13.38] Longo joined two slightly larger-than-life-size drawings of single figures by a cast aluminum relief of a simplified block of urban buildings. Longo is morbidly fascinated by evocations of authority in its most obdurate forms (from Albert Speer to General Motors) and he persistently leaves the viewer craning his or her neck up from below at the towering buildings that embody it. The figures lie contorted as though shot down but they float in a void, utterly without reference in time or space—not even the ground plane is articulated. Likewise, the relation of the relief to the figures is inexplicable, except in the intuitive sense that the emotionless objectivity of these powerless bodies is an acquiescence to the cold corporate authority expressed by the office block.

What became considerably clearer in the aftermath of pop art is that corporate culture and mainstream values were colonizing everyone's identity, undermining the sense that one has uniqueness or originality. For Eric Fischl, "the whole struggle for meaning since the 1970s has been a struggle

13.38 Robert Longo, *National Trust*, 1981. Two charcoal and graphite drawings on paper, one cast fiberglass and aluminum bonded sculpture, three panels, 5ft 3in × 19ft 6in (1.6 × 5.94m) overall. Walker Art Center, Minneapolis. Art Center Acquisition Fund, 1981.

for identity . . . a need for self."[68] But Fischl's subject was suburbia, where the veneer of normalcy forbids acknowledgement of what doesn't fit the community's image.

Fischl's works unfold like stories. His startling 1979 painting *Sleepwalker*, for example, shows a naked boy standing ankle-deep in a suburban backyard pool, masturbating. "What's an adolescent boy's masturbation about anyway," Fischl asked, "if it's not, in some sense, a separation technique? He's separating from his parents. He's becoming aware of himself."[69] Fischl's *Bad Boy* [fig. 13.39] is beautifully (indeed seductively) painted, drawing the viewer in as an accomplice to an act in which he or she may not wish to participate. Fischl has made explicit a common but normally unacknowledged situation—here one doesn't know if the title refers to the theft from the purse or the guilt the boy feels for his sexual curiosity, and we are left undecided about who's exploiting whom.

If Fischl dealt with suburbia and Longo with corporate culture, a painting like Robert Colescott's *Grandma and the Frenchman (Identity Crisis)* [fig. 13.40] deals with an inherited conflict that only became visible to the broader culture in the polyvalent postmodernism of the eighties and nineties. Colescott was a black artist who went to Egypt for two years in 1964 and discovered a 3,000-year-old history of African narrative art that catapulted him into an analysis of the complexity of his own identity and situation.[70]

Colescott trained in the French school, including a year in the atelier of Fernand Léger in Paris (1949–50). In *Grandma and the Frenchman* he used cubist fragmentation

13.39 Eric Fischl, *Bad Boy*, 1981. Oil on canvas, 5ft 6in × 8ft (1.68 × 2.44m). Private collection. Courtesy Mary Boone Gallery, New York.

in the description of the central figure's head and showed the influence of Léger in the monumentality of the composition. However, his expressive handling of the surface is unique and very un-French. In this painting the white doctor (who seems to have reached for his white-figured crucifix rather than his stethoscope) takes the black woman's pulse while staring fixedly at her breasts. Meanwhile, the African witch doctor's snake coils around the other side of her chair. It is ironic that the African doctor's mask and the head of Grandma herself derive from the African-influenced figure in the lower right corner of Picasso's famous *Les Demoiselles d'Avignon* (a landmark of the European art historical canon).

The cubist oscillation of Grandma's head, from black to Caucasian and back again, is amplified in the vignettes around the canvas showing her as she conceives herself in alternating aspects of black and white identities, brought out, presumably, by her ambivalent liaison with the Frenchman. This, of course, has important parallels with the artist's own conflicts about his French classical training.

13.40 Robert Colescott, *Grandma and the Frenchman (Identity Crisis)*, 1990. Acrylic on canvas, 7 × 6ft (2.13 × 1.83m). Collection of James and Maureen Dorment, Rumson, New Jersey. Courtesy Phyllis Kind Gallery, New York and Chicago.

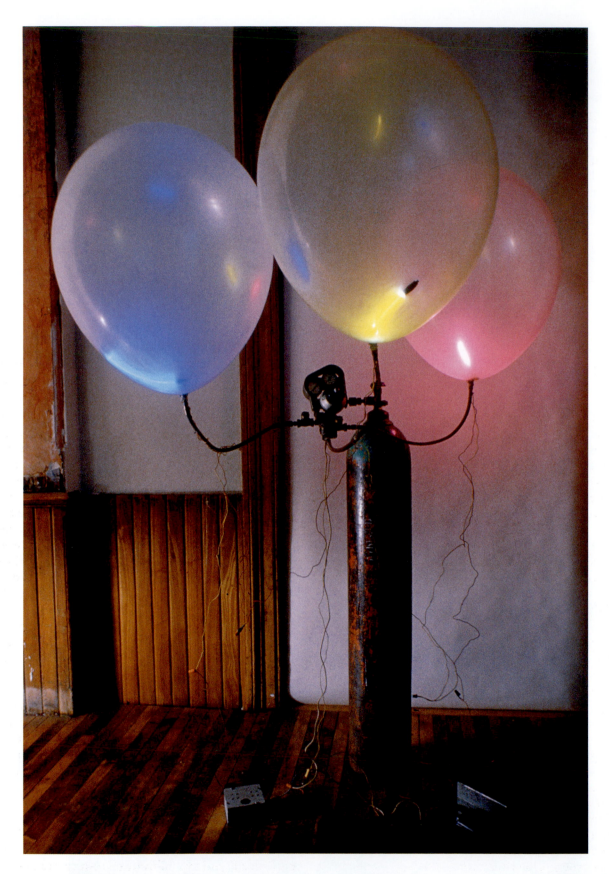

14.1 James Clark, *Hermes*, 1979. Helium, three latex balloons, argon lights, electrical mechanisms, 8 × 6 × 6ft (2.44 × 1.83 × 1.83m).

Courtesy Max Protetch Gallery, New York.

14 THE EIGHTIES

COMPLEXITY SETTLES IN

As the pluralism of the seventies morphed into postmodernism, the idea of dominant movements disappeared into a much more atomized and complicated cultural totality. There even ceased to be any defined sense of an art world in the eighties, and an increasing amount of the exciting new work in New York came from young artists who had been pushed by rising real estate costs to small storefronts on the gritty Lower East Side of Manhattan or at the end of the decade out to Brooklyn. Although it was just a short walk down from Avenues A, B, C or a quick ride over the bridge from Williamsburg to the chic galleries of SoHo, these artists had little to do with that world.

A Fresh Look at Abstraction

A remarkable generation of young abstract artists emerged toward the end of the seventies, characterized by an explicit eccentricity of style that announced the eccentricity of intellectual discourse generally in the eighties. Although James O. Clark, for example, showed in the established galleries, he built an aesthetic around the pervasive debris on the streets and empty lots of the Brooklyn waterfront where he lived, prefiguring the aesthetic of the rather self-contained artists' community that would emerge in Williamsburg at the end of the decade. He transformed materials such as the helium tanks, latex balloons, argon lights, and reused electrical mechanisms in *Hermes* [fig. 14.1] of 1979 into something exotically beautiful—the wires stream down like delicate hairs and the glow of red, yellow, and blue light from inside the balloons suggests an apparition.

Terry Winters, on the other hand, was very much a part of the SoHo and Tribeca (*Triangle Below Canal*) art scene. He stands out among an exceptional group of abstract painters who began attracting attention in New York in the late seventies. Winters found inspiration in Twombly's pictorial structure [see fig. 6.5], in the surface handling of Guston and Johns, and in the material presence of the surface in the late-sixties paintings of Brice Marden and in the drawings of Richard Serra. In *Good Government* [fig. 14.2] Winters did not balance the composition in the manner of traditional painting—rather, he gave it coherence through the continuity of his train of association. The forms derive from nature (developing organisms, primitive cell clusters, crystals, plant parts), but above all Winters seeks the invisible aspects of nature that are accessible only through the abstraction of technology. Whether the suggestions come from the intervention of the microscope or the theoretical configurations of computer-generated fractals, Winters projects the imagination beyond the knowable.

This aesthetic exploration of natural science has near antecedents in both Smithson and Aycock and in Buckminster Fuller, Frei Otto, and D'Arcy Thompson (two engineers and a biologist who provided specific sources for Winters); Winters is interested in those who have sought to imagine vivid form beyond what is literally visible in nature. Perhaps this ability to create sensual immediacy despite the distancing of technological intervention and emotional displacement is also a part of what gives Winters his virtuosity as a printmaker (a medium that imposes a distance in its technical processes).

The eccentricity of the structure in *Good Government* parallels a deliberately ungraceful sense of form, color, and surface. The organic origins of the materials are an important aspect of the content in these works too—Winters went back to the ancient naturalist Pliny to learn about the sources of pigments and this information contributes to the train of organic association that generates these works. Lisa Phillips aptly described his paintings as "totally uningratiating and visceral, they are nonetheless tactile and sensual. The paint

14.2 (left) **Terry Winters**, *Good Government*, 1984. Oil on canvas, 8ft 5¼in × 11ft 5¼in (2.57 × 3.49m). Whitney Museum of American Art, New York. Purchase, with funds from The Mnuchin Foundation and the Painting and Sculpture Committee, 85.15.

14.3 (below) **Anish Kapoor**, *Cloud Gate*, Millennium Park, Chicago, 2004. Stainless steel. Courtesy Gladstone Gallery, New York.

itself is a psychologically and sexually charged material. Its mucilaginous texture reeks of a sticky sexuality."[1]

That same eccentricity of form and visceral sensuality is evident in the strong crop of abstract sculptors who appeared in Britain at the end of the seventies, among them Tony Cragg, Richard Deacon, Bill Woodrow, and Anish Kapoor. They all use materials in novel ways. Kapoor, for example, made a number of works with powders of intensely saturated pigment over organic forms that look like overgrown gourds of an especially odd variety. Increasingly, his work has also involved highly polished reflective surfaces, as in the stainless steel *Cloud Gate* for the Millennium Park in Chicago (2004) [fig. 14.3].

Cragg's perceptually intriguing found plastic pieces engage several levels of content simultaneously. He is in one sense a materialist in scattering his motley collection of found plastic fragments on the floor or the wall, like a Carl Andre, emphasizing real space and real time, and also like Andre subordinating the individual elements to a larger system of ordering. However, Cragg has used plastic detritus, rather than natural materials, as his medium and his schemata involve both ordering by color and the creation of a representational silhouette that cuts to another level of perception and interpretation entirely, as in his 1981 wall piece, *Britain Seen from the North* [fig. 14.4], which also involves a third semiotic leap to the image of a map.

Informed by the ongoing vitality of conceptual art, Cragg explores these cognitive jumps as definitive of "Man's relationship to his environment and the objects, materials and images in that environment." Cragg described his subject matter as "celluloid wildlife, video landscapes, photographic wars, polaroid families, offset politics. Quick change, something new on all channels. Always a choice of second hand images." For this artist, such conceptual jumps are a matter of survival: "Reality can hardly keep up with its marketing image. The need to know both objectively and subjectively more about the subtle fragile relationships

14.4 Tony Cragg, *Britain Seen from the North*, 1981. Plastic and mixed media, 14ft 55¼in × 26ft 3in × 3ft 3⅓in (4.40 × 8.00 × 1.00m). Tate, London.

between us, objects, images and essential natural processes and conditions is becoming critical."[2]

The sculpture of the American artist Martin Puryear [figs. 14.5 and 14.6] lies at the other end of the spectrum from the plastic accumulations of Tony Cragg, although it shares the particularizing eccentricity of the English abstractionists and of Winters and Clark. Puryear's work relies above all on a unique style of working the surface of each object and maintaining the expressive integrity of that surface as distinct from (and at the same time in dialog with) the free, organic improvisation of the form. His working of the materials has a profoundly personal and spiritual character. In the late seventies the revitalized interest in expressionistic handling in painting made Puryear's subtlety of surface in sculpture newly relevant.

Martin Puryear created his first body of mature work when he settled in Brooklyn in 1973, where the stimulation of the New York art scene seems to have catalyzed the transition. Puryear's sculpture centers on a solid practice of making objects and its pronounced physicality represents a

14.6 Martin Puryear, *Maroon*, 1987–8. Steel wire mesh, wood, and tar, 6ft 4in × 10ft × 6ft 6in (1.93 × 3.05 × 1.98m). Milwaukee Art Museum. Gift of the Contemporary Art Society. Courtesy Donald Young Gallery, Seattle.

return to bodily experience. As in the work of Brancusi and that of the African carvers who influenced both Brancusi and Puryear, this expression of the body in connection to nature is an important facet of Puryear's sculpture and anticipates a more general reassertion of such concerns in the art of the nineties.

An Expressionism Beyond Medium: Jonathan Borofsky

Jonathan Borofsky finished graduate school at the Yale School of Art in 1966. At that time he turned away from making objects. Conceptual art dominated the scene when, sometime toward the end of 1968, Borofsky started counting and recording the numbers on sheets of paper. Whenever he returned to his work after a break he would check to see where he had left off and start up again from there. He explained:

> After counting for a few hours at a time I often found myself making little scribbles on the page—stick figures, heads attached to trees—but I let them go by. Then one day I looked at one of the past scribbles and thought, I'd like to make a painting of that . . . Then I took the number I had been on in my counting and put it in the corner of the painting. Something connected there. I had both a recognizable image and conceptual ordering in time . . . Looking back on it now I see it as a reaction to Minimalism.[3]

In 1973 Borofsky exhibited several stacks of the numbered papers as *Counting Piece* in a show curated by Sol LeWitt at the alternative Artists Space in New York. Borofsky had started painting again in 1972 and, as he told Kathy Halbreich, practically every work was a kind of self-portrait,

14.5 Martin Puryear, *To Transcend*, 1987. Stained Honduran mahogany, poplar, 169 × 13 × 90in (429.3 × 33 × 228.6cm). Walker Art Center, Minneapolis. Walker Special Purchase Fund, 1988. Courtesy Donald Young Gallery, Seattle.

14.7 Jonathan Borofsky, Installation, Philadelphia Museum of Art, October 7–December 2, 1984. Detail showing drawings pinned to the wall.

in the sense that he was attempting to represent the content of his head.[4] Moreover, his work became a continuous, total project. His first show at the Paula Cooper Gallery in 1975 was an overfilled installation into which he jammed everything he had been doing for the last year or so with relatively little selection. It included self-portraits, sketches on scraps of paper (often intermixed with notes of one kind or another), and dreams he had written down. This heterogeneity and informality continued to characterize subsequent exhibitions [fig. 14.7]. These shows aspired to give people "a feeling of being inside my mind."[5]

After installing virtually the entire contents of his studio in the Paula Cooper show, Borofsky started drawing directly on the floor and walls of his then-empty loft. He worked on this new piece solidly for over a month, doing all the drawing freehand. After this Borofsky created all his subsequent installations using an opaque projector to transfer his small notes and drawings onto the wall—he would arrive with only a briefcase of drawings instead of a truckload of objects and this is the origin of the black silhouette of a man with a briefcase that has appeared in so many of his works (see the center of fig. 14.7) and the hammering man (upper right). Borofsky felt that, by drawing directly on the walls in these installations, he was creating something that could not be purchased—the viewer had to be there out of a genuine interest in the experience.

Borofsky's installation in the Paula Cooper Gallery in 1983 was one of his greatest works. He created a baffling and chaotic environment of sounds, images, movement, and light as well as incorporating painting, drawing, and sculpture in a range of styles and states of completion [fig. 14.8]. The bare canvas stretcher, the walls of pinned-up notes and drawings (often on scraggly scraps of paper), the notations of dreams and childhood memories created an emotion-filled atmosphere that evoked not only the intimacy of the artist's studio but a revealing look straight into his psyche.

Borofsky painted *The Maidenform Woman, You Never Know Where She'll Turn Up at 2,841,779* in an illustrational style, as though straight out of the omnipresent underwear advertisement of the time. The free association from the line of faceless soldiers staring at the woman in her bra and panties to the featureless *Chattering Men* is the kind of

14.8 Jonathan Borofsky, Installation, Paula Cooper Gallery, November 5–December 3, 1983. View showing (left to right): *Chattering Man with Photograph at 2,845,312* (1983), *Painting with Hand Shadow at 2,841,780* (1981–3), *The Dancing Clown at 2,845,325* (1982–3), *The Maidenform Woman, You Never Know Where She'll Turn Up at 2,841,779* (1983), *Chattering Man with Two Stretcher Frames at 2,845,313* (1983), *Molecule Men at 2,945,318* (1982–3), *The Berlin Dream at 2,841,792* (1982–3), *Split Wire Dream with Chattering Man at 2,841,784* (1978–83), and (including neon loops and projection on ceiling) *Flying Frog with Chattering Men at 2,845,322* (1983).

associative structure with which Borofsky wove together the entire installation. Instead of painting in a single, signatory style of his own, he rendered each object in a fashion true to itself as a predefined, received image in his memory, so the jumps in style, subject, scale, and sound from work to work do, in the end, replicate a unified experience—that of the artist's mental landscape.

In this sense, the memory traces of quotidian existence are vividly evoked. The *Chattering Men* are featureless robots with mechanical jaws that repeat the same movements and (with a tape loop) emanate a constant din of meaningless chatter. *The Dancing Clown at 2,845,325*, with its twisting foot, seems to dominate the room intrusively, insistently singing "I did it my way"; a brilliantly colorful and gesture-filled canvas called *Sing* shows Borofsky transfixed by a glowing tablet with the commandment "sing" inscribed on it while the melodic sound from a tape behind the canvas plays songs composed and sung by the artist. The *Universal Groan Painting* recites facts and groans, while the perforated silhouettes of *Two Wrestlers* have an aggressive verbal exchange. With images projected onto the ceiling, a string of blue neon circles blinking on and off in a wave pattern overhead, and visitors wandering through the space, it was a truly Whitmanesque cataloging of contemporary experience. After this exhibition in New York, anything seemed possible.

Graffiti Art

Borofsky's installation opened the door to a graffiti aesthetic within the art world at precisely the moment when a new wave of expressionist graffiti emerged in the real cacophony of the city streets. Coming from the poor neighborhoods

14.9 Lee (Quinones), *Stop the Bomb,* 1979.
Whole car, spray paint, New York subway, destroyed.

of Brooklyn and the Bronx, the graffiti writers appropriated the train cars of the New York subway system like traveling exhibition walls that permeated the entire city with their influence [fig. 14.9]. The graffiti writers were not naive, either in theme or style, even though they had little formal education and gravitated toward forties and fifties gestural abstraction at just the moment when the more well-heeled art world was embracing postmodernism. Ramm-El-Zee, for example, wrote a manifesto of 1979–86 called *Ionic Treatise Gothic Futurism Assassin Knowledges of the Remanipulated Square Point One to 720° Rammellzee* which, as John Carlin described it, "reads like Jacques Derrida on acid linking the biophysical structure of the universe to the shape and evolution of letters."[6] The message is that symbolic creation can undermine institutional control, that the artist's manipulation of letters can change reality.

The start of graffiti art in the early seventies is usually attributed to TAKIS 183, as the first to "tag up" (i.e., write his alias and the street on which he hung out) repeatedly in the subway cars. The graffiti writers' simple script of names in black marker or spray paint moved to the outside of the cars around 1973. It then evolved into the more elaborate "bubble letters," inspired by underground comics (especially the "Cheech Wizard" cartoons by Vaughn Bodé), and in 1975 Caine and Fabulous Five painted the first "whole car" compositions. The eighties was the golden age of graffiti writing, with complex, abstract letter forms (called "Wild Style") as well as political and allegorical themes. Some of the other leading artists were Crash, Dondi, Futura 2000, Lady Pink, Lee, Phase II, Revolt, Seen, and Zephyr. When one of their cars rolled into the gray gloom of a New York subway station, it was, as Claes Oldenburg remarked, "like a big bouquet from Latin America."[7]

Keith Haring

Efforts were made to transplant the work of the graffiti writers into the art galleries, but it failed to survive that transition because the political appropriation of the city trains was integral to its character. However, Keith Haring, a twenty-two-year-old painter from rural Kutztown, Pennsylvania [fig. 14.10], inaugurated a major body of work in more conventional media in 1980 that was inspired by

graffiti writing. Haring came to New York in 1978 and went to the School of Visual Arts. He was painting in a brushy, abstract style when, toward the end of 1980, he noticed that the transit authority covered the posters on the subway platforms with black paper after the rental period on the advertisement expired. Haring found these black panels irresistible surfaces and his white chalk line drawings in the subways soon became a consuming passion [fig. 14.11].[8] The subway authorities would remove the drawings in a matter of days (arresting the artist if they caught him), but Haring replaced them as fast as new black frames appeared. The subject matter was a recurring repertoire of simple narrative images that travelers all over Manhattan began to recognize and look for: flying saucers with beams of energy empowering radiant babies and barking dogs, little androgynous people, composite monsters with some human, some animal body parts and often with television sets for heads.

Haring's drawings deal with the life of Everyman in our television culture. Sometimes he put dollar signs on the television screens (suggesting advertising) or showed a barking dog (perhaps politicians or moralizing preachers). Barry Blinderman described the artist's underlying subject matter as "the hallucinatory interface of biology and technology in our increasingly cybernetic society. Audio-visual surveillance, monitoring of bodily fluids as an employment prerequisite, genetic engineering, mass-media anesthesia that is beginning to seem as much inherited as culturally induced—these are

14.10 Keith Haring, *Radiant Baby Button,* 1982. Printed plastic button, with metal back and pin, 1in (2.4cm) diameter.

14.11 (left) **Keith Haring** drawing in the New York City subway, 1982.

14.12 (below) **Keith Haring**, all works untitled, black light installation for an exhibition in the Tony Shafrazi Gallery, New York, 1982.

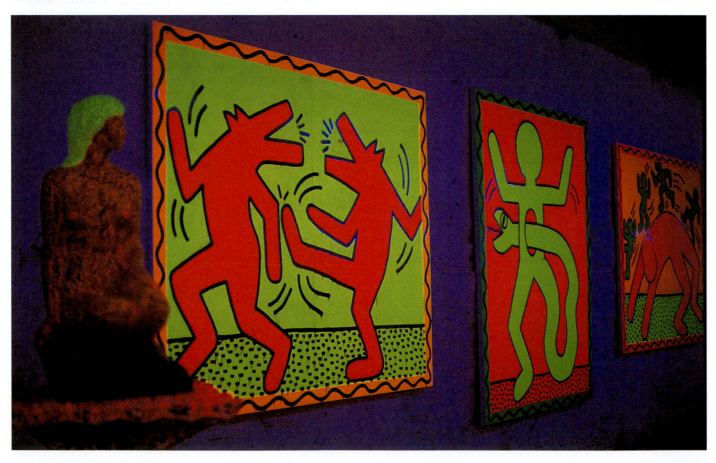

the conditions that characterize our so-called postmodern era."[9] The writing of William Burroughs was a formative influence on Haring in his efforts to come to terms with this postmodern condition. For Burroughs, experience comes in too much profusion and emotional intensity to attempt integration. Instead, he portrays himself as a neutral conduit through which all these psychic states pass: "I am a recording instrument . . . I do not presume to impose 'story' 'plot' 'continuity.'"[10] But where Burroughs is desperately alienated from himself, Haring's figures are life-affirming, taking comfort in their communal anonymity.

Some of Haring's subway drawings had obvious political themes, such as the one labeled "South Africa" in three narrative frames: a little figure leads a giant by a rope around the neck, then the big figure rubs its sore neck (evidently assessing the situation), and in the third frame the giant stamps on the small figure. Haring created icons of mass culture to which everyone could relate, using the same devices as advertising: repeated trademark images with simple, instantly understandable messages. He saturated his audience with them, painting on any surface at hand and even passing out free buttons and posters, as in an advertising campaign. He also mass-marketed his images as inexpensive souvenirs through the Pop Shop, which he opened on the edge of the SoHo gallery district in 1986.

In the work Haring did for the art galleries—as distinct from the public venues—he drew many overtly sexual subjects: copulating people and dogs (frequently mixed), masturbating figures (including that of Mickey Mouse, which in some sense represents American mass culture), and winged phalluses. He wanted to address sexuality as the driving force in life. But even in the work Haring made strictly for art audiences he also courted the taste for popular entertainment, as in the fluorescent works he painted for his show at the Tony Shafrazi Gallery in 1982 [fig. 14.12].

The East Village Scene of the Eighties

A series of early-eighties shows by Keith Haring at the downtown punk-rock Mudd Club inaugurated "fun art" and this in turn spawned the first East Village gallery—the Fun Gallery, run by Patti Astor. The seedy, low-rent East Village quickly blossomed as a boom town for new art, with young people in their twenties opening galleries in tiny storefronts side by side with the drug dealers, hookers, and gangs who had long occupied the neighborhood. This resulted partly from frustration about the inability of young artists to break into the SoHo galleries; the names of these East Village galleries—PPOW (written like a sound effect in a comic) and Civilian Warfare are examples—emphasize the difference between the East Village and SoHo, where most of the galleries are named, like law firms, after their founders. CASH gallery, which opened in 1983, suggests in its name the cynicism about commercial culture that pervaded the East Village. There was also a sophistication about language as a tool of political and social appropriation and about the

use of appropriation generally as the basis of art. Nature-Morte gallery, which opened in May 1982, took the French term for a still life (one of the most traditional artistic subjects and one associated with moral allegory) and made a *double entendre* on the literal meaning of "nature dead" as a comment on an age of reproduction and appropriation when no one paints from life any more and nature itself has come under attack as a viable term. Finally, the more visible presence of down-and-out people on the streets in the East Village made social issues—especially drug addiction and the emergent AIDS crisis—particularly poignant.

Jean-Michel Basquiat

Like his friend Keith Haring, Jean-Michel Basquiat made his network of art-world connections through the downtown clubs like CBGB's, the Mudd Club, and Hurrah, where he performed with his own "noise band" in 1979 and 1980. Haring and Basquiat also both burst onto the art scene with instantaneous celebrity in 1980 (they were twenty-two and twenty respectively) and then they were gone as suddenly as they had appeared: Haring died of AIDS in 1990 at the age of thirty-one and Basquiat of a drug overdose in 1988 at the age of twenty-seven. Finally, Basquiat also had a formative connection to graffiti writing, but for him it had the particular value of providing a coterie of other black artists. He was especially close to Ramm-El-Zee, Fab 5 Freddy, and Toxic.

Basquiat, however, grew up middle-class in Brooklyn, although he dropped out of high school and largely educated himself. At seventeen he left home and lived on the streets.[11] During this period of homelessness (1977–9) Basquiat collaborated with a schoolfriend named Al Diaz on a sequence of "SAMO" texts (originating from a combination of "Sambo" and "same old shit"), which they inscribed up and down the D-train and on walls around SoHo and the East Village. Unlike other graffiti, the SAMO texts were puzzling aphorisms like "SAMO as an end of mindwash, religion, nowhere politics, and bogus philosophy." By 1980 Basquiat had taken over the SAMO writings, and through them gained some degree of personal notoriety in the downtown art world. He also showed his art for the first time in 1980, in the countercultural "Times Square Show."

In February 1981 Basquiat installed a wall of paintings and drawings in the important "New York/New Wave" exhibition at P.S.1, then a highly visible alternative space on the Long Island side of the 59th Street Bridge. This exhibition included some of the graffiti writers, as well as Warhol, Haring, and his friend Kenny Scharf. Basquiat's contribution attracted the notice of the SoHo dealer Annina Nosei, who gave him the basement of her gallery as a studio and began to represent him.

From this point onward Basquiat's career followed a meteoric trajectory, driven by his relentless productivity. Nosei gave him a one-person show in March 1982 that drew considerable attention, but by fall he had split with her and organized a show at the Fun Gallery. It wasn't until March 1984 that he signed on with another New York dealer, Mary Boone, and although that relationship deteriorated too (in 1986) it firmly established his market. Meanwhile, Basquiat had formed a close friendship with Andy Warhol and had become an art celebrity in his own right. In the spring 1984 sale at Christie's a Basquiat painting sold for $19,000—an extraordinary price for a twenty-three-year-old artist—and in February 1985 his photograph appeared on the cover of the *New York Times Magazine*.

Basquiat was a brilliant success almost from the start but remained torn up by self-doubts to the end. In a painting like *Boy and Dog in a Johnnypump* of 1982 [fig. 14.13] one immediately feels an exalted exhaustion like that of Jack Kerouac whom Basquiat read avidly. The beauty of the color and the sublimely expressive brushwork overwhelm the viewer and, at the same instant, one experiences the terrifying vertigo of what the seventeenth-century philosopher Pascal referred to as "the eternal silence of these infinite spaces";[12] Basquiat's paintings portray a breathtaking existential absence. As a black artist in a white world, he was out there alone to an even greater degree than other major artists, and this was amplified by his alienation from his own family.

14.13 Jean-Michel Basquiat, *Boy and Dog in a Johnnypump*, 1982. Acrylic, oil paintstick, and spray paint on canvas, 7ft 10½in × 13ft 9½in (2.4 × 4.2m).
Courtesy Galerie Bruno Bischofberger, Zurich.

In this painting the black boy stands, palms out, in a gesture of supplication and spiritual disguise with a red-haloed familiar at his side. He has an ingratiating smile, but the face is a vacant mask with the inner person (of the artist?) hidden from view. Meanwhile, the boy's dreadlocks flash brilliant red, as though lit from within; the bones glisten against the black, animating the skeleton like a spirit brought back to life. Basquiat has raised every color and brushstroke to its maximum intensity, as in the rhythmic structure of jazz, giving the work what the art historian Robert Farris Thompson has called an "Afro-Atlantic vividness."[13]

The black gestural line in the left forearm of the figure in *Boy and Dog in a Johnnypump* is "written," as in a graffitero's script, and "NEEET" is inscribed as though on a wall to the left. Yet the broad gestures of red, yellow, and green reveal Basquiat's indebtedness to Franz Kline, Pollock's early work, and de Kooning's figures of the sixties. The expressive excess of the surface in this painting provides at once an outpouring of feeling and a wall through which the outsider cannot penetrate to the core of the artist's being. As bell hooks has written, "Basquiat's work gives that private anguish [of the black experience] artistic expression."[14]

Basquiat calls another painting of that year, *Portrait of the Artist as a Young Derelict* [fig. 14.14], a self-portrait. The roughly thrown-together wooden support (a common feature of his work) speaks to the "derelict" circumstances with which he identifies and accentuates the spontaneity and rebellious improvisation—half-graffiti, half-jazz. The fragmentation is a "cut-up" aesthetic like the literally cut-up texts of William

14.14 Jean-Michel Basquiat, *Portrait of the Artist as a Young Derelict*, 1982. Acrylic, oil, and oil paintstick on wood, 6ft 8⅜in × 6ft 10⅛in (204 × 208cm). Collection, Emmanuelle et Jerôme de Noirmont, Paris.

Burroughs.[15] The notational quality is another common feature of his work which he raises to masterful level in works like this. Below the self-portrait head he wrote: "Hic est rex," Latin for "This is the king," and in the central panel painted his crown.

Basquiat summarized his subject matter in an interview with Henry Geldzahler as "Royalty, heroism, and the streets."[16] *Charles the First*, also of 1982 [fig. 14.15], is a royal coronation of the great jazz saxophonist Charlie Parker and belongs to a recurring set of homages to black heroes with whom Basquiat identified—athletes, jazz musicians, writers. In an off-white square to the right Basquiat wrote

"Cherokee," the title of one of Parker's most famous tunes, right up there with the word "Opera," suggesting a parallel in artistic stature between "Cherokee" and this most aristocratic of musical genres. Below this he placed a crown, which is both a symbol of Parker's artistic royalty and Basquiat's own tag.

At the top of the left-hand panel of *Charles the First* the artist placed a crown labeled "Thor," suggesting a parallel with the mythological Norse god of thunder. The four feathers in the painting allude to Parker's nickname "Bird," and the black hand suggests the powerful bodily presence of both horn player and painter. Basquiat has also included the

14.15 Jean-Michel Basquiat, *Charles the First*, 1982. Acrylic and oil paintstick on canvas, triptych, 6ft 6in × 5ft 2¼in (1.98 × 1.58m). Courtesy Robert Miller Gallery, New York.

words "Marvel Comics" in two places, drawn the emblem of Superman, and written "X-Man." So here the fantasy world of the comics merges with history in supplying a spiritual genealogy for the artist. But in *Charles the First* Basquiat also expressed a pervasive ambivalence. "Hall of Fame" is also "Hall of Shame," as he notes in paintings like *Mitchell Crew* of 1983. In *Crowns (Peso Neto)* and elsewhere Basquiat pairs the royal crown with a crown of thorns and in *Charles the First* even the status of haloes is undercut by their price of "fifty nine cent."

The very ambition of Basquiat's painting *Charles the First*, and of his identification with the "royalty and heroism" of his personal black pantheon, comes with a corresponding anxiety; in the lower left corner of the painting he wrote: "Most young kings get thier [*sic*] head cut off." He crossed out "young," the qualifier that clearly refers to himself, only to enhance the self-referential overtone: "I cross out words so you will see them more; the fact that they are obscured makes you want to read them."[17] The same might be said of the impassiveness of all that one cannot read in the iconography of Basquiat's paintings and persona. His works cry out for connection and yet ward it off—Basquiat's *oeuvre* is a double portrait of absence and presence with an uncanny bodily and spiritual immediacy.

David Wojnarowicz

The art of David Wojnarowicz leaves no ambiguity about the identity of the artist. On the contrary, Wojnarowicz uses the sharp delineation of his identity, principally in its divergence from the culture's norms, to lay bare society's ethical flaws and dissimulation. The aesthetic he created out of this painfully uncompromising self-scrutiny and exposure nevertheless embodies the remarkable beauty of a complex and incisive mind.

Wojnarowicz had been a child prostitute in Times Square (his terrifying homosexual encounters in subway tunnels and sleazy hotel rooms are recounted in excruciating detail in his writings[18]) and he died of AIDS at the age of thirty-eight. At the same time he had one of the most brilliant collage sensibilities of the late twentieth century and used it in a lucid exposition of the layered interaction between nature, his personal identity, and contemporary cultural values.

> My whole life I've felt like I was looking into society from an outer edge, because I embodied so many things that were supposedly reprehensible—being homosexual or having been a prostitute when I was a kid, or having a lack of education. All my life I looked at the world with a longing to be accepted, but . . . the only way I could be accepted would be to deny all those things. At the moment of diagnosis [of AIDS] I fully gave up that desire to fit in, and started realizing that those places where I didn't fit and the ways I was diverse were the most interesting parts of myself. I could use that diversity as a tool to gain a sense of who I was.[19]

In *Water* [fig. 14.16], one of four paintings on the elements, a dark oceanliner surges into a vast night sea. A cutaway on the hull—as though we can see with Superman's X-ray vision—reveals a strange tangle of viscera in muted colors, all drawn with a comic book simplicity of style. Above and overlapping the ship is a frog, rendered with meticulous naturalism in a palette rich as only nature itself could conceive it. A window opens through the back of the frog and looks down on a black-and-white photograph of a trashed automobile hulk. Here the striking contrasts between the lush, human rendering of nature (the frog) and the starkly mechanical realism of the colorless photograph (recording the detritus of urban decay) set up one of the many charged levels of discourse within the composition.

Wojnarowicz filled the center of *Water* with an organically contoured grid of small black-and-white pictures in an illustrational style. Their subject matter relates to the various images around the periphery of the composition. Some frames contain energetically swirling spirals, like eddies of water; there are river and oceanscapes with a swimmer, fish, views of the steamship in daylight, superimpositions with other images; the frog recurs, once in a surreal scale looking over a railing, and in another section prefigured as eggs and tadpole; and other allusions to ontogenesis or to the biology of internal organs also crop up around the grid. Finally, there are three overtly erotic scenes.

In the upper right corner of *Water* the artist superimposed a colorful, circular vignette over this monochromatic checkerboard, showing an expressionistically painted hand swathed in bandages, reaching out through prison bars. A flower seems to drop from the hand into a snowy sky with tiny white figures scattered below like snowflakes. Finally, the inky blue water and night sky that form a perimeter around the painting are traversed by a school of sperm cells, animating the composition with a delicate pattern in their free profusion.

Part of the impact of this painting, and of Wojnarowicz's work generally, involves a radical insight into the complicated layering of impressions from nature, from subjective frameworks of interpretation, and from the languages of culture that make up what we understand today as "reality." Wojnarowicz seems to have experienced all these levels with remarkable distinctness, and yet that very analytical clarity also seems to engender a kind of detachment:

Inside my head behind the eyes are lengthy films running on multiple projectors; the films are images made up from information from media . . . some of the films are childhood memories of the forests I lay down in; the surfaces of the earth I scrutinized and some are made up of dreams. Sometimes the projectors run simultaneously sometimes they stop and start but the end result is thousands of feet of multiple films crisscrossing in front of each other thereby creating endless juxtapositions and associations.[20]

The career of Wojnarowicz resembles that of Basquiat and Haring to the extent that he first attracted notice on the downtown scene through the clubs, where he began playing with a post-punk noise band called "3 Teens Kill 4—No Motive" in 1979. But the core of his early work was a guerrilla-style political activism, stenciling images on walls (and gallery doors) that he derived from the tabloid media, politics, and the street—burning houses, dinosaurs, guns, muggers, soldiers, young male torsos, addicts shooting up. His aim was to call attention to the ethical state of emergency he found in American culture.

14.16 David Wojnarowicz, *Water*, 1987.
Acrylic, ink, collage on masonite, 6 × 8ft (1.83 × 2.44m).
Private collection, New York.

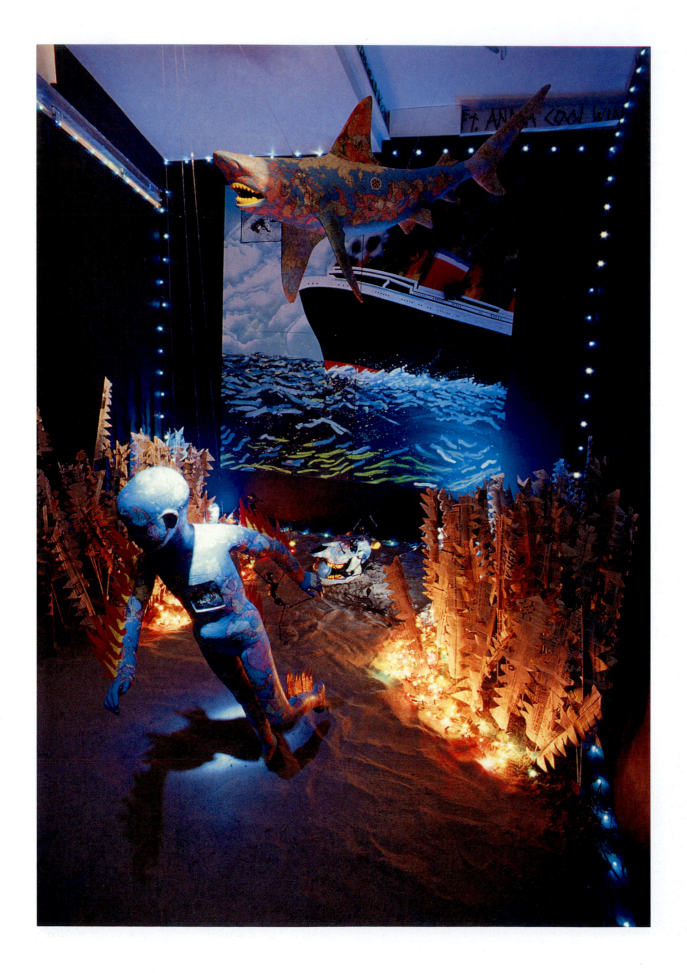

14.17 (opposite) **David Wojnarowicz**, Installation, November 1–25, 1984.
Gracie Mansion Gallery, New York.

Wojnarowicz frequently made powerful use of the media of performance and installation, sometimes in galleries [fig. 14.17] and at other times in derelict buildings [fig. 14.18] or other illegal sites like the abandoned piers on Canal Street in New York. As an act of conscience, he never permitted his art-world success (which had become considerable already by the mid-eighties) to overshadow his political and social statement. Sometimes he directly attacked the complacent ease of the art establishment—in 1980 he and his friend Julie Hare dumped a load of bloody cow bones from the Meatpacking District into the stairwell of Leo Castelli's chic SoHo gallery when it was full of visitors, and in 1982 they made an unsolicited contribution to the "Beasts" exhibition at P.S.1, releasing live cockroaches with tiny glued-on bunny ears and tails ("cockabunnies") into the galleries at the opening.[21]

Moved to a new kind of self-awareness by the writings of the French author Jean Genet and later by William Burroughs, Wojnarowicz developed a confrontational style of working that pushed his art out of the comfort zone. His work concerns the real immediacy of bodily experience and identity in a culture filled with unacknowledged violence, which society masks in a barrage of consumer fiction and contradiction. "You can turn and see some bum or some image of decay," he pointed out, "and then turn again and see some restaurant where it costs \$40 for a meal. So you're constantly superimposing images upon images and sandwiching them. TV, magazines, information, memory, grocery store signs—and there's all this suggestion of consumption . . . of images."[22]

The Death of American Spirituality [fig. 14.19] is a summarizing painting for Wojnarowicz, bluntly stating his grandest theme. He divided the composition into four panels, joined by the continuity of the bull across three of them, the mountains across another two, the sky across two others. Yet while the sky continues over the top and the red bolts of electricity join all four frames, the gray rocks in the upper right bluntly stop at the edges and the right border of the mountain is abruptly cut by the midline of the composition when other elements are not. This jarringly reinforces the multi-leveled reality of experience for Wojnarowicz, as in his painting *Water*.

The terrifying images of the Hopi snake charmer and the kachina with its radiating streaks of energy are the avatars of the ancient culture of the Americas and perhaps the purifying force of nature itself. The streaks of energy encircle the mechanical parts with bearings, wrapped in images from dollar bills (top center and center left), and lasso the arm of

14.18 David Wojnarowicz, "The Missing Children Show: 6 Artists from the East Village on Main Street," December 6–10, 1985, Louisville, Kentucky.
Courtesy Gracie Mansion Gallery, New York.

14.19 David Wojnarowicz, *The Death of American Spirituality*, 1987. Acrylic and mixed media on plywood, two panels, 6ft 8in × 3ft 8in (2.03 × 1.12m) each. Private collection, New Jersey.

the cowboy, who derives from Wojnarowicz's earlier graffiti stencil of Ronald Reagan as a nuclear "buckaroo." The gears painted on a political map of the American continents (below right) seem to emerge from flames of destruction out of which an apparition of a sickly green Christ with a crown of thorns emerges. Wojnarowicz despaired of this "diseased society,"[23] and yet he seems to have had a glimmer of hope that the directness of his confrontation with its moral failure might contribute to its salvation.

EIGHTIES INSTALLATION

For artists such as Wojnarowicz, the vividness of a totally immersive experience made installation increasingly important as a medium. But in the eighties and nineties, many installation artists moved toward a style that diffuses personality more than Wojnarowicz does. Despite the loaded subject matter evoked by the French artist Christian Boltanski, for example, his own character is not delineated or set into the foreground in an expressionist manner. Boltanski reconfigured simple, nostalgically aged objects from daily life and anonymous old photos into *tableaux* of fictive identities [fig. 14.20]. He even revised his own past: "I've recounted so many invented memories about my childhood," he said, "that now I have no real ones."[24]

Using archives of low-quality photos—dated snapshots of families on the beach; babies; people gathered around the dinner table; a soldier in uniform—he created the prosaic record that adds up to the intimation of a biography. He stacked rows of old biscuit tins as reliquaries or laid out the most undistinguished household items in a vitrine, like evidence. Some of the photos purport to be of prewar Jewish children who have disappeared into a terrifying anonymity; our response is shaped by our knowledge of the Nazi period. With the bare bulbs of cheap metal lamps turned into their faces, like an interrogation, the photos immediately evoke thoughts of the Holocaust. Boltanski's installations are still more poignant because of the way in which they take the viewer back to the indistinct and yet emotional vividness of childhood memory; not that one remembers these particular old photographs or objects—they were, of course, never part of our own individual pasts—but they evoke what is personal to each of us in our oldest memories and remind us of the experience of remembering our childhood past.

Yet Boltanski's work is not expressionist in that it insists on an act of interpolation from the viewer and maintains a distance by obscuring the personal identity of the artist. "I began working in the period of Minimalism," he explained,

and my vocabulary is often close to that. A biscuit tin is a minimal object but, if I use such tins rather than a steel cube,

The art audience is the worst audience in the world. It's overly educated, it's conservative, it's out to criticize, not to understand, and it never has any fun. Why should I spend my time playing to that audience? . . . I'll play with the street audience. That audience is much more human, and their opinion is from the heart. They don't have any reason to play games.[26]

Since his arrival in New York in the mid-seventies, Hammons has made installations and objects that deal directly with the African-American experience. He makes his works from found materials—frequently ones that have a heavy weight of association to the environment of the black inner city—such as tight curls of black hair gathered from the floor of neighborhood barber shops, bottle caps and wine bottles found on the street, *Greasy Bags and Barbecue Bones* (as one installation was called), or discarded chicken parts.

Hammons made *Higher Goals* (1982) [fig. 14.21] by fastening basketball hoops to the tops of unreachably high poles (in which there is the obvious metaphor, commenting

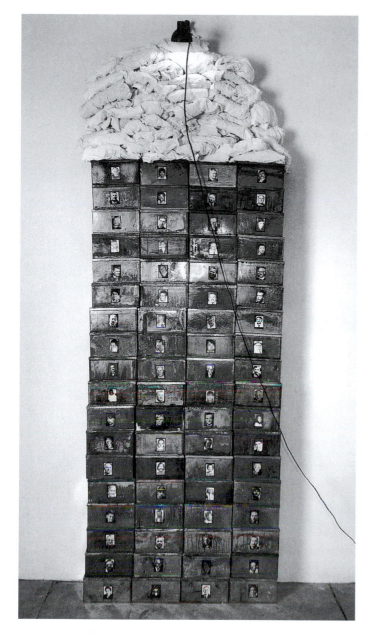

14.20 Christian Boltanski, *Reserve of Dead Swiss (Small)*, 1990. Photographs, fabric, tin boxes, and lamps, 116 × 37 × 13½in (294.6 × 94 × 34.3cm).
Private collection. Courtesy Marian Goodman Gallery, New York.

it's because the tin is also a sentimental object that evokes something familiar to all Westerners. It evokes the idea of basic protection (this is the box in which children keep their little treasures), of a funeral urn and, more generally, of storage. I don't want spectators faced with my work to discover but to recognize, to appropriate.[25]

Whereas Boltanski addresses an art audience, the installations and objects by David Hammons, an African-American artist living in Harlem, address the person on the street in the black community:

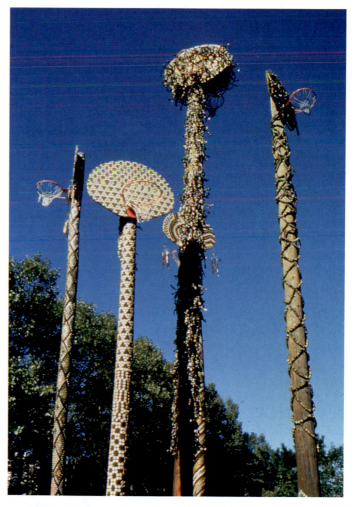

14.21 David Hammons, *Higher Goals*, 1982. Poles, basketball hoops, and bottle caps, 40ft (12.19m) high. Shown installed in Brooklyn, New York, 1986.
Courtesy Jack Tilton Gallery.

ironically on the frustration of black youth). He decorated the poles in highly patterned arrays of bottle caps and other materials that simultaneously clash and complement one another like beautiful African beadwork. As in all of his objects and installations, this cluster of poles has a powerful, bodily physicality, and the charismatic formal strength of his work lends value to these materials which have been marginalized both as inartistic detritus from the street and as belonging to aspects of the black experience which are not acknowledged precisely because of their difference. "There's nothing negative about our images," he pointed out. "It all depends upon who's seeing it, and we've been depending on someone else's sight . . . we need to look again and decide."[27] Thus Hammons's work is a homage to the black community and at the same time a direct reappropriation of the means of producing culture from the dominant sources of cultural production which for so long maintained the appearance of a "mainstream."

THE PECULIAR CASE OF THE RUSSIANS

No one could be less mainstream than the Russians in the eighties. Prior to the dissolution of the Eastern Bloc (symbolized by the 1989 dismantling of the Berlin Wall), the repressive climate made it impossible for Russian artists to exhibit anything that varied from the official formulas. In Moscow a tight-knit community of dissident artists staged one-night exhibitions in one another's apartments. They were almost totally cut off from developments in the West, so that the work of those who attempted to respond to the international scene looked anachronistic and derivative. They also existed in a strange limbo within their own society, cut off from entering their work into any form of public discourse on values.

An "unofficial" or "nonconformist" art movement arose from the reforms of the late fifties, but it was suppressed again after the fall of Khrushchev in 1964. Then in the early seventies an innovative vanguard of conceptual art emerged; it included performance artists such as "Red Star" and the "Collective Actions Group," as well as individuals such as the Gerlovins (Valeriy and Rimma), who both made objects and did ironic performances. In their 1977 *Zoo* [fig. 14.22] the Gerlovins appeared on display, nude and behind bars, with a plaque that read "Homo Sapiens, Group of Mammals, Male and Female." This work had a political edge as a commentary on the place of the individual in Soviet society, but it also exhibited a gloomy, Russian existentialism that does not originate in politics.

Some artists—Erich Bulatov, for example, or the team of Vitaly Komar and Alexander Melamid—appropriated the language of Socialist Realism (the official language of State-sponsored art). *Stalin and the Muses* (from the "Nostalgic Socialist Realism" series) [fig. 14.23] has the tenebrous light and palette of the poorly conserved Rembrandts and other old master paintings that hung in the gloomy Russian museums. The scantily clad muses approach a smiling Stalin,

14.22 Rimma Gerlovina and Valeriy Gerlovin, *Zoo*, performance February 17, 1977, Moscow. Gelatin silver print.
Photo by Victor Novatsky. State Tretyakov Gallery Moscow.

who accepts their offering of divine inspiration. Dressed in his gleaming white military uniform, with its highlights of red and gold and rich azure lining, he is an imperial presence of historical grandeur, not the bloodthirsty tyrant of the history books.

On the one hand this work satirizes the saccharine glorification of Soviet history that the style of Soviet realism was fashioned to depict, pushing the clichés to a ridiculous extreme in this ludicrous apotheosis of Stalin. Yet it also evokes a genuine nostalgia. Moreover, the fabulous invention of deities visiting Stalin, in an incongruous setting patched together from baroque and Renaissance paintings, creates a sense of displacement in time and social reality. This resonates with the surreal existence of the Soviet dissident artist of the seventies and eighties. The alienation in this work made it presciently relevant to issues that were emerging in the eighties in the mass culture of the West.

Komar and Melamid became close friends in art school and in 1972 decided on a collaborative career making what they dubbed "Sots" art. The term referred to socialist realism, but it also alluded to American pop art by lifting socialist realism out of its ideological context just as pop art took the clichés of consumer goods and popular media (the heart of American ideology) out of their commercial context in order to manipulate them as icons of the culture. Komar and Melamid emigrated to New York via Israel in 1978.

Ilya Kabakov

Ilya Kabakov, another "unofficial" Soviet artist, did not address ideology in his work of the seventies so much as the stolid inefficiency and oppressive drabness of quotidian existence in Russia. Kabakov's work grows out of painting and centers on the immediacy of lived experience and the flight of the creative imagination that transcends it. "It's not the artistic tradition but daily life that brings new ideas," he explained.[28]

In paintings of 1970–1 Kabakov already announced his use of fragments of prosaic text together with common objects mounted on spare, flatly painted canvases. His 1982 painting *Nikolai Ivanovich Kovin: The Kettle Is All Dirty* [fig. 14.24] exemplifies the simultaneous authenticity and irony in his approach. It consists of a rude, tin coffee pot, hanging in the center of a flat enamel panel; the panel is painted like any of the miles of drab, military green or gray walls in nondescript Soviet buildings, and the composition is crudely framed in a rustic wooden molding. In the upper corners small rectangles contain inscriptions recounting a conversation: "Nikolai Ivanovich Kovin: The coffee pot is all dirty." And from the other corner: "Maria Sergeevna Elaginskaya: That's Ana Fedorovna's."

14.23 Komar and Melamid, *Stalin and the Muses*, 1981–2. Oil on canvas, 6ft × 4ft 7in (1.82 × 1.4m).
Courtesy Ronald Feldman Fine Art, New York.

14.24 Ilya Kabakov, *Nikolai Ivanovich Kovin: The Kettle Is All Dirty*, May 1982. Coffee pot, enamel on masonite, 27⅝ × 47¼in (70 × 120cm). Private collection, Paris. Courtesy the artist.

In this most prosaic of exchanges over such a common object are embedded intimations of the trivial conflicts of everyday life in the kitchen of the communal apartment. The work uses the poorly made, familiar objects of Soviet existence to evoke the grim claustrophobia of these Moscow dwellings, extending painting into the space of the real world with commonplace objects. On another level it's hard not to read into this a sidelong critique of the idealism of Russian vanguard modernism; here these "real" objects have a deeply ironic resonance with Vladimir Tatlin's famous constructivist slogan of "Real Materials in Real Space," which at the beginning of the Russian experiment pointed to a future utopia in the marriage of art and industry. Nor is it hard

to see in the commonness of the placard-like "thought bubbles" in which this vulgar narrative is inscribed a formal parody of the banners in the constructivist drawings of the 1920s, which bear slogans of the Revolution's (now so painfully failed) utopianism:—slogans like "Proletariat!" (as in El Lissitzky's drawing for a *Lenin Podium* of 1924), or "The Press Is Our Weapon" (as in one of Alexander Rodchenko's advertising posters of 1923).

"It is our task to describe the state of mankind, of the world and of our own psyche in this post-utopian world,"[29] Kabakov told an interviewer in 1987, and he described this "state" for himself in an internal dialog of voices. Beginning in 1970, Kabakov invented characters and told their stories

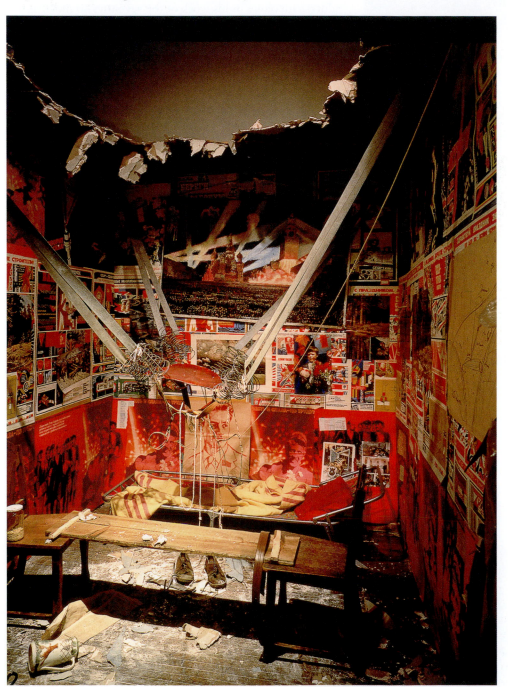

14.25 Ilya Kabakov, *The Man Who Flew into Space from His Apartment*, from *Ten Characters*, 1981–8. Installation at Ronald Feldman Fine Art, New York. Six poster panels with collage, furniture, clothing, catapult, household objects, wooden plank, scroll-type painting, two pages of Soviet paper, diorama; room 8ft × 7ft 11in × 12ft 3in (2.44 × 2.41 × 3.73m). Courtesy the artist.

in albums—the perfect vehicle for an "unofficial" art that was not permitted to be exhibited in public and for the life of a person living in a society that requires a harsh separation between public expression and private feeling. The very first of these albums concerns "Sitting-in-the-closet Primakov," a character who retreated into the dark for half a year as a child so that he could only imagine what went on outside from the sounds coming through the wall. The first eight pages of illustrations accompanying the text are merely black squares with yellow text blocks (implicitly offering an ironic "explanation" for Malevich's famous *Black Square* of 1915!). With age, Primakov became more eccentric and incoherent; "he pronounced only nonsensical words."[30]

With *Ten Characters* of 1988, Kabakov made the experience of this internal dialog still more real by creating a physical space within which the viewer is totally absorbed. Like "Sitting-in-the-closet Primakov," Kabakov himself mediates daily life and the real memories of formative experience by distancing himself from the "other" and creating an utterly free mental space in which the imagination can take in "what is heard through the wall." The seemingly chaotic and always open-ended narratives that generate the installations—which have become Kabakov's primary medium—are fantastic tales filled with irony and a profound sense of the absurd, but also with an almost childlike wish to believe, as in traditional Russian stories like Nikolai Gogol's "The Overcoat."

To accompany *The Man Who Flew into Space from His Apartment* [fig. 14.25], one of the visually overwhelming installations that belong to *Ten Characters*, Kabakov frames the setting with this explanation:

> The lonely inhabitant of the room, as becomes clear from the story his neighbor tells, was obsessed by a dream of a lonely flight into space, and in all probability he realized this dream of his, his "grand project." The entire cosmos, according to the thoughts of the inhabitant of this room, was permeated by streams of energy leading upward somewhere. His project was conceived in an effort to hook up with these streams and fly away with them. A catapult, hung from the corners of the room, would give this new "astronaut," who was sealed in a plastic sack, his initial velocity and further up, at a height of 40–50 meters, he would land in a stream of energy through which the Earth was passing at that moment as it moved along its orbit. The astronaut had to pass through the ceiling and attic of the house with his vault. With this in mind, he installed powder charges and at the moment of his takeoff from the catapult, the ceiling and roof would be wiped out by an explosion, and he would be carried away into the wide-open space. Everything was in place late at night, when all the other inhabitants of the communal apartment are sound asleep. One can imagine their horror, fright, and bewilderment. The local police are summoned, an investigation begins, and the tenants search everywhere—in the yard, on the street—but he is nowhere to be found. In all probability, the project, the general nature of which was known by the neighbor who told the investigator about it, was successfully realized.[31]

Kabakov in the West

Kabakov left the Soviet Union in 1988 for Western Europe. Although he had begun making installations in 1983, it was in the West that he began to construct completely immersive environments for his stories; to convey his ideas he felt he needed to create the context out of which they grew. With Emilia, a distant relative whom he rediscovered in the West and then married, he has created a *corpus* of now over 160 installations. The first was *Ten Characters*, constructed at the Ronald Feldman Gallery in New York in 1988. In this medium of "total installation,"[32] Kabakov emerged from a prominent role within the small underground of Moscow conceptualists in the early eighties into one of the most important international artists of the nineties.

The Kabakovs' 1998 *Palace of Projects* [figs. 14.26 and 14.27] exemplifies this phase of their work. It consists of a building with translucent walls, spiral in plan (like a snail shell), containing models and diagrams for sixty-five different ideal projects on how to improve yourself or the world, or how to increase creativity: they have invented a chauffeur from Kishinev who has designed wings that you strap on for

14.26 Ilya and Emilia Kabakov, *The Palace of Projects*, May 1998, London. Installation, approx. 23½ × 53½ × 76½ft (7.2 × 16.3 × 23.3m) overall, exterior view.
Courtesy the artist.

14.27 Ilya and Emilia Kabakov, *The Palace of Projects*, 1998, London. Interior detail. See fig. 14.26.
Courtesy the artist.

several sessions a day, in the privacy of your own room, to help you develop "in a better, more moral direction."[33] There is also a Mr. Sabirov from Vitebsk, whose instructions for sawing a hole through the floor of your apartment will liberate you from the "low, room, horizon" of your dull private life, and a V. Korneichuk (a writer from Ulan-Ude), who provides an elaborately furnished closet in which you can concentrate better. These are all replies both to the

grandiose projects of Soviet communism and to the history of modernism with its collection of personal utopias.

As in most of the Kabakovs' installations, each of the stories in the *Palace of Projects*, even each visual fragment, has a particular experiential truth, and the space of the installation provides the support for what seems to be an endless and unstructured collection of objects, images, and texts. We experience these details as though catching a few words of conversation overheard on the street. We order them, assign them meanings, and the process itself opens us to a further probing of our own stores of memory. The grand narratives described by Jean-François Lyotard as the pillars of modernism[34] dissolve in the postmodernism of the eighties and nineties, as people found themselves constructing experience in increasingly fragmented and unique vignettes. In part, this highlighting of the atomized and particular in the work of the Kabakovs is what has made their total installations so relevant.

THE AESTHETIC OF CONSUMERISM

For some of the artists emerging in the eighties, mass-market consumerism in itself offered imaginative possibilities. "Ali Baba's cave is not unlike Macy's," Haim Steinbach remarked, "but then it was more recognized as fantasy."[35] The East Village artists Steinbach, Jeff Koons, Peter Halley, Ashley Bickerton, and Meyer Vaisman found a genuine aesthetic pleasure in contemporary consumer culture. The commodification of art—art treated as an item for sale and consumption—attracted them as a fascinating new aspect of the present.

14.28 Haim Steinbach, *Ultra Red 1*, 1986. Mixed-media construction, 59 × 107 × 19in (149.9 × 271.8 × 48.3cm). Private collection. Courtesy Sonnabend Gallery, New York.

Steinbach [fig. 14.28] was visually excited by seeing the way things were presented in stacks in the store and built special shelves for lining up manufactured objects in repetitive rows. He was "taking pleasure in objects and commodities . . . being complicit with the production of desire."[36] Peter Halley painted reductive geometric abstractions derived from circuitry diagrams in a revival of geometric abstraction—an especially appealing style precisely because it was the ideologically empty form of the formalist abstraction against which abstract expressionism rebelled and which had finally become completely debased in the sixties as "op art." Halley used geometric abstraction as a metaphor of social confinement; we can't escape because our minds are imprinted with the system of thinking that confines us.

Meyer Vaisman's work is charged with a passion for the appropriation of simulated appearances, historical art styles, and subject matter that has deteriorated as an artistic language from overuse, while Ashley Bickerton produces objects which seem like high-tech consumer goods, covered in commercial logos, and yet oddly without identifiable function. Bickerton's *Solomon Island Shark* of 1993 [fig. 14.29] takes this instability of identity in an even stranger direction, constantly flipping from one line of association to another; at one moment this 9-foot, leather-clad, rubber creature seems like a fugitive from an S&M bondage dungeon, and at the next it evokes the exotic "natural" surroundings of the South Pacific to which the artist repaired. But then the beautiful blue-green "seawater" sacks hanging from the belts and cords are actually filled with Scope® mouthwash and the weirdly erotic coconuts are the only "natural" items included.

Allan McCollum probed the issue of commodified artistic language by making "art surrogates" or neutral "vehicles" to

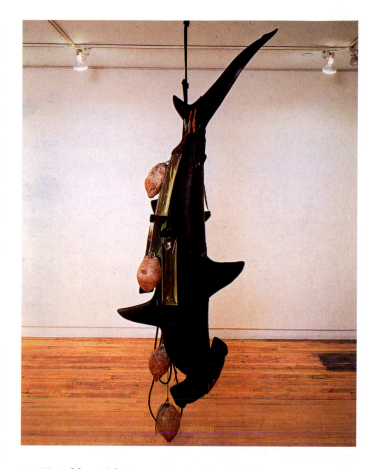

14.29 Ashley Bickerton, *Solomon Island Shark*, 1993.
Rubber, leather, canvas, rope, coconuts, acrylic, PVC, Scope®,
9ft 5in × 3ft 1in × 2ft 3in (287 × 94 × 68.5cm).
Neumann Family Collection, New York. Courtesy Lehmann Maupin, New York.

14.30 Allan McCollum,
*Collection of Forty Plaster
Surrogates*, molds made
1982–4, cast and painted
1990. Enamel on cast
Hydrostone, overall
71 × 110in (1.8 × 2.79m).
The Museum of Modern Art, New
York. Robert and Meryl Meltzer
and Robert F. and Anna Marie
Shapiro Funds, 417.1988a-nn.
Courtesy the artist.

14.31 Allan McCollum, *Drawings*, 1988–90. Installation at John Weber Gallery, New York, 1990. Over 2,000 framed drawings, pencil on museum board, various sizes.
Courtesy John Weber Gallery, New York.

see in what ways one could separate and perfect the forms in an artistic language as if they were mass-produced goods [fig. 14.30]. His *Plaster Surrogates* are "pictures" made of cast hydrocal objects with the "frames" (painted to look like wood) and the white "mats" all cast in a single piece. A collector could buy as many "paintings" as he or she wanted, hang them in any arrangement, and the artist painted the centers all black, suggesting that there does not actually need to be anything in the frame. His 1990 installation of *Drawings* [fig. 14.31] has a wonderful but different complexity embedded in its matter-of-fact treatment of the drawings as infinitely recombinable prefab units, stacked for sale in a store.

In "The New," the principal series of the early eighties by Jeff Koons, the artist explored not only modernism's perpetual hunger for "newness,"[37] but the sense of pristine newness that accompanies the acquisition of consumer goods and provokes such "a strange excitement in people."[38] The act of taking a utilitarian object like a vacuum cleaner out of

its functional context [fig. 14.32] owes a debt to Duchamp's readymades but for Koons this involved a somewhat different social critique. Koons gives the vacuum heroic status by enshrining it in an elegant Plexiglas vitrine with fluorescent showcase lighting. For Koons, it is both an aesthetic object— Duchamp insisted that his readymades were not—and a social icon. "One receives objects as rewards for labor and achievements," he theorized. "Everything one has sacrificed in life . . . in the effort to obtain these objects, has been sacrificed to a given labor situation. And once these objects have been accumulated, they work as support mechanisms."[39]

Koons then deliberately moved into kitsch [fig. 14.33], taking the inquiry into commercial pop culture, inaugurated by Andy Warhol in the 1960s. From there he went deeper into the desmesnes of consumerism and in 1990 he explored pornography. The "Made in Heaven" series consists of explicit blown-up photographs and sculptures of the artist performing sexual acts with an Italian porn star, whom he also briefly married. These cynical consumer icons for the rich were shocking both for their commercial ambition and for their bad taste. Yet in both respects the work forces the viewer into an uncomfortably raw confrontation with disturbing aspects of contemporary values.

14.32 Jeff Koons, *New Hoover Convertibles, New Shelton Wet/Drys, 5-Gallon Doubledecker*, 1981–7. Three Hoover Convertibles, two Shelton Wet/Drys, acrylic, fluorescent lights, 99 × 54 × 28in (251.5 × 137.2 × 71.1cm).

14.33 Jeff Koons, *Pink Panther*, 1988. Porcelain, 41 × 20½ × 19in (104.1 × 52.1 × 48.3cm). Private collection.

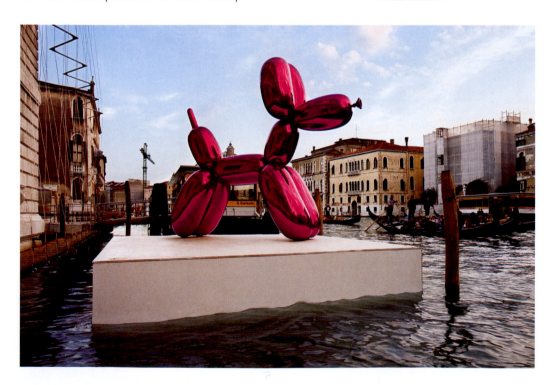

14.34 Jeff Koons, *Balloon Dog (Magenta)*, 1994–2000. Palazzo Grassi, Venice, 2006. High-chromium stainless steel with transparent color coating, 10ft 1in × 11 ft 11in × 3ft 11in (3.07 × 3.63 × 1.14m).

Koons also pushed the limits of public art in the nineties. His "scandalous" work garnered considerable financial support, making it possible to build works like his high-chromium stainless steel *Balloon Dog* (a 10-foot-high public sculpture based on the twisted balloon dogs that clowns make at children's birthday parties) [fig. 14.34] and his 43-foot-high topiary *Puppy* that bloomed in front of the Guggenheim Museum in Bilbao in 1992 (and Rockefeller Center in 2000). In his most recent paintings Koons superimposes, as in *Triple Elvis* (2007), appropriated images of a blow-up lobster pool toy over half-naked *Playboy* pin-ups on a backdrop of an H. C. Westermann print. The title is appropriated from Andy Warhol and the work deliberately violates the hierarchies of art, making us think about how far you can appropriate another artist's work or a commercial logo and what (or even whether) we learn about ourselves from carrying such images (which we know well, whether or not we like them) over acceptable boundaries of taste.

Political Appropriation

While Koons reveled in the consumer culture of the eighties, a forceful political counterculture also emerged within the New York art world, signaled by the founding of COLAB (in 1977) and Fashion/Moda and Group Material (both in 1979) as neighborhood-based art collectives. Like the British artists of the Independent Group in the fifties, these artists took in the whole range of cultural production from paintings to kitsch curios and the television news in their collaborative installations. Moreover, they included not only the imagery of contemporary popular culture but also its manner of presentation. They were more militantly political than their British precursors, however, in seeking to use popular culture to connect art with communities.

These artists wanted to intervene directly in events, serving as agents for social change, but as Tim Rollins, a founding member of Group Material, pointed out: "a political art can't really be made *at* working people or *for* the oppressed. A radical art is one that helps organize people who can speak for themselves."[40] COLAB's first major project was to take over an abandoned city building on the Lower East Side in order to stage an event that focused attention on tenants' rights issues. The "Real Estate Show," as it was called, opened on January 1, 1980 and was immediately closed by police. As Rollins remarked: "It's a radical art with a radical methodology, because it's illegal."[41]

Tom Otterness, John Ahearn, and other artists from COLAB and Fashion/Moda organized the 1980 "Times Square Show" [figs. 14.35 and 14.36] in an abandoned sex shop by Times Square, then the Manhattan porn district. They jammed the space with videos, graffiti, posters, installations, and ongoing performances, crystallizing the fusion of schooled art and Bronx graffiti that was taking place in the East Village with artists like Keith Haring and Jean-Michel Basquiat.

There were a number of reasons why such artists became so focused on political matters in the eighties. Prominent among them was the AIDS crisis, which first appeared,

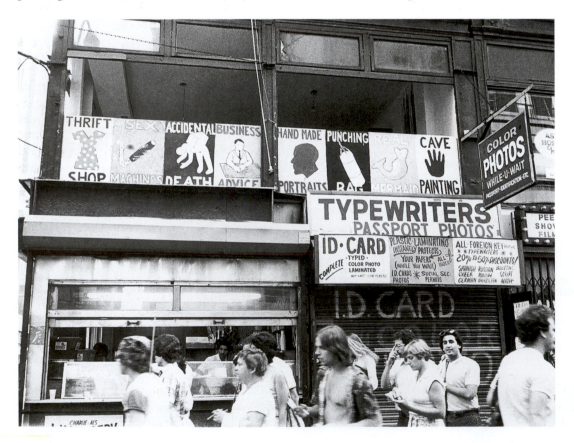

14.35 "Times Square Show," June 1980, second-floor window with paintings on masonite by Tom Otterness announcing attractions inside.
Photograph © by Lisa Kahane, New York.

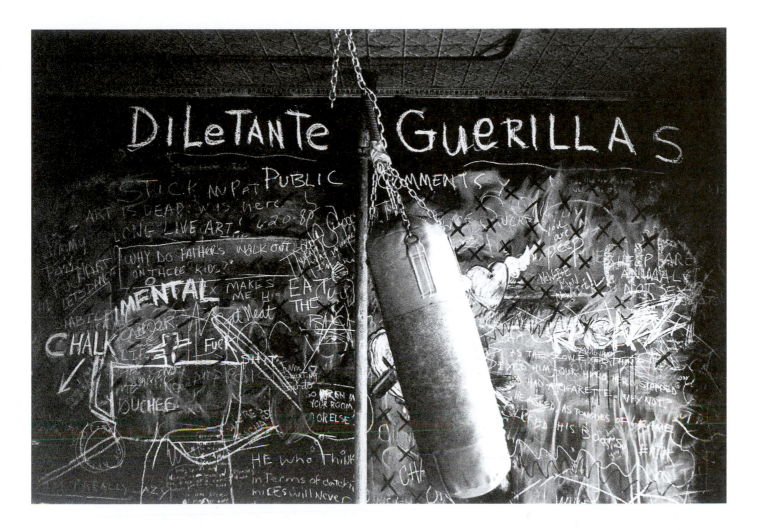

14.36 "Times Square Show," June 1980, anonymous chalk graffiti on the walls of the building's fourth floor, Tom Otterness's *Punching Bag*. Photograph © by Lisa Kahane, New York.

as though out of nowhere, in 1981 and escalated into an epidemic at a terrifying pace. The explosive growth in homelessness and unemployment also made many feel that government in the eighties served only the interests of the rich, a problem that became even more acute over the next two decades. Finally, there were fundamental new threats to freedom in America, in particular the consolidation of the media (daily newspapers, magazines, television, books, and motion pictures) into the hands of a few powerful corporations. In 1981 forty-six corporations controlled most of the business in media; by 1986 that number had shrunk to twenty-nine. By 2000 ownership of the American media industry and global communications was in the hands of only a few conglomerates and broad awareness of current affairs in any depth largely disappeared, saved only by the growth of the Internet and the inability (so far) of corporations and government to control it.[42] This takeover of the media seemed especially pernicious since the political events of the eighties had made it painfully clear that slick advertisements could sell the public a perspective

on a candidate or issue that might bear no resemblance to the truth.

Jenny Holzer, a participant in the "Times Square Show," appropriated the vehicles of advertising and graffiti for an ironic sociopolitical critique that undermines the stereotyped messages in the media [fig. 14.37]. She started her "truisms" in 1977, printing (and later electronically encoding) phrases such as "Murder has its sexual side," "Raise boys and girls the same way," "Abuse of power should come as no surprise" on posters, flyers, T-shirts, hats, and then electronic signs. Holzer's manipulation of "almost" familiar phrases displaces the clear presence of a personal voice—the words seem impersonal, underscoring the essential emptiness of the media and the strange isolation of people from one another in this society of mass-culture clichés.

Like Holzer, Barbara Kruger [fig. 14.38] combines ambiguous slogans with black-and-white images, pasted up together like a page of trendy graphic design from *Mademoiselle*, one of the magazines where she worked for eleven years learning her graphic design skills. She also hands out her messages on matchbooks, T-shirts, tote bags, posters, and photomontages, but hers is an angry and accusatory voice, with phrases like "We won't play nature to your culture," "We won't be our own best enemy," "You colonize

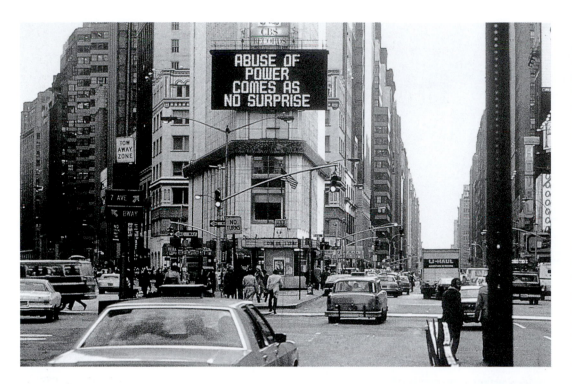

14.37 (left) **Jenny Holzer**, *Truisms, 1977–79: Abuse of Power Comes As No Surprise*, 1982. Spectacolor Board No. 1, Times Square, New York.

Sponsored by the Public Art Fund Inc. Courtesy Jenny Holzer.

14.38 (below) **Barbara Kruger**, *Untitled (You Rule By Pathetic Display)*, 1982. Photograph, 6ft 1in × 4ft 1in (1.85 × 1.25m).

Krannert Art Museum and Kinkead Pavilion, University of Illinois, Urbana-Champaign. Purchased by the Art Acquisition Fund. Courtesy Mary Boone Gallery, New York.

lacerated objects." Kruger also deliberately leaves both the voice in the text and the intended auditor in anonymity.

There is no such ambiguity in the texts of the Guerrilla Girls. After the Museum of Modern Art held its vast "International Survey of Contemporary Art" in 1984, in which almost no women or minorities were included, a number of professional women in the New York art world founded this collective organization. The Guerrilla Girls appeared on television (wearing rubber gorilla masks to maintain their anonymity), advertised, and distributed leaflets and posters to bring attention to the widespread race and gender discrimination that exists in the art world [fig. 14.39].[43]

Kryzsztof Wodiczko, an artist writing from communist Poland in the mid-seventies, pointed out that in a totalitarian state "individuals don't own images; the state does. The result is that it is impossible to change the context of images."[44] However, the observation also applies to the corporate control of the media in America today. Wodiczko's answer to this, like Christo's, is to create astonishing spectacles in the workaday setting of the city that will startle the casual passer-by out of his or her routine habits of thought.[45] In particular, Wodiczko insisted that "today more than ever before, the meaning of our monuments depends on our active role in turning them into sites of memory and critical evaluation of history as well as places of public discourse and action."[46]

Wodiczko fled to Canada in 1977 and then, in 1983, moved to New York. His best-known work involves the use of high-powered lanterns to project evocative images on public buildings, provoking his largely non-art audiences into a fresh encounter with the political and social forces that linger behind these structures. Just days before the

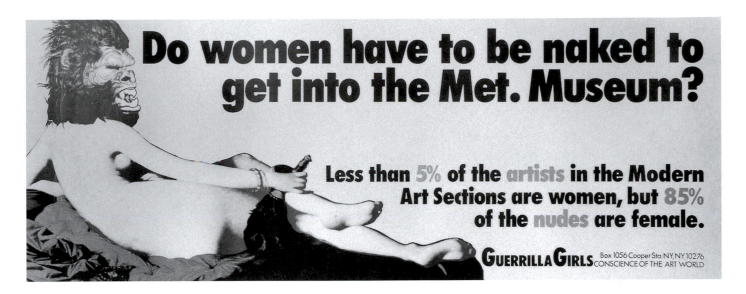

14.39 Guerrilla Girls, *Do Women Have to Be Naked to Get into the Met. Museum?*, 1989. Poster, 11 × 28in (27.9 × 71.1cm). Private collection.

1988 presidential election, for example, Wodiczko projected an ominous pair of hands on the Hirshhorn Museum on the Mall in Washington, D.C. [fig. 14.40]. The campaign had been marred by racist advertisements showing the face of a black convict named Willie Horton and attempting to scare the public into believing that the Democratic candidate would release dangerous black criminals from the prisons. In Wodiczko's projection one hand held a candle and the other a gun, symbolizing the rhetoric of hope and fear that had characterized the presidential campaigns of Michael Dukakis and George Bush respectively. In Kryzsztof Wodiczko's more recent work he has developed more direct ways of empowering the disempowered with a voice. In a powerful work of 2001 called Public Projection for InSite 2000, for example, he developed a headset that transmitted the face and voice of its wearer onto the building of a public cultural complex, allowing the workers in the factories that surround it to talk about the brutality of their social conditions. They become the monument, projecting themselves onto the "deaf and blind walls of the city."

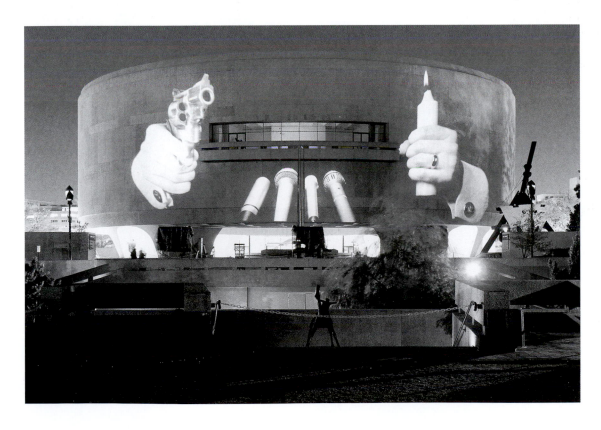

14.40 Kryzsztof Wodiczko, *WORKS*, October 25, 26, and 27, 1988. Projection on to the Hirshhorn Museum and Sculpture Garden, Smithsonian Institution, Washington, D.C.

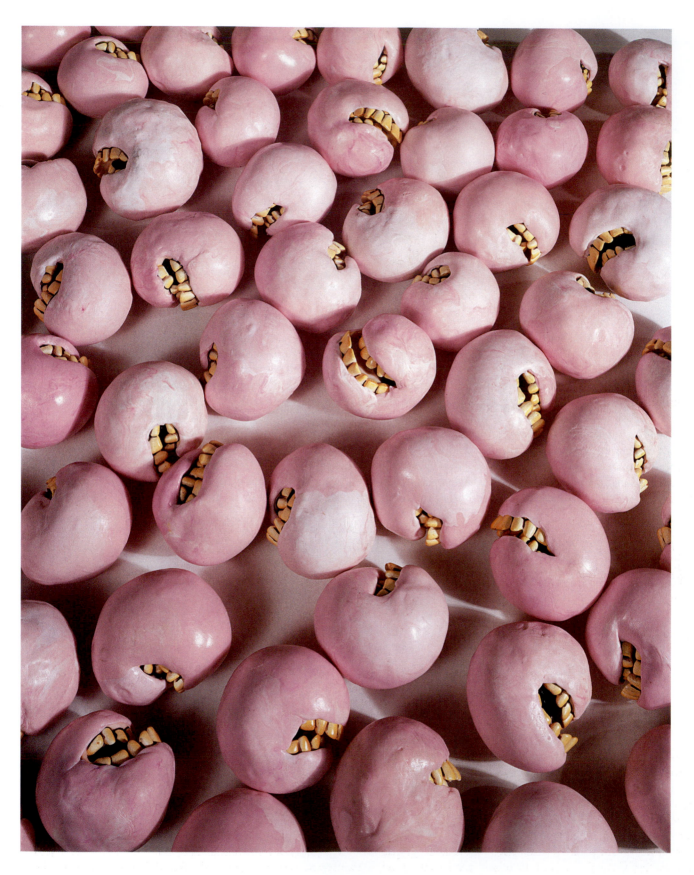

15.1 Rona Pondick, *Little Bathers* (detail), 1990–1. Wax, plastic, and rubber teeth,
3½ × 3 × 4in (8.9 × 7.6 × 10.1cm) each (500 pieces), dimensions variable.
Collection, Marc and Livia Straus. Courtesy Sonnabend Gallery, New York.

15 UNSTABLE DEFINITIONS

Any attempt at a traditional survey of the art of the last two decades is doomed to fail, because after 1990 the global art-world began to reconfigure itself into micro-ecologies of art —each with its own local concerns and discourse. There has continued to be a broad conversation across the increasingly porous boundaries that once defined isolated cultures, but the dominance that New York enjoyed roughly from 1940 to 1970 over the global art world dissipated and the electronic dissemination of information made it (among other things) possible to have an influential voice from anywhere. The instability of definitions of nations, of individuals, of cultures, of the self have made the last two decades of art extraordinarily dynamic and diverse. So here we will attempt to identify some important issues around which some of the most important innovations in art seem to coalesce.

KEEPING IT REAL

In the United States the nineties began as the decade in which the easy millionaires from the leveraged buyouts and junk bonds of the eighties lost their fortunes and started looking for real jobs. There was hope in the art world that art would also become less about fast money and careers and more about ideas again. But the voracious herds of Wall Street were soon replaced by a new generation of overnight millionaires, and the apotheosis of global consumerism continued. Marketing all but eliminated issues in both news reporting and political campaigns; television reporters stopped challenging even blatantly false claims by candidates on "the news," which had turned into an entertainment product in the U.S. There was so much manipulation of information by powerful interest groups from the eighties onwards that the average American no longer had enough reliable information to cast a responsible vote and the once vaunted public school system of the United States had by the last quarter of the twentieth century declined so precipitously that only the privileged had the analytical skills to evaluate the news anyway. The value of a stock portfolio soared, but the buying power of a schoolteacher's salary went down. Huge corporations got even bigger, local businesses disappeared (as did the American Main Street) in favor of global sameness in the shopping malls, airports, and commuter traffic jams where people increasingly lived their lives. The nineties became the decade in which everyone bought a cellular phone, logged onto the Internet, and found themselves endlessly on hold, listening to medleys of prerecorded menus and Muzak.

Despite all the money in the art world, serious artists persevered in trying to make sense of their experience in their work, and the variety of what they created reflects the many different complex issues that came to the fore all at once—not least, the overwhelming information flow itself. For some artists, a focus on immediate, bodily experience helped restore a sense of self in the increasingly anonymous culture. The particularizing features of one's identity also became important as a force against dissolution. The art world became more multicultural and global with worldwide consumer marketing. Above all, the years from 1990 to 2010 were transformed by a breathtaking advance in communications and computer technology.

One of the corollaries of the electronic revolution that has taken place is that people have begun losing touch with simple realities. The entertaining distractions of hyperreality on computers, televisions, and in film has left us with less time to talk to our families and neighbors, and even grave threats to our very survival, like global warming, nuclear proliferation, and the desperation of poverty that breeds international terrorism, seem unreal, as though they are just another line-up of TV shows.

RETURN TO THE BODY

A visceral preoccupation with the body was one way to make things "real" again. The performance work of Karen Finley, for example, relied on a raw, verbal evisceration of her audience. One writer described her performances this way:

> Wafting onto the stage in some polyester good-girl get-up at one or two in the morning, Finley first showed the audience her stage fright or self-doubt—the prelude to holding nothing back. Then, the deluge: monologues that erupted out of the gross forbidden subtext of everyday where grannies soak in their own piss, men force-feed boys to produce the perfect shit, and daddy works "his daughter's little hole." The monologues were disgusting and cathartic—like pus escaping from some subconscious wound. This was obscenity in its purest form—an attempt to explore emotions too primal for words.[1]

The shockingly explicit content of Finley's performances made her a target for censorship by the right wing of the U.S. Congress, which correctly perceived that her work challenged its moral self-righteousness. Vehement censorship battles were fought in the U.S. courts and Presidents Reagan and Bush (senior) even attempted to dismantle the broadly popular National Endowments for the Arts and Humanities as a way of winning the approval of the religious right and silencing dissent in America. The most visible battles centered on Finley, Andres Serrano (who juxtaposed his own bodily fluids with symbols of his quite genuine religious devotion, as in his notorious *Piss Christ* of 1987), and on the homoerotic content in the works of David Wojnarowicz and Robert Mapplethorpe.

The disconcerting objects by Rona Pondick, with their strong evocations of the body, were not as vulnerable to such attacks since they are not overt references to issues of sex or religion. But they nevertheless draw on primal sensations that exist in the recesses of the psyche and elicit a profoundly disquieting effect. *Little Bathers* [fig. 15.1] comprises dreamlike transformations of fetishized human mouths, and the viewer cannot distance him- or herself

15.2 Kiki Smith, *The Sitter*, 1992. Wax, pigment, papier-mâché, 28 × 36 × 24in (71.1 × 91.4 × 61cm). Collection of Emily Fisher Landau, New York.

from an uncomfortable, simultaneously physical and psychic engagement with them.

Kiki Smith's work also centered on the human body, but in a more directly allusive manner. Like Wojnarowicz, a close friend and sometime collaborator, Smith had an intense involvement with the most intimate functions and internal parts of the human body. In the mid-eighties she made a row of glass watercooler jars etched with the names of different bodily fluids (urine, tears, sweat, milk, oil, mucus, saliva, blood, vomit, semen, puss, diarrhea). Another piece consisted of eight jars of blood. She cast a stomach in glass, rendered a heart in plaster and silver leaf, cast bronzes of the uro-genital system (male and female), and made an iron cast of a digestive system from the mouth to the anus that has an odd resemblance to an old radiator. In the nineties she turned to the whole body, often rendered in fragile paper or in muslin and wax. The modest materials of Richard Tuttle (who had been a studio assistant to her father, the minimalist sculptor Tony Smith) and the organic use of latex, fiberglass, and rubber by Eva Hesse seem to have informed her choice of materials. In *The Sitter* of 1992 [fig. 15.2] Smith sliced into the back of a very lifelike wax figure to reveal an internal cross-section of raw tissue that elicits an empathic bodily discomfort.

Ann Hamilton

Ann Hamilton's work is always a powerful bodily experience—whether her medium is photography, video, installation, or even text—and it always arises from the artist's own desire for personal discovery. Hamilton wants "people to be absorbed into the physical experience of a piece."[2] She creates "situations which implicate you as an active participant,"[3] she explained, ". . . letting the work work on you up through your body instead of from your eyes down. So that you allow yourself to experience something before you try to name it."[4] Hamilton's work taps directly into a preverbal level of thought that has deep emotional roots in early childhood; it is the world of tactile reasoning and affective logic.

In *Malediction*, an installation of 1991–2 [fig. 15.3], for example, the viewer entered a gallery strewn with stiff rags. Stepping carefully through this field, she or he then came

15.3 Ann Hamilton, *Malediction*, December 7, 1991–January 4, 1992. Installation and performance: gesture of filling, molding, and emptying the mouth with raw bread dough; filling the wicker casket with the molds of the mouth, as performed in two rooms of the Louver Gallery, New York.
Courtesy Sean Kelly, New York.

into a second room to find Hamilton, sitting at a refectory table, slowly and methodically taking wads of bread dough from a large bowl and pressing them into the upper palate of her mouth, and then one by one filling a wicker casket with the impressions. She faced a wall of bed linens piled high and cascading down; behind the wall a recording played a woman quietly, blandly reading Walt Whitman's prose poems "Song of Myself" and "Body Electric." On one level the piece concerned the gender-stereotyped tedium and melancholy of domestic work. It is "the culture of domestic activity . . . comprised of small creative practices that privilege the cumulative power of iteration."[5]

Yet *Malediction* also brings to the fore other simultaneously cross-tracking emotions—self-absorption, tactile sensation, the feeling of straining to hear the voice (which is like an inner voice in one's own head), and at the same time an outer silence around. There is a sensuality mixed with the tedium, a sense of violation of the internal cavity of the mouth but, with that, the warmth of closeness, of contact. "The mouth is a negative space. The transgression of that border is a source of taboos and phobias . . . but it's just empty space."[6] The woven casket is of a nineteenth-century

type used to carry bodies from a battlefield and the wine stains on the rags also suggested blood; at the time she was making *Malediction* Hamilton was reading Civil War poetry.

Before leaving Yale art school in 1985, Hamilton began work on a series of sixteen black and white body-object photos (1984–93), which combine her own body with objects—hanging chairs front and back from her shoulders, engulfing the front of a shoe in her mouth, covering herself in a suit of toothpicks, like quills, with a chair fastened to her back [fig. 15.4]—in a manner that blurs the border between the human and the object and suggests an object-like character to the human sense of self. Gradually her work moved from objects and things put on the body into total environments which also had this diffuse identity, acquired variously from the artist, the materials, and the active participation of the viewer.

In *Mattering*, an installation of 1997–8 [fig. 15.5], Hamilton covered a vast room in a museum in Lyon, France, with an undulating, red-orange canopy of silk, rising and falling in waves and glowing from the brilliant light of the skylight above. Five male peacocks clipped across the hardwood floors, with the clicking sound of their talons and the swoosh of their long tails punctuated by an occasional screech. In the background one barely heard the sound of an opera singer giving lessons to a student. A telephone pole went up through a circular hole in the fabric ceiling; a man perched on a high seat attached to the pole pulled up an endless line of blue-black typewriter ribbon through the hole. He repetitiously wound the ribbon around one hand, creating a woven mitt which he would then cut free and drop in a pile at the base of the pole, only to begin winding again. The ceiling was like a skin—"that permeable edge of the body"[7]—and the artist described the sensation of rising into the orange silk with the line of blue typewriter ribbon (an outmoded carrier of language) as "coming up through language."[8] Like so many of Hamilton's installations, the piece is an open-ended peregrination through a number of very different tactile sensations and transformations of language into bodily experience.

Transgressive Dislocations of the Body

The work of Janine Antoni is also intensely physical. In creating *Gnaw* of 1992, the artist spent a month and a half both incorporating and destroying (figuratively and literally) two minimalist cubes. One cube was made of lard and the other of chocolate; the technique was to chew them bite by bite and then spit them out to make lipstick (from the lard) and confectionery packaging (out of the chocolate). In *Loving Care*, another art action of 1992, she painted the floor of a gallery using her long hair as a brush, slowly painting the people out of the space. Just as *Gnaw* took up the feminization of the minimalist cube from Eva Hesse and others of her generation, *Loving Care* (a play on the socially feminized role of caretaking and on the brand name of a woman's hair dye)

15.5 Ann Hamilton, *Mattering* (detail), 1997–8. Installation and performance: silk vellum canopy, peacocks, pole-sitting performer, typewriter ribbon, recorded voice, and music in several rooms of the Musée d'Art Contemporain, Lyon.

simultaneously restated Klein's "Anthropométries," as though from the point of view of the self-abnegating female models that he used as "living brushes," and ironically transformed the phallic power of the abstract expressionist brushstroke into a feminine labor. It is both a virtue and a vice of the canny graduate school training of younger artists in the nineties that works such as these so intelligently engage in a reinterpretation of recent art history. It makes such work instantly assimilable into the discourse of art but it also runs the risk of circumscribing the work within that discourse in a way that is not the case with the work of an artist like Hamilton.

Maurizio Cattelan's installation *Novecento* (1997) exploits the startling ability of a real taxidermed horse [fig. 15.6], hanging as though limply from the ceiling, to undermine the viewer's sense of aesthetic distance. His installation for the 1999 Venice Biennale consisted of a stone room filled with dirt, in which two human hands, palm to palm, seemed planted in the ground. But the hands were clearly alive—they sometimes moved slightly—so the viewer quickly realized that a human was buried underneath the dirt. This evoked both an intense claustrophobia and at the same time a visual experience of an elegantly minimal form that one could detach from its body context.

Robert Gober's work also explores this kind of detachment, both disconnecting common objects from their expected sites and focusing on parts and small objects recombined in ways that completely dislocate and objectify them. Gober first came to the attention of the art world with a series of beautifully handcrafted plaster sinks, made between 1983 and 1992. They looked at first sight identical to the real sinks on which he modeled them, except that they had no plumbing or hardware and they hung isolated on a gallery wall.

15.6 Maurizio Cattelan, *Novecento (Nineteenth Century)*, 1997. Taxidermied horse, 6ft 7in × 8ft 10½in × 2ft 3½in (2.00 × 2.70 × 0.70m).
Castello di Rivoli–Musee d'Arte Contemporaneo, Rivoli-Torino. Gift of the Sustaining Friends of the Castello di Rivoli.

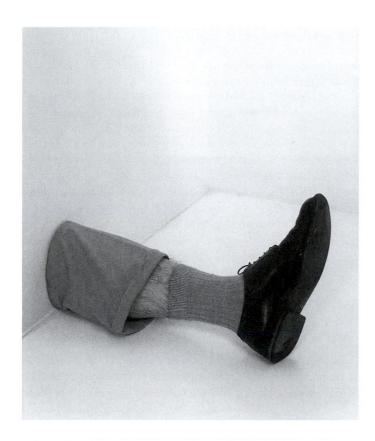

15.7 Robert Gober, *Untitled*, 1990. Beeswax, cotton, wood, leather shoe, and human hair, 10¾ × 20½ × 5in (27.2 × 52 × 14.2cm). Hirshhorn Museum and Sculpture Garden, Smithsonian Institution, Washington, D.C. Joseph H. Hirshhorn Purchase Fund, 1990.

In 1990 Gober began making fetishized body parts in wax—frequently legs [fig. 15.7] cut off below the knee, sticking out from the wall along the floor. The legs began, he told Richard Flood, when "I was in this tiny little plane sitting next to this handsome businessman, and his trousers were pulled above his socks, and I was transfixed in this moment by his leg."[9] Gober also made other anti-heroic objects and even large installations, all of which hovered ambiguously at this interface of verisimilitude and dysfunction. What is so provocative and interesting about this work is the intense, erotic focus on the simplest things, even fragments of things, in incongruous juxtapositions—the lovingly fabricated sinks, the hair-by-hair realization of an exposed twelve inches of leg, a leg with a candle projecting out of it—pointedly (and oddly) dissociated from the "normal" relations between things and the world; Gober makes three-dimensionally palpable the arbitrariness of the unconscious flux of images.

The French artist Orlan literally used her own face as a medium in the nineties, subjecting it to repeated plastic surgeries to give it a quite unnatural topography and videotaping the surgeries for exhibition. But the artist who made the objectification of the human body and the fetishization of body parts into an operatically grand spectacle on a vast scale was Matthew Barney. His fusion of installation, performance, and costuming into epic films dazzled the art world and culminated in a magnificently staged, multimedia installation that filled the Guggenheim Museum in New York in 2003. It was the perfect vehicle for the Guggenheim, which had redefined itself from a museum of modern art into an international franchise of art extravaganzas with Guggenheim museums in Bilbao (Spain), Venice (Italy), and Berlin (Germany), and ongoing plans for additional sites in the Middle East, South America, and the U.S. Its trademark was enormous art spectacles for the masses with catalogs the size of a valise that shoppers would carry home as trophies for their living rooms but probably never read.

Matthew Barney

Matthew Barney began using sophisticated prosthetics and make-up in the early nineties to create the peculiarly beautiful settings and human hybrid creatures in his films. Their visual sensuality is powerfully erotic and yet his actors are ambiguously gendered and their enigmatic actions and settings never explicitly show anything sexual in the normal sense. Barney's films evoke the buried, infantile sexuality which Freud called the "polymorphous perverse" of early childhood, because of its diffusion of sexual energy to the whole body in the stages of development that precede the genital organization of sexuality at puberty.[10] Barney seems to have reached this intuitively, not through psychological theory, just as he devised the exaggerated expressionism of the color and gesture of his films.

Barney graduated from Yale College in 1989. In his first one-person show, at the Barbara Gladstone Gallery in SoHo in 1991, he used mountaineering gear to climb the walls and ceiling of the gallery, nude, but festooned with tackle and bundles of steel climbing spikes. After the performance a video of the event played in the gallery, showing him crossing the ceiling like a fly and extruding shiny pellets from his rectum. The piece also included a refrigerated room, like a meat locker, maintaining chilled petroleum jelly sculptures of what seemed like mutated gym equipment crossed with medical specimens. Barney's toned naked body attracted attention and the transgressive bodily process of pressing pearls out of his anus elicited a simultaneously riveting prurience and repulsion.

From performance Barney quickly moved on to films which had big budgets and high production values from the start, as though both in emulation and perversion of Hollywood. They combined installation and performance into a hybrid medium on film. The five films in Barney's *Cremaster* series are his best-known work; he himself performs in them [fig. 15.8]; each shot is composed like a painting in brilliant colors and costumes. In these films Barney plays with stereotyped celebrities—Ursula Andress (famous for her role as a bikini-clad siren in the early James Bond film *Dr. No*); Richard Serra, the artist of seemingly dangerous and dramatic steel walls; and the writer Norman Mailer, who

15.8 Matthew Barney, *Cremaster 4: The Loughton Candidate*, 1994. Color photo, plastic frame, 12 × 14in (30.5 × 35.5cm).
Courtesy Barbara Gladstone Gallery, New York.

symbolizes a confrontational hybrid of fiction and journalism. The locations are over-the-top settings such as the famous art deco Chrysler Building in New York and the baroque Hungarian State Opera House. The scripts are hypertrophied adolescent fantasy built around a myth of an enlarged scrotum (among other things), with fragmented quotations from a wide range of story-types—musicals, *film noir* gangster movies, etc. Even in the medium itself Barney creates open-ended ambiguities of category between opera, dance, drama, installation, painting, sculpture, and art cinema.

Although an iconography is alluded to, the films are really about the lush profusion of impressions. Like shopping at a perfume counter with strong whiffs of this and that, the viewer is meant to consume an overwhelming bouquet. The experience of all these fragmentary allusions is extraordinarily rich visually and the system of symbols, though ultimately decipherable if you work at it, is beside the point. "Rather than reading *Cremaster*," one review tells us, "we are encouraged to consume it as high-end eye candy, whose symbolic system is available to us but hardly necessary to our pleasure: meaning, that is, is no longer a necessary."[11] But fragmented experience and consumption in rich profusion rather than depth was one of the core cultural issues of the nineties and that made these films important; we see across the shallow screen of images rather than penetrating content in depth.

FASHION (THE BODY FAÇADE)

Another great spectacle in the Guggenheim Museum was *Show* [fig. 15.9], a 1998 performance by Vanessa Beecroft. Beecroft arranged a formation of twenty nude or bikini-clad models to stand on display in the ground-floor rotunda (in full view not only to the elite invited audience inside the building, but to anyone looking in from Fifth Avenue through the plate-glass windows). Beecroft's work involves a heightened engagement, shared by a number of nineties artists, with the world of high fashion. She treats fashion as one of a number of languages with a syntax.

"Manolo shoes are like a paintbrush," she explained, "in red or blue or whatever,"[12] and Beecroft works with the models like a painter. In 2000 she opened the new Gagosian Gallery in London with girls wearing only bright red wigs to match their dyed, bright-red pubic hair and Manolo Blahnik mules. The impetus came from wanting to find a medium for formal aesthetics as well as personal expressive needs but, she said:

> the concept of beauty that they embody was not reproducible in painting or sculpture or drawing or photography ... The girls themselves are more ambiguous—they're half real and half fiction, part art and also part society, and their beauty is so painfully ephemeral. All this couldn't be in a painting or a photograph. Nudity in paintings looks refined, it looks glossy, but in real life there's something embarrassing or miserable about it. And at the same time, it's exciting and beautiful and attractive. I identify with the girls. I sympathize, and I don't really look at them when they're performing, because I feel so much empathy and stress.[13]

The models in Beecroft's works do not acknowledge the audience or perform in any way except to walk into position and stand there, as in *Show*, where they stood in a triangular formation with the apex at the front. The deliberate interplay of the formation in space (which sets up a schema) and the out-of-place elements (the occasional nude, individual models shifting from one foot to another) randomizes the structure at every level and suggests a lack of closure in the definition of the work. The overt sexuality of the beautiful young bodies also belies the disinterested expression of the models, who stand like fashion mannequins. In several respects these performances point the viewer to the explicit and yet denied sexuality of mass-marketing and indeed the strangely depersonalized commodification of sexuality in contemporary culture. Beecroft also paints on canvas (influenced stylistically by fashion drawings). The human image in her paintings seems so ephemeral that it nearly disappears into thin air, and the ephemerality mirrors the plethora of disposable "things" in our commodity culture.

The work of Karen Kilimnik also involves an investigation of the worlds of fashion and marketing, combined with teenage fantasy. In her crayon and pastel drawing *Nineteen Children of France* [fig. 15.10], for example, Kilimnik rendered a daydreaming adolescent girl with long, dark eyelashes in

15.9 Vanessa Beecroft, *Show*, April 1998. Live performance at the Guggenheim Museum, New York.

Courtesy Deitch Projects, New York.

the slight style of a fashion sketch. The girl is surrounded by a swan insignia, such as an adolescent might draw on a sheet of unplanned mark making, and fragmentary notes: "Nineteen children of France were born in this chamber" in the upper left; "MGM, Metro Goldwyn Mayer, Warner Brothers, Douglas Fairbanks Jr., Lillian Gish, Valentino" are listed to the right; and below (with incorrect orthography) "Sèvres porcelain, Baccarat." In the lower half of the sheet is another young girl, draped in a baroque swath of fabric and holding a lamb beside the inscription: "Chloe Sévigny, Sèvres, age 22, photograph by Guy Auroch Paris/the controversial indie kids/what added to her fame:/novelist Jay McInerey's [sic] proclaiming her/the new It girl./On exercise: 'I tried yoga, which Woody/showed me how to do. It felt great./But I only kept it up for about/three or four nights.' Why she's really/not an It girl after all: 'Right now/I'm wearing my pajamas at/3 o'clock and helping my mother put up Christmas wreaths.'/Hilary Sterne," and below: "Waterford."

These fragmentary inscriptions add up to a casual diary entry. Everything borders on the clichés of an adolescent girl's reveries and doodles, on the appropriated gossip and borrowed romance of kitsch. Yet there is also the radical suggestion of a democratization of art in the awkward drawing, the untutored composition, and the naive romanticism. It is as if to say any experience is valid, everyone is an artist, and the viewer completes the work with her or his own associations. The open-ended trajectories set in the brief allusions to vintage Hollywood, fancy porcelain, the momentary popularity of the "It" girl are provocatively polyvalent in a postmodern sense. Everything is sparkle and theater in Kilimnik's work.

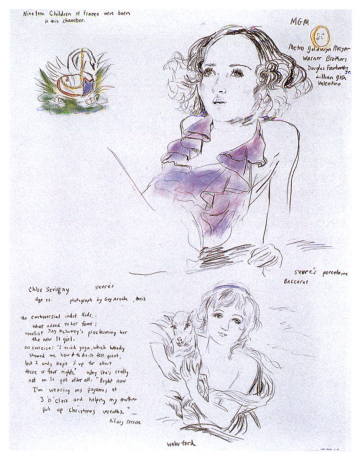

15.10 Karen Kilimnik, *Nineteen Children of France*, 1998. Crayon and pastel on paper, 34 × 26in (86.36 × 66cm).

Courtesy 303 Gallery, New York.

The New York and Tokyo-based Japanese artist Mariko Mori is a fashion school graduate and started, in the early nineties, using the techniques of fashion costuming, make-up, and photography to create a total, self-contained fantasy world around herself in installations, documented in photographs. In *Play with Me* of 1994 [fig. 15.11] Mori (a former fashion model) dressed herself like a sexy cyborg out of a science-fiction film—long ponytails of light-blue hair, hard-shell articulation of erotic body parts in metallic blue plastic, silver plastic gloves and dress—and stood outside a Tokyo toy store; the suggestive title has a double meaning, connecting her to the robotic toys inside but also to the fantasy of her sexual availability in a utopia of pure, unemotional sexuality. She entered a public space, transformed by costume, to explore different constructed identities (like Cindy Sherman); "when you wear clothes," she said, "you become a personality, you become the clothes."[14] But also like Cindy Sherman's works, the viewer can continually create new stories to explain the images, giving them a peculiarly post-modern open-endedness.

The 10-by-12-foot exhibition photograph of *Play with Me* achieves a kind of cinematic reality with its panoramic scale. Unlike the costumes of Cindy Sherman, Mori's outfit does not create an actor in an imagined real-life drama. Instead, it suggests the morphing of the human figure into a futuristic fantasy. Mori's work of 1995 features experiments in 3D effects, sound, and computer manipulation. The 1995 *Empty Dream* is an epic 24-foot-wide photo environment of a real public swimming place, constructed inside a building to look like a beach; it is a recreation facility that actually exists in Japan—strange though it is. But here the artist has manipulated the photograph to insert herself in a blue plastic mermaid costume in several locations within the scene. The self-replication, the high-tech manipulation of the

15.11 Mariko Mori, *Play with Me*, 1994. Fuji supergloss (duraflex) print, wood, pewter frame, 12 × 10 × 3ft (3.66 × 3.05 × 0.91m). Edition of three.

Courtesy Deitch Projects, New York.

15.12 Mariko Mori, *Burning Desire*, 1997–8. Glass with photo interlayer, five panels, 10ft × 20ft × ⅞in (304.8 × 609.6 × 2cm) overall.
Courtesy Deitch Projects, New York.

images, and the strangeness of the real simulacra of nature create a postmodern multivalency to the images, simultaneously connecting them to the hypervisuality of contemporary culture, to computer animation, to advertising, to nature, to the fantastic, and to the emerging technological and philosophical debate around the synthetic generation of human beings through biotechnology.

Dominic Molon pointed out a shift in Mori's work in 1996 and 1997, from what he called the "alluring but vapid vixens,"[15] the sensual worship of celebrity and fashion, to a cosmic spirituality, inspired by the fusion of Western pop culture and aesthetics with Buddhism. In these works Mori moved into an even more dazzling high-tech virtuosity with 3D virtual-reality videos accompanied by mesmerizingly cinematic photographs on a grand scale. In the 20-foot-wide *Burning Desire* of 1997–8 [fig. 15.12] Mori appears as an inspirational Buddhist deity levitating in Lotus position over the earth; the image recalls Glinda floating down in her bubble in *The Wizard of Oz*. She also replicates herself as four divine, flaming apparitions in attendance around the haloed goddess. The work crosses cultural boundaries (from Oz to Nirvana) and transcends human body boundaries into a futuristic virtuality that blends reality with Paradise. This is not a science-fiction dystopia of futuristic apocalypse but the blissful emptiness to which Buddhists aspire, blended into the sublime, plastic superficiality of contemporary culture.

SENSATIONAL METHODS

To some observers, the sensationalism of the celebrated "Freeze" show, held in the London Docklands in 1988, exemplified a climate of cynical and dispiriting exploitation. It announced a splashy new generation of British sculptors working with sensational materials and processes, most notoriously Damien Hirst, who announced himself with a 14-foot-long real shark, jaws open, suspended in a tank of formaldehyde. He also sliced cows, sheep, and pigs in various ways. *This Little Piggy Went to Market, This Little Piggy Went Home* [fig. 15.13] escalates the shock value with a title that alludes to a children's rhyme. Marc Quinn presented a portrait bust of himself in frozen blood (his own), and Rachel Whiteread cast the empty space of an entire room from a demolished Victorian house in plaster and titled it *Ghost*.

If the technical concept of Whiteread's castings derived from Nauman's *A Cast of the Space Under My Chair* (1965–8), her escalation in number and scale added a new twist. In 1993 Whiteread constructed her most ambitious and best-known work, *House* [fig. 15.14], which involved casting an entire house—the last remnant of a torn-down block of Victorian row houses in East London—in concrete. The myriad details of the house left in the cast impression elicited contemplation of the former life in the house—another set of issues taken over completely from Nauman's work. In addition, *House* was set in a public situation, like a Christo and Jeanne-Claude project, and the object was beautiful in itself. But it differs from Christo and Jeanne-Claude in that the public debate it triggered took place largely after the fact, rather than as part of the process, placing the emphasis on the object rather than on the dialectic between object and context.

15.13 (above) **Damien Hirst**, *This Little Piggy Went to Market, This Little Piggy Went Home*, 1996. Steel, GRP composites, glass, pig, formaldehyde solution, electric motor, two tanks, each 47 × 47 × 23½in (120 × 120 × 60cm). Courtesy Saatchi Gallery, London.

15.14 (left) **Rachel Whiteread**, *House*, completed October 23, 1993 and destroyed January 1994. Poured concrete. The 1993 Artangel/Beck's Commission. Grove Road, East London. Courtesy Artangel, London.

Whiteread completed the casting of *House* on October 25, 1993 and then the press started in on the piece; on November 23 Whiteread was awarded the prestigious Turner Prize and, on the same day, the local council voted for the immediate demolition of the project. As James Lingwood, one of the project organizers, said, that was "an incendiary combination,"[16] and heated debate in the press followed. But the debate was part of the intent. As one commentator remarked, the organizers chose a

> site where her project would fuse all the loose wires of potential catastrophe. House, seen from across the field, was a giant plug, feeding current into the madness of the city. Grove Road had the lot: a terrace house with three exploitable sides (and a sitting tenant), a hyperactive local politico, anarchist squatters, post-Situationist rock stars looking for the grand gesture, and wild-eyed psychogeographers prophesying war.[17]

House was torn down in January of 1994.

The work of Whiteread has deeper resonances quite apart from the controversy it has created around itself. In the details of *House* are the record of a human situation, the lives lived in that space left as palimpsests in the cast. In the Holocaust memorial she then conceived for Vienna, she cast a block from the space left behind the books on the shelves of a library; in this casting the absence of the books implied in the impression of their ends provides a poignant memorial. In 1998 she cast the inside of a water tower on the roof of a building in SoHo (the downtown art district in New York) using a translucent polymer that glowed with the sunlight in a very beautiful, ghostly transfiguration of the old wooden structure.

POSTMODERN CONCEPTUALISM

In the nineties, just as the border between art and a cynical exploitation of market capitalism was at times hard to draw, all the hierarchies of medium and method disintegrated in art, along with categories by movement, nationality, and all rules of "appropriate" subject matter or content. Eduardo Kac [fig. 15.15] used genetic modification to produce a phosphorescent, "transgenic" bunny that actually glowed green in the dark. The artist Larry Miller copyrighted his own DNA in 1989, after a Supreme Court ruling allowing the patenting of animals. Much of the new work of the nineties was based on a conceptual model in a wide range of mediums and methods as artists sought the most appropriate form in which to negotiate their experience of the decade. In the 1997 Documenta X exhibition the curator Benjamin Buchloh repositioned conceptualism as the core of the discourse in contemporary art.

But the conceptualism which had emerged was distinctly postmodern (different than the modernist conceptualism of the late sixties) in its assumption of the transcendence over hierarchies. The German artist Martin Kippenberger, for example, was at one moment creating painterly canvases and at the next constructing a full-scale subway entrance to nowhere. The Mexican artist Gabriel Orozco began rolling a large ball of Plasticine down the city streets (*Yielding Stone*, 1992) to collect the debris in each city in which he was having an exhibition. His work occupied the space without limitation, in order to annihilate the hierarchy of space.

The Los Angeles artist Charles Ray parked a full-scale fire truck—constructed like a toy, with its equipment painted

15.15 Eduardo Kac, *GFP Bunny*, 2000.
Alba, the fluorescent rabbit.
Courtesy the artist.

15.16 Charles Ray, *Oh! Charley, Charley, Charley . . .*, 1992. Mixed-media figures, all cast from the artist's body.
Courtesy Regen Projects, Los Angeles.

on it in the style of a children's book illustration—in front of the Whitney Museum in New York during the 1993 Biennial exhibition; *Oh! Charley, Charley, Charley . . .* of 1992 [fig. 15.16] consists of eight lifelike nude sculptures of himself engaged in having sex with himself. Ray's works all test the viewer's perception of reality in some strange way. He plays on stereotypes and fixed ideas in a critique of the surface of events. His work develops from perceptions of the cultural landscape around him rather than from a driving engagement with form or inner expression.

The Los Angeles-based artist Mike Kelley appropriated pop culture into performances, drawings, and sculpture in ways that crassly violated social taboos. The title of *Estral Star #1* (1989) [fig. 15.17] puns on *astral* and *estrus* (the term for animals in heat), imposing a sexual reference onto two sock monkeys—cuddly stuffed animals for children—refocusing our attention on the red, lip-like forms on these toys that his titles recontextualized as representations of the female genitalia. In Kelley's 1990 *Nostalgic Depiction of the Innocence of Childhood* a nude couple seem to have sexual relations with huge, furry toys, and to smear themselves with what looks like feces; the performance medium makes the same genre of crudely "inappropriate" subject matter as in *Estral Star 1* even more unsettling.

Kelley's performances have precedence in the highly sexualized, messy performance work of Paul McCarthy, another Los Angeles artist, who began performing in the seventies. Barbara Smith (a fellow performance artist) recounted McCarthy's 1974 *Hot Dog* [fig. 15.18] as beginning with him stripping to his underwear and shaving his body. Then he "stuffs his penis into a hotdog bun and tapes it on, then smears his ass with mustard . . . drinking ketchup and stuffing his mouth with hot dogs . . . Binding his head with gauze and adding more hot dogs, he finally tapes his bulging mouth closed . . . He stands alone struggling with himself, trying to prevent his own retching."[18] McCarthy's work continues to explore this grotesque encounter with the body, as in his 2004 bronze sculpture *Santa with Butt Plug* or his giant inflatable *Complex Shit* of 2008.

The French artist Gilles Barbier is also known for installations which critique social norms with a sarcastic wit and frequently involve multiple sculptural surrogates of himself (something Kippenberger also did), but the core of Barbier's work is revealed in his "dictionary pages" [fig. 17.1], an ongoing project of defining his own identity in relation to the highly traditional culture of France, by systematically copying (from start to finish) the Larousse dictionary of 1956 (the year of his birth). The Larousse has a centrality in French culture for which there is no parallel elsewhere. Once a year the forty members of the prestigious Académie Française (founded in 1635) meet under a dome across the river from the Louvre in Paris to decide which new words

15.17 Mike Kelley, *Estral Star #1*, 1989. Sock Monkeys sewn together, 31½ × 12 × 6½in (80 × 30.5 × 16.5cm). Courtesy Mike Kelley.

15.18 Paul McCarthy, *Hot Dog*, 1974. Still from performance, Oddfellows Temple, Pasadena, California. Mayonnaise, ketchup, hot dogs, hot dog buns, mustard, utensils, gauze, tables, chairs, dishes.

may be admitted officially into the French language; the Larousse is the definitive reflection of these deliberations. Barbier copies the dictionary by hand, page by page, going all the way across from left to right, and when he arrives at an illustration he copies that freehand too and then goes on until he fills a 7-by-7-foot sheet of paper. He then stops to read what he has done and makes "errata" sheets to emend miscopied or omitted text and illustrations, often adding notes of explanation like "I just wasn't paying attention."

CONSTRUCTING THE POSTMODERN SELF

Barbier's dictionary pages attempt to bind and master the totality of the language of the self; his gestural, handwritten pages have a bodily physicality, like skin. The paintings of Christian Schumann present a deliberately *unbounded* experience. In a painting like *Flatbush* (1998) [fig. 15.19] Schumann decenters the identity of the artist and of the subject by equating everything on the level of the sign; on the plane of images he juxtaposes all different kinds of styles and content, from the academic portrait head at top center to cartoon images, lettering, disjointed fragments of text, narrative vignettes, scientific diagrams, and even shifts in verbal language (as in the passages of French). The work defines itself as open-ended. But it is not without precedent.

Underlying the radical postmodernism of Schumann is the complex overlay of images in the work of artists from the late seventies like David Salle and Gary Panter [figs. 12.37 and 12.39] and the deeper simultaneous interpenetration of content in the works of Alice Aycock and Elizabeth Murray

15.19 Christian Schumann, *Flatbush*, 1998. Acrylic and mixed media on canvas, 7ft 3in × 9ft (2.21 × 2.74m). Courtesy Postmasters Gallery, New York.

15.20 Jimmie Durham, *Crazy for Life*, 1990. Performance, Dance Theater Workshop, New York City.
Courtesy Nicole Klagsbrun Gallery, New York.

[12.29–12.35 and 13.31–13.35]. What makes Schumann's work new is that he has assimilated this complexity into the even script of visual data flow and doesn't even seem to attempt coherence.

In the meantime the corporate conformity of nineties culture and the expansion of consumerism and marketing have left less and less mental space for a cohesive sense of self. In an article on the artist Jimmie Durham [fig. 15.20], who is part Cherokee Indian, Richard Shiff took up the issue of how mainstream culture "colonizes" the autonomous individuality of the Native American artist with stereotypes to which the artist is compelled to respond.[19] Durham's work centers on a postmodern dislocation of reductive logics used to classify individuals. To label his work "Native American" is to wipe out all intellectual and expressive independence in favor of a racial category. Durham engages in a kind of self-empowerment through the invention of a "trickster," inventing false "Native American" traditions and fictions of autobiography, and in general refusing to accept fixed identity. In some works he includes Cherokee texts but withholds untranslatable passages, in others he will appropriate skulls to tease the viewer's expectation of a "Native American" primitive tradition that isn't actually there as a way of subverting an attempt at reductively defining the work or the artist.

The use of the Internet for communicating, shopping, transferring data (including images and video), and "surfing" a virtually limitless sea of news and information without time, distances, or boundaries went from zero to nearly universal across the nineties, and its effect on our consciousness was perhaps the biggest new issue at the end of the century. Ik-Joon Kang, a South Korean artist, created an installation in 1994 called *Throw Everything Together and Add*; the title itself summed up the sense of the overwhelming quantity and complexity of information.

One response to the information explosion (which included an overwhelming collision of cultural perspectives and mores) was the atomization of people into smaller and more local subgroups, both geographically and simultaneously by self-selection on the Web. Already in the eighties the *New York Times* was reporting that "despite earlier predictions that television, radio, and the movies would exert a homogenizing influence on language in the United States,"[20] regional accents became stronger. The sociolinguists saw this as the "reflection of a new localism."[21] People were becoming global citizens, informed about the world to an

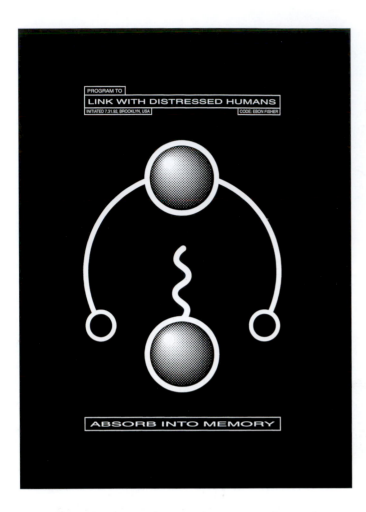

15.21 Ebon Fisher, *Social Program for Humans: Linkage with Distressed Human*, initiated in Brooklyn, 1992. Photographic print of computer-generated image, a behavioral inducement, to be disseminated via fax, modem, computer disk, hardcopy, slide projection, or video display.

unprecedented degree, and at the same time retreating into more and more localized communities.

The New York artist Ebon Fisher addressed himself directly to this issue in the early nineties. He inhabited the close-knit artists' neighborhood that existed in Williamsburg, Brooklyn at the start of the decade and his work involved the interface of media, technology, and industry with the human environment of a small community and with the individual. He was thrilled by the many possibilities of global communication in combination with the intimacy of the small artists' communities. "The web," he wrote in 1991, "has created the new Vienna."[22]

On the one hand Fisher focused on the immediacy of body experience and on community-based culture, organizing massive participatory art events in the neighborhood; his wildly sensual extravaganza, "Organism," held in an abandoned mustard seed factory near the Brooklyn waterfront in 1993, was a multisensory overcharge of several hundred people showing up to do installations, performances, play

music together, or just have a few drinks and shed all their inhibitions in the style of the contemporary "raves." On the other hand Fisher also began making digital art that had no fixed materiality; instead it had the flavor of contemporary cyberpunk fiction, as in William Gibson's 1984 novel *Neuromancer* where humans fuse with computers and communicate digitally in cyberspace. Fisher wrote utopian "social programs" on the computer [fig. 15.21], which he instructs his viewers to "absorb into memory" as templates for new social relations. Through community-based cultural enterprises and consumer technology he aspired to reclaim the production of culture from the mass-marketers and return it to each of us, one person at a time.

Tim Spelios's 1998 *Under the BQE* [fig. 15.22] is local in another way. Also a Williamsburg artist, his collages focus closely on the uniqueness of one person's vision—whether a scrap of crumpled paper, a Styrofoam container, a repair in the pavement that he finds under the Brooklyn–Queens Expressway by his studio, or images from the media. Spelios fits each prosaic item into a personal grid, asserting individuality as a pattern of seeing.

Gabriel Orozco has become one of the most celebrated recent practitioners of this kind of intimacy, using found

15.22 Tim Spelios, *Under the BQE*, 1998. Cut-and-pasted photographs on board, 80 × 60in (203.2 × 152.4cm). Edition of three. Courtesy the artist.

15.23 Gabriel Orozco, *Island Within an Island (Isla en la Isla)*, 1993. Cibachrome, 12⅞ × 18⅝in (32.70 × 47.3cm). Edition of five. Courtesy Marian Goodman Gallery, New York.

objects and making photographs that capture a definable vision. It is that identifiably personal way of seeing that matters most in *Island Within an Island (Isla en la Isla)* of 1993 [fig. 15.23], where Orozco poetically compares the distant view of the skyscrapers of Wall Street on the island of Manhattan with the washed-up boards and trash leaned against a concrete parking barricade in a lot by the Lower West Side docks. The trash in the foreground sits like an island in a puddle, a microcosm of the skyline, and yet this modest image engages a larger debate on the validity of marginalized perspectives that is at the heart of the multicultural and global sense of humanity on which the twenty-first century relies. As Jimmie Durham remarked: "We seem to want to approach everything with the knowledge of it already . . . I want to jumble up the expectations."[23] This, of course, is not an exclusively postmodern idea. It is—and perhaps always has been—the function of art to take us to the margins of contemporary experience, to try on what seems far-fetched, peculiar, different, and new so as to explore what may be on the verge of becoming essential to know.

LOUISE BOURGEOIS AFTER 1980

Sometimes our habits of seeing keep us from noticing something new even when it's right in front of us; just because it doesn't fit in, it's invisible. In 1982 the Museum of Modern Art in New York put on a major retrospective of the artist Louise Bourgeois.[24] Bourgeois was seventy years old when the show opened and it was not only *her* first retrospective but, remarkably, the first retrospective of *any* female artist at the Museum of Modern Art. Although she had had almost nothing exhibited since the early 1950s (see Chapter 2), no artist better exemplifies the complexity of a postmodern practice and, after this exhibition, the art world finally recognized this. When Lucy Lippard included Bourgeois's work in the 1966 "Eccentric Abstraction" show at the Fishbach Gallery in New York, the age difference between her and the younger rising stars in the show like Eva Hesse and Bruce Nauman made her seem more like a precursor. But she was actually their contemporary in that her new work broke the molds of minimalism and pop art. As Frances Morris has written, "Bourgeois's work of the 1960s, when first shown, appeared utterly different from anything she'd made before; but it also seemed absolutely counter to the reigning fashion in New York."[25] This pattern of divergence, driven by an inner compass, had always been a hallmark of Bourgeois's career and it has remained central to the work's meaning, its influence, and its reception.

Concurrent with her exhibition at MoMA, Bourgeois published an illustrated essay in *Artforum* magazine called "Child Abuse," in which she made public her deeply troubled childhood and its centrality in motivating her work. "My childhood," she later wrote, "has never lost its magic, it has never lost its mystery, and it has never lost its drama. All my work of the last fifty years, all my subjects, have found their inspiration in my childhood."[26] Bourgeois's work derives from a searing re-encounter with the traumas of her childhood; her stylistic restlessness reflects a perpetually unresolved search for forms that will lay that content to rest.

Perhaps the most disturbing of her early memories have to do with her relations with her father who, she said, "made fun of me." The damage to her self-esteem was early and profound but it became focused in memory on her father's flagrant infidelity. When she was ten her father hired a live-in English nanny and began sleeping with her, openly. "Sadie, if you don't mind, was mine," Bourgeois wrote in her autobiographical text for *Artforum*. "She was engaged to teach me English. I thought she was going to like me. Instead of which she betrayed me. I was betrayed not only by my father, damn it, but by her too."[27] This simultaneous rage and longing persist throughout Bourgeois's *oeuvre*.

Like Hedda Sterne, Bourgeois began as a painter, working in a surrealist-inspired idiom in the forties, before moving to sculpture in the later forties and early fifties. The intimacy of works like *Listening One* of 1947 [fig. 2.27] suggests that longing for a family of "personages" (as she called these totem-like sculptures) with whom she could interact. The physicality of *Untitled* [fig. 2.28] of the same year takes the viewer straight back to the bodily reality of childhood. The drawing is all about the sensation of mark making and shows no concern for the usual trained sense of symmetrical composition.

In works of the early sixties like *Double Negative* [fig. 10.24] the aggressiveness of the sexuality expresses the vehemence of the artist's rage. By the late sixties Bourgeois began to replace the organic messiness of the materials in this work with bronze and marble, although the vocabulary of forms continues. Nevertheless, she returned to these materials and to this vocabulary of organic sexuality when she ventured into installation for the first time in *The Destruction of the Father* of 1974. The work is set in a theatrical space and draws upon a childhood fantasy of murdering and eating her autocratic father at the dinner table—the theater of some of his most painful emotional transgressions against her.

In 1980, six years after *The Destruction of the Father*, Bourgeois moved her studio into a large open loft in Brooklyn and began building large installations that literally incorporate the viewer. "In order to get rid of the past I have to recreate it and then put it in a cage,"[28] she explained, and

15.24 Louise Bourgeois, *Spider Couple*, 2003, Bronze, silver nitrate patina, 90 × 142 × 144in (228.6 × 360.6 × 365.7cm). Courtesy Cheim & Read, Galerie Karsten Greve, and Hauser & Wirth.

many of these installations are literally framed inside wire cages. These spaces—into which we peer and sometimes physically enter—contain suggestively intimate forms and materials, such as articles of personal clothing, mirrors, erotic abstractions, and even severed mannequin limbs, set off against the harsh and cold cages. The enigmatic arrangements are dreamlike, with an essential open-endedness.

Around 2000, now eighty-nine years old, the physical limitations of the artist's age caused Bourgeois to work increasingly by directing assistants and to use less physically challenging materials. On the one hand this is the period of her monumental, frightening but also maternal spiders [fig. 15.24] that she modeled and had enlarged. At the same time she also turned to small fabric figures and heads, taking her back to her childhood experience in her father's tapestry repair workshops. *The Reticent Child* (2003) [fig. 15.25] is a tabletop installation of six red terrycloth figures, set off against marble, polished stainless steel, and aluminum pedestals and walls. The themes of birth, infancy, and motherhood intersect with a painful isolation in the figures and the profoundly tactile feel of their red terrycloth skins and the awkwardness of the handstitching give them a palpable "reticence."

Art is a privilege, a blessing, a relief . . . I had to pursue it, even more than the privilege of having children . . . The privilege was the access to the unconscious. It is a fantastic privilege to have access to the unconscious. I had to be worthy of this privilege, and to exercise it. It was a privilege also to be able to sublimate . . . A lot of people cannot sublimate. They have no access to their unconscious. There is something very special in being able to sublimate . . . and something very painful in the access to it. But there is no escape . . . and no escape from access once it is given to you, once you are favored with it, whether you want it or not.[29]

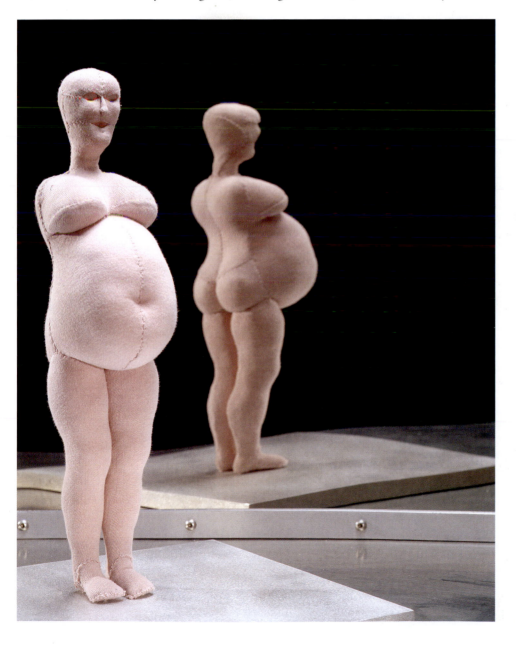

15.25 Louise Bourgeois,
The Reticent Child (detail), 2003.
Fabric, marble, stainless steel and aluminum: six elements, 72 × 112 × 36in (182.8 × 284.4 × 91.4cm).
Courtesy Cheim & Read, Galerie Karsten Greve, and Hauser & Wirth.

NEW USES OF THE CAMERA

In the 1960s photographers also faced a kind of invisibility problem in that the historic role of photography as documentation had made it hard to see as a medium of artistic expression. Even the most individualistic photographers, like Diane Arbus, were using straight photography to show us what we might have overlooked in the world around us. Experimentalists like Robert Heineken and Harry Callahan manipulated images in the darkroom but they too continued to work on the traditional scale for photography and, on the whole, the world of photography remained segregated from the contemporary art world. Robert Frank's aesthetic of the everyday was extended with the introduction of color by William Eggleston, and with the emergence of conceptual art, ephemeral art actions, and site specific art in remote places at the end of the decade, photography took on an important role documenting it (see Chapter 11). But it wasn't until the 1980s that the Bechers and then Cindy Sherman broke the ice with large-scale work. In the nineties

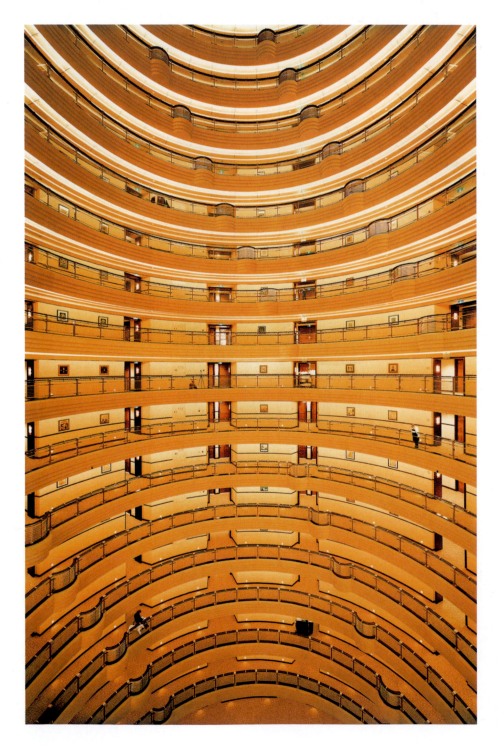

15.26 Andreas Gursky, *Shanghai*, 2000. Print mounted on Plexiglass in artist's frame, 9ft 10¾in × 6ft 9¼in (3.04 × 2.07m). Courtesy Matthew Marks Gallery, New York.

15.27 Candida Höfer, *Residenzschloss Weimar XIV 2006*, 2006.
C-print, edition of six, 5ft 1in × 5ft 1in (1.55 × 1.55m).
Courtesy HSL Fachlabor GmbH, Düsseldorf.

students of the Bechers like Thomas Ruff, Andreas Gursky [fig. 15.26], and Candida Höfer [fig. 15.27], and then a rapidly expanding number of others, made large-format photography and oversized prints familiar. The large scale creates the illusion of extraordinary realism and detail, but in fact they are highly manipulated digitally (as in the Gursky, for example, where the atrium in reality has only six stories). By 2000 interest in photography began to overshadow painting because; as the curator Okwui Enwezor has said, "photography and film [are] the quintessential mediums of modern documentary truth,"[30] and "truth" became one of the most challenging issues at the end of the twentieth century.

In 1969 William Wegman pushed the envelope in photography in another way with the side-splitting deadpan humor of his short, vaudevillian performance videos. They typically show the artist in his T-shirt and jeans, working

with minimal props and delivering an absurd monolog in a flat, emotionless tone. In 1970 he bought a Weimaraner puppy, which he named Man Ray, and in Ray he found his ideal collaborator. The dog made a perfect "straight man," accepting every command with absolute sincerity and transparent devotion. With phrases like "Bad dog" or "Who's coming?" Wegman prompted poignant expressions from the dog and began making photographs of him. Wegman drew goatees, glasses, and berets on the photographs, superimposed the dog's image on evocative settings, and in 1978 began using the newly developed large-format Polaroid camera, elaborating the ludicrously funny costumes, makeup, and sets for the dog into beautiful (if still quite funny) compositions, making full use of the Polacolor's visual richness and subtlety [fig. 15.28].

What makes Wegman's photographs and videos important—more than just entertaining, which they also are—is the way in which they undermined our expectations of the mediums. Wegman's use of straight photography, film, and video has at first the appearance of "documentation," albeit of an absurd activity. In documentation or in entertainment the medium is supposed to disappear. In the 1970s (before the existence of personal computers or the Internet) the point of reference was broadcast television and, unlike what audiences expected to see there or in the movies, Wegman made his viewers acutely aware of how the photograph or video was made. The visibility of his makeshift devices makes them even funnier, but in doing this he also undercut the illusion of narrative objectivity and destabilized our habits of seeing.

Alfredo Jaar's *Chile 1981, Before Leaving*—created as he fled Chile to live and work in New York—defined a deeply humanist political practice that forces us to question the control of images which, in our image-based global culture, has become a particularly postmodern form of power [fig. 15.29]. The photos comprising *Chile 1981, Before Leaving* provide, as Nicole Schweizer described them,

> a fleeting trace in the landscape of a country then under the dictatorship of General Augusto Pinochet. An alignment of small Chilean flags planted in the sand dunes, directed out to sea, disappearing into it, soon covered over by the waves, a frail line leading out of the country, but also pointing toward the sea as being this stretch of water in which so many murdered bodies had "disappeared."[31]

The work was shown for the first time as part of his first solo exhibition in his native Chile in 2006.

Jaar became well known for his project on the labors of the gold-miners in the Amazon—*Gold in the Morning* (1986)—for which he used billboards in the New York subway, and for *Real Pictures* (1995), which describes photographs of the horrific events of the Rwanda genocide by means of labels, placed on black pedestals in a black room; the pictures themselves are missing. In another work, *Untitled (Newsweek)* of 1994, he chronicles the events in Rwanda as text under a series of reappropriated covers

from *Newsweek* for those same dates. The headlines—like "How to Survive a Scary Market," "The Search for the Magic Pill: Better Than Vitamins," and "The Case Against O.J.: How Strong?"—seem glaringly banal against the parallel story in Jaar's captions, and they underscore the length of time before the story of Rwanda hit the magazine's cover in August 1994: "Hell on Earth: Racing Against Death in Rwanda."

Photography has, of course, long been the traditional medium for social issues. But with computer programs to alter photographs, the presumption of objectivity in photography is increasingly questionable. Gerhard Richter took up this issue, seeking to reinstate the "truth" of painting as early as the 1960s, and in recent works by Sigmar Polke abstract painting has even acquired visual effects from photography, paradoxically emulating its claim on "reality" in the realm of an explicitly constructed mode of abstraction [fig. 15.30]. In the meantime much large-format photography has moved closer to the fictions of painting. The photographer

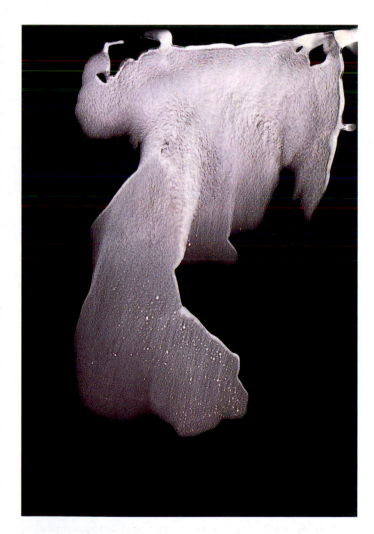

15.30 Sigmar Polke, *Untitled*, 1998–9. Mixed media on paper, 39⅞ × 26⅞in (101.2 × 68.2cm).

Courtesy Galerie Michael Werner, New York and Cologne.

15.31 Jeff Wall, *Outburst*, 1989. Transparency in lightbox, 7ft 6⅛in × 10ft 2⅞in (2.29 × 3.12m).
Courtesy Marian Goodman Gallery, New York.

Jeff Wall described his large, computer-altered, backlit images [fig. 15.31] as existing "in the gray area between the theatrical and the real."[32]

VIDEO

Video has had a particularly strong claim on "objectivity" since its inception in commercial television. Nam June Paik pioneered the use of video in art in the early sixties when Sony introduced consumer-priced equipment (see Chapter 8) and by the seventies a number of artists began experimenting widely with video as an art medium. Vito Acconci used it to bring the viewer into an unexpected (sometimes frightening) intimacy with performance actions under floors or behind walls. Bruce Nauman used video in a variety of ways, sometimes in a surveillance mode, as in his *Live Taped Video Corridor* of 1968–70, which shows the viewer her or his own location and movements, sometimes to magnify an installation, as in his *Rats and Bats (Learned Helplessness in Bats)* of 1985, where he immerses the viewer in the loud sounds of a drum, then of the artist pounding with a baseball bat, while watching live close-up projections all around of a rat moving through a yellow Plexiglas maze that sits in the center of the room.

In the mid-seventies Bill Viola [fig. 15.32] insinuated time, sound, and kinetics into contemplative subjects with video, conceiving the work like a moving painting. He also developed a dazzling technical virtuosity with the medium which made the most of the rapidly advancing commercial technology. In *Inasmuch As It Is Always Already Taking Place* [fig. 15.33] Gary Hill created a disorienting object with video monitors, dividing a near- (but not quite) motionless human body into sixteen segmented parts, each appearing

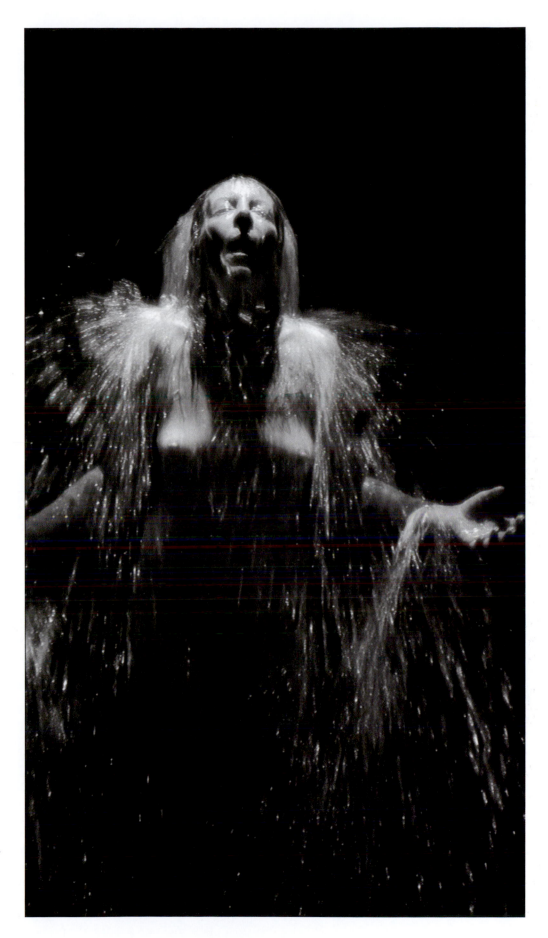

15.32 Bill Viola,
Impermanence, 2007. Black-and-white video on plasma display mounted vertically on wall. Performer: Pamela Blackwell.
Courtesy Bill Viola Studio.

on a separate video monitor and relying in part on the "truth" value of television to create a disconcertingly lifelike sense of a stretched-out body.

One of the most mesmerizing new uses of video has been in the work of William Kentridge, who exploits it to add a sense of time and movement to drawing. Kentridge makes animations with beautiful drawings that appear and then seem to mutate before your eyes on the video screen [fig. 15.34]. The subject is the violent landscape of South Africa under apartheid and its aftermath; the constant coming into being of the drawings on the screen followed by their mutation into other forms and scenes creates a disturbing instability and an act of erasure (with an inherent political critique).

As the art world became more global in the late nineties, video also increasingly explored uniquely local cultures and private memory. Shirin Neshat, for example, departed from Iran prior to the Islamic Revolution but her *oeuvre* of video and production stills centers on a Bergmanesque cinematic reverie on the culture she left behind [fig. 15.35]. The Swiss artist Pipilotti Rist, on the other hand, has abstracted the narrativity of video (which is inherently sequential) to tell stories built on visual impressions rather than on a logical story line. Tony Oursler has pushed the physical possibilities of video, using it to project human faces onto unlikely screens like pillows, rocks, and trees, distorting the faces and at the same time creating a surreal sense that these inanimate objects are speaking directly to the viewer.

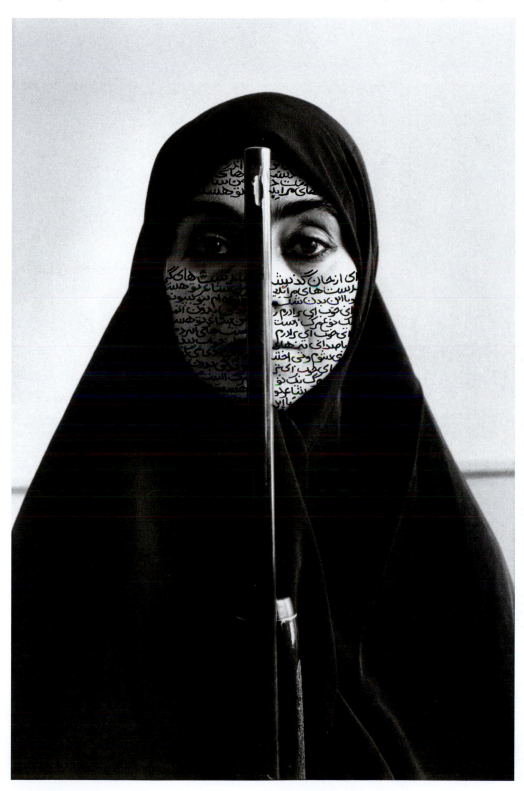

15.35 Shirin Neshat, *Rebellious Silence*, 1994. RC print and ink, 46⅝ × 31⅛in (118.4 × 79.1cm). Courtesy Gladstone Gallery, New York.

SLIPPAGE: FRED TOMASELLI

In Tony Oursler's trademark surreality, as in Mariko Mori's passion for the dislocated reality of artificial settings, technology takes us to a place where reality and fiction mingle. Fred Tomaselli's 1998 *Bug Blast* [fig. 15.36] is an eye-poppingly gorgeous hybrid of nature and artifice, op art, advertising, and the Los Angeles punk scene in which he came of age in the seventies and early eighties, blended as though in a simulated mind-altering drug high. Tomaselli grew up in Los Angeles, a mile from Disneyland, and remembers watching Tinkerbell fly off the Magic Mountain in Fantasy Land at night before he went to bed.[33] There was no affinity to art in his household; his aesthetic was fed on custom van painting, head shop designs, psychedelic posters, and theme parks.

15.36 Fred Tomaselli, *Bug Blast*, 1998. Photographs, collage, pills, leaves, insects, acrylic, and resin on panel, 5 × 5ft (1.52 × 1.52m). Private collection.

Nevertheless, the young Tomaselli took notice, like any rebellious adolescent, of how angry his mother would become reading in the newspaper about the outrageous body works of Chris Burden in the seventies, and this piqued his interest in contemporary art. The mother of a high school classmate took him to see several exhibitions in Los Angeles, among them the winter 1972–3 Bruce Nauman retrospective at the L.A. County Museum, which made him realize that "art" could be about anything! Until that point his idea of art had consisted of reproductions of "Salvador Dali and Michelangelo"; here, suddenly, Tomaselli saw a "wicked, bohemian, irrational, pathological" set of feelings and ideas in an art museum, and in his mind he compared the show to Disneyland.[34] He also encountered a James Turrell light projection (see Chapter 10) about this time in a Venice gallery while out skateboarding with some friends; he thought it was really stupid until he walked up to put his hand on the box in the corner and discovered to his astonishment that it wasn't there. Reference to the artificiality of theme parks, to these experiences that make you do a double-take (jumping from one perceptual frame of reference to another in the same object), and the sense that you could make art about anything you wanted persevere in Tomaselli's work.

Tomaselli went on to study painting in college near Los Angeles before, in 1985, moving to New York. His work of the late eighties consisted primarily of installations with a pointed artificiality: He made a piece in which he simulated waves by turning a fan on a plastic sheet and a field of Styrofoam cups, tethered to the floor with string so they would move in the patterns created by the air currents, and a work called *Cubic Sky* (1986–8) in which a light bulb inside a cube with holes in it projected stars around his studio. These works involve kinetic elements and lighting, referring back to the amusement parks in the way they immerse and absorb the viewer totally in the obviously artificial reality of a world that is both self-contained and completely dislocated from daily life.

That sense of dislocation has become increasingly prevalent at the start of the twenty-first century; manipulated media images have so thoroughly invaded our thoughts that it is often difficult to tell what is real. Tomaselli recounted the experience of taking a hike for the first time in the mountains with friends and coming across a beautiful waterfall; he couldn't believe it was real and went looking for the pipes and pumps—it was a shocking realization to find that reality was more dislocating conceptually for him than the artificial. The shift in our point of reference to the manmade world, rather than to nature, is increasingly common to people today, and as a painter Tomaselli deals with this perceptual slippage between reality and artifice in his work.

In 1997–8 Tomaselli made a series of collages that look, at first glance, just like the pages of a field guide to birds. But when you scrutinize them closely you see that the colorful patchwork on the birds is not made up of feathers, but of zippers, fabric, and stitching; he cut the forms from the

sportswear in Lands' End catalogs and reassembled them on pages from Perrin's *Illustrated Encyclopedia of Birds*. He titled the first of these collages *Land's End* and then began using the family names on the pages of the bird book as "readymade" titles, as in *Families Vireonidae* [fig. 15.37] of 1998. This destabilized form—which flips back and forth perceptually between the mental context of the snaps and pockets in the clothing and the representation of the birds—is a brilliant example of the unhinged language of postmodern form.

In *Bug Blast* the composition explodes out of the center, swirling in rings like a hypnotic mandala. Tomaselli made it out of actual pills, psychoactive plants, cutout pictures of butterflies, and an assortment of real bugs set in a deep plastic resin—a technique that recalls a kitsch hobbyist's "decoupage." The patterns and colors vibrate with optical intensity and at first seem to be painted. Then you come closer and realize they are real objects imbedded in the surface. The marijuana leaves and the pills can suddenly jump perceptually to become a star-filled night sky or a psychedelic pattern; this instability shifts the viewer back and forth from a romantic immersion in nature—as profound as the Hudson River School or the paintings of Casper David

15.37 Fred Tomaselli, *Families Vireonidae*, 1998.
Collage on paper, 11 × 8½in (28 × 21.6cm).
Private collection.

Friedrich—to a world of cultural simulacra (as in the cutout pictures of bugs).

Tomaselli continues to work with leaves, pills, and found images from print media imbedded in deep resin and overpainted with fine brushes. But in *Avian Flower Serpent* (2006) [fig. 15.38] and other more recent works the visual effects have become so rich that they take on a magical character. Whereas the conceptual dislocation in *Families Vireonidae* is epistemologically startling and conceptually provocative, the artist uses the same devices in *Avian Flower Serpent* for an effect that, instead of oscillating, seems to layer meaning. It is visually extraordinary and rewards close examination of the small collage fragments out of which he has built the larger forms; the falcon has a mystical presence with a depth of detail that is breathtaking, like a glimpse into the infinite space of a starry night.

ROXY PAINE'S TAXONOMY

The work of Roxy Paine also inspires a sense of awe in nature but it is the complexity of nature's systems and the epic struggle of the human mind to assimilate them that bring us to this point in Paine's work. "We desire and need to place things into nice, tight, little categories and classifications," he explained. "It's a comfortable thing, and it's a way we make sense of the madness all around us, and it also gets out of control."[35] So chaos ultimately engulfs us both in nature and in our efforts to make order out of nature.

Since the beginning of the 1990s Paine has explored the seemingly innate structures and logics of nature and the unstable certainties of the human mind, creating simulacra of nature parsed into highly elaborated systems and machines that perform what seem like human tasks. By the

15.38 Fred Tomaselli, *Avian Flower Serpent*, 2006. Leaves, photocollage, acrylic, gouache, and resin on wood panel, 7ft × 6ft ½in (2.13 × 1.84m). Courtesy of the artist and James Cohan Gallery, New York.

15.39 Roxy Paine, *Crop*, 1997–8. Epoxy, PVC, steel, wood, PETG, lacquer, oil paint, earth, 58 × 96 × 72in (147.3 × 243.8 × 182.8cm). Private collection. Courtesy Ronald Feldman Fine Art, New York.

age of twenty-five Paine was already widely respected among the community of artists working in the Williamsburg section of Brooklyn for a complex body of work that included, most famously, a group of remarkable machines, the movements of which crossed over into a disconcertingly human realm of gestures. In 1991 he and another artist organized an exhibition called "Tweeking the Human" in a tiny storefront gallery in this then-run-down artists' neighborhood. The title captures something of the unsettling poetry of these kinetic sculptures.[36]

In the mid-nineties Paine began studying psychotropic drugs and poisonous plants—extreme points of confrontation between the human mind and nature—making an astonishing group of artificial specimens and gardens, technically remarkable in their verisimilitude as well as in the unsettling ways in which they encroach on our psychic space. He cast them in polymer resin and meticulously painted them, one leaf at a time. *Poison Ivy Field (Toxicodendron Radicans)* of 1997—his perfectly rendered thicket of poison ivy, skunk cabbage, dandelions, beetles, scraggly grass, and a "Coney Island whitefish" (a discarded condom)—is set as though growing there on a fabricated patch of dirt in a table vitrine,

like something in a museum of natural history. For *Psilocybe Cubensis Field* of the same year he sited and glued each one of the 2,200 casts of psychedelic mushrooms in place right on the museum floor.

Crop, completed in 1998, is a 6-by-8-foot patch of waist-high opium poppies standing on a plot of artificial earth [fig. 15.39]. The plants seem at first to be disconnected from the machines. But the conceptually precise underlying logic of all the plant simulacra is aesthetically continuous with the machines in their engagement with systemic structures. In *Crop* we recognize Paine's predilection to classify in his systematic visual catalog of the various stages of the poppy's growth from young buds, to blooming flowers, to razor-slit seed pods oozing opium. The title makes clear that he intends to extend the work, as a metaphor, to the potential of the plants as narcotics, with all of the attendant social and economic systems around them. Paine has compared this

15.40 Roxy Paine, *SCUMAK (Auto Sculpture Maker)*, 1998. Stainless steel, polyethyline, extruder, cooling system, Teflon, and electronics, 13ft 7in × 6ft 10in × 4ft 8in (4.14 × 2.08 × 1.42m) overall.
Private collection. Courtesy Ronald Feldman Fine Art, New York.

overlay of opposing yet complementary impulses in his work—cataloging and metaphor—to Pieter Brueghel's allegory of *The Blind Leading the Blind* in which Brueghel visually catalogs the various causes of blindness known to the sixteenth century while simultaneously using his theme as a metaphor for human frailty.[37]

Paine's *SCUMAK (Auto Sculpture Maker)* of 1998 [fig. 15.40] is a remarkable machine that makes "expressively" modeled polyethylene sculptures according to directions from a computer. A laptop mounted on the wall next to a circuit box directs the extrusion of a molten polyethylene stream onto a conveyor belt for a precisely determined time, at a precisely determined rate. After a designated cooling time, the belt advances and the machine makes another sculpture. But these teasingly generic objects cannot actually be replicated even by this precise apparatus since the forces of chaos in nature continually act on the process. Two *SCUMAK* sculptures made according to precisely the same instructions will nevertheless turn out quite differently. This finely engineered and beautifully fabricated apparatus introduces an uneasy ambiguity between human and machine, laying bare the physical process of making the sculpture, as though

it were a mechanical act (which here it is—*sort of*). Yet the beauty of the machine and the eccentricity of the results are also a paean to the romantic. Paine positions both his gardens and his machines at a fluid interface between man, nature, and science; they take the viewer to an intuitive experience of the sometimes uncertain border of nature and invention at which scientists have arrived in the twenty-first century as they begin to redesign the human genome and connect living neurons with silicon chips.

In both *Crop* and *SCUMAK* Paine explores a concept he has gleaned from his avid interest in natural science. In *Crop* he has overlaid the life cycle of the plant from genesis to disintegration on the peculiar exploitation of it by humans, which in turn leads to individual and unexpected acts that ultimately coalesce into a system: the global drug culture. *Crop* hovers, like the new science of "complexity," on the boundary between the tendency toward disorder, dissolution, and decay (set out in the second law of thermodynamics) and the recognition that, simultaneously, systems that exhibit an inexorable tendency toward spontaneous self-organization exist at all levels of phenomena. The creative edge of new science today has shifted its focus from the Cartesian analysis of the fundamental units of matter—from molecules, atoms, nuclei, and quarks—to the observation that simple rules in physics, for example, can generate an interplay of forces which fundamentally and unpredictably differs from a simple sum of the parts.[38] Complexity is the science of how the individual pieces spontaneously fit together.

M. Mitchell Waldrop, in his book *Complexity: The Emerging Science at the Edge of Order and Chaos* (which Paine read), observes that after mapping and analyzing the components and mechanisms of the cell, science now is also asking how "several quadrillion such molecules organize themselves into an entity that moves, that responds, that reproduces, that is alive," or how individual acts of buying and selling by millions of individuals in different locations coalesce into an economy, or how "the genes in a developing embryo organize themselves in one way to make a liver cell and in another way to make a muscle cell."[39] In *Crop* Paine brings you to the genetic moment in this dynamically unfolding system of events. *SCUMAK* also has this suggestion of complexity with all of the independent sculptures which, in their resemblance to one another, begin to describe a spontaneous struggle between order and disorder on a different level. At the same time they contrast the immediacy of experience with the intensely depersonalizing commodification of an artist's work by the marketplace where it acquires a manufactured quality with a trademark style and is "normalized" by its reproduction and distribution.

For Paine, it is in art making (which he considers "inherently absurd") that the vestiges of our romantic selves survive in this increasingly standardized, "streamlined," and "efficient" corporate culture.[40] "What I love about these machines is that I establish the language, but I don't always know initially the complexities of that language and the nuances of using that language . . . to learn what that language can express takes time."[41]

At the end of the nineties Paine's work took a turn toward the abstract. He began to produce antiseptic panels of funghi on vertical Formica planes, even inventing some of the species (the "Abstracts"). *Amanita Muscaria* (1997–8) —a real species known for centuries as "the bloody mirror of the galaxy"—were legendarily eaten by the ancient Norsemen before their raids, transforming them into terrifying warriors; his rendering of them is flawless. In 1999 Paine embarked on a series of stainless steel trees and root systems. *Imposter* inaugurated the series of fourteen life-size trees, made over a period of eight years. Ranging up to 50 feet in height and set among live trees, these inventions bring together the artist's interest in the dynamic systems of nature with methods of industrial construction. Paine grinds and arc welds each branch; the sheer physical labor to make them is enormous. He made *Bluff* [fig. 15.41], the third full-scale tree, for the 2002 Whitney Biennial and set it in Central Park for the duration of the exhibition. At the recent end of this "dendritic" exploration is *Maelstrom*, a project for the roof of the Metropolitan Museum in New York which he said is "not quite a tree, it's a tree that is in the process of becoming abstract,"[42] a swirl of stainless steel roots or branches that seem to swirl out of control by some enigmatic force.

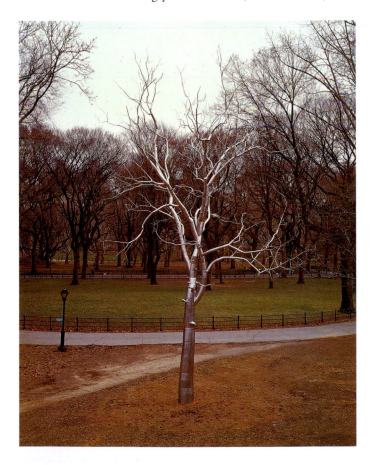

15.41 Roxy Paine, *Bluff*, 2002. Stainless steel, 50ft (15.25m) tall, installed as part of the Whitney Biennial in Central Park, New York, 2002.
Courtesy of the artist and James Cohan Gallery, New York.

CULTURAL IDENTITY

A new concern with local culture and cultural identities grew to prominence in the nineties—though it certainly had long antecedents in many places. This tendency arose simultaneously with (and with particular intensity in relation to) the increasingly global and image-based culture in which a connection to "nature" and the immediacy of individual experience and interaction tend to diminish in proportion to Internet and television use, and participation in disembodied conversations on cell phones. On plates in her 1991–2 "Sea Islands Series" Carrie Mae Weems inscribed across the top in bold type "Went Looking for Africa"; below she lettered a different experience on this psychic journey on each plate, as in: "and found it tightly woven in a woman's hair." This series involved her examination of the culture, language, and visual forms of the people of the Gullah Islands (derived from "Angola" = "golla" = "Gulla") off the coast of Georgia and South Carolina, thereby seeking her own cultural ancestry as an Afro-American.

In the "Kitchen Table Series" of 1990 Weems focused on the intimacy of events around the kitchen table as the locus of fundamental reflections on the private desires and circumstances of life. The sequence of photographs (accompanied by a text of reflections) tells the story of a black woman.

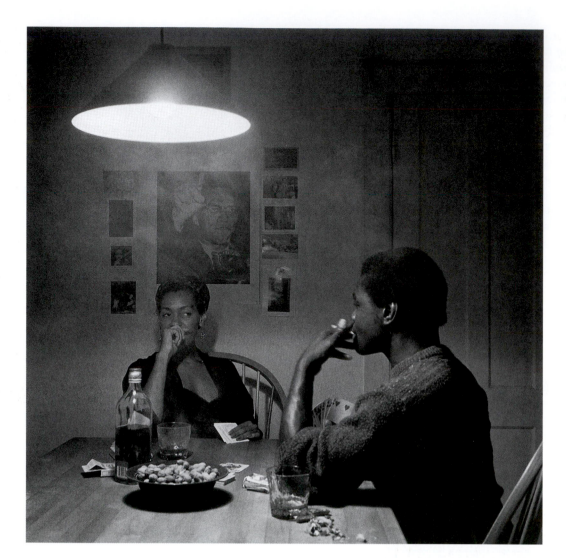

15.42 Carrie Mae Weems, *Untitled (Playing Cards)*, from the "Kitchen Table Series," 1990. Silver print, 28¼ × 28¼in (71.7 × 71.7cm). Courtesy P.P.O.W., New York.

In *Untitled* (*Playing Cards*) [fig. 15.42], for example, she sits at the table looking, analytically, at the man seated across from her. A photograph of Malcolm X, preaching with raised hand, is on the wall behind her, flanked by personal snapshots that reveal other parts of her sense of who she is—standards against which to measure this man. They are drinking and eating peanuts as they play a game of cards that stands in for the exploratory gambits of a human relationship.

In the last half of the twentieth century race was unavoidably central in America as a part of identity, and the exploration of racial stereotypes in the art of the nineties was more vigorous than ever before. But already by the beginning of the twenty-first century race in America began blending ambiguously and the election of an Afro-American President of the United States in 2008 was a dramatic expression of the erosion of this kind of perspective on difference. In some nineties works Weems, Robert Colescott, Lorna Simpson, and Kara Walker [fig. 15.43] all pushed racial stereotypes to extremes to deal openly with how they affect identity. "It took me quite some time," Kara Walker said, "before I realized . . . that the shadows (oh here we go) of the past, the deriding names and titles, in fiction and in fact, are continually informing, no, more like de-forming and re-forming who we think we are—who I think I am."[43] Walker's dramatic silhouettes, cut out in black paper and applied directly on the wall in large mural compositions, are her best-known works, although she is also a brilliant draftsman. In these large-scale wall pieces she depicts caricatured images of the treatment of slaves in the antebellum South. Some graphically (and shockingly) show white owners torturing and sodomizing slaves, particularly women. Other images caricature the slaves disparagingly as happy and simple-minded.

Kerry James Marshall

Kerry James Marshall's painting *Our Town* (1995) [fig. 15.44] also concerns cultural identity but Marshall approaches the subject by painting black people in all the ways that they have never been painted before. Here he depicts the American dream as a black American dream with nice houses in idyllic settings, kids playing, and the family dog running alongside. The mother, in an apron, waves from in front of the house and across the street is a grassy park with lush trees. The bluebirds with ribbons and the rays of the sunrise deliberately go too far; they seem as though they were lifted from a Disney cartoon and suggest the semiotic complexity of this work with symbolically laden references to different ways of painting from cartoon animation to abstract expressionism.

This work belongs to a series of paintings of garden housing projects beginning with *Nickerson Gardens* (the project into which Marshall's family moved in Los Angeles when he was nine). The perfection of the sanitized Walt Disney touch (in the cartoon-style lettering, the birds) is an ironic note, since these postwar garden utopias turned into

15.46 Kerry James Marshall, *Untitled (Pin-up)*, 2008. Acrylic on PVC panel, 6ft × 5ft (1.83 × 1.52m). Courtesy Jack Shainman Gallery, New York.

places of crime, hopelessness, and despair for most people. The collaged squares on top of the surface of this painting (set near the edges) remind us that this is a painting, a reality ordered by visual language. The references to abstract expressionist brushwork in the painterly white gestures and drips also cut to semiotics; indeed, the little girl's thoughts (in the bubble) are crossed out by these painterly gestures.

Marshall was born in Birmingham, Alabama in 1955 and lived there through the climax of the Civil Rights Movement in 1963 when Dr. Martin Luther King Jr. was arrested for demonstrating against segregated lunch counters and restrooms and wrote his famous "Letter from a Birmingham Jail." It was the Birmingham police chief, Eugene "Bull" Connor, who set police dogs and fire hoses against peaceful demonstrators that spring, and it was in Birmingham, after King negotiated a desegregation plan with city officials, that his hotel was bombed, followed by the bombing of the 16th Street Baptist Church, in which four children died. These events provided the impetus behind the next series of major paintings by Marshall, his "Souvenirs" [fig. 15.45], in which the artist eulogized great black artists, musicians, and writers as well as heroes of the Civil Rights Movement—especially King, John F. Kennedy, and Robert Kennedy. In the paintings in this series Marshall used glitter in the way that gold leaf was used in medieval religious paintings, but also in a tradition of high-affect decoration in Afro-American aesthetics, and he transformed the dignified black women in these stable middle-class interiors into angels with wings, tending the rituals of mourning for these deceased great figures and for the lost momentum of the movement itself.

One never sees black "pin-up" girls, the generally "white" stereotype of curvy girls in bathing suits that are the stuff of car repairshop calendars, so Marshall painted a series of them [fig. 15.46], and at the same time explored new ground formally by painting the figure in black on black. The result is quite startling: a powerful female nude with a large Afro hairstyle, head turned coquettishly. She straddles a giant Afro pik which is topped with a "Black Power" fist. The foreshortening of the right leg (derived from the syntax of comics) and the unstable tilt of the comb lend a dramatic dynamism to the composition. The delicate pink dots of nail polish on the toes echo the backdrop of glistening stars to convey a delicate eroticism set off against awesome power.

In 1999 Marshall embarked on a superhero comic strip for the Carnegie International exhibition in Pittsburgh. As a child he loved the comics and followed the adventures of Jack Kirby's "Fantastic Four" [fig. 15.47] but was disappointed to find no black superheroes. The hero of Marshall's comic is "RythmMastr" [fig. 15.48], a black superhero whose drumming brings to life African ancestral figures in a museum. They, in turn, have superpowers which are brought to bear on the perpetrators of crime in stories set against daily life in the ghetto. Just as Marshall's representation of black figures in his paintings is formally unprecedented in the rich depths of the black pigment itself, these comics break new formal ground as well. Marshall, one of greatest draftsmen of the turn of the century, makes a sophisticated appropriation of the language of action comics with dramatic foreshortening, narrative styles of lettering, the interplay of text and image within the frame, the strong graphic character of his line played off against the inking, the bold contrasts of line and tones, and the use of the framing to both contain and be transgressed in dialog with the imagery.

15.47 Jack Kirby, "Into The Jaws Of A.I.M," *A Captain America Story: Tales of Suspense*, 93 (Marvel Comics Group, September 1967), p. 5. Courtesy Jack Kirby Museum, Hoboken, NJ. © Marvel Entertainment Inc.

15.48 Kerry James Marshall, Page 1 of *RythmMastr*, 2006. Courtesy Jack Shainman Gallery, New York.

THE COMICS

Kerry James Marshall is hardly the first postwar artist to find inspiration in comics, but unlike predecessors such as Lichtenstein and Warhol who aestheticized them, Marshall disregarded the traditional hierarchies of "high art" and popular culture to see the formal genius of the comics masters like Jack Kirby. Kirby invented a dynamic style of storytelling with a set of formal devices to make every punch, every dive into space remarkably vivid. His figures and the expressively lettered words also play with the conventions of the frame, tumbling forward out of the picture or even across the page. The popularity of comic books alongside newspaper strips in America during World War II opened the space for the emergence of superheroes. Jerry Siegel and Joe Schuster created Superman in 1933 but it wasn't until 1938 that they persuaded Action Comics to publish his adventures. Their success led immediately to Batman and, in 1941, to Kirby's Fantastic Four.

Mad magazine (which commenced publication in 1953), and in particular the drawings of Harvey Kurtzman, spawned the emergence of a brilliant wave of underground comics in the sixties and also influenced such important painters as Peter Saul and, at the end of the decade, the Chicago Imagists Karl Wirsum and Jim Nutt. The irreverent text and drawings of *Mad* were in deliciously bad taste for the fifties and delighted the burgeoning counterculture. Saul's work in turn inspired S. Clay Wilson and R. Crumb [fig. 9.54] to found Zap Comix, a self-published vehicle for the beat generation's apotheosis of sex, drug culture, and neurotic anxiety, in San Francisco at the end of the sixties. They distributed the first issue walking through Haight-Ashbury, selling copies to hippies and stoners from a baby buggy.[44]

Art Spiegelman emerged from the underground comics scene in the early 1970s in New York and from the start made conceptually radical work. His comics functioned on many levels at the same time, both narratively and formally, and engaged with major art historical figures. As he wrote:

> Good comix are nourishing comix—unlike the Hostess Twinkies to be found in most children's comic books or in newspaper funny sections. The comix I like, and try to do, can be read slowly and often. Hopefully each reading serves up something new. I try to make every panel count and sometimes work as long as a month on a page. It's like concentrated orange juice. Although I'm still concerned with the narrative and comic aspects of comix I am also excited by the "secret language" of comix—the underlying formal elements that create the illusions.[45]

In Spiegelman's work it is the intellect and the structure of the language, rather than the expressivity of line, that distinguish it. *Maus: A Survivor's Tale*, published as a book in 1986, was perhaps less risky formally than some of Spiegelman's other work, but the power of the subject matter and the sustained depth of the narrative carried the genre of comics onto the same plane of reception as major painting

15.49 Art Spiegelman, *Maus: A Survivor's Tale and Here My Troubles Began*, vol. 2 (New York: Pantheon, 1991), p. 57.

for the first time. In this example [fig. 15.49] Spiegelman's formal control is nonetheless brilliantly nuanced: the five silhouetted figures marching off to the left in the background in the first frame beautifully balance the five prisoners marching right in the last frame; the cruel guard in the third frame looks down and across the frames to the agonized cries of Vladek in the penultimate frame (lower right). He balances the page as a whole using almost cinematic movement and expression, and yet instead of making one-of-a-kind gallery objects with this refined composition, Spiegelman wanted from the outset to make something intended for reproduction so it could be widely disseminated. *Maus* first began appearing in the second issue of *Raw* (a comics journal founded by Spiegelman and his wife Françoise Mouly) in 1980.

Maus is the story that Spiegelman's father, Vladek, tells the artist about surviving the Holocaust. It is also a glimpse into the cartoonist's own biography as he reflects on his creative struggles in drawing the story and on his relationship with his father. The radical idea of using the language of the comics for this searing tale gives this emotional narrative a gestural dimension that makes it all the more personal and powerful. A great master of visual form, Spiegelman used nuances of line and compositional structure to reinforce the layered threads of the narrative.[46] *Maus* won a Pulitzer Prize and crossed into the general book market with such success that it opened the door for a rich proliferation of graphic novels in the nineties.

Gary Panter's disjointed images and deliberately rough drawing style [fig. 12.39] in the mid-1970s in the Los Angeles punk-rock magazine *Slash* and in his *Jimbo* comic books pioneered a postmodern comic practice. Chris Ware's early-twenty-first-century comics [fig. 15.50] took this to the next step with a linguistically analytical and self-aware style in the standalone volumes of *The Acme Novelty Library*, notably *Jimmy Corrigan, The Smartest Kid on Earth* (2000).

"*Gasoline Alley* [by Frank King] changed a lot of my thinking about comics," Ware wrote. "It made me realize that the mood of a comic strip did not need to come from the drawing or the words. You got the mood not from looking at the strip, or by reading the words, but from the act of reading it. The emotion came from the way the story itself was structured."[47] Jimmy is Chris Ware, reading comics, losing himself in different layers of meaning within his own invented spaces. The leaps in time and logic, the random discontinuities, speak to the way in which everyone experiences life today.

GLOBAL CULTURE AND LOCAL MEANING

Chinua Achebe's 1958 novel *Things Fall Apart* precedes the nineties by over thirty years, but it provides a microcosm of what would happen in the arbitrary overlays of culture that had become commonplace at the turn of the century; the rules that the novel's protagonist, Okonkwo, thought he knew about how to live his life before British laws entered the life of his village suddenly no longer worked, and then "things fell apart." By the nineties the constantly shifting ground of postmodern culture had become so inherently difficult to grasp, except in local fragments, that events seemed to veer off unpredictably. Anticipating the future became increasingly difficult, history was constantly under revision, definitions of the things right in front of us seemed to be changing as we looked at them, the border between culture and nature blurred, and the stability of personal identity came under unprecedented pressure to accommodate perpetually evolving external demands. The explosion of information available on the Internet, the growth in international travel and communication introduced so many cross-tracking perspectives into our consciousness at any one time that conventions of all kinds were being thrown into flux.

The free flow of ideas across national borders after 1990 also complicated the prevailing dominance of West European and American cultures. Every five years the Documenta exhibition in Kassel, Germany (with a different curator each time) offers a critical lens through which to see culture at that moment. In 2002 Okwui Enwezor created Documenta XI around a series of discussion groups that took place across the globe and published them in volumes called "platforms." This groundbreaking "postcolonial" Documenta (as it came to be known) reset the assumptions of the art world by underscoring the radically plural, international culture which does not *a priori* privilege one culture over another. It also acknowledges the impossibility of encompassing the exponentially enlarged field of good artists and ideas that were cropping up from all directions after 1990.

For some artists, framing the context became their work. In the eighties Louise Lawler had already begun doing this by making stunningly beautiful photographs that focus the viewer on the institutional settings for works of art. Hers is a conceptual practice, looking at the appropriation of art (in particular, that by canonical artists) into corporate lobbies, major private collections, and museum galleries, as in her 1984 *Pollock and Tureen, Arranged by Mr. and Mrs. Burton Tremaine, Connecticut* [fig. 15.51]. Like the appropriationist photography of Sherrie Levine [fig. 12.38], she also uses photography to explore the meaning of our assumptions about originality and the way we normalize radical creativity.

15.50 Chris Ware, drawing for *Jimmy Corrigan, The Smartest Kid on Earth*, 1994–9. Pen and ink with brush, colored pencil, and opaque white, 23¼ × 15in (59.1 × 38.1cm).

Collection of the artist, courtesy John Carlin.

15.51 Louise Lawler, *Pollock and Tureen, Arranged by Mr. and Mrs. Burton Tremaine, Connecticut*, 1984. Cibachrome, 16 × 20in (40.6 × 50.8cm). Edition of five.

Courtesy of the artist and Metro Pictures.

15.52 Fred Wilson, *Metal Work, 1793–1880*, from *Mining the Museum*, 1992–3. Temporary installation, The Contemporary and Maryland Historical Society, Baltimore, April 4, 1992– February 28, 1993.

Courtesy PaceWildenstein Gallery, New York.

Fred Wilson literally appropriates objects and recontextualizes them, bringing to light alternative perspectives. In his 1992–3 *Mining the Museum* [fig. 15.52] he placed artifacts of the antebellum South in unexpected settings in the Maryland Historical Society. Setting shackles that were put on slaves in a display case next to the fine American silver of the period connects the one to the other and fundamentally complicates the meanings of both. This method of working is founded on a resurgence of conceptual-art practices in the nineties, altered for a postmodern world with a more social orientation.

The work of the Parisian-born Moroccan photographer Yto Barrada is contextual in another way. Her photographs capture the troubled youth of Tangier, her hometown, and the state of transience in this city to which Africans come hoping to cross into Europe. She explores this sadness and longing in her book of photographs *A Life Full of Holes: The Strait Project*.[48] One particularly poignant group of photographs is of details of the sides of buses; these seem at first like abstract designs until you realize you're looking at the painted panels of the bus bodies [fig. 15.53] and find out that young boys, longing to slip into Spain across the Strait of Gibraltar, sometimes die trying to stow away in the wheel wells of these Europe-bound tourist buses. This gives the seemingly abstract patterns an altogether different kind of meaning. Another image, *The Red Dress* [fig. 15.54], shows a girl playing jacks on a ledge; it represents the other side of things, the simple pleasures of life in Tangier. Her more recent *Iris Tingitana* project follows the interface where the botanical landscape meets the city, where flowers revolt against the encroaching urbanization. Like the bus pictures, the meanings are implicit, concerning borders and politics, and require a grasp of the social context.

Barada's projects highlight the remarkable interface between the local and the global, mirrored in her own transience; working in Paris, Morocco, New York, and Mexico, she instantiates an increasingly common transnationalism. As the Documenta and the Venice Biennale exhibitions began attracting rapidly escalating crowds (and dollars) in the nineties, international biennials began sprouting up in more and more places—Istanbul, Cairo, São Paulo, Johannesburg,

15.53 (above) **Yto Barrada**, *Figure 4 Autocar Series (Bus logos)*, Tangier, 2004. C-type, edition of five, 23⅔ × 23⅔in (60 × 60cm). Courtesy of the artist and Galerie Polaris, Paris.

15.54 (left) **Yto Barrada**, *The Red Dress*, 2004. C-type, edition of five, 23⅔ × 23⅔in (60 × 60cm). Courtesy of the artist and Galerie Polaris, Paris.

Cuenca, and Guanzhou, to mention only a few. International contemporary art fairs also proliferated in the nineties. Increasingly, important art dealers and collectors from around the world traveled to these expositions along with artists, who began reflecting the growing hybridity of global culture in general and at the same time its opposite—ever more emphasis on cultural specificity.

The Japanese artist Mariko Mori, who works in New York, explained that

> when you're in a place that everyone is different, then it's normal to be different … Since I came to New York I became aware that I am Japanese. I never thought about it, of course, when I'm in Japan … When I'm in Japan, it's normal to be Japanese … But while I'm in New York … I can be myself … If I make a circle … in Japan, it would have a meaning. So maybe they think she must be influenced by Zen calligraphy; it always has meaning … When I make a circle in New York, it's my circle.[49]

15.56 Ravinder G. Reddy, *Girija*, 2000. Painted and gilded polyester resin fiberglass.
The David and Alfred Smart Museum of Art, the University of Chicago. Gift of Susan and Lew Manilow, 2003.87.

15.55 Shahzia Sikander, *SpiNN 1* and *SpiNN 2*, details from *Digital Animation SpiNN*, 2003.
Courtesy of the artist and Gallery Sikkema Jenkins & Co., New York.

The freedom with which artists redefined styles and forms and categories of practice in the nineties, disregarding the meanings conventionally connected to them, led to surprising inventions. Shahzia Sikander went to art school in Lahore, Pakistan and became interested in the discredited genre of miniature painting after a curator from the Victoria and Albert Museum in London came to talk about historical Indian miniatures in her school. Sikander enrolled in a miniature painting program and mastered the techniques, subsequently transforming this ancient practice into an innovative language of postmodern mutability. The *gopis* (the traditional harem of the Hindu god Krishna) take over the patriarchal space; Sikander simplifies them into black dots multiplying dramatically into abstract patterns. In some, their bodies disappear, except for their hair, which floats off like a flock of birds [fig. 15.55]. She has also transgressed the style, developing from her mastery of miniature painting by using computer animation—still preserving all the beauty of the delicate miniaturist's touch and richness, or rather redefining it, as she explained:

> I was interested in violating the preciousness of the miniature as an equivalent to what might be considered an anti-heroic gesture. At the same time I was interested in process, labor, time, traditional skills, virtuosity of technique and formalism. Despite my investment in understanding and studying miniature painting, I was equally irreverent towards its traditions, mixing them in many unorthodox ways. If we were to equate "beauty" with "authenticity", then a subversive attitude, one that is open to contamination, would most accurately define my relationship to it.[50]

One of the striking features of the art world since 1990 has been its growing diversity. Interesting artists began emerging on the global scene from everywhere, from India [fig. 15.56] to Korea to Indonesia to Mexico, across Africa and South America. Islamic cultures have also produced a number of great artists in the last two decades. Mona Hatoum—a London-based Palestinian—is one of them. Her 1994 *Corps étranger* [fig. 15.57] addresses the political and psychological complexities of "foreign" identity. In this work she explores the exterior of her body with an endoscopic camera that magnifies the skin and hairs on video. When the camera encounters an orifice it dives directly inside her. The invasive camera also alludes to a surveillance camera that violates her bodily integrity (penetrating it) and

metaphorically the integrity of her identity. Her works engage bodily experience in a self-actualizing exploration. At the same time some critics and historians have framed her work (and in effect reified her identity) as one of the "authentic public voices of the Third World,"[51] at the expense of her individuality.

Ghada Amer, an Egyptian-born artist, raised and educated in France and working in New York, deliberately critiques fundamentalist Islamic practices in her erotic depictions of female sexuality. In *And the Beast* of 2004 [fig. 15.58] Amer used embroidery along with the more conventional techniques to "draw" multiple layers of sexual images on the canvas, including a particularly visible representation of a woman performing oral sex on another woman. The textural quality of the hair-like strings brings home the physicality of the work, making the image literally palpable. The images, taken from pornography, simultaneously attack the dogmas of both Islamic fundamentalism and radical feminism, provocatively suggesting their common ground and asserting the right of women to enjoy sexual pleasures. In *Encyclopedia of Pleasure* of 2001 she underscores the

15.57 Mona Hatoum, *Corps étranger* (details), 1994. Video installation with cylindrical wooden structure, video projector, video player, amplifier and four speakers, 11ft 5¾in × 9ft 10⅛in × 9ft 10⅛in (3.5 × 3 × 3m).
Musée National d'Art Moderne–Centre Georges Pompidou, Paris. Courtesy White Cube.

ancient tradition of celebrating sexuality in Islamic culture by referring back to a late-eleventh- or early-twelfth-century book entitled *Encyclopedia of Pleasure* by Ali Ibn Nasr al-Katib. The book, which catalogs sexual pleasures, is forbidden in the Arab world.

In Africa the art of the late twentieth century seemed to center on other issues, such as the relation of indigenous tendencies to colonial influences, racial identity, and social justice. When abstract expressionism came to South Africa in the 1980s it was seen as relevant because it was understood as a modernism that was race-blind. "Huit Facettes," an artists' group founded in 1996 in the lively art center of Dakar, Senegal, and "Le Groupe Amos," established in Kinshasa, Zaire in 1989, both grew out of sociopolitical concerns. Le Groupe Amos formed specifically in protest against the corrupt dictatorship of Mobutu Sese Seko, president of Zaire (which became the Democratic Republic of the Congo after his overthrow in 1997).

The London-born Nigerian artist Yinka Shonibare, MBE gave questions of colonial influence and African identity a provocative twist with his mannequins dressed in the brightly colored fabrics that are synonymous in people's minds with "African" dress. But the fabrics were actually invented in Indonesia by Dutch colonialists in the early twentieth century, manufactured in England and the Netherlands using the Dutch-Indonesian batik technique, and then sold by the British in Africa, where they became so popular that people worldwide now think of them as singularly African. "The fabrics are not really *authentically* African the way people think," Shonibare explained. "They prove to have a crossbred cultural background quite of their own. . . . And it's the fallacy of that signification that I like. It's the way I view culture—it's an artificial construct."[52]

Shonibare grew up in Lagos, Nigeria from the age of three. His father was a well-to-do lawyer who sent his son to an exclusive English boarding school. Barely into art school at the age of nineteen, he contracted a rare virus that left him permanently disabled. The artist is best known for his headless figures in Enlightenment and Victorian dress, made from these "African" fabrics. Many of the installations replicate famous paintings. He also borrows from literature for his subjects, and from Enlightenment thought. He took the pose for the headless skater in *Reverend on Ice* (2005) [fig. 15.59] from Sir Henry Raeburn's famous 1784 painting of *The Reverend Robert Walker Skating on Duddingston Loch*. He had his costumers make the eighteenth-century frock from Dutch batik, "African" fabric (probably made in England).

CHINA

Art in China since World War II was of little interest until the 1980s. The Cultural Revolution (1966–76), which began with Chairman Mao's reassertion of power in a severe campaign from 1966 to 1968, involved a wholesale attack on traditional culture. The "Four Olds: Old Custom, Old Culture, Old Habits, and Old Ideas" were strictly proscribed, so temples, books, even old family photo albums were destroyed by people fearful of reprisals from roving bands of the brutal, largely teenaged "Red Guard." In the 1942 Yan'an forum for artists and writers, Mao had already decreed that artistic creation should serve only peasants, workers, and soldiers and that oil painting was unnecessary. In the Cultural Revolution, individuality was further suppressed while history and memory were undermined by constantly changing official narratives.

Possibly the most traumatic aspect of the Cultural Revolution was the disruption of the family. Because of the disastrous condition of the economy, the cities could not sustain their populations, so Mao devised the idea of forcibly taking school-age children from their parents in the cities and "sending them down" to the countryside for "reeducation." They were harshly treated by the already impoverished peasants, who didn't want them; many were forced to live in caves and barns because there was no available housing. Everyone in China suffered the effects of the Cultural Revolution and just one month after the death of Mao in 1976 the Cultural Revolution was overthrown. A period of reflection and recovery followed. The youth went back to the cities but there were no jobs for them, so many returned to the parents they had denounced to the Communist Party.

For a decade, universities and art schools had been closed and intellectual endeavors were treated as treasonous.

When the schools reopened in the fall of 1976 there was a ten-year backlog of applicants and the competition was extraordinary. The artists who were accepted and graduated in those first classes at the end of the seventies were both remarkably talented and driven. This outstanding crop of new painters, photographers, installation, and performance artists included Xu Bing, Ai Weiwei, Cai Guo-Qiang, Zhang Xiaogang, Hai Bo, Yue Minjun, and Fang Lijun—all between thirteen and twenty-one years old at the end of the Cultural Revolution. Immediately behind them in age was another wave of remarkable artists including Zhang Huan, Wang Qingsong, Huang Yan, Yang Zhenzhong, Ma Liuming, Cui Xiuwen, and Yang Fudong—in their thirties by the turn of the century. These artists began to have an enormous impact on the global art world in the nineties.

Although China continued to be tightly controlled by the state, things did gradually begin to loosen up. Deng

15.60 Xu Bing, *Practicing Square Word Calligraphy*: top: *An Introduction to Square Word Calligraphy, Square Word Calligraphy*; bottom: *Red Line Tracing Book*, both "standard edition," 1996. 15⅓ × 9¼in (39 × 23.5cm) (closed).
Courtesy the artist.

Xiaoping outmaneuvred the notorious "Gang of Four" to take control, and in 1978 began a series of economic and political reforms aimed at promoting a market economy and some degree of political liberalization. The famous confrontation between the government and protestors (students and others) in 1989 in Tiananmen Square was the culmination of several years of demands for "rapid reform." Despite strong military suppression, things nevertheless moved toward freer expression almost immediately afterwards.

During the Cultural Revolution there were few books to read except the *Little Red Book* of aphorisms by Chairman Mao. Xu Bing was a "sent-down youth" and his lack of faith in this *Little Red Book* led to his broad attack on explicit meaning *per se* in writing. Xu Bing returned from the countryside in 1977 to study printmaking at the Central Academy of Fine Art in Beijing. He emigrated to New York in 1990, began a successful career in the West, and then in 2008 returned to China as Vice-President of the Central Academy.

Xu Bing's conceptual art practice has centered on his play with language. His childhood love of books played a role, but the introduction of *pinyin*, a simplified, Romanized, and phonetic form of Chinese in 1958, when he was three, instilled in him a sense of the instability of language. This feeling encouraged the aesthetic distance for him to create his *Practicing Square Word Calligraphy* [fig. 15.60], which both parodies and emulates all the highly ritualized practices of traditional Chinese calligraphy—training the apprentice to prepare the ink from an ink stick and stone in water, teaching him or her to hold the brush correctly with the correct posture, and rendering the brushstrokes properly.

"Square Word Calligraphy" looks like Chinese, but Xu Bing actually invented characters in a square, Chinese-looking format to render English words into blocks. He also produced a book of instructions and a practice book where the apprentice fills in the red outlined characters to learn how to write this new script. A Chinese viewer might expect to be able to read the words but cannot, whereas an English reader may puzzle over the blocks and then, perhaps while copying them, suddenly recognize the stylized English letters. The text in this illustration is "Little Bo Peep . . .", so the visual effect and the process of attempting to understand are complex whereas the overt meaning is finally banal, leaving us to wonder what kind of meaningful communication is possible with words anyway.

For Cai Guo-Qiang, who emigrated in 1995 to New York after a decade in Japan, it was important to integrate his Chinese cultural identity into the new crosscultural context of the contemporary art world. He often works with explosives in the landscape [fig. 15.61], modulating the shape and speed of the explosions in relation to the history, geography, and social conditions of the site; the scale, he ambitiously imagines, is such that any life form in the cosmos should be able to see it from space. Cai evokes the cosmic law of balance—*Yin* and *Yang* (creation and destruction)—in the momentary eternity of the explosion and uses principles derived from acupuncture and the ancient Chinese art of *feng shui* to reorient the energy of the elements in a place—their *Qi*, the life force—into better harmony with the totality of nature. His recurring use of fireworks and gunpowder introduces an uncontrollable element that contrasts with the suppression of individual expression in China. In 1999, he brought a team of craftsmen to the Venice Biennale to recreate a famous work of socialist realist propaganda sculpture, *The Rent Collection Courtyard* of 1965. This project forces to the surface issues of originality and ownership in art—in Mao's China collective practices and public ownership prevailed, but the creators of the original *Rent Collection Courtyard* protested Cai Guo-Qiang's work in Venice.

Zhang Xiaogang, one of the great painters to emerge in China in the nineties, sees 1992 as a turning point when China began opening up again. In *Red Baby* of 1993 [fig. 15.62] Zhang Xiaogang struggles to make sense of things, to deal with the traumas of the Cultural Revolution and of his own troubled family history. "For me," he explained, "the Cultural

15.61 Cai Guo-Qiang,
The Century with Mushroom Clouds—Projects for the 20th Century, 1996. Event at Nevada Nuclear Test Site.
Photograph by Hiro Ihara, courtesy of the artist.

15.62 Zhang Xiaogang, *Red Baby*, 1993. Oil on canvas,
4ft 9in × 5ft 1in (1.45 × 1.55m).
Courtesy of the artist.

Revolution is a psychological state, not a historical fact. It has a very strict connection with my childhood, and I think there are many things linking the psychology of the Chinese people today with the psychology of the Chinese people back then."[53]

The shocking color of *Red Baby* jumps out of its gray and black background. "On the television set you can see my mother's photo, a familiar image of Tiananmen, and also a throbbing heart. This box represents my past."[54] The baby is exposed and isolated on top of a crate full of memories. A patch of light hits his chest and a fine red blood vessel connects him, by the navel, to all the items in the picture. The baby has no mother to contain it and the images around it include an expression of rage (the knife), a nostalgic picture of his mother as a youth (distanced through the television representation), his heart, Tiananmen Square (the symbol of China), a pointing hand, and a book.

Zhang Xiaogang was born in Kunming, in the south of China, in 1958. He had an emotionally disturbed mother and at fourteen he lost both his parents when they were jailed for three years for their political beliefs, leaving the children to fend for themselves. In 1977, after his "reeducation" in rural Yunnan, Zhang Xiaogang entered the surrealist-influenced Sichuan Academy of Fine Arts and in 1986, four years after finishing, he joined the faculty. The growing availability of books from the West in the eighties nurtured his interest in Western existentialism and Freudian psychology and these interests fit in better in less doctrinaire Sichuan than in Beijing, where he moved in 1999.

For many, the 1989 "China/Avant Garde" exhibition in the National Museum in Beijing was the debut of contemporary art in China. Zhang Xiaogang participated in it with 186 other artists. Shortly thereafter he began exhibiting internationally, although his work was officially banned from shows in China until 1997, when he finally had a one-person show at the Central Academy of Fine Arts in Beijing. Still reacting to the events of Tiananmen Square, the 1993 *Red Baby* began Zhang Xiaogang's "Bloodline" series with the fine red vein that travels through all of his "Big Family" paintings [fig. 15.63]. The "Big Family"/"Bloodline" paintings were

15.63 Zhang Xiaogang,
Bloodline, 2004–5.
Courtesy of the artist.

inspired by his rediscovery of an album of family pictures, particularly photos of his mother as a young, attractive woman. "From the most private family photos you can actually view the effects of time and society on private life. . . . Every single one of us was living in a big family. Our relationships are a kind of mutual reliance and yet full of struggles." So he began to erase the individual traits as he painted these families staring blankly out of the picture. Yet somehow the turbulence and suppressed emotion below the surface seeps out.

In 2000, "while I was painting the *Big Family*," he said, "my own little small family had to split up. Therefore there was a big change in my life. I was unstable." At the same time he felt that the changes in China were

skidding faster and faster. If you hadn't been to a city for one month, the next time you went there you couldn't find a familiar street. The same thing with your personal life, if you didn't pay attention your life would have unexpected changes. That's why I felt that in this rapidly changing society the relationship between personal memories and the society had a very peculiar kind of relationship. On the one hand you must remember the things that are of value to you; on the other hand you really have to learn how to forget some of the things in your life. I felt that we were really living in a struggle between remembering and forgetfulness.

In 2004, he began a new series entitled "Amnesia and Memory" [fig. 15.64].

15.64 (left) **Zhang Xiaogang**, *Amnesia and Memory*, 2006. Oil on canvas, 6ft 6¾in × 8ft 6⅓in (2.00 × 2.60m). Courtesy of the artist.

15.65 (below) **Hai Bo**, *Bridge*, 1999. Two photographs, 24¼ × 35½in (61.6 × 90.2cm) each. Courtesy of the artist and Max Protetch Gallery, New York.

15.66 Fang Lijun, 1992, *Series 2, Number 2*.

Museum Ludwig, Cologne. Courtesy Arario Gallery, New York.

Memory is also at the heart of the photography of Hai Bo. As with Zhang Xiaogang, old photographs provided a fulcrum for his creative explorations in a series of works comparing past and present. The "comparison was meant not to reveal a change but to close the gap caused by change," the critic Leng Lin has written.[55] *I Am Chairman Mao's Red Guard* of 2000 is a diptych with an old photo of a pretty young woman dressed in the uniform of the Red Guard on the left and on the right a photograph of the same person taken perhaps thirty years later in her workaday flower print shift. Hai Bo had been attracted to the woman when they were young; when he went to find her many years later, it was as an exploration of the feelings aroused by confronting deep nostalgia for the past with the reality of the changes wrought by time.

The beginning of this series—the work that made Hai Bo so well known after it was shown at the Venice Biennale in 2001—is *Bridge* of 1999 [fig. 15.65]. The old photograph shows Hai Bo's mother, younger sister, and brother on a bridge over a lake in a park. They were a poor family and this was a rare leisure excursion made together to a beautiful park. Two months after the picture was taken, Hai Bo's brother fell off that same bridge and drowned. Hai Bo spent the next sixteen years trying to represent the trauma of this experience for himself. Finally, now living in Beijing, he returned to the park on a trip home and found that it had profoundly

changed. Once a barren park, it was now surrounded by modern buildings. He decided to photograph himself in precisely the spot and in the same posture as his brother had been in the old family photograph. "My hands are holding the same spot that my brother held," he later explained, "and I felt that I was holding his hands once again."[56]

Fang Lijun was the leading figure in a group of painters in the nineties dubbed by the art critic Li Xianting the "Cynical Realists." The bald-headed figure in a work like Fang Lijun's 1992 *Series 2, Number 2* [fig. 15.66] became a familiar protagonist in his work. It first appeared in 1988, while Fang Lijun was a graduate student in printmaking at the Beijing Academy. There was a spirit of optimism in the 1980s about the liberalization of China and the increasing freedom of expression that accompanied Deng Xiaoping's moves toward a Western-style market economy. In the aftermath of the events of 1989—not only the crushing of demonstrations in Tiananmen Square but the closure earlier that year of the "China/Avant Garde" exhibition which had been seen as announcing the rebirth of Chinese art—the disillusionment was palpable in the ironic imagery of these Cynical Realist painters.

The central figure in *Series 2, Number 2* could be yawning in boredom or shouting; the oafish, menacing figures in the background become a parade of the mindless, manipulated masses. In many of Fang Lijun's paintings endless populations

15.67 Fang Lijun, *Untitled (Red Head)*, 1997. Oil on linen, 5ft 4in × 4ft 3in (1.63 × 1.30m).
Courtesy Arario Gallery, New York.

of identical heads fill large sections of the canvas. The artist came from Handan (in southern Hebei), a provincial city in East Central China. His father worked as a low-level administrator for the Ministry of Railways until the Cultural Revolution, when he has demoted to labor on the trains. Fang Lijun watched his grandfather publicly humiliated in one of the regular denunciations of "counterrevolutionaries" and had his house ransacked by Red Guards. After the Revolution Fang Lijun studied ceramics and woodcuts at Hebei Light Industry College and began developing his ideas about art. After a brief stint in an advertising agency, he entered the Central Academy of Fine Arts in Beijing.

In the early nineties he occupied a prominent place in the artists' quarter around Yuanmingyuan (the old Summer Palace) but, in search of greater isolation to work, he left the very social Yuanmingyuan Artists' Village (later, in 1995, the police purged the neighborhood of its artists).

Fang Lijun's paintings explore the peculiar conditions of a world overrun with masses of people in which a sense of self is hard to articulate and social momentum is hard to steer. The cynical humor of his work speaks at the same time of a sincere idealism and genuine political commitment. Fang Lijun's *Untitled (Red Head)* of 1997 [fig. 15.67] resides in part in this conflict between the individual and mass culture. The repeated images of the same girl in the altered photographs of Cui Xiuwen [fig. 15.68] also connect to this tension, but it is the deeply personal nature of her subject matter, the powerful emotional expression of the wounded child that overpowers everything both as an exploration of the artist's own psyche and as a broad metaphor for the wounds of the Cultural Revolution. The same visceral emotionalism and social critique are evident in the work of the powerful group of performance artists that emerged in China in the nineties. In his 1997 performance piece *To Raise the Water Level in a Fish Pond* [fig. 15.69] Zhang Huan invited people who had lost their jobs in a recent ruthless modernization of Chinese industry to stand in a pond, raising the level of the water—a poetic assertion of their social presence. In *To Add One Meter to an Anonymous Mountain* of 1995 the piling of nude bodies one on top of another on a mountaintop has both ironic distance and a strong sense of human presence.

Free and At Leisure – 4 [fig. 15.70], a 2004 painting by Yue Minjun, sums up a number of the dilemmas of contemporary Chinese art. From the time the Soviet artists came to teach in China in the 1950s until the 1990s, all Chinese artists learned the soviet realist style in which this work is executed. Yet the eccentric and personal character of the subject matter with a signatory grinning self portrait belies that anonymous practice. Yue Minjun shows himself in quintuplicate, indecorously clad in the white socks and briefs made in China for export to the West. But for all its irony and individuality, the artist sets the picture in a Chinese landscape with reeds and water—the most canonical of

15.68 Cui Xiuwen, *Angel No. 2*, 2004. Chromogenic print.
Courtesy the artist.

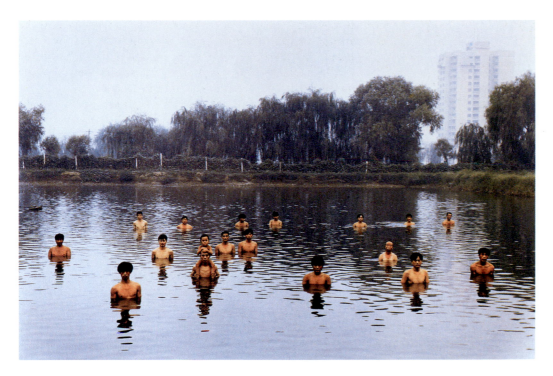

15.69 Zhang Huan, *To Raise the Water Level in a Fish Pond*, August 15, 1997. Performance documentation (middle-distance detail), Nanmofang Fishpond, Beijing. C-print on Fuji archival, 5ft × 6ft 6in (1.52 × 2.28m).
Courtesy Max Protetch Gallery. Photograph by Robyn Beck.

15.70 Yue Minjun, *Free and At Leisure – 4*, 2004. Oil on canvas, 13ft 1½in × 9ft 2⅛in (4 × 2.8m).

subjects for traditional Chinese painting—and poses himself in the positions of the classical Taoist symbol of the crane, who flies the immortals away from this world. (The Chinese title of the painting translates as "*Wandering Clouds, Wild Crane*.") Poignantly caught between past and future, between the "remembering and forgetfulness" to which Zhang Xiaogang points us, between the depersonalizing mass culture and the deeply individual realm of personal emotion, this painting by Yue Minjun raises so many of the crosscurrents of contemporary Chinese art.

16.1 Takashi Murakami, *Tan Tan Bo Puking—a.k.a. Gero Tan*, 2002.
Acrylic on canvas mounted on board, four panels, 11ft 9¾in × 17ft 8⅜in × 21ft 11¾in
(3.60 × 5.40 × 6.70m) overall.

Collection of Amalia Dayan and Adam Lindemann, courtesy of Galerie Emmanuel Perrotin, Paris and Miami.

16 COMPROMISED BOUNDERIES

This final chapter focuses on a single, but fundamental issue that seems at present to be the defining, emerging cultural issue of the last decade and may prove to be the central issue in coming decades: compromised boundaries. History is always being rewritten by the needs of the present. But in the twenty-first century, memory and history have become increasingly important points of cultural and personal reinvention as the stable boundaries between truth and fiction, past and present, nature and culture further erode. "Believability" has increasingly come to replace verifiable truth in the minds of many, a condition exacerbated by the Internet, television, and the digital manipulation of images. The television comedian Stephen Colbert introduced the term "truthiness" in 2005 to describe the practice of the Bush administration, for example, to make repeated assertions about events that defied logic and hard evidence but that nevertheless appealed to the public's "feelings" about what was true. Contemporary China has experienced a particularly pronounced dissonance between the official and the remembered past (with far-reaching effects on social and psychological conditions), but the issue has global resonance and this may be one of the reasons for the remarkable prominence of Chinese painting in the first decade of the twenty-first century. A mutability of boundaries which applies to many aspects of contemporary culture, including the boundaries that define personality as external standards play a greater and greater role in defining how we see ourselves. This instability has also undermined the definition of art as a protected realm in which we can explore the moral and psychological dilemmas that most disturb us, and nowhere is the integrity of the definition of art more challenged than at the interface with money.

ECONOMIES

Andy Warhol was the first artist to explore the market as an art form. Extending the territory opened by Warhol, British "bad boy" Damien Hirst pavé-set a platinum cast of a human skull (the teeth are real) with 8,601 diamonds in 2007 (entitling it *For the Love of God*) and sold it for the breathtaking price of $100 million; he was deliberately striving to make it the most expensive work of art ever made. His London dealer quotes the art historian Rudi Fuchs opining that the skull "proclaims victory over decay. At the same time, it represents death as something infinitely more relentless. Compared to the tearful sadness of a vanitas scene, the diamond skull is glory itself."[1] Nonsense! The meaning of this work has mostly to do with the price, which was, as suggested by the artist's title for the exhibition in which it was first shown, "Beyond Belief."

If we want to contextualize Hirst's work in art history and theology it is because that helps us to normalize the obvious meaning, which is too distasteful to admit to ourselves. The art market has come together with the hedge-fund billionaires, hijacking art into the entertainment industry and the world of luxury goods. The contemporary rooms of museums of modern art have begun looking like the pages of an auction catalog or the showcase for multinational corporate collections of expensive consumer trophies, rather than discursive spaces in which to explore meaningful issues and think deeply about our cultural past and present. The fact that an object such as Hirst's skull exists and that it could be sold at that price (even if there were complicated financial manipulations behind the scenes) forced the art public to think about the egregious surfeit of wealth among some individuals while others have so little. How is it that some people are homeless and starving in Europe and America, while others can afford to buy a $100 million *bibelot*? In this sense, the skull extends the disturbing line of inquiry about cruelty and excess that Hirst began in his sliced-up animals in formaldehyde tanks and in his preoccupation with drugs and macabre medical imagery.

"©Murakami": Branding the Self

Andy Warhol's remark "Well, I thought department stores were the new museums"[2] anticipates the growing tendency to define oneself in the act of shopping, to find our identity in what we own rather than built on an inner core of character and values. The Japanese artist Takashi Murakami has taken up the issue in a parallel but different direction from Hirst. On the one hand he has gleefully embraced popular culture in all its superficiality; he titled his pioneering exhibition of young Japanese artists in 2000 "Superflat,"[3] celebrating the addictively entertaining shallowness of contemporary culture. Murakami grew up with comics, television, and a world populated with plastic toys. His art draws on those cultural circumstances. He also pushes the definition of the artist into willful complicity with the world of entertainment and luxury consumption. "Murakami is now a distinct 'brand,'"[4] the director of the Los Angeles Museum of Contemporary Art wrote in his foreword to the 2007 catalog for "©Murakami," a large, comprehensive retrospective in the museum.

Whereas Warhol's "Factory" was a nostalgic metaphor marking our passage into the "postindustrial" era, Murakami's manufacturing business is for real. His Kaikai Kiki Co., Ltd. is a corporate powerhouse of international marketing and design. Since 1996 he has used commercial factory methods to produce his designs in everything from key chains to $5,000 handbags (in addition to his paintings and sculptures). He sells his products all over the world, not only in art galleries but in toy shops, boutiques, department stores, and in a special Louis Vuitton boutique set in the middle of the galleries of his big museum retrospective of 2007–8; the shop, selling Murakami-designed Louis Vuitton handbags and accessories, was an exhibited work in itself.

Murakami's work blends the deep roots of Japanese art history with the globally influential animation (animé) and comics (manga) of postwar Japan. This further complicates the hierarchies of "high" and "low" (an especially Western distinction between popular culture and what Westerners generally accept as "fine art"). But it also taps into a rapidly changing sense of what's real. The growing immersion of people in worlds of fantasy, assisted by the Internet, and their growing inability to see—and perhaps even their wish to see—the distinction between fiction and reality is one of the central issues of the new century, and it has very real consequences. The fictionalizing of political reality has become commonplace. On May 1, 2003 the media handlers for President George W. Bush (who had skipped out on his

military service during the Vietnam War) dressed him up in a pilot's jumpsuit with a parachute and had him do a "tailhook landing" on an aircraft carrier as the warm-up act to delivering a televised "victory" speech on his war in Iraq (which was still raging when he left office six years later). He was successfully packaged like a military hero (nobody

16.2 Takashi Murakami, *Miss Ko 2*, 1997. Oil, acrylic, synthetic resin, fiberglass, and iron, 73¼ × 26¾ × 25⅜in (186 × 68 × 65cm). Courtesy Marianne Boesky Gallery, New York.

pointed out that he didn't actually fly the plane) and people suspended disbelief, as if they were watching a movie; they even accepted the slogan on the banner behind him— "Mission Accomplished." As the film director Michael Moore stated in accepting the 2002 Oscar for best documentary feature: "We live in fictitious times."[5]

Murakami's entire project—the artworks, the products, the business protocols—all belong to an exploration of what it means to live in these "fictitious times." Artists help us see the fundamental dilemmas of existence in their historical moment and their insights have social value in helping us to understand the human concerns out of which they grow. Murakami's work is important because it makes these issues visible for us to think about. His 23-foot-wide painting *Tan Tan Bo Puking—a.k.a. Gero Tan*—of 2002 [fig. 16.1] is painted in "Superflat" decorative patterns and bright colors with cute little cartoon-style figures, like all of Murakami's work. But the subject matter is rife with violence, repulsion, and rage. In a small thought bubble in the painting the artist writes:

> Vomiting uncontrollably, together with the stench of my breath, my phlegm curdles. As my tongue flays to pieces, my headache intensifies, and my eyes have become blind. As shit and piss flow, an excruciating pain runs through my entire body and I sense death is near. As I cry for help, I regret my cowardly behavior, preventing others from loving me until now; as I feel the futility of my escape, my nausea continues endlessly.[6]

Mika Yoshitake has pointed out that Tan Tan Bo (which translates as "Phlegm Boy") is a character from Shigeru Mizuki's serial manga *Ge Ge Ge no Kitarō* (1966–70) about modern-day Japanese demons.[7] Murakami's recurrent images of happy cartoon mushrooms resonate with the horror of the World War II nuclear blasts that devastated the people of Nagasaki and Hiroshima. Other works center on consumerism (like the $5,000 handbags) and on sexual fetishism (as in the erotic, over-life-size "Miss Ko" dolls [fig. 16.2], which seem like "adult" sex toys); they are both endearingly cute and vulgar. Like Hirst's work, Murakami's is titillatingly entertaining and at the same time filled with anger.

Conrad Bakker—Parsing the Fictions of Real Economies

Instead of pushing us to the contradictory extremes of pleasure and repulsion in our fast-moving world of consumerism, many contemporary artists focus their practice on an analysis of our systems of exchange (economies). On a single, 10-foot-long shelf in an exhibition at the Krannert Art Museum at the University of Illinois in 2003, Conrad Bakker displayed about thirty chunky little blocks of composition board, each beautifully painted to copy a photograph of an Eames chair that had been listed for sale on eBay. The protocols for this *Untitled Projects: EAMES/EBAY* [fig. 16.3] involved listing each painting for auction (one for each day of the exhibition) on eBay, side by side with the "real" Eames chairs

16.3 Conrad Bakker, *Untitled Project: EAMES/EBAY*, 2003.

for sale. The label for the painting sold on November 25 was typical: "'EAMES, ORANGE, CHAIR, sideshell EXCELLENT!' is an oil painting on MDF, dimensions 4⅛ × 3⅛ × ¼'"" and "an Untitled Project by Conrad Bakker." As the auctions went ahead, the artist would go into the museum, take the painting in question off the shelf, and mail it to the buyer.

The "description" line on the eBay listing for the Eames chairs sums up the underlying aim of the project with a famous quotation: "'It is the relation between things that gives meaning to them and that formulates thought.' Hans Hofmann, The Search for the Real in the Visual Arts." For Hofmann, whose ideas of "push and pull" influenced the colors and designs of Charles and Ray Eames, this assertion referred to the compositional laws in painting. Bakker's appropriation and extrapolation to his own medium—the socioeconomic matrix in which the sale took place—would never have occurred to Hofmann.

Bakker's practice began modestly in 1997 with a yard sale in front of his house in Grand Rapids, Michigan. As in all of his work, the items laid out for sale—an old radiator, a pair of scissors, a toothbrush, a squash racket, a stuffed chair with a mismatched cushion, a KFC box left casually on the chair, and the like—were all hand carved and expressionistically painted wood objects that could scarcely pass for the real thing. Their awkward physicality expresses the specificity of the labor involved in making them. In *Untitled Project:*

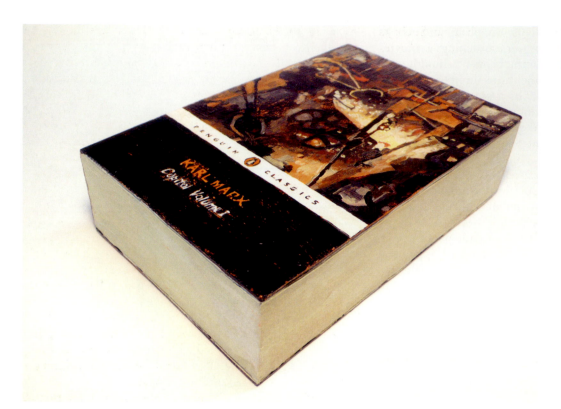

16.4 Conrad Bakker, *Untitled Project: COMMODITY [CAPITAL]*, 2007–8.

CONSUMER ACTIONS (2002) Bakker clandestinely "restocked" items on shelves in box stores like K-Mart with his to-scale wooden "almost" replicas of specific consumer goods normally found in those spaces for random customers to buy and take home (or not). As Miriam Kienle has written, "whether 'shop-dropped'[8] in a K-Mart, arranged in a gallery like designer furniture, sold in a yard sale, posted on eBay or bartered on Craigslist, Bakker's objects both call into question the authenticity of other commodities in their proximity and comment on how things are evaluated, marketed, and sold."[9]

Like many of the artists emerging around or after 2000, Bakker cultivates what Nicolas Bourriaud termed a "relational aesthetic," collaborating with his viewers. Their actions complete the work and in doing so the project illuminates the entire context of their encounter, bringing the social and the economic relations into view. Bakker's work has what Marx termed "use value" in so far as it serves to help viewers understand social processes, rather than standing as a simply "useless" object of consumption. Bakker takes Marx on directly in *Untitled Project: COMMODITY [CAPITAL]* [fig. 16.4] and *Untitled Project: rEpL1CA [SPAM]*. Carrying them out simultaneously in the fall of 2007–8, Bakker planned these two projects for exhibitions about art and commerce: "The Irresistible Force" at the Tate Modern in London and "Transactions" at the Blanton Museum of Art in Austin, Texas.

For the Tate, Bakker made painted wood replicas of the Penguin edition of Marx's *Capital*, volume 1 and sold them for £25 (the price of the Penguin paperback, plus shipping and handling) through mail-order forms slipped into the exhibition catalog. In Texas, Bakker marketed replicas of knockoff Rolex watches via fake spam emails that directed the recipients to an e-commerce website. On the site they could actually purchase a commodity sculpture (a wooden replica Rolex), but not without first reading a commentary from Marx's writings on commodity fetishism, such as:

> The usefulness of a thing makes it a use-value. But this usefulness does not dangle in mid-air. It is conditioned by the physical properties of the commodity, and has no existence apart from the latter . . . Exchange-value appears first of all as the quantitative relation, the proportion, in which use-values of one kind exchange for use-values of another kind. This relation changes constantly with time and place. Hence exchange-value appears to be something accidental and purely relative, and consequently an intrinsic value, i.e. an exchange-value that is inseparably connected with the commodity, inherent in it, seems a contradiction in terms. Let us consider the matter more closely.
> —Karl Marx, *Capital*, Volume 1, Section 1

Marx interests Bakker both for the actual texts and for the ways in which the fashions of contemporary criticism exploit Marx as a type of academic capital. *COMMODITY [CAPITAL]* serves as a fetish of Marx's "commodity fetishism."

Andrea Fraser: Context and Self

What does it mean for the individual, for one's sense of oneself, to live in a society so dominated by competitive consumerism and so saturated with mediated imagery that we sometimes wonder where reality ends and the artificial begins (to use Andy Warhol's famous phrase)? Society's commodification of female beauty and sexuality complicates these questions still more, especially (but not only) for women. How are these values institutionalized by society? How do they shape the nature of childhood in the twenty-first century?

The Los Angeles-based performance artist Andrea Fraser follows this inquiry with relentless intellectual rigor, using her own person as her medium. In *Official Welcome* (2001) she delivered, as Katie Stone wrote in *The Brooklyn Rail*, "a wickedly funny play on the self-congratulatory, aren't-we-all-fabulous nature of introductory remarks."[10] Fraser speaks as though she is the curator who has invited the artist (also herself, but not really her) to speak at this private dinner (the actual "private" nature of the venue made this performance particularly uncomfortable) and then she seamlessly morphs into the unspecified artist. "I am not a person today. I'm an object in an art work," she says, not for a moment pausing in her talk about herself ("the artist") as she takes off all her clothes and stands naked in front of the smartly dressed dinner guests.

Dissecting these art-world situations and the institutions that sustain them, Fraser has pioneered a powerful form of what has come to be known as "institutional critique." She first came to public attention for a performance of 1989 called *Museum Highlights*, in which the twenty-four-year-old artist, posing as museum docent "Jane Castleton," gave a tour of the Philadelphia Museum of Art that was funny, but with an edge. We have all experienced the ridiculously

hypertrophied language of a meaningless art history lecture, in which what is said might as easily apply to a bathroom fixture as to the painting on the wall; pointing to the water fountain, this docent described it as "a work of astonishing economy and monumentality . . . it boldly contrasts with the severe and highly stylized productions of this form!" Then, entering the museum cafeteria, she said: "This room represents the heyday of colonial art in Philadelphia on the eve of the Revolution, and must be regarded as one of the very finest of all American rooms."

One of the funniest of Fraser's works is a 2001 video called *Little Frank and His Carp*, in which hidden cameras show the artist in the foyer of the Guggenheim Museum in Bilbao (designed by celebrity architect Frank Gehry) listening to the official audio tour for the building. The absurd, suggestive, and self-serious language of the actual recorded tour provides a side-splitting soundtrack which the artist earnestly follows on camera. It describes the rapturous experience we're meant to be having from the forms and instructs us to engage in a sensual relationship with the building [fig. 16.5], which Fraser does quite literally in the film, caressing the walls and lifting her skirt to rub against the columns as other museum visitors turn in surprise.

In 2003, however, Fraser pushed her exploration of the power relations and market practices of the art world to a place where it became too uncomfortable to be funny. She asked her dealers, the Friedrich Petzel Gallery, to find a collector who would commission a film in which the artist would have sex with the collector on camera in a hotel room;

16.5 Andrea Fraser, still from *Little Frank and his Carp*, 2001. Video still, DVD NTSC. Duration six minutes.

Courtesy the artist and the Friedrich Petzel Gallery, New York.

they did, and then they editioned the video for sale. This extreme self-objectification was a logical outcome of Fraser's inquiry. The one-hour, $20,000 documentation video became "the work," and the first copy went to the private collector who "commissioned" it. She shot the piece in a generic upscale hotel and the single, immobile view resembled that of a high-definition security camera. By exhibiting it in an intensely lit gallery on a small single monitor (with no chairs available for viewers), Fraser further accentuated the simultaneous banality and discomfort of the piece. An artist who views art as a social field and comes to her investigation through cultural theory and psychoanalysis, she had to press this far in order to illuminate for herself the historically fraught relationship between patron and artist and the larger societal constructions it implied. What she found, of course, was a deep well of ambivalence in herself which has left the meanings of *Untitled 2003* to continue unfolding.

DETACHED SUBJECTIVITY

In a performance of 2001 called *Kunst Muss Hangen (Art Must Hang)* Andrea Fraser reenacted an impromptu 1995 speech by a drunken Martin Kippenberger, word for word, even replicating the gestures. In 2003 an artists' collective called Continuous Project (Bettina Funcke, Seth Price, Wade Guyton, and Joseph Logan) decided to start an art journal by selecting a publication from the past that they liked (the first issue of *Avalanche* magazine from 1970) and Xeroxing the entire magazine as their first issue. They also did a performance, appropriating the transcript of a panel discussion by several well-known critics held in the early seventies; Funcke et al. read the parts out loud in front of an audience without regard to expression or even the gender of the original participants. Like appropriating an entire magazine, taking this discussion out of its time and having

16.6 Candice Breitz, stills from *Mother*, 2005. Six-channel installation. Duration thirteen minutes, fifteen seconds. Edition of three + A.P. Courtesy Studio Breitz, Berlin.

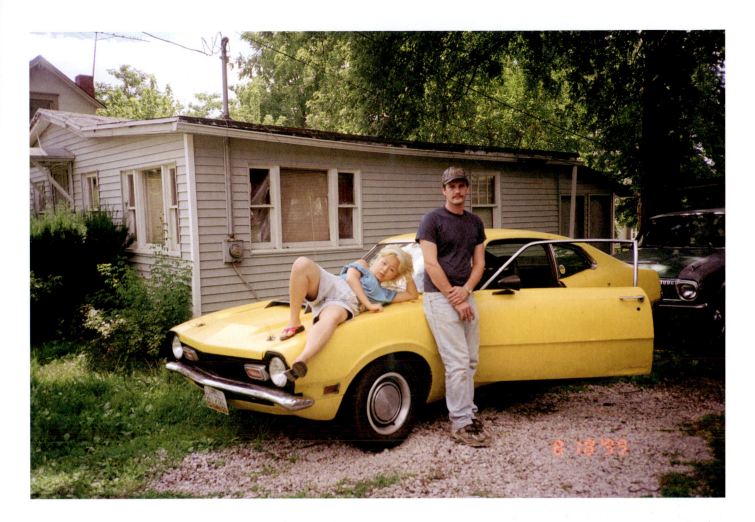

16.7 Nikki S. Lee, *The Ohio Project (6)*, 1999. Fujiflex print. Courtesy of Sikkema Jenkins & Co., New York.

the artists speak someone else's ideas not only changed the meaning completely but evoked a strange sensation of alienation and dislocation.

The choice of the seventies hardly seems coincidental since the concept of "appropriation" emerged in that decade as an overt working protocol. But "appropriation"—taking something wholly formed already and making it your own by recontextualizing it—is uniquely well adapted to the rearranging of images, text, and memory from TV, print, computers, and film. By 2000 this had become a cultural commonplace—and not just among artists.

Douglas Gordon caused an art-world sensation in 1993 with his video *24 Hour Psycho*, in which he showed Alfred Hitchcock's film *Psycho*, slowed down to run for twenty-four hours (instead of two), unhinging the viewer's sense of time and playing against our vivid memories of the famous film. In *Mother + Father* (2005) the South African artist Candice Breitz (who lives and works in Berlin) created a set of strong but detached emotions by lifting five- or ten-second fragments of Hollywood films and using them like expressive words in a sentence. She had six screens, playing one at a time, or a few at once, or all simultaneously, and featuring clips of Diane Keaton, Joan Crawford, Shirley MacLaine, Meryl Streep, Susan Sarandon, and Julia Roberts in roles as mothers, weeping or reciting phrases about their troubled

relationships [fig. 16.6]. Breitz rearranged the clips into powerful choruses of emotion but the feelings hang in the air without a narrative context. She did the same with well-known male leads as fathers, talking about their daughters and sex.

In a world where people interact increasingly with machines (simulated voices on frustrating corporate phone lines and hyperreal games on computers) we find ourselves more detached from ourselves and others in a deep way and more able to reinvent ourselves, as though we could consciously appropriate the parts we would like to have in life. The Korean artist Nikki S. Lee did a series of projects where she went cultural-identity shopping. Lee literally tried on different subcultures, making herself blend in as totally as she could among Hispanics, lesbians, skateboarders, yuppies, private-school girls, punks, and senior citizens. In *The Ohio Project* [fig. 16.7] she dyed her black hair platinum blonde, donned cutoffs, and moved in with trailer-park gun enthusiasts in small-town Ohio. Where Cindy Sherman made herself up for a photo that lived out a fantasy persona, Lee actually lived the parts and documented them. "My own identity has various identities," she told an audience at the Phillips

Collection in 2007. Lee came to the United States in 1994, her first trip out of South Korea; she was struck by "the gap between who I am and how I appear ... People have so many layers."[11]

Identity and Shopping: Sang-ah Choi

Sang-ah Choi also came to the United States from South Korea in the nineties and at first spoke almost no English. This fact set the contrast in cultures into particularly high relief for her. Unlike Nikki Lee who immersed herself in different subcultures, Choi embarked on a project of hybridization, appropriating what she liked in the commodity culture of America and making it her own. There is a drawing in Choi's sketchbook from 2000 for paper dolls with a variety of different costumes. The paper dolls of her childhood prefigure this drawing, which in turn connects to the paper cutout pop-up books that frequently occupy her today. Choi's work centers on a layering of cultural contrasts, seen with remarkable freshness, as she encounters the contemporary world (whether in traveling or on the Internet). Every impression seems to go through a rapid metamorphosis, flattened onto a "paper-thin" plane that in turn becomes a fairytale world of pleasures. Like the outfits for paper dolls, she can move things around, trying them on this way and that.

In *Snow White* of 2004 [fig. 16.8] Choi revisits the classic Western fairy tale (via the Walt Disney animation) about a beautiful princess who triumphs over death through the love of a handsome prince. But she retells the story as a tale of dress-shopping among images from the pages of *Vogue*. The same mirror which told the Wicked Witch that Snow White had displaced her as the "fairest" beauty in the land now shows Snow White which retro dress looks the most fabulous on her! Choi painted this work with pen and ink, acrylic, and glitter embedded in a deep layer of polymer resin on a wood panel. The thick, lacquerlike surface deliberately alludes to the inexpensive import furniture in Chinatown gift shops (another kind of culture shopping), which in turn evokes the stereotypes of "Asian" imports in America. On the other hand the large eyes on the figures and the use of white spots to represent light reflections in them come from the way that Japanese and Korean animé artists depict Caucasians.

As an art student in Seoul, Choi had to choose between two reductive stereotypes: a "traditional" and a "Western" curriculum. The former required students to make delicate sumi ink drawings of bamboo and the latter to paint after plaster casts of historical European sculptures like the *Venus de Milo*. This reinforced Choi's sense of detachment in cultural signifiers, as though one can simply select and arrange them at will. Just as you can buy a "Ralph Lauren look," you can also consume a package of values embedded in the entertainment or fashion products that you buy.

After the terrorist attacks of September 11, 2001 Choi's work turned toward issues of immortality (though still seen through commodity culture). In commercial mass consumerism if something is broken you get another one to replace it. In this sense it continues to be there, and this in turn gives it a serial permanence. This aesthetic of replaceable things, implied in continuing production, struck

16.8 Sang-ah Choi, *Snow White*, 2004. Acrylic, felt-tip pen, sumi ink, glitter, and polymer resin on wood, 16 × 32 × 1in (40.6 × 81.3 × 2.5cm).
Courtesy the artist.

Choi as an odd kind of immortality. The notion that you memorialize yourself in what you own (or a building named after you) struck her as particularly Western; as though through things, persevering as monuments, you last forever. This concept differs completely from the idea of spiritual immortality in Zen Buddhism. So Choi turned her attention to a series of paintings in which the unchanging Taoist symbols of long life find a new life in the commercial forms of the West: The turtle of long life morphs into a Teenage Mutant Ninja Turtle, the deer becomes Walt Disney's Bambi, the mushroom turns into a cartoon character from the enchanted forest of *Snow White*. Choi points to a longing for transcendent immortality in American pop culture through the act of consuming.

Dissolution, Dislocation, Displacement of Boundaries—An Autopsy on Identity

As we embark on the twenty-first century, the boundaries of death and immortality, of the body, of identity, the self, memory, reality, the object all seem fraught. As a remembrance and a cathartic coming to terms with the 1991 death of his lover, Felix Gonzalez-Torres made an installation that year, *"Untitled" (Portrait of Ross in L.A.)* [fig. 16.9], that consists of a pile of shiny Fruit Flashers (individually cellophane-wrapped candies) in a rainbow of colors. Visitors

are encouraged to help themselves and the supply can be maintained (or not) indefinitely at about 175 pounds (the body weight of his lover). The work literally dissipates and regenerates; it elides the boundaries of commodity and person, temporality and immortality. Even the title is left open-ended as "Untitled," with only a parenthetical note of something personal to the artist.

In the abstract paintings of Mary Heilman even the idea of abstraction has taken on a dislocated meaning as a "representation of abstraction."[12] It was the dislocation of subjectivity that made the work relevant. The Lebanese artist Walid Raad expressed this dislocated subjectivity in another way. In 1999 he founded the Atlas Group "to research and document the contemporary history of Lebanon,"[13] he writes on the website of his archive. The archive contains, for example, 229 notebooks and two short films bequeathed on his death by Dr. Fadl Fakhouri, "foremost historian of the Lebanese wars." There is also a section of photographs "attributed to Walid Raad who donated them to The Atlas

16.9 Felix Gonzalez-Torres, *"Untitled" (Portrait of Ross in L.A.)*, 1991. Multicolored candies individually wrapped in cellophane. Ideal weight 175lbs (79kg), installed dimensions variable. Collection, Donna and Howard Stone, on extended loan to the Art Institute of Chicago, 1.1999. Courtesy the Felix Gonzalez-Torres Foundation and Adrea Rosen Gallery, New York.

16.10 Walid Raad, *BEY82_City_II* from the series *"Untitled"*, 1982–2008. Archival color inkjet print, 44 × 67in (111.8 × 170.2cm). Edition of five. Courtesy the artist and the Paula Cooper Gallery, New York.

Group in 2002." Raad's archive does illuminate his subject even though all the carefully indexed documents and photographs [fig. 16.10] are fake. The archive challenges the boundary between truth and imagination and transgresses the very idea of stable hierarchies of "reality" in the world.

An Alternative History

The art of our times gives us another way of exploring what we perceive and feel in the present which in turn helps us shape our future. As children, we form our sense of ourselves by studying the powerful figures of those who care for us— our mothers and fathers and then teachers and mentors whose methods we emulate as we also build new methods and perspectives on the foundation of what we have acquired from them. One of the most important new developments in the new century concerns the way in which our society judges success ever more by wealth and power. Those who have it never feel satisfied because no amount of wealth and power can fill the inner void that comes from the failures of childhood to create a solid core. Whatever the causes, it is clear that much of the important new art of the early-twenty-first century concerns different implications of this epidemic of emptiness. "Relational art" focuses on artist–audience interactions, the work of artists like Murakami and Hirst press us to look at how consumerism defines us, the surge of formalist work simply suppresses the issue, and so much new work deals with identity itself in various ways.

Ilya Kabakov has made a career of taking on deliberately worked-out personas that simultaneously critique himself, history, and contemporary society. As Rob Storr pointed out, "The Man Who Describes His Life Through Personages"[14] (one of the Ten Characters whom Kabakov created before

his departure from the Soviet Union in 1988) seems to describe Kabakov himself. But this displacement of identity took an intriguing turn at the end of the nineties when Kabakov painted the entire *oeuvres* of three invented Russian artists: the interwar painter Charles Rosenthal, his 1970s spiritual follower Ilya Kabakov (not to be confused with the real Ilya Kabakov, making this all the more disconcerting), and Igor Spivak whose postmodern work of the 1990s completes a history of twentieth-century Russian art with a final nostalgic apotheosis of the past.

Kabakov exhibited the three *oeuvres* together for the first time under the title "An Alternative History of Art" in Moscow in 2008. With poignant irony Ilya Kabakov (the real one) and his wife Emilia Kabakov wrote an art historical commentary on Rosenthal's stylistic evolution—attempting to reconcile the irreconcilable styles of Soviet realism with Russian utopian abstraction. They also examine the teacher–follower relationship in the works of the invented Kabakov. "'Whom do I myself consider to be my teacher, who shaped my artistic 'personality'? . . . Although I spent almost 13 years pursuing artistic education (in school and in the institute), unfortunately, there is no one . . . That is why the need has arisen to create an artist-personage by the name of Kabakov who finally found his genuine teacher — C. Rosenthal."[15] The Kabakovs bypass the need for outside critics, teachers, or an art world; they invent them as needed in this autonomous "self"-defining system.

The Kabakovs describe the artists' individual projects in this way: Rosenthal attempted to fuse "minimalism with the . . . art of the 19th century." Kabakov combined "realistic painting with the rigid geometry of forms" and a premodern "'picturesque' significance." Spivak "combines a familiar avant-garde element—the unpainted white field—with photorealism."[16] These are ludicrous juxtapositions. The problem they describe as the animating obsession of a work like Rosenthal's 1930 painting *They Discuss the New Plan* (painted by the real Ilya Kabakov in 1997) [fig. 16.11] sounds like a docent tour by Andrea Fraser. The Kabakovs write:

> In the beginning of his creativity (the first hall of the exhibit) the theme of the "emptiness" and "whiteness" emerges and begins to "resound" distinctly among diverse plastic "experiments" of the young "artist." But it emerges in this period as more of a background, as a special quality and characteristic of this artist which the artist himself doesn't quite yet sufficiently realize and it isn't positioned as the main problem worthy of attention and elaboration.
>
> That's why it is easily muffled by other problems (the second hall) and among them, the "problem" of realism in art, the task of how accurately to reflect the current surrounding life in the form of that very life, i.e. the means of realistic depiction. Here emerge "realistic" subjects, real figures, a lofty perspective and other devices of "veracious" depiction of the surrounding world. That world "surrounding" the artist seized his imagination more and more.[17]

But then in the fifth hall, where Rosenthal's 1930 social-realist painting *They Discuss the New Plan* hangs, "white ruptures begin again,"[18] they tell us. "I have not managed to conquer the whiteness inside the canvas," Rosenthal is imagined to write; "like acid, it devours my depictions of actual reality to which I so aspired, which I managed to create with such difficulty for so long and with such tenacity.

(from a letter to Blum)."[19] Here the Kabakovs explore the artist's obsessive focus, the way in which all artists relentlessly pursue something very specific, a formal problem that keeps returning.

It is for us to unravel the metaphors in Kabakov's new work for our own lives and times. What does this persistent ventriloquism, the displacement of identity, tell us about our present and our future? To acknowledge that the formation of individual identity is challenged and shaped differently in the new century, that truth is more mutable, complicated, and plural than we might have thought in the past, that the pressures of society transgress the boundaries of the self in new ways, is necessary and self-evident. We have not transcended the need to form individual identities, nor is truth no longer susceptible to verification, nor has the human psyche's need to strive for integrity or wholeness in itself disappeared. This book went to press a year after the inauguration of the first African-American President of the United States. He stands as emblematic of this new, more complicated idea of what constitutes identity in the twenty-first century. His autobiography brings together a remarkably diverse collection of formative experiences in a way that seems to have captured the imagination of so many of us. But he also stands as testimony of our faith in human intelligence to build something new from all the disparate parts, something that is stronger and better than what we had before, even as we face the most daunting challenges in human history. The artists of our time help us to see that future and rethink how we shape our inheritance so we can act on that faith.

16.11 Ilya Kabakov, *Charles Rosenthal, They Discuss the New Plan, 1930*, 1997. Courtesy Emilia Kabakov.

17.1 Gilles Barbier, *De "Coordonnée" à "Cristallisation,"* 1995.
Dictionary page with errata sheet. Ink and gouache on paper,
84¾ × 84¾in (215 × 215cm) and 25 × 19⅝in (65 × 50cm).
Private collection, California. Courtesy Galerie Georges-Philippe and Nathalie Vallois.

EPILOGUE
TO SAY THE THINGS
THAT ARE ONE'S OWN

More than a thousand years ago a Chinese critic named Chang Yen-yüan lamented that "contemporary paintings are chaotic and meaningless."[1] In the year of Kandinsky's first abstract paintings and the most experimental moment of Picasso's cubism, a Munich critic brought out a book called *The Death of Art* in which he complained that "art is dying of the masses and of materialism . . . for the first time we have entered a period without direction, without an artistic style, without a young revolutionary generation."[2]

The most important contemporary art has perhaps always been difficult to recognize and understand. It requires hard work from the serious viewer. It baffles people, makes them uncomfortable and angry, it seems perpetually defeated by the overwhelming ills of every historical epoch, and it isn't even "politically correct." But it does offer a unique kind of truth, embodying an individual's struggle to come to terms with his or her inner thoughts and identity in relation to the constantly changing facts of existence in the world.

If we can imagine ourselves into the experience of the artist, suspend our point of view for the moment and attempt to assume the artist's frame of mind, we can understand and feel that truth and we can use it to understand ourselves and our world. "Look at any inspired painting," Philip Guston once told a reporter for *Time* magazine. "It's like a gong sounding; it puts you in a state of reverberation."[3]

For all sincere artists, their art is an evolving perspective on events, and it is who they are. "I realized that I had things in my head not like what I had been taught," Georgia O'Keeffe wrote to her friend Anita Pollitzer, "not like what I had seen—shapes and ideas so familiar to me that it hadn't occurred to me to put them down. I decided to stop painting, to put away everything I had done, and to start to say the things that were my own."[4]

Over the past forty years many critics have felt that the avant-garde has reached the end of the road because "the protest of the historical *avant-garde* against art as an institution is accepted as *art*"[5] now, eradicating its posture of opposition and defining it out of existence. Others have worried that the power of corporate culture has finally silenced dissent. But as Freud pointed out in *Civilization and Its Discontents*,[6] a permanent tension exists between the individual and society and the alienation that this tension engenders perpetuates an avant-garde (though we may not properly call it that any more) as the expression of an enduring human need. Art contributes to the ideals and models of thinking about important issues in a culture. We need to look beyond market influences and beyond the intellectual fashions of academia to see this spiritual dimension, because artists enter their ideas into the world, not just into books, collections, and art history classes.

BIBLIOGRAPHY

General Guidelines

This bibliography is intended to give readers a starting place for further information about the many artists and issues discussed in this book. The list includes a few standard books on each topic, some landmark essays that are not in the anthologies cited here, and, every now and again, something eccentric that takes up an aspect of an artist or issue from an unusual and interesting point of view. Many excellent books have been left out in order to keep the list short enough to read over a school year for a student who wants a balanced overview, and it defers to the bibliographies in the more specialized books cited for more detailed listings on particular topics. Essays in the anthologies listed are not cited individually; entries appear once where they first seem relevant and are not repeated later, even though they may also relate to issues or artists covered in later chapters. The reader is also encouraged to consult the databases JSTOR and Art Full Text (hosted by WilsonWeb), which offer electronic versions of articles from various art periodicals, as well as Art Bibliographies Modern (ABM) and The Bibliography of the History of Art (BHA) for references to books, articles, and catalogs. Many books and catalogs may be previewed on Google Books.

Anthologies of Criticism and Interviews

Foster, Hal, ed. *The Anti-Aesthetic: Essays on Postmodern Culture*. Port Townsend, Wash.: Bay Press, 1983.

Greenberg, Clement. *Art and Culture*. Boston: Beacon Press, 1961.

Greenberg, Clement. *The Collected Essays and Criticism*, vol. 1: *Perceptions and Judgements, 1939–1944*. Chicago, University of Chicago Press, 1986.

Greenberg, Clement. *The Collected Essays and Criticism*, vol. 2: *Arrogant Purpose, 1945–1949*. Chicago, University of Chicago Press, 1986.

Harrison, Charles and Paul Wood. *Art in Theory: 1900–2000*. Oxford: Blackwell Publishers, 2003.

Hills, Patricia. *Modern Art in the USA: Issues and Controversies of the 20th Century*. Upper Saddle Creek, N.J.: Prentice Hall, 2001.

Kuh, Katherine. *The Artist's Voice: Talks with Seventeen Artists*. New York and Evanston, Ill.: Harper & Row, 1962.

Lippard, Lucy. *Changing: Essays in Art Criticism*. New York: E. P. Dutton, 1971.

Robinson, Hilary. *Feminism-art-theory: an anthology, 1968–2000*. Malden, Mass.: Blackwell Publishers, 2001.

Rosenberg, Harold. *De-Definition of Art*. New York: Collier Books, 1972.

Rosenberg, Harold. *The Anxious Object, Art Today and its Audience*. New York: Horizon Press, 1966.

Rosenberg, Harold. *The Tradition of the New*. New York: Horizon Press, 1959.

Steinberg, Leo. *Other Criteria: Confrontations with Twentieth-Century Art*. London, Oxford, New York: Oxford University Press, 1972.

Stiles, Kristine and Peter Howard Selz. *Theories and documents of contemporary art: a sourcebook of artists' writings*. Berkeley: University of California Press, 1996.

Chapter 1

Different Directions in Recent Critical and Cultural Theory

Arato, Andrew and Eike Gebhardt, eds. *The Essential Frankfurt School Reader*. New York: Continuum, 1982.

Bal, Mieke and Norman Bryson. "Views and Overviews: Semiotics and Art History." *Art Bulletin*, vol. 73, no. 2, June 1991: 174–208.

Barthes, Roland. *Image-Music-Text*. Trans. Stephen Heath. New York: Hill & Wang, 1977.

Barthes, Roland. *The Pleasure of the Text*. Trans. Richard Miller. Garden City, N.Y.: Doubleday, 1972.

Baudrillard, Jean. *Jean Baudrillard: Selected Writings*. Ed. Mark Poster. Stanford: Stanford University Press, 1988.

Benjamin, Walter. *Illuminations*. Trans. Harry Zohn. New York: Harcourt, Brace and World, 1968.

Bryson, Norman. *Vision and Painting*. New Haven, Conn.: Yale University Press, 1983.

Buchloh, B. H. D. *Neo-Avantgarde and Culture Industry Essays on European and American Art from 1955 to 1975*. Cambridge, Mass.: MIT Press, 2000.

Bürger, Peter. *Theory of the Avant-Garde*. Trans. Michael Shaw. Minneapolis: University of Minnesota Press, 1984.

DeGeorge, Richard and Fernande, eds. *The Structuralists from Marx to Lévi-Strauss*. Garden City, N.Y.: Doubleday, 1972.

Deleuze, Gilles and Félix Guattari. *Anti-Oedipus: Capitalism and Schizophrenia*. Trans. Robert Hurley, Mark Seem, and Helen R. Lane, with a preface by Michel Foucault. Minneapolis: University of Minnesota Press, 1983.

Derrida, Jacques. *Of Grammatology*. Trans. Gayatri Chakravorty Spivak. Baltimore and London: Johns Hopkins University Press, 1974.

Eagleton, Terry. *Literary Theory*. Minneapolis: University of Minnesota Press, 1983.

Ellmann, Richard and Charles Feidelson, Jr., eds. *The Modern Tradition*. New York: Oxford University Press, 1965.

Foucault, Michel. *The order of things: an archaeology of the human sciences*. New York, Pantheon Books, 1971.

Foucault, Michel. *The archaeology of knowledge*. New York, Pantheon Books, 1972.

Harari, Josue V., ed. *Textual Strategies*. Ithaca, N.Y.: Cornell University Press, 1979.

Heidegger, Martin. *Poetry, Language, Thought*. Trans. Albert Hofstadter. New York: Harper & Row, 1975.

Huyssen, Andreas. *After the Great Divide*. Bloomington: Indiana University Press, 1986.

Jameson, Fredric. *The Political Unconscious*. Ithaca, N.Y.: Cornell University Press, 1981.

Jauss, Hans Robert. *Toward an Aesthetic of Reception*. Trans. Timothy Bahti. Minneapolis: University of Minnesota Press, 1982.

Krauss, Rosalind E. *The Originality of the Avant-Garde and the other Modernist Myths*. Cambridge, Mass. and London: MIT Press, 1986.

Lyotard, Jean-François. *The Postmodern Condition: A Report on Knowledge*. Trans. Geoff Bennington and Brian Massumi. Minneapolis: University of Minnesota Press, 1984.

Marcuse, Herbert. *Eros and Civilization*. Boston: Beacon Press, 1966.

Marx, Karl. *Grundrisse: Foundations of the Critique of Political Economy*. Trans. Martin Nicolaus. New York: International Publishers, 1970.

Massumi, Brian. *Parables for the Virtual: Movement, Affect, Sensation*. Chapel Hill, N.C.: Duke University Press, 2002.

Morris, Robert. "Words and Images in Modernism and Postmodernism." *Critical Inquiry* 15, winter 1989: 337–47.

Nancy, Jean-Luc. *The Inoperative Community*. Minneapolis: University of Minnesota Press, 1991.

Norris, Christopher. *Deconstruction: Theory and Practice*. London: Methuen, 1982.

Poggioli, Renato. *The Theory of The Avant Garde*. New York: Harper & Row, 1968.

Pollock, Griselda. *Vision and Difference*. London: Routledge, 1988.

Rancière, Jacques. *The Politics of Aesthetics: The Distribution of the Sensible*. London: New York: Continuum, 2006.

Said, Edward. *Reflections on Exile and Other Essays*. Cambridge, Mass.: Harvard University Press, 2000.

Sontag, Susan. *Against Interpretation*. New York: Dell, 1966.

Chapter 2

Altshuler, Bruce. *Isamu Noguchi*. New York: Abbeville, 1994.

Ashton, Dore. *The New York School*. New York: Viking, 1973.

Auping, Michael. *Abstract Expressionism: The Critical Developments*. Buffalo: Albright-Knox Art Gallery; New York: Harry N. Abrams, 1987.

Carmean, E. A., Jr., and Eliza Rathbone. *American Art at Mid-Century: The Subjects of the Artist*. Washington, D.C.: National Gallery of Art, 1978.

Christove-Bakargiev, Carolyn. *Franz Klien: 1910–1962*. Milano: Skira, 2004.

Conwill, Kinshasha Holman, Jacques Leenhardt, Giulio V. Blanc, Julia P. Herzberg, and Lowery Stokes Sims. *Wifredo Lam and his Contemporaries 1938–1952*. New York: Studio Museum in Harlem, 1992.

Doty, Robert and Diane Waldman. *Adolph Gottlieb*. New York: Whitney Museum of American Art, Solomon R. Guggenheim Museum, and Praeger, 1968.

Du Pont, Diana C. ed., *Tamayo: A Modern Icon Reinterpreted*. Santa Barbara, Cal.: Santa Barbara Museum of Art, 2007.

Eckhardt, Sarah. *Uninterrupted Flux: Hedda Sterne, A Retrospective*. Champaign, Ill.: Krannert Art Museum, University of Illinois at Urbana-Champaign, 2006.

Friedman, Martin. *Noguchi's Imaginary Landscapes*. Minneapolis: Walker Art Center, 1978.

Gaugh, Harry F. *The Vital Gesture: Franz Kline*. Cincinnati: Cincinnati Art Museum; New York: Abbeville, 1985.

Gordon, John. *Franz Kline: 1910–1962*. New York: Whitney Museum of American Art, 1968.

Graham, John D. *System and Dialectics of Art*. New York: Delphic Studios, 1937.

Guggenheim, Peggy. *Out of this Century: Informal Memoirs of Peggy Guggenheim*. New York: Dial Press, 1964; and *Confessions of an Art Addict*. New York: Macmillan, 1960; republished together as Peggy Guggenheim, *Out of this Century*. New York: Universal Books, 1979.

Guilbaut, Serge. *How New York Stole the Idea of Modern Art*. Chicago: University of Chicago Press, 1983.

Helfenstein, Josef. *Louise Bourgeois: The Early Work*. Champaign, Ill.: Krannert Art Museum, University of Illinois at Urbana-Champaign, 2002.

Hobbs, Robert C. *Lee Krasner*. New York: Abbeville, 1993.

O'Neill, John P. *Clyfford Still*. New York: Metropolitan Museum of Art, 1979.

Polcari, Stephen. *Abstract Expressionism and the Modern Experience*. Cambridge and New York: Cambridge University Press, 1991.

Rosenberg, Harold. *Discovering the Present*. Chicago: University of Chicago Press, 1973.

Rosenblum, Robert. *Modern Painting and the Northern Romantic Tradition: Friedrich to Rothko*. New York: Harper & Row, 1975.

Sandler, Irving. *The Triumph of American Painting: A History of Abstract Expressionism*. New York and Washington: Praeger, 1970.

Sims, Lowery Stokes. *Wifredo Lam and the International Avant-garde, 1923–1982*. Austin: University of Texas Press, 2002.

Sawin, Martica. *Surrealism in Exile and the Beginning of the New York School*. Cambridge, Mass.: MIT Press, 1995.

Tuchman, Maurice, ed. *New York School—The First Generation Painting of the 1940s and 1950s.* Los Angeles: Los Angeles County Museum of Art, 1965.

Turner, Elizabeth Hutton, ed. *Jacob Lawrence: The Migration Series.* Washington, D.C.: The Rappahannock Press and The Phillips Collection, 1993.

Waldman, Diane. *Joseph Cornell: Master of Dreams.* New York: Harry N. Abrams, 2002.

Photography

Marien, Mary Warner. *Photography: A Cultural History.* 3rd ed. Upper Saddle River, N.J.: Prentice Hall. 2010.

Purcell, Kerry William. *Weegee.* New York: Phaidon Press, 2004.

Rhem, James. *Aaron Siskind.* New York: Phaidon Press, 2003.

Thomas, Ann. *Lisette Model.* Ottawa: National Gallery of Canada, 1990.

Weegee. *Naked City.* New York: Da Capo Press, 1975.

Chapter 3

Alexander Calder

Calder, Alexander. *Calder: an Autobiography with Pictures.* New York: Pantheon Press, 1977.

Lipman, Jean. *Calder's Universe.* New York: Whitney Museum of American Art and Viking, 1976.

Marchesseau, Daniel. *The Intimate World of Alexander Calder.* New York: Harry N. Abrams, 1989.

Marter, Joan M. *Alexander Calder.* Cambridge and New York: Cambridge University Press, 1991.

Hans Hofmann

Goodman, Cynthia. *Hans Hofmann.* New York: Abbeville, 1986.

Hofmann, Hans. *Search for the Real and Other Essays.* Cambridge, Mass.: MIT Press, 1967.

Seitz, William C. *Hans Hofmann.* New York: The Museum of Modern Art, 1963.

Arshile Gorky

Levy, Julien. *Arshile Gorky.* New York: Harry N. Abrams, 1966.

Rand, Harry, *Arshile Gorky. The Implications of Symbols.* Montclair, N.J.: Allenheld and Schram, 1980 (reprinted Berkeley: University of California Press, 1991).

Rosenberg, Harold. *Arshile Gorky: The Man, the Time, the Idea.* New York: Sheep Meadow Press/Flying Point Press, 1962.

Waldman, Diane. *Arshile Gorky: A Retrospective.* New York: Solomon R. Guggenheim Museum and Harry N. Abrams, 1981.

Robert Motherwell

Arnason, H. Harvard and Dore Ashton. *Robert Motherwell.* New York: Harry N. Abrams, 1982.

Carmean, E. A., Jr. *The Collages of Robert Motherwell.* Houston: Museum of Fine Arts, 1973.

Fineberg, Jonathan. "Death and Maternal Love: Psychological Speculations on Robert Motherwell's Art." *Artforum,* September 1978: 52–7.

O'Hara, Frank. *Robert Motherwell.* New York: The Museum of Modern Art, 1965.

Willem de Kooning

Butler, Cornelia and Paul Schimmel. *Willem de Kooning: Tracing the Figure.* Princeton, N.J.: Princeton University Press, 2002.

Cummings, Paul, Jörn Merkert, and Claire Stoullig. *Willem de Kooning: Drawings, Paintings, Sculpture.* New York: Whitney Museum of American Art and W. W. Norton and Company, 1983.

Gaugh, Harry F. *Willem de Kooning.* New York: Abbeville, 1983.

Hess, Thomas B. *Willem de Kooning.* New York: The Museum of Modern Art, 1968.

Rosenberg, Harold. *Willem de Kooning.* New York: Harry N. Abrams, 1973.

Chapter 4

Jackson Pollock

Frank, Elizabeth. *Jackson Pollock.* New York: Abbeville, 1983.

Friedman, B. H. *Energy Made Visible.* New York: McGraw-Hill, 1972.

Landau, Ellen G. *Jackson Pollock.* New York: Harry N. Abrams, 1989.

O'Hara, Frank. *Jackson Pollock.* New York: Braziller, 1959.

Rose, Bernice. *Jackson Pollock: Works on Paper.* New York: The Museum of Modern Art, 1970.

Rushing, Jackson W. "Ritual and Myth: Native American Culture and Abstract Expressionism." In Maurice Tuchman and Judi Freeman, eds. *The Spiritual In Art: Abstract Painting 1890–1985.* Los Angeles: Los Angeles County Museum of Art; New York: Abbeville, 1986: 285ff.

Barnett Newman

Hess, Thomas. *Barnett Newman.* New York: The Museum of Modern Art, 1971.

Newman, Barnett. *Selected Writings and Interviews.* Ed. John P. O'Neill with an introduction by Richard Shiff. Berkeley and Los Angeles: University of California Press, 1992.

Richardson, Brenda. *Barnett Newman: The Complete Drawings 1944–1969.* Baltimore: Baltimore Museum of Art, 1979.

Rosenberg, Harold. *Barnett Newman.* New York: Harry N. Abrams, 1978.

Temkin, Ann and Richard Shiff. *Barnett Newman.* Philadelphia, PA: Philadelphia Museum of Art, 2002.

Mark Rothko

Ashton, Dore. *About Rothko.* New York: Oxford University Press, 1983.

Breslin, James E. B. *Mark Rothko: A Biography.* Chicago: University of Chicago Press, 1993.

Chave, Anna C. *Mark Rothko: Subjects in Abstraction.* New Haven and London: Yale University Press, 1989.

Clearwater, Bonnie. *Mark Rothko Works on Paper.* New York: Hudson Hills, 1984.

Waldman, Diane. *Mark Rothko, 1903–1970: A Retrospective.* New York: Solomon R. Guggenheim Museum, 1978.

David Smith and the Sculpture of the New York School

Fry, Edward F. and Miranda McClintic. *David Smith: Painter, Sculptor, Draughtsman.* Washington, D.C.: Hirshhorn Museum and Sculpture Garden, Smithsonian Institution; New York: Braziller, 1982.

Gray, Cleve, ed. *David Smith by David Smith.* New York: Holt, Rinehart, & Winston, 1968.

McCoy, Garnett, ed. *David Smith.* New York: Praeger, 1973.

Phillips, Lisa. *The Third Dimension.* New York: Whitney Museum of American Art, 1984.

Wilkin, Karen. *David Smith.* New York: Abbeville, 1984.

Chapter 5

Jean Dubuffet and Postwar Paris

Dubuffet, Jean. *Prospectus et tous écrits suivants,* 2 vols. Paris: Gallimard, 1967.

Glimcher, Mildred. *Jean Dubuffet: Towards An Alternative Reality.* New York: Abbeville, 1987.

Morris, Frances. *Paris Post War: Art and Existentialism 1945–55.* London: Tate Gallery, 1993.

Rowell, Margit. *Jean Dubuffet: A Retrospective.* New York: Solomon R. Guggenheim Museum, 1973.

Selz, Peter. *The Work of Jean Dubuffet.* New York: The Museum of Modern Art, 1962.

Viatte, Germain and Sara Wilson. *Aftermath: France 1945–54, New Images of Man.* London: Barbican Art Gallery, 1982.

The Existentialist Figuration of Alberto Giacometti

Fletcher, Valerie J., Reinhold Hohl, Silvio Berthoud. *Alberto Giacometti, 1901–1966.* Washington, D.C.: Hirshhorn Museum and Sculpture Garden, Smithsonian Institution, 1988.

Hohl, Reinhold. *Alberto Giacometti: A Retrospective Exhibition.* New York: Solomon R. Guggenheim Museum, 1974.

Klemm, Christian, Carolyn Lanchner, Tobia Bezzola, and Anne Umland. *Alberto Giacometti.* New York: Museum of Modern Art, Distributed by H.N. Abrams, 2001.

Lord, James. *A Giacometti Portrait.* New York: The Museum of Modern Art, 1965.

Selz, Peter. *Alberto Giacometti.* New York: The Museum of Modern Art, 1965.

Francis Bacon

Ades, Dawn and Andrew Forge. *Francis Bacon.* New York: Harry N. Abrams, 1980.

Alley, Ronald and John Rothenstein. *Francis Bacon.* London: Thames & Hudson, 1964.

Davies, Hugh and Sally Yard. *Francis Bacon.* New York: Abbeville 1986.

Russell, John. *Francis Bacon.* Greenwich Conn.: New York Graphic Society, 1971.

Sylvester, David. *Francis Bacon Interviewed.* New York: Pantheon, 1975.

Chapter 6

Purified Abstraction

Barthes, Roland. "Cy Twombly: Works on Paper." In *The Responsibility of Forms.* Trans. Richard Howard. Berkeley: University of California Press, 1991, 157–176.

Beeren, Wim, Nicholas Serota, et al. *Fontana.* London: Whitechapel Art Gallery, 1988.

Bois, Yve-Alain. "Fontana's Base Materialism." *Art in America,* April 1989: 238–497.

Borja-Villel, Manuel J. *Fundació Antoni Tàpies.* Barcelona: Fundació Antoni Tàpies, 1990.

Braun, Emily, ed. *Italian Art in the 20th Century: Painting and Sculpture 1900–1988.* Munich: Prestel Verlag; London: Royal Academy of Arts, 1989.

Carmean, E. A., Jr. *The Great Decade of American Abstraction: 1960–1970.* Houston: Museum of Fine Arts, 1974.

Dimitrijevic, Nina. "Meanwhile in the Real World." *Flash Art,* May 1987: 44–9 [Fontana].

Elderfield, John. *Morris Louis.* New York: The Museum of Modern Art; Boston: Little, Brown, 1986.

Reinhardt, Ad. *Art as Art: The Selected Writings of Ad Reinhardt.* Edited by Barbara Rose. New York: Viking (The Documents of Twentieth Century Art), 1975.

Rose, Barbara. *Frankenthaler.* New York: Harry N. Abrams, 1970.

Sandler, Irving. *The New York School: The Painters and Sculptors of the Fifties.* New York: Harper & Row, 1978.

Seitz, William. *The Responsive Eye.* New York: The Museum of Modern Art, 1965.

Szeeman, Harold, Demosthenes Davettas, Roberta Smith, and Cy Twombly. *Cy Twombly: Paintings, Works on Paper, Sculpture.* London: Whitechapel Art Gallery; Munich: Prestel Verlag, 1987.

"New Images of Man" in Europe and America

Albright, Thomas. *Art in the San Francisco Bay Area 1945–1980.* Berkeley and Los Angeles: University of California Press, 1985.

Alechinsky, Pierre. *Paintings and Writings.* Pittsburgh: Museum of Art, Carnegie Institute, 1978.

Alechinsky, Pierre and Michael Gibson. *Pierre Alechinsky: Margin and Center.* New York: Solomon R. Guggenheim Museum, 1987.

Atkins, Guy. *I Jorn in Scandinavia, 1930–1953.* London: Lund Humphries, 1968.

Atkins, Guy. *II Asger Jorn. The Crucial Years 1954–1964.* London: Lund Humphries; Paris: Yves Rivière—Arts et Métiers Graphiques, 1977.

Atkins, Guy. *III Asger Jorn: The Final Years 1965–1973.* London: Lund Humphries; Copenhagen: Borgens Forlag, 1980.

Beattie, Ann. *Alex Katz.* New York: Harry N. Abrams, 1987.

Cobra 1948–1951, complete facsimile edition. Paris: Éditions Jean-Michel Place, 1980.

Elderfield, John. *Richard Diebenkorn.* New York: The Museum of Modern Art, 1991.

Hughes, Robert. *Lucian Freud: Paintings.* New York: Thames & Hudson, 1987.

Lambert, Jean-Clarence. *Cobra.* New York: Abbeville, 1984.

Schimmel, Paul and Judith Stein. *The Figurative Fifties: New York Figurative Expressionism.* Newport Beach, Cal.: Newport Harbor Art Museum, 1988.

Selz, Peter. *New Images of Man.* New York: The Museum of Modern Art, 1959.

Chapter 7

"A Coney Island of the Mind": The Beats, John Cage

Burroughs, William S. *Naked Lunch.* New York: Grove Press, 1959.

Cage, John. *Silence*. Cambridge, Mass.: MIT Press, 1966.

Duberman, Martin. *Black Mountain: An Exploration in Community*. New York: E. P. Dutton, 1972.

Ferlinghetti, Lawrence. *A Coney Island of the Mind*. Norfolk, Conn.: New Directions, 1955.

Ginsberg, Allen. *Howl and Other Poems*. San Francisco: City Lights Books, 1956.

Harris, Mary Emma. *The Arts at Black Mountain College*. Cambridge, Mass.: MIT Press, 1987.

McLuhan, Marshall. *The Mechanical Bride, Folklore of the Industrial Man*. New York: Vanguard Press, 1951.

Patterson, David Wayne. *John Cage: Music, Philosophy, and Intention, 1933–1950*. New York: Routledge, 2002.

Tomkins, Calvin. *The Bride and the Bachelors*. New York: Viking, 1968.

Robert Rauschenberg

Ashton, Dore. *Rauschenberg: XXXIV Drawings for Dante's Inferno*. New York: Harry N. Abrams, 1964.

Feinstein, Roni. *Robert Rauschenberg: The Silkscreen Paintings, 1962–64*. New York: Whitney Museum of American Art; Boston, Toronto, London: Little, Brown, 1990.

Hopps, Walter. *Robert Rauschenberg, The Early 1950s*. Houston: Fine Art Press, 1991.

Hopps, Walter, *Robert Rauschenberg*. Washington, D.C.: National Collection of Fine Arts, 1977.

Rose, Barbara. *An Interview with Robert Rauschenberg*. New York: Vintage, 1987.

Saltz, Jerry. "Notes on a Drawing." *Arts Magazine*, November, 1988: 19–22.

Schimmel, Paul. *Robert Rauschenberg: Combines*. Los Angeles: Museum of Contemporary Art, 2005.

Seckler, Dorothy Gees. "The Artist Speaks: Robert Rauschenberg." *Art in America* 54, May/June 1966: 73–84.

Stuckey, Charles F. "Reading Rauschenberg." *Art in America* 65, March/April 1977: 74–84.

Tomkins, Calvin. *Off the Wall: Robert Rauschenberg and the Art World of Our Time*. Garden City, N.Y.: Doubleday, 1980.

Appropriating the Real: Junk Sculpture and Happenings

Friedman, Martin and Graham W. J. Beal. *George Segal: Sculptures*. Minneapolis: Walker Art Center, 1978.

Gordon, John. *Jim Dine*. New York: Whitney Museum of American Art, 1970.

Haskell, Barbara. *Blam! The Explosion of Pop, Minimalism, and Performance 1958–1964*. New York: Whitney Museum of American Art, 1984.

Kaprow, Allan. "The Legacy of Jackson Pollock." *Artnews* 57, no. 4, October 1958: 24–6, 55–7.

Kaprow, Allan, André Lepecki, Eva Meyer-Hermann, and Stephanie Rosenthal. *Allan Kaprow: 18/6 – 18 happenings in 6 parts*. Munich: Steidl/Hauser & Wirth, 2006.

Kirby, Michael. *Happenings: An Illustrated Anthology*. New York: E. P. Dutton, 1965.

Kostelanetz, Richard. *The Theatre of Mixed Means: An Introduction to Happenings, Kinetic Environments, and Other Mixed Media Performances*. New York: Dial Press, 1968.

Levin, Kim. *Lucas Samaras*. New York: Harry N. Abrams, 1975.

Meyer-Hermann, Eva, Andrew Perchuk, and Stephanie Rosenthal. *Allan Kaprow: Art as Life*. Los Angeles: Getty Research Institute, 2008.

Monte, James K. *Mark di Suvero*. New York: Whitney Museum of American Art, 1976.

Sandler, Irving. *American Art of the 1960s*. New York: Harper & Row, 1988.

Seitz, William C. *The Art of Assemblage*. New York: The Museum of Modern Art, 1961.

Shapiro, David. *Jim Dine*. New York: Harry N. Abrams, 1981.

Stein, Judith E., John Ashbery, and Janet K. Cutler. *Red Grooms, A Retrospective, 1956–84*. Philadelphia: Pennsylvania Academy of the Fine Arts, 1985.

Waldman, Diane. *John Chamberlain*. New York: Solomon R. Guggenheim Museum, 1971.

Underground Film

Boswell, Peter. *2000 BC: The Bruce Conner Story Part II*. Minneapolis: Walker Art Center, 2000.

Brakhage, Stan, *Essential Brakhage: Selecting Writings on Filmmaking*, Ed. Bruce R. McPherson. Kingston, N.Y.: McPherson & Co., 2001.

Deren, Maya. *An Anagram of Ideas on Art, Form and Film*. New York: The Alicat Book Shop Press, 1946.

Nichols, Bill, ed. *Maya Deren and the American Avant-Garde*. Berkeley: University of California Press, 2001.

Vogel, Amos. *Film as a Subversive Art*. Forward by Scott MacDonald. New York: Distributed Art Publishers, 2005.

Claes Oldenburg

Friedman, Martin. *Oldenburg: Six Themes*. Minneapolis: Walker Art Center, 1975.

Oldenburg, Claes. *Proposals for Monuments and Buildings 1965–9*. Chicago: Big Table Publishing Co., 1969.

Oldenburg, Claes. *Notes in Hand*. New York: E. P. Dutton, 1971.

Oldenburg, Claes and Emmet Williams. *Store Days*. New York: Something Else Press, 1967.

Rose, Barbara. *Claes Oldenburg*. New York: The Museum of Modern Art, 1969.

van Bruggen, Coosje. *Claes Oldenburg: Mouse Museum/Ray Gun Wing*. Köln: Museum Ludwig, 1979.

Jasper Johns

Bernstein, Roberta. *Jasper Johns' Paintings and Sculptures 1954–1974: "The Changing Focus of the Eye"*. Ann Arbor, Mich.: UMI Research Press, 1985.

Castleman, Riva. *Jasper Johns: A Print Retrospective*. New York: The Museum of Modern Art, 1986.

Cuno, James, ed. *Foirades/Fizzles: Echo and Allusion in the Art of Jasper Johns*. Los Angeles: Grunwald Center for Graphic Arts, Wight Art Gallery, University of California, 1987.

Francis, Richard. *Jasper Johns*. New York: Abbeville, 1984.

Geelhaar, Christian. *Jasper Johns: Working Proofs*. London: Petersburg Press, 1980.

Rosenthal, Mark. *Jasper Johns: Work Since 1974*. Philadelphia: Philadelphia Museum of Art, 1988.

Rosenthal, Nan and Ruth E. Fine. *The Drawings of Jasper Johns*. Washington, D.C.: National Gallery of Art, 1990.

Shapiro, David. *Jasper Johns Drawings 1954–1984*. New York: Harry N. Abrams, 1984.

Weiss, Jeffrey S. and John Elderfield. *Jasper Johns: An Allegory of Painting, 1955–1965*. Washington: National Gallery of Art, 2007.

Chapter 8

Nouveau Réalisme

Bodet, Aude, Sylvain Lecombre, et al. *1960: Les Nouveaux Réalistes*. Paris: Musée d'Art Moderne de la Ville de Paris, 1986.

McEvilley, Thomas et al. *Yves Klein 1928–1962: A Retrospective*. Houston: Institute for the Arts, Rice University, 1982.

Pontus Hulten, K. G. *Jean Tinguely: Méta*. London: Thames and Hudson, 1975.

Restany, Pierre. *Yves Klein*. New York: Harry N. Abrams, 1982.

Schimmel, Paul. "Leap Into the Void: Performance and the Object." In *Out of Actions: Between Performance and the Object, 1948–1979*. Los Angeles: The Museum of Contemporary Art, and London: Thames and Hudson, 1998.

Gutai

Schimmel, Paul. "Leap Into the Void: Performance and the Object," *Out of Actions*. [see above for full citation]

Yoshihara, Jiro. "The Gutai Manifesto," *Gennijutsu Shincho* (December 1956); See Stiles and Selz *Theories and documents of contemporary art: a sourcebook of artists' writings*. Berkeley: University of California Press, 1996.

Fluxus

Armstrong, Elizabeth and Joan Rothfuss. *In The Spirit of Fluxus*. Minneapolis: Walker Art Center, 1993.

Hanhardt, John G. *The Worlds of Nam June Paik*. New York: Guggenheim Museum, 2000.

Hendricks, Jon. *Fluxus codex*. Detroit: Gilbert and Lila Silverman Fluxus Collection; New York: Harry N. Abrams, 1988.

Higgins, Hannah. *Fluxus Experience*. Berkeley: University of California Press, 2002.

Joselit, David. *Feedback: television against democracy*. Cambridge, Mass.: MIT Press, 2007.

Munroe, Alexandra, Jon Hendricks, et al. *YES: Yoko Ono*. New York: Japan Society, 2000.

Stooss, Toni and Thomas Kellein. *Nam June Paik: Video Time—Video Space*. New York: Harry N. Abrams, 1993.

Joseph Beuys

Joachimides, Christos and Norman Rosenthal. *Zeitgeist, Internationale Kunstaustellung*. Berlin: Martin Gropius Bau, 1982; New York: Braziller, 1983.

Joachimides, Christos, Norman Rosenthal, and Wieland Schmied, eds. *German Art in the 20th Century*. London: Royal Academy of Arts; Munich: Prestel Verlag, 1986.

Mesch, Claudia and Viola Maria Michely, eds. *Joseph Beuys: The Reader*. Cambridge, Mass.: MIT Press, 2007.

Serota, Nick. *Joseph Beuys: The Secret Block for a Secret Person in Ireland*. Oxford: Museum of Modern Art, 1974.

Sharp, Willoughby. "An Interview with Joseph Beuys." *Artforum* 8, December 1969: 40ff.

Tisdall, Caroline. *Joseph Beuys*. New York: Solomon R. Guggenheim Museum, 1979.

Chapter 9

British Pop: From the Independent Group to David Hockney

Banham, Rayner. *The New Brutalism. Ethic or Aesthetic*. New York: Reinhold Publishing, 1966.

Friedman, Martin, ed. *Hockney Paints the Stage*. Minneapolis: Walker Art Center; New York: Abbeville, 1983.

Leffingwell, Edward et al. *Modern Dreams: The Rise and Fall of Pop*. New York: The Institute for Contemporary Art; Cambridge, Mass.: MIT Press, 1988.

Livingstone, Marco. *David Hockney*. New York: Thames & Hudson, 1988.

Massey, Anne. "The Independent Group: Towards a Redefinition." *Burlington Magazine* 129, no. 1009, April 1987: 232–42.

Paolozzi, Eduardo, and Robin Spencer. *Eduardo Paolozzi: Writings and Interviews*. Oxford and New York: Oxford University Press, 2000.

Russell, John and Susie Gablik. *Pop Art Redefined*. London: Thames & Hudson, 1969.

Russell, John. *Richard Hamilton*. New York: Solomon R. Guggenheim Museum, 1973.

Spencer, Robin. *Eduardo Paolozzi: Recurring Themes*. New York: Rizzoli, 1984.

Tuchman, Maurice and Stephanie Barron. *David Hockney: A Retrospective*. Los Angeles: Los Angeles County Museum of Art, 1988.

The Electronic Consciousness and New York Pop

Alloway, Lawrence. *American Pop Art*. New York: Collier Books, 1974.

Armstrong, Richard. *Artschwager, Richard*. New York: Whitney Museum of American Art, 1988.

De Salvo, Donna and Paul Schimmel. *Hand-Painted Pop: American Art in Transition 1955–62*. Los Angeles: Museum of Contemporary Art; New York: Rizzoli, 1992.

Livingstone, Marco. *Pop Art: A Continuing History*. New York: Harry N. Abrams, 1990.

McLuhan, Marshall. *Understanding Media: The Extension of Man*. New York: McGraw-Hill, 1965.

Venturi, Robert. *Complexity and Contradiction in Architecture*. New York: The Museum of Modern Art, 1966.

Andy Warhol

De Salvo, Donna M. *"Success is a job in New York . . .": The Early Art and Business of Andy Warhol*. New York: Grey Art Gallery and Study Center, New York University, 1989.

Goldsmith, Kenneth. *I'll Be Your Mirror: The Selected Andy Warhol Interviews, 1962–1987*. New York: Carroll & Graf Publishers, 2004.

McShine, Kynaston, ed. *Andy Warhol: A Retrospective*. New York: The Museum of Modern Art, 1989.

Michelson, Annette, ed. *Andy Warhol*. Cambridge, Mass.: MIT Press, 2001.

Ratcliff, Carter. *Andy Warhol*. New York: Abbeville, 1983.

Warhol, Andy. *The Philosophy of Andy Warhol (From A to B and Back Again)*. New York: Harcourt, Brace, Jovanovich, 1975.

Warhol, Andy and Pat Hackett. *Popism: The Warhol 60s.* New York: Harcourt, Brace, Jovanovich, 1980.

Wilcock, John. *The autobiography and sex life of Andy Warhol.* New York: Other Scenes Inc, 1971.

Roy Lichtenstein

Alloway, Lawrence. *Roy Lichtenstein.* New York: Abbeville, 1983.

Lobel, Michael. *Image Duplicator: Roy Lichtenstein and the Emergence of Pop Art.* New Haven, Conn.: Yale University Press, 2002.

James Rosenquist

Goldman, Judith. *James Rosenquist.* Denver: Denver Art Museum; New York: Viking, 1985.

Hopps, Walter and Sarah Bancroft. *James Rosenquist: A Retrospective.* New York: Guggenheim Museum, 2003.

H. C. Westermann, Peter Saul, and the Hairy Who

Adrian, Dennis and Richard Born. *The Chicago Imagist Print: Ten Artists' Works, 1958–1987, A Catalogue Raisonné.* Chicago: Smart Gallery, University of Chicago, 1987.

Adrian, Dennis et al. *Who Chicago? An Exhibition of Contemporary Imagists.* Sunderland, U.K.: Sunderland Arts Centre, 1980.

Adrian, Dennis. *Karl Wirsum.* Champaign, Ill.,: Krannert Art Museum, University of Illinois, 1991.

Barrette, Bill, ed. *Letters from H. C. Westermann.* New York: Timken, 1988.

Benezra, Neal. *Ed Paschke.* Chicago: Art Institute of Chicago, 1990.

Cameron, Dan. *Karl Wirsum: A Retrospective.* Chicago: Phyllis Kind Gallery, 1986.

Cameron, Dan, et al. *Peter Saul.* Ostfildern, Germany: Hatje Cantz; Newport Beach, Cal.: Orange County Museum of Art, 2008.

Halstead, Whitney. *Jim Nutt.* Chicago: Museum of Contemporary Art, 1974.

Halstead, Whitney and Dennis Adrian. *Made in Chicago.* Washington, D.C.: National Collection of Fine Arts, Smithsonian Institution; Chicago: Museum of Contemporary Art, 1974.

Haskell, Barbara. *H. C. Westermann.* New York: Whitney Museum of American Art, 1978.

Lawrence, Sidney. *Roger Brown.* Washington, D.C.: Hirshhorn Museum and Sculpture Garden, Smithsonian Institution, 1987.

Saul, Peter. *Peter Saul.* De Kalb, Ill.: Swen Parson Gallery, Northern Illinois University, 1980.

Saul, Peter. *Peter Saul: New Paintings and Works On Paper.* New York: Allan Frumkin Gallery, 1988 [letters to Allan Frumkin].

Schulze, Franz. *Fantastic Images: Chicago Art Since 1945.* Chicago: Follet, 1972.

Storr, Robert. *Peter Saul.* Aspen, Col.: Aspen Art Museum, 1989.

Warren, Lynne, and Michael Rooks. *H. C. Westermann.* Chicago: Museum of Contemporary Art in Association with Harry N. Abrams, 2001.

West Coast Pop

Auping, Michael, Robert J. Bertholf, and Michael Palmer. *Jess: A Grand Collage 1951–1993.* Buffalo, N.Y.: Albright-Knox Art Gallery, 1993.

Ayers, Anne. *L. A. Pop in the Sixties.* Newport Beach, Cal.: Newport Harbor Museum, 1989.

Beal, Graham W. J. and John Perrault. *Wiley Territory.* Minneapolis: Walker Art Center, 1979.

Hickey, Dave and Peter Plagens. *The Works of Edward Ruscha: Essays.* New York: Hudson Hills Press; San Francisco: SFMoMA, 1982.

Moser, Joann. *What's it all mean: William T. Wiley in retrospect.* Washington, D.C.: Smithsonian American Art Museum; Berkeley: University of California Press, 2009.

Plagens, Peter. *Sunshine Muse: Contemporary Art on the West Coast.* New York: Praeger, 1974.

Relyea, Lane. *Vija Celmins.* London: Phaidon, 2004.

Richardson, Brenda. *Wizdumb: William T. Wiley.* Berkeley: University Art Museum, 1971.

Tuchman, Maurice. *Edward Keinholz.* Los Angeles: Los Angeles County Museum of Art, 1966.

Weschler, Lawrence et al. *Edward and Nancy Reddin Kienholz: Human Scale.* San Francisco: San Francisco Museum of Modern Art, 1984.

Robert Arneson

Adrian, Dennis. "Robert Arneson's Feats of Clay." *Art in America,* September 1974: 80–3.

Benezra, Neal. *Robert Arneson: A Retrospective.* Des Moines, Iowa: Des Moines Art Center, 1985.

Kuspit, Donald B. "Arneson's Outrage." *Art in America,* May 1985: 134–9.

Marshall, Richard and Suzanne Foley. *Ceramic Sculpture: Six Artists.* New York: Whitney Museum of American Art, 1981.

Chapter 10

Back to First Principles—Minimal Art

Barris, Roann. "Peter Eisenman and the Erosion of Truth." *20/1 Art and Culture,* vol. 1, no. 2, spring 1990: 20–37.

Battcock, Gregory, ed. *Minimal Art.* New York: E. P. Dutton, 1968.

Berger, Maurice. *Labyrinths: Robert Morris, Minimalism, and the 1960s.* New York: Harper & Row, 1989.

Bourdon, David. *Carl Andre.* Austin: Laguna Gloria Art Museum, 1978.

Brown, Julia, ed. *Occluded Front: James Turrell.* Los Angeles: Museum of Contemporary Art, 1985.

Chave, Anna. "Minimalism and the Rhetoric of Power." *Arts Magazine,* 64, January 1990: 44–63.

Compton, Michael and David Sylvester. *Robert Morris.* London: Tate Gallery, 1971.

Foster, Hal. "The Crux of Minimalism." In *The Return of the Real.* Cambridge, Mass.: MIT Press, 1996, 34–69.

Garrels, Gary. *Sol LeWitt: A Retrospective.* New Haven, Conn.: Yale University Press, 2000.

Govan, Michael and Tiffany Bell. *Dan Flavin: A Retrospective.* New Haven, Conn.: Yale University Press, 2005.

Haskell, Barbara. *Donald Judd.* New York: Whitney Museum of American Art, 1988.

Suzanne Hudson, *Robert Ryman: Used Paint.* Cambridge, Mass.: MIT Press, 2009.

Irwin, Robert. *Robert Irwin.* New York: Whitney Museum of American Art, 1977.

Judd, Donald. *Complete Writings 1959–75.* Halifax: The Press of the Nova Scotia College of Art and Design; New York: New York University Press, 1975.

Koschalek, Richard, et al. *Robert Irwin.* Los Angeles: Museum of Contemporary Art, 1993.

Meyer, James. *Minimalism: Art and Polemics in the Sixties.* New Haven, Conn.: Yale University Press, 2001.

Meyer, James, ed. *Minimalism.* London: Phaidon, 2000.

Raskin, David. "Specific Oppositions: Judd's Art and Politics." *Art History* 24, no. 5 (November 2001): 682–706.

Richardson, Brenda. *Frank Stella: The Black Paintings.* Baltimore: Baltimore Museum of Art, 1976.

Rubin, William S. *Frank Stella.* New York: The Museum of Modern Art, 1970.

Serota, Nicholas. *Donald Judd.* London: Tate; New York: D.A.P., 2004.

Shearer, Linda. *Brice Marden.* New York: Solomon R. Guggenheim Museum, 1975.

Tucker, Marcia. *Robert Morris.* New York: Whitney Museum of American Art, 1970.

Wagstaff, Samuel, Jr. "Talking to Tony Smith." *Artforum,* December 1966: 14–19.

Waldman, Diane. *Carl Andre.* New York: Solomon R. Guggenheim Museum, 1970.

Weschler, Lawrence. *Seeing is Forgetting the Name of the Thing One Sees . . . Robert Irwin.* Berkeley and Los Angeles: University of California Press, 1982.

Eva Hesse and Investigations of Materials and Process

Armstrong, Richard and Richard Marshall. *The New Sculpture 1965–75.* New York: Whitney Museum of American Art, 1990.

Barrette, Bill. *Eva Hesse: Sculpture.* New York: Timken, 1988.

de Zegher, Catherine. *Eva Hesse drawing.* New York: The Drawing Center; New Haven, Conn.: Yale University Press, 2006.

Lippard, Lucy. "Eccentric Abstraction." *Art International* 10, no. 9 (Nov 1966): 28–40.

Lippard, Lucy. *Eva Hesse.* New York: New York University Press, 1976.

Nemser, Cindy. "An Interview with Eva Hesse." *Artforum,* May 1970: 63.

Sussman, Elizabeth. *Eva Hesse.* New Haven, Conn.: Yale University Press, 2002.

Sussman, Elizabeth. *Eva Hesse: sculpture.* New York: Jewish Museum; New Haven, Conn.: Yale University Press, 2006.

Wagner, Anne Middleton. *Three artists (three women): modernism and the art of Hesse, Krasner, and O'Keeffe.* Berkeley: University of California Press, 1996.

Bruce Nauman and Richard Serra

Adriani, Götz, Hans Albert Peters, and Clara Weyergraf, eds. *Richard Serra: Works 1966–77.* Baden-Baden and Tübingen, Germany: Kunsthalle, 1978.

Benezra, Neal. *Affinities and Intuitions: The Gerald S. Elliott Collection of Contemporary Art.* Chicago: Art Institute of Chicago; New York: Abbeville, 1990.

Foster, Hal, Gordon Hughes, and B. H. D. Buchloh. *Richard Serra.* Cambridge, Mass.: MIT Press, 2000.

Krauss, Rosalind. *Richard Serra/Sculpture.* New York: The Museum of Modern Art, 1986.

Lewallen, Constance, Robert R. Riley, Anne Middleton Wagner, and Bruce Nauman. *A Rose Has No Teeth: Bruce Nauman in the 1960s.* Berkeley: University of California Press, 2007.

Kraynak, Janet, ed. *Please pay attention please: Bruce Nauman's words: writings and interviews.* Cambridge, Mass.: MIT Press, 2003.

Richardson, Brenda. *Bruce Nauman: Neons.* Baltimore: Baltimore Museum of Art, 1982.

Simon, Joan, Neal Benezra, and Kathy Halbreich. *Bruce Nauman.* Minneapolis: Walker Art Center, 1994.

van Bruggen, Coosje. *Bruce Nauman.* New York: Rizzoli, 1987.

Weyergraf, Clara, ed. *Richard Serra: Interviews, Etc. 1970–1980.* Yonkers, N.Y.: Hudson River Museum, 1980.

Artists Working in the Landscape

Beardsley, John. *Earthworks and Beyond.* 2nd ed. New York: Abbeville, 1989.

Burnham, Jack. *Great Western Salt Works.* New York: Braziller, 1974.

Cooke, Lynne and Karen J. Kelly. *Robert Smithson: Spiral Jetty.* Berkeley: University of California Press; New York: Dia Art Foundation, 2005.

Hobbs, Robert. *Robert Smithson: Sculpture.* Ithaca, N.Y.: Cornell University Press, 1981.

Insley, Will. "Seriocomic Sp(i)eleology: Robert Smithson's Architecture of Existence." *Arts,* May 1978: 98–101.

Joosten, Ellen and Feliix Zdenek. *Michael Heizer.* Essen, Germany: Museum Folkwang, 1979.

Kastner, Jeffrey. *Land and environmental art: themes and movements.* London: Phaidon, 1998.

Roberts, Jennifer L. *Mirror-travels: Robert Smithson and history.* New Haven, Conn.: Yale University Press, 2004.

Smithson, Robert. *The Writings of Robert Smithson.* Ed. Nancy Holt. New York: New York University Press, 1979.

Tsai, Eugenie. *Robert Smithson Unearthed: Drawings, Collages, Writings.* New York: Columbia University Press, 1991.

Tsai, Eugenie and Cornelia H. Butler. *Robert Smithson.* Berkeley: University of California Press, 2004.

Arte Povera, and a Persevering Rapport with Nature in Europe

Auping, Michael, in Benezra, Neal. *Affinities and Intuitions: The Gerald S. Elliott Collection of Contemporary Art.* Chicago: Art Institute of Chicago; New York: Abbeville, 1990.

Braun, Emily, ed. *Italian Art in the 20th Century: Painting and Sculpture 1900–1988.* Munich: Prestel Verlag; London: Royal Academy of Arts, 1989.

Celant, Germano. *Arte Povera.* New York: Praeger, 1969.

Celant, Germano. *Mario Merz.* New York: Solomon R. Guggenheim Museum, 1989.

Celant, Germano. *Michelangelo Pistoletto.* New York: Rizzoli, 1989.

Flood, Richard, and Frances Morris. *Zero to Infinity: Arte Povera, 1962–1972.* Minneapolis: Walker Art Center, 2001.

Krane, Susan. *Mario Merz: Paintings and Constructions.* Buffalo, N.Y.: Albright-Knox Art Gallery, 1984.

Chapter 11

Re-Radicalizing the Avant-Garde

Acconci, Vito, Sarina Basta, and Garrett Ricciardi. *Vito Acconci: Diary of a Body, 1969–1973.* Milan and New York: Charta, 2006.

Alberro, Alexander and Blake Stimson. *Conceptual Art: A Critical Anthology.* Cambridge, Mass.: MIT Press, 1999.

Basualdo, Carlos. *Hélio Oiticica: Quasi-Cinemas*. Columbus, OH: Wexner Center for the Arts; Hatje Cantz, 2001.

Borja-Villel, Manuel J. *Lygia Clark*. Barcelona: Fundació Antoni Tàpies, 1997.

Brett, Guy et al. *Hélio Oiticica*. Minneapolis: Walker Art Center, 1992/3.

Campany, David. *Art and photography*. London; New York: Phaidon, 2003.

Cherix, Christophe. *In & Out of Amsterdam: Travels in Conceptual Art, 1960–1976*. New York: Museum of Modern Art, 2009.

Debord, Guy. *The Society of the Spectacle*. Revised English ed. Detroit: Black and Red, 1983.

Garrels, Gary. *Roth Time: A Dieter Roth Retrospective*. New York: Museum of Modern Art, 2004.

Goldberg, RoseLee. *Performance: Live Art 1909 to the Present*. New York: Harry N. Abrams, 1979.

Goldberg, RoseLee. *Laurie Anderson*. New York: Harry N. Abrams, 2000.

Goldwater, Marge et al. *Marcel Broodthaers*. Minneapolis: Walker Art Center and New York: Rizzoli, 1989.

Fusco, Coco. *Corpus Delecti: Performance Art of the Americas*. London and New York: Routledge, 2000.

Hall, Doug and Sally Jo Fifer. *Illuminating Video: An Essential Guide to Video Art*. New York: Aperture Foundation, 1990.

Horvitz, Robert Joseph. "Nature As Artifact: Alan Sonfist." *Artforum*, November 1973: 32–5.

Kardon, Janet. *Laurie Anderson: Works From 1969 to 1983*. Philadelphia: Institute of Contemporary Art, University of Pennsylvania, 1983.

Lippard, Lucy. *Six Years: the dematerialization of the art object from 1966 to 1972*. New York: Praeger, 1973.

Linker, Kate. *Vito Acconci*. New York: Rizzoli, 1994.

Osborne, Peter. *Conceptual Art*. London and New York: Phaidon, 2002.

Schimmel, Paul. *Out of Actions*. [see Chapter 8 for full citation]

Ramírez, Mari Carmen, Luciano Figueiredo, and Wynne Phelan. *Helio Oiticica: the body of color*. Houston: The Museum of Fine Arts, 2007.

Richardson, Brenda. *Gilbert and George*. Baltimore: Baltimore Museum of Art, 1984.

Vergine, Lea. *Body Art and Performance: The Body as Language*. Milan: Skira, 2000.

Viso, Olga M. *Ana Mendieta: Earth body: Sculpture and Performance, 1972–1985*. Washington, D.C.: Hirshhorn Museum and Sculpture Garden; Ostfildern-Ruit, Germany: Hatje Cantz, 2004.

Warr, Tracey and Amelia Jones *The Artist's Body: Themes and Motives*. London: Phaidon, 2000.

Christo and Jeanne-Claude

Bourdon, David. *Christo*. New York: Harry N. Abrams, 1970.

Christo. *Christo: Valley Curtain*. New York: Harry N. Abrams, 1973.

Christo. *Christo: The Pont Neuf, Wrapped*. New York: Harry N. Abrams, 1990.

Fineberg, Jonathan. "Theatre of the Real: Thoughts on Christo." *Art in America*, December 1979: 92–9.

Fineberg, Jonathan. *Christo and Jeanne-Claude: On The Way to The Gates*. New York: Metropolitan Museum of Art; New Haven, Conn.: Yale University Press, 2004.

Spies, Werner. *Christo: Surrounded Islands*. New York: Harry N. Abrams, 1984.

Spies, Werner. *The Running Fence—Christo*. New York: Harry N. Abrams, 1977.

Postmodernism: Richter, Polke, Baldessari

Buchloh, Benjamin, et al. *Gerhard Richter*. Cambridge, Mass.: MIT Press, 2009.

Caldwell, John. *Sigmar Polke*. San Francisco: San Francisco Museum of Modern Art, 1990.

Dietrich, Dorothea. "Gerhard Richter: An Interview." *The Print Collector's Newsletter*, vol. 16, September/October 1985: 128–32.

Rainbird, Sean. *Gerhard Richter*. London: Tate Gallery, 1991.

Richter, Gerhard. *The Daily Practice of Painting: Writings 1962–1993*, edited by Hans-Ulrich Obrist. Cambridge, Mass.: MIT Press, 1995.

Storr, Robert, "Polke's Mind Tattoos," *Art in America*, December 1992: 71.

Storr, Robert. *Gerhard Richter: October 18, 1977*. New York: Museum of Modern Art, 2000.

Storr, Robert. *Gerhard Richter: Forty Years of Painting*. New York: Museum of Modern Art, 2002.

Tucker, Marcia, ed. *John Baldessari*. New York: New Museum of Contemporary Art, 1981.

van Bruggen, Coosje. *John Baldessari*. New York: Rizzoli, 1990.

Chapter 12

A"New" Pluralism

Basilio, Miriam. *Latin American & Caribbean art: MoMA. at El Museo*. New York: El Museo del Barrio and the Museum of Modern Art: Distributed Art Publishers, 2004.

Bloom, Lisa. *With OtherEeyes: Looking at Race and Gender in Visual Culture*. Minneapolis: University of Minnesota Press, 1999.

Goldman, Shifra M. and Luis Camnitzer, eds. Special issue on "Latin American Art." *The Art Journal*, winter 1992.

Flomenhaft, Eleanor, et al. *Faith Ringgold: A 25 Year Survey*. Hempstead, N.Y.: Fine Arts Museum of Long Island, 1990.

Levin, Kim. *Rafael Ferrer: impassioned rhythms*. Austin: Laguna Gloria Art Museum, 1982.

Lippard, Lucy. *Mixed Blessings: New Art in a Multicultural America*. New York: Pantheon, 1990.

Mosquera, Gerardo. *Beyond the fantastic: contemporary art criticism from Latin America*. Cambridge, Mass.: MIT Press, 1996.

Powell, Rick. *The Blues Aesthetic: Black Culture and Modernism*. Washington, D.C.: Washington Project for the Arts, 1989.

Robins, Corinne. *The Pluralist Era: American Art, 1968–81*. New York: Harper & Row, 1984.

Sondheim, Alan. *Individuals: Post-Movement Art in America*. New York: E. P. Dutton, 1977.

Romare Bearden

Conwill, Kinshasha Holman, Mary Schmidt Campbell, and Sharon F. Patton, *Memory and Metaphor: The Art of Romare Bearden 1940–1987*. New York: Oxford University Press and the Studio Museum in Harlem, 1991.

Fine, Ruth. *The Art of Romare Bearden*. Washington D.C.: National Gallery of Art, 2003.

Art and Feminism

Bobo, Jacqueline. *Black Feminist Cultural Criticism*. Malden, Mass.: Blackwell, 2001.

Butler, Cornelia H. *WACK!: Art and the Feminist Revolution*. Los Angeles: Museum of Contemporary Art; Cambridge, Mass.: MIT Press, 2007.

Bird, Jon, Jo Anna Isaak, and Sylvère Lotringer. *Nancy Spero*. London: Phaidon Press, 1996.

Nettles, Bea. *Breaking the Rules: A Photo Media Cookbook*. 3d ed. Urbana, Ill.: Inky Press, 1992.

Nochlin, Linda. "Why Have There Been No Great Women Artists?" *Artnews* 69, January 1971: 22–39, 67–71.

Reckitt, Helena and Peggy Phelan. *Art and feminism*. London and New York: Phaidon, 2001.

Rosen, Randy and Catherine C. Brawer, eds. *Making Their Mark: Women Artists Move into the Mainstream, 1970–85*. New York: Abbeville, 1989.

Rossler, Martha. *Decoys and Disruptions: Selected Essays 1975–2001*. Cambridge, Mass.: MIT Press, 2004.

Photorealism

Storr, Robert. *Chuck Close*. New York: Harry N. Abrams, 1998.

Varnedoe, Kirk. *Duane Hanson*. New York: Harry N. Abrams, 1985.

Public Sites

Fox, Howard N. *A Primal Spirit: Ten Contemporary Japanese Sculptors*. Los Angeles: Los Angeles County Museum of Art, 1990.

Halbreich, Kathy, Thomas Sokolowski, Shinji Kohmoto, and Fumio Nanjo, *Against Nature: Japanese Art in the Eighties*. New York: Grey Art Gallery, University of New York; Cambridge, Mass.: MIT List Visual Arts Center; Tokyo: Japan Foundation, 1989.

Kwon, Miwon. *One place after another: site-specific art and locational identity*. Cambridge, Mass.: MIT Press, 2002.

Lee, Pamela. *Object To Be Destroyed: The Work of Gordon Matta-Clark*. Cambridge, Mass.: MIT Press, 2000.

Matta-Clark, Gordon. *Gordon Matta-Clark: works and collected writings*. Gloria Moure, ed. New York: Distributed Art Publishing, 2006.

Neff, John et al. *Charles Simonds*. Chicago: Museum of Contemporary Art, 1981.

Alice Aycock

Fineberg, Jonathan. *Complex Visions: Sculpture and Drawings by Alice Aycock*. Mountainville, N.Y.: Storm King Art Center, 1990.

Fry, Edward. *Alice Aycock: Projects 1979–1981*. Tampa: University of South Florida College of Fine Arts and Art Galleries, 1981.

Tsai, Eugenie. "A Tale of (At Least) Two Cities: Alice Aycock's Large Scale Dis/Integration of Microelectric Memories (A Newly Revised Shantytown)." *Arts* 56, June 1982: 134–41.

Dan Graham

Peltzer, Birgit, Mark Francis and Beatriz Colomina. *Dan Graham*. London: Phaidon Press, 2001.

Simpson, Bennett and Chrissie Iles. *Dan Graham: Beyond*. Los Angeles: Museum of Contemporary Art; Cambridge, Mass.: MIT Press, 2009.

Appropriation

Burton, Johanna and Craig Owens. *Cindy Sherman*. Cambridge, Mass.: MIT Press, 2006.

Crimp, Douglas. "Pictures," *October*, no. 8 (Spring 1979), pp. 75–88.

Cruz, Amada, Elizabeth A. T. Smith and Amelia Jones. *Cindy Sherman: Retrospective*. New York: Thames & Hudson, 1997.

Garrels, Gary, ed. *Amerika: Tim Rollins and K.O.S.* New York: Dia Art Foundation, 1989.

Eklund, Douglas. *The Pictures Generation, 1974–1984*. New York: Metropolitan Museum of Art; New Haven, Conn.: Yale University Press, 2009.

Galassi, Peter. *Cindy Sherman: The Complete Untitled Film Stills*. New York: Museum of Modern Art; London: Thames & Hudson, 2003.

Heiferman, Marvin and Lisa Phillips. *Image World: Art and Media Culture*. New York: Whitney Museum of American Art, 1989.

Kardon, Janet. *David Salle*. Philadelphia: Institute of Contemporary Art, 1986.

Lawson, Thomas. "Last Exit: Painting." *Artforum* (Oct. 1981): 40–47.

Olander, William. "Material World." *Art in America*, January 1989: 122–9, 167.

Phillips, Lisa. *David Salle*. New York: Whitney Musuem of American Art, 1987.

Phillips, Lisa. *Richard Prince*. New York: Whitney Museum of American Art, 1992.

Rian, Jeffrey. "Social Science Fiction: An Interview with Richard Prince." *Art in America*, March 1987: 86–95, cover.

Schjeldahl, Peter. *An Interview with David Salle*. New York: Vintage, 1987.

Spector, Nancy. *Richard Prince*. New York: Guggenheim Museum, 2007.

Chapter 13

Philip Guston's Late Style

Arnason, H. Harvard. *Philip Guston*. New York: Solomon R. Guggenheim Museum, 1962.

Ashton, Dore. *Yes, But . . . , A Critical Study of Philip Guston*. New York: Viking, 1976.

Hopkins, Henry. *Philip Guston*. San Francisco: San Francisco Museum of Modern Art; New York: Braziller, 1980.

Hunter, Sam, Harold Rosenberg, and Philip Guston. *Philip Guston: Recent Paintings and Drawings*. New York: Jewish Museum, 1966.

Mayer, Musa. *Night Studio: A Memoir of Philip Guston by His Daughter*. New York: Viking-Penguin, 1988.

Storr, Robert. *Philip Guston*. New York: Abbeville, 1986.

New Expressionist Painting in Europe

Arasse, Daniel. *Anselm Kiefer*. New York: Harry N. Abrams, 2001.

Auping, Michael. *Francesco Clemente*. Milano: Charta, 2000.

Benezra, Neal. *Affinities and Intuitions*. [see Chapter 10 for full citation]

Bromfield, David. *Identities: A Critical Study of the Work of Mike Parr, 1970–1990*. Nedlands, Australia: University of Western Australia Press, 1991.

Cowart, Jack. *Expressions: New Art from Germany*. St. Louis: Saint Louis Art Museum; Munich: Prestel Verlag, 1983.

Crone, Rainer and Georgia Marsh. *An Interview with Francesco Clemente*. New York: Vintage, 1987.

Fineberg, Jonathan and Daniel Thomas. *An Australian Accent*. New York: P.S.1, 1984.

Gallwitz, Klaus, ed. *Georg Baselitz*. Venice: German Pavilion, Biennale di Venezia, 1980.

Grisebach, Lucius, ed. *A. R. Penck*. Berlin: Nationalgalerie; Munich: Prestel Verlag, 1988.

Immendorff, Jörg. *Here and Now: To Do What Has to Be Done* [*Hier und Jetzt: Das tun, was zu tun ist*]. Köln and New York: Gebr. König, 1973; republished in *Immendorff's Handbuch der Akademie für Adler*. Köln: Walter König, 1989.

Jörg Immendorff's "The Rake's Progress". London: Barbican Art Gallery, 1995.

Joachimides, Christos M., Norman Rosenthal, and Nicholas Serota. *A New Spirit in Painting*. London: Royal Academy of Arts, 1981.

Kort, Pamela. *Jörg Immendorff: Early Works and Lidl*. New York: Gallery Michael Werner, 1991.

Kort, Pamela. *Jörg Immendorff: I wanted to Be an Artist 1971–1974*. New York: Gallery Michael Werner, 1992.

Krens, Thomas, Michael Govin, Joseph Thompson, eds. *Refigured Painting: The German Image 1960–88*. New York: Solomon R. Guggenheim Museum; Munich: Prestel Verlag, 1988.

Percy, Ann and Raymond Foye. *Francesco Clemente: Three Worlds*. Philadelphia: Philadelphia Museum of Art; New York: Rizzoli, 1990.

Ratcliff, Carter. *Komar and Melamid*. New York: Abbeville, 1989.

Rosenthal, Mark. *Anselm Kiefer*. Philadelphia: Philadelphia Museum of Art; Chicago: Art Institute of Chicago; Munich: Prestel Verlag, 1987.

Yau, John. *A. R. Penck*. New York: Harry N. Abrams, 1993.

Zweite, Armin. *Anselm Kiefer: The High Priestess*. New York: Harry N. Abrams; London: Anthony d'Offay Gallery, 1989.

Jennifer Bartlett, Susan Rothenberg: New Imagist Painting and Sculpture

Goldwater, Marge, Roberta Smith, Calvin Tomkins. *Jennifer Bartlett*. Minneapolis: Walker Art Center; New York: Abbeville, 1985.

Marshall, Richard. *New Image Painting*. New York: Whitney Museum of American Art, 1978.

Marshall, Richard and Roberta Smith. *Joel Shapiro*. New York: Whitney Museum of American Art, 1982.

Rifkin, Ned. *Robert Moskowitz*. Washington, D.C.: Hirshhorn Museum and Sculpture Garden, Smithsonian Institution, 1989.

Rosenthal, Mark. *Neil Jenney*. Berkeley: University Art Museum, 1981.

Simon, Joan. *Susan Rothenberg*. New York: Harry N. Abrams, 1991.

Stearns, Robert. *Robert Wilson: From a Theatre of Images*. Cincinnati: Cincinnati Arts Center, 1980.

Elizabeth Murray

Graze, Sue, Kathy Halbreich, and Roberta Smith. *Elizabeth Murray: Paintings and Drawings*. Dallas: Dallas Museum of Art; Cambridge, Mass.: MIT Committee on the Visual Arts, 1987.

King, Elaine A. *Elizabeth Murray Drawings 1980–1986*. Pittsburgh: Carnegie Mellon University Art Gallery, 1986.

Simon, Joan. "Mixing Metaphors: Elizabeth Murray." *Art in America*, April 1984: 140–7.

Storr, Robert. *Elizabeth Murray*. New York: Museum of Modern Art, 2005.

American Neo-Expressionism

Baker, Elizabeth C., ed. "Special Issue: Expressionism I." *Art in America*, December 1982.

Baker, Elizabeth C., ed. "Special Issue: Expressionism II." *Art in America*, January 1983.

Fox, Howard N. *Robert Longo*. Los Angeles: Los Angeles County Museum of Art; New York: Rizzoli, 1989.

Kuspit, Donald and Erich Fischl. *An Interview with Erich Fischl*. New York: Vintage, 1987.

McEvilley, Thomas and Lisa Phillips. *Julian Schnabel: Paintings 1975–1987*. London: Whitechapel Art Gallery; New York: Whitney Museum of American Art, 1987.

Schjeldahl, Peter. *Eric Fischl*. New York: Art in America and Stewart, Tabori, & Chang, 1988.

Chapter 14

A Fresh Look at Abstraction

Benezra, Noal. *Martin Puryear*. Chicago: Art Institute of Chicago; London and New York: Thames & Hudson, 1991.

Phillips, Lisa. *Terry Winters*. New York: Whitney Museum of American Art, 1991.

Schimmel, Paul et al. *Tony Cragg: Sculpture 1975–1990*. Newport Beach, Cal.: Newport Harbor Art Museum, 1990; London and New York: Thames & Hudson, 1991.

The East Village Scene of the Eighties

Blinderman, Barry. *David Wojnarowicz: Tongues of Flame*. Normal, Ill.: University Galleries, Illinois State University, 1990.

Blinderman, Barry. *Keith Haring: Future Primeval*. Normal, Ill.: University Galleries, Illinois State University; New York: Abbeville, 1990.

Cooper, Martha and Henry Chalfant. *Subway Art*. New York: Holt, Rinehart, & Winston, 1984.

Deitcher, David. "Ideas and Emotions." *Artforum*, May 1989: 122–7 [Wojnarowicz].

Fry, Edward F. *Robert Morris: Works of the Eighties*. Newport Beach, Cal.: Newport Harbor Art Museum, 1986.

Gruen, John. *Keith Haring: The Authorized Biography*. Upper Saddle River, N.J.: Prentice Hall, 1991.

Hooks, Bell. "Altars of Sacrifice: Remembering Basquiat." *Art in America*, June 1993: 68–75, 117.

Kardon, Janet. *The East Village Scene*. Philadelphia: Institute of Contemporary Art, University of Pennsylvania, 1984.

Marshall, Richard, ed. *Jean-Michel Basquiat*. New York: Whitney Museum of American Art and Harry N. Abrams, 1992.

Mayer, Marc and Fred Hoffman. *Basquiat*. Brooklyn: Brooklyn Museum of Art; London and New York: Merrell, 2005.

Pincus-Witten, Robert, Jeffrey Deitch, and David Shapiro. *Keith Haring*. New York: Tony Shafrazi Gallery, 1982.

Plous, Phyllis and Mary Looker. *Neo York: Report on a Phenomenon*. Santa Barbara: University Art Museum, 1984.

Prat, Jean-Louis and Richard Marshall. *Jean-Michel Basquiat*. Paris: Galerie Enrico Navarra, 1996.

Robinson, Walter and Carlo McCormick, "Report from the East Village: Slouching Toward Avenue D." *Art in America*, summer 1984: 134–61.

Rose, Matthew. "David Wojnarowicz: An Interview." *Arts*, May 1988: 60–5.

Rosenthal, Mark and Richard Marshall. *Jonathan Borofsky*. Philadelphia: Philadelphia Museum of Art; New York: Whitney Museum of American Art, 1984.

Saltz, Jerry. *Beyond Boundaries*. New York: Alfred Van der Marck Editions, 1986.

Saltz, Jerry. "Notes on a Painting: Not Going Gentle." *Arts*, February 1989: 13–14.

Wojnarowicz, David. *Memories That Smell Like Gasoline*. San Francisco: Artspace Books, 1992.

Wojnarowicz, David. *Close to the Knives: A Memoir of Disintegration*. New York: Vintage, 1991.

Wojnarowicz, David. "Spiral." *Artforum*, March 1992: 100.

Eighties Installation

Davies, Hugh Marlais and Ronald J Onorato. *Blurring the Boundaries: Installation Art 1969–1996*. San Diego, Cal.: Museum of Contemporary Art, 1997.

De Oliveira, Nicolas, Nicola Oxley, and Michael Perry. *Installation Art*. Washington, D.C.: Smithsonian Institution Press, 1994.

Finkelpearl, Tom. *David Hammons: Rousing the Rubble*. New York: Institute for Contemporary Art; Cambridge, Mass.: MIT Press, 1991.

Gumpert, Lynn and Mary Jane Jacob. *Christian Boltanski: Lessons of Darkness*. Chicago: Museum of Contemporary Art; Los Angeles: Museum of Contemporary Art; New York: New Museum of Contemporary Art, 1988.

Marmer, Nancy. "Boltanski: The Uses of Contradiction." *Art in America*, October 1989: 168–81, 233–5.

The Peculiar Case of the Russians

Ross, David. *Between Spring and Summer: Soviet Conceptual Art in the Era of Late Communism*. Boston: Institute of Contemporary Art; Tacoma, Wash.: Tacoma Art Museum; Cambridge, Mass. and London: MIT Press, 1990.

Stoos, Toni, ed. *Ilya Kabakov: Installations 1983–2000, Catalogue Raisonné*. 2 vols. Düsseldorf: Richter Verlag, 2003.

Wallach, Amei. *Ilya Kabakov: The Man Who Never Threw Anything Away*. New York: Harry N. Abrams, 1996.

Wallach, Amei. *Ilya Kabakov, 1969–1998*. Annandale-on-Hudson, N.Y.: Center for Curatorial Studies, 2001.

The Aesthetics of Consumerism

Bonami, Francesco. *Jeff Koons*. Chicago: Museum of Contemporary Art; New Haven, Conn.: Yale University Press, 2008.

Breuer, Rolf-E., Thomas Krens, and David Sylvester. *Jeff Koons: Easyfun – Ethereal*. New York: Guggenheim Museum Publications, 2000.

Kabakov, Ilya and Emilia. *An Alternative History of Art: Rosenthal, Kabakov, Spivak*. Cleveland: Museum of Contemporary Art; Bielefeld: Kerber Verlag, 2005.

Politi, Giancarlo. "Luxury and Desire: An Interview with Jeff Koons." *Flash Art*, February/March 1987: 71–6.

Political Appropriation

Ault, Julie. *Alternative art, New York, 1965–1985: A Cultural Politics Book for the Social Text Collective*. New York: Drawing Center; Minneapolis: University of Minnesota Press, 2002.

Boswell, Peter et al. *Public Address: Krzysztof Wodiczko*. Minneapolis: Walker Art Center, 1992.

Chapter 15

Return to the Body

Adams, Brooks. *Sensation: Young British Artists from the Saatchi Collection*. London: Royal Academy of Arts, 1997.

Bonami, Francesco et al. *Maurizio Cattelan*. London: Phaidon, 2003.

Deitch, Jeffrey. *Post Human*. Lausanne: FAE Musée d'Art Contemporain, 1992.

Finley, Karen. *A Different Kind of Intimacy: The Collected Writings of Karen Finley*. New York: Thunder's Mouth Press, 2000.

Flood, Richard, et al. *Robert Gober: Sculpture + Drawing*. Minneapolis: Walker Art Center, 1999.

Posner, Helaine. *Kiki Smith*. Boston: Bulfinch Press and Little, Brown, 1998.

Rogers, Sarah J. *The Body and the Object: Ann Hamilton 1984–1996*. Columbus, Ohio: Wexner Center for the Arts, Ohio State University, 1996.

Rugoff, Ralph, Kristine Stiles, Giacinto Di Pietrantonio. *Paul McCarthy*. London: Phaidon Press, 1996.

Simon, Joan. *Ann Hamilton*. New York: Harry N. Abrams, 2002.

Spector, Nancy, ed. *Matthew Barney: The Cremaster Cycle*. New York: Guggenheim Museum, 2002.

Sussman, Elizabeth. *Mike Kelley: Catholic Tastes*. New York: Harry N. Abrams and Whitney Museum of American Art, 1993.

Vance, Carole S. "The War on Culture," *Art in America* 47 (September 1989): 39–43.

Fashion

Deitch, Jeffrey. *Post Human*. Lausanne: FAE Musée d'Art Contemporain, 1992.

Hickey, Dave. *Vb 08–36 Vanessa Beecroft performances*. Ostfildern-Ruit, Germany: Cantz, 2000.

Molon, Dominic. *Mariko Mori*, Chicago: Museum of Contemporary Art, 1998.

Postmodern Conceptualism

Buchloh, Benjamin, David, Catherine, and Chevrier, Jean-Francois. "The Political Potential of Art," *Documenta X, the book*. Ostifeldern, Germany: Cantz Verlag, 1997.

Fineberg, Jonathan, ed. *Out of Town: The Williamsburg Paradigm*. Champaign, Ill.: Krannert Art Museum, 1993.

Fineberg, Jonathan. *Roxy Paine*. Chicago: Terra Museum of American Art; Giverny, France: Musée d'art americain, 1998.

Goldstein, Ann and Mary Jane Jacob. *A Forest of Signs: Art in the Crisis of Representation*. Los Angeles: Museum of Contemporary Art, 1989; Cambridge, Mass.: MIT Press, 1989.

Goldstein, Ann. *Martin Kippenberger: The Problem Perspective*. Los Angeles: Museum of Contemporary Art; Cambridge, Mass.: MIT Press, 2008.

Mulvey, Laura, Dirk Snauwaert, and Mark Alice Durant. *Jimmie Durham*. London: Phaidon Press, 1995.

Shiff, Richard. "The Necessity of Jimmie Durham's Jokes." *The Art Journal*, fall 1992: 74–80.

Temkin, Ann; Briony Fer, Benjamin Buchloh. *Gabriel Orozco*. New York: Museum of Modern Art 2009.

Louise Bourgeois

Gorovoy, Jerry, Danielle Tilkin, Josef Helfenstein, et al., *Louise Bourgeois: Memory and Architecture*. Madrid: Museo Nacional Centro de Arte Reina Sofía, 1999.

Helfenstein, Josef. *Louise Bourgeois* [see Chapter 2 for full citation]

Morris, Frances, et al. *Louise Bourgeois*. London: Tate Modern, 2007.

Wye, Deborah. *Louise Bourgeois*. New York: Museum of Modern Art, 1982.

New Uses of the Camera

Galassi, Peter. *Andreas Gursky*. New York: Museum of Modern Art, 2001.

Galassi, Peter. *Jeff Wall*. New York: Museum of Modern Art, 2007.

Lyons, Lisa and Kim Levin. *Wegman's World*. Minneapolis: Walker Art Center, 1982.

Schweizer, Nicole. *Alfredo Jaar: The Politics of Images*. Lausanne: Musée Cantonal des Beaux-Arts, 2007.

Enwezor, Okwui. *Archive Fever: Uses of the Document in Contemporary Art*. New York: International Center of Photography, 2008.

Wall, Jeff. *Jeff Wall: Selected Essays and Interviews*. New York: Museum of Modern Art, 2007.

Video

Benezra, Neal. *William Kentridge*. Chicago: Museum of Contemporary Art; New York: New Museum and Harry N. Abrams, 2001.

Horrigan, Bill. *Shirin Neshat: two installations*. Columbus, Ohio: Wexner Center for the Arts, Ohio State University; New York: Distributed Art Publishers, 2000.

Ross, David A., Peter Sellars, Lewis Hyde, et al. *Bill Viola*. New York: Whitney Museum of American Art, 1997.

Rothschild, Deborah. *Tony Oursler: introjection, mid-career survey, 1976–1999*. Williamstown, Mass.: Williams College Museum of Art, 1999.

Cultural Identity

DuBois Shaw, Gwendolyn. *Seeing The Unspeakable: The Art of Kara Walker*. Durham, N.C.: Duke University Press, 2004.

Kirsch, Andrea and Susan Fisher Sterling. *Carrie Mae Weems*. Washington, D.C.: National Museum of Women in the Arts, 1993.

Jacobs, Mary Jane. *Carrie Mae Weems*. Philadelphia: The Fabric Workshop, 1994.

Sultan, Terrie and Arthur Jafa. *Kerry James Marshall*. New York: Harry N. Abrams, 2000.

Tucker, Marcia. *The Decade Show: Frameworks of Identity in the 1980s*. New York: New Museum of Contemporary Art, Museum of Contemporary Hispanic Art, and Studio Museum in Harlem, 1990.

Weems, Carrie Mae. *In These Islands, South Carolina and Georgia*. Tuscaloosa: Sarah Moody Gallery of Art, University of Alabama, 1994.

The Comics

Carlin, John, Paul Karasik, and Brian Walker, *Masters of American Comics*. Los Angeles: Hammer Museum and the Museum of Contemporary Art; New Haven, Conn.: Yale University Press, 2005.

Raeburn, Daniel. *Chris Ware*. New Haven, Conn.: Yale University Press, 2004.

Global Culture and Local Meaning

Archer, Michael, Guy Brett, and Catherine de Zegher. *Mona Hatoum*. London: Phaidon, Contemporary Artists Series, 1997.

Enwezor, Okwui, and Olu Oguibe, eds. *Reading the Contemporary: African Art from Theory to the Marketplace*. Cambridge, Mass.: MIT Press, 1999.

Enwezor, Okwui. *Documenta 11*. Ostfildern-Ruit, Germany: Hatje Cantz, 2002.

Kasfir, Sidney Littlefield. *Contemporary African Art*. New York: Thames and Hudson, 2000.

Kent, Rachel and Robert Carleton Hobbs. *Yinka Shonibare, MBE*. New York: Prestel, 2008.

Oguibe, Olu. *The Culture Game*. Minneapolis: University of Minnesota Press, 2004.

China

Cai, Guo-Qiang. *Cai Guo-Qiang*. New York: Thames & Hudson, 2000.

Chiu, Melissa and Zheng Shengtian, *Art and China's Revolution*. New Haven, Conn.: Yale University Press, 2008.

Fineberg, Jonathan. *Revision: Zhang Xiaogang*. New York: PaceWildenstein, 2008.

Hung, Wu and Christopher Philips. *Between Past and Future: New Photography and Video from China*. Chicago: Smart Museum of Art, 2004.

Hung, Wu. *Chinese art at the crossroads: between past and future, between East and West*. Hong Kong: New Art Media; London: Institute of International Visual Arts, 2001.

Hung, Wu. *Transience: Chinese experimental art at the end of the twentieth century*. Chicago: Smart Museum of Art, 1999.

Minglu, Gao. *Inside Out: New Chinese Art*. San Francisco: Museum of Modern Art; New York: Asia Society Galleries, 1998.

Munroe, Alexandra. *Cai Guo-Qiang: I want to believe*. New York: Guggenheim Museum, 2008.

Silbergeld, Jerome. *Persistence-transformation: text as image in the art of Xu Bing*. Princeton N.J.: Princeton University Press, 2006.

Chapter 16

Economies

Fraser, Andrea. *Museum Highlights: The Writings of Andrea Fraser*. Cambridge, Mass.: MIT Press, 2005.

Hickson, Patricia, ed. *Conrad Bakker Objects & Economies*. Des Moines: Des Moines Art Center 2009.

Hirst, Damien. *For the Love of God: The Making of the Diamond Skull*. New York: Harry N. Abrams, 2007.

Schimmel, Paul, ed. *©Murakami*. Los Angeles: Museum of Contemporary Art; New York: Rizzoli International Publications, 2007.

Detached Subjectivity

Allen, Jennifer. *Candice Breitz: inner + outer space*. Köln: König; New York: Distributed Art Publishers, 2008.

Goldberg, RoseLee. *Nikki S. Lee: Parts*. Ostfildern-Ruit, Germany: Hatje Cantz; New York: Distributed Art Publishers, 2005.

Martin, Lesley A. *Nikki S. Lee: Projects*. Ostfildern-Ruit, Germany: Hatje Cantz; New York: Distributed Art Publishers, 2001.

Nakas, Kassandra, Britta Schmitz and Walid Raad. *The Atlas Group (1989–2004): A Project by Walid Raad*. Köln: Buchhandlung Walther König, 2006.

Dissolution, Dislocation, Displacement of Boundaries

Ault, Julie. *Felix Gonzalez-Torres*. Göttingen: SteidlDangin, 2006.

Armstrong, Elizabeth, Johanna Burton and Dave Hickey. *Mary Heilmann: To Be Someone*. Newport Beach, Cal.: Orange County Museum of Art; Munich: Prestel, 2007.

Kabakov

[see Chapter 14 for publications on Kabakov]

NOTES

Chapter 1

1. William Wordsworth, preface to *Lyrical Ballads*, 1802; in Stephan Gill, ed., *William Wordsworth*, The Oxford Authors Edition (Oxford and New York: Oxford University Press, 1984), 606.
2. Willem de Kooning, "Content Is a Glimpse," excerpts from an interview with David Sylvester broadcast on the BBC, Dec. 3, 1960; published as a transcript in *Location* 1:1 (spring 1963); reprinted in Thomas B. Hess, *William de Kooning*, exh. cat., Museum of Modern Art (Greenwich, Conn.: New York Graphic Society, 1968), 150. Cézanne also used this term; see for example John Rewald, *Post-Impressionism*, Museum of Modern Art (Boston: New York Graphic Society, 1978), 454; quoted from Octave Mirbeau, in Mirbeau et al., *Cézanne* (Paris: 1914), unpaginated (9). See also Richard Shiff, *Cézanne and the End of Impressionism* (Chicago: University of Chicago Press, 1984), in which the author discusses the meaning and context of this phrase at considerable length.
3. See Alfred Whitehead, *Adventures of Ideas* (New York: The American Library, A Mentor Book, 1955), 247.
4. Gustave Flaubert, "Style as Absolute," 1852; cited in Richard Ellmann and Charles Feidelson, Jr., eds., *The Modern Tradition* (New York: Oxford University Press, 1965), 126.
5. Clive Bell, "The Aesthetic Hypothesis," 1914; reprinted in Francis Frascina and Charles Harrison, eds., *Modern Art and Modernism: A Critical Anthology* (New York: Harper & Row, 1982), 69.
6. Clement Greenberg, "Avant-Garde and Kitsch," 1939; reprinted in *Art and Culture* (Boston: Beacon Press, 1961), 5–6. See also Clement Greenberg, "Modernist Painting," *Arts Yearbook* 4 (1961), 109–16.
7. See Peter Bürger, *Theory of the Avant-Garde*, trans. Michael Shaw, *Theory of Literature*, vol. 4 (Minneapolis: University of Minnesota Press, 1984); Jürgen Habermas, "Modernity—An Incomplete Project," in Hal Foster, ed., *The Anti-Aesthetic: Essays on Postmodern Culture* (Port Townsend, Wash.: Bay Press, 1983); and Renato Poggioli, *The Theory of the Avant-Garde*, trans. Gerald Fitzgerald (Cambridge, Mass.: Harvard University Press, 1968).
8. Charles Baudelaire, "The Salon of 1859," in *Art in Paris, 1845–1862: Salons and Other Exhibitions*, trans. and ed. Jonathan Mayne (London and New York: Phaidon, 1965), 156.
9. Harold Rosenberg, *The Tradition of the New* (New York: Horizon Press, 1959).
10. Jean-François Lyotard, "Introduction," in *The Postmodern Condition: A Report on Knowledge*, trans. Geoff Bennington and Brian Massumi (Minneapolis: University of Minnesota Press, 1984).
11. Gilles Deleuze and Félix Guattari, *A Thousand Plateaus* (*Mille Plateaux*), 1980.
12. Robert Rauschenberg, cited in Mary Lynn Kotz, *Robert Rauschenberg: Art and Life* (New York: Harry N. Abrams, 1990), 99.
13. Dan Flavin, "Several More Remarks," *Studio International* (April 1969), 175.
14. Barnett Newman, 1967; cited in Harold Rosenberg, *Barnett Newman* (New York: Harry N. Abrams, 1978), 28.
15. Thomas Jefferson, "A Bill for the More General Diffusion of Knowledge," 1778; in Merrill D. Peterson (ed.), *Thomas Jefferson: Writings: Autobiography/Notes on the State of Virginia/Public and Private Papers/Addresses/Letters* (New York, N.Y.: Literary Classics of the United States Library of America, 1984), 365.
16. Martin Heidegger, "The Origin of the Work of Art," 1935–6 (revised 1950); in *Poetry, Language, Thought*, trans. Albert Hofstadter (New York: Harper & Row, 1975), 57.

Chapter 2

1. André Breton, *Manifeste due surréalisme* (Paris: Editions du Safittai, 1924); cited in William S. Rubin, *Dada and Surrealist Art* (New York: Harry N. Abrams, 1968), 121.
2. Lowery Stokes Sims, *Wifredo Lam and the International Avant-garde, 1923–1982* (University of Texas, Austin Press, 2002), 47.
3. See Martica Sawin, *Surrealism in Exile and the Beginning of the New York School* (Cambridge, Mass.: The MIT Press, 1995), 318.
4. Joseph Cornell, letter to Alfred Barr, Nov. 13, 1936, Archives of the Museum of Modern Art; cited in Dawn Ades, "The Transcendental Surrealism of Joseph Cornell," in Kynaston McShine, ed., *Joseph Cornell*, exh. cat. (New York: The Museum of Modern Art, 1980), 19.
5. Joseph Cornell, Cornell Papers, Archives of American Art, 1059:276, Oct. 14, 1950; cited in Lynda Roscoe Hartigan, "Joseph Cornell: A Biography," in McShine, *Joseph Cornell*, 107.
6. Jackson Pollock, interview with William Wright, The Springs, Long Island, New York, late 1950. Broadcast on radio station WERI, Westerly, R.I., 1951. Transcribed and published in Pepe Karmel, ed., *Jackson Pollock: Interviews, Articles, Reviews* (New York: The Museum of Modern Art, 1998), 20.
7. Mary Coffey, "'I'm not the fourth great one': Tamayo and Mexican Muralism," in Diana C. Du Pont, ed., *Tamayo: A Modern Icon Reinterpreted* (Santa Barbara, Cal.: Santa Barbara Museum of Art, 2007), 247–67.
8. Harold Rosenberg, in conversation with Jonathan Fineberg in 1976.
9. Diego Rivera, *My Art, My Life*, ed. Gladys March (New York: Citadel Press, 1960), 124; cited in Linda Downes, "Introduction," in *Diego Rivera: A Retrospective*, Founders Society, Detroit Institute of Arts (New York: W. W. Norton and Company, 1986), 19.
10. See articles by Jacinta Quirarte, "The Coatlicue in Modern Mexican Painting," *Research Center for the Arts Review* 5 (April 1982), and Betty Ann Brown, "The Past Idealized: Diego Rivera's Use of Pre-Columbian Imagery," in *Diego Rivera: A Retrospective* (1986).
11. George Biddle, letter to President Franklin Roosevelt, May 9, 1933; reprinted in William F. McDonald, *Federal Relief Administration and the Arts* (Columbus, Ohio: Ohio State University, 1969); cited in Dore Ashton, *The New York School* (New York: Viking, 1973), 46.
12. Thomas B. Hess, *Barnett Newman* (New York: Walker & Co., 1969); cited in Ashton, *The New York School*, 44.
13. Lee Krasner recalled seeing the collection here in an interview with Gail Levin. See Gail Levin, *Miró, Kandinsky, and the Genesis of Abstract Expressionism: The Formative Years*, exh. cat. (Ithaca: The Herbert F. Johnson Museum of Art, Cornell University; and New York: Whitney Museum of American Art, 1978), 27.
14. Robert M. Coates, "The Art Galleries," *The New Yorker* 22:7 (March 30, 1946), 83.
15. Harold Rosenberg, in conversation with Jonathan Fineberg in 1977–8.
16. Harold Rosenberg, "The Herd of Independent Minds," *Commentary* (1948); in *Discovering the Present* (Chicago: University of Chicago Press, 1973), 19.
17. Harold Rosenberg, "The American Action Painters," *Artnews* (1952); in *Tradition of the New* (New York: Horizon Press, 1959).
18. Ann Eden Gibson, *Abstract Expressionism: Other Politics* (New Haven and London: Yale University Press, 1997), ix.
19. Jean-Paul Sartre, *Action* (Dec. 29, 1944). "En un mot, l'homme doit créer sa proper essence; c'est en se jetant dans le monde, en y souffrant, en y luttant, qu'il se définit peu à peu."
20. Friedrich Nietzsche, "Schopenhauer as Educator" (1874); in Friedrich Nietzsche, *Untimely Meditations*, trans. R. J. Hollingdale (Cambridge and New York: Cambridge University Press, 1983), 129.
21. See Martin Heidegger, *Being and Time*, trans. John Macquarrie and Edward Robinson (New York: Harper & Row, 1962).
22. Harold Rosenberg, "Introduction to Six American Artists," in *Possibilities* (New York: Wittenborn Schultz, 1947), 75.
23. Robert Motherwell, "Symposium: What Abstract Art Means to Me," *Bulletin of the Museum of Modern Art* 18:3 (spring 1951), 12.
24. Cited in Ashton, *The New York School*, 34.
25. Robert Motherwell, in conversation with Jonathan Fineberg, Jan. 15, 1979, Greenwich, Conn.
26. Mark Rothko, introduction to the catalog of the Clyfford Still exhibition at the Art of This Century Gallery, New York, Feb. 12–March 2, 1946, unpaginated; cited in Irving Sandler, *The Triumph of American Painting* (New York: Praeger, 1970), 67.
27. Clyfford Still, from diary notes of Feb. 11, 1956; cited in *Clyfford Still*, exh. cat., San Francisco Museum of Art (San Francisco: San Francisco Museum of Art, 1976), 122.
28. Letter of June 7, 1943 by Mark Rothko and Adolph Gottlieb (with unacknowledged help from Barnett Newman), in Edward Alden Jewell, "The Realm of Art: A New Platform and Other Matters: 'Globalism' Pops into View," *New York Times*, June 13, 1943, x9.
29. Elaine de Kooning, *Franz Kline Memorial Exhibition* (Washington, D.C.: Washington Gallery of Modern Art, 1962), 14; cited in Sandler, *The Triumph of American Painting*, 249.
30. Clement Greenberg, "A New Installation at the Metropolitan Museum of Art, and a Review of the Exhibition *Art in Progress*," *The Nation* (June 10, 1944); reprinted in Clement Greenberg, *The Collected Essays and Criticism*, vol. 1: *Perceptions and Judgements, 1939–1944* (Chicago: University of Chicago Press, 1986), 213.
31. Robert Motherwell, in conversation with Jonathan Fineberg, Jan. 10, 1976, Greenwich, Conn.
32. Mark Tobey, in Dorothy C. Miller, ed., *Fourteen Americans* (New York: The Museum of Modern Art, 1946), 70; cited in William C. Seitz, *Mark Tobey*, Museum of Modern Art (Garden City, N.Y.: Doubleday, 1962), 9.
33. Cited by Elizabeth Hutton Turner, ed., *Jacob Lawrence: The Migration Series* (Washington, D.C.: The Rappahannock Press and The Phillips Collection, 1993), 7.
34. Sarah Eckhardt, *Uninterrupted Flux: Hedda Sterne, A Retrospective* (Champaign, Ill.: Krannert Art Museum, University of Illinois at Urbana-Champaign, 2006).
35. Harold Rosenberg, *Saul Steinberg* (New York: Whitney Museum of American Art, 1978).
36. Josef Helfenstein, *Louise Bourgeois: The Early Work* (Champaign, Ill.: Krannert Art Museum, University of Illinois at Urbana-Champaign, 2002), 27.
37. Walter Benjamin, "The Work of Art in the Age of Mechanical Reproduction" (1936); in *Illuminations* (New York: Schocken, 1969), 217–51.

38. See Christopher Phillips, "The Judgement Seat of Photography," *October* 22 (fall 1982); reprinted in Richard Bolton, ed., *The Contest of Meaning: Critical Histories of Photography* (Cambridge, Mass.: MIT Press, 1992).

39. Kerry William Purcell, *Weegee* (New York: Phaidon, 2004), unpaginated.

40. Virginia Heckert, "Weegee's Story," in Margit Zuckriegl, ed., *Weegee's Story: From the Berinson Collection* (Salzburg: Rupertinum, 1999), 19–28; reprinted in *Weegee's Story*, exh. pamphlet (New York: Ubu Gallery, May 2004), 5

41. Ann Thomas, *Lisette Model* (Ottawa: National Gallery of Canada, 1990), 66–7.

42. Cited from a 1963 interview in James Rhem, *Aaron Siskind* (New York: Phaidon, 2003), 11.

43. See Abigail Solomon-Godeau, "The Armed Vision Disarmed: Radical Formalism from Weapon to Style," in Richard Bolton, ed., *The Contest of Meaning* (Cambridge, Mass.: MIT Press, 1996), 82–107. Solomon-Godeau emphasizes the break in style between the Bauhaus in Dessau, where the formalism of the photography was defined in opposition to expressionism, and that of the Chicago group, which explicitly embraced personal expression. But it is worth noting that both approaches rely on the exploitation of formal abstraction and that the expressionism of Siskind and Callahan grows naturally out of that formalism.

Chapter 3

1. Alexander Calder, *Calder: An Autobiography with Pictures* (New York: Pantheon Books, 1966), 54–5.

2. Thomas Wolfe, *You Can't Go Home Again*, book 1 (Garden City, N.Y.: Doubleday, 1942), 273–82.

3. Calder, *Calder: An Autobiography with Pictures*, 113.

4. *Ibid.*, 127, 130.

5. Calder, "What Abstract Art Means to Me," *Bulletin of the Museum of Modern Art* (1951); cited in Jean Lipman, *Calder's Universe*, exh. cat. (New York: Whitney Museum of American Art, 1976), 1.

6. Lipman, *Calder's Universe*, 262.

7. Camilla Gray, *The Great Experiment: Russian Art 1863–1922* (New York: Harry N. Abrams, 1962), 147.

8. Lipman, *Calder's Universe*, 32.

9. Albert Elsen, "Calder on Balance," in *Alexander Calder: A Retrospective Exhibition*, Museum of Contemporary Art (Chicago: Museum of Contemporary Art, 1974), 5.

10. Elizabeth Hutton Turner and Oliver Wick, "Calder and Miró: A New Space for the Imagination," in Elizabeth Hutton Turner and Oliver Wick, *Calder/Miró* (Washington: The Philips Collection and Basel: Foundation Beyeler, 2004), 49.

11. Katherine Kuh, *The Artist's Voice: Talks with Seventeen Artists* (New York and Evanston, Ill.: Harper & Row, 1962), 42.

12. Stuart Davis, letter to Henry McBride, reprinted in *Creative Art* 6 (Feb. 1930), supplement, 34–5; Stuart Davis, cited in James Johnson Sweeney, *Stuart Davis* (New York: The Museum of Modern Art, 1945), 23; cited in Diane Kelder, "Stuart Davis and Modernism: An Overview," in Lowery Stokes Sims, *Stuart Davis: American Painter* (New York: Metropolitan Museum of Art and Harry N. Abrams, 1991), 26.

13. Hans Hofmann, "The Search for the *Real* in the Visual Arts," in *Search for the Real and Other Essays*, ed. Sarah T. Weeks and Bartlett H. Hayes (Cambridge, Mass.: MIT Press, 1967), 40.

14. *Ibid.*, 64.

15. *Ibid.*, 43.

16. Clement Greenberg, *Nation* 160 (April 21, 1945), 469; cited in Cynthia Goodman, *Hans Hofmann* (New York: Abbeville, 1986), 9.

17. Cited in Goodman, *Hans Hofmann*, 49.

18. Kuh, *The Artist's Voice*, 124.

19. Hofmann, *Search for the Real*, 48.

20. Samuel M. Kootz, "Credibility of Color: Hans Hofmann," *Arts Magazine* 41 (Feb. 1967), 38; cited in Goodman, *Hans Hofmann*, 9–10.

21. Hans Hofmann, "The Color Problem in Pure Painting—Its Creative Origin," in *Hans Hofmann*, exh. cat. (New York: Kootz Gallery, 1955), unpaginated; cited in Goodman, *Hans Hofmann*, 110–11.

22. From "Hans Hofmann on Art," *Art Journal* 22 (spring 1963), 18; reprint of a speech delivered at the inauguration of Hopkins Center, Dartmouth College, Nov. 17, 1962; cited in Goodman, *Hans Hofmann*, 111.

23. Harold Rosenberg, *Arshile Gorky: The Man, the Time, the Idea* (New York: Horizon Press, 1962), 45; the personal impressions below come chiefly from Rosenberg.

24. *Ibid.*, 42.

25. See Nick Dante Vaccaro, "Gorky's Debt to Gaudier-Brzeska," *Art Journal* 23 (fall 1963), 33–4.

26. Ethel Schwabacher, *Arshile Gorky*, exh. cat., Whitney Museum of American Art (New York: Macmillan, 1957), 62.

27. Stuart Davis, "Arshile Gorky in the 1930s: A Personal Recollection," *Magazine of Art* 44 (Feb. 1951); in Diane Kelder, ed., *Stuart Davis* (New York: Praeger, 1971), 178–9.

28. Noted in the catalog for Gorky's first group show in New York, *An Exhibition of Works by 46 Painters and Sculptors Under 35 Years of Age* (New York: The Museum of Modern Art, 1930); cited by Lisa Dennison Tabak in her chronology for Diane Waldman, *Arshile Gorky: A Retrospective*, exh. cat., Guggenheim Museum (New York: Harry N. Abrams, 1981), 258.

29. Stuart Davis, "Arshile Gorky in the 1930s: A Personal Recollection," 178–9.

30. Marny George, quoted in Schwabacher, *Arshile Gorky*, 61.

31. Willem de Kooning, letter to *Artnews* (Jan. 1949); cited in Schwabacher, *Arshile Gorky*, 8.

32. Rosenberg, *Arshile Gorky: The Man*, 66.

33. Julien Levy, foreword to William C. Seitz, *Arshile Gorky*, exh. cat., Museum of Modern Art (Garden City, N.Y.: Doubleday, 1962), 7. A similar remark is cited by most of those who knew Gorky and wrote about him.

34. Satenig Avedisian, letter to Mrs. [Minna] Metzger, March 31, 1949, Whitney Museum of American Art files; cited in Harry Rand, *Arshile Gorky: The Implication of Symbols* (Montclair, N.J.: Allenheld & Schram, 1981), 74, n. 4.

35. Arshile Gorky, in Schwabacher, *Arshile Gorky*, 66.

36. André Breton, "The Eye Spring Arshile Gorky," introduction to the Gorky exhibition at the Julien Levy Gallery, 1945; cited in Irving Sandler, *The Triumph of American Painting* (New York and Washington: Praeger, 1970), 56.

37. See Schwabacher, *Arshile Gorky*, 118.

38. Arshile Gorky, letter to Vartoosh, April 22, 1944; in "The Letters of Arshile Gorky," ed. and trans. Karlen Mooradian, in "A Special Issue on Arshile Gorky," *Ararat* 12 (New York, fall 1971), 32; cited in Jim Jordan and Robert Goldwater, *The Paintings of Arshile Gorky: A Critical Catalogue* (New York: New York University Press, 1982), 84–5.

39. This iconography has been discussed in Rand, *Gorky: Implication of Symbols*, 183–4.

40. According to Julien Levy, *Arshile Gorky* (New York, 1966), 24.

41. Arshile Gorky, letter of Sept. 26, 1939; in "Toward a Philosophy of Art" (selected letters and trans. Karlen Mooradian), in *Arshile Gorky: Drawings to Paintings*, exh. cat., University of Texas (Austin, Tex.: University of Texas at Austin, University Art Museum, 1975), 31.

42. Arshile Gorky, letter of Jan. 17, 1947; in "The Letters of Arshile Gorky," 39; cited in Harry Rand, "Arshile Gorky Iconography," in *Arshile Gorky: Drawings to Paintings*, exh. cat. 67.

43. Arshile Gorky, letter to Vartoosh from Hamilton, Virginia, Aug. 1943; in *Arshile Gorky*, a film by Charlotte Zwerin (New York, 1982).

44. Agnes Magruder, interviewed by Courtney Sale, in *Arshile Gorky*, a film by Charlotte Zwerin.

45. Julien Levy, foreword to Seitz, *Arshile Gorky*, 9.

46. Harold Rosenberg reported this to Jonathan Fineberg in a conversation in 1975.

47. Robert Motherwell, in conversation with Jonathan Fineberg, Jan. 10, 1976 in Greenwich, Conn.

48. *Ibid.*

49. Robert Motherwell, "Preliminary Notice," in Daniel-Henry Kahnweiler, *The Rise of Cubism*, trans. Henry Aronson (New York: Wittenborn & Schultz, 1949), vii.

50. Robert Motherwell, exh. cat., "The School of New York," Perls Gallery, Beverly Hills, Jan. 1951, unpaginated; cited in Sandler, *The Triumph of American Painting*, 202.

51. See Stephanie Terenzio and Dorothy C. Belknap, *The Prints of Robert Motherwell: A Catalogue Raisonné 1943–1948* (New York: Hudson Hills Press, 1984).

52. Robert Motherwell, commentary to the illustration of *Pancho Villa, Dead and Alive*, in H. Harvard Arneson, *Robert Motherwell*, 2nd ed. (New York: Harry N. Abrams, 1982), 105.

53. I have discussed the specificity of this subject matter in relation to Motherwell's childhood and character in Jonathan Fineberg, "Death and Maternal Love: Psychological Speculations on Robert Motherwell's Art," *Artforum* (Sept. 1978), 52–7.

54. Robert Motherwell, in conversation with Jonathan Fineberg, Jan. 8, 1977, Greenwich, Conn.; see Fineberg, "Death and Maternal Love," 55.

55. Robert Motherwell, in conversation with E. A. Carmean, Aug. 17, 1977; cited in *American Art at Mid-Century: Subjects of the Artist* (Washington, D.C.: National Gallery of Art, 1978), 98.

56. Robert Motherwell, "Robert Motherwell: A Conversation at Lunch," in *An Exhibition of the Works of Robert Motherwell*, Jan. 10–28, 1963, to accompany the First Louise Linder Eastman Memorial Lecture, Jan. 14, 1963 (Northampton, Mass., 1963), unpaginated.

57. Robert Motherwell, in conversation with Jonathan Fineberg, Jan. 10, 1976, Greenwich, Conn.; see Jonathan Fineberg, "Death and Maternal Love," 55.

58. Willem de Kooning, "Content Is a Glimpse," excerpts from an interview with David Sylvester broadcast on the BBC, Dec. 3, 1960; published as a transcript in *Location* 1:1 (spring 1963); reprinted in Thomas B. Hess, *Willem de Kooning*, exh. cat., Museum of Modern Art (Greenwich, Conn.: New York Graphic Society, 1968), 148.

59. See, for example, Edwin Denby, "Willem de Kooning," in *Dancers, Buildings, and People in the Streets* (New York: Horizon Press, 1965), 269–70; or the account by Elaine de Kooning in Hess, *Willem de Kooning*, 22.

60. Willem de Kooning, interviewed by Courtney Sale, in a film by Charlotte Zwerin, *De Kooning on de Kooning* (New York, 1980).

61. Harold Rosenberg, "Interview with Willem de Kooning," *Artnews* (Sept. 1972); reprinted in Harold Rosenberg, *Willem de Kooning* (New York: Harry N. Abrams, 1973), 47.

62. Judith Wolfe, *Willem de Kooning: Works from 1951–1981*, exh. cat., Guild Hall Museum (East Hampton, N.Y.: Guild Hall Museum, 1981), 7.

63. Rosenberg, "Interview with Willem de Kooning"; reprinted in Rosenberg, *Willem de Kooning*, 51.

64. Willem de Kooning, cited in Hess, *Willem de Kooning*, 16.

65. Willem de Kooning, "What Abstract Art Means to Me," *Bulletin of the Museum of Modern Art* 18:3 (spring 1951), 7; reprinted in Hess, *Willem de Kooning*, 145.

66. Willem de Kooning, "Content Is a Glimpse"; in Hess, *Willem de Kooning*, 147.

67. Sally Yard, personal interview with Thomas Hess, Dec. 5, 1977; cited in Sally Yard, *Willem de Kooning: The First Twenty-Six Years in New York* (New York: Garland, 1985), 210, n. 121.

68. Willem de Kooning, interviewed by Courtney Sale, in *De Kooning on de Kooning*.

69. Hess, *Willem de Kooning*, 47.

70. Willem de Kooning, in James T. Valliere, interview with Willem de Kooning, "De Kooning on Pollock," *Partisan Review* (fall 1967), 604; cited in Yard, *Willem de Kooning*, 151.

71. Willem de Kooning, cited in Hess, *Willem de Kooning*, 78.

72. Harold Rosenberg, "Interview with Willem de Kooning," *Artnews* (Sept. 1972); reprinted in Rosenberg, *Willem de Kooning*, 43.

73. De Kooning, "Content Is a Glimpse"; in Hess, *Willem de Kooning*, 148.

74. Willem de Kooning, interviewed by Courtney Sale, in *De Kooning on de Kooning*.

75. De Kooning, "Content Is a Glimpse"; in Hess, *Willem de Kooning*, 148.

76. De Kooning ranked it as one of the three most important shows for him, along with the 1927 Dudensing Gallery show of Matisse and the 1939 Picasso retrospective at the Museum of Modern Art. Interview with the artist by Sally Yard on Aug. 14, 1976; cited in Yard, *Willem de Kooning*, 14.

77. Interview with Elaine de Kooning by Sally Yard, Aug. 5, 1979; cited in Yard, *Willem de Kooning*, 181.

78. Hess, *Willem de Kooning*, 73.

79. Interview with Judith Wolfe on April 24, 1981; cited in Wolfe, *Willem de Kooning: Works from 1951–1981*, 8.

80. De Kooning, "Content Is a Glimpse"; in Hess, *Willem de Kooning*, 148–9.

81. Selden Rodman, *Conversations with Artists* (New York: Devin-Adair, 1957), 102.

82. Rosenberg, "Interview with Willem de Kooning"; reprinted in Rosenberg, *Willem de Kooning*, 43.

83. Willem de Kooning, in an unpublished paper read at a Friday evening meeting on Feb. 18, 1949, at "Subjects of the Artist: A New Art School"; cited in Hess, *Willem de Kooning*, 15.

84. William Seitz asserted that abstract expressionism as a whole did not distinguish between representation and abstraction. See William C. Seitz, *Abstract Expressionist Painting in America: An Introduction Based on the Work and Thought of Six Key Figures*, Ph.D. diss., Princeton University, 1955, 286–7.

85. De Kooning, "Content Is a Glimpse"; in Hess, *Willem de Kooning*, 149.

86. Hess, *Willem de Kooning*, 25.

87. Harold Rosenberg, cited in Hess, *Willem de Kooning*, 74.

88. Hess, *Willem de Kooning*, 74.

89. Rodman, *Conversations with Artists*, 104.

90. Hess, *Willem de Kooning*, 77–8.

91. De Kooning, "Content Is a Glimpse"; in Hess, *Willem de Kooning*, 149.

92. Willem de Kooning, interview with Judith Wolfe, April 14, 1981; cited in Wolfe, *Willem de Kooning: Works from 1951–1981*, 14.

93. Willem de Kooning, interviewed by Courtney Sale, in *De Kooning on de Kooning*.

Chapter 4

1. Willem de Kooning, in Rudi Blesh, *Modern Art USA: Man, Rebellion, Conquest, 1900–1956* (New York: Alfred A. Knopf, 1956), 253.

2. Lee Krasner, "An Interview with Lee Krasner Pollock by B. H. Friedman," in *Jackson Pollock: Black and White*, exh. cat. (New York: Marlborough Gallery, 1969), 8.

3. B. H. Friedman, *Energy Made Visible* (New York: McGraw-Hill, 1972), 7.

4. John D. Graham, "Primitive Art and Picasso," *Magazine of Art* 30:4 (April 1937), 237–8; cited in Irving Sandler, *The Triumph of American Painting* (New York: Praeger, 1970), 106.

5. Friedman, *Energy Made Visible*, 62.

6. Jackson Pollock, radio interview with William Wright, taped 1950; in Francis V. O'Connor, "Documentary Chronology," in Francis Valentine O'Connor and Eugene Victor Thaw, *Jackson Pollock: A Catalogue Raisonné of Paintings, Drawings, and Other Works*, vol. 4 (New Haven: Yale University Press, 1978), 249–50.

7. See William S. Rubin, "Pollock as Jungian Illustrator: The Limits of Psychological Criticism," Part I, *Art in America* (Nov. 1979), 104–23; Part II, *Art in America* (Dec. 1979), 72–91. The most extensive treatment of Jungian themes in Pollock's work is Elizabeth Langhorne, *A Jungian Interpretation of Jackson Pollock's Art Through 1946*, Ph.D. diss., University of Pennsylvania, 1977.

8. See W. Jackson Rushing, "Ritual and Myth: Native American Culture and Abstract Expressionism," in Maurice Tuchman and Judi Freeman, eds., *The Spiritual in Art: Abstract Painting 1890–1985*, Los Angeles County Museum of Art (New York: Abbeville, 1986), 285ff.

9. Lee Krasner, in an interview by Courtney Sale, in a film by Charlotte Zwerin, *Jackson Pollock: Portrait* (New York, 1984).

10. Friedman, *Jackson Pollock*, 65.

11. Jackson Pollock, ibid., 176.

12. Christopher B. Crosman and Nancy E. Miller, "Speaking of Tomlin," interview with James Brooks and Ibram Lassaw, *Art Journal* 39:2 (winter 1979–80), 114.

13. Ibid., 114.

14. Jackson Pollock, "Unframed Space," *The New Yorker* (Aug. 5, 1950), 16.

15. Wassily Kandinsky, "Text Artista: Autobiography by Wassily Kandinsky," in *In Memory of Wassily Kandinsky*, exh. cat. (New York: Museum of Non-Objective Painting, 1945), 59.

16. Jackson Pollock, "My Painting," *Possibilities 1: An Occasional Review* (winter 1947–8), in the series *Problems of Contemporary Art*, no. 4 (New York: Wittenborn, Schultz, 1947), 79.

17. Harold Rosenberg, "The American Action Painters," *Artnews* 51:5 (Sept. 1952); reprinted in Rosenberg's anthology of essays *The Tradition of the New* (New York: Horizon Press, 1959).

18. See Jean-Paul Sartre, *Being and Nothingness*, trans. Hazel Barnes (New York: Pocket Books, 1956), 50.

19. Jackson Pollock, radio interview with William Wright, taped 1950; in O'Connor, "Documentary Chronology," 251.

20. Lee Krasner, quoted in Francine Du Plessix and Cleve Gray, "Who Was Jackson Pollock?" *Art in America* (May–June 1967), 48–59; cited in Friedman, *Jackson Pollock*, 88.

21. "Is Jackson Pollock the Greatest Living Painter in the United States?" *Life* (Aug. 8, 1949), 41–5.

22. "The Wild Ones," *Time Magazine* (Feb. 20, 1956), 70–5.

23. Richard Shiff, "Introduction," in John P. O'Neill, ed., *Barnett Newman: Selected Writings and Interviews* (Berkeley and Los Angeles: University of California Press, 1992), xiv–xv.

24. Barnett Newman, "The New Sense of Fate" (1945); in Thomas Hess, *Barnett Newman*, exh. cat. (New York: The Museum of Modern Art, 1971), 41.

25. Barnett Newman, "The Ideographic Picture," catalog foreword, Betty Parsons Gallery, New York (1947); cited in Harold Rosenberg, *Barnett Newman* (New York: Harry N. Abrams, 1978), 30.

26. Barnett Newman, "The Sublime Is Now," *The Tiger's Eye* 6 (Dec. 1948), 51–3; cited in Sandler, *Triumph of American Painting*, 149.

27. Barnett Newman, quoted in A. J. Liebling, "Two Aesthetes Offer Selves as Candidates to Provide Own Ticket for Intellectuals," *New York World Telegram* (Nov. 4, 1933); cited in Hess, *Barnett Newman*, 25.

28. Cited in Hess, *Barnett Newman*, 7–9.

29. *Zohar (Book of Splendor)*, an early sacred book of Cabbalists, cited in Hess, *Barnett Newman*, 56.

30. Robert Motherwell, an interview with Max Kozloff, *Artforum* 4:1 (Sept. 1965), 37; cited in Sandler, *Triumph of American Painting*, 156.

31. Barnett Newman (1967); cited in Rosenberg, *Barnett Newman*, 27–8.

32. According to Hess, *Barnett Newman*, 58.

33. Ibid., 58.

34. See John P. O'Neill, ed., *Barnett Newman: Selected Writings and Interviews* (Berkeley and Los Angeles: University of California Press, 1992), 216ff.

35. Ibid., 73.

36. Newman himself commented on this; cited in Hess, *Barnett Newman*, 93.

37. Barnett Newman, "Statement," in *Barnett Newman: The Stations of the Cross, Lema Sabachthani*, prepared by Lawrence Alloway (New York: Solomon R. Guggenheim Foundation, 1966), 9.

38. As suggested in Hess, *Barnett Newman*, 98.

39. Barnett Newman, "The Ideographic Picture," foreword to an exhibition catalog, Betty Parsons Gallery, New York (1947); cited in Sandler, *Triumph of American Painting*, 187.

40. Dore Ashton, "Art: Lecture by Mark Rothko," *New York Times* (notes by Ashton from a lecture delivered by Rothko at the Pratt Institute), Oct. 31, 1958, 26.

41. Dore Ashton, *About Rothko* (New York: Oxford University Press, 1983), 20.

42. Robert Motherwell, in conversation with Jonathan Fineberg, Jan. 15, 1979, Greenwich, Conn.

43. William Rubin, "Mark Rothko 1903–70," *New York Times* (March 8, 1970), 21–2.

44. Ashton, *About Rothko*, 51.

45. Mrs. John de Menil, *Address Made at the Opening of the Rothko Chapel in Houston*, Feb. 27, 1971, mimeograph distributed at the chapel.

46. See Stephen Polcari, "The Intellectual Roots of Abstract Expressionism: Mark Rothko," *Arts* (Sept. 1979), 124.

47. See the discussion of Rothko's relation to these events in Ashton, *About Rothko*.

48. John Fischer, "The Easy Chair: Mark Rothko: Portrait of the Artist as an Angry Man," *Harper's* 241:1442 (July 1970), 17.

49. Mark Rothko, "The Portrait and the Modern Artist," in *Art in New York*, a program on WYNC, New York, copy of broadcast transcript, Oct. 13, 1943, 1, 2, 3; cited in Maurice Tuchman, *New York School: The First Generation* (Greenwich, Conn.: New York Graphic Society, 1971), 139.

50. Mark Rothko, in Sidney Janis, *Abstract and Surrealist Art in America* (New York: Reynal & Hitchcock, 1944), 118.

51. Letter of June 7, 1943 by Mark Rothko and Adolph Gottlieb (with the unacknowledged help of Barnett Newman), in Edward Alden Jewell, "The Realm of Art: A New Platform and Other Matters: 'Globalism' Pops into View," *New York Times* (June 13, 1943), x9.

52. Ibid.

53. Dore Ashton, *The New York School* (New York: Viking, 1973), 98.

54. Mark Rothko, "Personal Statement," in *A Painting Prophecy—1950*, exhibition catalog for a group show, David Porter Gallery, Washington, D.C., 1945; cited in Waldman, *Mark Rothko*, 48–9.

55. "The Passing Shows: Mark Rothko," *Artnews* 43 (Jan. 15, 1945), 27.

56. According to Ernest Briggs (a student of Rothko's in the late forties)—Barbara Shikler, interview with Ernest Briggs, July 12 and Oct. 21, 1982, transcript on file at the Archives of American Art, Smithsonian Institution, Washington, D.C.; cited in Bonnie Clearwater, *Mark Rothko: Works on Paper* (New York: Hudson Hill Press, Mark Rothko Foundation, American Federation of the Arts, Viking Penguin, 1984), 33–4.

57. In letters written by Still to Betty Parsons; cited in Ashton, *About Rothko*, 103.

58. Ashton, *About Rothko*, 112.

59. Mark Rothko, "Statement on his Attitude in Painting," *The Tiger's Eye* 1:9 (Oct. 1949), 114.

60. Letter of June 7, 1943 by Mark Rothko and Adolph Gottlieb (with the unacknowledged help of Barnett Newman); cited in Waldman, *Mark Rothko*, 39.

61. Mark Rothko, some notes on art education in an unpublished notebook of the late thirties, collection of the George C. Carson family; cited in Clearwater, *Mark Rothko: Works on Paper*, 36.

62. Anna Chave, *Mark Rothko Subjects*, exh. cat., High Museum of Art, Atlanta, Oct. 15–Feb. 26, 1983, 21. She discusses the idea that Rothko intended the color blocks as disguised figures, entombment and pietà scenes in this catalog and in her Yale doctoral dissertation of 1981, published as Anna C. Chave, *Mark Rothko: Subjects in Abstraction* (New Haven and London: Yale University Press, 1989).

63. Dore Ashton, "Art: Lecture by Rothko," *New York Times* (Oct. 31, 1958), 26; cited in Clearwater, *Mark Rothko: Works on Paper*, 28.

64. Mark Rothko, "The Romantics Were Prompted," *Possibilities 1*, 84.

65. Ibid.

66. Cited in Ashton, *About Rothko*, 154.

67. Mark Rothko, statement delivered from the floor at a symposium of the Museum of Modern Art in New York, published in "A Symposium on How to Combine Architecture, Painting and Sculpture," *Interiors* 110:10 (May 1951), 104.

68. Mark Rothko, in Selden Rodman, *Conversations with Artists* (New York: Devin-Adair, 1957), 93–4.

69. Mrs. John de Menil, *Address*, unpaginated.

70. William Seitz asserted that abstract expressionism as a whole did not distinguish between representation and abstraction. See William C. Seitz, *Abstract Expressionist Painting in America: An Introduction Based on the Work and Thought of Six Key Figures*, Ph.D. diss., Princeton University, 1955, 274–5; and Ashton, *About Rothko*. Both discuss Nietzsche as an important influence on Rothko.

71. Friedrich Nietzsche, *The Birth of Tragedy*, trans. Francis Golffing (Garden City, N.Y.: Doubleday, Anchor Books edition, 1956), 19.

72. Rothko, "The Romantics Were Prompted," 84.

73. David Smith, "Who Is the Artist? How Does He Act?" *Everyday Art Quarterly*, Walker Art Center, no. 23 (1952); cited in Jane Harrison Cone, *David Smith*, exh. cat. (Cambridge, Mass.: Fogg Art Museum, 1966), 99.

74. Ibid.

75. Smith file, reel 2, frame 578, 1950–4; in Archives of American Art, Smithsonian Institution, Washington, D.C.; cited in Cleve Gray, ed., *David Smith by David Smith* (New York: Holt, Rinehart, & Winston, 1968), 130.

76. David Smith, a paper delivered in "The New Sculpture," a symposium held at the Museum of Modern Art, New York, Feb. 21, 1952; cited in Garnett McCoy, ed., *David Smith* (New York: Praeger, 1973), 84.

77. *Art in America* 1 (1966); cited in Gray, *David Smith by David Smith*, 16.

78. Robert Motherwell, in conversation with Jonathan Fineberg, Jan. 15, 1979, Greenwich, Conn.

79. David Smith, "Economic Support of Art in America Today," speech delivered at the American Federation of Arts conference at Corning, New York, Oct. 30, 1953; McCoy, *David Smith*, 107–8.

80. David Smith, a paper delivered in "The New Sculpture" symposium; cited in McCoy, *David Smith*, 82.

81. Maude Riley, "Sewer Pipe Sculpture," *Cue* (March 16, 1940); cited in Stanley E. Marcus, *David Smith: The Sculptor and His Work* (Ithaca, N.Y.: Cornell University, 1983), 51.

82. "Screw Ball Art," *Time* 35:17 (April 22, 1940), 70; cited in Marcus, *David Smith: The Sculptor and His Work*, 51.

83. David Smith, "On Abstract Art," Feb. 15, 1940, lecture to Local 60 of the United American Artists, New York; cited in McCoy, *David Smith*, 40.

84. Clement Greenberg, "American Sculpture of Our Time—Group Show," *Nation* 156:4 (Jan. 23, 1943), 140–1; cited in Marcus, *David Smith: The Sculptor and His Work*, 63.

85. David Smith, speech delivered on WNYC radio, New York, Dec. 30, 1952; in Smith file, reel 4, frame 363, in Archives of American Art, Smithsonian Institution, Washington, D.C.; cited in Marcus, David *Smith: The Sculptor and His Work*, 117.

86. David Smith, interview with Katherine Kuh, in Katherine Kuh, *The Artist's Voice* (New York: Harper & Row, 1960), 229.

87. Smith was quite familiar with them at least since 1948, when a reproduction of Giacometti's 1947 *Man Pointing* was featured in *The Tiger's Eye* along with a work and two poems by Smith. See "The Ides of Art, 14 Sculptors Write," *The Tiger's Eye* (June 1948), 72ff.

88. David Smith, "Perception and Reality," a speech given at Williams College, Dec. 17, 1951; cited in McCoy, *David Smith*, 78.

89. According to Robert Motherwell, in conversation with Jonathan Fineberg on Jan. 15, 1979, Greenwich, Conn. Clement Greenberg destroyed them. However, Garnett McCoy (in a telephone conversation with Jonathan Fineberg on Feb. 1, 1989) recounted that he also found a pile of such photographs—perhaps the same ones or another stack—a short time later and that Ira Lowe (another of the executors) was there at the time and took the pictures away with him.

90. See for example Karen Wilkin, *David Smith* (New York: Abbeville, 1984), 99.

91. David Smith, *New York Herald Tribune* forum in April 1950, Smith file, Archives of American Art, Smithsonian Institution, Washington, D.C.; cited in Gray, *David Smith by David Smith*, 132.

92. Smith file, reel 4, frame 695–730, in Archives of American Art, Smithsonian Institution, Washington, D.C.; cited in Gray, *David Smith by David Smith*, 42.

93. David Smith, "Report on Voltri," notes written after 1963; cited in McCoy, *David Smith*, 162.

94. David Smith, sketchbook 36, 1952, Smith file, reel 3, frame 174, in Archives of American Art, Smithsonian Institution, Washington, D.C.; cited in Marcus, *David Smith: The Sculptor and His Work*, 172.

95. Smith file, reel 4, frame 484–6, 1952–9, in Archives of American Art, Smithsonian Institution, Washington, D.C.; cited in Gray, *David Smith by David Smith*, 60.

96. David Smith, "The Language Is Image," *Arts and Architecture* (Feb. 1952); cited in Cone, *David Smith*, 96.

97. David Smith, "Aesthetics, the Artist, and the Audience," speech delivered at Deerfield, Massachusetts, Sept. 24, 1952; cited in McCoy, *David Smith*, 107.

Chapter 5

1. Friedrich Wilhelm Nietzsche, "Schopenhauer as Educator"; cited in Walter Kaufmann, *Existentialism from Dostoyevsky to Sartre* (New York: World Publishing Co., 1956), 104.

2. Bataille defines *l'informe* in his *Dictionaire, Documents* 1:7 (Paris, 1929). See also the discussion in Rosalind Krauss, *The Originality of the Avant-Garde and Other Materialist Myths* (Cambridge and London: MIT, 1985), 63–4. Subsequently, Krauss and Yve-Alain Bois curated an exhibition with a book based loosely on Bataille's idea of *l'informe*—Yve-Alain Bois and Rosalind E. Krauss, *Formless: A User's Guide* (New York: Zone Books, 1997)—but they took the position that anything implying an attack on binary thought was an example of *l'informe* (thus taking in nearly all advanced art of the twentieth century), but this has little to do with the narrower use of the term by Bataille or Dubuffet's interest in the concept. For an excellent brief discussion of this period and issue see Sarah Wilson, "Paris Post-War: In Search of the Absolute," in Frances Morris, ed., *Paris Post-War: Art and Existentialism* (London: Tate, 1993), 25–52.

3. Jean Dubuffet, *Prospectus aux amateurs de tout genre* (Paris: Gallimard, 1946), 17; cited in Peter Selz, *The Work of Jean Dubuffet* (Garden City, N.Y.: Doubleday; and New York: The Museum of Modern Art, 1962), 10.

4. Jean Dubuffet, *Anti-Cultural Positions*, originally delivered as a lecture in English at the Arts Club of Chicago, Dec. 20, 1951; this version adapted from Dubuffet's French text by Joachim Neugroschel in Mildred Glimcher, *Jean Dubuffet: Towards An Alternative Reality* (New York: Pace Publications, Abbeville, 1987), 127.

5. Jean Dubuffet, "Memoir on the Development of My Work from 1952," trans. Louise Varese; in Selz, *The Work of Jean Dubuffet*, 97–102.

6. *Ibid.*, 102.

7. Jean Dubuffet, "Apercevoir," in *Prospectus et tous ecrits suivants*, vol. 2 (Paris: Gallimard, 1967), 62; trans. Margit Rowell in Margit Rowell, "Jean Dubuffet: An Art on the Margins of Culture," in *Jean Dubuffet: A Retrospective* (New York: Solomon R. Guggenheim Museum, 1973), 15.

8. Marcel Duchamp, interviewed by James Johnson Sweeney in "Eleven Europeans in America," *Bulletin of the Museum of Modern Art* 13:4–5 (New York, 1946), 19–21; cited in Herschel B. Chipp, *Theories of Modern Art* (Berkeley and Los Angeles: University of California Press, 1968), 394.

9. André Breton, *Les Pas perdus* (Paris: Editions de la Nouvelle Revue Française, 1924), 174; trans. Margit Rowell in Rowell, "Jean Dubuffet: An Art on the Margins of Culture," in *Jean Dubuffet: A Retrospective*, 20.

10. Jean Dubuffet, *Anti-Cultural Positions*; in Glimcher, *Jean Dubuffet: Towards An Alternative Reality*, 131.

11. Jean Dubuffet, "Honneur aux valeurs sauvages," in *Catalogue des travaux de Jean Dubuffet*, Max Loreau, fascicule 6, *Corps de dames* (Paris and Lausanne: Jean-Jacques Pauvert, 1965), 109; cited in Reinhold Heller, "'A Swan Only Sings at the Moment It Disappears': Jean Dubuffet and Art at the Edge of Non-Art," in *Jean Dubuffet: Forty Years of His Art*, exh. cat. (Chicago: Smart Gallery, University of Chicago, 1984), 24.

12. Jean Dubuffet, "Landscaped Tables, Landscapes of the Mind, Stones of Philosophy," catalog introduction, trans. the artist and Marcel Duchamp, Pierre Matisse Gallery (New York, 1952); cited in Selz, *The Work of Jean Dubuffet*, 63.

13. *Ibid.*, 66.

14. André Breton, "Seconde manifeste du Surréalisme" (1929), in André Breton, *Manifestes du surréalisme* (Paris: Jean-Jacques Pauvert, 1962), 154; trans. Margit Rowell in Margit Rowell, "Jean Dubuffet: An Art on the Margins of Culture," *Jean Dubuffet: A Retrospective*, 19.

15. See Wilson, "Paris Post War: In Search of the Absolute," 30.

16. Jean Dubuffet, "Note pour les fins-lettres" ("Note for the Well-Read"), in *Prospectus et tous ecrits suivants* (Paris: Gallimard, 1967); trans. Joachim Neugroschel in Glimcher, *Jean Dubuffet: Towards An Alternative Reality*, 8.

17. Hans Prinzhorn, *Artistry of the Mentally Ill* (*Bildnerei der Geisteskranken*), trans. Eric von Brockdorff (New York: Springer-Verlag, 1972), 13.

18. Jean Dubuffet, "Landscaped Tables, Landscapes of the Mind, Stones of Philosophy"; in Selz, *The Work of Jean Dubuffet*, 71.

19. Jean Dubuffet, "Empreintes," in *Les Lettres nouvelles* 5:48 (Paris, April 1957), 507–27; trans. Lucy R. Lippard, in Chipp, *Theories of Modern Art*, 613.

20. Glimcher, *Jean Dubuffet: Towards An Alternative Reality*, 15.

21. Jean Dubuffet, letter to Arnold Glimcher, Sept. 15, 1969; cited in Rowell, "Jean Dubuffet: An Art on the Margins of Culture," in *Jean Dubuffet: A Retrospective*, 26.

22. Jean Dubuffet, in Max Loreau, *Catalogue des travaux de Jean Dubuffet*, vol. 25, Arbres, Murs, Architectures (Lausanne, 1974), xvi; cited in Andreas Franzke, *Dubuffet* (New York: Harry N. Abrams, 1981), 159.

23. Jean Dubuffet, "Closerie Falbala and the Cabinet Logologique," preface to an exhibition catalog of 1978; trans. Joachim Neugroschel in Glimcher, *Jean Dubuffet: Towards An Alternative Reality*, 249.

24. Jean Dubuffet, letter to Arnold Glimcher, April 19, 1985; trans. Joachim Neugroschel in Glimcher, *Jean Dubuffet: Towards An Alternative Reality*, 301.

25. Alberto Giacometti, letter to Pierre Matisse, 1947; first published in *Exhibition of Sculptures, Paintings, Drawings* (New York: Pierre Matisse Gallery, 1948); cited in *Alberto Giacometti*, exh. cat., Museum of Modern Art (Garden City, N.Y.: Doubleday, 1965), 16.

26. Alberto Giacometti, "Palais de 4 heures," *Minotaure* 3–4 (Paris, December 1933), 46.

27. Alberto Giacometti, letter to Pierre Matisse, 1947; in *Alberto Giacometti*, 16.

28. Reinhold Hohl, "Form and Vision: The Work of Alberto Giacometti," in *Alberto Giacometti: A Retrospective Exhibition*, Solomon R. Guggenheim Museum (New York: Praeger, 1974), 23.

29. Alberto Giacometti, letter to Pierre Matisse, 1947; in *Alberto Giacometti*, 28.

30. Alberto Giacometti, cited in James Lord, *A Giacometti Portrait* (Garden City, N.Y.: Doubleday, 1965), 10, 11.

31. *Ibid.*, 8.

32. Hohl, "Form and Vision: The Work of Alberto Giacometti," 24.

33. Alberto Giacometti, cited in Lord, *A Giacometti Portrait*, 26.

34. Francis Bacon, Oct. 1962, in David Sylvester, *Interviews with Francis Bacon* (London: Thames & Hudson, 1975), 26–8.

35. Francis Bacon, October 1973, *ibid.*, 100.

36. Francis Bacon, cited in John Russell, *Francis Bacon* (Greenwich, Conn.: New York Graphic Society, 1971), 20.

37. Letter from Bacon, Jan. 9, 1959, in Ronald Alley and John Rothenstein, *Francis Bacon* (New York: Viking, 1964), 35.

38. Aeschylus, *The Eumenides*, line 252, as translated in a book well known to Bacon: W. B. Stanford, *Aeschylus in His Style: A Study in Language and Personality* (Dublin: The University Press, 1942); cited in Dawn Ades, "Web of Images," in Dawn Ades and Andrew Forge, *Francis Bacon* (London: Tate in association with Thames & Hudson, 1985), 17.

39. Francis Bacon, Oct. 1962, in Sylvester, *Interviews with Francis Bacon*, 11.

40. Francis Bacon, Oct. 1962, *ibid.*, 23.

41. Francis Bacon, May 1966, *ibid.*, 48.

42. He had seen the work only in reproduction, according to Alley and Rothenstein, *Francis Bacon*, 13. He kept the film still from *Potemkin* in his studio; *Francis Bacon*, May 1966, in Sylvester, *Interviews with Francis Bacon*, 34.

43. Francis Bacon, Dec. 1971, in Sylvester, *Interviews with Francis Bacon*, 72.

44. Francis Bacon, May 1966, *ibid.*, 30–2.

45. Francis Bacon, April 3, 1973, interviewed by Hugh Davies, in Hugh Davies and Sally Yard, *Francis Bacon* (New York, Abbeville Press, 1991), 106–7, n. 83.

46. Francis Bacon, Oct. 1962, in Sylvester, *Interviews with Francis Bacon*, 12.

47. Francis Bacon, May 1966, *ibid.*, 56.

48. Francis Bacon, Oct. 1973, *ibid.*, 92.

49. Francis Bacon, May 1966, *ibid.*, 56.

Chapter 6

1. Lucio Fontana, *Manifesto Blanco* (Buenos Aires, 1946); cited in Yve-Alain Bois, "Fontana's Base Materialism," *Art in America* (April 1989), 244. The manifesto is anthologized as "The White Manifesto" in Charles Harrison and Paul Wood, eds., *Art in Theory: 1900–1990* (Oxford: Blackwell Publishers, 1992).

2. Cited in Harold Rosenberg, *Barnett Newman* (New York: Harry N. Abrams, 1978), 27–9.

3. Elaine de Kooning, "Subject: What, How or Who?" *Artnews* (April 1955); cited in Irving Sandler, *The New York School: The Painters and Sculptors of the Fifties* (New York: Harper & Row, 1978), 55.
4. Friedel Dzubas, statement, in Irving Sandler, "Is There a New Academy?", Part II, *Artnews* (Sept. 1959), 37.
5. Clement Greenberg, "'American Type' Painting," *Partisan Review* (spring); reprinted in Clement Greenberg, *Art and Culture* (Boston: Beacon Press, 1967), 208.
6. Barbara Rose, in William C. Seitz, moderator, *Art Criticism in the Sixties*, A Symposium of the Poses Institute of Fine Arts, Brandeis University (New York: October House, 1967), unpaginated.
7. William S. Rubin, "Younger American Painters," *Art International* 1 (1960), 20; cited in Irving Sandler, *American Art of the 1960s* (New York: Harper & Row, 1988), 17.
8. Clement Greenberg, "Modernist Painting," *Arts Yearbook* 4 (1961); reprinted in Gregory Battcock, ed., *The New Art* (New York: E. P. Dutton, 1966), 101–2.
9. Sandler, *American Art of the 1960s*, 118.
10. Kenworth Moffett, "Pop Art: Two Views," *Artnews* (May 1974), 31; cited in Sandler, *American Art of the 1960s*, 127, n. 60.
11. Michael Fried, in William C. Seitz, moderator, *Art Criticism in the Sixties*, unpaginated.
12. Michael Fried, "Modernist Painting and Formalist Criticism," *The American Scholar* (autumn 1964), 648; cited in Sandler, *American Art of the 1960s*, 50.
13. Rosalind Krauss, "A View of Modernism," *Artforum* (September 1972), 49–50; cited in Sandler, *American Art of the 1960s*, 48.
14. Sandler, *American Art of the 1960s*, 128, n. 61.
15. He was publicly taken to task for this by many historians and critics. For example, see Rosalind Krauss, "Changing the Work of David Smith," *Art in America* (Sept.–Oct. 1974), 31–4.
16. Diane Upright Headley, *Morris Louis: The Mature Paintings 1954–1962*, Ph.D. diss., University of Michigan, 1976, 50, n. 78; cited in Sandler, *American Art of the 1960s*, 140, n. 4.
17. Michael Fried, "Some Notes on Morris Louis," *Arts Magazine* (Nov. 1963), 25; cited in Sandler, *American Art of the 1960s*, 29.
18. Michael Fried, "New York Letter," *Art International* (May 25, 1963), 69; cited in Sandler, *American Art of the 1960s*, 30.
19. Harold Rosenberg, conversation with Jonathan Fineberg in 1977. The quotation by itself later appeared in Rosenberg, *Barnett Newman*, 21.
20. Constant, cited in Jean-Clarence Lambert, *Cobra* (New York: Abbeville, 1984), 82.
21. Pierre Alechinsky, cited in Lambert, *Cobra*, 183.
22. Pierre Alechinsky, "Abstraction faite," *Cobra* 10; cited in Lambert, *Cobra*, 186.
23. Lucian Freud, quoted in Lawrence Gowing, *Lucian Freud* (London: Thames & Hudson, 1982), 190–1.
24. Robert Hughes, *Lucian Freud: Paintings* (New York: Thames & Hudson, 1987), 7.
25. Elaine de Kooning, "Subject: What, How or Who?" 26 and 27 respectively; cited in Sandler, *The New York School: The Painters and Sculptors of the Fifties*, 96.
26. Leon Golub, Bloomington, Indiana, March 1959; cited in Peter Selz, *New Images of Man*, exh. cat., Museum of Modern Art (Garden City, N.Y.: Doubleday, 1959), 76.
27. An idea frequently repeated by Rauschenberg; see, for example, G. R. Swenson, "Rauschenberg Paints a Picture," *Artnews* (April 1963), 46.

Chapter 7

1. Allen Ginsberg, *Howl and Other Poems* (San Francisco: City Lights Pocket Bookshop, 1956), 9, 14.
2. Lawrence Ferlinghetti, "Dog," in Lawrence Ferlinghetti, *A Coney Island of the Mind* (New York: New Directions, 1955), 67–8.
3. Harold Rosenberg, "The Herd of Independent Minds," *Commentary* (Sept. 1948); reprinted in Harold Rosenberg, *Discovering the Present* (Chicago: University of Chicago Press, 1973), 28.
4. Marshall McLuhan, *The Mechanical Bride, Folklore of the Industrial Man* (New York: Vanguard Press, 1951), v.
5. Ibid., 3.
6. Ferlinghetti, *A Coney Island of the Mind*, 1955.

7. Cited in many places; see for example Jill Johnston, "Tracking the Shadow," *Art in America* (October 1987), 135.
8. John Cage, an address to the convention of the Music Teachers National Association in Chicago, 1957; reprinted in *Silence* (Cambridge, Mass.: MIT Press, 1966), 10.
9. John Cage, cited in Harvey Stein, *Artists Observed* (New York: Harry N. Abrams, 1986), 93.
10. Merce Cunningham, *Dance in America*, transcript of a program for WNET/13, New York, 1978, 2–3; cited by Melissa Harris in a senior art history thesis on the Merce Cunningham Dance Company written under the direction of Jonathan Fineberg at Yale University, April 1982.
11. Martin Duberman, *Black Mountain: An Exploration in Community* (New York: E. P. Dutton, 1972), 278.
12. Ibid., 352–4.
13. William S. Burroughs, *Naked Lunch* (New York: Grove Press, 1959), 221.
14. Robert Rauschenberg, interviewed in Barbara Rose, *An Interview with Robert Rauschenberg* (New York: Elizabeth Avedon Editions, Vintage, 1987), 72.
15. Ibid., 53.
16. Some art historians have attempted to "read" these objects in Rauschenberg's work as a systematic iconography. Kenneth Bendiner, for example, argued in 1982 that *Canyon* of 1959 was a homoerotic reinterpretation of Rembrandt's *Ganymede* and in an article of 1977 Charles Stuckey turned all the images in *Rebus* of 1955 into words through free association and then attempted to "read" them like a sentence. Lisa Wainwright has successfully followed specific trains of association through sequences of permutations. See Kenneth Bendiner, "Robert Rauschenberg's 'Canyon,'" *Arts Magazine* (June 1982), 57–9; Charles F. Stuckey, "Reading Rauschenberg," *Art in America* (March–April 1977), 82–3; Lisa Susan Wainwright, *Reading Junk: Thematic Imagery in the Art of Robert Rauschenberg from 1952 to 1964*, unpublished doctoral dissertation, University of Illinois at Urbana-Champaign, 1993. Two other provocative essays on the meaning of the imagery in Rauschenberg's work are: Roger Cranshaw and Adrian Lewis, "Re-Reading Rauschenberg," *Artscribe* 29 (London, June 1981), 44–51; and Graham Smith, "Robert Rauschenberg's 'Odalisque,'" *Wallraff-Richartz Jahrbuch* 44 (Köln, 1983), 375–82.
17. Dorothy Gees Seckler, "The Artist Speaks: Robert Rauschenberg," *Art in America* (May–June 1966), 81.
18. See Lisa Susan Wainwright, *Reading Junk: Thematic Imagery in the Art of Robert Rauschenberg from 1952 to 1964*.
19. Cited in Duberman, *Black Mountain*, 346.
20. Seckler, "The Artist Speaks: Robert Rauschenberg," 76.
21. Calvin Tomkins, *Off the Wall: Robert Rauschenberg and the Art World of Our Time* (Garden City, N.Y.: Doubleday, 1980), 72.
22. Robert Rauschenberg, quoted in Andrew Forge, *Rauschenberg* (New York: Harry N. Abrams, 1972), 10.
23. Robert Rauschenberg, interviewed in Rose, *An Interview with Robert Rauschenberg*, 50.
24. John Cage, an address to the convention of the Music Teachers National Association in Chicago, 1957; reprinted in *Silence*, 12.
25. Robert Rauschenberg, in an interview with Dorothy Seckler, Dec. 21, 1965, transcript from the Archives of American Art; cited in Wainwright, *Reading Junk*, 16.
26. Michael Newman, "Rauschenberg Re-evaluated," *Art Monthly* (London, June 1981), 9.
27. Robert Rauschenberg, interviewed in Rose, *An Interview with Robert Rauschenberg*, 96.
28. Robert Rauschenberg, cited in G. R. Swenson, "Rauschenberg Paints a Picture," *Artnews* (April 1963), 46.
29. Robert Rauschenberg, in Jeanne Siegel, *Artwords: Discourse on the 60s and 70s* (Ann Arbor, Mich.: UMI Research Press, 1985), 155.
30. According to Ileana Sonnabend, who was married to Leo Castelli at the time and later became Rauschenberg's dealer in her own gallery; Ileana Sonnabend, conversation with Jonathan Fineberg, Sept. 8, 1988.
31. See Dore Ashton, *Rauschenberg: XXXIV Drawings for Dante's Inferno* (New York: Harry N. Abrams, 1964); and Jerry Saltz, "Notes on a Drawing," *Arts Magazine* (Nov. 1988), 19–22.

32. Robert Rauschenberg, talking about *Broadcast* of 1959, in Swenson, "Rauschenberg Paints a Picture," 45.
33. Tomkins, *The Bride and the Bachelors*, 204, 232.
34. Robert Rauschenberg, interviewed in Rose, *An Interview with Robert Rauschenberg*, 85.
35. Robert Rauschenberg, in Robert Hughes, *The Shock of the New* (New York: Alfred A. Knopf, 1981), 345; cited in Mary Lynn Kotz, *Robert Rauschenberg: Art and Life* (New York: Harry N. Abrams, 1990), 99.
36. Robert Rauschenberg, interviewed in Rose, *An Interview with Robert Rauschenberg*, 74.
37. Robert Rauschenberg, cited in Swenson, "Rauschenberg Paints a Picture," 67.
38. Robert Hughes, "The Most Living Artist," *Time* (Nov. 29, 1976), 54.
39. John Cage, address to the convention of the Music Teachers National Association in Chicago, 1957; reprinted in *Silence*, 12.
40. Richard Stankiewicz, remarks made on a panel at "The Club," on March 25, 1955, as recorded by Irving Sandler; cited in Irving Sandler, *The New York School: The Painters and Sculptors of the Fifties* (New York: Harper & Row, 1978), 147.
41. For a fuller discussion of the term see William C. Seitz, *The Art of Assemblage*, exh. cat., Museum of Modern Art (Garden City, N.Y.: Doubleday, 1961), 93, 150, n. 5.
42. For example, Shelley Rice, *Inverted Odysseys: Claude Cahun, Maya Deren, Cindy Sherman* (Cambridge: M.I.T. Press, 1999) and Amelia Jones, "Tracing the Subject with Cindy Sherman," in *Cindy Sherman Retrospective* (Chicago: The Museum of Contemporary Art; Los Angeles: The Museum of Contemporary Art, 1997), 33–53.
43. Stan Brakhage, "Metaphors on Vision," *Film Culture*, no. 30 (fall 1963), 12.
44. John Cage, address to the convention of the Music Teachers National Association in Chicago, 1957; reprinted in *Silence*, 12.
45. Allan Kaprow, "The Legacy of Jackson Pollock," *Artnews* (Oct. 1958), 56–7.
46. Allan Kaprow, cited in Michael Kirby, *Happenings: An Illustrated Anthology* (New York: E. P. Dutton, 1965), 48.
47. Allan Kaprow, "'Happenings' in the New York Scene," *Artnews* (May 1961), 59.
48. Claes Oldenburg, transcript from a panel entitled "New Uses of the Human Image in Painting," Judson Gallery, Dec. 2, 1959, Judson Memorial Church Archives, New York; cited in Barbara Haskell, *Blam! The Explosion of Pop, Minimalism, and Performance 1958–1964*, exh. cat., Whitney Museum of American Art (New York: W. W. Norton and Co., 1984), 27.
49. Haskell, *Blam! The Explosion of Pop*, 27.
50. Jim Dine, in Kirby, *Happenings: An Illustrated Anthology*, 188.
51. Claes Oldenburg, as cited in Tomkins, *Off the Wall*, 154.
52. Haskell, *Blam! The Explosion of Pop*, 27.
53. George Segal, in Henry Geldzahler, "An Interview with George Segal," *Artforum* (Nov. 1964), 26.
54. Jim Dine, in John Green, "All Right Jim Dine, Talk!" *World Journal Tribune, Sunday Magazine* (Nov. 20, 1966), 34.
55. Claes Oldenburg, notebook entry of 1961; cited in Barbara Rose, *Claes Oldenburg*, exh. cat., Museum of Modern Art (Greenwich, Conn.: New York Graphic Society, 1970), 48.
56. Claes Oldenburg; cited in Rose, *Claes Oldenburg*, 30.
57. Claes Oldenburg, notebook entry, Dec. 1–7, 1960; cited in Claes Oldenburg and Emmet Williams, *Store Days* (New York: Something Else Press, 1967), 65.
58. Claes Oldenburg, notebook entry, 1960; cited in Rose, *Claes Oldenburg*, 62.
59. Claes Oldenburg, notebook entry, 1962; ibid., 192.
60. Claes Oldenburg; ibid., 154.
61. Claes Oldenburg, notebook entry, 1960; ibid., 189.
62. Claes Oldenburg; ibid., 46.
63. Claes Oldenburg; ibid., 31.
64. Claes Oldenburg; ibid., 31.
65. Claes Oldenburg, "Extracts from the Studio Notes (1962–64)," *Artforum* (Jan. 1966), 33; cited in Ellen H. Johnson, *Claes Oldenburg*, Penguin New Art 4 (Baltimore, 1971), 20.
66. Claes Oldenburg, notebook entry; in Oldenburg and Williams, *Store Days*, 60.

67. Claes Oldenburg, notebook entry, New York, 1961; cited in Coosje van Bruggen, *Claes Oldenburg: Mouse Museum/Ray Gun Wing* (Köln: Museum Ludwig, 1979), 16.
68. Claes Oldenburg, cited in Rose, *Claes Oldenburg*, 69.
69. Claes Oldenburg, summer 1963; *ibid.*, 92.
70. Claes Oldenburg, "America: War & Sex, Etc.," *Arts Magazine* (summer 1967), 36.
71. Claes Oldenburg, notebooks; in Oldenburg and Williams, *Store Days*, 62.
72. Claes Oldenburg; cited in Martin Friedman, *Oldenburg: Six Themes*, exh. cat. (Minneapolis: Walker Arts Center, 1975), 14.
73. Claes Oldenburg interview with Paul Carroll, Aug. 22, 1968; in Claes Oldenburg, *Proposals for Monuments and Buildings 1965–9* (Chicago: Big Table Publishing Co., 1969), 14.
74. Marshall McLuhan, *Understanding Media: The Extension of Man* (New York: McGraw-Hill, 1965), 7.
75. John Ciardi, *How Does a Poem Mean?* 2nd ed. (Boston: Houghton Mifflin, 1975 [1959]), 6.
76. In particular see Joan Carpenter, "The Infra-Iconography of Jasper Johns," *Art Journal* 36:3 (spring 1977), 221–7.
77. Jasper Johns, in Walter Hopps, "An Interview with Jasper Johns," *Artforum* (March 1965), 33.
78. Jasper Johns, interviewed by Leo Steinberg, in Leo Steinberg, "Jasper Johns: The First Seven Years of His Art" (1962), in *Other Criteria* (New York: Oxford University Press, 1972), 32.
79. David Sylvester, "Interview," in *Jasper Johns: Drawings* (London: Arts Council of Great Britain, 1974), 19.
80. Jasper Johns, cited in "His Heart Belongs to Dada," *Time* 73 (May 4, 1959), 58.
81. Michael Crichton, *Jasper Johns* (New York: Harry N. Abrams, 1977), 66, n. 18.
82. Tatyana Grosman, cited in Crichton, *Jasper Johns*, 19.
83. Jasper Johns, in Crichton, *Jasper Johns*, 27.
84. Jasper Johns, in Vivian Raynor, "Jasper Johns: 'I have attempted to develop my thinking in such a way that the work I've done is not me,'" *Artnews* (March 1973), 22.
85. Entry of April 3, 1970 in unpublished journal by Roberta Bernstein; cited in Roberta Bernstein, *Jasper Johns' Paintings and Sculptures 1954–1974: "The Changing Focus of the Eye"* (Ann Arbor, Mich.: UMI Research Press, 1985), 21.
86. A mental processing conflict occurs when one tries to read the name of a color written in the wrong color, as in such paintings as *False Start, Jubilee,* and *Diver.* This has come to be known as "the Stroop effect" after the discoveries published by J. Ridley Stroop, "Studies of Interference in Serial Verbal Reactions," *Journal of Experimental Psychology* 18:6 (Dec. 1935), 643–61. Stroop showed that delays in processing can be caused by such dissonances and learned something about the relative speed of processing words and color from this work. This is the kind of thing that might well have caught Johns's interest but we have no evidence beyond the paintings themselves that he knew of this. The reference was pointed out to me by Jami Dowd, a student at the University of Illinois, in 1995.
87. Jasper Johns, cited in Crichton, *Jasper Johns*, 46.
88. Jasper Johns, in Hopps, "An Interview with Jasper Johns," 36.
89. Jasper Johns, in G. R. Swenson, "What Is Pop Art? Part II: Jasper Johns," *Artnews* 62:10 (Feb. 1964), 66.
90. Richard S. Field, *Jasper Johns: Prints 1970–1977*, exh. cat. (Middletown, Conn.: Wesleyan University, 1978), 33, n. 14.
91. Ludwig Wittgenstein, *Philosophical Investigations*, trans. G. E. M. Anscombe (Oxford, 1953), 19e, no. 38; cited in Bernstein, *Jasper Johns' Paintings and Sculptures 1954–1974: "The Changing Focus of the Eye,"* 94.
92. Ludwig Wittgenstein, *The Blue and Brown Books* (Oxford, 1958), 39; cited in Bernstein, *Jasper Johns' Paintings and Sculptures*, 94.
93. Sylvester, "Interview," in *Jasper Johns: Drawings*, 16–17.
94. Bernstein, *Jasper Johns' Paintings and Sculptures*, 108.
95. Roger Cranshaw and Adrian Lewis, "Re-Reading Rauschenberg," *Artscribe* 29 (London, June 1981), 49; they cite Johns as quoted in Brian O'Doherty, *American Masters* (New York: Random House, 1973), 202.
96. Hart Crane, "Cape Hatteras," cited in Alan R. Solomon, "Jasper Johns," *Jasper Johns*, exh. cat., Jewish Museum (New York, 1964), 16.

97. Philip Horton, *Hart Crane: The Life of an American Poet* (New York: Viking, 1957), 302; cited in Bernstein, *Jasper Johns' Paintings and Sculptures*, 109.
98. Crichton, *Jasper Johns*, 50.
99. Jasper Johns, in John Coplans, "Fragments According to Johns, An Interview with Jasper Johns," *Print Collector's Newsletter* 3:2 (May–June 1972), 29–32; cited in Field, *Jasper Johns: Prints 1970–1977*, 35, n. 27.
100. Jasper Johns, statement, in Dorothy C. Miller, ed., *Sixteen Americans*, exh. cat., Museum of Modern Art (Garden City, N.Y.: Doubleday, 1959), 22.
101. Sylvester, "Interview," in *Jasper Johns: Drawings*, 9.
102. "Interview with Jasper Johns," in Christian Geelhaar, *Jasper Johns: Working Proofs* (London: Petersburg Press, 1980), 39.
103. Sylvester, "Interview," in *Jasper Johns: Drawings*, 13–14.
104. Peter Fuller, "Jasper Johns Interviewed: II," *Art Monthly* 19 (London, Sept. 1978), 7; cited in Mark Rosenthal, *Jasper Johns: Work Since 1974*, exh. cat. (Philadelphia: Philadelphia Museum of Art, 1988), 60.
105. Judith Goldman, *Jasper Johns: The Seasons*, exh. cat. (New York: Leo Castelli Gallery, 1987), unpaginated.
106. Cited in Jill Johnston, "Tracking the Shadow," *Art in America* (Oct. 1987), 135.
107. Jasper Johns, letter to Jonathan Fineberg, Sept. 20, 1994.
108. Sylvester, "Interview," in *Jasper Johns: Drawings*, 14.

Chapter 8

1. This is discussed in careful detail in Thomas McEvilley, "Yves Klein: Conquistador of the Void," in *Yves Klein 1928–1962: A Retrospective* (Houston: Institute for the Arts, Rice University; New York: Arts Publisher, 1982); and in his "Yves Klein and Rosicrucianism," *ibid.*
2. Yves Klein, cited in McEvilley, "Yves Klein: Conquistador of the Void," 48.
3. Pierre Restany, *Yves Klein*, trans. John Shepley (New York: Harry N. Abrams, 1982), 22.
4. Yves Klein, cited in Restany, *Yves Klein*, 47.
5. Restany, *Yves Klein*, 49.
6. McEvilley, "Yves Klein: Conquistador of the Void," 50.
7. Nan Rosenthal, "Assisted Levitation: The Art of Yves Klein," in *Yves Klein 1928–1962: A Retrospective*, 119.
8. Yves Klein, "Truth Becomes Reality," trans. Thomas McEvilley, in *Yves Klein 1928–1962: A Retrospective*, 229–30.
9. Yves Klein, cited in Restany, *Yves Klein*, 90.
10. Rotraut Klein-Moquay, cited in McEvilley, "Yves Klein: Conquistador of the Void," 62.
11. Jean Tinguely, cited in *ibid.*, 27.
12. Thomas McEvilley, "Yves Klein: Conquistador of the Void," 74.
13. Calvin Tomkins, *The Bride and the Bachelors* (New York: Viking Press, 1965), 173.
14. *Ibid.*, 180.
15. Marcel Duchamp, cited in *ibid.*, 15.
16. Paul Schimmel chronicled this history in a brilliant exhibition catalog, *Out of Actions: Between Performance and the Object 1949–1979* (Los Angeles: Museum of Contemporary Art, 1998).
17. See Paul Schimmel, "Leap Into the Void: Performance and the Object," in *Out of Actions: Between Performance and the Object, 1949–1979*, 24.
18. Ray Falk, "Japanese Innovators," *New York Times*, Dec. 8, 1957, section 2, 24.
19. John Cage, Michael Kirby, and Richard Schechner, "An Interview with John Cage," *The Tulane Drama Review* 10:2 (winter 1965), 67. See also Hannah Higgins, *Fluxus Experience* (Berkeley: University of California Press, 2002), 1–2.
20. Barbara Haskell, *Blam! The Explosion of Pop, Minimalism, and Performance 1958–1964*, exh. cat., Whitney Museum of American Art (New York: W. W. Norton and Co., 1984), 53.
21. Robert Watts, cited in Rene Block, "Fluxus and Fluxism in Berlin 1964–1976," in Kynaston McShine, ed., *Berlinart 1961–1987* (New York: Museum of Modern Art; Munich: Prestel Verlag, 1987), 66.
22. Al Hansen, "Some More Thoughts/Notes on the Fluxus Phenomenon" (Dec. 1990); in Heike Hoffmann, ed., *Al Hanson: Introspective* (Köln: Kölnisches Stadt Museum, 1996), 44.

23. Joseph Beuys, cited in Caroline Tisdall, *Joseph Beuys*, exh. cat. (New York: Solomon R. Guggenheim Museum, 1979), 21.
24. See John Anthony Thwaites, "The Ambiguity of Joseph Beuys," *Art and Artists* 6:7 (Nov. 1971), 22; and Willoughby Sharp, "An Interview with Joseph Beuys," *Artforum* 8 (Dec. 1969), 43.
25. Joseph Beuys, cited in Tisdall, *Joseph Beuys*, 17.
26. Joseph Beuys, in Nick Serota, *Joseph Beuys: The Secret Block for a Secret Person in Ireland*, exh. cat. (Oxford: The Museum of Modern Art, 1974), unpaginated.
27. Joseph Beuys, cited in Tisdall, *Joseph Beuys*, 18.
28. *Ibid.*, 7.
29. Joseph Beuys, cited in John Russell, "The Shaman as Artist," *The New York Times Magazine* (October 28, 1979), 103.
30. Beuys as a practitioner of the occult and in particular his connection with Steiner has been explored at length (if not sympathetically) in J. F. Moffitt, *Occultism in Avant-Garde Art: The Case of Joseph Beuys* (Ann Arbor, Mich.: UMI Research Press, 1988).
31. Though men's felt hats are more often made of rabbit fur than of lamb's wool.
32. Joseph Beuys, in George Jappe, "Joseph Beuys soll gehen. Soll er?", *FAZ* (Nov. 28, 1969); cited in Irene Von Zahn, "By Way of Introduction," in *Some Artists, For Example Joseph Beuys*, exh. cat. (Riverside: University of California, 1975), unpaginated.
33. Joseph Beuys, cited in Tisdall, *Joseph Beuys*, 94–5.
34. *Ibid.*, 7.
35. *Ibid.*, 10.
36. Nam June Paik, cited in Douglas Davis, "Electronic Wallpaper," *Newsweek* (Aug. 24, 1970), 54.
37. Yoko Ono, "The Word of a Fabricator" (1962, trans. Yoko Ono 1999, Anthology 12); cited in Alexandra Monroe, "Spirit of YES: The Art and Life of Yoko Ono," Alexandra Monroe with Jon Hendricks, *YES: Yoko Ono*, exh. cat. (New York: Japan Society, 2000), 13.
38. Yoko Ono, "To the Wesleyan People," Anthology 14, 1966; cited in Monroe, "Spirit of YES: The Art and Life of Yoko Ono," 16.
39. Monroe, "Spirit of YES: The Art and Life of Yoko Ono," 17.
40. D. T. Suzuki, *Zen and Japanese Culture*, 212; cited in Monroe, "Spirit of YES: The Art and Life of Yoko Ono," 17.
41. See discussion in Monroe, "Spirit of YES: The Art and Life of Yoko Ono," 21.
42. *Ibid.*, 26.
43. *Ibid.*, 29.

Chapter 9

1. William L. O'Neill, *Coming Apart: An Informal History of America in the 1960s* (Chicago: Quadrangle Books, 1977), 3; cited in Irving Sandler, *American Art of the 1960s* (New York: Harper & Row), 81.
2. Allan Kaprow, "Should the Artist Become a Man of the World?", *Artnews* 63 (Oct. 1964), 34.
3. Claude Lévi-Strauss, "The Structural Study of Myth," in *Structural Anthropology* (New York: Basic Books, 1963), 217. This is also at the heart of Lévi-Strauss's critique of Sartre; see Claude Lévi-Strauss, *The Savage Mind* (London: Weidenfeld & Nicolson, 1966), 253ff.
4. Reyner Banham, "Vehicles of Desire," *Art 1* (Sept. 1955), 3; cited in *Modern Dreams: The Rise and Fall of Pop*, exh. cat. (New York: The Institute for Contemporary Art, 1988), 66.
5. Alison and Peter Smithson, "But Today We Collect Ads," *Ark* 18 (Nov. 1956); reprinted in *Modern Dreams*, 57.
6. Commentary by Richard Hamilton, in *Richard Hamilton*, exh. cat. (New York: Solomon R. Guggenheim Museum, 1973), 24.
7. Richard Hamilton, note from 1956, cited in *Richard Hamilton*, 24.
8. See Simon Frith and Howard Home, *Art into Pop* (London, 1987).
9. David Hockney, cited in Marco Livingstone, *David Hockney* (New York: Thames & Hudson, 1988), 40.
10. David Hockney, in Nikos Stangos, ed., *David Hockney by David Hockney* (New York: Harry N. Abrams, 1977), 61.
11. David Hockney, in *ibid.*, 93.
12. David Hockney, quoted in Lawrence Weschler, *Cameraworks: David Hockney* (New York: Alfred A. Knopf, 1984), 11.

13. Gert Schiff, "A Moving Focus: Hockney's Dialogue with Picasso," in *David Hockney: A Retrospective*, exh. cat. (Los Angeles: Los Angeles County Museum of Art, 1988).

14. John Carlin and Sheena Wagstaff, "Beyond the Pleasure Principle: Comic Quotation in Contemporary American Painting," in *The Comic Art Show*, exh. cat., Whitney Museum of American Art (New York: Fantagraphics Books, 1983), 55.

15. Tom Wesselmann, in G. R. Swenson, "What Is Pop Art? Part II: Jasper Johns," *Artnews* 62:10 (Feb. 1964), 41.

16. *Time* 80 (Oct. 12, 1962), 85; cited in Sidra Stich, *Made in USA*, exh. cat., University Art Museum, University of California (Berkeley and Los Angeles: University of California Press, 1987), 89.

17. Adam Gopnik, "The Art World: The Innocent," *The New Yorker* (April 10, 1989), 109.

18. Andy Warhol, in *Andy Warhol*, exh. cat. (Stockholm: Moderna Museet, 1968), unpaginated.

19. According to Benjamin Buchloh, "Andy Warhol's One-Dimensional Art: 1956–1966," in Kynaston McShine, ed., *Andy Warhol: A Retrospective*, exh. cat. (New York: The Museum of Modern Art, 1989), 39.

20. According to Warhol, in Barry Blinderman, "Modern Myths: An Interview with Andy Warhol," *Arts Magazine* 56 (Oct. 1981), 145; cited in Marco Livingstone, "Do It Yourself: Notes on Warhol's Techniques," in McShine, *Andy Warhol*, 66.

21. Andy Warhol and Pat Hackett, *Popism: The Warhol 60s* (New York: Harcourt Brace Jovanovich, 1980), 7.

22. Cited in *ibid.*, 16.

23. *Ibid.*, 7.

24. Andy Warhol, *The Philosophy of Andy Warhol* (New York: Harcourt Brace Jovanovich, 1975), 100–1.

25. Kynaston McShine, "Introduction," in McShine, *Andy Warhol*, 14–15.

26. Irving Blum gave an engaging account in Laura de Coppet and Alan Jones, *The Art Dealers* (New York: Potter; distributed by Crown, 1984), 150–8.

27. Isabel Eberstadt, in Jean Stein, ed. with George Plimpton, *Edie: An American Biography* (New York: Alfred A. Knopf, 1982), 208.

28. Andy Warhol, in Gene Swenson, "What Is Pop Art? Part I," *Artnews* 62 (Nov. 1963), 26.

29. Warhol, *Andy Warhol*, unpaginated.

30. Warhol, *Philosophy of Andy Warhol*, 7.

31. Warhol and Hackett, *Popism*, 50.

32. Warhol, *Andy Warhol*, unpaginated.

33. Henry Geldzahler, in Stein, *Edie*, 201.

34. Warhol and Hackett, *Popism*, 133.

35. Daniel Bell, *The Coming of Post Industrial Society* (New York: Basic Books, 1976).

36. Calvin Tomkins, *Off the Wall: Robert Rauschenberg and the Art World of Our Time* (Garden City, N.Y.: Doubleday, 1980), 261.

37. Warhol, *Philosophy of Andy Warhol*, 92.

38. Tomkins, *Off the Wall*, 260–1.

39. Brigid Polk, *Time* (Oct. 17, 1969), 48.

40. Andy Warhol, in Phyllis Tuchman, "Pop! Interviews with George Segal, Andy Warhol, Roy Lichtenstein, James Rosenquist, and Robert Indiana," *Artnews* 73 (May 1974), 26. See also Livingstone, "Do It Yourself," 77, n. 9; and Warhol and Hackett, *Popism*, 248, in which Warhol explains that his assistant's remark was a deliberately outrageous joke.

41. See Trevor Fairbrother, "Warhol Meets Sargent at Whitney," *Arts Magazine* 61 (Feb. 1987), 71, n. 12.

42. Warhol, *Philosophy of Andy Warhol*, 91.

43. *Ibid.*, 146.

44. Warhol, *Andy Warhol*, exh. cat., Kunsthaus (Zurich, 1978), 106.

45. Roy Lichtenstein, in Bruce Glaser, "Oldenburg, Lichtenstein, Warhol: A Discussion," *Artforum* (Feb. 1966), 22.

46. Roy Lichtenstein, in Lawrence Alloway, *Roy Lichtenstein* (New York: Abbeville, 1983), 105–6.

47. Roy Lichtenstein, in Swenson, "What Is Pop Art? Part I," 62.

48. Roy Lichtenstein, in Diane Waldman, *Roy Lichtenstein* (New York: Chelsea House, 1971), 25.

49. Roy Lichtenstein, in Alloway, *Roy Lichtenstein*, 106.

50. Roy Lichtenstein, in Swenson, "What Is Pop Art? Part I," 63.

51. Roy Lichtenstein, in Glaser, "Oldenburg, Lichtenstein, Warhol: A Discussion," 23.

52. James Rosenquist, in Judith Goldman, *James Rosenquist* (Denver: Denver Art Museum; New York: Viking Penguin, 1985), 13.

53. James Rosenquist, in Swenson, "What is Pop Art? Part II," 63.

54. James Rosenquist, in G. R. Swenson, "The New American 'Sign Painters,'" *Artnews* 61 (Sept. 1962), 61.

55. James Rosenquist, in Goldman, *James Rosenquist*, 16.

56. *Ibid.*, 27–8.

57. *Ibid.*, 35.

58. James Rosenquist, cited in John Rublowsky, *Pop Art* (New York: Basic Books, 1965), 93.

59. James Rosenquist, "Art: Pop: Bing Bang Landscapes," *Time* 28 (May 1965), 80; cited in Sandler, *American Art of the 1960s*, 162.

60. See David McCarthy, "H. C. Westermann's Brinksmanship," *American Art* 10:3 (fall 1996), 50–69.

61. H. C. Westermann, letter to Tom Armstrong, May 3, 1978; in Bill Barrette, ed., *Letters from H. C. Westermann* (New York: Timken, 1988), 163.

62. Peter Saul, letter to Allan Frumkin, Mill Valley, California, 1972; in *Peter Saul: New Paintings and Works on Paper* (New York: Allan Frumkin Gallery, 1988), unpaginated.

63. *Ibid.*, unpaginated.

64. *Ibid.*, unpaginated.

65. Peter Saul, letter to Allan Frumkin, Mill Valley, California, 1967; cited in *Peter Saul*, unpaginated.

66. *Ibid.*

67. *Ibid.*

68. Whitney Halstead, "Made in Chicago," in *Made in Chicago*, exh. cat. (Washington, D.C.: National Collection of Fine Arts, Smithsonian Institution, 1974), 14.

69. Roger Brown, in Sidney Lawrence, *Roger Brown*, exh. cat. (Washington, D.C.: Hirshhorn Museum and Sculpture Garden, Smithsonian Institution, 1987), 93.

70. See Robert George Reisner, "The Parlance of Hip," in *The Jazz Titans* (Garden City, N.Y.: Doubleday, 1960), 156.

71. Jess, cited in Michael Auping, *Jess: Paste-Ups (and Assemblies) 1951–1983*, exh. cat. (Sarasota, Fla.: John and Mabel Ringling Museum of Art, 1983), 10; cited in Stich, *Made in U.S.A.*, 147.

72. Peter Voulkos, cited in Thomas Albright, *Art in the San Francisco Bay Area 1945–1980* (Berkeley and Los Angeles: University of California Press, 1985), 135.

73. William Wiley, cited in Albright, *Art in the San Francisco Bay Area 1945–1980*, 119.

74. John Donne, *Devotions upon Emergent Occasions*, 1624, no. 17.

75. Stuart Morgan, "The Hard Way," in James Lingwood et al., *Vija Celmins: Works 1964–1996* (London: Institute of Contemporary Arts, 1996), 77.

76. Robert Arneson, in Chiori Santiago, "Portrait of Bob," *The Museum of California* 10:4 (Jan.–Feb. 1987), 6.

77. Robert Arneson, transcript of a tape-recorded conversation with Maddie Jones, 1978, Archives of American Art, unpaginated; cited in Neal Benezra, *Robert Arneson: A Retrospective*, exh. cat. (Des Moines: Des Moines Art Center, 1985), 23.

78. Robert Arneson, telephone conversation with Jonathan Fineberg, June 27, 1990.

79. Robert Arneson, transcript of a tape-recorded conversation with Maddie Jones, 1978, Archives of American Art, 44–6; cited in Robert C. Hobbs, "Robert Arneson: Critic of Vanguard Extremism," *Arts Magazine* (Nov. 1978), 89.

80. Robert Arneson, conversation with Jonathan Fineberg at Yale University, Feb. 3, 1981.

81. Robert Arneson, quoted in Cecile N. McCann, "About Arneson, Art and Ceramics," *Artweek* (Oct. 26, 1974), 1; cited in Benezra, *Robert Arneson: A Retrospective*, 93, n. 30.

82. This and the following remarks come from a telephone conversation between Jonathan Fineberg and the artist on June 27, 1990, in response to the sources for the work put forward in Dennis Adrian, "Robert Arneson's Feats of Clay," *Art in America* (Sept. 1974), 81.

83. See Benezra, *Robert Arneson: A Retrospective*, 53, 56.

84. As in the Roman *pasquinade*. See Irving Lavin, "Bernini and the Art of Social Satire," in[?] *History of European Ideas*, vol. 4, no. 4 (Oxford and New York: Pergamon, 1983), 365–420; reprinted with corrections from Irving Lavin et al., *Drawings by Gianlorenzo Bernini from the Museum der bildenden Künste, Leipzig*, exh. cat. (Princeton: Art Museum, Princeton University, 1981).

85. Robert Arneson, telephone conversation with Jonathan Fineberg, June 27, 1990.

86. Donald B. Kuspit, "Arneson's Outrage," *Art in America* (May 1985), 135.

Chapter 10

1. Barbara Rose, "ABC Art," *Art in America* (Oct.–Nov. 1965), 58.

2. Donald Judd, "Specific Objects," *Arts Yearbook* 8 (1965), 74–82; reprinted in Donald Judd, *Complete Writings 1959–75* (Halifax: The Press of the Nova Scotia College of Art and Design; New York: New York University Press, 1975), 181–9. Robert Morris's term "unitary forms" conveyed roughly the same idea; see Robert Morris, "Notes on Sculpture," Part I, *Artforum* (Feb. 1966); reprinted in Gregory Battcock, ed., *Minimal Art* (New York: E. P. Dutton, 1968), 228.

3. Lucy R. Lippard, "New York Letter: Recent Sculpture as Escape," *Art International* (Feb. 20, 1966), 50.

4. Hal Foster, "The Crux of Minimalism," in Howard Singerman, ed., *Individuals: A Selected History of Contemporary Art 1945–1986*, exh. cat. (Los Angeles: Museum of Contemporary Art, 1986), 174. See also Anna Chave, "Minimalism and the Rhetoric of Power," *Arts Magazine* (Jan. 1990), 56.

5. Donald Judd, "Kenneth Noland," *Arts Magazine* (Sept. 1963); reprinted in Judd, *Complete Writings 1959–75*, 93.

6. Morris, "Notes on Sculpture," Part I; reprinted in Battcock, *Minimal Art*, 224.

7. Clement Greenberg, "Recentness of Sculpture," in Maurice Tuchman, ed., *American Sculpture of the Sixties*, exh. cat. (Los Angeles: Los Angeles County Museum of Art, 1967), 25.

8. Michael Fried, "Art and Objecthood," *Artforum* (summer 1967), 20.

9. Ad Reinhardt, "Art-as-Art," *Art International* (Dec. 20, 1962); cited in Dorothy C. Miller, *Americans 1963*, exh. cat. (New York: The Museum of Modern Art, 1963), 82.

10. Ad Reinhardt, "Twelve Rules for a New Academy," *Artnews* (May 1957), 38; excerpted in Dorothy C. Miller, *Americans 1963*, exh. cat. (New York: The Museum of Modern Art, 1963), 83.

11. According to Irving Sandler, *American Art of the 1960s* (New York: Harper & Row, 1988), 21.

12. Frank Stella, in William S. Rubin, *Frank Stella*, exh. cat. (New York: The Museum of Modern Art, 1970), 12.

13. Carl Andre, "Frank Stella," in Dorothy C. Miller, *Sixteen Americans*, exh. cat. (New York: The Museum of Modern Art, 1959), 76.

14. Brenda Richardson, *Frank Stella: The Black Paintings*, exh. cat. (Baltimore: Baltimore Museum of Art, 1976), 3–4.

15. Michael Fried, "Frank Stella," in *Towards a New Abstraction*, exh. cat. (New York: Jewish Museum, 1963), 28; and Michael Fried, "New York Letter," *Art International* (April 25, 1964), 59.

16. Walter Darby Bannard, "Present-Day Art and Ready-Made Styles," *Artforum* (Dec. 1966), 30; cited in Sandler, *American Art of the 1960s*, 19.

17. Frank Stella, quoted in Bruce Glaser (interviewer) and Lucy R. Lippard (ed.), "Questions to Stella and Judd," *Artnews* (Sept. 1966), 59–9; reprinted in Battcock, *Minimal Art*, 158.

18. See Chapter 9, note 8.

19. Barbara Haskell, *Donald Judd*, exh. cat. (New York: Whitney Museum of American Art, 1988), 21.

20. Donald Judd, "In the Galleries: Frank Stella," *Arts Magazine* (Sept. 1962); reprinted in Judd, *Complete Writings 1959–1975*, 57.

21. Donald Judd, in John Caplans, "An Interview with Don Judd," *Artforum* (June 1971), 49.

22. *Ibid.*, 40.

23. Tony Smith, cited in Morris, "Notes on Sculpture," Part II; reprinted in Battcock, *Minimal Art*, 228, 230.

24. Carl Andre, in Phyllis Tuchman, "An Interview with Carl Andre," *Artforum* (June 1970), 61.

25. Carl Andre, informal discussion with Jonathan Fineberg's students at Yale University in 1981.

26. Don Flavin, ". . . in daylight or cool white: an autobiographical sketch," *Artforum* (Dec. 1965), 24.

27. For a detailed discussion of the dependence on Duchamp see Maurice Berger, *Labyrinths: Robert Morris, Minimalism, and the 1960s* (New York: Harper & Row, 1989).

28. Jonathan Fineberg, "Robert Morris Looking Back: An Interview," *Arts Magazine* (Sept. 1980), 111, 114. See also Robert Morris, "Anti-Form," *Artforum* (April 1968), 33–5.

29. Sol LeWitt, "Paragraphs on Conceptual Art," *Artforum* (summer 1967), 80.

30. *Ibid.*, 80.

31. For a more thorough discussion of minimalism and critical theory see Roann Barris, "Peter Eisenman and the Erosion of Truth," *20/1 Art and Culture* 1:2 (spring 1990), 20–37; and Robert Morris, "Words and Images in Modernism and Postmodernism," *Critical Inquiry* 15 (winter 1989), 337–47.

32. Robert Irwin, "Notes Toward a Model," in *Robert Irwin*, exh. cat. (New York: Whitney Museum of American Art, 1977), 30.

33. Robert Irwin, cited in Jan Butterfield, "Robert Irwin: On the Periphery of Knowing," *Arts Magazine* (Feb. 1976), 74.

34. James Turrell, in Josef Helfenstein, "First Light and Catso White," in *James Turrell; First Light*, exh. cat. (Bern: Kunstmuseum, 1991), 11.

35. James Turrell, "Interview with James Turrell," in Julia Brown, ed., *Occluded Front: James Turrell*, exh. cat. (Los Angeles: Museum of Contemporary Art, 1985), 41.

36. James Turrell, statement to Julia Brown, 1985, cited in Helfenstein, "First Light and Catso White," 14.

37. Ellsworth Kelly, in Harvey Stein, *Artists Observed* (New York, 1986), 46.

38. Robert Ryman, cited in Nancy Grimes, "White Magic," *Artnews* (summer 1986): 87.

39. Suzanne Hudson, *Robert Ryman: Used Paint* (Cambridge, Mass.: MIT Press, 2009).

40. P. Adams Sitney, *Visionary Film: The American Avant-Garde, 1943–1978* (New York: Oxford University Press, 1979), 368–97.

41. Lynn Gumpert, Ned Rifkin, and Marcia Tucker, *Early Work: Lynda Benglis/Joan Brown/Luis Jimenez/Gary Stephan*, exh. cat. (New York: New Museum, 1982), 8.

42. Eva Hesse, cited in Lucy R. Lippard, *Eva Hesse* (New York: New York University Press, 1976), 24–5.

43. Tom Doyle confirmed that Hesse was impressed with Ücker and Beuys, in Lucy R. Lippard, *Eva Hesse*, 33.

44. As noted in Bill Barrette, *Eva Hesse Sculpture, Catalogue Raisonné* (New York: Timken Publishers, 1989), 62.

45. Eva Hesse, in Cindy Nemser, "An Interview with Eva Hesse," *Artforum* (May 1970), 59.

46. Eva Hesse, a sheet of pencil notes from her last year, in Linda Shearer, "Eva Hesse: Last Works," in Robert Pincus-Witten and Linda Shearer, *Eva Hesse: A Memorial Exhibition*, exh. cat. (New York: Solomon R. Guggenheim Museum, 1972), unpaginated.

47. Bill Barrette pointed out that she even titled her one-person show at the Fischbach Gallery in Nov. 1968: "Eva Hesse: Chain Polymers." See Barrette, *Eva Hesse Sculpture, Catalogue Raisonné*, 15.

48. *Ibid.*, 218.

49. *Ibid.*, 14; Lippard, *Eva Hesse*, 115, 210.

50. Eva Hesse, in Nemser, "An Interview with Eva Hesse," 60.

51. *Ibid.*, 63.

52. Bruce Nauman, in Willoughby Sharp, "Nauman Interview," *Arts Magazine* 44:5 (March 1970), 26.

53. Bruce Nauman, in Jane Livingston and Marcia Tucker, *Bruce Nauman: Works from 1965 to 1972*, exh. cat. (Los Angeles: Los Angeles County Museum of Art, 1973), 10.

54. Bruce Nauman, in Sharp, "Nauman Interview," 27.

55. Brenda Richardson, *Bruce Nauman: Neons*, exh. cat. (Baltimore: Baltimore Museum of Art, 1982), 17.

56. Bruce Nauman, in Sharp, "Nauman Interview," 25, n. 5.

57. Robert Arneson, in conversation with Jonathan Fineberg, Benicia, California, Feb. 19, 1989.

58. Bruce Nauman, cited in Richardson, *Bruce Nauman: Neons*, 20.

59. Richard Serra, "Document: 'Spin Out '72–73 for Bob Smithson,'" *Avalanche* (summer–fall 1973); reprinted in Clara Weyergraf, ed., *Richard Serra: Interviews, Etc. 1970–1980* (Yonkers, N.Y.: The Hudson River Museum, 1980), 36.

60. First published in Grégoire Müller, *The New Avant-Garde: Issues for the Art of the Seventies* (New York: Praeger, 1972); reprinted in Weyergraf, *Richard Serra: Interviews, Etc. 1970–1980*, 9–11.

61. Richard Serra, "Play it Again, Sam," *Arts Magazine* (Feb. 1970); reprinted in Weyergraf, *Richard Serra: Interviews, Etc. 1970–1980*, 18.

62. Richard Serra, "Extended Notes from Sight Point Road," in *Richard Serra: Recent Sculpture in Europe 1977–1985* (Bochum, Germany: Galerie m, 1985), 12; cited in Douglas Crimp, "Serra's Public Sculpture: Redefining Site Specificity," in Rosalind Krauss, *Richard Serra/Sculpture*, exh. cat. (New York: The Museum of Modern Art, 1986), 47.

63. Heizer's term. Telephone conversation with Jonathan Fineberg, Oct. 18, 1993.

64. Michael Heizer in a brochure for Galerie H, Graz, 1977, unpaginated; cited in Sandler, *American Art of the 1960s*, 333.

65. Michael Heizer, "The Art of Michael Heizer," *Artforum* (Dec. 1969), 34; cited in John Beardsley, *Probing the Earth: Contemporary Land Projects*, exh. cat. (Washington, D.C.: Hirshhorn Museum, Smithsonian Institution, 1978), 10.

66. Conversation between Jonathan Fineberg and John Weber in Oct. 1982.

67. Robert Hobbs, *Robert Smithson: Sculpture* (Ithaca, N.Y.: Cornell University Press, 1981), 12.

68. Robert Smithson, "Entropy and the New Monuments," *Artforum* (June 1966), 26–31; reprinted in Nancy Holt, ed., *The Writings of Robert Smithson* (New York: New York University Press, 1979), 9–18.

69. Tony Smith, in Samuel Wagstaff, Jr., "Talking with Tony Smith," *Artforum* (Dec. 1966), 19; reprinted in Battcock, *Minimal Art*, 386.

70. Robert Smithson, in "The Symposium," *Earth Art*, exh. cat. (Ithaca, N.Y.: Andrew Dickson White Museum of Art, Cornell University, 1970), unpaginated.

71. Robert Smithson, "The Spiral Jetty," in Gyorgy Kepes, ed.. *Arts of the Environment* (New York: George Braziller, 1972), 231, n. 1; reprinted in Holt, *The Writings of Robert Smithson*, 115, n. 1.

72. As discussed by Hobbs, *Robert Smithson: Sculpture*, 30.

73. Eugenie Tsai, "The Sci-Fi Connection: The IG, J. G. Ballard, and Robert Smithson," in *Modern Dreams: The Rise and Fall of Pop*, exh. cat. (New York: The Institute for Contemporary Art, 1988), 71–6.

74. Smithson, "The Spiral Jetty," in Holt, *The Writings of Robert Smithson*, 111; cited in John Beardsley, *Earthworks and Beyond* (New York: Abbeville, 1984), 22.

75. *Ibid.*, 22.

76. Smithson, "The Spiral Jetty," in Holt, *The Writings of Robert Smithson*, 111.

77. Robert Smithson, "A Sedimentation of the Mind: Earth Projects," *Artforum* (Sept. 1968), 50; reprinted in Holt, *The Writings of Robert Smithson*, 82; cited in Beardsley, *Probing the Earth*, 85.

78. Michael Heizer, "The Art of Michael Heizer," *Artforum* (Dec. 1969), 37.

79. They included Giovanni Anselmo, Alighiero Boetti, Luciano Fabro, Jannis Kounellis, Mario Merz, Giulio Paolini, Giuseppe Penone, Michelangelo Pistoletto, and Gilberto Zorio.

80. Jannis Kounellis, in Kathan Brown, *Italians and American Italians* (Oakland: Crown Point Press, 1981), unpaginated; cited in Michael Auping, "Primitive Decorum: Of Style, Nature, and the Self in Recent Italian Art," in Neal Benezra, *Affinities and Intuitions: The Gerald S. Elliott Collection of Contemporary Art*, exh. cat. (Chicago: Art Institute of Chicago, 1990), 163.

81. Mario Merz, in Germano Celant, "The Organic Flow of Art," *Mario Merz*, exh. cat. (New York: Solomon R. Guggenheim Museum, 1989), 15.

82. Mario Merz, in Richard Koshalek, "Interview with Mario Merz," in *Mario Merz*, exh. brochure (Minneapolis: Walker Art Center, 1972), 3; cited in Celant, "The Organic Flow of Art," 29.

83. Mario Merz, in Susan Krane, *Mario Merz: Paintings and Constructions*, exh. cat. (Buffalo: Albright-Knox Art Gallery, 1984), 6.

Chapter 11

1. Douglas Heubler, statement in Seth Sieglaub, *January 5–31, 1969*, exh. cat. (New York: published by the author, 1969); in Lucy R. Lippard, *Six Years: The Dematerialization of the Art Object from 1966 to 1972* (New York: Praeger, 1973), 74.

2. Sol LeWitt, "Paragraphs on Conceptual Art," *Artforum* (June 1967), 83.

3. Lucy R. Lippard and John Chandler, "The Dematerialization of Art," *Art International* (Feb. 1969), 31–6; and Lippard, *Six Years*.

4. There were over thirty of the most popular bands and singers of the day performing live at Woodstock, including: Joan Baez; Creedence Clearwater Revival; Crosby, Stills, & Nash; The Grateful Dead; Arlo Guthrie; Blood, Sweat & Tears; Joe Cocker; Jimi Hendrix; The Incredible String Band; Jefferson Airplane; Janis Joplin; Melanie; Santana; Sha-Na-Na; and The Who.

5. For one discussion of this change see Robert Morris, "Words and Images in Modernism and Postmodernism," *Critical Inquiry* 15 (winter 1989), 337–47. An emblematic example is Joseph Kosuth, "Art After Philosophy," part one, *Studio International* (Oct. 1969), 134–7; part two (Nov. 1969), 160–1; part three (Dec. 1969), 212–13; reprinted in Gregory Battcock, ed., *Idea Art* (New York: E. P. Dutton, 1973).

6. Joseph Kosuth, "Art After Philosophy," part one, 135.

7. Lawrence Weiner, in "Art Without Space," a symposium on WBAI-FM, New York, Nov. 2, 1969, moderated by Seth Sieglaub with Lawrence Weiner, Robert Barry, Douglas Heubler, and Joseph Kosuth; cited in Lippard, *Six Years*, 130.

8. Jordana Moore Saggese, "The Myth of Neutrality: Reconsidering Conceptual Art Photography," in *Exposure* (The Journal of the Society for Photographic Education) 40:1 (spring 2007), 33–42.

9. Diane Arbus, in *Diane Arbus: An Aperture Monograph* (Millerton, N.Y.: Aperture, 1972), 15; cited in Sandra S. Phillips, "The Question of Belief," in Elizabeth Sussman and Sandra S. Phillips, eds., *Diane Arbus: Revelations* (New York: Random House and San Francisco: San Francisco Museum of Modern Art, 2003), 50.

10. Piero Manzoni, "Libera dimensione," *Azimuth 2* (Jan. 1960); cited in Giuliano Briganti, "Cultural Provocation: Italian Art of the Early Sixties," in Emily Braun, ed., *Italian Art in the 20th Century: Painting and Sculpture 1900–1988* (Munich: Prestel Verlag; London: Royal Academy of Arts, 1989), 302.

11. To use Harold Rosenberg's term: Harold Rosenberg, *The De-Definition of Art* (New York: Macmillan, 1973).

12. Helen Mayer Harrison and Newton Harrison, in Michel de Certeau, "Pay Attention: To Make Art," in Helen Mayer Harrison and Newton Harrison, *The Lagoon Cycle*, exh. cat. (Ithaca, N.Y.: Herbert F. Johnson Museum of Art, Cornell University, 1985), 19.

13. The quotations from Vito Acconci in this and the next three paragraphs come from a conversation with Jonathan Fineberg and students at the Pierson College Master's Residence, Yale University, Jan. 25, 1982.

14. Cited in Avis Berman, "A Decade of Progress, But Could a Female Chardin Make a Living?" *Art News* 79:8 (Oct. 1980), 77.

15. Adrian Piper, in Lucy R. Lippard, "Catalysis: An Interview with Adrian Piper," in *From The Center: Feminist Essays on Women's Art* (New York: Dutton, 1976), 167.

16. Ana Mendieta, in John Perreault, "Earth and Fire: Mendieta's Body of Work," in *Ana Mendieta: A Retrospective* (New York: New Museum of Contemporary Art, 1987), 10.

17. Amilcar de Castro, Ferreira Gullar, Franz Weissmann, Lygia Clark, Lygia Pape, Reynaldo Jardim, and Theon Spanudis, "Neo-Concretist Manifesto," Rio de Janeiro, March 1959; reprinted in *October 69* (summer 1994), 93.

18. Lygia Clark, *Trailings*, 1964; reprinted in *October 69* (summer 1994), 99. See also *Lygia Clark*, exh. cat. (Barcelona: Fundació Antoni Tàpies, 1997).

19. Lygia Clark, *Concerning the Instant*, 1965; reprinted in *October 69* (summer 1994), 100.

20. Hélio Oiticica, "Tropicália," March 4, 1967, in Guy Brett et al., *Hélio Oiticica*, exh. cat. (Minneapolis: Walker Art Center, 1992–3), 124.

21. *Ibid.*, 24.

22. Hélio Oiticica, *Aspiro ao Grande Labirinthe* (Rio de Janeiro: Rocco, 1986), 73; trans. by Paula Braga in Paula Braga, "Hélio Oiticica and the Parangolés: (Ad)Dressing Nietzsche's Übermensch," *Third Text* 17:1 (March 2003), 43–52.

23. RoseLee Goldberg, "Performance: The Golden Years," in Gregory Battcock and Robert Nickas, eds., *The Art of Performance: A Critical Anthology* (New York: E. P. Dutton, 1984), 87.

24. Janet Kardon, *Laurie Anderson: Works from 1969 to 1983*, exh. cat. (Philadelphia: Institute of Contemporary Art, University of Pennsylvania, 1983), 25.

25. Michel Serres and Craig Owens, in Craig Owens, "Sex and Language: In Between," in Kardon, *Laurie Anderson: Works from 1969 to 1983*, 53.

26. Daniel Buren, "Is Teaching Art Necessary?" (June 1968) *Galeries des Artes*, September 1968: n.p. text reprinted in Lucy Lippard, *Six years: the dematerialization of the art object from 1966 to 1972* (Berkeley: University of California Press, 1997), 51–53.

27. There is a full account of the episode in Jack Burnham, "Hans Haacke's Cancelled Show at the Guggenheim," *Artforum* (June 1971), 67–71.

28. Marcel Broodthaers, quoted in *Piero Manzoni*, exh. cat. (Brussels: Galerie des Beaux-Arts, 1987); cited in Michael Compton, "In Praise of the Subject," in Marge Goldwater et al., *Marcel Broodthaers* (Minneapolis: Walker Art Center; and New York: Rizzoli, 1989), 21.

29. See Christopher Phillips, "Homage to a Phantom Avant-Garde: The Situationist International," *Art in America* (Oct. 1989), 182–91, 239; and *Arts Magazine* (Jan. 1989), which contains four articles on situationism by Edward Bail, Bill Brown, Myriam D. Maayan, and Kristine Stiles.

30. Guy Debord, *The Society of the Spectacle*, 1967 (New York: Zone Books, 1995), 12.

31. *Ibid.*, 13.

32. *Ibid.*, 16.

33. Jean Dubuffet, "Rough Draft for a Popular Lecture on Painting," 1945; trans. Joachim Neugroschel in Mildred Glimcher, *Jean Dubuffet: Towards An Alternative Reality* (New York: Pace Publications, Abbeville, 1987), 46.

34. Willem de Kooning, "What Abstract Art Means to Me," *Bulletin of the Museum of Modern Art* 18:3 (spring 1951), 7; reprinted in Thomas B. Hess, *Willem de Kooning* (New York: The Museum of Modern Art, 1968), 145–6.

35. Yves Klein, cited in Pierre Restany, *Yves Klein* (New York: Harry N. Abrams, 1982), 8.

36. Joseph Beuys, in Willoughby Sharp, "An Interview with Joseph Beuys," *Artforum* (Nov. 1969); cited in Lippard, *Six Years*, 121.

37. President Dwight David Eisenhower, "Farewell Radio and Television Address to the American People," Jan. 17, 1961; in Robert L. Branyan and Lawrence H. Larsen, eds., *The Eisenhower Administration 1953–1961*, vol. 2 (New York, 1971), 1375.

38. Christo, in an interview with Jonathan Fineberg at the University of Illinois at Urbana-Champaign, 1977; cited in Fineberg, "Theatre of the Real: Thoughts on Christo," *Art in America* (Dec. 1979), 96; reprinted in Jonathan Fineberg, *Christo and Jeanne-Claude: On the Way to the Gates* (New Haven & New York: Yale University Press & The Metropolitan Museum of Art, 2004), 130.

39. Christo, cited in Fineberg, "Theatre of the Real," 97; reprinted in Jonathan Fineberg, *Christo and Jeanne-Claude*, 143.

40. Christo, cited in Fineberg, "Theatre of the Real," 98; reprinted in Jonathan Fineberg, *Christo and Jeanne-Claude*, 138.

41. Robert Arneson, in conversation with Jonathan Fineberg, 1981.

42. Christo, in conversation with Jonathan Fineberg, 1983; cited in "Meaning and Being in Christo's *Surrounded Islands*," in *Christo: Surrounded Islands* (New York: Harry N. Abrams, 1986), 27; reprinted in Jonathan Fineberg, *Christo and Jeanne-Claude*, 162.

43. See Charng Jiunn Lee, *Watering, That's My Life: The Symbolism and Self-Imaging of Marcel Duchamp*, unpublished doctoral dissertation, University of Illinois at Urbana-Champaign, 1993. Dr. Lee has shown that Duchamp's entire oeuvre after 1912 centered on the practice of Ch'an Buddhist and Taoist philosophy. Although the many artists influenced by Duchamp's work over the course of the twentieth century appear to have had no inkling of this (with the possible exception of John Cage), they did recognize that his use of a discourse among real objects to provoke enigmatic, conceptual experiences was his characteristic mode of interacting with the viewer.

44. Neil Postman, *Amusing Ourselves to Death: Public Discourse in the Age of Show Business* (New York: Penguin Books, 1986), 99–100, 110; cited in Marvin Heiferman, "Everywhere, All the Time, for Everybody," in Marvin Heiferman and Lisa Phillips, *Image World: Art and Media Culture*, exh. cat. (New York: Whitney Museum of American Art, 1989), 27. See also Erik Barnouw, *Tube of Plenty: The Evolution of American Television* (New York: Oxford University Press, 1975), 114.

45. Robert Storr, "Polke's Mind Tattoos," *Art in America* (Dec. 1992), 71. Wim Beeren, "On the 'Werkgruppe', Three Paintings by Sigmar Polke in the Collection of the Boymans-van Beuningen Museum," in *Sigmar Polke*, exh. cat. (Rotterdam: Museum Boymans-van Beuningen, 1983; Bonn: Städtisches Kunstmuseum, 1984), 16, referred to the relationship of the preprinted images to the ones created by the artists as "hallucinatory." John Caldwell went still further, proposing a literal reading of *Alice in Wonderland* as referring to watching TV sports on a drug high, in John Caldwell, "Sigmar Polke," in *Sigmar Polke*, exh. cat. (San Francisco: San Francisco Museum of Modern Art, 1991), 11.

46. See Grandville, *Un Autre Monde* (Paris: H. Fournier, 1844); cited in Gary Garrels, "Mrs Autumn and Her Two Daughters," in *Sigmar Polke* (Amsterdam: Stedelijk Museum, 1992), 68.

47. Gerhard Richter, "Notes 1966," in Gerhard Richter, *The Daily Practice of Painting; Writings 1962–1993*, ed. Hans-Ulrich Obrist (Cambridge, Mass.: MIT Press, 1995), 58.

48. Gerhard Richter, "Notes 1964–1965," in Gerhard Richter, *The Daily Practice of Painting*, 35.

49. *Ibid.*

50. Gerhard Richter, interview with Benjamin H. D. Buchloh, 1986; in Gerhard Richter, *The Daily Practice of Painting*, 160.

51. Gerhard Richter, letter to E. de Wilde, Feb. 23, 1975; in *Gerhard Richter*, exh. cat. (London: Tate, 1991), 112.

52. Gerhard Richter, interview with Rolf Shoen, 1972; in Gerhard Richter, *The Daily Practice of Painting*, 72–3.

53. Rainald Schumacher, "Gerhard Richter," *Flash Art* 199 (March–April 1998), 86–7.

54. Gerhard Richter, *Documenta VII* (Kassel: Documenta, 1982); cited in *Gerhard Richter*, exh. cat. (London: Tate, 1991), 112–113.

55. John Baldessari, cited in Coosje van Bruggen, *John Baldessari* (New York: Rizzoli, 1990), 19.

56. *Ibid.*, 35.

Chapter 12

1. Calvin Tomkins, "The Art Scene," *The New Yorker* (May 19, 1980), 134–6.

2. Barbara Rose, *American Painting: The Eighties*, exh. cat. (New York: Grey Art Gallery, New York University, 1980).

3. Rafael Ferrer, in Kim Levin, "Rafael Ferrer: In the Torrid Zone," in *Rafael Ferrer: Impassioned Rhythms*, exh. cat. (Austin, Tex.: Loguna Gloria Art Museum, 1982), 12.

4. See Robert Farris Thompson, "Betye & Renee, Priestesses of Chance and Medicine," in *The Migrations of Meaning: A Source Book*, exh. cat. (New York: INTAR Gallery, 1992), 19–31.

5. Romare Bearden, in Charles Childs, "Bearden: Identification and Identity," *Artnews* 63 (Oct. 1964), 24, 54, 61; cited in Sharon F. Patton, "Memory and Metaphor: The Art of Romare Bearden," in Kinshasha Holman Conwill, Mary Schmidt Campbell, and Sharon F. Patton, *Memory and Metaphor: The Art of Romare Bearden 1940–1987* (New York: Oxford University Press and the Studio Museum in Harlem, 1991), 38.

6. Romare Bearden, in M. Bunch Washington, *The Art of Romare Bearden: The Prevalence of Ritual* (New York: Harry N. Abrams, 1972), 9.

7. Patton, "Memory and Metaphor: The Art of Romare Bearden." See also Mary Schmidt Campbell, "Romare Bearden: A Creative Mythology," Ph.D. dissertation, Syracuse University, 1982, 50–3.

8. Patton, "Memory and Metaphor: The Art of Romare Bearden," 22.

9. Romare Bearden, in Patton, "Memory and Metaphor: The Art of Romare Bearden," 40.

10. *Ibid.*, 39.

11. *Ibid.*, 38.

12. Romare Bearden, in Mary Schmidt Campbell, "History and the Art of Romare Bearden," in Conwill, Campbell, and Patton, *Memory and Metaphor*, 9.

13. Nancy Spero, in *Jon Bird, Jo Anna Isaak, and Sylvere Lotringer* (London: Phaidon, 1996), 12.

14. Carolee Schneeman, in Bruce McPherson, ed., *Carolee Schneeman: More Than Meat Joy: Complete Performance Works and Selected Writings, 1963–1978* (New Paltz, New York: Documentext, 1979), 239–40; cited in Norma Broude and Mary D. Garrard, *The Power of Feminist Art* (New York: Harry N. Abrams, 1994), 162–3.

15. Anne Middleton Wagner, *Three Artists (Three Women): Modernism and the Art of Hesse, Krasner, and O'Keeffe* (Berkeley, Los Angeles, London: University of California Press, 1996), 20.

16. Richard Estes, quoted in Harvey Stein, *Artists Observed* (New York: Harry N. Abrams, 1986), 32.

17. Richard Haas et al., "The Exuviae of Visions: Architecture as a Subject for Art," *Perspecta: The Yale Architectural Journal* 18 (1982), 95.

18. See Martin Filler, "The Writing on the Wall: Richard Haas and the Art of Architecture," in *Richard Haas: Architectural Projects 1974–1988*, exh. cat. (New York: Brooke Alexander; Chicago: Rhona Hoffman Gallery, 1988), 5.

19. Jackie Ferrara, in conversation with Jonathan Fineberg, Oct. 4, 1986.

20. Jackie Ferrara, letter to Jonathan Fineberg of Oct. 27, 1993.

21. See "Interview," in Mika Koike, Motoi Masaki, and Makoto Murata, eds., *Tadashi Kawamata* (Tokyo: Gendaikikakushitsu Publishing, 1987), 37.

22. Mary Miss, in Deborah Nevins, "An Interview with Mary Miss," *The Princeton Journal: Thematic Studies in Architecture 2* (1985), 99.

23. As stated by the artist in *14 Americans: Directions of the 1970s* (New York: Michael Blackwood Films, 1980).

24. Charles Simonds, "Microcosm to Macrocosm/Fantasy World to Real World," *Artforum* (Feb. 1974), 38.

25. Gordon Matta-Clark, interview with Donald Wall, "Gordon Matta-Clark's Building Dissections," *Arts Magazine* 50 (May 1976), 79.

26. Gordon Matta-Clark, in Joan Simon, "Gordon Matta-Clark 1943–1978," *Art in America* (Nov.–Dec. 1978), 13.

27. Gordon Matta-Clark, cited in Mary Jane Jacob, "Introduction and Acknowledgements," in *Gordon Matta-Clarke: A Retrospective*, exh. cat. (Chicago: Museum of Contemporary Art, 1985), 8.

28. *Ibid.*, 8.

29. Susan Rothenberg, cited in Joan Simon, "Interviews," in *Gordon Matta-Clarke: A Retrospective*, 73.

30. Alice Aycock, "Alice Aycock, Reflections on Her Work, An Interview with Jonathan Fineberg," in *Complex Visions: Sculpture and Drawings by Alice Aycock*, exh. cat. (Mountainville, N.Y.: Storm King Art Center, 1990), 16–17.

31. Alice Aycock, "Conversation Between Alice Aycock, Tilman Osterwold and Andreas Vowinckel," in *Alice Aycock: Retrospective der Projekte und Ideen 1972–1983, Installation und Zeichnungen*, exh. cat. (Stuttgart: Württembergischer Kunstverein, 1983), unpaginated.

32. Alice Aycock, "Work 1972–74," in Alan Sondheim, ed., *Individuals: Post-Movement in Art in America* (New York: E. P. Dutton, 1977), 106.

33. She talks about such experiences in Alice Aycock, *Project Entitled "The Beginnings of a Complex . . ."* (New York: Lapp Princess Press and Printed Matter, 1977), unpaginated.

34. Alice Aycock, lecture to students at Yale University, 1981.

35. Alice Aycock, "Alice Aycock, Reflections on Her Work," 13.

36. *Ibid.*

37. Alice Aycock, "Conversation Between Alice Aycock, Tilman Osterwold and Andreas Vowinckel," unpaginated.

38. Alice Aycock, "Alice Aycock, Reflections on Her Work," 13.

39. *Ibid.*, 30–2.

40. *Ibid.*, 9.

41. Roland Barthes, "The Death of the Author," in *Image-Music-Text*, trans. Stephen Heath (New York: Hill & Wang, 1977), 143, 146. Previously published as "La mort de l'auteur," *Mantéia* 5 (1968).

42. Roland Barthes, "The Death of the Author," 142–3, 146–7.

43. John Carlin, Pop Apocalypse, exh. brochure (New York: Grade Mansion Gallery, 1988), unpaginated.

44. Thomas Lawson, "Last Exit: Painting," Artforum (Oct. 1981), 42.

45. Peter Schjeldahl, "An Interview with David Salle," in Salle (New York: Vintage, 1987), 48.

46. David Salle, in Richard Marshall, 50 New York Artists (San Francisco: Chronicle Books, 1986), 96.

47. Lisa Phillips, "His Equivocal Touch in the Vicinity of History," in Janet Kardon, David Salle (Philadelphia: Institute of Contemporary Art, 1986), 22.

48. See Jonathan Fineberg, " 'A long time ago in a galaxy far, far away . . . ,'" in Jonathan Fineberg, ed., Out of Town: The Williamsburg Paradigm (Champaign, Ill.: Krannert Art Museum, 1993), unpaginated.

49. Richard Prince, letter to Craig Owens, 1982; cited in Lisa Phillips, "People Keep Asking: An Introduction," in Lisa Phillips, Richard Prince (New York: Whitney Museum of American Art, 1992), 33. For an interesting autobiographical account see J. G. Bollard's interview with Prince, published in Punch magazine as "Extraordinary," Sept. 1967, revised from Bollard's notes by Prince and published in ZG; reprinted in Vicente Todoli, Spiritual America: Richard Prince (Valencia, Spain: Institute Valenciano de Arte Moderno, 1989).

50. Richard Prince, in Jeffrey Rian, "An Interview with Richard Prince," Art in America (March 1987), 90.

51. Ibid., 94.

52. Cindy Sherman, in Marshall, 50 New York Artists, 109.

53. Cindy Sherman, in Els Barents, "Introduction," in Cindy Sherman (Munich, 1982), 11; cited in Peter Schjeldahl, "Introduction: The Oracle of Images," in Peter Schjeldahl and I. Michael Danoff, Cindy Sherman (New York, 1984), 10.

54. Cindy Sherman, in "Cindy Sherman," American Photographer (Sept. 1983), 73; cited in I. Michael Danoff, "Afterword: Guises and Revelations," in Schjeldahl and Danoff, Cindy Sherman, 196.

55. Cindy Sherman, interview with Lisbet Nelson, "Q & A: Cindy Sherman," American Photographer (Sept. 1983), 77; cited in Lisa Phillips, "Cindy Sherman's Cindy Shermans," in Cindy Sherman, exh. cat. (New York: Whitney Museum of American Art, 1987), 14.

Chapter 13

1. Lecture at the Cooper Union, March 1974. Cited in Dore Ashton, Yes, But . . ., A Critical Study of Philip Guston (New York: Viking, 1976), 1.

2. Harold Rosenberg, "Liberation from Detachment: Philip Guston," in The De-Definition of Art (New York: Collier Books, 1973), 132–40.

3. Philip Guston, letter of Oct. 1974 to Dore Ashton; cited in Musa Mayer, Night Studio: A Memoir of Philip Guston by His Daughter (New York: Viking Penguin, 1988), 104.

4. Ashton, Yes, But . . ., A Critical Study of Philip Guston, 87.

5. Peter Schjeldahl, "Philip Guston," in Art of Our Time: The Saatchi Collection, vol. 3 (New York: Rizzoli, 1985), 12–13.

6. Mercedes Matter, interview with Musa Mayer, 1987; cited in Mayer, Night Studio, 65–6.

7. Philip Guston, cited in Ashton, Yes, But . . ., A Critical Study of Philip Guston, 74.

8. Philip Guston, in Philip Guston: A Life Lived, a 16mm. film (Michael Blackwood Films: New York, 1982).

9. Philip Guston, "Philip Guston's Object: A Dialogue with Harold Rosenberg," in Philip Guston: Recent Paintings and Drawings, exh. cat. (New York: The Jewish Museum, 1966), unpaginated.

10. Philip Guston, in William Berkson, "Dialogue with Philip Guston, November 1, 1964," Art and Literature. An International Review 7 (winter 1965), 66; cited in Robert Storr, Philip Guston (New York: Abbeville, 1986), 43.

11. Philip Guston, cited in Ashton, Yes, But . . ., A Critical Study of Philip Guston, 154; a more complete version of the statement is reprinted in Magdalena Dabrowski, The Drawings of Philip Guston, exh. cat. (New York: The Museum of Modern Art, 1988), 29.

12. "Philip Guston Talking," a lecture given by Philip Guston at the University of Minnesota in March 1978, edited by Renee McKee in Philip Guston: Paintings 1969–80,

13. Philip Guston, in Philip Guston: A Life Lived.

14. "Philip Guston Talking," a lecture given by Philip Guston at the University of Minnesota in March 1978, edited by Renee McKee in Philip Guston: Paintings 1969–80, 52

15. Philip Guston, in Philip Guston: A Life Lived.

16. He made reference to this in "Philip Guston's Object: A Dialogue with Harold Rosenberg," unpaginated. For a discussion of the golem see Gerschom G. Scholem, The Kabbalah and Its Symbolism (New York: Schocken Books, 1969), 158–204; and Jorge Luis Borges, Seven Nights (New York: New Directions Books, 1980), 95–106; cited in Robert Storr, Philip Guston, 60.

17. Philip Guston, in Philip Guston: A Life Lived.

18. Philip Guston; cited in Ashton, Yes, But . . ., A Critical Study of Philip Guston, 177.

19. Pamela Kort, Jörg Immendorff: Early Works and Lidl, exh. cat. (New York: Gallery Michael Werner, 1991), unpaginated.

20. Jörg Immendorff, Here and Now: To Do What Has to Be Done (Hier und Jetzt: Das tun, was zu tun ist) (Köln and New York: Gebr. König, 1973); republished in Immendorff's Handbuch der Akademie für Adler (Köln: Walter König, 1989).

21. Trans. from Pamela Kort, Jörg Immendorff: I Wanted to Be an Artist 1971–1974 (New York: Gallery Michael Werner, 1991), unpaginated.

22. Arthur Rimbaud, "Correspondance, XII, À Paul Demeny, 15 mai, 1871," in Oeuvres complètes (Paris: Bibliothèque de la Pléiade, 1963), 270.

23. See Jörg Immendorff, in Siegfried Gohr and Pamela Kort, "Interview with Jörg Immendorff," May 1994, in Jörg Immendorff, The Rake's Progress, exh. cat. (London: Barbican Art Gallery, 1995), 119.

24. Jörg Immendorff, interview with Pamela Kort, "On Gyntiana as an Imaginary Land," in Immedorgg-Gyntiana, exh. cat. (Berlin: Neuer Berliner Kunstverein, 1996), 37.

25. Jörg Immendorff, cited in Alexander Tolnay, "Gyntiana," in Immedorgg-Gyntiana, 11.

26. Jörg Immendorff commented on this to Jonathan Fineberg in conversation over dinner after the opening in Berlin, Sept. 2005.

27. See Thomas McEvilley, "The Work of 'Georg Baselitz'?," in Georg Baselitz: The Women of Dresden, exh. cat. (New York: Pace Gallery, 1990), 10; and Mariette Josephus Jitta, "Drawings: A. R. Penck," Tekeningen: A. R. Penck (The Hague: Gemeentemuseum, 1988), 180.

28. Donald Kuspit, "Flak from the 'Radicals': The Case Against Current German Painting," in Jack Cowart, Expressions: New Art from Germany, exh. cat. (St. Louis: Saint Louis Art Museum and Munich: Prestel Verlag, 1983).

29. Anselm Kiefer, interview with Mark Rosenthal in April 1986; cited in Rosenthal, Anselm Kiefer, 95.

30. Francesco Clemente, in Giancarlo Politi, "Francesco Clemente," Flash Art 117 (April–May 1984), 17; cited in Michael Auping, "Primitive Decorum: Of Style, Nature, and the Self in Recent Italian Art," in Neal Benezra, Affinities and Intuitions: The Gerald S. Elliott Collection of Contemporary Art, exh. cat. (Chicago: Art Institute of Chicago, 1990), 164.

31. Francesco Clemente, in Donald Kuspit, "Clemente Explores Clemente," Contemporanea 2:7 (Oct. 1989), 40; cited in Raymond Foye, "Madras," in Ann Percy and Raymond Foye, Francesco Clemente: Three Worlds, exh. cat. (Philadelphia: Philadelphia Museum of Art; New York: Rizzoli, 1990), 51.

32. Michael Auping, tape-recorded conversation with Clemente, May 11 and 12, 1984; cited in Michael Auping, "Fragments," in Francesco Clemente, exh. cat. (Sarasota, Wash.: John and Mabel Ringling Museum of Art, 1985), 18.

33. Kathy Halbreich, Culture and Commentary: An Eighties Perspective, exh. cat. (Washington, D.C.: Hirshhorn Museum, Smithsonian Institution, 1990), 38.

34. See Rainer Crone and Georgia Marsh, An Interview with Francesco Clemente (New York: Vintage, 1987).

35. Ibid., 42.

36. According to Calvin Tomkins, "Profiles: Getting Everything In," The New Yorker (April 15, 1985), 55; reprinted in Marge Goldwater, Roberta Smith, and Calvin Tomkins, Jennifer Bartlett, exh. cat. (Minneapolis: Walker Art Center; New York: Abbeville, 1985).

37. As pointed out in Marge Goldwater, "Jennifer Bartlett: On Land and At Sea," in Goldwater, Smith, and Tomkins, Jennifer Bartlett, 75, n. 3.

38. Michael Hurson, "Thurman Buzzard—An Essay on Fiction," in Artists' Architecture: Scenes and Conversations (London: Institute of Contemporary Art, 1983), 69.

39. Michael Hurson, in conversation with Jonathan Fineberg about the "New Image Painting" show, Chicago, Sept. 1979.

40. Neil Jenney, in Richard Marshall, New Image Painting, exh. cat. (New York: Whitney Museum of American Art, 1978), 38.

41. See Linda Shearer, "An Interview with Robert Moskowitz," in Ned Rifkin, Robert Moskowitz, exh. cat. (Washington, D.C.: Hirshhorn Museum and Sculpture Garden, Smithsonian Institution), 51.

42. Susan Rothenberg, in conversation with Jonathan Fineberg in her studio, New York, April 11, 1986.

43. Ibid.

44. This is the way Susan Rothenberg explained the work in ibid.

45. Joan Simon, Susan Rothenberg (New York: Harry N. Abrams, 1991), 33.

46. Ibid., 24.

47. The details of Rothenberg's personal life come from ibid., unless otherwise noted.

48. Susan Rothenberg, in ibid., 79.

49. Ibid., 88.

50. Joel Shapiro, tape-recorded interview with Richard Marshall, May 3 and 6, 1982, in Richard Marshall and Roberta Smith, Joel Shapiro, exh. cat. (New York Whitney Museum of American Art, 1982), 96.

51. Alice Aycock, in conversation with Jonathan Fineberg in her studio, July 9, 1992.

52. Elizabeth Murray, in Deborah Solomon, "Celebrating Paint," New York Times Magazine (March 31, 1991), 40.

53. Elizabeth Murray, in Kay Larson, "One from the Heart," New York Magazine (Feb. 10, 1986), 43.

54. Elizabeth Murray, quoted in Roberta Smith, "Motion Pictures," in Kathy Halbreich and Sue Graze, Elizabeth Murray: Paintings and Drawings (New York: Harry N. Abrams, 1987), 13.

55. Ibid., 122.

56. Elizabeth Murray, in 14 Americans: Directions of the 1970s (New York: Michael Blackwood Films, 1980).

57. Elizabeth Murray, in Halbreich and Graze, Elizabeth Murray: Paintings and Drawings, 44.

58. Ibid., 42.

59. Elizabeth Murray, in Richard Marshall, 50 New York Artists (San Francisco: Chronicle Books, 1986), 82.

60. Elizabeth Murray, in Halbreich and Graze, Elizabeth Murray: Paintings and Drawings, 130.

61. Elizabeth Murray, in ibid., 118.

62. See, for example, Robert Hughes, "Careerism and Hype Amidst the Image Haze," Time (June 17, 1985), 81.

63. Julian Schnabel, cited in Jeanne Siegal, "Julian Schnabel," Arts Magazine (June 1983), 15.

64. Julian Schnabel, "Writings," Nov. 21, 1985; in Thomas McEvilley and Lisa Phillips, Julian Schnabel: Paintings 1975–1987, exh. cat. (London: Whitechapel Art Gallery; New York: Whitney Museum of American Art, 1987), 104.

65. Julian Schnabel, "Writings," July 11, 1986; in McEvilley and Phillips, Julian Schnabel: Paintings 1975–1987, 104.

66. Julian Schnabel, conversation with Jonathan Fineberg and a few of Fineberg's Yale University students in Schnabel's studio, New York, fall 1981.

67. Julian Schnabel, "Writings," from the Madrid notebooks, 1978; in McEvilley and Phillips, Julian Schnabel: Paintings 1975–1987, 104.

68. Eric Fischl, in Donald Kuspit and Erich Rischal, "An Interview with Erich Fischl," in Fischl (New York: Vintage, 1987), 62.

69. Eric Fischl, in Nancy Grimes, "Eric Fischl's Naked Truths," Artnews (Sept. 1986), 72.

70. Robert Colescott, in conversation with Jonathan Fineberg, Champaign, Illinois, Feb. 17, 1992.

Chapter 14

1. Lisa Phillips, "The Self Similar," in Lisa Phillips, Terry Winters (New York: Whitney Museum of American Art, 1991), 17.

2. Tony Cragg, cited in *Tony Cragg* (London: Tate, 1989), 11–12.

3. Jonathan Borofsky, in Joan Simon, "An Interview with Jonathan Borofsky," *Art in America* 69 (Nov. 1981), 157–64.

4. Jonathan Borofsky, in Kathy Halbreich, *Jonathan Borofsky: An Installation*, exh. brochure (Cambridge, Mass.: MIT Press, 1980); cited in Mark Rosenthal, "Jonathan Borofsky's Modes of Working," in Mark Rosenthal and Richard Marshall, *Jonathan Borofsky*, exh. cat. (Philadelphia: Philadelphia Museum of Art; New York: Whitney Museum of American Art, 1984), 14.

5. Jonathan Borofsky, note to the illustrations, in Rosenthal and Marshal, *Jonathan Borofsky*, 106.

6. John Carlin, "Bombing History: Graffiti and Art of the Eighties," unpublished paper read at the meeting of the College Art Association in Boston in 1987.

7. Claes Oldenburg, quoted in the *New York Times*, 1984; cited by John Carlin, "Bombing History: Graffiti and Art of the Eighties."

8. Barry Blinderman, "Close Encounters with the Third Mind," in Barry Blinderman, *Keith Haring: Future Primeval*, exh. cat. (Normal, Ill.: University Galleries, Illinois State University, 1990), 18.

9. *Ibid.*, 16.

10. William S. Burroughs, *Naked Lunch* (New York, 1959), 221.

11. See Richard Marshall, "Repelling Ghosts," in Richard Marshall, *Jean-Michel Basquiat*, exh. cat. (New York: Whitney Museum of American Art and Harry N. Abrams, 1992), 16. Also see the detailed chronology at the back of the catalog.

12. "Le silence éternel de ces espaces infinis m'effraie." Blaise Pascal, *Pensées* (1670), 206.

13. Robert Farris Thompson, "Royalty, Heroism, and the Streets: The Art of Jean-Michel Basquiat," in Richard Marshall, *Jean-Michel Basquiat*, 32.

14. bell hooks, "Altars of Sacrifice: Re-Membering Basquiat," *Art in America* (June 1993), 72.

15. See Jordana Moore Saggese, *Jean-Michel Basquiat's Language*, doctoral dissertation, Urbana-Champaign, Ill.: University of Illinois, 2008, forthcoming as a book in 2010.

16. Henry Geldzahler, "Art: From Subways to Soho, Jean-Michel Basquiat," *Interview* 13 (Jan. 1983), 46; cited in Thompson, "Royalty, Heroism, and the Streets," 32.

17. Jean-Michel Basquiat, in Thompson, "Royalty, Heroism, and the Streets," 32.

18. See David Wojnarowicz, *Memories That Smell Like Gasoline* (San Francisco: Artspace Books, 1992) and David Wojnarowicz, *Close to the Knives: A Memoir of Disintegration* (New York: Vintage, 1991).

19. David Wojnarowicz, in Barry Blinderman, "The Compression of Time: An Interview with David Wojnarowicz," in Barry Blinderman, ed., *David Wojnarowicz: Tongues of Flame*, exh. cat. (Normal, Ill.: University Galleries, Illinois State University, 1990), 49.

20. David Wojnarowicz, in Lucy R. Lippard, "Out of the Safety Zone," *Art in America* 78 (Dec. 1990), 134.

21. See Walter Robinson and Carlo McCormick, "Report from the East Village: Slouching Toward Avenue D," *Art in America* (summer 1984), 160.

22. David Wojnarowicz, in Matthew Rose, "David Wojnarowicz: An Interview," *Arts Magazine* 62 (May 1988), 62.

23. David Wojnarowicz, *Close to the Knives*, 114. For a more detailed discussion of the iconography of this painting see John Carlin and Jonathan Fineberg, *Imagining America: Icons of Twentieth-Century American Art* (New Haven: Yale University Press, 2004) and the documentary film of the same title for PBS Television.

24. Christian Boltanski, interview with Jacques Clayssen, *Identité/Identifications*, exh. cat. (Bordeaux: Centre d'Arts Plastiques Contemporains, 1976), 24; cited in Nancy Marmer, "Boltanski: The Uses of Contradiction," *Art in America* (Oct. 1989), 175.

25. Christian Boltanski, interview with Béatrice Parent, in Christian Boltanski, *Dernières Années*, exh. cat. (Paris: Musée d'Art Moderne de la Ville de Paris, 1998).

26. David Hammons, interviewed by Kellie Jones, *Real Life* 16 (autumn 1986), 8; in Tom Finkelpearl, *David Hammons: Rousing the Rubble* (New York: Institute for Contemporary Art; Cambridge, Mass.: MIT Press, 1991), 28.

27. *Ibid.*, 34.

28. Ilya Kabakov, in Katrina F. C. Cary, "Ilya Kabakov: Profile of a Soviet Unofficial Artist," *Art and Auction* (Feb. 1987): 86–7; cited in Robert Storr, *Dislocations*, exh. cat. (New York: The Museum of Modern Art, 1991), 22.

29. Ilya Kabakov, in Claudia Jolles, "Interview with Erik Bulatov and Ilya Kabakov, Moscow, July 1987," in *Erik Bulatov* (London: 1989), 40–1; cited in Amei Wallach, *Ilya Kabakov: The Man Who Never Threw Anything Away* (New York: Harry N. Abrams, 1996), 56.

30. Ilya Kabakov, *Five Albums* (Helsinki: Museet för Nutidskonst, The Museum of Contemporary Art, 1994; and Oslo: Museet for Samtidskunst, National Museum of Contemporary Art, 1995), 33.

31. Ilya Kabakov, *Ten Characters*, text accompanying an installation at Ronald Feldman Fine Art, New York, 1988; cited in David Ross, ed., *Between Spring and Summer: Soviet Conceptual Art in the Era of Late Communism* (Boston: Institute of Contemporary Art; Tacoma, Wash.: Tacoma Art Museum; Cambridge, Mass, and London: MIT Press, 1990), 25–7.

32. See Toni Stoos, ed., *Ilya Kabakov: Installations 1983–2000, Catalogue Raisonné*, 2 vols. (Düsseldorf: Richter Verlag, 2003).

33. Ilya Kabakov, *The Palace of Projects*, exh. cat. (Madrid: Museo Nacional Centro de Arte Reina Sofia, 1998), 1.

34. See Jean-François Lyotard, *The Postmodern Condition: A Report on Knowledge*, trans. Geoff Bennington and Brian Massumi (Minneapolis: University of Minnesota Press, 1984).

35. Haim Steinbach, in Gary Garrels, *New Sculpture: Robert Cober, Jeff Koons, Haim Steinbach* (Chicago: The Renaissance Society at the University of Chicago, 1986), unpaginated.

36. Haim Steinbach, in Peter Nagy, moderator, "From Criticism to Complicity," *Flash Art* 129 (summer 1986), 46, n. 1.

37. See Roberta Smith, "Rituals of Consumption," *Art in America* (May 1988), 164–71.

38. Jeff Koons, in Alan Jones, "Jeff Koons, 'Et qui libre,'" *Galleries Magazine* (Nov. 1986), 94.

39. Jeff Koons, in Giancarlo Politi, "Luxury and Desire: An Interview with Jeff Koons," *Flash Art* (Feb.–March 1987), 71.

40. Tim Rollins, cited in William Olander, "Material World," *Art in America* (Oct. 1989), 124.

41. Tim Rollins, quoted in Suzi Gablik, "Report from New York: The Graffiti Question," *Art in America* 70 (Oct. 1982), 37.

42. See Ben H. Bagdikian, *The Media Monopoly* (Boston: Beacon Press, 1987), 4; cited in Marvin Heiferman, "Everywhere, All the Time, for Everybody," in Marvin Heiferman and Lisa Phillips, *Image World: Art and Media Culture*, exh. cat. (New York: Whitney Museum of American Art, 1989), 32.

43. See Randy Rosen and Catherine C. Brawer, eds., *Making Their Mark* (New York: Abbeville, 1989).

44. Krzysztof Wodiczko (with Douglas Crimp, Rosalyn Deutsche, and Ewa Lajer-Burcharth), "Conversation with Krzysztof Wodiczko," *October* 38 (winter 1986), 39; cited in Peter Boswell, "Krzysztof Wodiczko: Art and the Public Domain," in *Public Address: Krzysztof Wodiczko* (Minneapolis: Walker Art Center, 1992), 13.

45. Peter Boswell has also cited the Situationist International as an important source. See Guy Debord, *The Society of the Spectacle*, rev. English edition (Detroit: Black and Red, 1983), unpaginated; Jonathan Crary, "Spectacle, Attention, Counter-Memory," *October* 50 (fall 1989), 97–106; and Ken Knabb, ed., *Situationist International Anthology* (Berkeley: Bureau of Public Secrets, 1981); all cited in Boswell, "Krzysztof Wodiczko: Art and the Public Domain," 19.

46. Krzysztof Wodiczko, in *Krzysztof Wodiczko: WORKS*, exh. catalogue (Washington, D.C.: Hirshhorn Museum and Sculpture Garden, Smithsonian Institution, 1988), unpaginated; cited in Boswell, "Krzysztof Wodiczko: Art and the Public Domain," 19.

Chapter 15

1. C. Carr, "Rehearsals for Zero Hour: Performance in the Eighties," in *The Decade Show: Frameworks of Identity in the 1980s*, exh. cat. (New York: New Museum of Contemporary Art, 1990), 204.

2. Ann Hamilton, "A Conversation with Ann Hamilton," interview by Hugh Davies and Lynda Forsha, in *Ann Hamilton* (San Diego: San Diego Museum of Contemporary Art, 1991), 66.

3. Ann Hamilton, "Ann Hamilton: Temporal Crossroads," interview by Joan Simon, in *Art Press* (Dec. 1995), 24.

4. Ann Hamilton, cited in Dave Hickey, "In the Shelter of the Word: Ann Hamilton's Tropos," in *Ann Hamilton, Tropos* (New York: Dia Center for the Arts, 1995), 141.

5. Ann Hamilton, "A Conversation with Ann Hamilton," 61.

6. Ann Hamilton, lecture at the University of Illinois at Urbana-Champaign, Sept. 1997.

7. Ann Hamilton, "A Conversation with Ann Hamilton," 64.

8. Ann Hamilton, conversation with Jonathan Fineberg, Columbus, Ohio, Dec. 18, 1998.

9. Robert Gober, in Richard Flood and Robert Gober, "Interview 2 (January 15, 1993)," in Richard Flood et al., *Robert Gober: Sculpture + Drawing*, exh. cat. (Minneapolis: Walker Art Center, 1999).

10. See Sigmund Freud, *Three Essays on the Theory of Sexuality*, in *The Standard Edition of the Complete Psychological Works of Sigmund Freud*, vol. 7, trans. James Strachey (London: Hogarth Press and the Institute for Psychoanalysis, 1953), 123–245. I am also indebted to the work of Nancy Blake on Matthew Barney and the issue of the polymorphous perverse.

11. Alexandra Keller and Frazer Ward, "Matthew Barney and the Paradox of the Neo-Avant-Garde Blockbuster", *Cinema Journal* 45:2 (winter 2006), 3–16.

12. Vanessa Beecroft, cited in Dodie Kazanjian, "The Body Artist," *Vogue* (April 2001), 376.

13. Vanessa Beecroft, in *ibid.*, 376.

14. Mariko Mori, "We've Got Twenty-Five Years," interview with Dike Blair, *Purple Prose* (summer 1995), 100; cited in Dominic Molon, "Countdown to Ecstasy," in *Mariko Mori*, exh. cat. (Chicago: Museum of Contemporary Art, 1998), 3.

15. Molon, "Countdown to Ecstasy," 7.

16. James Lingwood, "Introduction," in James Lingwood, ed., *House* (London: Phaidon, 1995), 7.

17. Iain Sinclair, "The House in the Part: A Psychogeographical Response," in James Lingwood, ed., *House*, 18.

18. Barbara Smith, in Ralph Rugoff, "Survey," in Ralph Rugoff, Kristine Stiles, and Gaicinto Di Pertantantino, *Paul McCarthy* (London: Phaidon, 1996), 43.

19. See Richard Schiff, "The Necessity of Jimmie Durham's Jokes," *The Art Journal* (fall 1992), 74–80.

20. William K. Stevens, "Study Finds Blacks' English Increasingly Different," *New York Times* (March 15, 1985), A14.

21. William K. Stevens, "Stronger Urban Accents in Northeast Are Called Sign of Evolving Language," *New York Times* (July 21, 1985), 36. These two articles in the *New York Times* were grounded in the landmark research, done over three decades, by William Labov, a University of Pennsylvania researcher whose data demonstrated that linguistic change does not originate in high or low classes, but in centrally located groups in the socioeconomic hierarchy and that, despite the expansion of the media, regional accents in America have become more diverse and divergent than they were a century earlier. See William Labov, *Principles of Linguistic Change* (Oxford: Blackwell Publishing, 1994).

22. Ebon Fisher, telephone conversation with Jonathan Fineberg, fall 1998.

23. Jimmie Durham, "Convert Operations: Excerpts from a Discussion Between Jimmie Durham and Michael Taussig with Miwon Kwon and Helen Molesworth," 1993; in Laura Mulvey, Dirk Snauwaert, and Mark Alice Durant, *Jimmie Durham* (London: Phaidon, 1995), 119.

24. Deborah Wye, *Louise Bourgeois* (N.Y.: Museum of Modern Art, 1982).

25. Francis Morris, "I Do, I Undo, I Redo," in *Louise Bourgeois*, exh. cat. (London: Tate, 2007), 14.

26. Louse Bourgeois, 1994, unpublished notes, cited in *Louise Bourgeois*, 81.

27. Louise Bourgeois, "Child Abuse," *Artforum* 20:4 (Dec. 1982), 40–7; cited in *Louise Bourgeois*, 80.

28. Louise Bourgeois, filmed interview, Marion Cajori and Amei Wallach, *Louise Bourgeois: The Spider, the Mistress, and the Tangerine* (New York: Zeitgeist Films, 2008).

29. Louise Bourgeois, in Donald Kuspit, "Bourgeois (an interview with Louise Bourgeois)," 1988, 67–8; cited in *Louise Bourgeois*, 48.

30. Okwui Enwezor, *Archive Fever: Uses of the Document in Contemporary Art* (New York: International Center of Photography, 2008), 11.
31. Nicole Schweizer, "An Introduction," in *Alfredo Jaar: The Politics of Images*, exh. cat. (Lausanne: Musée Cantonal des Beaux-Arts, 2007), 7.
32. Jeff Wall, in Vicki Goldberg, "Photos That Lie—and Tell the Truth," *New York Times*, "Arts and Leisure" (March 16, 1997), 34.
33. Fred Tomaselli, conversation with Jonathan Fineberg in Tomaselli's Williamsburg studio, Jan. 30, 1999.
34. Fred Tomaselli, telephone conversation with Jonathan Fineberg, Oct. 8, 1999.
35. Roxy Paine, conversation with Jonathan Fineberg, Nov. 7, 2007.
36. Roxy Paine and Kit Blake, "Tweeking the Human," in "Brand Name Damages" and "Minor Injury" galleries, Williamsburg, Brooklyn, 1991.
37. Phone conversation with Jonathan Fineberg, April 8, 1998.
38. Conversation with Gordon Baym, Department of Physics, University of Illinois at Urbana-Champaign.
39. M. Mitchell Waldrop, *Complexity: The Emerging Science at the Edge of Order and Chaos* (New York: Simon and Schuster, 1992), 16, 11.
40. When "the artist formerly known as Prince" (as he briefly came to be called) had his very name legally taken away by lawyers at Warner Brothers Records as the price of his contractual freedom, the resulting dislocation of his identity (into a kind of cold void that your computer might call a file with no label) is a form of disconnectedness in which we can all feel a resonance.
41. Roxy Paine, interview with Jonathan Fineberg, Nov. 7, 2007.
42. Roxy Paine, telephone conversation with Jonathan Fineberg, Feb. 10, 2008.
43. Kara Walker, "Interview with Sydney Jenkins, 1995"; cited in Jo Anna Isaak, *Looking Forward Looking Black* (Geneva, N.Y.: Hobart and William Smith Colleges Press, 1999), 6.
44. See John Carlin, "Masters of American Comics: An Art History of Twentieth-Century American Comic Strips and Books," in John Carlin, Paul Karasik, and Brian Walker, *Masters of American Comics* (New Haven and Los Angeles: Yale University Press with the Hammer Museum and the Museum of Contemporary Art, 2005), 120.
45. Art Spiegelman, from *The Apex Treasury of Underground Comix*, 1974; reprinted in *Art Spiegelman: Comix, Essays, Graphics and Scraps (From Maus to Now to MAUS to Now)* (Rome: Sellerio Editore-La Centrale dell'Arte, 1999), 7.
46. See John Carlin, "Masters of American Comics," 128–39.
47. Chris Ware, in Daniel Raeburn, *Chris Ware* (New Haven: Yale University Press, 2004), 13; cited in John Carlin, "Masters of American Comics," 158.
48. Yto Barrada, *A Life Full of Holes—The Strait Project* (Berlin: Autograph ABP, 2005).
49. Mariko Mori, unreleased filmed interview with Jonathan Fineberg in the artist's New York studio, Nov. 22, 2002.
50. "Shahzia Sikander in conversation with Fereshteh Daftari," in *Shahzia Sikander: Intimate Ambivalence/ Shahzia Sikander: Interstitial: 24 Faces and the 25th Frame*, catalog for two exhibitions (Birmingham, England: Ikon Gallery, 2008, and Berlin: Daad Galerie, 2008), 56.
51. See the discussion in Caren Kaplan, *Questions of Travel: Postmodern Discourses of Displacement* (Durham, N.C.: Duke University Press, 1996), 123–4.
52. Yinka Shonibare, interview, in Pernilla Holmes, "The Empire's New Clothes," *Art News* 101:9 (Oct. 2002), 118.
53. From an interview with the artist conducted by Francesca Dal Lago, May 2, 1999, cited on http://www.legacy-project.org/index.php?page=art_detail&artID=870/.
54. This and the following quotations from Zhang Xiaogang are from a recorded lecture at the University of Illinois at Urbana-Champaign, Oct. 23, 2007.
55. Leng Lin, "Foreword," in *Hai Bo* (New York: Max Protetch Gallery, 2006), 7.
56. The quotations from Hai Bo come from a recorded lecture he gave on his work at the Phillips Collection, Washington, D.C., Sept. 17.

Chapter 16

1. Cited on the White Cube website: http://www.whitecube.com/exhibitions/beyond_belief/.
2. Andy Warhol, in Kenneth Goldsmith, *I'll Be Your Mirror: The Selected Andy Warhol Interviews, 1962–1987* (New York: Carroll & Graf Publishers, 2004), 301. See also Andy Warhol, *America* (New York: Harper & Row Publishers, 1985), 22: "When you think about it, department stores are kind of like museums."
3. Takashi Murakami, *Superflat*, exh. cat. (Tokyo: MDRA Publishing, 2000).
4. Jeremy Strick, "Director's Foreword," in Paul Schimmel, ed., ©*Murakami*, exh. cat. (Los Angeles: Museum of Contemporary Art and New York: Rizzoli International Publications, 2007), 6.
5. Michael Moore, acceptance speech for best documentary feature, Sunday, March 23, 2003. See http://www.youtube.com/watch?v=M7Is43K6lrg.
6. Cited in Mika Yoshitake, "The Meaning of the Nonsense of Excess," in Paul Schimmel, ©*Murakami*, 111.
7. Yoshitake, "The Meaning of the Nonsense of Excess," 111.
8. "Shop-dropping" involves taking a object and surreptitiously putting it on the shelf of a store for customers to find and perhaps attempt to purchase from the store.
9. Miriam Kienle, "The Decoy: Objects and Economies of Conrad Bakker's *Untitled Projects*," unpublished master's thesis, Urbana, Ill.: University of Illinois, 2008, 1.
10. *Brooklyn Rail* online posting for July 2004: http://www.thebrooklynrail.org/arts/july04/5-fraser.html.
11. Nikki S. Lee, "Conversations with Artists: Nikki Lee," Illinois at the Phillips and the Center for the Study of Modern Art at the Phillips Collection, Feb. 28, 2007.
12. Johanna Burton, in conversation with Jonathan Fineberg while walking through a Mary Heilman show together, and implied in, especially, part II of Johanna Burton, "Mountain Wave: Mary Heilmann's 'Mary Heilmann Phase,'" in *Mary Heilmann: To Be Someone* (Newport Beach, Cal.: Orange County Museum of Art, 2007), 56ff.
13. The Atlas Group Archive is located at http://www.theatlasgroup.org/index.html.
14. Rob Storr, "Blinded by the Light," in Ilya and Emilia Kabakov, *An Alternative History of Art: Rosenthal, Kabakov, Spivak* (Cleveland: Museum of Contemporary Art and Bielefeld: Kerber Verlag, 2005), 142
15. Ilya Kabakov, "Ilya Kabakov and His Teacher, Charles Rosenthal," in Ilya and Emilia Kabakov, *An Alternative History of Art*, 153.
16. Ilya and Emilia Kabakov, "An Alternative History of Art: C. Rosenthal, I. Kabakov, I. Spivak," in Ilya and Emilia Kabakov, *An Alternative History of Art*, 6.
17. Ilya Kabakov, text from the first exhibition in 1999 of *The Life and Creativity of Charles Rosenthal*, in *Ilya Kabakov: Installations 1983–2000, Catalogue Raisonné* (Düsseldof: Richter Verlag, 2003), 376–7.
18. Ilya Kabakov, "The Life and Creativity of Charles Rosenthal," in Ilya and Emilia Kabakov, "An Alternative History of Art," 76.
19. Charles Rosenthal, cited in Ilya Kabakov, "The Life and Creativity of Charles Rosenthal," 76.

Chapter 17

1. Chang Yen-yüan, c. 847, *Li-tai-ming-hua-chi*, 1/6; see William Acker, *Some T'ang and Pre-T'ang Texts on Chinese Painting* (Leiden: E. J. Brill, 1954), 149.
2. Victor Aubertin, *Die Kunst Stirbt* (Munich, 1911); cited in Klaus Lankheit, ed., *Blue Rider Almanac* (New York: Viking, 1974), 11.
3. Philip Guston, *Time* (Jan. 7, 1952); cited in Musa Mayer, *Night Studio: A Memoir of Philip Guston by His Daughter* (New York: Viking Penguin, 1988), 63, and in Dore Ashton, *Yes, But . . . , A Critical Study of Philip Guston* (New York: Viking, 1976), 105.
4. Georgia O'Keeffe, writing to Anita Pollitzer from South Carolina in the teens, cited in Doris Bry, *Georgia O'Keeffe: Some Memories of Drawings* (Albuquerque: University of New Mexico Press, 1988), unpaginated.
5. Peter Bürger, *Theory of the Avant-Garde*, trans. Michael Shaw, *Theory of Literature*, vol. 4 (Minneapolis: University of Minnesota Press, 1984), 53.
6. Sigmund Freud, *Civilization and Its Discontents* (London: Hogarth Press, 1930).

PICTURE CREDITS

The publisher, the author and the picture researcher wish to thank the institutions and individuals who have kindly provided photographic material for use in this book. Museum and gallery locations are given in the captions. Sources for illustrations not supplied by museums or collections, additional information, and copyright credits are given below. Numbers are picture numbers unless otherwise indicated.

1.1 Photograph by David Mathews © President and Fellows of Harvard College; **1.2** Photograph by Jonathan Fineberg.

2.1 © 2009 Digital image, The Museum of Modern Art, New York/Scala, Florence. **2.2** Photograph Erik Gould. © ADAGP, Paris and DACS, London 2010; **2.3** Photograph by Hickey-Robertson. © ADAGP, Paris and DACS, London 2010; **2.4** © The Joseph and Robert Cornell Memorial Foundation; **2.5** Photograph by Geoffrey Clements, New York. © Estate of Ben Shahn/DACS, London/VAGA, New York 2010; **2.6** Photograph by E. Irving Blomstrann. © T.H. Benton and R.P. Benton Testamentary Trusts/DACS, London/VAGA, New York 2010; **2.7** © 2009 Digital image, The Museum of Modern Art, New York/Scala, Florence. © D.R. Rufino Tamayo / Herederos / México / 2009. Fundación Olga y Rufino Tamayo, A.C.; **2.8** Photograph Detroit Institute of Arts, USA/The Bridgeman Art Library. © 2010 Banco de México Diego Rivera Frida Kahlo Museums Trust, Mexico, D.F. / DACS; **2.10** © Succession Picasso/DACS 2010; **2.11** © The Pollock-Krasner Foundation ARS, NY and DACS, London 2010; **2.12** Photograph by Geoffrey Clements, New York; **2.13** © Dedalus Foundation, Inc./DACS, London/VAGA, New York 2010; **2.14** © Adolph and Esther Gottlieb Foundation/DACS, London/VAGA, New York 2010; **2.15** Photograph by Geoffrey Clements, New York. © ARS, NY and DACS, London 2010; **2.16** Photograph by Robert E. Mate. © DACS, London/VAGA, New York 2009 Est. Represented by the Michael Rosenfeld Gallery; **2.17** Photograph by Geoffrey Clements, New York; **2.18** Photograph by Lee Stalsworth. © ARS, NY and DACS, London 2010; **2.19** © 2009 Digital image, MOMA/Scala, Florence © ARS, NY and DACS Escobar 2010; **2.20** © Estate of Mark Tobey, ARS, NY/DACS, London, 2010; **2.24** © 2009 Digital image, MOMA/Scala, Florence. © ARS, NY and DACS, London 2010; **2.25** © ARS, NY and DACS, London 2010; **2.27** Photograph Christopher Burke, courtesy Cheim and Read/© Louise Bourgeois. DACS, London/VAGA, New York 2010; **2.28** Photograph Eeva Inkeri. © Louise Bourgeois. DACS, London/VAGA, New York 2010; **2.29** International Centre of Photography/Getty Images; **2.30** The Lisette Model Foundation, Inc. (1983). Used by permission. **2.31** © Aaron Siskind Foundation, courtesy Bruce Silverstein Gallery, New York.

3.1 © Calder Foundation, New York / DACS London 2010; **3.2** Photo © Estate of André Kertesz/Higher Pictures. © Calder Foundation, New York / DACS London 2010; **3.3** © Calder Foundation, New York / DACS London 2010; **3.4** Photography © Museum of Contemporary Art, Chicago © Calder Foundation, New York / DACS London 2010; **3.5** Photograph by Ellen Page Wilson. © Calder Foundation, New York / DACS London 2010; **3.6** Photograph by Ellen Page Wilson © Calder Foundation, New York / DACS London 2010; **3.7 – 3.9** Calder Foundation, New York / DACS London 2010; **3.10** Photograph courtesy of Christie's, New York. © Calder Foundation, New York / DACS London 2010; **3.11** Photograph by Jonathan Fineberg. © Calder Foundation, New York / DACS London 2010; **3.12** Photograph by Geoffrey Clements, New York. © Estate of Stuart Davis/DACS, London/VAGA, New York 2010; **3.13** Photo © 2005 The Philadelphia Museum of Art/Art Resource/Scala, Florence. **3.14** © ARS, NY and DACS, London 2010; **3.15** © 2009 Image copyright the Metropolitan Museum of Art/Scala, Florence. © Succession H Matisse/DACS 2010; **3.16** © ARS, NY and DACS, London 2010; **3.17** © ADAGP, Paris and DACS, London 2010; **3.18** Photography © The Art Institute of Chicago. © ARS, NY and DACS, London 2010; **3.20** Photograph by Geoffrey Clements. © ADAGP, Paris and DACS, London 2010; **3.21** © ADAGP, Paris and DACS, London 2010; **3.22** © 2009 Digital image, The Museum of Modern Art, New York/Scala, Florence. © Succession Picasso/DACS 2010; **3.23** © 2009 Digital image, The Museum of Modern Art, New York/Scala, Florence. © ADAGP, Paris and DACS, London 2010; **3.24 & 3.25** © ADAGP, Paris and DACS, London 2010; **3.26 & 3.28** © Dedalus Foundation, Inc./DACS, London/VAGA, New York 2010; **3.29** Photograph by Peter A. Juley & Son, New York. © Dedalus Foundation, Inc./DACS, London/VAGA, New York 2010; **3.30 – 3.32** © Dedalus Foundation, Inc./DACS, London/VAGA, New York 2010; **3.33** Photograph by Geoffrey Clements, New York. © The Willem de Kooning Foundation, New York/ ARS, NY and DACS, London 2010; **3.34 – 3.37** © The Willem de Kooning Foundation, New York/ ARS, NY and DACS, London 2010; **3.38** Photography © The Art Institute of Chicago. © The Willem de Kooning Foundation, New York/ ARS, NY and DACS, London 2010; **3.40** © Estate of Hans Namuth. © The Willem de Kooning Foundation, New York/ ARS, NY and DACS, London 2010; **3.41 – 3.43** © The Willem de Kooning Foundation, New York/ ARS, NY and DACS, London 2010.

4.1 © The Pollock-Krasner Foundation ARS, NY and DACS, London 2010; **4.2** Photography © The Art Institute of Chicago. © The Pollock-Krasner Foundation ARS, NY and DACS, London 2010; **4.3 & 4.4** Digital image, The Museum of Modern Art, New York/Scala, Florence © The Pollock-Krasner Foundation ARS, NY and DACS, London 2010; **4.5** Photograph © Hans Namuth Estate. © The Pollock-Krasner Foundation ARS, NY and DACS, London 2010; **4.6 & 4.7** Photograph by Geoffrey Clements, New York. © The Pollock-Krasner Foundation ARS, NY and DACS, London 2010; **4.8** Digital image, The Museum of Modern Art, New York/Scala, Florence. © The Pollock-Krasner Foundation ARS, NY and DACS, London 2010; **4.9** © The Pollock-Krasner Foundation ARS, NY and DACS, London 2010; **4.10 – 4.12** Digital image, The Museum of Modern Art, New York/Scala, Florence. © ARS, NY and DACS, London 2010; **4.13 & 4.14** © ARS, NY and DACS, London 2010; **4.15** © 1995 Board of Trustees, National Gallery of Art, Washington, D.C. © ARS, NY and DACS, London 2010; **4.16, 4.18, 4.19** © 1998 Kate Rothko Prizel & Christopher Rothko ARS, NY and DACS, London **4.17** Photograph courtesy the National Gallery of Art, Washington, D.C. © 1998 Kate Rothko Prizel & Christopher Rothko ARS, NY and DACS, London; **4.20** Photograph by Geoffrey Clements, New York. © 1998 Kate Rothko Prizel & Christopher Rothko ARS, NY and DACS, London ; **4.21** Digital image, The Museum of Modern Art, New York/Scala, Florence. © 1998 Kate Rothko Prizel & Christopher Rothko ARS, NY and DACS, London; **4.22** Photograph by Christopher Burke © 1998 Kate Rothko Prizel & Christopher Rothko ARS, NY and DACS, London; **4.23** Digital image, The Museum of Modern Art, New York/Scala, Florence. © ADAGP, Paris and DACS, London 2010; **4.25, 4.26 & 4.28** © Estate of David Smith/DACS, London/VAGA, New York 2010; **4.29** Photography © The Art Institute of Chicago. © Estate of David Smith/DACS, London/VAGA, New York 2010; **4.30 – 4.32** © Estate of David Smith/DACS, London/VAGA, New York 2010; **4.33** Photograph © 2010 Museum of Fine Arts, Boston. © Estate of David Smith/DACS, London/VAGA, New York 2010; **4.34** © Estate of David Smith/DACS, London/VAGA, New York 2010; **4.35** © The Henry Moore Foundation, 1994.

5.1 Digital image, The Museum of Modern Art, New York/Scala, Florence. © ADAGP, Paris and DACS, London 2010; **5.2 & 5.3** © ADAGP, Paris and DACS, London 2010; **5.4** Photograph by F. W. Seiders. © ADAGP, Paris and DACS, London 2010; **5.5** © ADAGP, Paris and DACS, London 2010; **5.6** © ADAGP, Paris and DACS, London 2010; **5.7** Digital image, The Museum of Modern Art, New York/Scala, Florence. © ADAGP, Paris and DACS, London 2010; **5.8** Digital image, The Museum of Modern Art, New York/Scala, Florence. © ADAGP, Paris and DACS, London 2010; **5.9** © ADAGP, Paris and DACS, London 2010; **5.10** Magnum Photos/Henri Cartier-Bresson, 1994; **5.11 – 5.13** Digital image, The Museum of Modern Art, New York/Scala, Florence. ADAGP, Paris/© Succession Giacometti 2010; **5.14** ADAGP, Paris/ © Succession Giacometti 2010; **5.17** © Succession Picasso/DACS 2010; **5.18 – 5.20** © The Estate of Francis Bacon. All rights reserved. DACS 2010.

6.1 Photo: Jens Ziehe © 2005 Scala, Florence/BPK, Bildagentur für Kunst, Kultur und Geschichte, Berlin. © ADAGP, Paris and DACS, London 2010; **6.2** Photography © The Art Institute of Chicago. © Georges Mathieu; **6.3** © Fondazione Palazzo Albizzini "Collezione Burri", Città di Castello, Italy; **6.4** © Lucio Fontana/SIAE/DACS, London 2010; **6.5** Photograph courtesy the collectors; **6.6** © Estate of Joan Mitchell; **6.7** Photograph by Lee Stalsworth. © Guston estate; **6.8** © ARS, NY and DACS, London 2010; **6.9** Photograph by Geoffrey Clements, New York; **6.10** Photograph by Geoffrey Clements, New York. © Estate of Kenneth Noland. DACS, London/VAGA, New York 2010; **6.11** Photograph by Geoffrey Clements, New York. © The Josef and Anni Albers Foundation/VG Bild-Kunst, Bonn and DACS, London 2010; **6.12** © ARS, NY and DACS, London 2010; **6.13** Photograph by Tibor Franyo. © ADAGP, Paris and DACS, London 2010; **6.14** Photograph by Robert E. Mates © The Solomon R. Guggenheim Foundation, New York 78.2518. © Estate of George Rickey/ DACS, London/VAGA, New York 2010; **6.15** Photograph by David Heald © The Solomon R. Guggenheim Foundation, New York 83.3040. © Donation Jorn, Silkeborg/ DACS 2010; **6.16** © Karel Appel Foundation, courtesy www.vanlennepproducties.nl; **6.17** © ADAGP, Paris and DACS, London 2010 **6.18** © DACS 2010; **6.19** Photo John Riddy courtesy Goodman Derrick; **6.21** Photograph by Lee Stalsworth; **6.22** © Estate of Larry Rivers/ DACS, London/VAGA, New York 2010; **6.23** © Alex Katz, DACS, London/VAGA, New York 2010; **6.27** Photograph by Geoffrey Clements, New York; **6.29** © Wayne Thiebaud/ DACS, London/VAGA, New York 2010; **6.30** Photography © Museum of Contemporary Art, Chicago.

7.1 © Robert Frank, courtesy PaceWildenstein MacGill, New York; **7.2** © Succession Marcel Duchamp/ADAGP, Paris and DACS, London 2010; **7.4 & 7.5** © Estate of Robert Rauschenberg. DACS, London/VAGA, New York 2010; **7.7** Photograph courtesy Rheinisches Bildarchiv, Köln. © Estate of Robert Rauschenberg. DACS, London/VAGA, New York 2010; **7.8** Digital image, The Museum of Modern Art, New York/Scala, Florence.© Estate of Robert Rauschenberg. DACS, London/VAGA, New York 2010; **7.9** Photograph Smithsonian American Art Museum/Art Resource/Scala, Florence © Estate of Robert Rauschenberg. DACS, London/VAGA, New York 2010; **7.10** Photograph © Estate of Peter Moore/ VAGA, NYC. © Estate of Robert Rauschenberg. DACS, London/VAGA, New York 2010; **7.11** © Estate of Robert Rauschenberg. DACS, London/VAGA, New York 2010; **7.12** © Estate of Robert Rauschenberg. DACS, London/VAGA, New York 2010 and Gemini G.E.L.; **7.13** © Zabriskie Gallery, New York. © Collection Centre Pompidou, Dist. RMN / Droits réservés; **7.14** Photograph by Glenn Steigelman. © ARS, NY and DACS, London 2010; **7.15** Courtesy Oil and Steel Gallery, New York; **7.16** Photograph by Geoffrey Clements, New York. © ARS, NY and DACS, London 2010; **7.17** Courtesy Anthology Film Archives; **7.18** Courtesy of the Estate of Stan Brakhage and Fred Camper (www.fredcamper.com); **7.21** Photograph courtesy the artist; **7.22** © ARS, NY and DACS, London 2010; **7.23** Photograph courtesy Mrs. Robert B. Mayer, Chicago. © The George and Helen Segal Foundation/DACS, London/VAGA, New York 2010; **7.24** © Marisol Escobar. DACS, London/VAGA, New York 2010; **7.25** Digital image, The Museum of Modern Art, New York/Scala, Florence; **7.26** Photograph by Jerry L. Thompson; **7.27** Photograph by Squids & Nunns, courtesy of Contemporary Art, Los Angeles; **7.28** Digital image, The Museum of Modern Art, New York/Scala, Florence; **7.29 & 7.30** Photograph by Geoffrey Clements, New York. **7.31** Photograph by Bob Kolbrener; **7.33** Photography © The Art Institute of Chicago; **7.35** Photograph © by Jonathan Fineberg; **7.36** Photograph courtesy Leo Castelli Gallery, New York. © Jasper Johns / VAGA, New York / DACS, London 2010; **7.37** Photograph by Geoffrey Clements, New York. © Jasper Johns / VAGA, New York / DACS, London 2010; **7.38** © Jasper Johns / VAGA, New York / DACS, London 2010; **7.39** Photograph Paul Macapia, Seattle Art Museum. © Jasper Johns / VAGA, New York / DACS, London 2010; **7.40** Photograph courtesy Rheinisches Bildarchiv, Köln. © Jasper Johns / VAGA, New York / DACS, London 2010; **7.41** Photograph by Rudolph Burckhardt, courtesy Leo Castelli Gallery, New York. © Jasper Johns / VAGA, New York / DACS, London 2010; **7.43** Photograph courtesy Leo Castelli Gallery, New York. © Jasper Johns / VAGA, New York / DACS, London 2010; **7.44** Photograph by Rudolph Burckhardt. © Jasper Johns / VAGA, New York / DACS, London 2010; **7.45** Photograph by courtesy Gagosian Gallery. © Jasper Johns / VAGA, New York / DACS, London 2010; **7.46** Photograph courtesy of the artist. © Jasper Johns / VAGA, New York / DACS, London 2010; **7.47** Photograph by Dorothy Zeidman. © Jasper Johns / VAGA, New York / DACS, London 2010.

8.1 Photograph by Hickey-Robertson. © ADAGP, Paris and DACS, London 2010; **8.2** Collection Centre Pompidou, Dist. RMN / Adam Rzepka. © ADAGP, Paris and DACS, London 2010; **8.3** © ADAGP, Paris and DACS, London 2010; **8.4** Photograph by Paul Hester. © ADAGP, Paris and DACS, London 2010; **8.5** © ADAGP, Paris and DACS, London 2010; **8.6** Photograph by eeva-inkeri, courtesy the artist. © ADAGP, Paris and DACS, London 2010; **8.7** © ADAGP, Paris and DACS, London 2010; **8.8** Photograph courtesy Rheinisches Bildarchiv, Köln. © ADAGP, Paris and DACS, London 2010; **8.9** © ADAGP, Paris and DACS, London 2010; **8.12 – 8.15** © DACS 2010; **8.16** Photograph by Mary Donlon, © The Solomon R. Guggenheim Foundation, New York. © DACS 2010; **8.17 & 8.18** © Estate of Peter Moore/ VAGA, NYC; **8.19** © Collection Centre Pompidou, Dist. RMN; **8.20** Photograph by Geoffrey Clements. © Copyright by Henmar Press Inc., New York. Reprinted by permission of Peters Edition Ltd, London; **8.21 & 8.22** Courtesy Lenono Photo Archive © Yoko Ono.

INDEX